This book is dedicated to **Dan O'Bannon**, who passed away while I was completing it. He added much to the genre both as a director and a writer, creating some of the most beloved characters, stories and films in the genre. I only wish he could have done more, but he will definitely be missed.

9/30/46 - 12/17/09

Horror, I love it. Books, games, anything horror, especially movies. I consider horror to be a very broad genre, and you don't have to be a masked killer or a flesh eating zombie to be considered horror. Horror seeps into Science Fiction, Fantasy, Mystery, Action, Comedy, and on. It can be quite the chameleon. So I place many split genre movies in here too, because what would be a horror book without non-straight up horror like Alien, The Thing or Shaun of the Dead? And it also tends to hold hands with the Suspense genre, hence why I include that genre among the horror. I also "tag" each movie to give it a subgenre for those of you just looking for maybe zombie flicks or vampire movies. Here's a breakdown of that list:

Aliens – Beings from another world, meaning outer space, not another dimension.

Animals – Movies dealing with regular animals, which may or may not be genetically enhanced, but are standard in real life.

Animated – A movie that is not live action but rather computer generated or more traditionally animated. Also includes Claymation.

Anthology – A movie comprising of multiple stories, not necessarily connected.

Biological – This covers plants, organisms, slimes and oozes.

Cannibals – Deals with humans who hunt and eat the flesh of other humans.

Cults – Groups of people, usually with social and theological ideals well outside the norm.

Demonic Possession – When a dark force, sometimes unholy, takes control of a human and forces them to do their bidding.

Demons – Creatures from Hell or some other nether region. Can come in a true form or can transform others into their kind. There is a fine line between true demons and demonic possession.

Devil – Movies dealing directly with the granddaddy of all evil.

Ghosts – Spirits of those who have died but not fully passed over into any kind of afterlife.

Horror Related – Not exactly a straight horror movie, but something horror fans would enjoy, could be a documentary or a movie with a horror subtext.

Infection – Afflicts humans much like regular everyday infections, but with much more dire results, and is usually transmittable between humans.

Mechanical – Movies dealing with machines.

Monsters – A term to describe creatures that do not fit neatly into another category.

Mummies – People who have died, been mummified, and returned to life. Usually Egyptian in origin.

Sea Monsters – The same deal as regular monsters, but aquatic in nature.

Serial Killer – Deals with the exploits of a real life serial killer.

Serial Killer (Fictional) – Deals with the exploits of a fictional serial killer.

Short Film Compilation – This is basically a DVD with multiple short movies on it.

Slasher / Survival – I lumped both together because they usually go hand in hand. Deals with situations where a person or people, sometimes of a supernatural nature, stalk and kill other people, or where people are placed into a survival situation that may not include stalking.

Suspense – This is a general term I use for human horror. This covers tales of obsession, madness, stalking and usually involves murder, kidnapping, torture, rape, etc.

Vampires – Most of the time these are undead creatures that can only come out at night and must drink the blood of the living.

Werewolves – Humans that have the ability or curse of turning into a half man, half wolf, or just a wolf either during full moons or at will.

Witchcraft – I am referring to black magic in general here, witches, warlocks, or just people with magical properties. Also refers to rituals, satanic or otherwise, and curses.

Zombies – Humans that have returned from being dead, usually to feast on the flesh and/or brains of the living.

[Hidden to conceal spoilers] – This means that if I was going to tell you what was going on in the movie, it would reveal twists in the storyline or secrets I would not want to spoil for the first time viewer.

And now that brings me to the topic of spoilers, I hate them. I don't know how many times I've gone to read a review about a movie that interested me, and the son of a bitch writing it tells me about half the movie and now I know what will happen and where. They think that just because they don't reveal the ending, they're doing a good job. But I don't want anything revealed. So I try to limit giving any detailed information, and sorry if some slips out. This includes sequels. You may notice that I don't give out much information in the synopsis, but I don't want to ruin what happened in the previous movie. Reviewers also tend to do that. They'll say, "And in the end of the last movie when the killer did this…" Thanks prick, because I haven't seen that one yet. So I just perform a basic paragraph long review that includes a synopsis and my thoughts on the important stuff like story, acting, direction, FX and various other little tidbits. I think anything longer than a paragraph or two is too much anyway, then people tend to drag on and get into the spoiler territory. Short and sweet is the way I like it.

As for my movie selections, when I first started collecting DVDs, I focused mainly on the movies I grew up with and newer stuff that interested me. So you may see some glaring oversights in this book and maybe some of your favorites are missing. Well, I am but one man and buy movies when I can, so I just don't have everything yet. But that's what Volume II is for. I swear next time I'll get into the Universal Monsters, Hammer films, more foreign stuff, independent stuff, new releases, gialli and maybe even Godzilla. Also, I didn't want to limit this book to just good horror because someone's trash is another person's treasure, and I want to give people a wide view on horror unlike anything they've seen before. And just because I didn't like it, if it sounds interesting to you, try it out, you may like it.

Now I'd like to talk about my rating system. It's a five point scale with half points, which I know is essentially a ten point scale, but I just have a preference to the look of the five point scale. Not a single person in the world is going to agree with my rating of every movie, but it's just my opinion and I try to put words behind it to help convey why I gave a certain movie a certain score. But if you do agree with all of my ratings, then we need to hang out. My scale is as follows:

5 – Masterpiece
4.5 – Classic
4 – Excellent
3.5 – Very Good
3 – Good
2.5 – Average
2 – Below Average
1.5 – Bad
1 – Terrible
0.5 – Worthless

Please note that I do take budget into account when making my review, but I will usually state low budget works when they come up. It's just not fair to evenly compare the twenty million dollar movie with the twenty dollar movie. When it comes to low budget and better still, microbudget movies, I can look past bad acting because that really is par for the course. When you have a tiny budget, sometimes your friends have to be your actors, and your friends can't act, and I understand that.

I also realized that I use some terminology that might not be instantly recognizable to genre newbies so I'll try and explain some of it here:

FX – This is just an abbreviation for special effects. When I say practical FX that means special effects that were created by hand while on the other end CGI stands for Computer Generated Images, which are essentially fake images created by a computer that actors have to pretend to interact with.

Genre Actor – A genre actor is someone who has appeared prominently in at least three horror movies.

Genre Vet – A genre vet is someone who has appeared in either several horror movies or in a few really great horror movies.

Genre Legend – A genre legend is someone who has pretty much devoted their entire acting career to horror and who are also deceased. I don't believe in living legends.

Gorehound – A gorehound is someone who enjoys watching horror movies that feature a large amount of bloodshed.

But enough about all this, let's just move on to the meat of book with one thousand movies all lined up in alphabetical order for ease. And before you start I just want to say that I am very confident that everyone who reads this book will hate it. Why you ask? Well, it's quite simple really. I'm sure that somewhere within I'm going to trash your favorite movie and rain accolades upon what you consider to be a piece of trash, but it's just opinions, just me giving my thoughts on a genre I have loved for so long. So even though you'll hate me for something I'm about to say in the next few hundred pages, try to like me for that one movie you've never heard of and now thanks to me you don't know how you lived without out it. Come on, there's a thousand movies in here, there's got to be at least one.

P.S. You'll also find several sections in the back of the book that will lump all the movies together by director, year, rating and sub genre for your ease of reference. And sorry for any spelling or grammatical errors contained within, I tried to keep it to a bare minimum.

3 Extremes (Sam Gang Yi)

Year – 2004
Director – Fruit Chan, Chan-Wook Park, Takashi Miike
Tags – Anthology, Suspense

This anthology features three stories and no wraparound. The first is about an aging woman and her attempt at being more youthful by ingesting some curious dumplings. The second is about a successful director and a man who despises him for all he has. The third is about a young woman and her sordid past dealing with her sister and a small box. This is a great anthology, and usually it's easy to pick a favorite and a least favorite but each story is just so equally excellent, which is surprising given the very different nature of each. The acting and direction are superb on each production and there is a nice mix of atmosphere and gore throughout the entire movie. This anthology shows why I like foreign horror so much because this movie deals with subject matter that you would never see in the States. A great time.

4/5

3 Extremes II (Saam Gaang)

Year – 2002
Director – Peter Chan, Ji-Woon Kim, Nonzee Nimibutr
Tags – Anthology, Ghosts, Suspense

This "sequel" also features three stories and no wraparound. The first is about a woman who wakes up in the street with no memory and her husband can not recall why his wife left him. The second is about a puppeteer and his cursed puppets. The third is about a man and his son who move into a new apartment only to have trouble with the neighbors. I really liked the first one (even though this movie actually came out first but was released as a sequel in the States), but this one obviously suffers from the use of second string talent because it's about half as good as the first. Every section looks great but the stories are all fairly weak and the direction also takes a hit because of this and makes for some pretty boring sections. The first story is much too predictable, the second too dull and the third is probably the best and most interesting but still comes off slow. I wasn't pleased with this entry but I guess it wasn't all bad, still, it could have been much better. Just stick with the first.

2/5

4th Floor, The

Year – 1999
Director – Josh Klausner
Tags – Suspense

A woman inherits rent control apartment and soon afterward is terrorized by her downstairs neighbor. But there's more afoot than it appears. I bought this mainly due to the caliber of actors in the movie because I have to be honest, this didn't sound very appealing. But it turned out to be a good if somewhat mundane thriller with a wonderful open ended final scene. Not open ended as in open for a sequel, but it made you wonder just what happened after the credits rolled. Very nice. The acting and direction were fine, nothing wrong there. The story was a bit bland but overall a satisfying affair. This movie certainly won't break down any boundaries in the suspense genre but it is a good little thriller to occupy your time with.

3/5

5ive Girls

Year – 2006
Director – Warren P. Sonoda
Tags – Demonic Possession

Years after a girl mysteriously disappears at a Catholic school, the school reopens to take care of troubled young women. Five girls come to the school for what they believe to be an attitude readjustment but soon they learn they each have special powers and are at the school for much more diabolical purposes. From the beginning of this movie, I was really digging it, the acting was very good and the direction was smooth. The problem is that the story doesn't really go anywhere and it plays out in a somewhat mundane way. That's not to say that it was bad by any means, it was just a little thin is all. And toward the end the movie started to drag as well, which was weird because that's when the demonic possession and violence came to full swing. But it's overall a good movie it just didn't blow me away.

3/5

8MM

Year – 1999
Director – Joel Schumacher
Tags – Suspense

A private detective is hired by a wealthy widow to discover the origins of a snuff film that she found in her husband's belongings. His investigation leads him into the seedy world of pornography, and depths which he could have never fathomed. I found this to be a rather compelling movie. It's so dark and evil in its nature with a truly gripping story of mystery and suspense. The acting is great and such a wonderful cast was assembled. The direction is really good and there weren't many pacing issues, I was pretty interested the entire way through the movie. I don't think this could be much better, sure it could be gorier and had even more sexual depravity, but I don't think that would have added much to my entertainment factor. This is just a great thriller with an extreme dark side.

4/5

8MM 2

Year – 2005

Director – J.S. Cardone
Tags – Suspense

This fake sequel has nothing at all to do with the original. Here a couple deep in the political game are secretly filmed having sex with a prostitute and then blackmailed. Now they're on the hunt to find out who is blackmailing them before the video can be released, and their journey takes them into the underground world of pornography. From snuff to porn, kind of a massive step down, don't you think? I don't fault the movie because it doesn't have anything to do with the original. I fault it because it just isn't very good. The story is weak and it seems to be an excuse to show lots of sex and nudity. The direction is also pretty slow but not entirely bad. The acting is pretty good, which surprised me, pleasantly might I add. This may be worthwhile to someone looking for a soft thriller featuring a lot of soft core porn, it wasn't terrible, but I didn't really like it.

2/5

13: Game of Death (13 Game Sayawng)
Year – 2006
Director – Chukiat Sakveerakul
Tags – Suspense

A man very down on his luck gets a strange call asking him to be a part of a game show. All he must do is complete thirteen challenges and he will receive $100,000,000 (or one million if you watch this movie dubbed). I like the concept, but it does have the potential to fail if the challenges are lame. So I decided to play along and for every challenge he performed, I wondered aloud if I could do it. Once the movie came to challenge five, I wondered if I could even physically do it, so therefore they planned the challenges out very well. The movie does lag at times, but not too bad, and I loved the end even though I could see it all coming. Overall I love the way it played out and greatly enjoyed the progression of challenges and how they all tied together in the end. This is a very well done thriller.

4/5

13 Tzameti
Year – 2005
Director – Gela Babluani
Tags – Suspense

A hard working young man looses his latest construction contract when the man who employed him suddenly dies and no one is left to pay him. But he comes across a piece of mail meant for the man that contains a train ticket and hotel voucher. The young man steals the mail and ends up traveling into a place where people are gambling on the ultimate game of chance, and he's the next contestant. I found this to be an extremely gripping and well accomplished movie. The game itself doesn't even take up half the movie, and since that is the main draw, the movie had the potential to be boring, but I found it to be a very well crafted and taught thriller that kept my attention throughout. But I also have to say that when the game was played it was done so in such a suspenseful way that I was literally on my feet while I was watching it. Well acted and directed with a very suspenseful and well written story. Thrillers don't get much better than this.

4.5/5

28 Days Later
Year – 2002
Director – Danny Boyle
Tags – Infection

When an animal rescue group tries to free some primates from a research lab, they unknowingly unleash the Rage virus, which turns people into murderous psychopaths. The virus is transmitted through blood and saliva, and soon all of London is infected. This movie follows a small group of people as they try to survive. First off, let me set the record straight, this is not a zombie movie! The villains in this movie are not dead, rather they are still alive and infected with concentrated rage, which makes them want to kill and destroy whatever they come across. Zombies are dead (undead), the infected are still alive. Ok, now that I have had my dork moment, I shall get on with my thoughts. This movie is brilliant, it really is. The way it was shot was so gritty and realistic that it really lends to the terror facing England. The transformation from human to infected is almost instantaneous, which is truly frightening because you have little time to react. The movie is brutal and unforgiving and this type of direction really allows you to feel like you're a part of things. The human element of the story is also very welcome, and it shows the many flaws we have in full luster and is an unflinching look at the light and dark parts of the soul. The shots of an abandoned London are very chilling as are the places the survivors visit on their journey. The acting is about real as it gets and the story moves along fluidly. The blood factor is very high here and the tension and pulse pounding chase sequences only make the horror greater. Inventive and well made, this movie is an instant classic.

5/5

28 Weeks Later
Year – 2007
Director – Juan Carlos Fresnadillo
Tags – Infection

Six months after the initial infection, the US Army has occupied England and begins the clean-up effort to restore the ravaged country. The infection is gone and survivors begin to repopulate London. But a woman is discovered inside the quarantine zone that is immune to the virus, but also a carrier, and through her the infection begins anew. I was wary of a sequel to such a great movie, but I was pleasantly surprised with what this movie was: excellent. The sequel to 28 Days Later is nothing short of an achievement.

We get to see the infection consume the masses, and experience the wide spread chaos and panic only spoken of in the original film. Drastic measures by the Army are taken and I feel that was a smart plot point because that is what would really happen in a situation like this, and it's that unflinching take that really makes this sequel work. That, and the increased loads of blood and gore that saturate the movie. I would like all filmmakers to take note of this movie, because this is how you make a sequel to a masterpiece. You go full bore into it, never pull any punches, and stay true to the original formula while adding your own unique touches. This movie is one hell of a ride.

4.5/5

30 Days of Night
Year – 2007
Director – David Slade
Tags – Vampires

Ravenous vampires descend upon a small Alaskan town just as it about to plunge into one month of complete darkness. Two things I really love about this movie are the plot itself, which is brilliant, and the fact that vampires here are not suave and sexy, they are vicious killers. Maybe even the most vicious vampires ever. One thing I did not like about the movie was the time span. The movie goes through the entire month, but it just doesn't feel like anything more than a single night aside from beard growth on the male actors. I know it must have difficult to try and cram a month into a ninety minute run time, but that part of the movie just always irked me. Aside from that, the movie plays out nicely and there are a ton of bloody kills, which is great to see. I like this movie a lot but it may just have been too big of a concept to pull off in one go.

4/5

100 Feet
Year – 2008
Director – Eric Red
Tags – Ghosts

After a woman kills her abusive husband she is forced into house arrest and can not leave her residence. The problem is that she is now trapped in the house with her husband's ghost, and he wants revenge. I love the concept of this movie, and for the most part the script lives up to it. There are a few minor annoyances in the story, like how she keeps opening her door all stretched out with her foot in the threshold even though she has three minutes to get back to where she needs to be. The direction is very good with only a few lags in pacing. The acting is also very good, especially from Famke Janssen, which is good since she has to carry pretty much the whole movie by herself. The FX were also very nice and not overused either. This is just a really good ghost movie with only minor flaws that do not inhibit the overall entertainment value.

3.5/5

976-EVIL

Year – 1988
Director – Robert Englund
Tags – Demonic Possession

After people call for their horoscope at 976-Evil, things begin happening, sometimes good, but eventually ending up bad, including becoming a henchman for the Devil. This movie has some good originality to it, but the script isn't very strong. You can also tell this is a first time director because the direction, while it is good, could use some work. But I can tell that Englund has natural talent, it just needs to be honed to be in full effect. The acting is fairly good as well. I don't think anyone plays the creepy weird kid quite like Stephen Geoffreys. This is a fun '80's flick that could have used a heavy dose of fine tuning, but I still found good entertainment value from it.

3/5

1408

Year – 2007
Director – Mikael Hafstrom
Tags – Ghosts

A writer travels around and stays in supposedly haunted places, effectively debunking most establishments. But when he is invited to stay at room 1408 in an old hotel, which has an incredibly sordid past, he learns that it has claimed the lives of several people along the way. Once he enters the room, the haunting begins, making a believer out of him. But will he survive long enough to tell his tale? This is one of the more memorable Stephen King adaptations to come out in awhile. From the beginning of this movie, especially once he gets to the hotel it quickly becomes one of the best ghost movies I have ever seen. The haunting occurrences are unique, extravagant and very well done. This was a very edge of your seat experience, and then about two-thirds into the movie you get completely sucked out of the story and everything just stops. I couldn't believe it was happening, it was like approaching the climax during intercourse and then the woman just leaves, what the hell? In all fairness the movie ended strong, was terrifically acted and well directed to that point, but I just can not forgive it. Still, this is one of the best ghost movies I have ever seen for the most part. Just expect a huge speed bump along the way.

3.5/5

2001 Maniacs

Year – 2005
Director – Tim Sullivan
Tags – Slasher / Survival

This is a remake of the movie Two Thousand Maniacs and follows the same plotline. I like this movie because it feels like it could have been made in the 80's right next to all the other cheesy slasher flicks. I'm not a huge fan of the original, but I liked it to some degree, and I feel that this update kept the core of the original movie and improved upon it greatly. It added what it needed to add in the form of lots of gore and lots of nudity, but I do have to say that even I think this movie is a bit too cheesy. The acting is a mixed bag but the direction is really great. I loved the kills and there were some great FX on most of them. The characters are a bit better in this version, more of the townsfolk come to the forefront but the visitors are just as disposable as they were in the original. This is fun movie and I enjoyed it.

3.5/5

Abandoned, The
Year – 2006
Director – Nacho Cerda
Tags – Ghosts

A woman returns to her homeland to visit the home of the family she never knew to uncover a secret buried there. But then she starts to see ghosts all around her, including her own. The atmosphere in this movie is top notch, and the location is amazingly cool. The acting is good as well, but I think that the problems in this movie lie within the script and subsequently the direction. I was bored by this movie on more than one occasion as it is very slow and somewhat uneventful. But even then I still managed to enjoy it quite a bit because it just had so much original stuff going on and just so much going for it. The direction and script could have been tighter, but the atmosphere trumps all, making this one very unique ghost story with its share of flaws, but one that is still very good in the realm of other similar tales.

3.5/5

Abominable
Year – 2006
Director – Ryan Schifrin
Tags – Monsters

A crippled man and a group of women partying in the cabin next to his are under attack by a giant creature deep in the woods. This is a very fun throwback to the monster movies of yesteryear. The monster is pretty cheesy but that just goes along with the vibe of the movie. The acting is actually very good and features a handful of genre vets as well. The direction is also very good with limited hiccups. One thing that kind of annoyed me was the lack of good kills for the first half of the movie because in the second half the kills were just downright awesome. Lots of blood, a bit of nudity and a hulking abominable snowman ripping people to shreds, you can't ask for much more from a monster movie. Good times.

Abyss, The
Year – 1989
Director – James Cameron
Tags – Aliens, Suspense

A submarine crashes in the deep ocean after coming into contact with some unknown force. A drilling team is dispatched with some Navy personnel to the sub where they encounter the same force, and must deal with the Navy's paranoid suspicions that the Russians are behind everything. This is the one time that I think I may have preferred the original cut over the director's cut. The special edition of this movie is ungodly long and is loaded with completely unnecessary scene after scene. The movie itself has a decent story, nothing special, but does have great FX and acting. The movie is much too slow to be called great, but enough going for it that it's far from bad. Skip the director's cut and instead view the much cleaner chopped version, still not great but it will save nearly an hour of your life.

3/5

Against the Dark
Year – 2009
Director – Richard Crudo
Tags – Vampires

Stephen Seagal versus vampires, 'nuff said! That's really all it is and if you're a fan of Seagal or vampires, you should still skip it. I didn't have much hope for this movie but even my lowest expectations were not met. The acting is pretty bad and the direction is about as horrible as it comes. The story is a joke. Essentially what we have here is 28 Days Later meets Underworld. People are infected and become vampires, this movie follows some uninfected folks in a hospital who are regularly attacked by vampires and then Seagal and his band of pansy ass vampire hunters come along and kick ass in poorly choreographed fashion. And that's all that happens, over and over again. There was some good gore, so I'll give the movie that, but overall this pathetic attempt at a horror movie is just that, pathetic.

1/5

Alien
Year – 1979
Director – Ridley Scott
Tags – Aliens

A mining ship discovers a distress signal in deep space and goes to investigate. Upon their exploration of a seemingly abandoned planet, they come across a strange creature unlike anything else they have ever seen. The funny thing about this movie is that it plays out like a haunted house story. The spaceship that comprises most of the setting for the movie is almost like an old mansion, with the alien being a malevolent spirit. When it begins to kill people they just vanish with little trace. There is a constant tension and dark atmosphere here that is pretty unexpected from an alien movie. The direction is quite simply put, flawless. This is supported by some incredible acting from the entire cast. The FX in this movie are really something special, and the creature design for the alien has now become legendary. The story is just so unique and compelling because of one simple fact, it was just thought out well. The evolution of the alien is probably the high point for me, as that was very fleshed out and original. In the end, this is just one of the best sci-fi/horror movies to ever be released with a terrific cast and crew performing a well written story to its full potential.

5/5

*Alien 2 can be found under Aliens.

*Alien 4 can be found under Alien: Resurrection

Alien 3
Year – 1992
Director – David Fincher
Tags – Aliens

This movie continues some amount of time after the second one and takes place in a maximum security prison on an isolated planet. I like the way the story continues here, it was a good place for the franchise to go, and it went there with continuity in tact. The acting is really great and the setting is very dark and dismal, which is a great thing for this movie. I'm not a fan of the direction though. Actually, I think my problem is a mix of the script as well as the direction. This movie is just too slow. When something happens, it's pretty great, there's just a long drawn out period of time between each such occurrence. This movie also depends too heavily on CGI for the alien, and let me tell you, the CGI is terrible and it makes the alien look too cartoonish. But the final act in the movie is fast paced and features some really great stuff, which almost redeems everything leading up to that point. Still, even though this movie could have used a fair amount of tightening, I still found it to be very good.

3.5/5

Alien Raiders
Year – 2008
Director – Ben Rock
Tags – Aliens, Infection

A small town grocery store is invaded by a band of masked individuals, but they want more than money, they're looking for the source of an alien infection very few know about. This movie has an interesting set-up. It dives straight into the action giving little explanation as to what exactly is going on, and really that's the way it should be. I've always been a little irritated with the movies that conveniently find a way to spill out the entire synopsis in the first five minutes. Here everything unfolds over the course of the movie, and by the end, you still have a few questions, but those will probably be revealed in a sequel. The pacing is top notch, as it never gives you time to catch your breath. Something is always happening and the movie never gets dull. I think the script could have been tweaked because about halfway through the movie you can figure out just what's going to happen, and it kind of tarnishes an otherwise fine production. And one more thing, the character Kane is just plain annoying. Yeah, you're a badass, we get it. Other than a few minor issues, this was a very enjoyable flick.

4/5

Alien Resurrection
Year – 1997
Director – Jean-Pierre Jeunet
Tags – Aliens

This fourth Alien movie takes place many years after the last one, and revealing anymore would spoil the ending of the third movie. I actually consider this one to be kind of opposite of Alien 3 in terms of storytelling. I really liked the fast pace of the first two-thirds of the movie, but the latter act was really hokey. This one has some great performances, but for the first time in the series, it also has some fairly bad ones. There's also a lot of bad dialogue here, and I said earlier, the story really gets lame toward the end. The direction is great though, persevering even through that rough final third. This movie definitely has the weakest story of the bunch, but it's still pretty damn entertaining and I can say with great confidence that I have enjoyed every movie in this franchise, and that's not a common thing to be able to say.

3.5/5

Aliens
Year – 1986
Director – James Cameron
Tags – Aliens

This sequel takes place 57 years after the original with a group of space marines going to the planet of the original alien sighting. This movie is a perfect example of how to make a sequel, and the formula created really works but for some reason it has never really been duplicated. This movie keeps great continuity but makes a movie that is incredibly different from the original, which is very refreshing considering that so many sequels tend to just reuse the formulas of their predecessors. The direction and acting are just as good as the original, which only helps it gain that legendary perfect sequel status. The FX work is once again monumental, and now that we are dealing with aliens instead of just one alien, it adds a whole new level to the terror. There's a constant debate as to which movie is better, this one or the original, and I guess it just really depends on your preference of movie style. If you prefer suspense, go with the original, if you prefer action, go with this one. I'll take the original personally, but isn't it nice to be able to debate on which two movies of a franchise are more perfect?

5/5

Aliens vs. Predator
Year – 2004
Director – Paul W.S. Anderson
Tags – Aliens

During an archaeological expedition to an island in the Antarctic Ocean, a group of scientists get caught up in a battle between two alien species. Aliens AND Predator together? This is going to be awesome right? Nope. The first big mistake is that the lead character isn't very likeable, and played by a bad actress. The rest of the acting is a mixed bag, but none of it is what I would call great. The CGI looks fairly bad most of the time too. When the battles between the Aliens and Predators happen, they're pretty undramatic and not well choreographed. The movie moves along decent enough but the story is just pretty crappy. This movie should have been epic but the script made sure that it wouldn't be. Overall I still found this movie to be watchable, but it's just much dumber than it should have been.

2.5/5

Aliens vs. Predator Requiem
Year – 2007
Director – Colin Strause, Greg Strause
Tags – Aliens

This movie takes place immediately after the first one. The original should have been much better than it was, just look at the movies it was based on. So after it came out and people said it was crap, they only had to fix a few things to make this one awesome. So why in the hell is this movie such a steaming pile and manages to be worse than the original. Well, first off the acting is still pretty bad. Second, the direction is much worse. Third, the story is even worse still. Need I go on? Ok, the CGI is awful, and even though they amped up the gore considerably, most of it is that same awful CGI. This is just an ugly movie that's boring, stupid and even worse than the original, if they do a third, they better spend some money to get competent people involved because this is pretty ridiculous.

1.5/5

All Soul's Day: Dia de los Muertos
Year – 2005
Director – Jeremy Kasten
Tags – Zombies

On the day of the dead, the past residents of a Mexican town rise up, seeking vengeance for being wronged in the past and now some people passing through are caught up in the zombie nightmare. This movie is so terrible, I actually sat in disbelief and wondered how anyone could think was good enough to release. The story is horrendous, and the way the movie unfolds is awful. If you ran into a funeral procession, and the people carrying the coffin dropped it, and then a live, nude woman with her tongue cut out fell out of the coffin, would you shrug your shoulders and walk across the street to go stay in the local hotel? Ridiculous. The direction is just as bad. Poor pacing, bad acting, lame zombies, precious little gore. This is by far one of the worst zombie movies ever made, but sadly enough not the worst. Although it does come close.

1/5

Alone in the Dark
Year – 2005
Director – Uwe Boll
Tags – Monsters

This movie follows a paranormal detective who slowly unravels the mystery behind an ancient civilization and what it has to do the presence of some strange monsters today. This movie baffles me. How could anyone think this was worthy enough to be made, let alone given a theatrical run? First off, the acting is terrible and everyone is miscast. For example, Tara Reid as a scientist? She can't even pronounce Newfoundland properly! The movie is incredibly slow and boring as well, which is never good, obviously. The FX work is garbage, especially the CGI. The monsters look like crap not only because they are CGI, but because their design is just boring and uninspired. The costume choices also made me laugh because the bullet proof vest had muscles on them. Why didn't they just put nipples on them too?! The story is the only mildly interesting thing about this movie, but it is based on a video game so I can't really give anyone involved in the movie any credit. This is terrible and it's just a shame that money goes to a movie like this instead of financing half a dozen smaller budget genre movies that would obviously be better than this. Well, they wouldn't have to try hard to be better anyway.

1/5

Alone With Her
Year – 2006
Director – Eric Nicholas
Tags – Suspense

Shown from the perspective of hidden cameras, Alone With Her is the tale of a voyeur and the young woman he has chosen to stalk. In this electronic age, it has become even easier for stalkers to spy on their victims, and voyeurism is at a definite all time high. Showing the story from the perspective of the multiple video cameras the stalker has placed in his victim's apartment is chancy, but actually works perfectly. He watched her constantly and uses everything he learns about her to weasel his way into her life. The acting is perfectly natural in this movie, which lends a ton of believability to what's going on, and that's exactly what is needed to make it work. I also have to commend the ending because it is an unexpected and welcome change from the norm. I always appreciate a movie more when it takes chances instead of following the tried and true formula, and this one does it on several levels and still manages not to disappoint. Truly one of the most poignant stalker films ever made. Unparalleled realism.

4.5/5

Along Came a Spider
Year – 2001
Director – Lee Tamahori
Tags – Suspense

This is not a direct sequel to Kiss the Girls, rather it is a new story using some of the same characters. Here a senator's daughter is kidnapped not for ransom, but for fame, and now it's up to a damaged cop to try and figure out how to save her from a man who wants to play a dangerous cat and mouse game. This movie is good, but everything about it is just not as good as Kiss the Girls. Maybe I just preferred the subject matter in that movie more but the story here is fairly average, and while the acting and direction give it more life, it still only barely holds up. A slightly above average tale of suspense is what is delivered here, and while I wasn't even close to loving it, I still found some enjoyment in it, which is good.

3/5

Alphabet Killer, The
Year – 2008
Director – Rob Schmidt
Tags – Serial Killer

This movie is loosely based on a serial killer in Rochester, New York who would kill young girls who had the same first initial in their name as the last initial. When a crime has never been solved, and you make a movie about it, it opens up a lot of ways that you can tell the story. This is an interesting movie that quite frankly just comes up short. The acting is pretty good all around, and even features a few genre vets. The direction is good as well, with some fairly consistent pacing and good shot structure. The identity of the killer is much too obvious and when the reveal came along, it garnered only a shrug from me. The made-up story inside the real story isn't that great, focusing on a troubled detective who really isn't that likeable. This is a good movie but there are much more entertaining serial killer flicks to watch.

3/5

Altered

Year – 2006
Director – Eduardo Sanchez
Tags – Aliens

A group of men capture an alien and bring it back to a mutual friend's house. As the night goes on as they try to keep the alien captive while it tries its best to escape. The high point of this movie is the great make-up and practical FX work, the alien looks pretty awesome and there are some other noteworthy FX as well. Unfortunately that's about it. The acting is decent, but the story is just plain uninteresting. Most of movie is uneventful and we aren't even treated to some sort of tension or atmospheric tone, it's just uneventful. It's essentially the equivalent of watching two people sit in a room and talk about dust bunnies. And since nothing much happens during the movie, it's slow and ultimately boring. I wish I had more good things to say about it, but I can't think of any, which sucks because I did feel that this movie had the potential to do more with its material.

2/5

Altered States
Year – 1980
Director – Ken Russell
Tags – Suspense

A doctor begins tests involving psychotropic drugs and sensory deprivation, using himself as the subject. But when he finds himself beginning to change physically, he must question if it is actually happening, or is it all in his head? This movie, even by today's standards, has some impressive visual FX. They're just so out there and dreamlike that you can't help but admire the thought that went into those sequences. Outside of these visions however, the movie can be fairly dull. Perhaps it would appeal to those in the scientific community more, but for me, the movie did get a bit boring on more than one occasion. While I do think that parts of the story and the pacing did hold this movie back from greatness, the excellent acting, FX and everything else overall make this a pretty damn good movie. It feels like a drug induced nightmare at times, and I can really appreciate that.

3.5/5

American Crime, An
Year – 2007
Director – Tommy O'Haver
Tags – Suspense

This movie tells the true story of woman who tortured a young girl in her basement with the help of her children and other children from the neighborhood. So this movie and The Girl Next Door came out around the same time and both deal with the same event, but The Girl Next Door is actually based on a book by Jack Ketchum which was based on the same event and this one is based more on the crime itself. Ok, just wanted to clear everything up. It's very clear that the people behind this movie were really afraid of this story because practically nothing is shown, and I'm sorry but if you're going to cover such a disturbing crime, you need to make a disturbing movie. This movie not only did not show the torture but left the rape aspect of the story completely out, which left me feeling pretty indifferent. The movie failed to elicit any emotion from me because it was just very watered down. The acting and direction were very good, but the story lacked the substance to make me feel any hatred for the woman or pity for the child, and with this kind of crime, you are supposed to feel all that and more. Still a very good movie, but check out The Girl Next Door instead, as I feel they handled the same material much better.

3.5/5

American Haunting, An
Year – 2005
Director – Courtney Solomon
Tags – Ghosts

A landowner is cursed by his neighbor, a supposed witch, which he believed to be nonsense until his daughter begins to be attacked by unseen spectral forces on a nightly basis. This movie is perfect… perfect as a cure for insomnia. This movie is so completely boring and not scary, it's ridiculous. I believe that ghost movies have the potential to scare more than any other sub genre of horror and when a movie completely misses that mark by a mile, it is felt much harsher than in other sub genres of horror. The acting is good but restrained, most likely due to a lack of good material in this supposed true story. Just because something really happened or an amalgamation of things happened doesn't mean it's a good fit for a movie, and An American Haunting is proof positive of that. This movie is just uninteresting and its only use is to put you to sleep faster than a plate of turkey and a glass of warm milk.

1.5/5

American Psycho
Year – 2000
Director – Mary Harron
Tags – Serial Killer (Fictional)

Set in 1987, this movie follows an investment banker in New York City who tries to hide his psychotic alter ego from his coworkers and friends. But as he delves deeper into his violent and sexual fantasies, he begins to lose control. This movie is a masterwork of fiction, plain and simple. I also believe that since the screenplay was written by women, and directed by one, that it lends a certain amount of elegance to the movie that men really can not create. And that elegant nature matched with the complete brutality and depraved actions of the main character really make for a unique movie. The acting is wonderful and Christian Bale puts on a wonderfully brilliant performance as the psychotic killer. Beside the fact that the movie has a lovely tone to it, it also happens to be immaculately paced and features not only some graphic violence, but hinted violence that really allows the imagination to flourish. This is a perfect movie, plain and simple.

5/5

American Psycho 2: All American Girl
Year – 2002
Director – Morgan J. Freeman
Tags – Serial Killer (Fictional)

The relationship to the first movie is very, very miniscule and was most likely tacked on so they could call this a sequel for name recognition. Here a young woman is trying to get a TA job at her college and begins to kill off the competition. I actually don't consider this to be a bad movie; I just really hate the name. If this had been a stand alone movie I would have more respect for it. The story isn't bad, just tired and done to death in some form or another. The acting is a mixed bag of good and bad and direction is decent. This is just an average movie that induces yawns over chills but is still perfectly watchable.

2.5/5

American Werewolf in London, An
Year – 1981
Director – John Landis
Tags – Werewolves

Two friends backpacking through Europe find themselves alone in the wilderness during a full moon and are promptly attacked by a werewolf. One dies and the other survives, only to become infected with lycanthropy himself. When his dead friend appears to him, urging him to kill himself, he thinks himself mad, until he starts to change. Often billed as a horror/comedy, An American Werewolf in London really isn't. It does have comedic moments, but they are more subtle and sometimes morbid, ensuring that not everyone will "get it". I like that about the movie, and it does work most of the time. Of course I have to talk about the transformation since it is regarded as one of the best, if not the best of all time. The make-up won an Oscar for crying out loud, one of the few horror movies to possess one, so you know it has to be good. Everything about this movie is great, really no complaints, from the acting to the direction and everything in between. This is a must watch for horror and werewolf fans.

4.5/5

American Werewolf in Paris, An
Year – 1997
Director – Anthony Waller
Tags – Werewolves

This isn't exactly a remake or even a sequel of An American Werewolf in London as it's just kind of set in the same universe. Here a man rescues a woman as she is about to kill herself, and ends up getting mixed up in her world of werewolves. So the wonderful werewolf FX from London are replaced here by awful CGI, and all the werewolves look exactly the same, there is just no character to any of them. The story is ok, the acting is fairly good, but the whole movie is just mundane, as if there was no real effort put into it. I think the people behind this movie were just hoping to bank on a similar name to make a couple of bucks. Not all bad, but a below average attempt.

2/5

Amusement
Year – 2009
Director – John Simpson
Tags – Slasher / Survival

A man stalks three young women whom he has had a grudge against since childhood. You know, when a movie sits on a production company's shelf for a long time it can only mean one of two things. It's either misunderstood or it just plain sucks, and Amusement falls under the latter category for sure. The story is set up much like an anthology with a different section for each woman, and that only adds to the many issues with the direction and pacing. The acting isn't very good either, not terrible, but far from being good. The FX are ok, there is some decent gore but it's CGI for the most part, and not very good looking. This movie is slow and the story is severely lacking, and there are only a couple of good points that keep it from being horrible, so I definitely do not recommend this movie. It's the kind of slasher movie that make people look down upon slasher movies.

1.5/5

Anaconda
Year – 1997
Director – Luis Llosa
Tags – Animals

A documentary group gets hijacked along the Amazon by a hunter who is trying to catch a massive anaconda alive. But the anaconda has other ideas, including making everyone lunch. This movie is as crappy as it is good. That statement doesn't make sense? Neither does casting non-actors like Ice Cube and Jennifer Lopez in any movie, even a B movie like this. Fortunately the rest of the cast does a good job in making the silly plot acceptable. The movie may be dumb, but it's dumb fun and well paced. The direction is fine and the FX are pretty laughable, but that just adds to the B movie charm. It's pretty funny at times, especially watching Lopez bumble through the movie and Ice Cube trying to be a badass with his tiny little knife, so the unintentional humor makes it passable in my book.

2.5/5

*Anaconda 2 can be found under Anacondas: The Hunt for the Blood Orchid.

Anaconda 3: The Offspring
Year – 2008
Director – Don E. FauntLeRoy
Tags – Animals

Two genetically enhanced anacondas have escaped from the research lab where they were housed and now it's up to a tracking team and a poacher to recover them. I knew this movie was going to be bad but I didn't think it could possibly suck this hard. The CGI is horrendous and it's used constantly in the movie, including during kills which just look terrible. Most of the acting is also pretty bad and the lead actress is especially horrible. Her line delivery is off and she has trouble pronouncing words, which was really flabbergasting since they allowed these errors to be in the movie. I guess those were her best takes. The story is also garbage and the direction is slow and boring. About the only good thing in this movie is the gory aftermath of the kills and Hasslehoff's sense of humor. Everything else about this movie is worthless.

1/5

Anacondas: The Hunt for the Blood Orchid
Year – 2004
Director – Dwight H. Little
Tags – Animals

In this name only sequel to Anaconda we find a group of scientists traveling deep into anaconda territory to try and find a rare flower that could be the key to a medical miracle and big money for all involved. This movie is only slightly better than the last one. The story is different, which is commendable because the last thing anyone wants is a complete rehash of the last movie. But even with a different story, it still kind of plays out the same and everything I liked and disliked about the first one is here. Some crappy actors, some good direction but a paper thin story. If you liked the last one you'll probably like this, and vice versa. It's different while still being more of the same, go figure.

2.5/5

Anatomy (Anatomie)
Year – 2000
Director – Stefan Ruzowitsky
Tags – Slasher / Survival

A medical student learns that the school she is attending houses an Antihippocratic society whose sole purpose in the field of medicine is to advance the research of medicinal science by any means necessary, even if it means the murder of fellow students. I really enjoyed this German horror flick because it went about things differently than most slasher flicks. Instead of just brutalizing people, the kills here are slow and torturous, requiring a lot of finesse. The story is nice and the acting and direction are very good. The main point of interest is in the FX work, which looked great during the "surgeries", but I don't think they employed it enough and could have definitely shown more. This is quite simply a very good movie and I have nothing bad to say about it, I just wish they had done more in places.

3.5/5

Anatomy 2 (Anatomie 2)
Year – 2003
Director – Stefan Ruzowitsky
Tags – Suspense

Now this is how you make a sequel. This movie continues on a couple of years after the original, and while related to the first, the story is vastly different. Here, instead of the Antihippocratics killing others in the name of advancing medical science, they experiment on each other with synthetic muscles, but there is murder and drug use behind it all and one young intern is caught up in the middle. The story is great, and while the first one was pretty much a slasher movie done up to medical standards, this is much more based in the realm of suspense. The acting and direction are very good, and the movie flows very nicely. I was fascinated by where the story went and it was easy for me to become engrossed by it. I actually like this one a little better than the original, but for different reasons.

3.5/5

Angel Heart
Year – 1987
Director – Alan Parker
Tags – Suspense

A detective is hired by a mysterious man to try and track down another man with whom he has a contract with. But the deeper he looks for the man, the more people start dying and strange happenings occur. I love it when classic noir is mixed with supernatural horror and this is a prime example of a successful blending of the genres. Much more than a suspense movie, Angel Heart is really a one of a kind supernatural, psychological horror movie with some terrific acting and direction. The story is great, and as it goes on, you can pretty clearly see who's who and what's really going on, but that's not to its detriment in the least. I love this movie for all its originality and plot devices, and while I don't feel it's perfect, it's still a damn fine experience.

4/5

Apocalypse and the Beauty Queen

Year – 2005
Director – Thomas Smugala
Tags – Suspense

Set in a post apocalyptic world dominated by cruel leaders and food whores, this movie focuses on a former beauty queen who runs her province with kindness on the outside, but unbeknownst to her subjects, she has young woman kidnapped for her so she can use their blood to keep herself beautiful. An apocalyptic Elizabeth Bathory tale? Sign me up! It's just too bad the movie was a nearly complete failure in every way it could be. Gunnar Hansen is the only actor here and his role is pretty small, so you'll have to put up with a lot of bad acting if you watch this. The direction is very slow at times and then painfully slow at others, making for a very dull experience. The plot is good but the story doesn't match up and a professional writer should have been hired to pen this. This movie is an unfortunate waste of a good idea and ends up being pretty bad in the end.

1.5/5

April Fool's Day
Year – 1986
Director – Fred Walton
Tags – Slasher / Survival

A group of rich kids take a ferry to the island home of one of their other rich friends and are then promptly stalked by a killer. It's obvious that the focal point for this movie was it's ending, and everything else came after the fact. The ending is something that has been debated by horror fans since the movie's release. I liked it personally, I felt it was a good twist and something different. The kills are kind of bland, but not bad. The acting is fairly good, and the direction is about the same. In truth this is just a throwaway slasher that's claim to fame is its ending and nothing more. It isn't a bad movie, it's just standard stuff that's only mildly different from everything else that came before it.

3/5

April Fool's Day [Remake]
Year – 2008
Director – Mitchell Altieri, Phil Flores
Tags – Slasher / Survival

The plot of this remake is a little bit different from the original. In this one, a group of kids are being stalked one year after the accidental death of a young girl while at their party. The original movie is hardly a great slasher, so this had the potential to be better, so why, oh why, is it so awful? First off, instead of sticking true to the original story, it goes off and pretty much steals the plot from I Know What You Did Last Summer. Why anyone would steal the plot from that movie I'll never know, there are far better plots to rip off if you feel you must do that. Second, the actors are all pretty much crap and to top things off, this movie has no good kills or blood. Add terrible pacing and a bad story and you have this mess. There is extremely little to enjoy in this horrible knock off and it makes the original look like one of the greatest movies ever filmed. This is definitely one to avoid.

1/5

Arachnophobia
Year – 1990
Director – Frank Marshall
Tags – Animals

On a South American expedition, a photographer gets bitten by a deadly spider and dies, with the spider hitching a ride in his coffin to the US where it begins to breed in a small town and kill the citizens. I've always enjoyed the horror movies with small villains. You can always see the big monsters and killers coming, but a tiny spider with a deadly bite? You'll never see it coming, you're just dead, and that is a far more horrifying thought than any slasher or fanged beast. This movie plays out nicely, but you do have to suspend disbelief on more than one occasion to believe things are happening as they are in the movie. There is also great direction and some very good acting, which only aids the story. The spiders are pretty cool looking, especially the original ones found in the jungle. I know that people who don't like spiders just hate this movie, so you should know that ahead of time because there are plenty of creepy spider moments. This is a very entertaining flick even if it is pretty unbelievable at times. Good stuff.

3.5/5

Arcade
Year – 1993
Director – Albert Pyun
Tags – Mechanical

A new virtual reality arcade game is killing off children and it's up to two friends to kill the heart that runs the machine before it can kill again. This is just good 'ol B-movie fun right here, but with a twist, there's some actual good actors in the movie who would go on to bigger and better things. The story is pretty weak but still fun and the direction is actually pretty good, not a whole lot of slow points. The FX are pretty bad, like Lawnmower Man bad, but we are talking about a nineties video game world. One thing that I've always found funny about Arcade is that the video game wouldn't even work as a video game and the way you play it just makes no sense. Arcade is just dumb fun, nothing brilliant or mind blowing here, but a good time nonetheless. I'm sure I'll be the minority in my viewpoint however.

3/5

Army of Darkness
Year – 1992

Director – Sam Raimi
Tags – Zombies, Demonic Possession

This movie picks up directly after Evil Dead 2, but a little bit different from how that movie ended. The slapstick factor has been upped greatly from the last two movies but it actually works out very well, making this over the top gorefest into a hilarious slice of comedy as well. The FX work is a mix of awesome stuff and absolute cheese, but the cheese definitely goes with the overall theme of the movie. The acting is the same here as in past installments, but maybe a bit more dramatic for extra effect as this movie is much larger in scale than the previous ones. The camera work is pretty great and the harsh zooming adds even more drama. It's rare to see a franchise be so consistently good, but it happened here, three Evil Dead movies, three undeniable classics. This trilogy is a must own for any fan of horror.

4.5/5

Arrival, The
Year – 1996
Director – David Twohy
Tags – Aliens

An astronomer discovers a signal of alien origin but gets shut down every time he tries to tell someone about it. Not being able to let it go, he investigates further only to discover that the signal is not in outer space, but from Earth. Part alien movie, part suspense thriller, this had a lot going for it but ended up becoming an overly long and extremely uneven affair. I like the story, but only at times. I like the direction, but only at times. I like the acting, well, you get the idea. I can not fathom why this movie was two hours long because it would have been much smoother with at least half an hour trimmed off. Still, it has its moments and isn't all bad, and I did like the mix of aliens and suspense, I just wish it had reached its full potential.

2.5/5

Arrival II, The (The Second Arrival)
Year – 1998
Director – Kevin Tenney
Tags – Aliens

This movie takes place not too long after the first, but with a different set of characters. The first movie was a passable attempt at making a suspenseful alien film and probably made a couple of bucks at the box office, hence the sequel. But the sequel is nothing but bad. The acting is second rate and the direction is pretty bad too, which is surprising because Tenney has made some good movies in the past. The FX are even worse than those in the first and the story is just as sloppy as a mindless rush job can get. This movie is proof positive that not every movie needs a sequel, in fact, most don't. But as long as studios exist, they always make a sequel to any movie that makes any money for them, whether it's good or not.

1/5

Audition (Odishon)
Year – 1999
Director – Takashi Miike
Tags – Suspense

A lonely man is looking to get remarried years after his wife dies. He holds an audition for a movie in order to meet women and finds one that he could see himself being with. But the more he finds out about her, the more he realizes that she isn't entirely truthful and may not be what she seems. This movie goes beyond your normal tale of obsession, so far beyond in fact, it seems as though you're in an alternate reality, and that's why I like it so much. The movie can be a little slow at times, but that time is used for some masterful character development. I think what sets this apart from similar tales, besides the intense third act, is that the guy who is the object of obsession isn't a piece of shit. Most of time the man is unfaithful or much worse and you feel like he has something coming to him, here this guy just wants to find love again and when things start to happen to him, you really feel bad for him. This is a great movie that chugs along slowly but pays off in spades. Definitely a must see at least once.

4/5

Automaton Transfusion
Year – 2006
Director – Steven C. Miller
Tags – Zombies

Three teens find their town overrun by zombies as they fight their way tooth and nail to try and find safety. This movie is very low budget but the FX work is nice, the acting is good, the story is strong and the zombies look good… and I hate this movie. Why you ask? It had so much going for it, could have been one of the greatest low budget zombie movies ever, but the direction and camerawork are some of the worst I have ever seen. Every damn scene is plagued by shaky cam. Whoever thought this was a good idea (I'm guessing the director), needs to have some sense knocked into them. The camera was moving up and down violently for about half the movie, and for the other half it was still pretty jittery. This movie makes The Blair Witch Project look steady. I love what the movie could have been and I hate the end product. Words of wisdom to the director, next time you make a movie, whether it be sequel to this turd or otherwise, put the damn camera on a tripod or something. A huge disappointment.

2/5

Autopsy

Year – 2008
Director – Adam Gierasch
Tags – Slasher / Survival

Five people get into a bad car accident and are picked up by an ambulance and taken to a nearby hospital. What they don't know is that the hospital staff is not there to help them, but to kill them. This has the feel of your typical slasher movie but with a flair all its own. There are some excellent death sequences and lots of blood mixed with some strange bedside manner that I won't go into and instead let you see for yourself. The characters aren't that good though, the car crash victims are all undeveloped and I really didn't care if they lived or died. The hospital staff however was a different story, they each had their own unique personality and I think that may be attributed to the fact that they were played by a higher class of actors. The pacing could have used a little bit more tightening but overall it was pretty solid. In the end the flaws didn't kill the movie for me and this is a pretty damn good slasher with loads of gore and cool visuals.

3.5/5

Awake
Year – 2007
Director – Joby Harold
Tags – Suspense

A wealthy young man goes in for heart surgery and ends up being awake after being administered anesthesia. It's only then that he finds out that his doctors plan to kill him during surgery for money. Now he is paralyzed and at the mercy of his killers. I can pretty much figure out just how the idea came about for this movie. Someone read an article about anesthetic awareness and decided that would make a good movie. And obviously no thought was put into it afterward. The second rate script and director took what was only a mildly interesting idea to begin with and turned it into an absolutely boring, nearly worthless movie. The acting was dull and lacking any kind of passion whatsoever, and when the twist in the storyline came about, I couldn't help but laugh because you could see it coming practically from the opening credits. A word to the wise for whoever came up with this idea, next time just flush the toilet and forget about it.

1/5

Awaken the Dead
Year – 2007
Director – Jeff Brookshire
Tags – Zombies

A priest with a sordid past gets caught up in a world that has been suddenly overtaken by zombies. Now he tries to find his friend who would stand the best chance of surviving all this while simultaneously trying to figure out who the man is who seems to be able to walk among the dead. This is a surprisingly good microbudget zombie flick. It has an actual story attached to it, which is a nice change from the usual zero character development, zombies rise, zombies kill type of movie. It's still not the best, but pretty good. The acting isn't too bad either. Well, some is real bad but there are a few people that put on good performances. The FX are pretty good too as the zombies look interesting and there's a fair amount of gore. The direction isn't bad and I like the graininess of the movie, the pacing is fair. If you can get past the budget shortcomings, you might just find a good zombie movie here, I did.

3/5

Baby's Room, The (La Habitacion del Nino)
Year – 2006
Director – Alex de la Iglesia
Tags – Ghosts

This is part of the DVD box set "6 Films to Keep You Awake". A young couple moves into a new house with their baby and begin experiencing some odd phenomenon. The baby monitor reveals strange voices and soon the husband becomes obsessed with discovering just who or what is in the baby's room. This is a great movie with a very unique and well done twist on your typical ghost story. The acting is great and the direction is just as good. I love the story and have found it difficult to find another one that is as competent. Ghost stories are a dime a dozen anymore, so it's always nice to find one that actually makes strides to not only do something different but do it well.

4/5

Backwoods, The (Bosque de Sombras)
Year – 2006
Director – Koldo Serra
Tags – Suspense

Set in 1970's Spain, two couples go on holiday deep in the woods. During a hunting trip, the two men find a mutant girl locked in an old house, and take her back to their cabin. But when the locals find out she's gone, they come looking for her armed with shotguns. The whole backwoods thing has been done multiple times but never really with a mature group of people and actors of this caliber, unless you count Deliverance, but there were no women in that one. The acting is really great and the backwoods themselves are beautiful and gloomy all at the same time. It's just too bad the story isn't up to snuff. It seems like a rush job because there isn't a whole lot of cohesive or interesting material on display. When the movie reaches its climax it's really not that good because at this point I don't care very much. The direction is decent but the lack of material does create some pacing issues. I wish I had more to say in the movie's defense because it does have a great set-up but fails to execute.

3/5

Bacterium

Year – 2006
Director – Brett Piper
Tags – Biological

Some friends playing paintball happen upon a house that has a secret lab in it, a lab that contains a deadly organism that's not only growing, it's multiplying. This is another one of those low budget movies that suffers from too much ambition for such a tiny budget. The CGI is horrible and used way too much. Fortunately the practical FX almost balance it out because these slimy organisms they created do look pretty damn good. The acting is fairly bad but some is passable, par for the course I suppose. The direction and story are ok but there is definitely room for improvement. This is an average movie that probably would have been pretty good if the filmmakers had some money, so I look forward to seeing something else from the director, I just hope he recognizes his budget better and rolls with it.

2.5/5

Bad Channels

Year – 1992
Director – Ted Nicolaou
Tags – Aliens

A UFO heads to Earth and hijacks a radio station in order to kidnap women for their own nefarious uses. And how will they do it? With Rock N' Roll of course! This movie is a lot like The Howling II in that it's so bad it's almost passable. This uber-cheesy alien movie from Full Moon is bad in every way it could be but it's also pretty hilarious at times. The aliens look so lame that they made me laugh and the segments where the women are kidnapped play out like cheap music videos. A band will play a song and the woman will dance around, then poof, she's gone and under the alien's control. What? Sure, this is a movie to mock, but sometimes that can be more fun than the movie itself. As cheesy as alien movies can get.

2/5

Bad Dreams

Year – 1988
Director – Andrew Fleming
Tags – Slasher / Survival

After a cult had committed mass suicide by setting their home ablaze, the sole survivor falls into a coma for thirteen years. She awakens in a mental hospital and soon believes that the cult leader has returned and is after her. The staff automatically dismisses her until people start dying. It initially seemed as if this movie would be a rip-off of A Nightmare on Elm Street, what with the burned up dead guy being the villain, and the fact the movie is called Bad Dreams. But the plot is much different and when the kills happen, it happens when the victim is awake. And speaking of kills, they do look pretty good here with lots of blood to go around. And while I stated that the plot is different, maybe it shouldn't have been because the story isn't that great, except for that twist towards the end, which was nice. The acting is ok as there are a handful of genre actors in the movie. The direction is pretty damn slow, and boy did I feel it. This movie is decent and I enjoyed it for the most part. I garnered some entertainment value out of it, which is a success in my book, even if it isn't a big one.

2.5/5

Bad Moon
Year – 1996
Director – Eric Red
Tags – Werewolves

A man gets attacked by a werewolf and survives, thus becoming infected with the werewolf curse. Now he struggles to restrain himself from killing his sister and her child. As far as werewolf movies go, this one is pretty standard, offering little in the way of ingenuity, but definitely having entertainment value. I really like the dog angle of the movie, because the dog is the real star of the movie. The dog knows what the man is and strives for nothing but the defense of his owners. It's a nice look at how great dogs can be. The rest of the acting is ok but nothing special. The direction is straightforward and the pacing is good, so I have no complaints there. The transformation FX are pretty lame but the end result is one very cool looking werewolf. The story is nothing new and it feels like several other movies that came before it which makes this movie pretty forgettable. There's nothing really bad about this flick, it just doesn't have the power to leave any kind of lasting impression.

2.5/5

Bad Reputation
Year – 2005
Director – Jim Hemphill
Tags – Suspense

A young girl is an outcast at her high school, sticking pretty much to herself until she is invited to a party by a popular boy in school. Once there she is slipped a ruffie and gang raped by some of the boys at the party. To make matters worse, the girlfriends of the boys duct tape her to a tree and then spread rumors about her being a slut. After trying to seek justice but not getting any help, she takes matters into her own hands. This microbudget film is really impressive. The revenge plot has been done before, but the way this movie allows it to unfold is really something special. The rape scene is really long and graphic, which allows you the time to truly hate the boys, and then the humiliation handed down by the girls afterward really just adds insult to injury and makes you hate the people even more. When the victim starts getting her revenge, it feels so good you just want to cheer. Angelique Hennessy does an incredible job as both the sweet victim and then finally the cold hearted killer. The director / writer will be a force to be reckoned with one day, he just needs a budget and a decent FX department. Hemphill has made a compelling and unflinching tale of the cruelty that not only shows talent, but knowledge on how to make people care about fictional characters, which is very difficult to do. This movie doesn't pull any punches, the flaws are minor and mostly budget related, and this is a just a great movie.

4/5

Bad Seed, The
Year – 1956
Director – Mervyn LeRoy
Tags – Suspense

A woman has growing suspicions that her adolescent daughter may not be the sweet and kind girl she seems to be and instead may be a cold hearted killer. Now she is torn between protecting her daughter and exposing her for what she is. This is a pretty remarkable movie, especially for the time period. The acting here is nothing short of amazing, especially by Patty McCormack, who put on easily one of the best performances as a child ever. I really liked the story as well, as you could fully see just how heart wrenching it was for the mother to be put into such a situation. And it all culminated into a very memorable plot twist and finally, a great ending. I did think the movie was a bit long though and it really hurt the pacing in some places. Still, this is an awesome blast form the past and yet another reason to sleep with one eye open if you have a child.

4/5

Badlands
Year – 1973
Director – Terrence Malcik
Tags – Serial Killer (Fictional)

This is a dramatization of the Charles Starkweather murders where a young man and his teenage girlfriend go on a cross state killing spree. I really liked this movie and even though it is not a true account of the Starkweather murders per se, it is still the best movie about them. The very dark drama that unfolds whilst all of these murders are taking place is remarkable. I could hardly imagine growing up in such an environment and being in love with a killer at such a young age. The acting is remarkable and the direction is very good with only a few slow points, but even those don't drag too badly. The demeanor of the killer is really very different from anything else I've seen, as he thought of everything as a sort of adventure and nothing more. Killing was natural and in the face of the law and an inevitable execution, he was in good cheer, like he was some sort of celebrity. This is a fascinating movie of almost true crime and if you're a follower of serial killers, this is a must have for your collection.

Basic Instinct
Year – 1992
Director – Paul Verhoeven
Tags – Serial Killer (Fictional)

A retired rock star is brutally murdered with an ice pick, and the police believe it was done by his girlfriend, a brilliant writer, who plays a dangerous game with the lead detective. This is just a very well crafted thriller. The story is very tight and well done, the characters are fleshed out nicely, and it's heavily erotic, which works perfectly in the context of the film. I actually saw this in the theatre when I was eleven, and I found it to be competent then, now that I can fully grasp everything that's happening, I found even more enjoyment, kind of the same thing that happened with The Silence of the Lambs. The acting is superb, especially by Sharon Stone, and the direction is very well paced. This movie manages to be suspenseful, bloody, thought-provoking and sexual all at the same time, and that's the recipe for a classic movie.

4.5/5

Basic Instinct 2
Year – 2006
Director – Michael Caton-Jones
Tags – Serial Killer (Fictional)

This movie takes place years after the original. Making this movie seemed like a pretty pointless thing to do, especially so many years after the original, and unfortunately I was proved right, this movie is just pointless. The script must have been written with crayon, complete with backwards Rs for effect, because it really is that childish and stupid. It tries to copy the original on just about every level, but seems to fail at every corner. Even a straight carbon copy could be more compelling than this. The acting is ok, but with transparent characters and shoddy design, there's not much that can be done. The direction is also very poor, as the movie is incredibly slow and uneventful. There is very little to enjoy here, so just skip it altogether.

1.5/5

Bats
Year – 1999
Director – Louis Morneau
Tags – Animals

Genetically enhanced bats escape from the research lab they are housed in and compile a new roost in the southwest, attacking and devouring humans at night. Now it's up to a bat expert and the local sheriff to put a stop to them. So the plot is derivative of multiple killer animal movies that came before it, only now we have bats, which has the potential to be cool, but it's not. The acting is decent, but I hated the comic relief character. The actor who played him was fine, but the dialogue he had to spew out was horrendous. The direction isn't too bad as the movie moves along nicely with only a few hiccups. The FX though, are all pretty bad. The CGI bat sequences are terrible, and even the practical bats look like garbage, like tiny little rubber gargoyles. There were some cool sets though, like the roost itself and the river of guano. It's not a terrible movie, in fact I found it to be quite average, but bats are awesome creatures and they deserve something better than this.

2.5/5

Bats: Human Harvest
Year – 2007
Director – Jamie Dixon
Tags – Animals

I'm not sure if this was meant to be a sequel to Bats, since it has no relation to that movie other than a name. Here we find a group of soldiers traveling to Russia and coming across a group of genetically engineered bats bred to be weapons. Blah, blah, blah, whatever. This movie may just singlehandedly have the worst CGI I have ever seen, which is an accomplishment since I have seen a lot of bargain basement FX. The bats just look like little black blobs floating around on the screen, and the rendered environments are just ungodly bad. And speaking of ungodly bad, let me tell you about the acting, direction and story, or better yet, I won't. There is nothing to enjoy here, the entire movie is a festering sore and a blight upon the world.

0.5/5

Bay Cove (Bay Coven)
Year – 1987
Director – Carl Schenkel
Tags – Cults

A couple buy a house on a remote island and discover that the people on the island are all part of a secret coven that delves into witchcraft. I was surprised that I enjoyed this movie as much as I did because to be honest it just didn't seem that interesting. But fortunately the story was pretty strong and aided by some well done direction. The acting was actually a mixed bag despite there being some good actors involved. The movie had some good suspense going for it and I was really digging it because it also got kind of weird at times, which worked. Unfortunately it did get really cheesy toward the end and the acting became pretty hammy. This is good stuff and I enjoyed it regardless of the flaws, hardly the best thing out there but I've seen a whole lot worse.

3/5

Beast, The

Year – 1996
Director – Jeff Bleckner
Tags – Animals

A giant squid is roaming the waters of a small fishing community, and once it has run out of fish to eat, it starts to kill and eat the people who happen into the water. This Peter Benchley novel adaptation plays out way too much like a more popular adaptation, Jaws. It's all here, the marine biologist coming to investigate, locals trying to make money by killing the creature itself, and on and on. Just change out the shark for a squid and the local sheriff with the local fisherman. No, it's not quite that bad, there are some differences but there are enough similar events to let you know how the movie is going to play out before you're done watching the first part. The acting ranges from very good to pretty bad, and the direction is ok, but I think the main problems with the direction stem from the movie being too long and thus, the pacing is damaged. The squid looks pretty cool and I like that they used practical FX most of the time. This is nothing great but it's still pretty fun, flawed but entertaining.

3/5

Beetlejuice
Year – 1988
Director – Tim Burton
Tags – Ghosts

A couple dies and are forced to stay in their home for the duration of their afterlife. The problem is that a new family is moving into their home, a terribly annoying new family and the couple are forced to enlist the aid of a ghost that specializes in exorcizing the living to get them to vacate the house. When Tim Burton handles original material, I think he is at his peak, which is very true with this movie here. It's nice to see a very comical take on how ghosts exist because we usually only see their effects on the living, but what they do when they're not terrorizing humans. The acting is great and the direction is very smooth but it's the visuals that make this movie so appealing for me. There is lots of originality here and a fair amount of humor, which really adds a lot. This is a fun look into seeing how the other half lives… er, dies I guess.

4/5

Behind the Mask: The Rise of Leslie Vernon
Year – 2006
Director – Scott Glosserman
Tags – Slasher / Survival

In a world where Freddy, Jason and the rest actually lived and killed, a documentary team follows a slasher as he prepares for his coming out killing spree. The concept on this movie is great, and it's pulled off the way it should be, very informative with a bit of humor to it. Unfortunately for me, since I know how the stereotypical slasher goes, there were some dull points for me. Despite that this movie is still a winner in my book. The direction is great, the acting believable, and the kills were nothing special, but this wasn't the kind of movie for extravagance. Your long time horror fan may find the material redundant but entertaining, and for those newbies out there, this is a great way to familiarize yourselves with the genre, as it hands out the "rules" and in turn kind of mocks the slasher movies of yesteryear for being so one-dimensional (Which many were). Overall, a great time.

4/5

Believers
Year – 2007
Director – Daniel Myrick
Tags – Cults

Two paramedics attempting to save a man are kidnapped by a religious cult who believes that the end of the world is coming and only if they kill themselves and others will they truly be saved. Awful, just awful. I found myself to be incredibly bored by this movie. The pacing was horrible, the acting very wooden, and the storyline so incredibly predictable it was ridiculous. There was hardly any blood, no inventive kills and one incredibly boring and pointless sex scene. It had a lot of potential to be something interesting, but fell flat on its face, and I can not recommend this movie at all. It was bad, and while not entirely unwatchable, this snore fest nearly put me to sleep. Oh, and you will be able to figure out the ending before you even see the movie, pretty sad.

1.5/5

Below
Year – 2002
Director – David Twohy
Tags – Ghosts

Set during World War II, a US submarine crew picks up survivors from a British hospital boat and soon afterward begin experiencing strange occurrences on board that seem to be tied with their dead captain. I was really looking forward to this because a haunting underwater is a fabulous idea, but I just wasn't impressed by it. Everything was just so middle of the road. But I do have to say that there was nothing really bad about it. The story is good, the acting is good, the direction is good and the FX are good. It all makes for an above average movie, but honestly I think they could have done much more with the idea.

3/5

Beowulf
Year – 2007
Director – Robert Zemeckis

In this legendary tale of dark fantasy a man comes to a foreign kingdom to try and slay a monster that has been terrorizing the king's mead hall. But that is only beginning of Beowulf's grand adventure. Yeah, I know this is more fantasy than horror, but anytime a giant creature breaks into a building crushing people and biting off their heads, I think that automatically moves it into horror territory. I like that they animated this in a way, because a story so grand in scale as this would have to feature heavy CGI usage, so they figured you might as well animate the whole damn thing. And the CGI does look pretty amazing most of the time, but sometimes it gets a little cartoonish. The voice work really gives the movie life, and while the action was pretty much non-stop for the first half of the movie and towards the end, there was a definite lag in the middle and I think a half hour could have easily been trimmed off. Still, with loads of gore and lots of action, it makes for a very entertaining monster movie.

3.5/5

Beowulf & Grendel
Year – 2005
Director – Sturla Gunnarsson
Tags – Monsters

After a king kills a troll but spares his child, that child grows and expends his wrath upon his people. Now Beowulf and his men have come to destroy this vengeance seeking troll, but end up finding out more about Grendel than they were led to believe. I originally read the tale of Beowulf in elementary school and always loved it for all its gore and monsters. And with this adaptation, hardcore fans might be a little miffed about the changes made, but I still liked it. Sure it was a little too blatant in showing that the king was the real monster and I didn't really like that Grendel was so human in appearance, but there is much more good than bad going on here. The movie is just gorgeous, beautifully shot and beautifully situated. The acting is great and I really enjoyed the mix of bloody violence and drama, with a little humor thrown in for good measure. The FX were really good as well. The direction was also good but the pacing was slightly uneven at times, nothing too detrimental though. Despite the changes in the original story (I can not fathom why anyone doesn't just make a true adaptation, the original story is marvelous), this is still a very respectable attempt and I enjoyed it quite a bit.

3.5/5

Beyond, The (Seven Doors of Death)
Year – 1981
Director – Lucio Fulci
Tags – Zombies

Fulci dips into Lovecraft lore for this movie of terror and the unknown. A Louisiana hotel is under new ownership, but what the new owner doesn't realize is that it houses one of the seven gateways to Hell. This is such a surreal experience. If you are not well versed in Lovecraft, or just unfamiliar in how Lovecraftian filmmaking works, then this movie will probably not make much sense to you, so be forewarned. The gore here is just extraordinary. Every death scene is graphic as hell which each death being carefully thought out and performed. I wish more filmmakers would put this much effort into their work. The movie runs smoothly and is well acted to top things off. This is a very different movie and might make some people's heads explode, but the same goes for people reading Lovecraft, it can be difficult to follow for some and for others it may not make any sense at all. But if you can handle a ramshackle story packed to the gills with close up shots of graphic death scenes, then you'll discover one of the best horror movies to ever be released.

4.5/5

Beyond Re-Animator
Year – 2003
Director – Brian Yuzna
Tags – Zombies

Herbert West finds himself arrested after another incident of reanimation, this time a boy's older sister dies and the boy himself gets a hold of the Re-Agent. Fast forward thirteen years and we find West in prison and the boy now resident doctor of the prison. They team together to find a way to perfect reanimation with less than savory results. I like the fact that the bulk of the movie takes place in prison, because that is a great place for a zombie outbreak. This movie has a much larger zombie population than previous installments and also has more gore, unfortunately that was a trade-off for a pretty poor story and some very mixed acting. The way the movie plays out is just too cut and dried and lacks the flair of the two previous movies. They also could have done a lot more with the zombie uprising. But the movie is paced well this time around, and that's always good. I would say this movie is on par with the second one, but for different reasons. Another very good installment.

3.5/5

Beyond the Wall of Sleep
Year – 2006
Director – Barret J. Leigh, Thom Mauer
Tags – Suspense

After a serious of brutal murders, a backwoods man is brought to the local asylum. A young intern sees him as more than an inbred killer and instead sees him as the harbinger of a dark and malevolent force. Lovecraft must be turning over in his grave. This movie is the equivalent of having food poisoning. While watching it you feel sick and feverish, completely drained, like the movie is sucking out all of your brain cells. You just want to kill yourself before you have to endure anymore of it. Afterward you're in pain and you can still taste vomit in your mouth. Needless to say, it takes a long time to recover. That's this movie in a nutshell, by far one of the worst I have ever subjected myself to. The acting was unbearably terrible. The direction was a very poor attempt at Lovecraftian filmmaking, relying too heavily on flashy editing and nonsensical sequences of garbage. It felt like my eyes were bleeding. The FX are pretty awful too. This movie was a literally painful experience for me, and unless you're a glutton for punishment or a straight out masochist, you don't ever need to see this festering pile of shit.

0.5/5

Big Bad Wolf
Year – 2006
Director – Lance W. Dreesen
Tags – Werewolves

Six friends go on a camping trip that is cut short by a bloodthirsty beast. And while two of them survive, they are not out of danger yet as they discover that the werewolf is very close to home. I have to admit, I wasn't expecting much here. Once I saw a group of six kids going to a cabin in the woods, I just expected this to be a run of the mill, werewolf picks off one kid at a time, type of movie. Well, I was very wrong. Four of the six get picked off in about five minutes, one even being brutally raped by the werewolf, and don't think I've seen that before in a movie. And that was just the first unique perspective thrown into the very tired werewolf genre. This movie does not follow the boring standard of many films that came before it. It switches gears so often I'm not really sure what's about to come next. Awesome graphic kills, a high body count, and some pretty solid acting as well. Once the two survivors get out of the woods, then a mystery aspect is also introduced, as they try to uncover who the werewolf is, all while the werewolf is trying to stop them. While Big Bad Wolf does have its slow points, overall I found it to be a very well done movie. Horror fans will definitely appreciate its strides taken to avoid being clustered in with other B movies of the same nature.

3.5/5

Bio-Zombie (Sun Faa Sau Si)
Year – 1998
Director – Wilson Yip
Tags – Zombies

An elixir has been created that can re-animate the dead. After a deal to purchase the elixir is made by some shady individuals, things go wrong and one becomes infected, turning into a zombie. Now a marketplace has become a breeding ground for the undead. I had read that this was the Japanese answer to Shaun of the Dead, which amused me since this came out years before that movie. But anyway, this horror/comedy is an amusing and gory low budget flick that I can't help but like. This is definitely more comedy than horror, as this movie isn't all about flesh eating fiends and focuses instead on a couple of bumbling clerks and their activities. The direction is really good as the movie transitions smoothly from joke to joke to gore shot to back again nicely. The acting is definitely where most of the comedy comes in. The story is typical b-movie zombie stuff, but the FX are nice. Overall this is a fun movie that I enjoyed.

3.5/5

Birds, The
Year – 1963
Director – Alfred Hitchcock
Tags – Animals

A woman visiting a man in the small town of Bodega Falls is suddenly subjected to massive bird attacks along with the rest of the town. Now they must try and survive against the avian hordes as they attempt to make their way to safety. The thought of killer birds may sound cheesy on the outside, but we are talking about the master of suspense here, and if you really think about it, humankind is far outnumbered by birds and if they wanted us gone, I don't think it would be that hard for them. The FX here are just spellbinding, it's funny how almost fifty years later, with all of our technology, and we still struggle to make them look as good as what we see here, amazing. The acting is also exceptional, and the actors really add a human touch to a movie based around animals. The direction is great as always, but I really would have preferred to get into the business with the birds sooner. Even though the human element of the first hour or so was good, the bird sequences were so great I just wanted more of them. I did love the ending though. This is an astounding movie so grand on scale I can't help but appreciate it. This is a great film.

4/5

Black Christmas
Year – 1974
Director – Bob Clark
Tags – Slasher / Survival

In a sorority house, one of the women living there has gone missing and her sisters fear she might be dead. Little do they know that the man responsible for her disappearance is the attic. This slasher flick takes the high road and offers up a tight story over gory kills, which I can appreciate, but I can't help but think that if the kills were graphic, this easily could have been the best slasher ever. But still, I really did enjoy the story because it was far from a straightforward slasher movie and instead contained elements of suspense and drama in addition to the horror, which really worked well. The acting was also very good and I especially liked the housemother, who was hilarious and I loved Margot Kidder and her awesome potty mouth. There's just something about women with a dirty mouth that never ceases to make me smile. The direction is also great and the movie moves along very nicely. I love this movie despite the lack of blood, definitely one of the finer slasher movies ever made.

4/5

Black Christmas [Remake]
Year – 2006
Director – Glen Morgan
Tags – Slasher / Survival

This remake follows the same essential plot as the original. But here's the thing about this movie. They added the gore that was absent from the original, which was nice but not completely necessary, especially since they sacrificed the story for it. The first movie was creepy and tense, while this one just plays out like your standard slasher flick. That really has its pluses and minuses. On the one hand you get some good kills, but on the other the movie isn't nearly as interesting to watch. The acting was fine and the direction was good, but I definitely wasn't as engrossed by this one. I still managed to be entertained though. The new story is just a throwaway and the provided back story was completely pointless and took the mystery out of the killer. This remake took out many of the good elements that made the original work so well, and while it added something as well, it just wasn't nearly enough.

3/5

Black Sheep
Year – 2006
Director – Jonathan King
Tags – Animals

Some genetic testing is performed on a New Zealand farm, and now flocks of sheep are infected. The once docile animals are now feral and craving human flesh. Now this is a unique and fun idea that could only work in a horror/comedy. While I like the movie a lot, the humor doesn't always work for me. The violence on the other hand, is awesome. The FX work by WETA is amazing and the mixture of FX with real sheep is pretty seamless. This movie is also gory as hell, which is awesome. The acting is great and the direction is fairly tight. This is just a very fun movie. I think its funny that when you see flocks of sheep running after the actors because they're just so damn cute, but in the context of the movie, they're hungry for flesh, and that really amused me. Also, this movie tends to play out like a zombie flick, complete with people bitten by the sheep turning into sheep themselves. This is a really great movie with some of the best FX I have ever seen.

4/5

Blade
Year – 1998
Director – Stephen Norrington
Tags – Vampires

A half vampire, with all of their strengths and none of their weaknesses, hunts full fledged vampires, searching for the one that killed his mother and made him what he is. I've always liked Blade and the Nightstalkers as they were some pretty cool comic books. So after losing interest in comics, I was glad to see a movie coming out, even though it was kind of a strange pick for them to adapt. Fortunately what we have here is a very well done movie packed with loads of action, killing and blood. The acting is very good, the direction is well done, and the FX is a mix between some great make-up and practical work, along with some decent CGI. This is probably one of my favorite action/horror split genre movies, and they are becoming much more prevalent today, so the makers of said movies should take note of Blade's formula, because it works. A great movie, not a classic, but very enjoyable.

4/5

Blade II
Year – 2002
Director – Guillermo del Toro
Tags – Vampires

In the first sequel we find Blade teaming up with an elite group of vampires to stop a vampire mutation from destroying everything. The plot behind this movie is a good idea but in the end the script just isn't that great. The direction is awesome and the acting is on par with the original. There are some familiar faces returning and some new ones that put on a good show. There's an increase in action sequences and blood, which is great. The story isn't bad, in fact, it starts out very good, but then it just feels thrown together toward the end. Still, with better direction and more action, this one is almost as good as the first, coming up a little short but still a very fine addition to the budding Blade franchise.

3.5/5

Blade: Trinity
Year – 2004
Director – David S. Goyer
Tags – Vampires

Blade returns in this third movie and now he is having trouble with humans as they think he is just a murderer and that vampires don't exist. At the same time, a group of vampires have sought out Dracula and helped him rise from his tomb. I think this movie is slightly better than the first. There is added humor here, which is great because Ryan Reynolds is in the cast, and when he's involved, you can pretty much count on a slew of funny one liners. There's a lot of action to be had here, things move along quickly, and there's the addition of some great new characters. The whole movie plays out great in the beginning and then kind of falls from grace in the third act. The whole fight between Dracula and Blade is not that great and I was expecting something a bit more epic. Still, everything leading up to that point is wonderful and the third act isn't bad, it's just average. Overall though, I really liked this movie.

Blair Witch Project, The
Year – 1999
Director – Daniel Myrick, Eduardo Sanchez
Tags – Ghosts

Three student filmmakers went missing in the woods near Burkittsville, Maryland. One year later their footage was found, and this movie is made from their film. Well, not really, but much like another notorious cinema verite film that came before it, Cannibal Holocaust, it was thought to be real when it was released. And it was thought to be real not only because of the wonderful marketing behind it, but because it is just a brilliantly crafted film. The acting is this faux documentary was very natural and well accomplished, much like the direction. I've heard a lot about the shaky filming style but I didn't find it at all distracting and thought it was well done. The movie is an aural masterpiece, wisely forgoing music and instead depending on wonderful sound effects for some nice genuine scares. This movie probably has more mixed reviews than any other horror movie, but I think it's a great story with a wonderful style and the realism they created here is trumped only by the aforementioned Cannibal Holocaust. It may not be for everyone but I love it.

4.5/5

*The Blair Witch Project 2 can be found under Book of Shadows: Blair Witch 2.

Blame, The (La Culpa)
Year – 2006
Director – Narciso Ibanez Serrador
Tags – Suspense

This is part of the DVD box set "6 Films to Keep you Awake". Here a nurse and her daughter move in with a woman who runs a clinic out of her home. Soon she starts to become troubled by the woman's possessive nature and begins to wonder just what happened to her last nurse. And that's only part of the story, the second aspect I will leave for you to discover yourself. While this is probably my least favorite of the box set, it's still pretty damn good. The story is intriguing but also a bit muddled with a somewhat dubious ending. However, it is still an entertaining watch with some great acting and very good direction. I wasn't completely pleased by this entry but I still found enjoyment in the unusual tale, I just wish it was a bit more of a straightforward take.

3.5/5

Bleeders
Year – 1997
Director – Peter Svatek

This quasi adaptation of Lovecraft's Lurking Fear is about a man coming back to his hometown to find out why he has a strange blood disease, only to find out that his relatives died long ago, or have they? Bleeders had a lot going for it, but somehow failed and I'm unsure who to blame. The story is there but never gets executed in the manner it should have been. The acting is at times very good and then at other I'm wondering if somehow I'm watching a different movie. The direction is up then down so many times I lost count. At least the creatures were cool looking. Sometimes ridiculous, sometimes great, Bleeders is probably the most inconsistent movie I've ever seen. Oh well, better luck next time.

2/5

Blood and Chocolate
Year – 2007
Director – Katja Von Garnier
Tags – Werewolves

A woman is torn between keeping her family's secret and finding love with a human man. This movie is absolute dreck. It's obvious that the director has no business being behind the lens just as the writers of this garbage have no excuse for churning out such a horrible screenplay. The acting is uninspired but I place no blame upon the actors and instead blame those behind the scenes who had them perform such awful dialogue and participate in such badly choreographed scenes. The CGI is terrible and the transformation sequences are total, utter shit. The human spins around in the air, add some sparkles, and then they're a wolf. Atrocious. It's also boring as hell, one of the most poorly paced movies I have ever seen, and I never thought it was going to end. This movie has no redeeming value whatsoever and I just can't think of a positive thing to say about it.

0.5/5

Blood Feast
Year – 1963
Director – Herschell Gordon Lewis
Tags – Slasher / Survival

A woman hires a caterer to provide food for her daughter's party. The caterer intends an Egyptian Feast, which requires him to kill young women and use their body parts. Ok, that's a little weird. Not weird because it's strange, but more or less weird because it's pretty senseless. Surely there are better ideas out there for loads of gore than this. But anyway, I believe this is Gordon's first splatter-horror movie, and it's definitely one of the worst. Quite frankly none of them are good, but at least most of the others had nice ideas behind them, this one is just a load of crap. It is mildly amusing in a way, so I have to give it credit there, but as usual this is just another movie made up of terrible acting, shoddy direction and fake as can be FX.

2/5

Blood Feast 2: All U Can Eat
Year – 2002
Director – Herschell Gordon Lewis
Tags – Slasher / Survival

This movie takes place many years after the original. Herschell Gordon Lewis returns to making movies and a collective groan can be heard among the horror community. I kid, because I know some people really dig his work. I actually had some hopes for this movie because maybe after a long period of downtime, Lewis could turn out a good movie and hire a great FX group. Nope. He uses the same brand of non-actors, well, one actor and then a group of talentless fools. And the FX still aren't very good. The story is a decent progression on the previous movie but not anything truly worthwhile. It's not all bad though, the gratuitous gore and nudity were really amusing and the movie did offer up a few laughs. A typical Lewis movie for a new generation.

2/5

Blood Gnome
Year – 2004
Director – John Lechago
Tags – Monsters

A pack of invisible gnomes are killing people involved in the BDSM community, more specifically those involved in bloodsports. Now it's up to a forensic photographer to prove that the gnomes exist, because only he can see them through his camera lens. Yeah, this movie is very poorly acted and directed, but there's no shock there. I expected this movie to just show some nudity and blood and just end up being completely worthless otherwise. But to my shock, there was actually a pretty good story behind all the junk. There aren't many horror movies dealing with the fetish community, and none that I can think of dealing with bloodsports, so there is actually some originality here. I expected a crappy rip-off of Ghoulies, which was just a crappy rip-off of Gremlins, but the story was actually interesting and original in its own way. The FX weren't bad either, and the gnomes themselves looked pretty cool. This is soft core porn loaded with gore, but with a little more depth than I'm used to seeing. Overall, not bad.

2.5/5

Blood Moon (Wolf Girl)
Year – 2001
Director – Thom Fitzgerald
Tags – Suspense

A boy becomes friends with a girl from a traveling sideshow who is afflicted with hypertrichosis, a rare genetic condition that covers her body and face with hair. She is tormented by some local kids, and when her new friend offers her a cosmetic solution, she dives in and ends up becoming more of animal on the inside as her outside appearance changes. This movie reminds me of the classic Freaks because while the stories are very different, the message is still the same, more often than not, the real freaks are the ones who appear "normal" on the outside. The story is really good and the characters are really brought to life by some great acting. The direction was also well done with few pacing problems. I love how the story progressed and it just felt deeply personal at times, which I could really get behind. This is a very solid movie that I enjoyed a great deal. It's not particularly exciting but it's just a very good movie all around.

3.5/5

Bloodrayne
Year – 2005
Director – Uwe Boll
Tags – Vampires

Based on the video game of the same name but not following its story, this movie instead focuses on a young half vampire woman during medieval times instead of Nazi Germany. This movie is crap, there's really no other way to describe it. The story is incredibly poor, even for a Boll movie. The acting is beyond bad, but then again the dialogue is just so terrible that how could anyone actually even attempt to make it sound good? The direction isn't good at all, but it's definitely an improvement over some other movies Boll has directed. There's a sloppy sex scene that doesn't really fit, but there is a ton of blood, which would be good but it doesn't seem to fit either. The many fight scenes in the movie are very badly choreographed as well. I guess I could say that the movie is watchable, even if you're watching it just to find out how NOT to make a movie. It's awful, but there are actually much less appealing movies out there.

1.5/5

Bloodrayne 2: Deliverance
Year – 2007
Director – Uwe Boll
Tags – Vampires

This movie continues on centuries after the last one and takes place in the Wild West. I didn't think this movie could be worse than the last one, but it is. There are a couple of decent performances but most are very bad and the new Rayne is a horrendous actress, I literally winced when she would "act". The direction is terrible. The movie is so incredibly boring I just could not wait for it to be over, more so than others. The FX are pretty bad to boot. The story is also very weak and I can't think of a single good thing to say about it. I can't say I had high hopes for this movie but I was expecting something a little better than this. Boll seemed to be making slight improvements with each movie he made but this is definitely a step back.

1/5

Blue Velvet
Year – 1986
Director – David Lynch
Tags – Suspense

A young man home from college finds a human ear in a field. Due to his inquisitive nature, he investigates the matter outside of the law and ends up getting caught up in an odyssey of sexual depravity and shady figures. No matter how many times I see this movie, it's just brilliant. The acting is top notch and the direction is so artistic and well accomplished. The story is one of a kind and I just wonder how it was created. What were the circumstances? What was the setting? I would love to be able to write such a wide open and unique story. This is more accessible than some of Lynch's other works in my opinion, of course I have a somewhat twisted sensibility and sometimes the bizarre just makes sense to me. Either way, I love this movie and I found it to be a timeless classic.

4.5/5

Body Bags
Year – 1993
Director – John Carpenter, Tobe Hooper
Tags – Anthology, Slasher / Survival, Suspense

This anthology has three stories with a wraparound story concerning a morgue attendant searching the body bags for stories to tell. The first story is about a gas station attendant and her run in with a maniac. The second story is about a man with thinning hair who goes to a hair restoration clinic and gets more than he bargains for. And the third story is about a baseball player that loses an eye during an accident and has an experimental surgery to receive a cadaver eye, with disastrous consequences. The best part of this movie is the wraparound story, Carpenter himself plays the morgue attendant and he is just hilarious. But each segment is enjoyable as well. The first is probably my favorite, it's just a simple slasher plot but the execution is really well done. The other two segments have probably the most inventive plotlines and are very good. In all, this is an excellent anthology, it may not be the best, but it's still pretty damn good.

3.5/5

Body Snatchers
Year – 1993
Director – Abel Ferrara

This second remake of Invasion of the Body Snatchers is a bit different from the other two movies as this one takes place on a military base almost exclusively. While this movie doesn't quite reach the greatness of the previous two movies, it does come damn close. The acting is very good from everyone. The direction is awesome as the story progresses very quickly, just like in the first remake, wasting little time getting to the heart of it all. The new story isn't very different from how the previous ones played out, it just has a different location, but I definitely prefer the city over the base. The FX are great though, showing the viewer how the pod people take over in more detail. This is another great movie in a stellar series and I definitely recommend it.

4/5

Bone Snatcher, The
Year – 2003
Director – Jason Wulfsohn
Tags – Animals

A mining team is attacked by a swarm of insects that use the bones of the dead to form together into humanoid creatures. The story is interesting and a little different from anything else out there, but the good elements were unfortunately underused and the movie was much too dialogue heavy in situations that could have been better spent on insect attacks. The acting and direction are good, and the FX are good, even the CGI. I really wish I had more good things to say because the movie did have a lot of good things going for it, but there was just too much missed potential to call it great. But it is still a good movie and nice break from the low budget garbage that clogs the marketplace.

3/5

Bones
Year – 2001
Director – Ernest R. Dickerson
Tags – Ghosts

A betrayed man is murdered in his home, and now his spirit can not rest and will attack anyone who dares to enter. Twenty years later someone new owns the house and begins to renovate it into a nightclub, unwittingly allowing the murdered man to take form and seek revenge on those who killed him. The plot of the movie is ok, nothing all that new, but with some nice plot twists that mildly set it apart from similar movies. The acting is better than I thought it would be, as some people do a good job while others are pretty terrible. The FX are a sticky point with me because there are some excellent visuals and there are times when the FX look great. But then the blood looks exactly like red paint and there are some awful CGI shots. The movie also seemed to drag on, but when the murdered man comes back to seek out his killers, it definitely takes an upswing, only to be drug down by a fairly lame ending. This was almost an average attempt at horror, but just came up a little short.

2/5

Boogeyman
Year – 2005
Director – Stephen T. Kay
Tags – Ghosts

A man has devoted his life to avoiding the spectral figure that killed his father when he was a child. But now he is forced to face it. Zzzzzzz. Huh, what? Oh yeah, sorry, this movie put me to sleep. Wow, what a piece of crap. You would think that Sam Raimi had an eye for good horror, but this movie released under his Ghost House shingle is anything but. This movie is far from being scary or creepy and is instead a boring and trite take on the legend of the boogeyman. Everyone knows about the boogeyman, because the story has been in circulation for a very long time in one form or another, so why is it that here the most incompetent screenwriter they could find has been put in charge of bringing the legend to life? The story is absolutely worthless and direction is boring as hell. The acting isn't too bad though, and I guess some of the FX are good, but the CGI is horrendous. Definitely a bad movie in almost every way, but I think that most the most shocking thing of all about this flick is that is actually spawned sequels.

1.5/5

Boogeyman 2
Year – 2007
Director – Jeff Betancourt
Tags – Slasher / Survival

This movie is only minutely related to the last one. Here a girl witnessed her father being killed by a shadowy figure and years later she must check herself into a fear clinic. But once there people start to die mysteriously. I think it was a good idea to move the franchise in a different direction than the original since that one was so bad, but it also seems silly to make a sequel at all. Fortunately I can say with certainty that this movie is much better than the original. The story is somewhat more interesting and there are several graphic and gory kill sequences, which were a very nice treat. The acting and direction are just ok though. This is a decent enough slasher light on story but heavy on blood. Still not good, but at least it's average.

2.5/5

Boogeyman 3
Year – 2008
Director – Gary Jones
Tags – Ghosts

This sequel is a bit more tied to the last one than the previous movie was to the original and continues shortly after Boogeyman 2. Here we also see a spectral killer return as opposed to a slasher and with the upswing in quality that came between the first and second movie, I was hoping for something above average, alas I did not receive it. The movie isn't bad so much as it was just very mundane. Very amateurish acting, off camera kills, a cheesy killer and a fairly weak story comprise this third movie in the franchise. There's nothing I can honestly say that is bad here but everything is very much below average. I didn't enjoy this movie but I didn't hate it either, at least it was better than the original.

2/5

Book of Shadows: Blair Witch 2
Year – 2000
Director – Joe Berlinger
Tags – Ghosts

This sequel to The Blair Witch Project follows a group of people who go on a Blair Witch Tour into the woods where the original movie was made, which is now a tourist hot spot. They end up blacking out some time in the night and try to piece together what happened to them and all of the strange occurrences that now plague them at every turn. I was a bit wary of a sequel, as it seemed like a silly idea, but I do have to admit that this is an interesting progression of the story. It doesn't completely work but it does have some good elements to it. The direction is also pretty good with some rather good pacing. The acting is ok, not too bad but it could have been a lot better. I have to admit that I was entertained by this movie, it was far from being great but I enjoyed myself while watching it.

3/5

Bordello of Blood
Year – 1996
Director – Gilbert Adler
Tags – Vampires

A private investigator discovers that a funeral home doubles as a whorehouse filled with the undead, and now it's up to him and a religious woman to stop their killing spree. This is the second Tales from the Crypt movie to be released, and after Demon Knight turned out to be an exceptional horror movie, I was excited to see this. Unfortunately it turned out to be a cheesy vampire flick that really lacks substance. The acting and direction are decent, and the same goes for the story. It's a little different but not particularly well made. The movie plays out like a comedy but is only mildly amusing. The make-up and FX are pretty good though. The saving grace here are the loads of blood and nudity that permeate every corner of the movie. Still, this is an average movie and while completely watchable, it's just not very good.

2.5/5

Borderland

Year – 2007
Director – Zev Berman
Tags – Cults

Based on a true story, Borderland tells the tale of a three friends on vacation in Mexico and how they came into contact with a cult specializing in human sacrifice. As if I needed another reason not to visit Mexico, Borderland may make you think twice about walking the streets down there alone after dark. The scenes of murder and sacrifice are especially graphic and well done. The FX work is extraordinary and the acting really sets the mood. The movie is very slow, which is understandable since this isn't exactly the kind of story that moves along quickly, but it still had me squirming around in my seat in boredom. The dark and grimy look of the movie works very well with the overall atmosphere. This is a great movie, even if it is slow, the realism is great, and I look forward to seeing more from this director because I can tell he really has some skill.

4/5

Botched

Year – 2007
Director – Kit Ryan
Tags – Slasher / Survival

After the botched heist of a priceless heirloom, three thieves find themselves trapped inside a building with their hostages all while an insane descendant of Ivan the Terrible stalks them. This movie is a lot of fun and it has some good jokes peppered throughout along with some incredibly gory kills. There's not much more I could have asked for from the movie, but I wish it was more consistent in its attempts at humor. The acting is good and comedic, the direction is good, and pacing is good, everything about the production is at least above average. Where the movie does shine is in the kills, some we get to see and others we get to see the aftermath. Overall this is a very good flick just shy of true greatness.

3.5/5

Bottom Feeder

Year – 2006
Director – Randy Daudlin
Tags – Monsters

A scientist is injected with his own experimental creation, thus turning him into a ravenous rat monster who is hunting people in a series a tunnels near a University. Yeah, the story is about as compelling as it sounds. This is just a throwback to the monster movies of yesteryear and is just a cheesy, entertaining romp through very familiar territory. The acting ranges from good to very, very bad. The direction is ok but the pacing isn't very good, nothing unmanageable though. The FX are decent, and it's nice to see a monster movie with a dude in a suit instead of a CGI beast. There is a fair amount of blood as well. Bottom Feeder isn't a bad movie, it's just a very average one, but I can think of worse ways to spend my time.

2.5/5

Boy Eats Girl
Year – 2005
Director – Stephen Bradley
Tags – Zombies

Wishing to declare his love for one of his friends, a teenage boy ends up seeing her with another guy and thinks the worst. Later that night he dies by accident, and his mother resurrects him using an ancient tome, but ends up doing it incorrectly and makes him a flesh hungry zombie. This is a teen horror flick made in Ireland, and while it was pretty light on story, it made up for it with loads of gore and just being an entertaining watch. The acting is good, and the direction is pretty solid too. There are a couple of laughs and a little bit of blood to begin with which later culminates into a massive splatter fest of entrails and body parts, got to love that. The story is just standard stuff, but at least pulled off well. When all is said and done this movie is just a very good zombie flick that I enjoyed quite a bit. It's not a classic redefining the genre, it's just good fun.

3.5/5

Bram Stoker's Dracula
Year – 1992
Director – Francis Ford Coppola
Tags – Vampires

The vampire king comes to England is hopes of seducing a woman who looks remarkably like this former love. The story of Dracula has been told many times, but not quite as well as it is done here. I'm sure the advancements in technology have a lot to do with making this movie so visually appealing over other, older versions. Add a bunch of great actors to the mix, in particular Gary Oldman, who nails the role of Dracula, easily making his performance one of the best in the cinematic history of the character. The story of Dracula at its core is a love story, and that really takes the forefront here, deservedly so as well. But fret not because there are still plenty of bloodletting moments and carnal pleasures. The movie manages to never lag and flows so smoothly, even with a 2+ hour runtime. Visually impressive, dark, ominous, heartbreaking and powerful, this is Dracula as it was meant to be seen.

5/5

Breaking Dawn
Year – 2004
Director – Mark Edwin Robinson
Tags – Suspense

A student doctor is assigned a mental patient as a subject who does not respond to anyone. She begins to get through to him and learns that he has many secrets to tell. This is an incredibly dull movie with really nothing much going for it. The story is transparent and uninspired with your typical twist ending that's way too obvious. The direction reflects this and is slow and painful. The acting isn't that good either, I've seen a lot worse but most of the actors were just unconvincing. It's not all bad but there's nothing so good I would call it redeeming. This is just a bland, cardboard cut-out thriller that's instantly forgettable the second you're done watching it.

1.5/5

Breed, The
Year – 2001
Director – Michael Oblowitz
Tags – Vampires

A detective and a vampire try to track down a killer. Actually, that's about the whole movie wrapped up in one sentence. The paper thin plot is definitely an attempt at something new but I don't think the writer had the skills to actually create a worthwhile story, nor did the director have the skills to make an interesting movie because The Breed is almost unbearably slow and uneventful. The action sequences are really lame and all of the actors do a very poor job in their roles. It seems as though everyone was miscast because I've seen some good performances from some of the actors in other roles. One good thing I will say is that the movie looks good with some great locales and a nice dark sheen covering the production. I can't even say that this is a nice attempt at something new because there isn't much worthwhile here.

1.5/5

Breed, The
Year – 2006
Director – Nicholas Mastandrea
Tags – Animals

Five young people fly to a secluded house on an island for vacation. Unfortunately they are not the only inhabitants, and now a pack of genetically engineered dogs are hunting them. The plot sounds like a loser and for the most part, the movie is. I do have to award the people behind this movie points for using real dogs instead of CGI ones. Also, there are some great, tense moments in the movie. But every time the pace picked up, it's shot right back down and the movie went right back to being boring. The characters are actually pretty unlikeable and a couple of them you just want to die so you don't have to look at them anymore. And the end was so lame I can't believe they used it, because you could see it coming a mile away and it's not the least bit clever. This movie is about as uneven as they come, but at least it's an average attempt.

2.5/5

Breeders
Year – 1986
Director – Tim Kincaid
Tags – Aliens

All over New York City, virgins are being attacked and raped. Later on a detective and a doctor find out that are being used as breeders for an alien living under the streets. The story is somewhat interesting, of course the way it's made is nothing but absolutely cheesy crap, but come on this is low budget 80's horror. The acting is terrible, I mean really terrible. The direction isn't bad but this movie could have used a whole lot of polish. The FX are pretty good though, all except the alien which is just a crappy rubber suit coated in slime. There's some blood but not really enough, what there is an abundance of however is nudity. Lots of it. There's even a drawn out sequence of six nude women in a nest of what I could only call semen. It was pretty gross for me but I guess if you're into bukkake you'll probably dig it. Overall I enjoyed the movie somewhat as it's not bad, but just not good either.

2.5/5

Bride of Chucky
Year – 1998
Director – Ronny Yu
Tags – Slasher / Survival

The fourth movie in the Child's Play series takes place a couple of years after the last one. Now this is what I'm talking about. This is just what the series needed, a completely fresh coat of paint. The movie is no masterpiece but it is incredibly entertaining. The acting and direction are very good and match the new story perfectly. This installment definitely has more comedic elements in it than previous movies in the series, and the horror does take a backseat, which kind of sucks. The movie does pay a little bit of homage to other iconic horror franchises, which is fun. This movie may not be a brilliant and original genre flick but it is a well paced and entertaining time killer if nothing else.

3.5/5

Bride of Re-Animator
Year – 1990
Director – Brian Yuzna
Tags – Zombies

Herbert West is back months after the incidents of the first movie and now he has plans to not only reanimate the dead, but to create new life from the body parts of various women. Hmmm, that plot sounds familiar. Clearly an homage to the golden age of horror, this movie increases the gore, and with the help of KNB, the FX look marvelous. The make-up stands out, especially on the "Bride" herself. The way the parts were put together made for a fascinating if not truly morbid sight. The pacing of the movie does leave something to be desired, but the trade off for increased blood almost makes it worth it. This is a very good movie and a worthy sequel to a classic, even if it is fairly slow, I still enjoyed it quite a bit.

3.5/5

Broken
Year – 2006
Director – Simon Boyes, Adam Mason
Tags – Suspense

A woman wakes up in the woods and begins a series of games that a psychopath has created. She plays along, hoping to find the whereabouts of her daughter. In all of the torture movies that have come out, this one is rather bland. There are some definitely bloody moments, but only a couple and the rest of time the viewer is subjected to some boring domestic situations, which are twisted, but not very interesting. The acting is good though, and like I said, when it does get bloody, it's pretty graphic, so the FX are good, but there's just too many lags to really make it anything great. This would have been a good concept before the torture flicks flooded the horror marketplace, but as it stands, this isn't a bad movie, just pretty much a forgettable one.

3/5

Broken, The
Year – 2008
Director – Sean Ellis
Tags – [Hidden to conceal spoilers]

A woman's life spirals into madness after she sees herself drive by in her own car on the street. I need to be vague because I don't want to reveal too much. This movie has its fair share of flaws, namely in the pacing and storytelling areas, but it almost makes up for it with a great, original story (which is somewhat muddled), and some great acting. I really love this movie at times but it's just so disjointed at others that it really kills the atmosphere that had been building and takes me out of the movie. I'm a little disappointed because this probably could have been a classic if more care was put into it, but it's still pretty damn good in the end.

3.5/5

Brood, The

Year – 1979
Director – David Cronenberg
Tags – Monsters

A husband investigates the unusual techniques of a psychologist's treatment of his institutionalized wife while at the same time a horde of mutant children are killing the people around him. Cronenberg is known for his bizarre imagery and gory details, which are present here but not enough. The first two thirds of the movie focus on the husband's investigation, which is very slow going, punctuating only a couple times by attacks from the children. However when the final act unfolds, it is pure Cronenberg, loaded to the gills with gore and twisted occurrences. It's almost enough to redeem everything before it. This is a good movie but a little too dull overall to be anything more.

3/5

Brotherhood of Blood
Year – 2007
Director – Michael Roesch, Peter Scheerer
Tags – Vampires

This is a movie about vampire hunters. And it sucks, real bad. Let me get the good out of the way, and don't worry, I'll be brief. Sid Haig and Ken Foree. Now on to the bad. First, the direction is some of the worst I have seen. The movie jumps around to different points in time, but it's not at all clever, it's actually quite annoying. It's also unnecessary. I feel this movie could have at least been slightly better if they would have kept things more coherent. I guess they filmed it that way to throw you off from the twist ending, which was easy to figure out, and lame on top of that. The set design looked like cardboard, the fangs looked like too white plastic, and the FX was shoddy. Haig and Foree are the only saving grace here, but their parts are small, so they're not enough of a saving grace in my opinion. Probably one of the worst vampire movies ever made.

1/5

Brotherhood of the Wolf (Le Pacte des Loups)
Year – 2001
Director – Christophe Gans
Tags – Monsters

A beast is roaming the French countryside, killing many in 18th century France. The king sends a man and his Native American friend to put a stop to it. This movie is an astonishing mix of horror, drama and martial arts the likes of which I had never seen before or since. The movie is just plain beautiful and the direction style is one of a kind. The fight scenes are wonderfully choreographed and fit well with the movie's style. The acting is also noteworthy. The story is well done and brilliantly accomplished. The beast looks great but unfortunately the CGI that gives it life isn't very good. The director does do an admirable job of masking it though. There's not much I can say for the movie other than it being a brilliant and gorgeous genre bending experience. But I think that's enough. A must see.

4/5

Bruiser
Year – 2000
Director – George A. Romero
Tags – Slasher / Survival

A man dumped on by everyone in his life wakes up one day to find that his face is gone and replaced by a stark white mask. Now with his new found anonymity he has found the courage to make things right in his life by killing off everything that's wrong. I like the concept a lot, because who hasn't dreamed of killing off all of the assholes in his or her life and being anonymous while doing it? For those of you that haven't, you're probably the asshole so watch out. Unfortunately the story isn't very good and the writers could have done a lot more with the subject matter. The direction is good though, the movie moves along fairly well. The acting ranges from well done, to overdone, to complete crap for some truly mixed performances. This is a decent movie that I just wanted more out of, but it wasn't entirely unpleasant.

2.5/5

Brutal Massacre: A Comedy
Year – 2007
Director – Stevan Mena
Tags – Horror Related

This movie is not an outright horror movie rather it is a mockumentary about the horror industry. This movie follows a Z grade horror movie director as he begins working on his newest movie. The production however, is fraught with disaster after disaster. This movie is hilarious in my opinion. And to have a bunch of genre vets mixed with comedic actors was a great idea. The plot behind the movie is an ambitious one, and most likely destined to fail, but it manages to work here. There are a few slow points in the movie where nothing funny and nothing of consequence occurs, but they're not prevalent enough to keep me from enjoying this movie. The humor may or may not be for you, but I would call it required viewing for horror fans.

4/5

Bubba Ho-Tep
Year – 2002
Director – Don Coscarelli
Tags – Mummies

Geriatric Elvis and a black JFK unite to stop an ancient mummy from killing the resident of their nursing home. No, you read that synopsis right. In the hand of a less capable director, that ridiculous premise would have been a complete failure, but Coscarelli makes it work, most of the time. Bruce Campbell and Ossie Davis are a brilliant match here and pull off both their unique roles splendidly. Davis especially gets some killer lines and the comedy is off the wall great. And that brings me to my problem with the movie, there's just too much dead space between the punctuations of comedy and the mummy action. Still, I love this movie for its great moments and dare-to-be-different attitude. I just wish it was a little better paced.

3.5/5

Buffy the Vampire Slayer
Year – 1992
Director – Fran Rubel Kuzui
Tags – Vampires

A cheerleader gets a visit from a mysterious man just as creatures of the night begin to overtake her town. She finds out it is up to her to stop the vampires and rid her community of the undead. So the story of Buffy the Vampire Slayer is about as vapid as the main character herself, but that doesn't mean it isn't entertaining, stupid can be fun too. This movie is pretty unremarkable as a whole, but its silly plotline does have a certain charm that is able to carry it above being labeled as garbage. Buffy is good, mindless fun whose appeal wears off promptly after viewing it, but I can think of many worse ways to spend an hour and a half.

3/5

Bug
Year – 2006
Director – William Friedkin
Tags – Suspense

A lonely woman gets mixed up with a man who claims to have been experimented on by the military, wherein they placed bugs inside his body as a means of surveillance. While everyone around her says the man is crazy, she begins to be drawn in by his delusions. There are such exceptional performances here for such an unremarkable film. The concept of the movie, while interesting, does not fully fill out the runtime associated with it. The movie is very slow at times and I know it is not from the direction but rather due to the story just not having enough substance. There is a definite upswing toward the end of the movie when the occurrences reach their peak, but getting there feels a bit like a chore. This is definitely a good movie and if you have the patience for it, you'll be rewarded with some amazing acting and a great (short) story that just unfortunately overstayed its welcome.

3/5

Buried Alive
Year – 2007
Director – Robert Kurtzman
Tags – Slasher / Survival

A group of college kids decide to spend some time at a secluded desert house and end up fighting for their lives against a malevolent axe wielding spirit. The story is pretty standard stuff and it plays out like a normal slasher, no surprises, no twists. The concept is good, but the script doesn't match up with it too well. The direction is good, the acting is fairly bad, but the FX are where the movie really shines. There are some great, bloody kills here. There's also some good nudity to mix things up as well. At the end of the day this a completely watchable, mildly entertaining slasher flick with a supernatural vibe, and I enjoyed it, but not enough to call it anything more than average.

2.5/5

Buried Alive [Web Series]
Year – 2007
Director – Paul Etheredge
Tags – Suspense

A group of friends are all kidnapped and placed into various underground boxes, each rigged with ways to kill them. Now the kidnapper has made streaming online videos of his captives and it's up to another friend and her brother to find them before they're buried alive. This originally appeared on FEARnet as a series of shorts before being combined together and released on DVD. The story is derivative of many feature length movies that came before it, but it does have some interesting aspects to it, and the character interaction is pretty good. The acting is also good for the most part, which did surprise me a little bit. The direction is also good, and it damn well better be with an hour long run time. The twist in the story is pretty obvious, but this makes for an entertaining movie nonetheless.

3/5

Burning, The
Year – 1981
Director – Tony Maylam
Tags – Slasher / Survival

Years after a prank on a camp caretaker goes terribly wrong, the now horribly burned caretaker returns to a nearby camp to take his revenge. I figured this movie would just be another Friday the 13th clone, but the camp setting is the only thing in common with that movie. The story is much different and pretty good, especially for a slasher flick. The characters have some actual depth as well, and are played by some good actors, you'll even see a few people who are big names in the industry now. The direction is also awesome with great pacing and a nice shot structure. The FX work is done by Tom Savini, who also did the FX for Friday the 13th, so you know they look great. The kills are wonderful and very bloody. There's even a group kill, which is extremely rare, as usually slashers pick people off one by one. The body count is also surprisingly high for a first movie, usually we don't get to see this much death until a sequel. The killer's weapon of choice is a pair of hedge clippers, which offers up a nice variety of death scenes. This is one my favorite slasher flicks because it was created with care and a lot of thought was placed into it to diversify it from the rest. Lots of blood, lots of nudity, and all wrapped up in a great production, this is highly recommended.

4.5/5

Burnt Offerings
Year – 1976
Director – Dan Curtis
Tags – Suspense

A couple and their young son move into an old gothic manor to be summer caretakers, but something about the house isn't quite right and soon begins to affect the mother of the boy in strange ways. This overly long and fairly dull thriller does have some good points, but not enough to allow me to say that I actually liked it. The acting is great but the direction needs quite a bit of work. The movie is much too slow and feels pretty stale. And the fact that this movie is nearly two hours long only drags things out worse. It's not really a bad movie because it does have good things going for it, just not enough to make me call it anything better than average.

2.5/5

Butterfly Effect, The
Year – 2004
Director – Eric Bress, J. Mackye Gruber
Tags – Suspense

A young man suffering from random blackouts realizes that he has the ability to travel back to certain points in his life with his mind. But every time he jumps back, he alters his timeline and the timelines of others drastically. I love this movie because while it treads on familiar ground, it does so in such a refreshingly original way. I was a little worried about having Ashton Kutcher in the lead given his past roles, but he pulls off a dramatic performance with ease, and like the rest of the cast, he does a remarkable job. The direction is also clean and concise, which is always a pleasure to see. The story is great and the timeline alterations are well thought out and executed. There are some definite plot holes, and while you do get that in every time travel movie and it is to be expected, there are a few more than usual here. Still, this is an awesome movie and I definitely recommend it.

4/5

Butterfly Effect 2, The
Year – 2006
Director – John R. Leonetti
Tags – Suspense

This movie focuses the same idea of the original on a new person. And I'm fine with that. This movie is like Final Destination, the story has a certain gimmick that needs to be revisited in each movie, and just as long as they vary it up and keep it interesting, everything's cool. Unfortunately here the story is incredibly weak to the point where it becomes predictable and dumb. The acting is passable and the direction isn't too bad, but ultimately the movie fails from the aspect of the script. In the original we saw a line of varied occurrences that happened whenever the main character altered the timeline, here everything is very mundane and doesn't offer up much variety. It was somewhat enjoyable, I definitely wouldn't call it bad, but it's close. I will say it's definitely not as bad as I was led to believe it would be when I first heard of it.

2/5

Butterfly Effect 3: Revelations, The
Year – 2009
Director – Seth Grossman
Tags – Suspense

Same deal here with a new guy having the power of the previous two, but here he uses his power to observe crimes and find those responsible, but not to get involved and keep the timeline in tact. But when he breaks the rules and intercedes on a murder that affected his own life, things get out of control once again. The new twist on the story is nice and it also makes sense that someone would try and solve crimes with it. The story here is much better than the last one, despite it being fairly open and predictable. The acting and direction are also better. There was also a ton of gore and nudity which was fun to see but it wasn't completely necessary. Can't say it didn't fit though because the murders were especially brutal and the added sexuality was very prevalent. I actually wasn't looking forward to watching this because the second movie was so underwhelming but I pleasantly surprised to find a good movie here.

3/5

C.H.U.D.
Year – 1984
Director – Douglas Cheek
Tags – Monsters

The title stands for Cannibalistic Humanoid Underground Dweller, just so you know. Anyway, the movie involves a diverse group of people each searching for a reason as to why the homeless population of New York City appears to be dwindling. What they find are a horde of subterranean monsters feeding upon human flesh. The name of this movie is probably the most entertaining thing about it, I kid of course. C.H.U.D. has all of the trappings of a cheap B movie but features several actors who actually have talent. The acting is very good and somewhat wasted on the sub par story, but it is welcome nonetheless. The direction is also pretty good. There could have been a lot more done with the movie, more monsters, more gore, less conversation, more killing. But it's still a fun flick, it just could have been a whole lot more.

3.5/5

Cabin Fever
Year – 2002
Director – Eli Roth
Tags – Infection

A group of college kids decide to take a vacation to an isolated cabin in the woods (sounds familiar). While partying they come across a man who is very sick from an unknown illness. After driving him off, they find similar symptoms amongst themselves. Eli Roth takes your typical "kids in the woods" tale and throws a nice spin on it. I wish I could say it works, but unfortunately he also tries to ram humor and general weirdness down the viewer's throats, and it just doesn't work. For the most part the movie is great, and if it had taken itself more seriously, it could have very well been a modern classic. Still, it is a very good watch with great FX and a nice plot. This movie showed that Eli Roth has a lot of potential and he proved down the road that he only gets better with time. A good time, but a bit lacking overall.

3/5

Cadaverella
Year – 2007
Director – Timothy Friend
Tags – Zombies

A young woman is murdered by her step-mother's lover so that she can collect on her trust fund, but the woman is given the opportunity to return from the grave and exact her revenge by a malevolent spirit. The story has pretty much been done before, but this microbudget zombie flick does have a charm about it. It's not in the crappy acting or the slow direction. It's not in the cheap but effective FX or the mounds of gore. The story actually has some depth to it and a sense of humor. The movie is so cheesy and fun that it can definitely be construed as a horror/comedy. I can't say I loved it, or even really liked it, but it was a better effort than I'm used to seeing from Brain Damage Films, and while I can't even call it average, it's not all bad.

2/5

Call of Cthulhu, The [Silent]

Year – 2005
Director – Andrew Leman
Tags – Monsters

The classic tale by H.P. Lovecraft about a man who follows his great uncle's research into a mysterious creature known to be an ancient god that lives under the sea. The most interesting part of the movie is that the filmmakers filmed this as if it were made in the 1920's, during Lovecraft's life. So the film is silent and has a very old feel, which cleverly hides the low budget. The movie is very short and flows nicely, also making it easily the most faithful Lovecraft adaptation ever made because the filmmakers didn't string anything out. The set design, costumes and visual FX were really awesome and given the nature of the film, they didn't feel cheap and instead worked wonderfully within the context of the old silent movie feel. The score is also really well done and adds a lot to the movie. The concept behind this movie is brilliant, and fortunately all the other elements also come together perfectly. If I had any complaints it would be that the movie is too crisp and should have been grainier, maybe even filmed using an old box camera, but still, this is a very inventive and unique way to adapt a Lovecraft story of such high caliber.

4.5/5

Calvaire (The Ordeal)
Year – 2004
Director – Fabrice Du Welz
Tags – Slasher / Survival

A young man's van breaks down deep in the woods. He manages to find a place to stay, and the man who owns the inn pledges to fix his vehicle, but letting the young man leave is the last thing on the innkeeper's mind. This is an extremely well crafted survival horror movie. It's incredibly creepy throughout its entire runtime and the lack of a musical score only adds to the tension in my opinion. Without music it allows the movie to be genuinely frightening instead of relying of cheap jump scares. The acting and direction are also very good. I like how they didn't show everything, but still definitely let you know just what was happening. This is a great movie that ends up being pretty bizarre and still retains its brutality despite not showing too much, which is the mark of a gifted filmmaker.

4/5

Camp Blood
Year – 1999
Director – Brad Sykes
Tags – Slasher / Survival

Two couples go camping in a set of woods that is supposedly the domain of a killer in a clown mask. It doesn't take long for them to find out that it isn't just a legend. First it must be said that this is a microbudget horror movie shot with a camcorder, so of course there are some issues. First off, the acting ranges from decent to terrible, everyone involved are probably just friends with the director, so that's fine. The story is just pointless, but this is slasher movie so you don't really need one to make an effective flick. The movie is kind of slow, but not bad, especially given the short run time. The movie starts out good with boobs and blood in the first couple minutes, letting you know that the director is a student of horror. The FX are ok, utilizing a fair amount of blood. This movie isn't very worthwhile to be honest, but it is a somewhat impressive microbudget flick. If you're a fan of slasher movies, this is a good example of how to make a decent one for little to no money.

3/5

Camp Blood 2
Year – 2000
Director – Brad Sykes
Tags – Slasher / Survival

This movie takes place one year after the original. There are some pluses and minuses to this sequel. First off, while the first story was fairly pointless, the set-up for this one is just plain ludicrous. But on the plus side it appears as though Sykes has improved as a director because this movie has much better pacing. The acting is still pretty terrible, but the FX have definitely improved with this installment. More blood, more realistic kills, just better all around. I'm not going to say this is a good sequel, but it's definitely not bad, in fact this one is almost as good as the original, and if you liked it I recommend you watch this one as well. If you didn't, then this one is just more of the same.

2.5/5

*Camp Blood 3 can be found under Within the Woods.

Candyman
Year – 1992
Director – Bernard Rose
Tags – Slasher / Survival

This is an adaptation of a written work by Clive Barker that follows a woman as she works on a thesis based on myths and legends. One in particular is based on the Candyman, and the legend goes that if you say his name five times into a mirror, he will appear behind you with a hook and slit you from groin to gullet with a rusty hook. But she will soon find out that the Candyman is no myth. This is one of my favorite horror movies for a lot of reasons, firstly due to the great story. Second is Tony Todd, who plays the Candyman and gives the character such immense personality that I was absolutely enthralled by his performance. Lastly, the direction is perfect and really manages to keep a dark, almost gothic atmosphere throughout the entire movie, punctuated by very graphic and gory kills. It really doesn't get much better than this movie, it's a rare glimpse in seeing how a movie can be both atmospheric and creepy but also pull off tremendous gore as well. Usually the two don't mix well and can often seem forcefully placed together, but here they are natural. Candyman is also a love story at heart, as about as dark as one can get anyway. Chilling and powerful, this is one of the greatest horror movies ever made.

5/5

Candyman 2: Farewell to the Flesh
Year – 1995
Director – Bill Condon
Tags – Slasher / Survival

Some time after the events of the first movie we find the Candyman terrorizing New Orleans. This sequel feels very forced. The story is a bit too similar to the last one, the pacing isn't very good and the atmosphere that made the last one so great is now all but gone. The lead actress is no Virginia Madsen and she, as well as others, bumble through the movie making nothing but bad impressions. Tony Todd is excellent once again though, and there is a good amount of blood. And while the story does feel much too similar, it's not bad and does offer at least a little bit of variety on the original tale. There are also some scenes involving Candyman's origins, which were only spoken of in the original, so actually seeing what happened was nice. Still, this movie is barely average and a big disappointment.

2.5/5

Candyman 3: Day of the Dead
Year – 1999
Director – Turi Meyer
Tags – Slasher / Survival

This third movie in the Candyman franchise occurs at an indeterminate amount of time after the last one. The last Candyman movie was at least passable, but this one is just so incredibly bad it's unforgivable. Tony Todd is about the only good thing here, but even he looks disillusioned by the Candyman now. The rest of the acting is just so terrible that it just about makes the movie unwatchable. Of course if you add in the horrendous direction and awful story, well I guess that would make this movie pretty much unwatchable. You should only ever see this crap if you are a die hard fan of the series, or a die hard fan of Tony Todd, otherwise don't bother, it really is that bad.

1/5

Cannibal Holocaust
Year – 1980
Director – Ruggero Deodato
Tags – Cannibals

Four documentary filmmakers go missing in the South American jungle, and an anthropologist follows their trail in the hopes of finding them. All he ends up finding though is their camera footage, which he takes back to the US to view. This movie is not campy, there is no humor, this is not a lighthearted affair, instead, this is by far the most disturbing and sick movie ever made. Now that being said, I do have to say that this movie is really a work of art due to the absolutely unabashed style of filmmaking seen here. No taboo is left untouched, and things that have never been in any other movie are here. There is actual animal death in this movie on several occasions, and it is incredibly graphic, so be prepared for that. The violence in this movie is about as real as it gets, there are several brutal rape scenes, a lot of killing, and a lot of torture with just loads of gore. To give you an idea of the realism of this movie, the director was arrested because authorities believed he really did kill the people in the movie, it's just that intense. I have to say out of every movie I've watched, this is the only one I had a problem with, not because of the human death scenes, but because I love animals and the animals in this movie really do die terrible deaths. This is a one of a kind movie and I know there will probably never be anything as graphic as this again. It can be tough to handle, but if you can stomach it, you'll be treated to one of the most realistic and well made movies ever put out into the world.

4.5/5

Captivity
Year – 2007
Director – Roland Joffe
Tags – Suspense

A model is kidnapped and now finds herself a part of some demented individual's twisted games and torture devices. After movies like Saw and Hostel were released, there were plenty of imitators wanting to get in on some torture flicks. The thing is, those aforementioned movies have good stories, and this does not. The story is just not good at all and a complete throwaway plot. The direction is also pretty bad to boot, making this one incredibly boring movie with one lame torture technique after another. Well, there are a couple of cool ones, but that's about it. The acting is also pretty bad. The FX are ok for the most part but there are some really terrible looking sequences as well. This just seems like yet another crappy movie that After Dark Films picked up for cheap and tried to turn into a quick buck. But in the end there's just nothing here all that interesting or entertaining.

1.5/5

Carrie
Year – 1976
Director – Brian De Palma
Tags – Suspense

An outcast girl is relentlessly tormented at school by her classmates and kept under the sadistic thumb of her overly religious mother at home. But as she enters womanhood she discovers that she has telekinetic powers and slowly learns how to use them. The classic Stephen King novel was made into a classic movie here, and I really could not be happier with it. The acting is great and the direction is very tight. During one iconic scene, I loved how the action was shown in a split screen format, allowing the viewer to see Carrie and her powers working at their peak. This is much more than a horror film because it really is a coming of age film at its heart, albeit a very dark one. But I'm sure at some point in our lives at school we wished we could harness such powers. This is a wonderful movie with a great story and it deserves its classic status.

4.5/5

*Carrie 2 can be found under Rage: Carrie 2, The.

Carrie [Remake]
Year – 2002
Director – David Carson
Tags – Suspense

This remake follows the original movie and then adds more, mainly to fill the miniseries run time, and yes, most of it is rather stupid. This movie doesn't have much going for it, so let me get the good things out of the way so I can properly trash this mess. In my opinion no one can do a better job than Sissy Spacek, and that statement still holds true. But I do have to commend the filmmakers for using Angela Bettis because she is the best choice to play Carrie nowadays and she did a fantastic job. Katherine Isabelle was also good but underused much like P.J. Soles was in the original. Now onto the bad. The way the story was told through flashbacks was unappealing, much like the rest of the actors in the movie. None of them seemed to really fit. The direction was very mixed up as well. At times the movie would run smoothly and then the rest of the time I was just bored to tears. The use of horrible CGI was also uncalled for. They didn't need it to make the original effective so why use it now? It's just lazy. I think without Bettis this movie would have been completely worthless but it has just enough going for it to keep it out of the trash can.

2/5

Castle Freak
Year – 1995
Director – Stuart Gordon
Tags – Monsters

A troubled family inherits a castle and go to visit their new acquisition. What they don't realize is that the castle has another inhabitant, locked away deep within the depths of the castle. And now it's loose. This seldom seen Lovecraft movie is definitely one of the best adaptations of his work ever made. I tag this as a monster movie because even though the castle freak is human, it lost its humanity long ago through years of torture and is now a completely twisted beast. The make-up and FX are wonderful, and this is a pretty bloody movie to boot. You also have to love the locale, such a beautiful old castle. The acting is great and I think Jeffrey Combs puts on his best performance ever here. The direction is great as well, with only a few lags during the character development and back story phase of the movie. The freak itself is hideous and wonderfully made up. The story itself is great and very well adapted (still kind of loose, but I dig it). The movie has some mild flaws, mainly due to budget and I think this is just an amazing movie in the genre that needs more recognition.

4/5

Cat's Eye
Year – 1985
Director – Lewis Teague
Tags – Anthology, Suspense, Monsters

This anthology follows a cat on three adventures comprising of a company using extreme methods to get people to quite smoking, a gambling man offering another man who stole his wife a small wager, and finally a small troll that tries to steal the breath of a little girl. Cat's Eye is a fun movie that I like but don't love. I do love the first segment of the movie though as James Woods does a great job with his role, the story is not only excellent but very original. The second story, while well done, felt a little mundane and wasn't that interesting to me. And the last story also felt too plain, but it did have great FX work and the little troll looked awesome. There's nothing I would call bad here, just two average stories and one great one. The screenplay by Stephen King is good but not one of his finer works, but it's still better than average.

3/5

Cave, The
Year – 2007
Director – Bruce Hunt
Tags – Monsters

A scientific expedition into an unexplored cave system goes horribly wrong when a cave-in shuts them off from the only known exit. To make things worse, unknown creatures stalk their every move as they search for a way out. This moderately entertaining flick suffers from a few issues I'll just dispense of right now. First, the cave system looks nice, but too nice, giving it a very artificial feel. The creatures are poorly rendered CGI and very much uninspired in their creation. The cast is uniformly bad, none of them really believable in their roles. Also, this movie is very watered down to receive a PG-13 rating and would have been much more enjoyable as a bloody gorefest than the virtually bloodless affair we have before us. All that being said, it does move along quickly and never gives the viewer a chance to become really bored with it. With some tweaking it could have a lot better, now it is just very average.

2.5/5

Cellar Door, The
Year – 2007
Director – Matt Zettell
Tags – Suspense

A woman is kidnapped by an obsessed man who places her in a wooden box of his own design and hopes that she'll eventually fall in love with him. Yeah, this movie is redundant of other similar movies and doesn't really add much new to the sub genre, but it does have its entertainment value. The acting by the female lead is very poor and her character was pretty unlikeable, so I actually wanted bad things to happen to her, but everyone else is fine in their acting duties. The direction is ok and the pacing is fine for the most part, but there are just too many dull spots in the story to truly hold my interest. There are some punctuations of graphic violence, which is nice. This movie has its good points and bad points, which makes for a fairly average ride, but I've definitely seen a whole lot worse.

2.5/5

Cemetery Gates
Year – 2006
Director – Roy Knyrim
Tags – Monsters

Some kids filming a zombie movie in a graveyard, as well as some other people, are attacked by a giant, mutated Tasmanian devil who was unwittingly freed by an animal rights group. This is a pretty fun old school style monster movie. The creature looks awesome and fortunately the filmmakers did the right thing by barely using CGI and then when they did use it, only using brief flashes. The gore was also off the charts, massive amounts of blood and entrails flying around, and they looked good. But there were bad parts of the movie too. Like the acting, most of the acting was pretty bad. The story isn't bad per se, but it's fairly empty and lacks any real initiative. The direction was ok. The movie had some pacing issues but nothing so bad that it crippled the experience. And all that put together makes for a pretty average flick. Not bad, not good, but really glad it wasn't bad.

2.5/5

Cemetery Man (Dellamorte Dellamore)
Year – 1994
Director – Michele Soavi
Tags – Zombies

This is about a man in a cemetery. Sorry, couldn't resist. The story revolves around a cemetery caretaker and his simple minded assistant. Their job is to put the dead back into the ground after they return as flesh hungry zombies, this time permanently. This is by far one of the most unique zombie movies ever made. Amidst the walking undead is a menagerie of love stories, each one more bizarre than the next. The movie seems to flip between the genres at will and combining the two at times, making for a very different experience. Those expecting constant zombie action may be let down, but the dark humor and brilliant FX work should more than make up for it. I liked this movie a great deal, if for nothing more than daring to be different, the movie plays out like poetry. But, it can be kind of slow, so be prepared for that. No zombie fan should be without this movie in their collection, it breaks the traditional trend of the sub genre and then goes even further into left field.

4/5

Chair, The
Year – 2007
Director – Brett Sullivan
Tags – Ghosts

A woman moves into a house with a sordid past and begins to experience strange phenomenon. As she slowly slips into madness she feels compelled to create a chair in her attic for a rather dubious use. I like this movie even for all of its budget shortfalls. I liked the story, the direction was pretty good and the acting was respectable. The movie carried about a nice atmosphere and had a lot of good ideas, not all of which reached fruition. It's pretty rough but my second viewing allowed me to appreciate more because I knew going into it again that it would be kind of slow. But in the end I liked it for its sparse but effective creepy moments and overall vibe.

3.5/5

Children of the Damned
Year – 1964
Director – Anton Leader
Tags – Suspense

In this sequel to Village of the Damned we find special children from various nations coming together once again. This doesn't really feel like a sequel because it doesn't make much sense as a sequel. The story is definitely lacking and the direction reflects this by being slow and seemingly unsure. The acting is still good but I was troubled by the fact that the children were not all of the fair haired variety. Also, their eyes did not glow when they used their powers until much later in the film, which was a little weird. The way things happened in the original only seemed to be an afterthought on how things would happen here. It's not a bad movie, but it seems as though it's just a bad excuse to make a sequel to a classic.

2.5/5

Children of the Living Dead
Year – 2001
Director – Tor Ramsey
Tags – Zombies

Zombies had risen in a small town years ago and now they are coming back, quietly raising their numbers and being led by a super zombie named Abbot Hayes. This movie started out good enough with Tom Savini and a bunch of good 'ol boys roaming the fields blowing away any zombie they come across. The zombies looked good and there were some nice FX and blood, and then the movie devolved into a showcase of terrible scriptwriting and acting. There is a massive absence of zombies for the bulk of the movie and they only show back up toward the end. I liked the zombie action that bookended the movie but everything else is completely worthless. Ah well, at least the zombies looked pretty good, and in particular the make-up for Hayes. Maybe they shouldn't have tried to create a story and instead just made this into a zombie hunting movie with loads of gore. It would have undoubtedly been more entertaining.

1.5/5

Children of the Night
Year – 1991
Director – Tony Randel
Tags – Vampires

In a sleepy US town, there is a ritual that all kids must go through. They must swim the flooded crypt below a church said to house the body of a very evil man and the corpses of the children he killed. Two girls find out that the legend is true and awaken a vampire from his watery grave. Now it is up to one of the girls and a teacher to send him back and free the town. This is an interesting one. Vampires have been written about and shown on screen for a long time, but never quite like this. Here they do not use coffins, but instead sleep underwater or in a strange mucus cocoon, with their lungs outside their body. I've got to give up some points for originality there. The make-up and FX are pretty good and the acting is ok, but I have to say that the direction is a bit schizophrenic. Sometimes the movie is dark and serious and other times it's just downright silly. There are some flaws in Children of the Night, but I really did enjoy it as a whole. If they had focused more on the atmosphere and cut the cheese factor out, I think they could have made a very scary movie. As it is, not so much but it's still pretty entertaining, especially for a sub-genre that has been used an abused heavily over the years.

3.5/5

Child's Play
Year – 1988
Director – Tom Holland

A killer is taken down by a police detective but before he dies he uses a black magic ritual to transfer his soul into the body of a doll, which ends up in the hands of a young boy as a birthday present. Now the killer has some loose ends to tie up and to find a new body. What sounds like pure 80's cheese actually goes beyond that and ends up being a damn fine slasher flick. With the killer as a seemingly harmless doll, it allows the identity of the killer to be hidden from everyone, and even if the child knows, who would believe him? I like that. And since Brad Dourif voices Chucky, it really gives the doll a lot of personality. Too bad such a great actor didn't get the chance he deserved because he would be forever tied with the killer doll. The rest of the acting is great as well as the direction. But it's the FX I love the most, when Chucky really comes to life and we get to see him, he really does look like a doll come to life, very realistic. It sounds silly on paper and translated much better than it should have on screen. Child's Play is a definite classic of the genre.

4.5/5

Child's Play 2
Year – 1990
Director – John Lafia
Tags – Slasher / Survival

This movie picks up not long after the events of the first movie. I like how the story progresses here because it feels natural and it is the most sensible direction for the franchise to go. I'm not saying the story is great, but it is good and feels right. The acting is fine, nothing wrong there. The direction is good as well, nothing extraordinary but it works. There is a fairly low body count and the kills that aren't really that special, but I guess to add more for the sake of more blood wouldn't make much sense. This is a good sequel that doesn't do anything badly, it's just nothing great. But I do like it because it's just fun and has great dark comedy in it.

3/5

Child's Play 3
Year – 1991
Director – Jack Bender
Tags – Slasher / Survival

This movie continues on several years after the last one. Well, here the story shows some serious strain and this budding franchise is in serious need of some retooling. The acting and direction are fine, nothing special, but nothing terrible. This movie is just so blah though. The setting is interesting and I guess it makes sense, but it's clear that Don Mancini was in no position to write another movie so quickly after the last one. It is a rush job and it just feels like a rush job every inch of the way. Still, it's not bad and it fits with the rest of series, so even though it's the worst installment thus far, it's still completely watchable. If you like the others, you'll probably like this too.

2.5/5

*Child's Play 4 can be found under Bride of Chucky.

*Child's Play 5 can be found under Seed of Chucky.

Chopping Mall
Year – 1986
Director – Jim Wynorski
Tags – Mechanical

A group of people stay overnight in a shopping mall to have a party, but unfortunately for them, the new security system has malfunctioned and now three robots are killing everything that moves. This movie is deliciously cheesy and heavily flawed, but still a good ride. The robots look ok, but most of their kills are pretty standard. The pacing is fine, there are plenty of people to kill and they die at regular intervals. The acting is your typical 80's low budget horror style as is the FX work. While this movie is hardly anything great, you have to admire the dedication to the silly plot and at least having the balls to try something new. The entertainment value is there, but don't go into this expecting the next big thing.

3/5

Christine
Year – 1983
Director – John Carpenter
Tags – Mechanical

A nerdy boy buys a junk car and begins to fix it up. The further along he gets, the more he begins to change, and then car begins to fix itself and gain a mind of its own. An evil car may not sound like much of a premise, but it did come from the mind of Stephen King and this is directed by John Carpenter, so it has more than just a chance of being good. And fortunately it excelled beyond my expectations. This movie isn't scary in the least but it is rather suspenseful and backed by great characters and their relationships. The acting is great, especially by Keith Gordon who plays a nerd, then a badass, and then a psychopath with such a wonderfully seamless transition. The direction is excellent, with the pacing being nearly flawless. The FX are really cool, the way they made the car regenerate is awesome, no doubt this would be done with CGI today, so its nice to see some hard work go into an FX shot, which really makes look that much more special. There's only so much you can do with a killer car, and I kept saying to myself that anyone it chases could just climb a ladder to the top of a building and get away, so you do have to suspend some disbelief when the car goes out killing people, but this is still a pretty awesome movie.

Christmas Tale, A (Cuento de Navidad)
Year – 2006
Director – Paco Plaza
Tags – Suspense

This is part of the DVD box set "6 Films to Keep You Awake". Five children find a woman dressed as Santa Claus that has fallen into a hole in the woods. When one goes for help, he finds out that she is a wanted robber, so instead of setting her free, they decide to extort the money she stole from her by refusing her food and a means of escape. This is one of the most original and well executed movies I've seen in awhile. It's set in the 80's and it even feels like it was made in the 80's as well. The movie is pretty funny at times, genuinely so, and that's surprising given the incredibly dark nature of the story. Here we see children being very cruel and vicious, and pulling off the acting duties very well. The direction is also exceptional, nearly flawless. This movie is almost like a demented version of The Goonies, but better in so many ways. This is far more than a simple suspense story as it unfolds into other genres of horror that I will not ruin for you. Best to just watch it yourself and see some brilliant Spanish horror.

4.5/5

Church, The (La Chiesa)
Year – 1989
Director – Michele Soavi
Tags – Demons

Centuries after a group of knights slaughtered an entire town of people and buried their bodies in a mass grave, the church that was built over top of the grave will now be the site of a demonic uprising. Technically meant to be Demons 3, but the director did not approve of that title and preferred it to a be a stand alone movie, as he felt this movie was more of an atmospheric gothic horror tale as opposed to the gorefests that were Demons and Demons 2. So at least this movie isn't yet another rehash of the original Demons movie. However it is a pretty slow movie with great visuals and FX but no real payoff. The pacing is definitely off but everything else about the movie is great. It's a great piece of horror, but just be sure you're fully awake before watching it.

3.5/5

Citizen X
Year – 1995
Director – Chris Gerolmo
Tags – Serial Killer

This movie is based on serial killer Andrei Chikatilo, who between the years of 1978 and 1990, raped, killed, and mutilated over fifty children in the Soviet Union. This movie focuses on the investigation of Chikatilo and does not show much of the killer's actions. For that you'll have to see the movie Evilenko, which focuses more on the killing and the killer himself and while not quite as good as this movie, is still very good. Anyway, despite the lack of killing on screen for a movie about a serial killer, this is still a pretty amazing film. The acting is tremendously effective and the direction is tight. The way the investigation unfolds is so frustrating that it elicits such emotion from the viewer. While politics soil the investigation the killing keeps going on for years with no end in sight. This is an incredible look into one of the most dreaded serial killers in history and this is definitely a movie I recommend to everyone.

4/5

City of the Living Dead (The Gates of Hell)
Year – 1980
Director – Lucio Fulci
Tags – Zombies

After a priest commits suicide in the small town of Dunwich, strange occurrences begin to happen, culminating in the dead rising from their graves. First I have to start by saying this anything but your standard run of the mill zombie movie. The zombies here move about like they aren't even material, more like ghosts, and they appear to have some sort of psychokinetic abilities too. The direction of this movie takes a little getting used to, as Fulci definitely has a style all his own that will not be for everyone. But you will be treated to a massive amount of unique gore and incredible FX. There was more than one occasion where I was astonished with how they accomplished certain scenes. The story is really very different from everything else out there, which always is a big plus for me when it's done right, and Fulci definitely does it right. Don't go into this expecting a Romero type zombie flick and instead prepare yourself for a thrillingly unique tale with lots of twisted gore and a great story behind it.

4.5/5

Clawed: The Legend of Sasquatch (The Unknown)
Year – 2005
Director – Karl Kozak
Tags – Monsters

A group of poachers are brutally slaughtered by what the locals believe to be a grizzly bear, but when some local kids venture into the woods by themselves, they discover a Sasquatch instead. Yeah, this is just a cliché excuse for a Sasquatch movie and I expected to just hate it, but instead I was actually mildly entertained. The story doesn't offer up anything that hasn't been done in a hundred other movies, but at least it's not bad. The acting is surprisingly adequate as well, not particularly great but at least it didn't have me ripping my eyes out of my head like so many other low budget horror movies. The direction is ok, once again, nothing special. There's some gore and the Sasquatch is fairly cool looking to boot. A strictly average Bigfoot tale but that's better than a bad Bigfoot movie any day.

2.5/5

Cloverfield
Year – 2008
Director – Matt Reeves
Tags – Monsters

A giant creature suddenly begins attacking New York City and the night unfolds through a first person perspective via camcorder. It's about time we got our own Godzilla, but instead of being a cheeseball monster movie, what we got was a very human drama that just happens to have a very unique monster surrounding it. For being a camcorder type movie, the screen remains smooth instead of jerky, which is appealing for the audience, and a very small sacrifice at realism. Unfortunately the PG-13 rating also takes away a bit of the realism, you're going to tell me a giant monster attacks New York and no one's screaming expletives? Very minor of course, but I just had to mention it. The CGI is great here, and the monster is refreshingly original. The acting is smooth and the direction is tight. After about a fifteen minute intro, the monster arrives and it never gets boring at all after that, the story is constantly moving, which is great. I think this movie is done exceptionally well, but be warned that since this told from a first person perspective, virtually no explanation is given for any of the occurrences. I like it, some people may not. But you can figure things out on your own through DVD special features and the viral marketing campaign behind this movie, which I had fun doing. This was just a great moviegoing experience.

4.5/5

Club Dread
Year – 2004
Director – Jay Chandrasekhar
Tags – Slasher / Survival

A killer targets the staff of an island paradise resort, threatening to kill everyone if they try to tell anyone. I was excited see that Broken Lizard was delving into horror because I found their comedies to be pretty damn funny. Yes, I watch more than horror, shocking isn't it? And this movie definitely has its funny moments, but not many. The kills are pretty standard for the most part, good blood, but nothing extraordinary, except for the last kill of the movie, which is pretty awesome. Other than that, the pacing is great, the acting is great, and when it does manage to be funny, it is pretty damn funny. If they had worked a bit more on the comedy and maybe had some more blood and gory kills, this movie could have been amazing, but as it stands, it's still pretty good. Oh, and the life size Pac-Man game was great.

Congo
Year – 1995
Director – Frank Marshall
Tags – Animals

Congo is the tale of an African expedition by a very diverse group of people. One is going into the heart of Africa in the name of science, one for the love of her former fiancé, and another for wealth. In addition to having to deal with a nation in perpetual civil war, they must also deal with a colony of murderous, ravenous apes. This is a very good flick, filled with interesting plot points and a great pace. Special mention must be paid to the various apes in the movie, as they are a mix of animatronics and people in cleverly designed suits, and in this regard, the FX work is absolutely astounding. I'm very glad they did not try to use CGI for the apes, as it just would not have looked nearly as slick. The cast does an exceptional job in their very diverse roles and the direction is very smooth. When the killer grey apes finally come into play for the expedition, their methods of murder are exceptionally brutal, and the final showdown in the diamond mines displays this fact with great vigor. Now, the production is not without its flaws. First off, everything unfolds much too conveniently for my tastes, and second, you know who's making it out of the jungle right away as the rest of the cast is obviously cannon fodder. But that's just a minor annoyance in an otherwise great movie. And I don't just consider this horror because Bruce Campbell is in it, come on, killer apes!

3.5/5

Constantine
Year – 2005
Director – Francis Lawrence
Tags – Demons

Constantine, based on the comic book Hellblazer, follows a man spending his time smoking and sending demons back to Hell. But now stricken with a very aggressive Cancer, he now stands a chance of going to Hell himself, and to be surrounded by everyone he has sent there. I have to say I wasn't expecting much here, a lot of comic book adaptations are notoriously bad, and especially so when it comes to lesser known comics. I do have to say though that I was pleasantly surprised with how much I enjoyed this. Shia LaBeouf is definitely the bane in this movie as his annoying presence is certainly a hindrance, but other than his awful acting, everyone else is really quite good. The story moves along at a quick pace and gives you some great visual eye candy. The movie is always moving forward and never sticks to over explaining situations and it always leaves some things in the dark. Kind of a fan's inside joke thing going on. If they had recast that one part I could have rated it higher, because really that's my only complaint, but since his part is kind of big, it just brought the movie down a peg or two for me. Still great though.

Copycat
Year – 1995
Director – Jon Amiel
Tags – Serial Killer (Fictional)

A serial killer begins a murdering rampage in San Francisco and the police seek the aid of an agoraphobic psychologist to put an end to reign of terror. Then he begins to change how he kills, copying the style of serial killers from the past. This is a really well done movie, the concept is fresh and interesting, and overall it's a great production. The actors do a great job, the script is tight and well thought out. It isn't the kind of movie that just blows me away and redefines the serial killer sub genre like other movies have, but it's just a damn fine thriller and I honestly have no complaints about it. It may not be the end all be all, but it is awesome enough for me.

4/5

Cottage, The
Year – 2008
Director – Paul Andrew Williams
Tags – Slasher / Survival

Deep in the countryside, a bungled kidnapping turns into a nightmare when the people involved are attacked by a murderous backwoods man. This horror/comedy features some excellent gore and some pretty funny moments, but not enough of them. I was left wanting more because the moments I enjoyed were great, and I felt a little let down when I didn't get more. Don't get me wrong, this is a great movie, but I just think they could have done more with it. The direction is very good as the movie moves along smoothly and never really lags. The FX and acting are great as well. I like the story and the movie as a whole, and while I felt there could have been more humor and more gore, what we have here is still a great slasher flick.

3.5/5

Cradle of Fear
Year – 2001
Director – Alex Chandon
Tags – Anthology, Suspense

While I mark this as an anthology because it does have four different stories, in a way it also isn't because it still flows like a regular movie and is very cohesive, each section ultimately relating to one another. Here, different groups of people all come into contact with someone known simply as "The Man", who appears to working for an imprisoned serial killer in some capacity. And as the tagline says, "It's not if they die… its how." This is a fascinating recipe for a horror movie. It's an anthology, but also a regular movie. It's kind of cheesy and silly but also features graphic gore sequences, soft core porn moments, loads of nudity and more. I have to say I've never really seen a movie quite like it. The story and direction really fit well in the movie and come out great. The acting seems to be bad but I found it to work, maybe the British accents made it sound better than it was, I'm not sure. This movie is rather interesting and compelling, especially for such a low budget movie. Gorehounds, prepare to have a goregasm. Oh, and this is not just for Cradle of Filth fans as the movie goes above and beyond just being the movie that stars the lead singer.

4/5

Craft, The
Year – 1996
Director – Andrew Fleming
Tags – Witchcraft

A teenage girl with some personal anguish and now living in a new town falls in with three other teenage girls who practice witchcraft. Now with a fourth, their circle is complete and they begin castings spells and curses to fill their hearts content. The Craft is one of those movies you can't help but like even though the storyline is about as linear and transparent as they come. The acting is pretty good, especially by Fairuza Balk, who just oozes talent. The FX work is also pretty good for the most part. The story however, is typical fair. There are no surprises here, you can pretty much guess how the movie is going to play out in the first few minutes, but the film is ultimately entertaining and just good fun all around.

3/5

Crazies, The
Year – 1973
Director – George A. Romero
Tags – Infection

A mind altering chemical finds its way into the water supply of a small Pennsylvania town. The military are quick to shut the town down before the infection can spread. Now a group of people are trying to escape only to be stuck between the infected crazies and the military personnel who have shot to kill orders. Between the creations of his zombie epics, George Romero shot this lesser known movie. In a lot of ways this is kind of like another zombie movie, but instead of an undead infection, the protagonists in the story must deal with an infection that causes insanity and homicidal behavior. I like this movie for a lot of reasons, but first I have to say that this movie is also pretty slow. Other than the pacing and the overly long feel of the movie, I have very little to complain about. The direction and acting are pretty natural, the action sequences are modest and have a realistic feel to them. There is one particularly twisted moment that was very daring and I appreciate its inclusion in the movie. This is about madness after all, and to fully portray that, you really need to get into some taboo territory. The Crazies is slow but rewarding and the legendary director proves he can do more than just zombies.

3.5/5

Crazy Eights
Year – 2006
Director – James K. Jones
Tags – Ghosts

Six childhood friends are brought back together by the death of an old friend, and they are forced to bring up a secret they all share, when the secret brings itself to light. I just can not recommend this movie as I just found it to be incredibly boring and formulaic. The cast is really good but they just look bored, and if they were bored making it, just imagine what kind of fun you're in line for. Nothing of consequence really happens in this movie. There's some blood and off camera kills, nothing special occurs there either. The plot is far from anything new but this movie still could have been something more besides this utter disappointment. And I must say that if it wasn't for the great cast, this movie would have been worth nothing at all.

1.5/5

Creature
Year – 1998
Director – Stuart Gillard
Tags – Sea Monsters

The military has been experimenting with mixing shark and human DNA, and now their experiment is loose in the open ocean. Now it's up to a scientist to find a way to stop a vicious creature that possesses the intelligence of a man. Wow, this movie is pretty crazy, but not necessarily in a good way. The story is just so over the top it ends up being so dumb that it's actually entertaining. The acting is fine, for the most part, but the movie is way too long though and instead of being a miniseries, it should have just been a regular movie. Because of this fact the movie is slow and the direction is greatly hindered. The FX are also somewhat cheesy, a little too much so. I had hoped that this would be at least somewhat interesting, and I guess it does have its entertainment value, just not as much as I would have liked.

2.5/5

Creature from Black Lake
Year – 1976
Director – Joy N. Houck Jr.
Tags – Monsters

Two college students head off into a small town to investigate reports of a sasquatch-like creature. This movie kind of blows. The acting isn't very good and the direction is really slow, sitting through this was difficult. The story isn't a bad set-up, pretty standard stuff really but it has some really good moments, just not enough of them strung along to make the movie interesting. When they finally show the creature I wish they hadn't because when it was cloaked in shadows it looked cool and mysterious but when you get to see it in full light, it's so obviously a costume and make-up and the movie isn't campy enough to make that work. Overall this is a very unsatisfying Bigfoot movie.

1.5/5

Creep
Year – 2004
Director – Christopher Smith
Tags – Slasher / Survival

A woman using the subway to meet up with a friend finds herself trapped after nodding off on the platform. Now someone, or something, is following her as she tries to escape, leaving a bloody trail of death in its wake. The subway is such an underused locale in the horror genre. It has tons of possibilities to it but we rarely see a horror movie based completely in it. Fortunately here the subway is used to great effect. The Creep is just that, creepy, but I won't say more because I want you to see it for yourself. The acting is very good and it's always nice to see Franka Potente in a genre flick. The direction is also very good but there are some pacing issues. The story is great stuff though and nothing is ever fully explained, which I like because nothing is more annoying than when a character conveniently just knows things that they really have no business knowing. There is also a fair amount of gore, which is always welcome in a movie like this. This may not be a redefining genre movie but it sure is a damn good time.

3.5/5

Creepshow
Year – 1982
Director – George A. Romero
Tags – Anthology, Zombies, Biological, Monsters, Animals

This anthology has five stories and a wraparound. The wraparound story concerns a boy whose father hates that he reads comic books. The first segment sees a murdered man coming back for his Father's Day cake. The second concerns a meteorite that causes extreme plant growth. The third is about a scorned husband whose revenge scheme goes wrong. The fourth is about an old crate found locked away and what's inside it. And the last story is about an old man and his fear of roaches. It's hard to find an anthology where every story is just top notch, and undoubtedly that is due to the fact that Romero directed, King wrote, and Savini handled the FX. That trio has made a comic book come to life with this movie. The stories are all very good, the cast is remarkable, and of course, the direction is smooth. The FX work does deserve extra attention as there was such a varying degree of elements used in the stories, and that meant a lot of different FX. Savini rose to the challenge and made them all work. And extra kudos go to King himself for his starring role in the second story, he played a bumpkin so well you would never guess the man was actually a genius. This is a timeless horror classic and easily one of the best anthologies ever made.

4.5/5

Creepshow 2
Year – 1987
Director – Michael Gornick
Tags – Anthology, Slasher / Survival, Biological, Zombies

This sequel to the original has three new stories and a new wraparound. This time the wraparound story is mostly animated, giving the movie an even bigger comic book feel whilst following a boy for the day. The first story is about a robbery turned murder and the revenge that ensues when a wooden Native American statue comes to life. The second story follows a group of college kids as they visit a lake inhabited by a strange substance. And the last story involves a woman involved in a fatal hit and run accident who is mercilessly followed by the hitchhiker whom she killed. I like this movie but it just doesn't have the same appeal as the original. The second story is my favorite because it is just so awesome with some really great FX. The first story is very good and the last one is just ok. I'm glad to see Romero back, but here he wrote the screenplay from King's stories and had someone else direct. And while the direction is good, it would have undoubtedly been better with Romero at the helm. I'm also disappointed there are only three stories. But still, this is a really good anthology and a nice follow up to one of the best.

3.5/5

Creepshow 3
Year – 2006
Director – Ana Clavell, James Glenn Dudelson
Tags – Anthology, Mechanical, Serial Killer (Fictional), Ghosts

The third Creepshow movie has five new stories and no wraparound story. The first is about a universal remote that works on more than electronics. The second is about a man and his special radio. The third is about a hooker who happens to be a serial killer. The fourth is about a professor and his bride to be. And the last segment is about a doctor who is haunted by someone he has wronged. What in the blue hell did I just watch? This has got to be one of the worst pieces of shit ever constructed. A lobotomized raccoon could make a better movie than this. The writers / directors need to be sterilized immediately before they get a chance to breed and spread their stupidity among the masses. There is not a single good point in this movie. Every story sucks, is poorly written and is predictable, nonsensical, or just plain moronic. The movie is also boring as hell and very poorly shot. The acting is some of the worst I have ever seen as well. There's no humor, no scares, and absolutely nothing worthwhile here. They try to connect the stories as well but there's no point to it and there's even continuity errors. You read that right, continuity errors in the same movie. The people who made this should be shot.

0.5/5

Crush, The
Year – 1993
Director – Alan Shapiro
Tags – Suspense

A man lands a new job at a trendy magazine and rents a guest house from a nice couple upon his arrival to the city. The couple has a 14 year old daughter who is intelligent, attractive, and just a little bit out of her mind. A deep obsession on her part begins, with disastrous consequences. This was a fun film, centering on Cary Elwes and Alicia Silverstone, who carry the movie quite well. You really have to feel bad for the guy once the obsession really kicks into high gear, as things in his life simply spiral out of control. To be honest, I really enjoyed this movie, and it's a great time killer, but it just seems all too familiar. There's no new ground here to speak of, and this has all been done before, so while it does lose some points with me for total lack of originality, the movie more than makes up for things with an excellent script, wonderful direction, as stated before, great acting from the two leads. You've seen it all before, but don't you just want to see it again, especially when it's done this well?

3.5/5

Cry of the Banshee
Year – 1970
Director – Gordon Hessler
Tags – Witchcraft

The hunt for witches takes a turn for the worse as a coven fights back against Christian savagery with supernatural means. This movie definitely has a cheese factor to it, but honestly, I really liked it. It shows just how barbaric Christians could be back in the day in charging innocent people with witchcraft just so they could rape and kill them. I'm not even exaggerating. And there's plenty of barbarism on display here with sex and violence, the only difference is that the witches fight back. I liked the acting despite the fact that the cast could really ham it up at times and the direction was a bit uneven, but this is still a pretty entertaining movie with lots of boobs and blood set in a time that modern day religious folks love to pretend never happened.

3.5/5

Cry_Wolf
Year – 2005
Director – Jeff Wadlow

A group of rich kids at a posh boarding school decide to play a game of lies and deception, but when the real terror comes into play, no one will believe them. And who really cares about them anyway? Not me, that's for sure. The story is very plain and boring, obviously written from the plot twist backwards, and speaking of that twist, it actually made the movie even more unappealing. The acting and direction are ok, nothing special. The kills are pretty much all standard and not very bloody either. This is just a throwaway slasher flick that you'll forget right after watching it. Wait a minute, what movie am I writing about? Ha ha, hey at least I amuse myself, which is more than this movie did. Bad, but still somewhat better than a lot of other movies out there, which is actually pretty sad if you stop to think about it.

1.5/5

Cube
Year – 1997
Director   Vincenzo Natali
Tags – Mechanical

A group of strangers awaken to find themselves trapped inside a matrix of cubes, some of which contain deadly traps. Now they must discover a way to escape before they die of dehydration .This movie gets major points for originality and execution. Even with such an ambitious idea, the minimalist set-up really works out well. Limited cast, small location, etc. There aren't many traps shown, but the ones that are come off pretty sinister and lead to some excellent death sequences. The pacing is a small issue though, as the movie does tend to lag a few times, but that is really the only issue I had. This is a very nice mix of Sci-Fi, Horror, Mystery and Suspense all rolled into a giant killing machine. This is a great movie.

4/5

Cube 2: Hypercube
Year – 2002
Director – Andrzej Sekula
Tags – Mechanical

In the second Cube movie, we have not only new people but a new kind of Cube, a Hypercube. While the first movie was more about math, this takes on a more science and physics role. The plot is more complex, but I think they were trying to make it a little too complex. The traditional traps of the first Cube movie are replaced here with rooms having different aspects like time alterations and gravitational shifts, which are interesting, but I miss the traps. I appreciate that the people behind the sequel took a different route instead of just rehashing the original with new people and new traps, but it is a slightly less effective movie. I still enjoyed it because they kept the same production quality as the original, and added an engaging plot that has a similar, but not too similar formula.

3.5/5

Cube Zero
Year – 2004
Director – Ernie Barbarash
Tags – Mechanical

This is a supposed prequel to the Cube series, but doesn't quite feel like it. This movie does give some behind the scenes type stuff though, showing us how and why things are happening the way they are. I have mixed feelings about this movie. I like that the whole Cube experiment was left in the shadows and we're not sure why any of it is happening, and this movie explains away most of those shadows. At the same time I liked seeing what was happening while everyone is running around, trying to avoid traps and searching for a way out. The way the film was done though is kind of boring as it plods along trying to be clever but not doing the job very well. We are treated to more traps and a new jumble of people, but they really do take a backseat to the over explaining of the Cube. It's not bad, but may disillusion fans of the series and that's really something you don't want to do in my opinion.

2.5/5

Cujo
Year – 1983
Director – Lewis Teague
Tags – Animals

A woman and her son become trapped in a car that won't run by a rabid St. Bernard. I guess that one line pretty much sums it up. You would think that that plot would be rife for a boring experience, but this did come from the master of terror mind you. And the director did do a great job with the movie because in the wrong hands it could have easily been extremely dull. There are great character interactions, back stories, and very good acting to back all of it up. The best actor of all is the dog, and that's not a slam against the actors, they were all great, but that dog was just something special. And the make-up they put on that dog was just crazy, he really did look rabid. The dog just had such a personality, like how at the beginning when he was just turning rabid, you could see him struggle to remain sane, and then he was like a completely different dog overtaken by madness. This is a very tense movie with a lot of great moments and I just like it a lot. I think somebody once said don't work with children or animals, well, both are here, and both did a stellar job, making this a really one of a kind movie.

4/5

Curse, The

Year – 1987
Director – David Keith
Tags – Biological

Loosely based on the H.P. Lovecraft tale, The Colour Out of Space, this movie is about a comet that crash lands in a farmer's field, carrying with it a sort of bacteria that gets into the water supply and starts to change the farmer's crops, and eventually the people as well. I wish I could say that this is a great movie but it just isn't. Even though it's based on a great story, the way it plays out here is just not very good. The acting is fine, but the direction is slow and kind of boring. I was worried about the FX when the comet "crash landed" because you could clearly see the pole it was attached to, and then when the comet was idle it just looked like a giant testicle. But then when the fruit and vegetables became infected they looked absolutely revolting, and then the make-up and other FX looked great as well, which totally redeemed it. This is ok and if you're a hardcore Lovecraft fan you could do a lot worse.

2.5/5

Curse 2: The Bite

Year – 1989
Director – Frederico Prosperi
Tags – Infection

A man gets bitten by a strange snake and suddenly his arm begins to change into a snake itself, as his mind slowly deteriorates and he begins to lose control. Yeah, this doesn't have anything to do with the original Curse movie, but that's ok. This one is actually a little better than the original, if only for the grand FX sequences toward the end of the movie. And that really is the high point of the movie, the FX. Everything else is decent, the acting, direction and story, but it's the FX that really pull this movie into being better than average. It works really well as an off beat 80's horror flick where pretty much anything went back then. Good stuff.

3/5

Curse of the Puppet Master

Year – 1998
Director – David DeCoteau
Tags – Slasher / Survival

I can't even tell anymore where each Puppet Master installment falls in with the rest. This sixth movie is just a movie, and I'm not sure when it happens in the series. And honestly I don't care either. This is definitely the worst of the series thus far, which is quite the feat given the crap that's been put out up to this point. The acting isn't very good, the direction is slow and plodding, and the story just doesn't fit well in the series. I don't think I've ever had quite as difficult a time figuring out when the hell the movies in a series are actually happening. There are just so many continuity errors and unclear directions in the storyline that I can't help but get completely confused by this point. Another issue with this movie is that there is hardly any puppet action as well, and come on, the puppets are the only reason we watch these movies. Skip it.

1.5/5

Cursed
Year – 2005
Director – Wes Craven
Tags – Werewolves

After a nasty car accident, two siblings find themselves attacked by a huge wolf, but escape with only a couple of flesh wounds. But then they begin to change and find out that what attacked them was no wolf, but a werewolf and they must find out who the werewolf is and kill it or be forever cursed. Yawn. That word pretty much sums up the movie for me. It's really not that good at all, and here's why: The actors just don't seem to fit their roles for the most part. The story is also pretty weak and therefore the direction suffers. The werewolf is ok looking but the kills and blood are benign. If you watch the unrated version you get to see some really bad CGI kills and one awesome kill though. This werewolf movie just isn't anything special and while it's not the worst one, it is still definitely below average.

2/5

Dagon
Year – 2001
Director – Stuart Gordon
Tags – Monsters

The bulk of this Lovecraft adaptation is from The Shadow Over Innsmouth. A young entrepreneur and his girlfriend are on the sea with friends when a freak storm damages their boat. He must paddle to shore for help, and instead finds a small fishing village who worship a sea god, and are themselves turning into creatures of the sea. So the synopsis sounds strange, I know, doesn't sound like much in the way of startling horror, but this is Lovecraft we're talking about here. This is definitely one of the more effective adaptations I've seen, and in all fairness, it is very difficult to adapt Lovecraft. But Stuart Gordon crafts an absolute classic here. The CGI can get pretty bad at times, but I'm sure budget constraints are the main cause. Everything else however is at the top of its game. The make-up and practical FX work are unbelievably great. They made the people of the village look absolutely horrifying. The set design is grandiose and the acting is very well done and natural, especially by Ezra Godden, who carries the bulk of the movie on his own. If you are a Lovecraft fan, you owe it to yourself to see this movie, and as for horror fans, treat yourself to something different. Amazing job.

4.5/5

Dahmer
Year – 2002
Director – David Jacobson
Tags – Serial Killer

This tells the true life story of Jeffrey Dahmer, who killed 17 men and boys over a period of 13 years. The movie focuses on one small portion of Dahmer's life while telling the bulk of his story in flashbacks. I liked this and it was interesting to tell his story this way, but also kind of unnecessary. I also feel that the filmmakers really chickened out in making this movie because Dahmer was known for doing some incredibly sick things to his victims including torture, mutilation and cannibalism, none of which are really shown. They focused more on the murder and rape aspect, leaving out the gory details. I don't know, I just think that if you're going to make a movie about a depraved individual, you better go all the way. The direction is ok but the movie does feel a little long. The acting is very good and Jeremy Renner is pretty creepy as the title character. Overall this is an ok movie, average really does it justice. With hardly any blood and violence, this just seems like a very tame take on a very violent serial killer.

2.5/5

Damien: Omen II
Year – 1978
Director – Don Taylor
Tags – Devil

This movie continues on several years after the original Omen. I love the progression of the story here. Sequels to box office successes tend to have a habit of being rushed and not thought out well, but here I think the story is very well made, and on top of that the acting and direction are great. There are also some more great death scenes that compliment those of the original nicely. And while I did enjoy this movie a great deal, and I liked everything about it, I did like it less than the original, but that's fine, I don't expect every sequel to top the first, I just want a good progression on the original, and this movie definitely accomplished that.

4/5

Dance of the Dead
Year – 2008
Director – Gregg Bishop
Tags – Zombies

On the night of the big high school dance, zombies rise from their graves to attack the living, and now the towns only hope are the kids who couldn't get dates to the prom. I'll tell you, Gregg Bishop is becoming a headliner in the horror community, and if he keeps putting out great movies like this, he's on the fast track to becoming a genre legend. Dance of the Dead is funny, gory and just plain awesome. It definitely has an 80's horror feel to it, but instead of being cheesy, it's just genuinely funny. I like the fact that actual teenagers were used to play the part of the kids, as that really made the movie more believable. There was one exception, Justin Welborn is obviously not a teenager but he played his role well and given his character, I believe that he could have been held back a grade or ten. The FX work is excellent, the zombies are wonderful, and the loads of blood work wonders. This is what low budget horror is all about, showing that you can make a truly great movie without millions of dollars and big name actors, at least big names in the commercial sense. One of the best zombie movies I've ever seen, keep up the great work Gregg.

4.5/5

Dark, The
Year – 2005
Director – John Fawcett
Tags – Ghosts

A young girl is visiting her father with her mother when she mysteriously disappears into the ocean. Now there is a new girl in their lives, but this girl has been dead for fifty years. I just don't like this movie. The movie is very slow and doesn't have much to show for it. It just doesn't go anywhere. The acting is good, except by Maria Bello who can't put on a good performance to save her life it seems. I guess I can't blame the director because even though the movie was slow, he did an admirable job at trying to make it interesting, and there were some interesting visuals, but the story is just so bland it was doomed from the beginning.

2/5

Dark Angel: The Ascent
Year – 1994
Director – Linda Hassani
Tags – Demons

A female demon escapes Hell to try and live on Earth. Along the path she takes, she ends up killing "sinners" and even manages to fall in love. This is another one of those movies I remember watching back in the day on late night cable and being delighted with the bits of blood and nudity that came with it. The story is a pretty good one to boot as it has some originality to it and manages to cross genres by adding an awkward but interesting love story in with her bloody punishment of bad people. The acting here is decent, and the direction is about the same. The FX looked good most of the time, but there are some pretty shoddy moments. This is a movie with a good story and an average everything else. Nothing special but nothing bad either.

3/5

Dark City

Year – 1998
Director – Alex Proyas
Tags – Aliens

Beings from another world play with the lives of people by changing the city they live in and even their own personalities. But one man has broken free and tries to sort out the mystery of who the beings are and what exactly they want. This movie is a very ambitious venture into very original territory, and although it is not a terribly exciting movie, it is a very entertaining watch. The acting is good but nothing overwhelming, but the direction however, is very tight and offers up very few lags. The story is the real star here as the movie plays out like an old detective story set in a fantastic world of soul sucking creatures with telekinetic powers. I really liked the architecture of the city and the old style it had as well, all of which made for a visually appealing film if nothing else. Dark City is a very good and well made movie and if you're into wildly original tales, then this is definitely the movie for you.

3.5/5

Dark Floors
Year – 2008
Director – Pete Riski
Tags – Ghosts, Monsters

A man and his autistic daughter emerge from a hospital elevator with three other people to find out that suddenly the hospital is abandoned, except for the spirits and monsters that now lurk the hallways. This is a movie that had tons of potential but failed to really deliver anything significant. Everything about this movie was great except for one thing, the script, and that's a pretty big thing. The movie was just not very well put together. The story is muddled and doesn't make much sense. On the plus side the viewer is treated to some really cool looking ghosts and monsters, I just wish there was a decent story behind all the good stuff. You'll enjoy the visuals for sure, they are a treat, but there's nothing behind them to make the movie the outstanding experience it could have been. Disappointing, but not a bad effort.

3/5

Dark Half, The
Year – 1993
Director – George A. Romero
Tags – Suspense

A writer who has written his most successful works under a pen name is blackmailed by a man who threatens to tell the world his secret. When the writer "kills" his alter ego instead of paying the man, his pen name takes form and begins to kill all those in contact with the writer, setting him up in the process. The story is interesting but it just isn't one of my favorites. It has some good elements to it but it just ends up playing out like so many movies that have come before it. Fortunately there is some great acting and direction to help bolster the somewhat weak story. When Romero and King got together, I was hoping for a different adaptation, but for what it is, it's pretty good, I would just like to see them team up on something with a little more meat to it.

3/5

Dark Hours, The
Year – 2005
Director – Paul Fox
Tags – Slasher / Survival

A psychiatrist decides to spend a relaxing weekend with her husband and sister in their isolated cabin in the woods when a patient of hers escapes from the asylum and seeks retribution for what he believes is unfair treatment. So the territory of this movie is nothing new, and when something like this comes along, I want to be wowed or there's just no point in making it. Well, I was wowed, but not at first. The movie starts off on shaky ground as it was a little slow and I really disliked the main character, but once things started to happen, the movie moved along very briskly and never let up. There's a twist in the storyline that I could see coming because I think the filmmaker's foreshadowed too much, but when it came I still wasn't disappointed because it was just pulled off that well. The story is awesome, the acting is very good, the direction is excellent, and to top things off, there's nice FX work as well. This is just a great survival horror movie with wonderful psychological overtones and I highly recommend it.

4/5

Dark Remains
Year – 2005
Director – Brian Avenet-Bradley
Tags – Ghosts

After the brutal murder of their young daughter, her parents temporarily move out into an isolated cabin to escape the madness of their lives. But once there they discover that their new retreat is anything but safe. The story here isn't exactly the best but it definitely has some very good moments, what really helps out the movie is that fact that it is a genuinely scary time. The acting is pretty good and the direction is well done. The FX are really nice with some creepy make-up that really sells the ghosts. I can always appreciate a movie like this because the filmmakers don't make it cheap, they use good scares, not bullshit jump scares, and they give the movie a great creepy atmosphere. This movie does have some issues but the overall appearance greatly outshines those issues and makes for a fantastic film.

4/5

Dark Ride

Year – 2006
Director – Craig Singer
Tags – Slasher / Survival

A van load of friends decide to take a detour on their trip to visit a carnival ride with a checkered past. It was the sight of a grisly double murder, and it turns out that the murderer may not actually be gone. Dark Ride is not unique or original in any way shape or form, it adds nothing to the slasher genre, but hey, how much could you possibly add at this point and time anyway? That being said, Dark Ride is entertaining. It's a turn-your-brain-off-and-enjoy-the-blood movie. Nothing outstanding here, but it wasn't trying to be either. This movie wanted to be a fun and bloody ride, and it was, even if it wasn't in the least bit memorable.

2.5/5

Dark Water (Honoguari Mizu No Soko Kara)
Year – 2002
Director – Hideo Nakata
Tags – Ghosts

A single mother and her daughter move into a new apartment and almost immediately the woman begins to see visions of a child and is disturbed by the curious water stain growing on her ceiling. I've heard a lot of good things about this movie, and while I like it, I can't say I loved it. The story is pretty good but fails to be anything compelling and the direction reflects this as the pacing can get pretty slow at times. I love how it ended though, which made for a unique twist and heightened my enjoyment. It had many good things going for it but it was just too slow for me. Enjoyable if somewhat laborious in its journey.

3.5/5

Dark Water [Remake]
Year – 2005
Director – Walter Salles
Tags – Ghosts

This remake of the foreign Dark Water follows the same essential plot of the original. American remakes of foreign are always interesting to watch even though the majority of them are quite inferior, and this one is no different. This isn't a shot for shot remake and it does make a couple of small tweaks to the story, but even so it manages to be even slower than the original. It's also dumbed down quite a bit, like most foreign remakes and lacks any good flair. But fortunately the filmmakers did the right thing in throwing a lot of good actors into the movie, which ended up being it's only highlight. Another disappointment in a long line of disappointments.

2/5

Dark Waters

Year – 1993
Director – Mariano Baino
Tags – [Hidden to conceal spoilers]

After her father's death, a woman travels to a mysterious island to try and find out why he funded a monastery for many years. What she finds there is nothing short of evil. This movie was crafted in a very grand Lovecraftian fashion, whether intentional or not. But while it delves deep into that style of filmmaking, it also manages to be very cohesive, which is a difficult thing to accomplish. The story is great and the FX are marvelous, loaded with creepy visuals and a fair amount of gore. The direction and acting are also very good with only minor annoyances along the way that did not profoundly affect my feelings toward the movie. This movie is definitely a visual feast for those out there who like their horror dark and bloody, and the Lovecraftian angle gives it an even better staying power in my eyes. Great stuff.

4/5

Darkness

Year – 2002
Director – Jaume Balaguero
Tags – Ghosts

A family moves into a new home with a very dark past and now the darkness held in the walls of the house is looking to claim the new resident's lives. I love contemporary Spanish horror but this was obviously made to have American appeal and dumbed down a bit from what it could have been. Despite the attempt at giving the movie a wider appeal, it does have some good stuff going for it. The back story of the house is very nice but the present day situations just aren't scary and end up culminating into some very yawn inducing moments. The direction is good but very slow at times, the movie does pick up in the third act and it does end nicely however. The acting is very good so there are no complaints there. It's disappointing to see a movie with potential like this be toned down to placate your average audience, but the world is run by money and when it comes down to pleasing the fans with a well done movie or pleasing the masses with average fare, the cash-in will win almost every time.

3/5

Darkness Falls

Year – 2003
Director – Jonathan Liebesman
Tags – Ghosts

In the town of Darkness Falls, a vengeful spirit has returned after being murdered 150 years ago, and she has come back in the form of an evil tooth fairy. After a boy survives an attack, he is forced to come back and help the little brother of an old friend who is being visited by the same spirit. This movie is an excellent take on how to make a completely average horror movie. The script isn't that great, the acting and characters are ok, the pacing is decent, the ghost and other FX work are blah and everything else about the production is more of the same. It certainly is somewhat entertaining and watchable, but there is nothing at all special about this movie. That's all I have to say for this, the vanilla of horror movies, not my favorite but it will do when I'm hungry.

2.5/5

Dawn of the Dead
Year – 1978
Director – George A. Romero
Tags – Zombies

While not a direct sequel to Night of the Living Dead, Dawn of the Dead is rather a continuation of the zombie uprising. Here we find a group of four people escaping by means of helicopter from a city that is falling apart. They come across a mall that is abandoned, save for the undead, and try to fortify it from the growing number of zombies. This is still, after all these years, one of the best horror movies ever made. Romero is known for putting comments on society in his movies, and here that comment is still prevalent today. The way the zombies mindlessly went to the mall, have you been to a mall lately? Everyone there really does look like a zombie. But the movie is not a classic just because of that, there are multiple reasons. The FX work is great, especially during a particular helicopter scene; you'll know which one it is when you see it. The zombies may just be blue faced, but back then, it worked, of course you couldn't get by with that nowadays, but the blue faced zombie has a nostalgic appeal for me. The scale of the movie is probably what most impressed me, the mall is huge, and so is the army of the undead, which always managed to get my imagination brewing and let me think about what was happening outside of what was shot in the movie. I think the direction in this movie is also Romero at his finest, because I found it to be absolutely flawless. Even if you're not a fan of zombie movies, you owe it to yourself to watch this work of art.

5/5

Dawn of the Dead [Remake]
Year – 2004
Director – Zack Snyder
Tags – Zombies

This remake follows the original to a degree, with people holing up in a mall to evade a zombie uprising, but has different characters, more characters and follows a different chain of events. Remaking a classic will always get people in a tizzy, but fortunately Zack Snyder made a movie that is a more than competent retelling of the original masterpiece. There are many differences between the two movies, but this remake definitely has the essence of the original. First, the zombies here are fast, which does a lot to update the fear factor. The inclusion of more characters allows for a more diversity and plot points. The FX in this movie are particularly awesome, very bloody. The acting is where I had my issues with this movie. Ving Rhames and Mekhi Phifer don't have much range as actors and know how to really only play one kind of person and here it feels pretty stagnant. Everyone else is fine though. The direction is tight and the pacing is wonderful, I couldn't have asked for anything more in that respect. My gripes are minor and they didn't hurt the movie too badly in my opinion. This is an excellent movie and it gives me hope that remakes of the classics will not be made for mere dollar signs and instead may be put in someone's hands that actually cares how it will turn out.

4.5/5

Day of the Dead
Year – 1985
Director – George A. Romero
Tags – Zombies

The third Romero zombie movie takes us even further into the zombie apocalypse, where the undead greatly outnumber the living. In an underground bunker, a small army unit and a group of scientists search for explanation behind the crisis and try to survive. This is an interesting movie because it focuses on the humans far more than the zombies. But on the flipside, this is also the goriest Romero movie even though the zombie action is fairly minimal. This movie attempts to explore the reason behind the zombie apocalypse and the scientific explanations held within. I have great respect for Romero because he took a smaller budget for this movie so he could release it as is in an unrated format, rather than edit the movie down for an R rating. That's the mark of a true artist, and it shows through in his work. I like how the breakdown of the human mind, when tested with such stressful angles and isolation, is fully on display here. A lot of people don't like this movie because of a lack of zombies, but in a lot of ways I find the human horror a little more unsettling. And believe me, Romero more than makes up for the lack of zombies within the final act of the film, which features some incredibly graphic content. Another great zombie movie from the master.

4.5/5

Day of the Dead 2: Contagium
Year – 2005
Year – Ana Clavell, James Glenn Dudelson
Tags – Zombies

First things first, this has nothing to do with Romero's Day of the Dead, nothing. Much like this team of "directors" did with Creepshow 3, they spent the majority of their budget to buy rights to a name so they could pawn off their crap as a sequel to a classic rather than make it its own movie that of course no one would care about. Oh, and by the way morons, contagium isn't even a word! Remember those names up there, when you see them attached to any movie, just avoid it. This movie is stupid, boring and pointless. The acting is terrible, the direction is ungodly, the FX are bad and the story is nonexistent. I'm not even going to bother with a synopsis because no one should ever watch this movie for any reason. Even if you want to rent a movie and this is the only one the store has, go stare at a wall instead for an hour and a half, it will be a much more rewarding experience.

0.5/5

Day of the Dead [Remake]
Year – 2008
Director – Steve Miner
Tags – Zombies

The remake bears very little resemblance to the original movie. In this version, we find the zombie outbreak barely beginning in a small Colorado town. A quarantine is put in place after a strange illness begins effecting the people, but when they start to change, the Army finds out they are far from prepared for what is about to come. This movie sucks, seriously. After such great remakes for the other "Dead" movies, I had my hopes, but this is just horrible. The acting is half and half, for example, Mena Suvari is good, and Nick Cannon is pretty much the worst actor ever, you get the idea. The zombies in this movie are not only fast, but they can leap through the air and run across the ceiling like a spider. Yeah, it's pretty ridiculous. I have to say that I appreciate them trying to do something new, but that just does not work, making zombies run is kind of pushing it, turning them into Spiderman is just asinine. And another problem with the zombies is that when the infection takes over, the people are instantly decayed, which is pretty stupid. The FX work is crap, lots of lame CGI kills. On the plus side, there is some great zombie action, especially at the hospital, and the movie is paced fairly well at times, which saves it from being lumped in with movies like House of the Dead. But still, this movie is a travesty and I wish the honor of remaking such a horror classic fell into competent hands.

1.5/5

Day Watch (Dnevnoy Dozor)
Year – 2006
Director – Timur Bekmambetov
Tags – Vampires

This movie takes place not terribly long after the last movie. And I definitely appreciate how the story moves on from the original. The same director and many actors return for the sequel to Night Watch, so everything is on par with the original in that respect. Once again the story does have difficulty being confined into a single movie, but this one is longer and it does give the story more room to stretch its legs. The visuals are once again very grandiose and large scale, making for some truly memorable moments and lots of "wows". The sequel had some big shoes to fill and I feel they did an admirable job in doing that. If you were a fan of the original, there is probably no reason why you wouldn't enjoy this one as well.

Days of Darkness
Year – 2007
Director – Jake Kennedy
Tags – Zombies

A comet passes over earth, and fragment falls to the ground, unleashing a virus that transforms nearly everyone into flesh eating zombies. Now it's up to a rag tag group of uninfected people to try and find a cure. I expected about an average zombie movie, and what I received was an average zombie movie. Yay for me. I can appreciate the strides that were made to make this movie different from other zombie movies, and it does have some intriguing ideas, but unfortunately there is too much focus on making the movie different and not enough focus on making the movie entertaining. It's too dialogue heavy and slow at times, but there are some great moments of violence and gore. The practical FX are really good, but the acting isn't the greatest. I did find some of the characters to be pretty funny, like the old porn star who blurts out that she has been with over eight thousand guys. It's funny because she says it for no reason and the statement has no bearing on anything going on. This movie is equal parts good and bad but ultimately ends up being a passable low budget zombie movie.

2.5/5

Dead & Breakfast
Year – 2004
Director – Matthew Leutwyler
Tags – Zombies

An RV full of friends making their way to a wedding decide they should stop at a bed & breakfast for the night. But after the owners are brutally murdered they end up getting stuck in the town, and to make matters worse, the dead are returning to life. This movie takes multiple stabs at comedy and completely fails in its attempts. This movie is just not funny at all, and to make matters worse, there is an incredibly annoying band doing musical numbers throughout the movie. The acting isn't great but there are enough good performances from some genre actors to make it passable. The direction isn't good either. The movie is slow and often times boring. But the FX are great. Loads of gore and great kills all around, but just not enough to truly make this movie worthwhile. And the musical sequences are dreadful. I'm all for horror/comedies and zombie flicks, but this one is just not very good at being either.

2/5

Dead & Buried
Year – 1981
Director – Gary Sherman

A small town sheriff is overwhelmed when a series of gory murders take place. The strangest part of all is that those people who are murdered are coming back as friendly townsfolk. This is a zombie movie, but it really is unlike any other zombie movie made. They don't eat flesh and for all intents and purposes, they're just normal people who work, say good morning and are generally good natured, when they're not brutally murdering people of course. The story is one of a kind and really written out well, with a wonderful ending to boot. The acting is very good, the direction is great. The FX work is really something because there are some incredibly brutal kills and they do not shy away from showing them. Dead & Buried is a very good movie that I definitely love, I just don't love it above all others, and for a very unique tale that's well executed, you really don't have to look much further.

4/5

Dead Above Ground
Year – 2002
Director – Chuck Bowman
Tags – Slasher / Survival

An outcast teenage boy dies at the hands of a fellow student accidently and then one year later people begin to be killed. Could it be his vengeful spirit returned, or is someone else killing in his name? Who cares? This movie is such a piece of crap. The story is just pathetic and riddled with stereotypical characters and situations. The acting is beyond terrible and you just hope the people in the movie will hurry up and die so you don't have to be subjected to their awful dialogue and horrendous delivery. But then when the kills come, they're lame and the FX are just plain bad. This is an awful movie that's barely watchable and I don't recommend it to anyone.

1/5

Dead Alive (Braindead)
Year – 1992
Director – Peter Jackson
Tags – Zombies

A man's mother is bitten by a Sumatran rat-monkey and dies from the wound, but it doesn't take long for her to come back to life and begin feeding on the flesh of the living. This movie isn't brilliant because the director went on to do bigger things, it is just brilliant. The story is not only pretty hilarious, but it's also original, which is very difficult to find in a zombie film. The movie moves along nicely by blending good humor with some fun gross out moments until it culminates into a major gorefest. This is definitely one of the goriest movies ever made. The acting has a good cheesy quality and the FX are nothing short of amazing. Definitely one of the most unique, fun and bloody zombie movies ever made.

4.5/5

Dead Birds
Year – 2004
Director – Alex Turner
Tags – Ghosts

Set in 1863, after a bank robbery, a group of outlaws go to hide out in an old plantation house. But once there they discover it is not abandoned and instead houses the spirits of the former residents, as well as some strange creatures that roam out in the cornfield. This is a pretty impressive low budget feature with some actual actors, so that's a nice change of pace. And those actors are great here fortunately. The story is also well conceived but comes off a little cheap during the middle of the movie. It's almost as if the writer thought of a great set-up and a wonderful conclusion and everything else was just an afterthought. The direction also reflects this as it gets a little slow at times during the middle segment, but for the most part it's a great job. The FX are also pretty slick, especially for the creatures in the cornfield, which look pretty awesome. Overall this is a pretty creepy and well made movie and with a stronger story it could have been a classic, but it's still pretty damn good the way it is.

3.5/5

Dead Calm
Year – 1989
Director – Phillip Noyce
Tags – Suspense

After a tragedy befalls them, a man and wife decide to sail the open seas in their yacht to escape the world. During their voyage they come across another boat with only one man aboard. He claims he is the only survivor and that everyone else has died of severe food poisoning, but by the time the husband finds out the truth, it is already too late. Dead Calm is a great movie, and what makes it even better in my mind is that the bulk of the film is supported by three actors who never let it get dull. Billy Zane and Sam Neil are really amazing in this movie, while I felt Nicole Kidman played her role out in a painfully average kind of way. I like that the director didn't pull any punches and showed you everything including a fairly graphic child death and a very uncomfortable quasi-rape scene. The movie moves along very nicely which surprises me because I didn't expect it to paced so well with such a small cast and locale. I also have to speak of the soundtrack composed by Graeme Revell, because it is just so incredibly well done and fits perfectly with the movie. Graeme comes from an industrial music background, which I am pretty well versed in, and some of that background leaks into his score, making it very haunting and just extra special for me. Really my only complaint is Nicole Kidman, I feel she was miscast, but I must tell you, I am not a big fan of hers to begin with, so if you are a fan, you'll probably love her in this. And she also gets naked in this movie, if that's your thing. Overall, Dead Calm is a stellar thriller.

Dead End
Year – 2003
Director – Jean-Baptiste Andrea, Fabrice Canepa
Tags – [Hidden to conceal spoilers]

For the first time in twenty years, a man driving his family to his mother's house for Christmas takes a shortcut. But he'll wish he hadn't as the never ending road he travels upon conceals many terrors. I love this movie. It's almost Lovecraftian in its own way because it deals so much with the weird and unknown. You never know exactly what is going on until the end, which is always fun because that really allows your imagination to flourish. The acting is excellent and really lends a lot to the movie. The direction is also great but to be honest I wanted more. I wanted more strange occurrences and I wanted to see more of what was happening because everything was just so well done. This is a one of kind movie which is pretty rare nowadays and the way it was pulled off was nothing short of great.

4/5

Dead End Road
Year – 2004
Director – Jeff Burton
Tags – Serial Killer (Fictional)

The FBI chase a killer who patterns his murders based on the death scenes from the works of Edgar Allen Poe. I was intrigued by the concept of this movie and I did really like the story at times, but this movie has a lot of problems. The acting is terrible, I mean awful. It's so bad that I can't even fully blame the budget. The direction also left much to be desired, as the movie could get kind of slow at times. There was some good gore though, so that's something. I feel a bit generous calling this average, but it's really not bad. If the movie had a budget to hire a better director and some actual actors, I'm confident that this could have been something pretty good. As it stands, average.

2.5/5

Dead Heat
Year – 1988
Director – Mark Goldblatt
Tags – Zombies

There's a new gang in town robbing businesses and it's up to a couple of wild cops to stop them. But that might be hard to accomplish, since this gang of hoodlums is already dead. This movie is a nice addition to the zombie sub genre with a pretty original plot and decent enough story to carry it through. The direction is pretty good, but the acting is quite the mixed bag. It ranges from good to ungodly bad. This movie is also about as cheesy as they come with bad joke thrown in after bad joke I thought my eyes were going to fall out of my head from rolling them around so much. The FX work is where the movie really stands out because there are some seriously awesome moments. There is a scene in a butcher shop that I particularly found to be brilliant. Overall this is a fun movie that has some good things going it that outweigh the incredible cheese factor. But nothing could ever outweigh Joe Piscopo's mullet, that thing is hypnotic.

3/5

Dead Life
Year – 2005
Director – William Victor Schotten
Tags – Zombies

Zombies rise in a small town and a group of friends try to survive the onslaught. Yeah, there's no story here whatsoever. It's your typical microbudget fare as in zombies show up, and then people try to survive against said zombies while heavy metal music is blasting. Nothing really wrong with that, I like zombies and metal, but this movie is still pretty bad. The acting is worse than usual, and I understand there is no kind of budget here but it's almost unwatchable. The FX are really weak and the zombies look like crap. The direction is aimless and while trying to follow a non-story, I guess I shouldn't expect anything more. I can only blame the budget so much, but there are some good things to be said. I can sense the effort here and for all the parts that suck, it does make for a pretty funny movie. Like when the guy finds a zombie woman munching on some other guy. The dude almost throws up and then does what any normal person would do: he of course has sex with the zombie woman doggy style. I almost died laughing. It's not so bad that it's good, but it's just bad enough for some laughs.

2/5

Dead Man's Shoes
Year – 2004
Director – Shane Meadows
Tags – Suspense

A man leaves to join the military, and while away his younger, mentally challenged brother is brutalized by a gang of thugs and forced to do things he doesn't want to do. When his brother returns, he sets into motion a brutal revenge scheme. What I really like about this movie is how the revenge starts out almost comical and the man starts out by ridiculing the gang, but as flashbacks show just what the gang did, and those actions become more severe, so does the man's revenge. I would have liked to have seen the story fleshed out a bit more, because I do think that is the only thing holding this movie back from absolute greatness. The direction is excellent and the acting is brilliant, although you may want to watch with subtitles because there are some rather thick Irish accents in this movie. It's nice to see that someone besides Chan-Wook Park can make an exceptional modern day revenge movie, and I really look forward to seeing more films by the people involved here, genre based or not.

4/5

Dead Mary
Year – 2007
Director – Robert Wilson
Tags – Demonic Possession

A group of college friends gather at a cabin to relax. After talk of relationships and other sticky matters, they decide to play a game called Dead Mary, and now one of them is possessed by an evil spirit and they are killing the others, but which one is the killer? This movie attempts to blend The Evil Dead with The Thing, which would be awesome, but they don't quite achieve that. What they do achieve is a mildly entertaining movie with some very interesting and promising aspects, but ultimately it overstays its welcome and then leaves the viewer with a half assed ending. The acting is ok, but definitely not what I would call great. The direction could have used some fine tuning as well. The story is good and has some great elements that don't really pay off. There are some excellent FX and make-up work though. I think that with some different people involved, a few tweaks to the story, and maybe a bigger budget, this could have been a killer horror flick, but as it is, it's just a little better than average.

3/5

Dead Meat
Year – 2004
Director – Conor McMahon
Tags – Zombies

A zombie outbreak hits the Irish countryside and a city woman teams up with the local gravedigger to try and find safety. This is a pretty fun movie, and that's good to see after picking up so many bad zombie movies. Here we see the filmmakers keep it simple and allow the movie to work. There are lots of zombies, quite a bit of gore and even some good laughs. The outbreak is a result of mad cow disease, which is a concept I don't believe I've seen before. The acting and direction are good, nothing special but more than passable. It may play out like dozens of other zombie movies but this one is better than those for the reasons I mentioned above, so for some good zombie action, check out Dead Meat, you'll be happy you did.

3.5/5

Dead Men Walking
Year – 2005
Director – Peter Mervis
Tags – Zombies

A man is arrested for murder and placed into a prison for holding by order of the CDC. But he didn't actually kill anyone, they were undead flesh eating zombies and now he himself is infected. Now the zombie virus is infecting the other inmates and all hell has broken loose. I love the whole zombies in prison thing, which was a little underdone in Beyond Re-Animator so I had some hopes for this low budget effort, and I have to say I wasn't really let down either. The story is straightforward and doesn't offer up much variety on the sub genre, but that's ok because it's fairly entertaining. The acting is really bad, a little worse than usual, and the direction isn't the best but it was still somewhat enjoyable. I think the main downfall here is that they tried to attach a story were there needn't be one. If they had just given us a zombie mob and a handful of survivors killing them off in gory fashion, it would have been even more mindless fun. All of the dialogue struck me as a bit trite and forced. The FX are very good and the gore is great so if they had just laid off the lame conversations and focused on headshots, this good movie could have been a great gorefest.

3/5

Dead Moon Rising
Year – 2007
Director – Mark E. Poole
Tags – Zombies

A zombie apocalypse hits Louisville and it's up to a rag tag band of survivors to escape the onslaught. Emblazoned across the front of the DVD artwork for this movie were the words "The largest zombie scene ever filmed". That's a gimmick, and that automatically lets me know that this movie is going to suck. I give a lot of leeway to microbudget movies because they don't have the resources of other, bigger budget movies, but this here is quite simply pathetic. The movie is billed as a horror/comedy, but it's not the least bit funny. The acting is beyond terrible and the lead "actor" was so annoying that I just wanted to wring his scrawny little neck. And when they unleashed the obligatory "badass chick" character, it was so lame that I just wanted to shut the movie off, but I continued on punishing myself and kept watching. The FX were unbelievably bad and I can't imagine that anyone would think they looked good enough to display in a final product. When it came to that supposed largest zombie scene, uh, yeah right, not even close. This crap is horrible on every level and then some. This is a bona fide worthless waste of time.

0.5/5

Dead Next Door, The
Year – 1989
Director – J.R. Bookwalter
Tags – Zombies

After the world became rampant with zombies, the remaining bits of the government set up a zombie extermination squad and a lab for scientists to work up a cure. This microbudget flick from days past is actually pretty awesome. The FX work is pretty cool and there's loads of blood to satisfy most gorehounds. The acting is incredibly cheesy, but it works for the most part. There are some very cool scenes like when the zombies are climbing the gates of the actual White House lawn, and I have to wonder how they pulled that one off. This movie also pays homage to the great horror movies of the past and even names several of its characters after icons of horror. The fact that this movie was made over a period of four years for very little money is pretty astounding. The movie definitely has a huge cheese factor to it, but for me, this is a great microbudget zombie movie that's just a lot of fun.

4/5

Dead Pit
Year – 1989
Director – Brett Leonard
Tags – Zombies

A mental hospital has a secret locked away underneath it. Many years ago a doctor was performing grotesque experiments on people and another doctor killed him for it, locking him away with his test subjects underneath the hospital. But now they're free, and they're hungry. The story here is pretty good, nothing outstanding but it has some good moments that set it apart from other zombie flicks. There's also some great FX, gore and even some gratuitous nudity. The acting on the other hand, is pretty bad, and the direction is average at best. The movie is probably just too long for its own good. I had hoped for a little more out of this, because it really is just barely above average, but I wasn't completely dissatisfied.

3/5

Dead Ringers
Year – 1988
Director – David Cronenberg
Tags – Suspense

This is the tale of twin gynecologists who share more than just the office workload. Being identical twins they take advantage by sharing women but their relationship deteriorates over one woman in particular, leading to drug addiction and other dire issues. This is very fascinating movie. I can imagine that this movie would mostly terrifying for women, given the profession of the twins, and especially when one of the reveals his gynecological instruments for mutant women. This movie definitely has the Cronenberg feel with a few sequences of kinky sex and weird visuals, but it is definitely one of his more straightforward films. The acting is great, but the dual performance by Jeremy Irons is quite simply monumental, how he didn't receive an Oscar nomination is beyond me. This is an excellent movie sure to appease the viewer's appetite for the bizarre as well as the average viewer just looking for a well done thriller.

Dead Silence
Year – 2007
Director – James Wan
Tags – Ghosts

A widower returns to his home town to try and figure out the circumstances of his wife's murder, which he believes may be tied to the ghost of an old ventriloquist. This movie has two flaws as far as I can see. The first is the story, which is eerily reminiscent of the movie Darkness Falls, in which many circumstances are the same, including the lore of the ghost. Sure, there are minor differences, but it's just too similar. And the direction is terrible because this movie is incredibly slow. I guess those are two pretty big things. But I will say that there are some nice visuals in this movie and the acting is fairly good. But still, the movie feels very unoriginal and it's just boring as hell, the good things only make it less bad, and could never make it good.

2/5

Dead Space: Downfall
Year – 2008
Director – Chuck Patton
Tags – Animated, Aliens, Infection

Meant to be a prequel to the video game Dead Space, this movie shows the exploits of the space craft Ishimura as it brings aboard an alien artifact from a distant planet. Soon people become sick and madness begins to take over, then they begin to change into strange creatures. I wasn't expecting much here, just a promotional tool for a video game, but I am pleased to say that some actual thought went into this movie. The animation is nice, nothing groundbreaking, but it's good. The creatures are like something out of John Carpenter's The Thing, only there's a lot more of them and they're a lot more aggressive. The gore factor is massive in this movie, there are plenty of disembowelments, decapitations, dismemberments and basically any other way you can kill someone violently and with a lot of blood. The movie is just too damn short though, clocking in at a mere 74 minutes. It left me wanting more, but I guess that was the idea to get you to buy the game. If you like the game, you'll probably like this, and I like both.

3.5/5

Deadlands: The Rising
Year – 2006
Director – Gary Ugarek
Tags – Zombies

An attack on the city ends up creating a horde of flesh hungry zombies. Yes, this is a microbudget zombie movie and it has no story at all. And that's ok just as long as I get what I want out it, zombies. The acting ranges from natural to god awful and they end up sort of balancing each other out. The movie is only a shade over an hour long so the direction is good and the pacing is quick. The FX are ok, dime store variety make-up and gore, but not bad considering the meager funds involved. Like I said, there's really no story here besides zombies appear and zombies kill, but I did rather enjoy the scene where the motorists trapped on the road were attacked by the horde. The zombies are also somewhat fast and cunning, which was nice. This movie was just mindless zombie fun and if you can overlook the budget shortcomings you'll find a quick and concise zombie movie.

3/5

Deadly Friend
Year – 1986
Director – Wes Craven
Tags – Mechanical

A teenage boy has mastered artificial intelligence and begins work on the human brain at a nearby university. Things start out well for him until the robot he has created is destroyed and then the girl he is falling for mysteriously dies. He steals her body and implants her brain with his robot's computer, effectively bringing her back to life. But this girl now has a mind of her own and sets off to kill everyone who has wronged her and the robot. Wow, so the story is obviously destined for B movie land given its utter ridiculousness, but it ended up being a very entertaining movie. The acting is ok, I did find Kristy Swanson to be rather robotic though (ha ha). The direction is good but could have been better. The FX work is the highlight though. This movie doesn't have a huge body count, but when the kills come, they sure do look great, especially the infamous basketball scene. And the robot was pretty badass looking too. The ending of this ridiculous story is so crazy and over the top that you can't help but laugh, but in a way I also had to appreciate it for going so far into left field. This is a flawed movie but an entertaining one for sure.

3/5

Deadwood Park
Year – 2007
Director – Eric Stanze
Tags – Ghosts

A man returns to his old home town, the place where a serial killer abducted and murdered his twin brother. The killer was never found and now the ghosts of his victims, twenty-six children are trying to lead the man into solving the identity of the killer. This is by far one of the most impressive low budget movies ever made. I liked how the story was told in the modern day and then also through flashbacks. There was also a twist in the storyline I didn't see coming and could probably never see coming in a hundred years. The beauty part was that it wasn't just an "out there" twist, it actually made sense too. The acting was really good for a low budget movie and the direction was tight and featured a very beautiful and somber shot structure. The locations they used were gorgeous (in a very dark way) and the dilapidated amusement park and house were especially creepy. And that's another thing about the movie, as it was genuinely scary and creepy at times. This is an exceptional and beautifully done movie, and the fact that it's a low budget work is even more impressive. This is a must see.

4.5/5

Death Proof
Year – 2007
Director – Quentin Tarantino
Tags – Slasher / Survival

This is part two of the theatrical experience called Grindhouse. A man stalks two sets of women, but not with a knife, with a turbo charged muscle car. This movie definitely has the feel of the 70's era grindhouse, much like its partner movie, Planet Terror, but in a very different way. I like this movie a lot but also feel it is much too dialogue heavy, as the movie introduces two separate sets of characters. And while the fleshing out of the characters is done well, it's just too much. But that is a relatively small complaint and I understand that the women just couldn't be glossed over. I do have to mention that this movie has probably the greatest car crash scene ever, and well as one the best car chase scenes ever. The cinematography is amazing, and the movie as a whole is stellar. My complaints are few, and I do have to recommend watching the Grindhouse as a whole, because I believe that only stands to heighten this great movie.

4/5

Death Sentence
Year – 2007
Director – James Wan
Tags – Suspense

After a man's son is brutally murdered as part of an initiation ritual, rather than seek out legal justice (which he feels is insufficient), he instead takes matters in his own hands in the form of bloody vengeance. But taking on an entire gang may be more than he bargained for. This movie sounded cool, but to be honest I wasn't expecting a whole lot, and it's nice to be pleasantly surprised. Right off the bat the story is remarkable and unfolds in a very exciting and twisted way. The story is pretty straightforward, which is fine, I don't expect an Oldboy kind of story in every revenge flick, and being straightforward worked here. The acting is great and the direction is also very well done. In the unrated version you can definitely expect loads of gore as well, which was another pleasant surprise. This tale of revenge can definitely hold its own with the big boys and was a very well made movie overall.

4/5

Death Tunnel

Year – 2005
Director – Philip Adrian Booth
Tags – Ghosts

Five college girls are locked in an abandoned hospital as part of an initiation ceremony, it's just too bad that the hospital is the site of over sixty thousand deaths, and some of those dead still linger in the hallways. But what's really too bad is anyone who has to sit through this crap for even a minute. The location is awesome, too bad there was no talent involved to make it worthwhile. The acting is painful, really painful. Not a single decent performance in the whole movie and definitely a few that I would consider some of the worst and downright laughable. The story is horrid and comes across as trying to be intelligent, and it would be intelligent, if written by someone who was brain dead. The direction is slow, uninteresting and ugly. The FX are also pretty bad. As I wrote this I thought about giving the movie points for its great location, but the fact of the matter is, it's just a place that was already there and the hacks involved in this travesty just used it. So yeah, this movie may have a great location, but in the end the whole production is worthless.

0.5/5

Deathbed

Year – 2002
Director – Danny Draven
Tags – Demonic Possession

A couple moves into a new apartment and come across an attic that was locked away and forgotten. Inside was a bed that the couple began to use, but this bed was the site of many perverse acts and murders, and now the spirit of an evil man is trying to take over the woman's body. Why Stuart Gordon would ever attach his name to this crap is beyond me. The idea behind it isn't that great to begin with, and the execution is just so poor it's practically vomit inducing. The lead actress actually isn't too bad, but the rest of the cast is fairly awful. The story is weak and the direction is slow and boring. There really aren't many FX to speak of, and what we do get to see are not very good. The slight sleaze factor works in the movie's favor but with this kind of movie there should have been more, because that's really all that will keep the audience entertained.

1.5/5

Deaths of Ian Stone, The

Year – 2007
Director – Dario Piana
Tags – Monsters

A man goes about his everyday life when he is viciously murdered by horrific creatures, only to wake up again the next day to be murdered again, and again, and again. A horror version of Groundhog Day? Count me in! This excellent premise is unfortunately only pulled off half-heartedly. The visuals are very nice and the acting is good but the storyline gets so muddled eventually everything just loses all meaning. Some good blood here and there, definitely not a gory movie, but some nice violence sprinkled throughout. This is an average movie that could have been so much more, it may have come up short but it was still pretty entertaining.

2.5/5

Deathwatch
Year – 2002
Director – Michael J. Bassett
Tags – Ghosts

Set during World War I, this movie follows a group of British soldiers as they overtake a forward German trench. But this trench is far from normal and holds a deadly supernatural secret. This is a very impressive low budget movie. The shooting location looks amazing and is quite creepy by itself, but when the paranormal occurrences are added, it gives it even more of a dark appeal. The acting is great and has more than a few familiar faces. The direction is also top notch and there really aren't any pacing issues. The FX are also really good and even the CGI looks good, probably because it was used in near darkness and sparingly. The story is also really good and even though there were some parts that I didn't particularly love, overall it was a very intriguing and well written. In a way this isn't so much a ghost movie but instead ghostly location, with constant rain and fog covering the deaths and disappearances of the British soldiers. It almost swallows them up in a way. This movie is a little rough around the edges but still remains an extremely satisfying experience.

4/5

Decoys
Year – 2004
Director – Matthew Hastings
Tags – Aliens

Aliens posing as conventionally attractive women seduce young college boys in the hope of impregnating them with their alien seeds. Unfortunately they have not been able to implant any of the boys properly and they always end up frozen from the inside out. Now there's an interesting premise for a low budget flick, pretty much guaranteeing your quota of bare breasts and dead bodies. The movie is definitely entertaining to a degree but does suffer from a few flaws. The first being that it's very slow at times, then add ugly CGI, and top it off with some bad acting. Now most of that tends to be par for the course but it's still noticeable. Decoys ends up being a fun movie that has an interesting premise and manages to be somewhat well done.

Decoys: The Second Seduction
Year – 2007
Director – Jeffery Scott Lando
Tags – Aliens

Here we have the second installment in the Decoys series, which follows the plot of the first movie, just in a different place this time, and with some returning characters as well. Even though the first one had a certain kind of charm, I can not say that for the second. Why? Well, it's just more the same. Not quite a carbon copy of the first, but pretty damn close. Add on top of that some shoddy acting and some pretty awful CGI and you have the recipe for a terrible movie. Still, it wasn't really bad, and I actually found myself somewhat entertained by this sequel. Not terribly boring, not terribly exciting, fun, but not too much fun. Fans of the original will probably find this to be a passable flick.

2.5/5

Deep, The
Year – 1977
Director – Peter Yates
Tags – Suspense

A couple on a vacation discovers some treasure in a sunken ship and takes it to a local expert for identification. But they also found an ampoule of morphine in the ship as well, which gained the interest of a local drug lord. Now the couple is torn between treasure hunting and fighting for their lives. To me there's not much more suspenseful than dealing with precarious situations underwater, and this movie has plenty of them as almost half of the movie takes place under the sea. There are incidents with underwater explosives, diving drug dealers, undersea creatures and more. The story itself is very good and features a bevy of different situations to vary up the action. The acting is great and the direction is quite good as well. If you're as fascinated with the ocean as I am then this just may be the thriller for you, I sure as hell enjoyed it. Most of it anyway.

3.5/5

Deep Blue Sea
Year – 1999
Director – Renny Harlin
Tags – Animals

On an isolated research facility in the ocean, scientists work toward a cure for Alzheimer's through sharks. The cure lies in the shark's brain so they genetically engineered the sharks to make their brains larger, and now these highly intelligent fish have a plan to escape, and begin killing their creators. The whole set-up for this movie could only happen in Hollywood. It is just way out there. The shark models look great and the CGI isn't that bad either. The cast however, is a very interesting mix, I mean seriously, LL Cool J? Whose bonehead idea was that? The set is probably the most impressive feature of the movie as it was well done and well thought out. I like this movie but the whole plot and the way it plays out had me shaking my head the entire time. It's entertaining, nothing special, but if you like shark movies or movies dealing with the water in general, you'll probably get a kick out of this.

2.5/5

Deep Red (Profondo Rosso)
Year – 1975
Director – Dario Argento
Tags – Serial Killer (Fictional)

A pianist gets caught up in the actions of a serial killer brutally murdering people and joins up with a feisty reporter to try and uncover the identity of the killer. While I love this movie and its brutal and bizarre nature, I also feel that the movie is much too long for its own good and thus suffers from some slow pacing. But honestly that's the only issue I have with Deep Red. The story is incredible and the murders are quite remarkable. The acting is also well done and there's even some well placed humor that works exceedingly well. It's always nice to be able to watch a movie like this and have no idea who the killer is because so many movies of this ilk are entirely much too predictable. Even though I don't feel it's a masterpiece as many other people do, I still enjoyed this greatly.

4/5

Deep Rising
Year – 1998
Director – Stephen Sommers
Tags – Sea Monsters

A boat crew is hired to take a group of men to the middle of the ocean where they find an ocean liner sitting idle, upon their entry to the vessel, they find that everyone on board has vanished, and that there is something on the boat with them. As schlocky as this movie is, it sure is entertaining. The CGI is lacking, the characters are typical, the humor is cheesy, but damn, it sure is fun. I do have a soft spot for sea monster movies and this one, as riddled with flaws as it is, just flows so nicely and always kept me interested. This is just a fun movie that doesn't exercise your brain and it just allows you to have a good time watching it.

3.5/5

Deepstar Six
Year – 1989
Director – Sean S. Cunningham

A group of scientists and naval personnel are setting up a missile base underwater when they unleash a creature from an underwater cavern the likes of which no one has ever seen. This is a guilty pleasure for me because there really is no basis for a good movie here. The characters are stereotypical, the storyline employs too many moments of convenience, and it's not really that original either. But I like the feel of it. The few kills that are shown are done well and have some good originality to them. The monster is nice, not extravagant, something you may actually expect to see hidden away 5000 fathoms underwater. It's just a good time killer with little to no thought needed to enjoy it.

3/5

Deliverance
Year – 1972
Director – John Boorman
Tags – Suspense

Four men decide to go canoeing down a river deep in the woods but their ideal vacation turns into a nightmare when they come under attack by some backwoods locals who some very terrible plans for them. While I think Deliverance is a good movie, it's also one of the most overrated. Sure, this movie has some twisted and violent stuff going on in it, but it's all very much censored. There's hardly any blood where there should have been gore and when the camera pans away from certain actions, it should have zoomed in. The acting is very good but the movie is pretty slow at times. If the filmmakers had the stomach for it, this movie could have been great, but it ends up being pretty watered down for mass appeal. But if nothing else, Deliverance is a good movie and the template for all backwoods horror movies that would come after it.

3/5

Demon Knight
Year – 1995
Director – Ernest R. Dickerson, Gilbert Adler
Tags – Demons, Demonic Possession

A man must protect an ancient key from a being known as The Collector or the demons will take back Earth and plunge the world into darkness once again. This is the first movie put out under the Tales from the Crypt flag, which was a seminal horror TV series. Here we are treated to an extended intro from the Cryptkeeper, which was nice. The movie itself is just one of my favorite horror flicks ever. The story is great and the way the plot unfolds is just awesome. The acting is also top notch all around with William Sadler and Billy Zane pulling out extra special performances. The demons look great and the rest of FX work is equally impressive. There's a lot of blood and gore too, which works out great. From the opening of this film, where we see a car chase with Hey Man,

Nice Shot by Filter playing in the background, I knew I was in for something special, and from the opening credits, the action started and never let up. This is a great movie in every way it could be.

4.5/5

Demon Pond (Yasha-Ga-Ike) [Stage]
Year – 2005
Director – Takashi Miike
Tags – Monsters

This piece of theatre is about a small Japanese village that fears the ancient evil inside of the Demon Pond. The bell ringer of the village is rumored to keep the evil at bay with his bell, but the villagers do not believe this and fear the drought that has besieged them. I almost didn't put this in the book because it's much more fantasy than horror, despite the horror elements, but I think the fans will really dig this. The story is brilliant, even if you can see where it's going at times and it plays so smoothly that you can barely tell it was over two hours long. The acting is great and features some excellent humor from both the story and some wonderful improvisation. This is the only theatre production in the book and it was nice change of pace. Great all around and beautifully captivating, I would love to see this in person someday.

4/5

Demons (Demoni)
Year – 1985
Director – Lamberto Bava
Tags – Demons

People are invited at random to attend a premiere at a movie theatre. One of the patrons puts a demon mask on and is cut by it, a short while later she transforms into a demon and begins attacking people, and those people as well turn into demons. Soon the remaining humans find themselves trapped in the theatre and must fight their way out. Demons, it's such an awesome movie. The FX work is spellbinding, the transformations look great and you really get a feel for how painful they are. The make-up on the demons is equally impressive, and all the kills are amazing. This movie is chock full of blood and bile so gorehounds should be appeased. It doesn't take long for the movie to bring on the demons, which is smart, and when they do come, the action rarely lets up from there. This is one of the highlights of Italian horror in my opinion, and should not be missed.

4.5/5

Demons 2: The Nightmare Continues (Demoni 2: L'incubo Ritorna)
Year – 1986
Director – Lamberto Bava
Tags – Demons

The second Demons movie plays out very similar to the first, instead of a movie theatre though, it takes place in an apartment building. This time the movie is less effective, maybe because we've seen it all before. This movie uses some of the same actors in this one as the first, as well as some of the same occurrences, and it just feels like cheating in a way. However, they did amp up the number of people and thus also increased the potential number of demons quite considerably. That's pretty impressive seeing as how many people were in the theatre in the first movie. You don't get to see but one full-on transformation and it looks nice, but not as good as the last movie. This is still a worthwhile movie; it just lacks in a few areas and feels too familiar. But the people-transforming-into-demons market is pretty slim, so have a go at this sequel.

3/5

*Demons 3 can be found under Church, The.

Dentist, The
Year – 1996
Director – Brian Yuzna
Tags – Slasher / Survival

After a well to do dentist sees his wife cheating on him with the pool guy, he goes insane and begins killing his patients. This is such an awesome movie, and you really wouldn't expect it to be. People who have a fear of the dentist will probably soil themselves whilst watching this. It plays on all of the fears associated with the dentist, like when he's cleaning a boy's teeth and you can hear that tell-tale scrape of the instrument on his teeth before the hook is plunged into his gums. And that's just the tip of iceberg. The direction is really good, and probably some of Yuzna's most concise. The acting is also very good, especially by Corbin Bernsen, who does an excellent job with his role as the dentist. The FX are very well done and there's plenty of blood and cool kills. This is a slasher movie unlike the others, because the killer here is just a normal person who snapped instead of some masked murderer. The Dentist is a great movie that explores new ground in the slasher sub genre.

4/5

Dentist 2: Brace Yourself, The
Year – 1998
Director – Brian Yuzna
Tags – Slasher / Survival

This movie continues on not long after the last one. I was expecting just another rehash of the last movie because I think the whole dentist thing was covered enough in one movie. Surprisingly this movie was not and instead the story is a good progression off the last one and manages to be fairly different. The dentist is obviously twisted from the start and the movie begins with a bang but then it slows down as he tries to get control over himself and start a new life, which is kind of boring. But then he gives in (of course) and the killing comes in to full swing, redeeming the movie somewhat. The acting and direction are still good but not as good as the first movie. There are some great gore shots and great visuals again, but not enough in my mind. This isn't a bad follow up, in fact I found it to be somewhat good, but it really does lack the punch of its predecessor.

3/5

Descent, The
Year – 2005
Director – Neil Marshall
Tags – Monsters

Six women go spelunking in a US cave system, only to have an unexpected cave-in trap them inside with no way out. Upon their further exploration of the cave, in a desperate search for a way out, they find out they are not alone in the cave. One of the best, if not the best horror movie ever made. Did that get your attention? Good. This incredibly original and well done movie blows my mind. First, the idea of having an all female cast is great, it worked for the opposite gender in John Carpenter's The Thing, and it works here. The feeling of fear and claustrophobia just oozes out of the screen, you really feel like you're there, and you just feel helpless. The creatures inside the cave system are great, and the director's decision to use actors instead of stunt people or dancers was a great move that really gives character to them. The set design was completely believable, I actually thought they shot this in a cave, and the make-up and FX work is equally satisfying. Genuine scares, a smooth as silk pacing structure, loads of appropriate gore, and just about the best ending ever makes this an incredible horror movie worth every bit of your attention. Go see it now!

5/5

Desperation
Year – 2006
Director – Mick Garris
Tags – Demonic Possession

Something in the mines of an old Nevada town has escaped and now possesses the town sheriff, who is gathering people in the jail and killing others, but for what reason is yet unknown. Well, here we see Garris slaughter yet another Stephen King story. This incredibly boring adaptation is only a sliver of the potential the original novel held. But the fault can not be completely placed upon the director because many of the actors were just not up to snuff. While people like Ron Perlman were in their element, others were just plain terrible, especially the religious boy, who was completely without talent. The story was butchered in a way that really removed many of the good points it had, which is sad. There are a lot of great visuals though and the locales were used well, especially in Bisbee, a town I have been to many times. This is just another wasted King miniseries and another Mick Garris bowel movement.

Devil's Advocate, The
Year – 1997
Director – Taylor Hackford
Tags – Devil

A young lawyer who has never lost a case lands an opportunity to work for a very prestigious law firm that happens to be run by the devil himself. Not only is this movie a great court drama, but when you add supernatural elements that work in the context of the film, you have a truly excellent thriller. This movie constantly kept me interested with wonderful pacing and terrific characters. The CGI is very subtle and creepy, and not overused, which is a pleasant surprise. Also, I have to commend the writers who penned a very engaging theological movie with a splendid human feel. The devil being a lawyer may not be much of a stretch (Ha ha, get it? It's a joke!), but this movie is just great on every level.

4.5/5

Devil's Backbone, The (El Espinazo del Diablo)
Year – 2001
Director – Guillermo del Toro
Tags – Ghosts

Set in 1939 during the Spanish civil war, the son of a dead soldier is dropped off at a makeshift orphanage and is soon seeing visions of a dead boy. I really hate like hell to give away too much of the story, hence the shoddy synopsis, because this is really one of those movies that you just need to see. Like many of del Toro's films, especially the more independent ones, this is much more than just a horror movie. The war aspect actually plays a somewhat large role in the movie as well, which makes for a very unique experience. Another unique aspect is the ghost of the boy, who probably ends up looking like what a real ghost would, it's just that cool. Let me sum things up for you like this: Brilliant story, great acting, and uncanny direction. This is unique and wonderful film of a certain caliber that you're not likely to see again, well that is until you watch del Toro's next instant classic, Pan's Labyrinth.

4.5/5

Devil's Chair, The
Year – 2006
Director – Adam Mason
Tags – [Hidden to conceal spoilers]

A man watches his girlfriend get mutilated by a strange chair in an old asylum, and thinking that he himself had killed her, he gets locked away for murder. But a professor gives him a second chance and returns with him and a group of students to the asylum to try and convince him that there is nothing wrong with the chair. Yeah, the set-up for the story is hardly the likeliest of scenarios so you definitely have to suspend some disbelief right off the bat. To be honest, I was very bored with this movie, all the set-up was very slow to unfurl and the first half of the movie was just plain uninteresting for the most part. But then a twist comes along, and even though it was pretty predictable, the way it was carried out almost made up for the earlier snail's pace. The acting is also somewhat lacking and the old guy was just terrible, and when the movie paused so the main character could do a voiceover, well, that got old real quick. Still, the third act is a tremendously twisted and gore soaked romp and I really dug it, too bad most everything before it was so slow.

3/5

Devil's Rejects, The
Year – 2005
Director – Rob Zombie
Tags – Slasher / Survival

This sequel to House of 1000 Corpses picks up a couple of years after the original. One thing I always appreciate is making a sequel much different than the last one, and here Rob Zombie does that. We already know the family and the last thing I wanted to see was another van load of people falling prey to them. The movie is much more brutal and twisted this time around and pretty damn funny as well, which all works great together. The introduction of more genre actors makes for a good time as well. Zombie's direction also improved with this movie, but the style of the first movie is gone and it takes a more traditional style, which still works for me. The story is great and a good direction to go in, but I must admit that I did not like the final third of the story as much as what had come before it. But the movie's final sequence was sheer poetry. So I actually liked this one a bit more than House of 1000 Corpses and I really wish Rob Zombie would get behind the lens with new original material more often.

4/5

Diary of Ellen Rimbauer, The
Year – 2003
Director – Craig R. Baxley
Tags – Ghosts

This is the prequel to Rose Red, showing how the house was built, and just generally dealing with the back story of the family. I find this movie to be quite superfluous because pretty much everything shown here was shown in Rose Red, some footage even taken from that movie. There's not a whole lot that this movie delves into that wasn't explained in the first movie. Also, even though we have the same director here, the direction is well below average and the pacing is pretty bad. The acting, especially by the woman playing Ellen Rimbauer, is awful. This movie does have a couple of interesting moments, but for the most part it's just a rehash of everything that was gone over in Rose Red. Not really worth your time.

1.5/5

Diary of the Dead
Year – 2007
Director – George A. Romero
Tags – Zombies

The fifth Romero zombie movie does not continue on but rather takes everything back to an initial outbreak. This movie follows a group of college students and their professor, who were out shooting a horror movie in the woods when the outbreak occurred. One student obsesses with shooting a documentary while the rest just try to survive. I'm always excited when Romero releases a zombie movie and have yet to be disappointed, and while I feel this is the weakest entry in the Dead series, I still like it quite a bit, which is saying something. The social commentary is a bit more overt here than in previous movies, and crybaby bloggers are likely to take offense. The movie is great as a whole but does have some flaws. First off, the acting isn't always good, especially from the female lead as she can get kind of annoying. Second, the majority of kills are CGI, and not even very good CGI, which is sad seeing as how the series has had such a good track record. Not all of the kills are bad, but they all could have benefited more from practical FX. The direction and story are great, the zombies look good, and the camera work is very good as well, which bears mentioning since this movie is shot in a documentary, handheld style. Overall this is a very good movie that could have used some tweaking. Some people may complain that this isn't good for a Romero movie, well, it's a pretty damn good zombie movie and Romero or not, that's what really matters.

3.5/5

Die, Monster, Die!
Year – 1965
Director – Daniel Haller
Tags – Biological

This Lovecraft adaptation of The Colour Out of Space is about a wheelchair bound man who discovers a meteorite that cause the plants in his greenhouse to grow to monstrous sizes, but then it affects his wife in disastrous ways as well. I'm all for a Lovecraft adaptation even thought most are rubbish, and this one definitely falls into that category. The pacing is atrocious and almost singlehandedly killed the movie, which is a shame since the core story is pretty good, the acting is at least comparable and the FX are great, well ahead of their time. This movie is so slow that it almost causes me physical pain to sit through it, and that really is a shame. At least other aspects of the movie kept it from being complete garbage.

2.5/5

Disturbia
Year – 2007
Director – D.J. Caruso
Tags – Suspense

A boy on house arrest spies on his neighbors and comes to believe that one of them may be a killer. If that synopsis sounds familiar to you, then you've seen Alfred Hitchcock's Rear Window, which this movie pretty blatantly rips off. While the creators tried to say that they changed enough of the story that they didn't need to buy the rights, well, that still didn't prevent them from getting sued. There is a thin line between homage and plagiarism, and this movie definitely falls into the latter category. Viewing it just as a movie I would say that it is an average attempt at suspense. The acting is decent but the characters are unlikeable. The direction isn't great as the movie can get pretty boring and stale quickly. The story is of course nothing original, just more of a technological update. There is a scene in the beginning of the movie that is pretty badass, but just everything goes downhill from there. If they had admitted that this was a remake of Rear Window, I would have called it average (2.5), but given the blatant plagiarism, you can see my score below.

1/5

Disturbing Behavior
Year – 1998
Director – David Nutter
Tags – [Hidden to conceal spoilers]

In the town of Cradle Bay, there are cliques in the high school, just like anywhere else, the only difference is that here, one clique in particular appears to be comprised of upstanding young kids, until they start killing people. And now they're looking for new members. On the outside this movie may seem like a rip-off of Invasion of the Body Snatchers, and while there are elements of that movie present, this one is definitely its own animal. I don't want to reveal too much about why the unruly students are suddenly becoming such great kids, because that would ruin the surprise, and I really liked how the story played out, so I'll just leave it at that. The acting in this movie is mostly decent with a few very good performances, some average ones and then some bad ones as well. For instance I feel that Katie Holmes was miscast as the bad girl. The direction is ok, pretty average stuff there. The whole movie feels like your typical teen horror flick but this one has a different story that I genuinely enjoyed.

3/5

Dog Soldiers
Year – 2002
Director – Neil Marshall
Tags – Werewolves

A routine military exercise turns bad in the Scottish woods when a military team comes across a camp of soldiers who have been ripped to shreds. Now the team must try to survive against a pack of flesh hungry werewolves. This is easily one of the best werewolf movies ever made. And I mean ever. The script shows a good deal of originality and is just expertly constructed as to avoid the typical mundane pitfalls of the sub genre. Here we have lots of action, buckets of gore, great acting, smooth as silk direction and even some humor. Add some great FX and some magnificent looking werewolves and we have a nearly perfect action/horror movie that belongs in everyone's library.

4.5/5

Dolores Claiborne
Year – 1995
Director – Taylor Hackford
Tags – Suspense

A woman is accused of killing the elderly woman she works for, which brings together her and her estranged daughter. It also brings back a man from her past, a detective who accused her of murdering her husband years before, and he's back to make this charge stick. I love Dolores Claiborne, both the movie and the character. You really do have to respect both. The acting here is tremendous as everyone involved is perfectly cast. The story itself is told in the present day and then shown through flashbacks as well. I really loved how the modern day feel was very dark and gloomy and the flashbacks were vibrant and colorful, it worked extremely well. This also goes beyond you typical abused woman story which are cranked out onto cable TV at a rate of two a day, this one has multi-faceted angles and deals with many issues. The direction is also well done and paced very well. This is the kind of movie I can pop in anytime and be satisfied with it, great all around.

4/5

Dominion: Prequel to the Exorcist
Year – 2005
Director – Paul Schrader
Tags – Demonic Possession

This is the first take on making a prequel to The Exorcist, which I guess the studio execs were so displeased with that they completely reshot the movie with someone else. This original version eventually was released on DVD anyway, allowing the public to decide which version was better. I was expecting a complete abomination of a movie here, but what I watched ended being a slightly better than average attempt. The acting is really good, but the direction is not, as the movie is pretty slow throughout its entire run time. I like the story but its execution could have used some more finesse. The CGI is horrible but not used too much fortunately. This is a good attempt and not the rotting pile of garbage we were led to believe it would be. I'll still take Exorcist: The Beginning over this version, but only by a small margin.

3/5

Donnie Darko
Year – 2001
Director – Richard Kelly
Tags – Suspense

After a teenage boy narrowly escapes a bizarre accident, he is urged to commit a series of crimes by a large rabbit who tells him that the world is about to end. Well, the movie definitely gets points for originality, and as silly as it all sounds, this is actually a very good thriller. The movie is fairly slow in the beginning but once it finds its groove it runs very smoothly. The story has a lot going on but is not overly complicated, which is nice, and it offers up a lot of interesting ideas, some of which are tripe, but for the most part it's pretty cool. The acting is also very well done and I definitely have no complaints there. The movie starts out as a dark comedy but ends up being a rather twisted little thriller. Not perfect by any means, but still a great time.

4/5

*Donnie Darko 2 can be found under S. Darko.

Doom
Year – 2005
Director – Andrzej Bartkowiak
Tags – Demons

Based on the popular video game Doom (Actually follows Doom 3 more), this is the story of a group of Space Marines who go to a Mars research center after some trouble, only to find the center overrun by demons. The video game, while fun, never had much of a story, which is pretty much true for the movie as well. There is an excellent first person shooter sequence which was a lot of fun, but for the most part, it's like they tried to make this movie into the next Aliens. They tried to over explain things and too much of the movie was spent with pointless dialogue. Had they just had a bunch of Space Marines shooting at demons for an hour and a half, that would have been a more enjoyable movie and really that was all that this movie needed to be. Demons from Hell on Mars, got it, now let's see some killing. Overindulged, but still somewhat fun.

2.5/5

Doomsday
Year – 2008
Director – Neil Marshall
Tags – Infection, Cannibals

A sudden killer virus nicknamed "Reaper" sweeps through Scotland, forcing England to completely wall off and quarantine the entire country. Thinking the virus dead, officials are shocked to discover that it has returned some years later, and this time it is in England. The government quickly assembles a team to enter Scotland in hopes of finding a cure, because there are still survivors in the country. But the team soon finds out they haven't been surviving on canned goods. It must be a great feeling to be given the money to direct a dream project, and here Neil Marshall is given license to pay homage to all his old favorites. You'll see shades of Escape from New York, The Road Warrior, and many more classics sewn together into this post-apocalyptic tale. That's its only downfall in fact as it just feels like too much in one movie, but that doesn't detract from the fact that this is one highly entertaining flick. The gore runs high in this feature and the FX work is just excellent. It never lets up and keeps you gasping for breath, and while it may seem like a bit of an overload, when it's over, you still want more.

4/5

Dorothy Mills
Year – 2008
Director – Agnes Merlet
Tags – Suspense

A psychiatrist is assigned to a troubled young girl after she hurt the child she was babysitting. She is believed to be mentally ill, but there may be much more wrong with Dorothy Mills. This movie has a lot going for it. It's well acted, has a nice plot with a bit of originality to it, well written, well shot, the recipe for a stellar movie. Unfortunately I also found it to be quite dull. The movie is very somber, and meant to be as such, but it was just so grey, it kind of made me tune out at times. Nothing more I can say about it really, it has a multitude of good points, but just came off a little slow. Still recommended though.

3/5

Dr. Jekyll and Mr. Hyde
Year – 1931
Director – Rouben Mamoulian
Tags – Suspense

A doctor who adores his fiancée creates an elixir that changes him not only physically, but mentally, allowing him to seek out another life and embellish his dark side. This classic tale is told almost to its full luster here. The movie is a bit racy for the time period, which was interesting to see. I also liked the point of view camera shots, which were really awesome. The direction is very good for the most part, and loaded with exceptional acting. The FX look incredible, especially for the time. The transformation sequences alone are astounding, and the set design is remarkable. This is a great movie for a great story.

Dr. Jekyll and Mr. Hyde [Remake]
Year – 1941
Director – Victor Fleming
Tags – Suspense

This remake follows the same story as the original and is almost exactly the same. This movie follows the original a little too closely for my tastes, but at least it isn't a complete shot for shot remake, they do vary it up a bit. The acting is excellent and even tops the 1931 version, but one issue I had was with the transformation. Mr. Hyde was almost indistinguishable from Jekyll, they just looked much too similar and I don't think the slight changes would have fooled anyone. The direction is very good here as well, and overall this is just a well done movie. Though I would have preferred a unique flair to this version, I still enjoyed it and definitely recommend it.

3.5/5

Dreamcatcher
Year – 2003
Director – Lawrence Kasdan
Tags – Aliens, Infection

Four lifelong friends tied together by the strange powers they received as children are camping in the woods when parasitic aliens attack, using humans as breeding grounds. This is another Stephen King adaptation and I have to say really is a great story and a nice concept, but it didn't translate too well to the big screen. It's overly long for starters, and the pacing is pretty bad. On the plus side, it is well acted for the most part, and the visuals are nice most of the time. But in all of the CGI usage there are some occasions when it looks pretty bad. This is an average movie with some near fatal flaws, but the positive aspects certainly increase the entertainment value.

2.5/5

Driftwood
Year – 2006
Director – Tim Sullivan
Tags – Ghosts

A boy is sent to an attitude adjustment camp that is run by a cruel taskmaster. The boy has his issues with certain people there, as well as a ghost who haunts him. This movie is really about the camp and the inhumane treatment that the so-called troubled kids have to endure. The ghost part of the story really just opens up the mystery aspect of the movie, which is quite good. The acting and direction are very nice, the story is also good, but it just wraps up a little too neatly in my opinion. Driftwood is definitely something different, which is pretty much always appreciated, and the camp itself is definitely a slice of true life because I know a lot of the cruelty that you'll see in the movie does actually happen in the camps themselves. The horror does take a backseat to the human drama that unfolds, but that works for the most part. This is a very good movie that didn't quite reach greatness but is still definitely a good watch.

3.5/5

Duel
Year – 1971
Director – Stephen Spielberg
Tags – Suspense

A man on the road for a business trip is suddenly, and for seemingly no reason, toyed with by a trucker. As the day progresses, the trucker increases the dangerous nature of his games, to the point where things become deadly. This is a fun adaptation of a work by Richard Matheson, but it's not without its flaws. The acting is handled mostly by one man and everyone else involved are just secondary characters with few lines that don't really add much to the movie. And the acting by that one man is fortunately more than adequate. The real star of the movie however is the truck, which is a rusty beast and gives the film an almost monster movie quality. The direction is good but the movie does get dull at times, fortunately there are some suspenseful moments that help progress the story. This is a very good movie but far from perfect.

3.5/5

Dunwich Horror, The
Year – 1970
Director – Daniel Haller
Tags – Witchcraft

A university student gets mixed up with a man who practices the dark arts and wishes to gain possession of her professor's copy of the Necronomicon by any means necessary to perform and evil ritual. Part Lovecraft adaptation, part 70's psychedelic acid trip, The Dunwich Horror is an entertaining but terribly uneven movie. The acting is really good, but the direction takes forever to find its place. By the end of the movie it achieves a certain amount of brilliance but it's a laborious journey to that point. The FX are, uh, interesting to say the least. I can appreciate not showing the beasties of the movie too much, but I would have liked more. I did enjoy the multi-colored monster vision however. This adaptation is far from great but still somewhat enjoyable. I do hope to see the story done justice someday however.

3/5

Dying Breed
Year – 2008

Director – Jody Dwyer
Tags – Slasher / Survival

Four people travel into Tasmania looking for the thought to be extinct Tasmanian tiger, and one of them looks for information on her sister's death while looking for the same animal. This is a pretty standard slasher flick. The back story is about the only original aspect of it, but that is really only a minor portion of the movie. The rest of the movie deals with familiar ground and your typical slasher movie trappings, making it just seem like more of the same. The acting is good and the same goes for the direction. The FX are nice, but underused. It's not a bad movie, I did enjoy watching it, but it is just that it really didn't offer up anything new or interesting so I just toss it into the pile of other competent and forgettable slasher flicks.

3/5

Ed Gein (In the Light of the Moon)
Year – 2000
Director – Chuck Parello
Tags – Serial Killer

Ed Gein was a very disturbed man who had an affinity for dead bodies and making garments out of human skin. Though he only actually killed two people, he is one of the most talked about serial killers due to his grisly usage of human bodies for various reasons. He is also the inspiration for such classic films as The Texas Chainsaw Massacre and Psycho. This movie is really done justice by Steve Railsback who plays Ed Gein in such a creepy manner that it really hits home. The movie itself though is fairly dull. I was bored several times while viewing this because it's just so uneventful. I feel that there could have been much more shown and that the makers of this movie could have delved much deeper into his depravity. The end result feels watered down. It does have its moments though, and as I said, Railsback does a great job, but it's just not enough to raise this movie above average.

2.5/5

Ed Gein: The Butcher of Plainfield
Year – 2007
Director – Michael Feifer
Tags – Serial Killer

Here we have another take on the notorious serial killer, Ed Gein. When I watch a movie I'm not a big stickler on historical accuracy, but when it comes to serial killers, you just can't make a movie about them and completely change everything. This movie plays out like a cheap slasher movie and not only has Kane Hodder play Ed Gein, which is ridiculous since Gein was nowhere near his size and stature, but also has him killing many random people, which just never happened. The movie also happens to be poorly directed and just very boring. The acting ranges from passable to downright bad. I do like that they delved into his more gruesome hobbies a bit, but it seemed to be more for shock value. While the other Ed Gein movie wasn't terribly well done, this was just garbage, and while the killer may have inspired many iconic horror movies, it seems as though he is undeserving of the horror treatment himself.

1.5/5

Eden Lake
Year – 2008
Director – James Watkins
Tags – Suspense

A couple decides to take a vacation in the woods but end up being accosted by youths, and when confronted, it leads to terrible consequences. The idea isn't exactly new, but the execution of said idea certainly deserves merit. This movie can be pretty brutal at times, but unfortunately it also tends to lag between scenes of brutality and tension, there's just some dead space floating around. But the acting is great, the FX look exceptional, the story is good, and it ends strong. There are a few hiccups along the way, but in all this is a very well done thriller with some great looking violence, and since the offenders are kids, it makes it just that much better.

3.5/5

Eden Log
Year – 2007
Director – Franck Vestiel
Tags – Monsters

A man wakes up in cavern with a dead man next to him and has no memory of who he is or how he got there. To make matters worse, he is being chased by a strange creature and must travel deeper into the subterranean catacombs. This is a very flawed and impressive movie at the same time. It may be that Eden Log is just too ambitious for its budget which is a common problem in independent horror. The movie is a very dark and industrial odyssey into the unknown with great performances and FX. The direction could have used some polish but is overall pretty satisfying. The creatures look awesome and not quite like anything else out there, which is always pleasant. With a tighter story and a bigger budget, this easily had the potential to be a classic, but it's still a very unique and well done movie.

3.5/5

Edge, The
Year – 1997
Director – Lee Tamahori
Tags – Animals, Suspense

A billionaire and two of his companions survive a plane crash deep in the wilderness. To make matters worse, they have attracted the attention of a man eating bear. This movie is really a double edged sword because it plays out two genres at once. First you have your human drama side, and then you have your killer animal side. Rather than both elements of the film melding cohesively, they tend to clash at times, and that drops the bear story into the background. I feel that was a mistake because the bear angle was more interesting than the human angle, and since it took a backseat, I feel the movie suffered a bit from that. When the bear is on screen, it's very menacing, and I'm glad they used a real bear as that will always be more effective than a CGI one. It's vicious and cunning, and that means the blood is going to flow. The acting is excellent and the direction is better than average. I just wish the bear was a bigger part of the story, because that was main draw of the movie. Still, very nice.

3/5

Eight Legged Freaks
Year – 2002
Director – Ellory Elkayem
Tags – Animals

A man housing all kinds of rare spider breeds accidently exposes them to some chemicals that caused the spiders to grow out of control and now they're loose in the town, hunting down humans. This ultra cheesy throwback to the giant animal movies of yesteryear is a lot of fun, but could have been so much more. If they had not gone for commercial appeal, they could have made this an ultra gory, nudity filled visceral epic. Instead we get a very watered down giant spider movie that while entertaining in its own right, just feels way too timid. The CGI is passable but there are moments of really bad looking spiders that seem to be floating along a wall instead of climbing up it. The acting is good, also cheesy, which fits. The direction is decent, as the movie is kept moving along at a nice pace. I like this but could never love it, it's the bastard child of greedy minds just looking for a quick buck instead of making this what it should have been.

3/5

Empty Acre, The
Year – 2007
Director – Patrick Rae
Tags – Suspense

A couple with a young baby moves into a farmhouse that has a curiously barren acre of land near it. Strange things begin to happen, but when the baby disappears, the mother finds herself trapped between a malevolent supernatural force and her alcoholic husband. This is a pretty awesome low budget movie. The originality is immense and the story itself is more than competent. Not quite as grandiose as it could have been but very good all the same. The acting is pretty good and the direction is fairly tight. There's a few red herrings thrown up as to what exactly is going on and the ending is thankfully masked by those. A very satisfying supernatural thriller.

3.5/5

End of Days
Year – 1999
Director – Peter Hyams
Tags – Devil

At the end of the new millennium, Satan comes to New York City in search of a bride that has been unwittingly groomed for him. Now it's up to an alcoholic security guard with a troubled past to stop him. Ok, do me a favor, stop for a second and re-read that synopsis. Now that it has sunk in, really, just how stupid does this movie sound? The story is just riddled with flaws and errors, and in the end is just not good at all. The direction reflects that, as Hyams doesn't seem to really know where to go with this crap. The acting is good enough, and Gabriel Byrne plays a good Satan, but it's not enough to save this movie. What does come close to saving it though are the great FX and bloody visuals, but in the end it's just not enough. In the Devil sub genre, this is one to watch if you don't have any other options.

2/5

Entrance, The
Year – 2006
Director – Damon Vignale
Tags – Demons

A police detective is drawn into a world where sinners are punished in a series of games, and when they lose, they lose everything. This movie really is pathetic. First off the actors are terrible, and worse than usual for a low budget movie. The story has an element that is supposedly based on a true story, but that doesn't have much of anything to do with the movie, which is rather lame. The story itself is also garbage and while I can see the tiniest bit of potential in it, it is still a complete failure. And the games they play for their lives… musical chairs, bingo? Are you kidding me? You couldn't think of anything better? The direction is also really bad as the movie was incredibly boring and never really went anywhere interesting. This is a terrible movie full of flaws and damn near completely worthless.

1/5

Event Horizon
Year – 1997
Director – Paul W.S. Anderson
Tags – Ghosts

A ship that had been lost in deep space seven years ago mysteriously reappears and a crew is put together to recover it. Once there however, the crew realizes they are not alone and now the ghosts from their past have come back to haunt them. Here's a unique take on the old haunted house story, set it in the future and exchange the house for a spaceship, brilliant! The acting is excellent all around and I really enjoyed the diverse cast. The direction is also very tight and the movie never gets boring in the least. The FX are very good for the time but do look a bit dated now. The ship itself looks incredible and has a nice creepy atmosphere to it. The movie is also heavy on the gore side which was a pleasant surprise. If you're a fan of haunted house movies, you need to see this, even if you don't like sci-fi, the unique take on the sub genre is worth every second of your time.

4.5/5

Evil Aliens
Year – 2005
Director – Jake West
Tags – Aliens

A news team doing a fluff piece on alien encounters ends up face to face with some real aliens, and they're not here for peace. This low budget movie is undeniably fun. The acting is pretty good and the direction is well done. There is an overload of blood and other bodily fluids which range from great gore shots to slapstick comedy. And there is some good comedy in the movie, even a clever use of a banana peel, which I haven't seen in a long time. The practical FX are great and the aliens are pretty cool looking. There is quite a bit of CGI usage in the movie, which is some of the worst I've ever seen. And while I could have forgiven it and chalked it up to the low budget, it was used in places where practical FX could have been used and it would have looked better. This movie could have been better but it's still a funny and gory romp that I enjoyed very much.

3.5/5

Evil Dead, The
Year – 1981
Director – Sam Raimi
Tags – Demonic Possession

Five friends travel to a cabin in the woods for some rest and relaxation. Upon their exploration of the cabin, they find a book called the Necronomicon and a recording of a man who was studying it. Through this they unleash an ancient demonic horror that begins to possess them one by one. Evil Dead is a labor of love and it shows. Filmed over a year and a half with a fairly meager budget, this movie has stood the test of time as one of the horror greats. The acting may not be the greatest, but that's to be expected in low budget horror, what you do get is incredible FX work, loads of gore, awesome direction, a great story and a general flair for filmmaking that can only come from people who care about their task at hand. And did I mention loads of gore? This is a phenomenal movie and a good study of how to make a movie cheap but still incredibly effective.

5/5

Evil Dead II: Dead by Dawn
Year – 1987
Director – Sam Raimi
Tags – Demonic Possession

This movie picks up immediately after the original right after a short recap of what transpired beforehand. And speaking of the recap, it's funny to me how wrong it is since the same people are involved with this movie as the original. But since this movie is a lot of comedy and slapstick, it also fits. The sequel is so over the top in everything that it does that you can't help but admire it. The gore, the humor, the drama, the acting everything is pretty outrageous. I really liked where they went with the sequel, ensuring that the story would progress instead of letting it stagnate. There's not much more I can say without giving away key information to this and the original's happenings so I'll just say that this is a great follow up to a timeless classic.

4.5/5

*Evil Dead III can be found under Army of Darkness.

Evilenko
Year – 2004
Director – David Grieco
Tags – Serial Killer

This movie is loosely based on the life and times of serial killer Andrei Chikatilo, who between the years of 1978 and 1990, raped, killed, and mutilated over fifty children in the Soviet Union. Such a depraved killer we have here, and such an elusive one as well. Malcolm McDowell does an amazing job here as the killer, and the rest of the cast is admirable as well. The movie is very slow however, and while graphic at times, the movie focused more on the manhunt than the actual killings. Don't get me wrong, the movie still shows many kills, and while I enjoyed the hunt aspect, I would have preferred to see his crimes explored further. Obviously given the nature of the material, the movie is incredibly dark, so be prepared for that, and while it could have been done better it's still a very comparable effort.

3.5/5

Evil's City
Year – 2005
Director – Tom Lewis
Tags – Demons

A group of reporters seek out a mysterious town that no one can seem to find. Once there they discover that the inhabitants are all dead and now have become some sort of demonic creatures. Trust me, the synopsis sounds much more interesting than this movie really is. The acting is bad but not too bad for a low budget movie. The story is complete garbage, as well as the direction. It takes about half the movie for the people to reach the town and then even longer for the first demon-zombie thing to appear. The make-up is ok and the gore looks good, but it is rarely used, and I'm sorry but if you're going to make a movie like this, it needs to be drenched in gore, not just have maybe two bloody moments. It was painful to sit through this and only has very minor things going right for it. Skip this festering pile of dung altogether.

1/5

Exorcism of Emily Rose, The
Year – 2005
Director – Scott Derrickson
Tags – Demonic Possession

Based on actual events, this movie shows the trial of a priest for negligent homicide after an attempted exorcism goes wrong. No, this isn't just a rip-off of The Exorcist, despite the similar theme it is a completely different movie. The story is good and the way it plays out in a courtroom, with the horror shown through flashbacks, is well done. But the movie can get pretty slow at times, especially with several unnecessary scenes. The acting is great, but none better than Jennifer Carpenter, who plays the title character and not only does a great acting job, but also does an amazing physical performance contorting her body and face. This is a very good movie with some definite creepiness to it and it's a great addition to the genre.

3.5/5

Exorcist, The
Year – 1973
Director – William Friedkin
Tags – Demonic Possession

An actresses' daughter becomes very ill, but when things start happening that can not be explained, she fears her daughter is possessed and turns to a couple of priests for help. The Exorcist is a classic horror movie for a lot of reasons. First off, it really is pretty shocking to hear the filth that comes out of a little girl's mouth and the vile acts she commits while possessed. Still today it's pretty much unheard of to have such things in a movie. Second comes the great acting, especially by Linda Blair, who plays sweet innocence just as well as she plays a sick and depraved demon. The direction is also very tight and well done. The FX work, both in make-up and sound, are probably the highlight of the movie for me. The way the little girl transforms is great, along with all of the phenomena that occurred around her. Everyone needs to see this movie at least once, as it can illicit a multitude of reactions from various people and it's just one of those movies you'll always remember for one reason or another.

4.5/5

Exorcist II: The Heretic, The
Year – 1977
Director – John Boorman
Tags – Demonic Possession

This movie takes place years after the original. I don't think there's been such a terrible follow up to iconic horror movie. The story is complete garbage and the direction is abhorrent. The acting is very good and there are some decent visuals, but for the most part this is a horrid movie. This movie could have been interesting with a different script and a different director. I don't think it could have been worse. If it wasn't for a grown up Linda Blair looking pretty hot and some good performances aside from her own, this would have been an easy candidate for worst horror movie ever. But it may be worth watching once to see how ridiculous it can get.

1/5

Exorcist III, The
Year – 1989
Director – William Peter Blatty
Tags – Demonic Possession

This third Exorcist movie is an adaptation of the novel Legion, written by William Peter Blatty, who directs and writes here. This is the true sequel to The Exorcist, taking place years after the original. Ignoring the second movie, as everyone should rightly do, this movie was probably Blatty's way of stepping in and saying: "No, this is how you make a sequel to a classic." This movie is very deep and atmospheric, with some excellent acting and very bizarre and wonderful visuals. If I had a complaint to make I suppose I could say that the pacing could have used a little work in the first half of the movie, but at least the second half of the movie, most notably the final third, is very tense and just plain evil looking, I like that. The killing in the movies is especially graphic and sick, but you don't get to see it, you don't even see much of an aftermath, but the way the deaths are told through the characters is very well done and you actually don't need to see it to get the full effect, and that's pretty damn special in my book. This movie is almost as good as the original and a very worthy follow-up.

4/5

Exorcist: The Beginning
Year – 2004
Director – Renny Harlin
Tags – Demonic Possession

Presented with a rare opportunity here, this is the second try on making a prequel to The Exorcist, the first of course being Dominion: Prequel to the Exorcist. I would have to say that I prefer this one, at least slightly over the other one. The actors are mostly the same as the other movie, so the performances are pretty equal here (good). This movie is almost as slow as the other one as well. The CGI is also just as bad here but used way too often. And while both movies have the same story at its core, this one is just told better. Add that this version also amps up the gore and that made this movie more appealing for me. I think that The Exorcist is definitely good ground for a prequel and the fact that we get two versions is pretty intriguing. Overall I think they did a good job, nothing great, but good.

3.5/5

Eyes of a Stranger
Year – 1981
Director – Ken Wiederhorn
Tags – Serial Killer (Fictional)

A serial killer is at large in the city and a newswoman believes she knows who he is. But upon her investigation of the man, the killer sets his sights on her blind and deaf sister. This movie is a good watch even if there isn't really anything special about it. Everything is good, the direction, acting, story, it's all fairly average and enjoyable, but definitely lacking any staying power. The FX are really cool though, but definitely underused. There's a fair amount of blood and nudity, but there could have been more. I liked watching this movie but it just left no kind of lasting impression for me. It could have been more, a lot more, but it's not bad for what it ended up being.

2.5/5

Faculty, The
Year – 1998
Director – Robert Rodriguez
Tags – Aliens

Alien organisms take control of the faculty of a small town high school. Soon the aliens begin taking over the student body and the rest of the town and it's up to a group of uninfected students to stop the invasion. Out of all the teen horror movies to come out after Scream (and there were a lot), this is by far one of the best. The characters are shown as stereotypical from the start, but they are fleshed out very well and evolve beyond what you'd expect, which is very refreshing. The faculty themselves are great characters as well. This movie starts out strong and is paced extremely well, never allowing for dull moments. The acting is very good, and the FX are done well. The CGI looks shoddy at times, but not too bad. This movie could have easily been viewed as a rip off of past sci-fi/horror efforts, but they actually acknowledge the similarities in the movie and further use one student's knowledge of them as a plot point, nicely done. This is a very enjoyable movie helmed by a great director and supported by a wonderfully diverse cast. Excellent work.

4/5

Fatal Attraction
Year – 1987
Director – Adrian Lyne
Tags – Suspense

A man has an affair with a woman who turns out to be mentally unstable and begins stalking him after he tries to break things off with her. This is not the first tale of obsession to be seen in the movies, but it is one of the better known tales. I guess that's because it has commercial appeal, but in my opinion it really lacks any staying power. For one thing, the movie is very tame, and the things she does are for the most part, annoyances, nothing more. She does get a bit more extreme toward the end, but nothing that hasn't been done better elsewhere. But the movie is very well acted and the direction is good. I don't want to sound like I'm bashing the movie, but it's just not all that it's cracked up to be. I can recommend a dozen movies that are better tales of obsession, but as this one goes, Fatal Attraction is a very good flick for those of you out there that want to watch a taste of the dark side but are afraid to go all the way.

3.5/5

Fear
Year – 1990
Director – Rockne S. O'Bannon
Tags – Serial Killer (Fictional)

A young woman is a psychic helping police find serial killers and making a career out of it. Now a new serial killer has surfaced who is always ahead of the police, and when the woman gets involved, she discovers that he too is psychic, and now plays a dangerous game with her. I like the idea, even though it is pretty silly, it's a little something different. The story is just unfortunately not very good, and when you add some pretty poor direction, the viewer is subjected to a fairly boring and uneventful movie. The acting is fine but nothing special. This is a mildly enjoyable movie with too many flaws to call it good, and I would just as soon skip it.

2/5

Fear
Year – 1996
Director – James Foley
Tags – Suspense

A young girl falls for a charming young man, but it doesn't take long for him to show his true colors and a penchant for violence and manipulation. I have to say, it's nice to see a guy get obsessed for once, the ladies have been getting the raw deal for years. This is a well done, if not somewhat cardboard thriller with little originality but good direction. Mark Wahlberg does a great job at being creepy, which is good since the whole movie really rode on his shoulders. I think I may have felt bad for the family if the father wasn't such a prick, because in reality, he brought a lot of the problems on himself. I also have to say that I hate the way the movie ended, it was pretty weak. But as far as tales of obsession go, I feel this is a competent entry into the genre, just nothing to write home about.

3/5

Fear, The
Year – 1995
Director – Vincent Robert
Tags – Slasher / Survival

Some people gather for a study of fear in a cabin nestled in the woods, using a full sized wooden dummy as an outlet. But when the dummy comes to life, it begins using their fears against them, and then slowly kills them off while driving others mad. This slasher flick actually has a lot going for it. The unique angles of the killer and the fear factor are interesting but I don't think they were used to their full potential. The story is also really good and has a lot of weird moments that set it apart from other slashers. Unfortunately the kills are rather dull and the acting isn't very good, along with some very uneven direction. If it wasn't for those issues, this easily could have been a great slasher, but I still have enough respect for it to call it good.

3/5

Fear 2: Halloween Night, The
Year – 1999
Director – Chris Angel
Tags – Slasher / Survival

This movie continues on some time after the original and features a new set of people. I enjoyed the first movie to some degree, but this one is pretty bad. It takes almost an hour for anything to really happen, and even when things do start to happen, they're not all that interesting. The acting isn't all bad, the direction is mostly bad, and the story is weak at best. There are some decent FX I suppose, but there's just nothing here that could make this a good movie. Even if you're a fan of the original or slasher movies in general, I still can't recommend this.

1.5/5

Feardotcom

Year – 2002
Director – William Malone
Tags – Ghosts

A detective and a health department worker try to solve the mystery behind a killer website and a dead girl that haunts all of those who visit it. So this movie is a pretty blatant rip off of Ringu / The Ring, and not even a good one at that. There are a handful of genre actors and vets that do a good job, and the rest of the cast is decent too, but that's where my praise for the movie ends. The story is unoriginal, poorly written and just plain bad. The direction is slow and boring but I'm not sure if I can place all the blame on the director since the script is downright terrible. Well I do place some blame on Malone because he was obviously going for some kind of David Lynch type storytelling which did have some interesting visuals, but overall was pretty forced and a bit pretentious on top of that. This is a really bad movie and I just did not care for it in the least. There is little to enjoy here.

1.5/5

Feast
Year – 2005
Director – John Gulager
Tags – Monsters

Bar patrons lock themselves in after the appearance of some bizarre monsters one night, and now the fight for survival begins. I love how Feast has not only has stereotypical characters, but tells the audience why they are stereotypical and if they will survive, and then completely turns every expectation on its head. The characters are truly great, as are the actors portraying them. The monsters are very different from anything else that has graced horror movies as they look different and act different, very nice. The humor works here in every way as it's not overdone in the least and is incredibly effective. And the gore, oh the gore, I love it, and it is exceptional here. Feast is one of those movies that horror fans pray will come along and rekindle their faith in the genre. So many pointless thrillers and flat monster flicks get pumped out by the studios in the hope that they can make a quick buck, you never expect another classic to come out again. But here we see a movie with boundless creativity and substance, and you just have to smile, because some people out there understand what the fans want, and they're not afraid to give it to them. Highly recommended.

5/5

Feast II: Sloppy Seconds
Year – 2008
Director – John Gulager
Tags – Monsters

This movie picks up right where the last one left off and moves into the town that is close to the bar. What the hell happened here? The same people are behind this movie as the last one, yet this is nowhere near as good as the original. First off, this one focuses too much on comedy, and there are some definitely funny moments, but for the most part the comedy is the equivalent of fart jokes. Also, there is some truly terrible CGI and green screen work, and they use it a lot, which really blows. And finally, a good chunk of this movie takes place during the day, where you can see the monsters in full daylight, thus making them much less effective. On the plus side though, there is still plenty of gore, and the dead bodies strewn everywhere are great. There is also a very precious scene with a baby that I will treasure forever, as it was one of greatest experiences of my movie watching life. I literally sat there and said to myself: "Did they actually just do that? So awesome." So yeah, I'm still disappointed by this, but I guess it wasn't that bad. It certainly had some good moments, and they threw in some nudity for good measure. So while I'm not happy with my sloppy seconds, it'll have to do.

2.5/5

Feast III: The Happy Finish
Year – 2009
Director – John Gulager
Tags – Monsters

Once again this movie picks up right where the last one left off. This is pretty much more of the same as the last movie, lacking the raw and brutal nature of the first movie, but still entertaining. This one is a little more focused on the blood and gore than fart jokes, which makes it slightly better than number two in my book. The introduction of new characters is about as random as the characters themselves. The ending is just about as strange as they come, but it does fit with the overall theme of randomness that has become the Feast franchise. I'll always treasure the original movie and as for the sequels, well, they may not have been up to snuff, but I guess in the end they could have been a hell of a lot worse.

3/5

Feed
Year – 2005
Director – Brett Leonard
Tags – Serial Killer (Fictional)

An Australian cop who specializes in bizarre sexual crimes involving the internet happens upon a site dealing with morbidly obese women and the desire to make them bigger. The deeper he explores, he finds out that there have been others who died from being overfed, and he travels to the US to find and put a stop to the site owner before he can kill his newest star. This is a great movie definitely not made for the mainstream, and that's what I like about it. You know going in that this will have limited appeal, and yet the movie is made anyway to its full gross-out potential, you've got to respect that. The story is very sound and I rather enjoyed the complete juxtaposition of the relationships on display. The cop's relationship with his skinny girlfriend is completely sick and dysfunctional, while the feeder and gainer have a relationship based on mutual gratification and real love. The acting is great, as well as the direction. There are plenty of sick moments here that all fall into a very unexpected and welcome ending. If you have a strong stomach you'll be treated to one of more interesting thrillers to be released in a long time.

4/5

Feeding the Masses
Year – 2004
Director – Richard Griffin
Tags – Zombies

A news team tries to cover a zombie uprising to full effect while the government attempts to suppress all instances of zombie attacks. The thing that made Romero's zombie movies so good was that he added social commentary, and the filmmakers here did the same thing, but were just much more blatant about it. The social commentary here is about how America doesn't even get news anymore, and they just get "spin". Watch one news network, you hear one thing, watch a different news network, you'll hear something completely different about the same damn thing. I get that, and they do a good a good job of conveying it, even if it is a tad bit obvious. The acting is good for a low budget movie, and the direction is very good. There's a fair amount of blood but that's where the filmmakers went wrong. Romero's movies worked because of the perfect balance, here, the zombie action is sacrificed for additional social commentary, and that doesn't work as well. Still, this is one of the better low budget zombie movies I have seen with a solid script and very nice direction.

3.5/5

Fido
Year – 2006
Director – Andrew Currie
Tags – Zombies

Set in the 50's, this movie offers up a different idea on what happens in the world. Here, zombies have risen due to radiation, and a company devised a way to domesticate the flesh hungry beasts, turning them into loyal servants and quelling their need for human flesh. This movie is great. The story is such an original take on the tired zombie sub genre, but it's not just a great concept, it's also pulled of splendidly, which is what really matters. It's pretty funny, but not as funny as it could have been. Don't get me wrong, I was definitely laughing, but I do feel there were some missed opportunities. The movie is very cute, but then it also features some great gore, and the mix of the two makes for one unique movie. The acting is great and the direction is very good with only a couple of small missteps. This horror/comedy is a definite breath of fresh air and a wonderful story of a boy and his dog… er, zombie.

4/5

Final Destination
Year – 2000
Director – James Wong
Tags – Slasher / Survival

A teenage boy receives a premonition that the plane he has boarded is about to explode, so he and group of others exit the plane, only to see it erupt into a ball of flames from the windows of the terminal. Now that Death's design has been skewed, the people who exited the plane start dying by mysterious circumstances. I love this movie for the wonderful plot device alone. The fact that the kids in this movie are being killed off one by one by an unseen force is blissful. You could never see anyone coming to get you, and you're just dead, nice. And the deaths are really good all around, they happen fast, which gives you just a quick glance at what happens. That's probably a good thing since the CGI probably wouldn't look good if it was drawn out. The acting is good, nothing incredible. The direction is fast paced though, which is always good. This is one of my favorite teen horror movies to come out of this era because it just has a wonderful plot and story to it. Very original and very fun.

4/5

Final Destination 2
Year – 2003
Director – David R. Ellis
Tags – Slasher / Survival

In this sequel we find a young woman having a premonition about a deadly car crash, and she saves a group of people from their demise, which sets Death in motion again. I can forgive this movie for following a similar plot as the original because that's its gimmick, and just as long as it has a strong story and good death scenes, I'm satisfied, and this one delivers. The acting and direction aren't quite on par with the original, but the story is strong and it connects several elements between this movie and the previous one. There is also an extended premonition scene which is gloriously graphic, and they also stepped up the deaths, which makes up for the movie being a bit shallow in other areas. This is a very worthy sequel and if you enjoyed the original, you'll almost certainly find entertainment value in this as well.

4/5

Final Destination 3
Year – 2006
Director – James Wong

Tags – Slasher / Survival

In the third Final Destination movie, a teenage girl has a premonition about a fatal accident involving a roller coaster, and you know the rest from there. The original director returns for this movie, and right off the bat the movie runs smoother than the last one. Unfortunately the opening roller coaster sequence is just meh at best. There isn't much in the way of graphic death and the CGI looks fairly crappy. Now afterward there are some good deaths, but once again they rely too heavily on CGI and some of them just don't look good. The acting is decent enough to be passable. The story is ok, but nothing special. In all this movie is entertaining, but just isn't as good as the other two. Still worth your time if you're a fan though.

3/5

First Born
Year – 2007
Director – Isaac Webb
Tags – Suspense

A woman becomes pregnant with her first child and during and after the birth begins experiencing strange phenomenon. This movie is just bad. The story is absolutely worthless, the character development is nil, nothing scary or creepy or suspenseful happens at any point during the movie. The acting is good, but wasted, and the direction reflects the poor storytelling. Nothing of consequence happens, the movie is incredibly dull and boring and it just never goes anywhere. The production values were high and it carries a shiny outer shell that looks good, but that's the only worthwhile thing here. This movie is like biting into a delicious looking apple and finding it full of maggots. Pretty, but pretty worthless too.

1.5/5

Flatliners
Year – 1990
Director – Joel Schumacher
Tags – Suspense

In Flatliners, we find a group of medical students searching for an afterlife, or basically proof of something beyond death. One by one they flat line and then after a set period of time, they are brought back to life, the problem is that they also bring something back with them. In my mind, this movie only half works, I can understand them bringing back the dead with them in a way, but why would they bring back issues with the living? Beyond that point of fact though, it's a great plot for a movie and it is very entertaining, but honestly, it could have been a whole lot more. Great cast though, they really pull off the movie well, but definitely needed some tweaking if it wanted to reach greatness.

3.5/5

Flesh for the Beast
Year – 2003
Director – Terry West
Tags – Demons, Zombies

A group of people investigate a supposedly haunted mansion only to face death itself in the form of undead creatures and demons straight from hell. Was this movie supposed to be a joke? If so I guess I just didn't get it. I suppose this was just some super geek's masturbatory fantasy that he dreamed up after years of living in his mother's basement. This movie isn't really much more than soft core porn mixed with a very poorly written horror story. Oh and the soft core segments are also poorly done. The acting is atrocious, the direction is sloppy and boring, the FX look terrible, and there still manage to be even more issues with the movie. I actually had hopes for this one because it had the potential to be cool, but in the hands of such talentless individuals, it ends up being one of the worst horror movies ever made.

0.5/5

Flesh Freaks
Year – 2000
Director – Conall Pendergast
Tags – Zombies

A man comes back to America as the sole survivor of a vicious attack by a zombie, deep in the South American jungle. Now there is another zombie outbreak, only this time it's at the university, and it appears the nightmare isn't over for him yet. Microbudget horror, I just can't get enough of it. Flesh Freaks is like a student film, so grainy and raw you know it's not going to be good, but does it show promise? I think that it does. I think the director did the best he could with most likely a twenty dollar bill and some pocket lint. The acting is typical for microbudget stuff, terrible. The direction however, while not great, showed a definite artistic flair and was more than your typical point and shoot filmmaking, this movie has some creativity to it. The story is ok, it does show some ingenuity and isn't just a "zombies appear and then zombies kill" kind of flick, they try to add some originality, some of which is fairly good. The FX are just funny because they are unbelievably fake, but you know, budget constraints and all. I do think they did a good job with what they had. I would like to see what this director can do with a bigger budget, hell, any budget, but this isn't bad at all.

2.5/5

Flight of the Living Dead: Outbreak on a Plane
Year – 2007
Director – Scott Thomas
Tags – Zombies

A passenger plane heading to Paris is carrying some very hazardous cargo. When rough turbulence disrupts the cargo, a zombie is let loose, and soon begins infecting others. I love the concept of a zombie outbreak on a plane, because there really is no place to hide, and really, not even much room to run. The movie is very bloody, which is nice, and the zombies look good with their minimal make-up (they are fresh after all). It takes about half the movie for the chaos on board to really begin, but the front half isn't exactly boring, it takes the time to introduce some characters, some of which seem pointless. The kills are fairly violent, although some of the kills were crap CGI, which is always annoying. But I must say I very pleased with this movie even though it did have a few rough spots.

3.5/5

Flowers in the Attic
Year – 1987
Director – Jeffrey Bloom
Tags – Suspense

After the death of their father, four children and their mother are forced to go live with their mother's parents, who never approved of the marriage to begin with. The grandfather is ill and the grandmother insists that he not know that the children exist, so they are forced to live in the attic. The grandmother while stern at first soon becomes more sadistic. I'm not going to compare this movie to the book, so I'm just going to review the movie itself. It's good, nothing incredibly grand, but a very solid effort. It runs smoothly, although the ending does have an expedited feel in my opinion, like they had to pare it down to meet time constraints. Everyone knows this story revolves around incest and sadism, which are more alluded to than actually explored. The kids tend to overact quite severely in this movie, but the adults put on great performances. Suspenseful at times, but definitely has a couple of spotty moments. Still, a better than average movie.

3/5

Fog, The
Year – 1980
Director – John Carpenter
Tags – Ghosts

On the centennial celebration of a small town's founding, a dense fog bank rolls in carrying with it a group of ghosts who were wronged by the founding fathers of the town. I like this movie, but it feels much too tame and I think I would have enjoyed this movie more had it been graphic instead of shying away. The story is really awesome with great characters supported by wonderful acting. The direction is also top notch, but no real shock there. I like the FX too, especially the way the zombie-like ghosts look, very original and creepy. This is a well told tale that I wish had some blood in it, but in the end that's not that big of a deal, and for some it may not matter at all. Recommended viewing for a well done ghost movie.

3.5/5

Fog, The [Remake]
Year – 2005
Director – Rupert Wainwright
Tags – Ghosts

This remake follows the basic plot of the original with a somewhat different story. And that's where the failure of the movie comes into play. Whoever wrote this crap probably not only didn't watch the original, but has never seen a horror movie before. The filmmakers here took a great adult horror movie and turned it into a terrible teen-esque throwaway slasher flick. The new characters introduced into the movie are poorly thought out and the original characters still present are somewhat sullied. The casting is also off, I mean, I like Selma Blair but I don't believe she has a ten year old kid. The acting is ok from some of the leads, but most of it is just really bad. The direction is also horrible as the movie is painfully slow, but they may be more of a script issue than anything. This is a pitiful attempt at a remake but at least it's a good study on what not to do.

1/5

Forest of the Dead
Year – 2007
Director – Brian Singleton
Tags – Zombies

Some friends plan a camping trip in the woods, only to have their laid back vacation ruined when some zombies crash the party. Ahh Forest of the Dead, what can I say about this movie? Do me a favor and open your wallet right now. How much money is in there? It doesn't matter, whatever you have is more than the budget of this entire movie. I understand the constraints of the low budget horror movie, like you can't have real actors, so you use your friends. You can't afford a real camera, so you use a camcorder. And why build sets when you can just find a place and shoot. This movie sucks, and I liked it a lot. Why you ask? Because these people took all they had and just had fun with it. This movie had to of been shot over a long period of time because, for example, one of the actors had a beard and braces and then in another scene they were gone. There were many things like this going on that were just so ridiculous you couldn't help but laugh. It's an Evil Dead like movie that is nowhere near as good, but still has some nice (sometimes obviously fake) gore and tons of laughs. It's nothing great, but it really wasn't meant to be either. I had a lot of fun watching this movie and I am proud to put it in my collection.

3/5

Forsaken, The

Year – 2001
Director – J.S. Cardone
Tags – Vampires

A man driving cross country to his sister's wedding comes across a hitchhiker on the hunt for vampires, but after they find a victim of the vampires still alive, they end up being hunted themselves. This is a very entertaining vampire flick, even if it does have a crap story thrown onto it. I'll be honest here, the story is in no way anything new or terribly exciting, but fortunately it is acted and directed very well, which still makes it worthwhile in my book. This is shown off like a teen horror movie but it really is much more mature than that. The actors are actually in their twenties and playing people in their twenties, how refreshing. There's a fair amount of blood and gore and even some nudity too. This may not be the best vampire movie out there, definitely not the most original, but still pretty damn good.

3.5/5

Fortress

Year – 1986
Director – Arch Nicholson
Tags – Slasher / Survival

A teacher and a group of students are kidnapped by four masked men from their small schoolhouse and taken to a cave as part of a ransom attempt. But the kids and their teacher refuse to let it happen and try their best to escape. This Australian survival horror movie is a gem from my childhood that I loved but for the life of me I could not remember the name of it. When I figured it out in my adult life and watched it again, I was still amazed by it. After being through such an ordeal, you could just see how the children became such a savage product of their new environment. The acting and direction were very good and the way the story played out was excellent. This is something dramatically different that the usual survival fare, mainly due to the people involved being children, and I appreciate it for the attempts it made to be a stand-out movie.

4/5

Frailty

Year – 2001
Director – Bill Paxton
Tags – Suspense

A loving single father of two boys receives visions from God saying he must hunt down and kill demons. The demons are wearing human suits to disguise themselves from sight. One of his sons believes him and the other thinks his father is just a serial killer. Religious thrillers are a tough sell, because more often than not they fail, but then a movie like this comes along and makes all the failures worth it. This is well done for many reasons, the first being, you don't know if the father really is talking to God or if he's completely insane. It's really interesting how the movie plays out and it's just a unique production in general, so big kudos goes to Paxton in that regard. I would have liked to have seen more though, maybe had some of the "demons" fleshed out more, so to speak. Still, this is an excellent thriller that keeps you guessing and it just oozes with originality, which is always welcome.

4/5

Freak Out
Year – 2004
Director – Christian James
Tags – Slasher / Survival

An escaped mental patient who is very docile and well mannered is taken in by a couple of guys who wish to train him into their own personal slasher and hi-jinks ensue. This movie had high potential for being a pretty cool horror/comedy but unfortunately fell a bit flat. Despite the great plot the movie just wasn't funny. Sure it had a couple of moments that made me chuckle but the comedy just wasn't there. The horror was also kind of lacking as this movie could have been much better with buckets of gore. Still, the story and direction are good and the acting is very good, especially for a low budget movie so it's not all bad, I just wish it could have been more.

2.5/5

Freaks
Year – 1932
Director – Tod Browning
Tags – Suspense

A woman working at a carnival marries a little person and then tries to poison him in order to gain his wealth, using another carnival worker as an accomplice. Once the plan is figured out it invokes the wrath of the sideshow workers who band together for revenge against those who had wronged one of their own. I love this movie, and I think what makes it so poignant is that it lays out the intolerance of people and shows that normal folks are the real freaks, not these people with the physical abnormalities. And that fact that this was made in '32 makes it even more poignant. This is just so well done and engrossing, the story was extremely well written and planned out. The fact that they used actual people with these abnormalities instead of make-up just gives the movie the extra something special. This is a must see for everyone, and the fact that this movie was banned for so long reaffirms my beliefs as to who the real freaks are.

4.5/5

Freddy vs. Jason

Year – 2003
Director – Ronny Yu
Tags – Slasher / Survival

Two slasher movie icons go head to head in a battle for horror supremacy, with many victims along the way. It's obvious that this movie was just a concept and the premise for how it would go down was just an afterthought. In that respect, the set-up is pretty stupid. The acting is also very mixed from the kids. For example Katharine Isabelle is great while Kelly Rowland (What is she, like 38 playing a teenager?) is just god awful. The dialogue in the movie is probably the worst thing of all, like when Rowland says in response to finding out they are being hunted by both Freddy and Jason, "We're not safe asleep or awake!" That is just the stupidest line ever uttered, why would you be safe from Jason if you were asleep? What is he, a bear? Play dead and he'll go away? I'm sure whoever came up with that line thought it was brilliant but in truth that person needs a lobotomy in order to have more interesting thoughts. I may seem like I'm bashing the movie but I really did like it. There were tons of kills, lots of blood and everything moved along nicely. It was cheesy as hell but who could take this seriously? I just can't wait until Chucky vs. Leprechaun.

3.5/5

Freddy's Dead: The Final Nightmare
Year – 1991
Director – Rachel Talalay
Tags – Slasher / Survival

All the kids in Springwood are dead, and Freddy needs new victims, but he also wants his child from when he was human back in his life. So, the series had a good run, and even the worst one in the series wasn't bad, it just wasn't that good, and I can appreciate the people behind it wanting to give Freddy a find send off with a sixth movie. This movie reveals a lot of Freddy back story through flashbacks, which was done very well, the current timeline plot though, feels a bit forced. Not that I can blame the writer though, there's not much left in the franchise by way of story, and I'm just glad they ended it here than drag it out forever. This movie is definitely the most cheeseball of the bunch, which is understandable because that's where the movies have been heading since the third installment. The movie is good even though the production feels a bit thrown together, and it's a decent way to end the series.

3/5

Friday the 13th
Year – 1980
Director – Sean S. Cunningham
Tags – Slasher / Survival

Camp counselors are murdered one by one when they attempt to re-open a camp that was the site of a child's drowning and then a double murder the following year. Some people call this a classic and I can't understand why. The story and the characters just aren't very good and the script is not well written at all. But I don't hate the movie, and in fact I actually like this one because it has some good kills, a fair amount of blood and some nudity, which is the recipe for any good slasher flick. The direction is good and the acting is great for a low budget flick. The movie also ends very strong, and these are all factors that aid the movie a great deal. I know that in slasher movies the story really is an afterthought, but I think a lot more care could have been taken with the lore of the camp as well as the development of the characters. Still, as far as slasher movies go, this isn't the best, but it's still pretty damn good.

4/5

Friday the 13th Part II

Year – 1981
Director – Steve Miner
Tags – Slasher / Survival

Camp Crystal Lake is closed after the events of the first movie and now a group of new camp counselors are working at a new camp, only to be hunting down in the same fashion. I don't think there's much new ground to be had in this franchise. Killer stalks counselors, killer murders counselors, lather, rinse, and repeat. And that's pretty much what we get here. The story is essentially the same as the original with almost indistinguishable tweaks, and thusly plays out pretty much the same. It's a little early in the franchise for repetition on such a massive scale don't you think? Unfortunately this time around the direction is kind of sloppy and the kills aren't as exciting. But there's still a definite entertainment factor here that makes the movie watchable, even with the carbon copy feel and the flaws. So it's not a bad movie, it's just not very good.

2.5/5

Friday the 13th Part III

Year – 1982
Director – Steve Miner
Tags – Slasher / Survival

This movie picks up shortly after the second one. I was into this movie up until at least the half way point. Miner showed an improvement on his direction between these two movies and found much more enjoyment in this one than the last one. But then the story took a nosedive when it began to copy the original movie in more ways than one. And I mean completely copying from kills to scenarios. On top of that, this movie was also to be 3-D, and the 3-D sequences are so forced it's pretty ridiculous. The acting is pretty bad once again, but I guess that's just to be expected. A nice start and a dismal finish make this movie just another average, but watchable attempt at propelling forth an already tired franchise.

2.5/5

Friday the 13th Part IV: The Final Chapter
Year – 1984
Director – Joseph Zito
Tags – Slasher / Survival

This movie picks up immediately after the third movie, giving the franchise some much needed continuity. If this really was the final chapter, the franchise would have gone away on a high note, because this installment is actually a bit better than the original. There are some really great kills in this one, and I think that's why it stands out so much for me. There was some actual humor too, for example, check out the reaction from Corey Feldman when he sees a neighbor undress through a window. Or Crispin Glover's dancing. Classic! The pace is also very good, the acting is above par for this kind of movie and to top things off, the story is actually pretty damn good, like someone took the time to actually think this one out. It's still no masterwork, but it's still a bright point in a rather dismal movie series that refuses to die.

4/5

Friday the 13th Part V: A New Beginning
Year – 1985
Director – Danny Steinmann
Tags – Slasher / Survival

This movie takes place several years after the last one at a reform camp for troubled kids. I've always kind of liked this one, and I liked it for the reason most people hated it, the ending. I won't go into detail of course, but I actually found it to be very refreshing and it injected a little something different into the franchise. Now beyond that, the movie isn't very good. The kills are standard for the most part, nothing special. The acting is as bad as usual, but this time since we are dealing with a reform camp, so there's a bit more diversity in the characters, and I especially liked the Goth girl, Violet. The story is just more of the usual stuff again, but at least they're continuing on with the story and adding more continuity to the series. The direction is ok and the movie moves along decent enough. This is a slightly better than average installment, and I don't care what the fans say, I like it.

3/5

Friday the 13th Part VI: Jason Lives
Year – 1986
Director – Tom McLoughlin
Tags – Slasher / Survival

This movie is a continuation of number five, taking place an indeterminate amount of time after that movie. And here we have the first bona fide turd of the series. It hasn't been a great series so far, but at least the worst ones were still average movies. This one just isn't good at all. The story starts off nice enough but then just devolves into a typical knock off of the other movies. The kills are sub par and nothing to write home about, the direction is sloppy, the acting is worse than usual and it's just a chore to sit through this. The series was already repeating itself by the third movie and now there's just no originality left it seems. Like I said, the movie starts off on a good note, but then just becomes more of the same and makes no attempt to add anything different.

2/5

Friday the 13th Part VII: The New Blood
Year – 1988
Director – John Carl Buechler
Tags – Slasher / Survival

This movie takes place an indeterminate amount of years after the last one. There is a character here that has psychic and telekinetic abilities, and I have to give props to the writers for adding a little variety to this series. The rest of the movie plays out the same as the others but that element really does make a big impact. The kills here aren't bad and do switch things up a bit, which is good. The acting is more of the same however as there are no stand out performances once again. The direction is ok, nothing special, but at least I wasn't completely bored with the movie. This is just another average installment in this geriatric series, but hey, at least it's better than having another below average movie, right?

2.5/5

Friday the 13th Part VIII: Jason Takes Manhattan
Year – 1989
Director – Rob Hedden
Tags – Slasher / Survival

This movie takes place some amount of time after the last one. I can appreciate that they finally moved Jason out of the woods and lake setting, but this movie is so incredibly stupid that the effort is for naught. I have to speak of the ending of the movie first because it is just so incredibly dumb and nonsensical it blows my mind that anyone would be allowed to film it, even as a joke. And another major issue is that Jason doesn't act like Jason. Here he is, mindless killing machine walking around New York, and he's not killing everyone, he's just following some people and ignoring everyone else, which just doesn't make any sense, he should be slaughtering everyone. The acting is as bad as usual, no stand out kills, boring direction and a shoddy story. This is easily the worst installment in the series and the last one Paramount would make, fortunately.

1.5/5

*Friday the 13th Part IX can be found under Jason Goes to Hell: The Final Friday.

*Friday the 13th Part X can be found under Jason X.

Friday the 13th [Remake]

Year – 2009
Director – Marcus Nispel
Tags – Slasher / Survival

This was described more as a reboot than a remake, as it encompasses the first three or four movies instead of just the first. This movie is just not very good, and they missed out on a golden opportunity. If you are going to restart a crappy slasher franchise, then you need to make it all about boobs and blood, because in a Friday the 13th movie, nobody cares about the plot. There were plenty of conventionally attractive women bearing their assets, and I'm not talking about their acting skills, but there was actually not a whole lot of blood. The kills were boring and uninventive for the most part, the rest simply stolen from other movies, and I'm not even talking about F13 movies either, some kills were blatantly stolen from other horror movies. This is a piss-poor attempt in breathing new life to a dead franchise. The movie was overall pretty boring and the entertainment value was mild at best. Let's hope a more talented group of people get a hold on the inevitable sequel to this mess.

1.5/5

Frighteners, The

Year – 1996
Director – Peter Jackson
Tags – Ghosts

A conman who employs ghosts to scare up business for his paranormal investigations comes across a real threat as a rogue apparition begins killing the living. Now this is a fun movie. Originality in a ghost movie is very difficult to find, but this movie has it. This is a great story brought to life by a great director. The acting is also excellent, especially by Jeffrey Combs who is as hilarious as he is twisted in his role. The FX are also very good and the CGI is nothing short of impressive, especially for the time period. CGI nowadays doesn't even look this good. In a way this is a family film but it also has some rather dark elements as well, and in that respect I feel the movie is like Gremlins. Any way you slice it this is just an excellent film and a very respectable addition to the ghost genre as well as the horror/comedy genre.

4/5

Frogs

Year – 1972
Director – George McCowan

A family has gathered in their country estate on an island to celebrate the 4th of July when the surrounding wildlife suddenly takes on murderous tendencies. My first thought behind this movie was that it was just impossible for it to be good, frogs do not illicit fear, and in fact I found them to be pretty cute. But somehow this movie was good. The movie doesn't focus completely on frogs though, as all of the swamp creatures get in on the action. Snakes, spiders, alligators, lizards, hell, even snapping turtles. The acting was actually really good, the main stars having numerous acting credits to their name. The direction was also good, and the movie was well paced for the most part. The story is still incredibly silly and the deaths even more so. A good third of the movie is just wildlife footage of animals moving around, and when the death scenes come they are usually just a person is peril then a quick cut of an animal, back to person and so on. This is good cheesy B-movie fun and worth at least one watch.

3/5

From Beyond
Year – 1986
Director – Stuart Gordon
Tags – Monsters

Scientists create a device that stimulates the pineal gland in humans and opens up a doorway to an alternate dimension that houses strange and horrible creatures. Now this is how you turn a very short story into a feature length movie. The Lovecraft story is very short but Gordon and company managed to turn it into an impressive feature while still keeping a core Lovecraftian feel to the film. The FX are the highlight here, displaying some wonderfully creative visuals. The acting is great, highlighting a trio of genre vets at the forefront of the movie. The direction is also great and the movie flows smoothly and beautifully. The movie is as sexual as it is gory and everything just fits together so well that it makes for a very unique and brilliant genre flick.

4.5/5

From Beyond the Grave
Year – 1973
Director – Kevin Connor
Tags – Anthology, Ghosts, Witchcraft

This movie has four stories and a wraparound. The wraparound story is about an antique shop and that sets up each segment as people buy things from it. The first story is about a mirror containing a ghostly apparition that craves blood. The next is about a man who becomes friendly with a father and daughter, but the daughter is far from normal. The third one is about a guy who gets a malevolent spirit called an elemental stuck on his shoulder. And the last story is about a door that does not lead to any earthly place. The anthology starts out on a good note with the first story being the best. I didn't really like any of the others a whole lot, but I didn't hate them either. The third one was pretty funny and at least the fourth had an awesome set. This is a pretty underwhelming anthology but definitely not bad, there's great acting and very good direction, the stories just weren't completely up to snuff.

3/5

From Dusk till Dawn
Year – 1996
Director – Robert Rodriguez
Tags – Vampires

Two brothers are on the run from the law, trying to escape into Mexico, when they are forced to kidnap a family of three to reach their destination. Once there, in the relative safety of Mexico and then at a rowdy bar called the Titty Twister, they find little time to relax as they soon learn the bar is inhabited by bloodthirsty vampires. This is such a fun movie as it is off the wall, bloody, sexy, and just plain brilliant. First I have to mention the cast, as they really do make this movie. Quentin Tarantino plays a great mental case opposite his cool, calm and collected brother, George Clooney. Add to that the talents of Juliette Lewis, Harvey Keitel, Tom Savini and more, and you end up with one hell of an ensemble. The practical FX work bears mentioning as well, as it is just beyond awesome. KNB do not disappoint here. The blood flows freely and the body parts fly, quite literally as well. And in writing about this movie, it would be a travesty not to mention that Salma Hayek unleashes pretty much the hottest dance ever seen on film here. All said this is an interesting twist on a tired subgenre of horror, and it is pulled off with great success. Highly recommended.

4.5/5

From Dusk till Dawn 2: Texas Blood Money
Year – 1999
Director – Scott Spiegel
Tags – Vampires

This sequel concerns a group of bank robbers who run into some vampires and are turned, much to the chagrin of the local police. Wow, this movie sucked, seriously. The story is pretty pathetic and is not only one of the weakest vampire tales ever, but one of the weakest heist tales as well. It could have been interesting in a lot of ways, but it just failed. Of course it doesn't help that the direction was terrible as well, as the movie was very slow and uninteresting. There were some good performances in this movie at least, but it's just too bad most of the cast was pretty awful. The first movie was a prime example of genre blending, but this one turned out to be a complete mess. There was some decent blood, but underused, and there was a fairly pointless nudity scene to boot. This movie is bad, plain and simple.

1.5/5

From Dusk till Dawn 3: The Hangman's Daughter
Year – 1999
Director – P.J. Pesce
Tags – Vampires

This prequel is set one hundred years before the first movie. The last movie was bad but this one is just a whole new level of bad. Most of the actors are no name people, and that's because they have no talent. The ones who do have talent just look bored here and don't really even try. The story is just terrible and completely uninteresting. The direction is about the same, there are few movies that have bored me quite as much as this one. And the FX, they're just laughably bad. And I guess that was the only good part in the movie, laughing at the terrible looking bats and make-up. Several scenes from the original are stolen here, but they're just so lame they can't even steal other people's ideas properly. It's a shame that such a great movie had two terrible sequels, I just hope there won't be another.

1/5

From Hell
Year – 2001
Director – Albert Hughes, Allen Hughes
Tags – Serial Killer

This movie, while about Jack the Ripper, a notorious serial killer of prostitutes in 1888 London, is actually based on a graphic novel. Here they explore a theory of the unsolved crime. And what a thought provoking theory it is. The story is well crafted and while historical enthusiasts may boo-hoo upon it, I enjoyed it because I realize it is a movie, which is a form of entertainment and not even based on the actual crimes, rather a graphic novel's interpretation of them. The acting is very well done and the direction is very good with only minor issues. The Ripper killings were especially brutal in real life, but not here. Here it is mostly watered down and they don't really show much, which does hurt the story a bit because come on, we're all adults here, show us, you don't need to be scared. When I watch a movie based on such a notorious serial killer, I expect something gruesome, not this. But it's still a great movie and very enjoyable.

4/5

From Within
Year – 2008
Director – Phedon Papamichael
Tags – [Hidden to conceal spoilers]

Residents of a small religious town begin committing suicide one by one. But there is more to the deaths than just suicide, something is making them kill themselves, and it's moving from body to body and won't stop until everyone is dead. I like this movie. It borrows small elements from several other movies to make something new, which is an interesting way to go about it. I do think that by the filmmakers showing so much negativity toward organized religion, and laying out everything wrong with it, they end up coming off a bit too bitchy and the movie does suffer a bit from this. It's like yeah, I know you hate religion and all the bad things it promotes, now will you please get back to the horror? But as for the horror, it's pretty cool. A fair amount of bloody and grisly suicides all tied together by a very good story that has a few nice twists and turns for good measure. I really liked the ending too. This movie is a little something different with good acting and direction, and I had a great time watching it.

3.5/5

Frontiere(s)
Year – 2007
Director – Xavier Gens
Tags – Slasher / Survival

A set of robbers head to the countryside to escape the law but instead come across a Neo-Nazi family who wants the woman in the group to continue on their bloodline. So essentially what we have here is the French version of The Texas Chainsaw Massacre. But this isn't a rip off by any means, as it just has the same shell. Here the story is good but ends up being just a run of the mill slasher in the end. Nothing wrong with that because the movie has some incredibly brutal and gory scenes that really make the movie stand out. It's just too bad that in between the scenes of intense bloodletting, the movie can get pretty dull. There are some pacing issues but nothing that kills the movie, just some noticeable hiccups. The acting is pretty good overall but I didn't really care for the lead actress. This is a very good movie that relies heavily on gore sequences to make it interesting and that works for it, I just wish it had more going on.

3.5/5

Gacy
Year – 2003
Director – Clive Saunders
Tags – Serial Killer

This movie is based on the life of John Wayne Gacy, who killed over thirty men and boys, most of which he buried in the crawlspace under his house. I've heard a lot of bad things about this movie and while I do feel this isn't as good of a portrayal of Gacy as it could have been, it is still a very well done movie. Mark Holton is great as the title character and the rest of the actors did a good job as well. The story really lacks the murder and rape aspect of his crimes, only showing very few of these instances and focuses instead the stink coming from under his house. The direction is great and the movie runs smoothly. While the story wasn't strong enough for a serial killer movie, it made for a good dark drama and overall I thought this was a very good movie.

3.5/5

Gate, The
Year - 1987
Director – Tibor Takacs
Tags – Demons

A boy finds a gate to Hell in his back yard, and he and his friend unwittingly open it just a crack, and then strange things start happening as the demons held within try to reclaim Earth for themselves. This movie, while seemingly cheesy and typical of 80's B movie territory, is actually a multi-faceted mostly serious horror film with loads of ingenuity. This is anything but a straightforward demon flick, there are many occurrences in the movie that use many horror elements and I don't want to say too much and reveal some good scares ahead of time. But speaking of demons, I watched this movie a lot as a kid and I always wanted my own little demon minion because they were cute but sinister at the same time. Yeah, that's right, most kids wanted a dog, but I wanted a demon minion. The FX really are great, and even through some definitely old CGI tactics were used and look really bad, there's so many good practical FX and make-up that it more than makes up for the other shortcomings. The acting is also really good, look for Stephen Dorff as the child lead. The direction is excellent as well, good pacing and never a dull moment. Fans of 80's horror and horror in general owe it to themselves to see this inventive horror movie that really is like no other.

4.5/5

Gate II: Return to the Nightmare, The
Year – 1990
Director – Tibor Takacs
Tags – Demons

This sequel takes place a few years after the original. This movie definitely lacks the inventive style of the original and instead ops for a more straightforward movie of demons and black magic. The FX are pretty much the same as the original, just not used as much. The story is ok, I do have a certain amount of respect for it because it does seem like a likely direction for a sequel to go and isn't just a rehash of the original, it just lacks any real ingenuity. Maybe I'm just feeling generous but I legitimately liked this movie, not nearly as much as the original, but I do like what it is. The acting is fine and the direction is just as good as it was in the first movie with maybe only a couple of lags in the pacing. I really do like the end sequence of the movie however, that's the highlight for me, everything leading up to it just happens to be kind of average. This is a good follow up to a classic 80's horror flick that is definitely lacking in certain areas but holds a charm that I appreciate.

3/5

Gates of Hell II: Dead Awakening, The (Through the Fire)

Year – 1988
Director – Gary Marcum
Tags – Cults

I think this is supposed to be a sequel to City of the Living Dead / tribute to Lucio Fulci. In this movie a woman seeks the help of a cop to find her missing sister, but instead finds a medallion that a cult of demon worshippers will stop at nothing to possess. This movie is more of an insult to Fulci than any kind of homage, as this nonsensical mess is almost unwatchable. The acting is pathetic and the direction is just as bad, I guess the only decent part of this movie is actually the FX. For example, the prosthetics that made up a demon in the movie are really pretty cool, and there are a couple other moments of good FX work, but that's about it. Some people will say that the movie is disjointed because Fulci's work could also be hard to follow, but at least his movies culminated into something, this is just a complete mess.

1/5

Ghost and the Darkness, The
Year – 1996
Director – Stephen Hopkins
Tags – Animals

An engineer is hired to build a bridge over a river in Africa for a wealthy man's railroad, but his plans run into trouble when a pair of lions begin killing the workers, lions that the locals say are not lions at all, but malevolent spirits. This is a very beautiful movie with grand, sweeping shots of Africa. I just wish that the rest of the movie was as engrossing. It is a very good movie bordering on excellent with great performances and good direction, but I wish the story had more meat to it because it comes off a little too lean. It's not a bad story at all though as it has many good elements but I feel that none are embellished upon as well as they could have been. There's even some good gore, which makes sense since we are talking about man eating lions, and some excellent tension to boot. In some ways I want to rate this movie higher because it does deserve it, but the current rating just feels right.

3.5/5

Ghost Ship
Year – 2002
Director – Steve Beck
Tags – Ghosts

Here we have a group of maritime scavengers who are tipped off to the whereabouts of a boat of some size that is adrift in the ocean, and they set off to find it. Upon arrival, they find that the boat is a luxury liner that has long since been lost at sea. When they board the vessel, they find out that the inhabitants are definitely dead, but not gone. This movie is interesting because it takes away the typical haunted house and replaces it with an ocean liner. Unfortunately the movie mirrors a similar movie by the name of Deep Rising a bit too closely. Everything is just too familiar to the aforementioned film and even though they have different plotlines, I just can't ignore it. So what you're left with after the stolen locale and scenarios is a miscast and somewhat boring attempt at a ghost movie. There are some fairly graphic kills, which is a bit unexpected for a ghost movie and also welcome. The practical FX are great, but unfortunately they are mixed with some awful green screen work and generally uneven CGI. The movie isn't a complete loss, but still a below average attempt.

2/5

Ghostbusters
Year – 1984
Director – Ivan Reitman
Tags – Ghosts

Three unemployed psychology professors start a business in which they remove hostile spirits for a fee. At first they are met with cynicism, but when an ancient demon from another world invades New York City, they may the city's only hope. This movie is a classic, and a great example of genre blending that results in an excellent horror/comedy. The comedy aspect of the movie is great, pulled off extremely well by the entire cast involved. The horror aspect is not only pulled off well, but is actually fresh as well. The FX are great, especially for the time, and the direction is very tight and well managed. Great gadgets, awesome ghosts, funny dialogue, an excellent story, and easily one of the most memorable villains in horror movie history, you would have to look cross-eyed at this movie to find any major flaws. And this movie really has stood the test of time as well, as I found it to be just as entertaining today as I did in my childhood. Highly recommended.

4.5/5

Ghostbusters II
Year – 1989
Director – Ivan Reitman
Tags – Ghosts

Years after the events of the first movie, we find the Ghostbusters scrounging for work by performing at birthday parties just to try and make ends meet. And when spectral activity suddenly increases, they investigate, finding a river of ectoplasm underneath the city. There is a similar formula between this movie and the original. However, the story just isn't up to par. It's definitely still good, but it's only good, nothing great. The cast returns and are as great as they were in the first film, and even the director returned, who also does a great job. This outing is a bit slower, less inventive, not quite as funny, and it just appealed to me less. But it's still a very good movie, it was just lacking a little bit of that magic that made the first work so well.

3.5/5

Ghosts of Mars

Year – 2001
Director – John Carpenter
Tags – Ghosts, Infection

A group of officers on Mars are sent to a small mining town to escort a very dangerous criminal back to the main city for prosecution. Only when they get there, they end up finding half the miners brutally murdered and the other half turned into sadomasochistic lunatics. This movie, in a lot of ways, plays out like a western, which is interesting, and the concept lays the groundwork for what could be yet another unique John Carpenter masterpiece. But that doesn't happen. First off, Ice Cube is top billed actor here, and he can't act his way out of a paper bag. He is particularly bad here. And Pam Grier and Natasha Henstridge, who have showed acting chops in the past, also fail to impress here. There's some pretty bad CGI, and the fight scenes between the heroes and the ghost-infected horde are surprisingly lackluster and way too obviously staged, as there's really nothing natural about them. Still, for all its flaws, it moves along briskly and Carpenter is able to make a somewhat enjoyable film with what he had. Disappointing? Sure, but I actually still somewhat enjoyed it.

2.5/5

Ghoul, The

Year – 1933
Director – T. Hayes Hunter
Tags – Zombies

A terminally ill man buys an Egyptian artifact fabled to give its owner eternal life. When he dies, his butler places him in the crypt with the artifact and upon the next full moon he rises from grave. Here's a lost gem I'm happy was found. This movie is a brisk gothic feature with an excellent performance by genre legend Boris Karloff. The rest of the acting is very good in its own right, but Karloff once again steals the show. His after death make-up only increased his menace. This is a very well done movie, nothing overly exceptional but very good nonetheless. The story is more or less just an excuse to make a horror movie as it really isn't the best but I'm not really going to complain either. If you're a fan of the golden age of horror you'll probably dig this.

3.5/5

Ghoulies

Year – 1985
Director – Luca Bercovici
Tags – Demons

A man inherits a large manor and becomes obsessed with the dark arts, ultimately raising diminutive demons in an attempt for power. This movie is so awful it's actually watchable in a way. The Ghoulies themselves are kind of cool looking but they don't really do much, or you don't get to see them doing much actually. The story is incredibly lame and stupid, with acting to match the cheesy 80's vibe. The direction is pretty bad too as the movie is just one long bore fest. While I should probably rate it lower because it is a terrible movie, it's just so bad that it made me laugh and so weird and pointless that it at least stands as a testament as how to not make a movie.

2/5

Ghoulies II
Year – 1987
Director – Albert Band
Tags – Demons

This movie follows the Ghoulies as they join a traveling carnival and take up residence in the spook house. That's also where they decide to kill carnival goers. People will make a sequel to just about anything, won't they? I was pretty generous with my rating of Ghoulies but the sequel won't get off so lightly. This one is definitely worse and has all of the same elements that made the first one so awful, but it also lacks the little bit of charm the original had as well. The story, acting and direction are all very bad, but at least the Ghoulies get a little more action this time around. If you're one of three people out there who actually liked the original, you'll probably like this too, but for the rest of us, just skip it and watch something worthwhile.

1.5/5

Ghouls, The
Year – 2003
Director – Chad Ferrin
Tags – Zombies

A stringer journalist with a very troubled life comes across a woman being attacked by a group of bums. When he runs into the alley with his camera, instead of finding a group of bums raping a woman, he instead finds a pack of zombies eating her flesh. After a narrow escape he tries to uncover what's going on in that part of the city. People expecting a straight zombie movie will surely be disappointed. This is a very dark drama that happens to feature zombies as a somewhat small but very integral part of the movie. This is definitely one of the best microbudget movies I've seen. The story is unorthodox and very solid, featuring a great deal of originality. The acting is also surprisingly good and even more surprisingly features a couple of genre vets. The direction could have used some tweaking though. I can see a lot of potential with this guy, but he just didn't really reach it with this movie. But this is a damn fine movie overall and most of the flaws are budgetary.

3.5/5

Gift, The
Year – 2000
Director – Sam Raimi
Tags – Suspense

A psychic uses her abilities to make ends meet by reading people's futures, but when a young woman goes missing, she helps the police to find her, which will start up a grand mystery as to what actually happened to her. So this movie is a rather clever crime drama wrapped up neatly with supernatural elements, making for a rather unique a compelling tale. The acting is great by a rather diverse cast, even Katie Holmes, who is usually pretty lackluster, puts on a good performance, which I think is just a testament as to how good of a director Sam Raimi really is. And speaking of which, the direction is wonderful, never a dull moment. This is a great multi genre film that seamlessly blends horror, mystery and drama together for an excellent time.

4/5

Ginger Snaps
Year – 2000
Director – John Fawcett
Tags – Werewolves

This film follows two inseparable sisters obsessed with death. While out one night, one of the sisters gets her first period and is promptly attacked by a creature. After a narrow escape, the girl finds herself changing, and craving blood. This is an unbelievable film that just came out of nowhere. I'll go out on a limb and say this is probably the greatest werewolf movie ever made. The story is very original and crafted with such care that the fact that this is a labor of love is evident. Beyond the great werewolf aspect of the story there is such a human drama element present here that makes it truly one of a kind. The acting is outstanding, the FX work is fresh and unique, the direction is superb, the score is haunting, quite simply said, this movie is a work of art. Ginger Snaps is a rare feat, an actual perfect movie in my mind. I've seen this dozens of times and it never ceases to amaze me.

5/5

Ginger Snaps 2: Unleashed
Year – 2004
Director – Brett Sullivan
Tags – Werewolves

Here in the sequel we pick up shortly after where the last movie left off. I'll leave it at that to refrain from revealing spoilers. Making a sequel to such a highly regarded movie is tricky work, fortunately we have a worthy sequel that doesn't quite reach the mark the first one hit, but comes close. While I feel the same care was taken with the sequel as the original, there is just something missing from this one. It lacks a bit of the human element that made the first one so outstanding, it's still there, but just to a lesser degree. I do feel that is a result of the outcome of the first movie however and this new director just moved forward with what he had, trying to stay true to the storyline. Again, the production as a whole is outstanding and I really enjoyed it. I'm happy to see a continuation in the story that's not only worthwhile, but pretty great as well.

4/5

Ginger Snaps Back: The Beginning
Year – 2004
Director – Grant Harvey
Tags – Werewolves

This movie is actually a prequel to the Ginger Snaps story, going way back to Colonial times and showing how the curse began. I was a little leery going into this movie for a couple of reasons. The first is that it's a prequel, and those don't have the best track record. And second, it was made so quickly after the second movie, which made me think that it was rushed. Fortunately what we have is a very dark and well made movie that comes close to the majesty of the original. Right off the bat you know the FX are going to be even better since KNB is involved, and they are really amazing. Second, both women reprise their roles as Brigitte and Ginger (albeit ancestral roles), which is also a very good thing. The movie takes place in a fort surrounded by forest and snowfields, which gives the movie a very cold and somber feel, excellent location. The acting from the rest of the cast is also quite good, and while some of the characters do have a stereotypical feel, the actors do a great job of giving them personality. This is a well directed, well scripted third chapter in a thus far impressive series of movies and I look forward to hopefully seeing more in the future. Sure, it is hardly historically accurate either but I don't really care about that with a movie this good.

4.5/5

Girl Next Door, The
Year – 2007
Director – Gregory Wilson
Tags – Suspense

Based on the Jack Ketchum novel and inspired by real events, The Girl Next Door is about two sisters who are forced to live with their aunt in 1958. During the summer, the older of the two young girls is subjected to being tied up in the basement by her sadistic aunt. Over a period of time the girl is raped, beaten, tortured and more by her relatives and other local children. The story behind this movie is just unimaginable, and the fact that it actually happened makes it that much more painful. Sometimes the worst horror of all is right in our own backyard. The movie is extremely graphic and didn't pull many punches. The acting is incredible, and this is especially poignant since most of the cast is comprised of children. The best acting of all is by Blanche Baker, who pays the aunt. She plays such a despicable role that it kind of makes you sick. And either that's raw talent or she needs to be locked up, but I'm guessing it's the former. The girl in the movie goes through so much you actually want her to die so she doesn't feel anymore pain. This movie is a visceral experience that should not be missed and it is a display of human horror the likes of which most minds couldn't even fathom.

4.5/5

Good Son, The
Year – 1993
Director – Joseph Ruben
Tags – Suspense

A young boy goes to live with his aunt and uncle and befriends his cousin who is the same age as him. But it doesn't take long for him to see that his new friend displays some ever increasing psychotic behavior. I like movies with kids acting like the evil little shits they are, only increased tenfold. And this is a good thriller, but ultimately it is very tame. Macaulay Culkin does a good job of trying to shed his good boy image here by acting like a twisted mental case, and he does do some evil things, but they are hardly anything as sick and demented as it could have been. Like I said, the movie is very tame and probably only received its R rating for bad language, so don't expect any graphic scenes of murder or anything. But I must say that the movie is well acted and directed, and it certainly is entertaining. I like this but it's just too watered down to truly be a classic. Still good if you're looking for something to pass the time though.

3/5

Gore Gore Girls, The
Year – 1972
Director – Herschell Gordon Lewis
Tags – Serial Killer (Fictional)

A serial killer is brutally murdering strippers and a ditzy reporter hires a pompous investigator to help her unravel the story and solve the crime. I actually liked this movie and I wasn't really expecting to since I wasn't a fan of Lewis, but I feel that this is his best work that I've seen. The movie contains an overabundance of nudity and gore and at least this time around the gore is more inspired. The acting is still terrible but I liked the lead actor. I liked how he was such a douchebag you couldn't help but admire the guy. This has the feel of an Italian movie and I just liked it. It still has tons of flaws but this is a good movie nonetheless.

3/5

Gothika
Year – 2003

Director – Mathieu Kassovitz
Tags – Ghosts

A psychiatrist leaves work one night and then wakes up inside the asylum where she used to work, but now she's a patient. With her husband dead and her being blamed for the crime, she races to solve the mystery of his murder as well as that of the girl who is haunting her. On the outside this looks like an interesting thriller with a supernatural aspect to it. Upon viewing it though, all I see is missed potential. The acting is pretty good for the most part, but there are some bad performances. The story is just not very good, for example, this psychiatrist is placed in the asylum with all the people she used to treat? That's like putting a corrections officer in with all of the inmates he used to guard, it would just never happen. At least she would have been put into a solitary cell and away from the general population. It's things like that, real world things that would never actually happen in the real world that dragged down this movie for me. The direction is decent but the movie is just too slow to unravel for my tastes. Overall this movie just didn't do anything for me, which is sad because this could have been pretty good.

2/5

Gravedancers, The
Year – 2006
Director – Mike Mendez
Tags – Ghosts

After the funeral of a long time friend, the three remaining friends perform a grand send off by having a party in the cemetery and dancing on graves. Unfortunately for them, this act angered the spirits of those graves that were danced on, and these were the kind of spirits you would not want to make angry. The idea behind this movie is sound, the execution however, not so good. Ghost movies really require a good atmosphere and an air of creepiness to make them work best, this unfortunately had neither. The movie just wasn't the least bit scary, but it did have some good moments. The ghosts looked cool, even if for some reason they all had the same face. There is some horrendous CGI as well, but the practical FX were nice. The acting is good, nothing great. I just found this to be an average attempt at a ghost movie, it could have been a lot more, but it just didn't do that good of a job.

2.5/5

Graveyard, The
Year – 2006
Director – Michael Feifer
Tags – Slasher / Survival

A young man dies after a practical joke goes wrong, and five years after his death, the people involved gather together in remembrance, only to be killed off by a masked murderer. Wow, that plot sounds familiar. Seriously, if you can't come up with anything new or anything at least exciting, why even bother to make the movie? And the story behind the derivative plot isn't very good either. Add to that the slow direction and the poor acting, and you definitely have a contender for worst horror movie ever. But what's this? There just happen to be some nice FX and some pretty great kills as well. There's even an awesome electrocution that was very well done. So that's the only saving grace here, because everything else is run of the mill or just plain bad.

2/5

Graveyard Shift
Year – 1990
Director – Ralph S. Singleton
Tags – Monsters

Workers at a textile mill begin to die, and when a crew is put together to clean out the basement of the mill, they find out there is a lot more than just rats in the basement. This Stephen King adaptation, much like the short story, is really nothing special or unique, but it sure is entertaining. This is a monster flick like so many that have come before it, but it is just so much fun. There's a great cast, most notable is the performance by Brad Dourif, which I thought was one if the genre vet's best. The direction was also great, as the movie moved through its hour and a half run time so fluidly it felt like a short rather than a feature. The FX are also really good and the monster is pretty cool. I don't know what it is about this movie, but I just really like it a lot. This may not be the best monster movie out there but it sure entertained me.

3.5/5

Gremlins
Year – 1984
Director – Joe Dante
Tags – Monsters

A man buys his son a strange creature for Christmas and soon it begins to multiply and then they begin to change into terrible monsters. This is a great movie with an unbelievably cute critter that takes center stage. The movie is very lighthearted and cutesy but it also has a dark side to it. Just think about Phoebe Cates telling her story about why she hates Christmas, it's pretty dark, and there are other things happening that I can say aren't really kid friendly, but it's still considered a children's flick, go figure. The acting is good and the direction is great, and the only real problems I had with this movie were story related. Like the rules of the creature. No feeding after midnight, on what time zone? No contact with water, but the food he is eating contains water. Just minor things like that that kind of irked me but didn't detract from my overall enjoyment of a very fun movie.

4/5

Gremlins 2: The New Batch
Year – 1990
Director – Joe Dante
Tags – Monsters

This movie takes place a few years after the last one. This movie is so ridiculous and so over the top that I couldn't help but love it. It doesn't quite have the same charm as the last one but it's still pretty funny. Add the cornucopia of new gremlins thanks to a conveniently placed gene splicing lab, and you have family horror gold. The acting is on par with the original, and it was nice to see Christopher Lee in the movie. The direction is also just as good as the original. I really appreciate the way they made this movie because if it wasn't as ridiculous as it ended up being, I wouldn't have enjoyed it as much. Silly and equally endearing, Gremlins 2 is a great follow up to a great movie.

4/5

Grim Reaper
Year – 2007
Director – Michael Feifer
Tags – Slasher / Survival

After a woman is hit by a car, she ends up in facility for troubled individuals, and it's there that she and the other residents are stalked by a cloaked figure wielding a scythe. The story here is pretty nonsensical and dumb, and I definitely believe that there could have been a different reason to make a slasher movie than this contrived crap. But there are some positive aspects. The acting isn't too bad and the direction is ok. There's definitely a lot of blood and few good kills, which is nice, but there is a lack of nudity which is pretty much a prerequisite for low budget slashers. This is actually a passable attempt at a movie despite the lame story and other pitfalls, but I still found some minor entertainment value.

2.5/5

Grudge, The
Year – 2004
Director – Takashi Shimizu
Tags – Ghosts

This movie is an American remake of the movie Ju-On and follows the same plot. I heard so many bad things about this remake and for the life of me I can not figure out why. This movie is just as creepy as the original, and even has the same director and some of the actors. I even think this movie is a bit better because it most likely had a bigger budget, and thus, better FX. I do like how this movie does use a lot of similar occurrences as the original, but also branches out into other territories and expands upon the story. Of course for all I know this may have something to do with both the Ju-On and Ju-On: The Grudge movies, as I have only seen one set. But anyway, the acting is very good and as I stated earlier, the FX are awesome and a bit better than those in the original movie. I also feel that the direction is a little better here as well. In all I think this is a very worthy remake of an excellent Asian horror movie with genuine scares and a great style that transcends the original.

4/5

Grudge 2, The
Year – 2006
Director – Takashi Shimizu
Tags – Ghosts

This sequel to the American remake of Ju-On does not follow Ju-On 2 but instead uses some elements from the original Ju-On to move the story to the United States. Most of the movie still takes place in Japan, but I can see where they're going with it. And to be honest, I didn't really care for it. I think this is just another step in Americanizing this franchise, and I don't like that because I felt the original Grudge still held true to the Japanese style, and this just seems like another lame retelling of an Asian horror movie. The scares aren't nearly as effective this time, and the atmosphere just isn't there. I still liked this movie to some degree though, as it did have a couple of good moments and it is completely watchable. The acting is ok and the direction is still good, and even if I didn't like the story as a whole, it still had some good points. Overall though, this movie is pretty average and kind of disappointing since I really did like the original remake a lot.

2.5/5

Gruesome Twosome, The
Year – 1967
Director – Herschell Gordon Lewis
Tags – Slasher / Survival

An elderly woman and her retarded son lure college women to their wig shop where the son scalps them and the woman transforms their actual heads of hair into wigs. The story is an interesting one, as usual with a Lewis movie, and it's also pretty terrible, which is also typical. But this one is just so terrible that it tends to be pretty hilarious. The acting is just some of the worst ever, the best being by the stuffed cat, Napoleon. The direction is pretty bad as per usual, but the movie is thankfully short and at least it's not drawn out. The gore is really cheap, and the dead women are blinking and breathing, which made me laugh. This movie is just so weird that I had to appreciate it on some level, and it did make me laugh several times. There's random dancing with fried chicken, a stuffed cat that has more personality than any of the actors, and a lot more. Not a good movie by any means, but a great flick to laugh at for sure. Wouldn't you say Napoleon?

2.5/5

Halloween

Year – 1978
Director – John Carpenter
Tags – Slasher / Survival

Fifteen years ago, young Michael Myers murdered his sister and has been institutionalized ever since. But now he's escaped and returns to his hometown to relive that night of murder again and again. Psycho may have really pioneered the slasher sub genre, but Halloween molded it into the formula still in use today. This movie stands head and shoulders above all others that came after it because it just really is that damn good. The direction is tight and the pacing is immaculate, keeping a thick atmosphere of tension ever present. The killer is voiceless, faceless and merciless, a creature that can not be reasoned with, and that's pretty damn scary. Myers doesn't even seem to be human and is more like a machine than anything. The acting is very good, especially for such a low budget, independent movie. I think the most impressive detail is that the movie really isn't very violent, but rather suspenseful, replacing blood with atmosphere. Carpenter made a masterpiece that is still impressive today, often imitated but never duplicated; Halloween is the king of modern slasher movies.

5/5

Halloween II
Year – 1981
Director – Rick Rosenthal
Tags – Slasher / Survival

This movie takes place immediately after the original. As far as sequels go, I don't think I've ever seen one blend so seamlessly with the movie prior to it. It's nice to see familiar faces return and it just seems like these movies were shot back to back instead of three years apart. Very nice. This one is also almost on par with the original, which is definitely quite the feat. The story is great and really needed to be told because the saga of Michael Myers could not be encapsulated in just one movie. This one has the same great acting, the lovely air of tension and the direction is great, similar in ways to Carpenter. This is a truly excellent sequel to a quintessential horror movie and you really couldn't ask for more than that.

4.5/5

Halloween III: Season of the Witch
Year – 1982
Director – Tommy Lee Wallace
Tags – [Hidden to conceal spoilers]

A mask making corporation is the target of investigation by a sheriff after a man holding secrets of the company is brutally murdered. What the sheriff uncovers is that the popular masks that the company manufactures have a very deadly secret. First off I have to justify the existence of this movie. There is no Michael Myers and there was never supposed to be. The original idea behind the Halloween franchise was to have a different story in each movie, all revolving around Halloween. Michael Myers was the first story, which properly encompassed two movies, and then came this movie, which was a new story. There was a public outcry because this movie was sans Myers, hence his return in the fourth movie. The problem is that this is the last excellent movie in the franchise, and when Myers returned, it was forced, and the whole series was ruined. I can only imagine what great stories we would have received had the franchise continued as planned. Anyway, with that geeky little rant out of the way let me tell you about this great movie. The story is very unique and plays out in a way that I found very appealing. And once you get to the secret of the mask, I was blown away. The direction is very smooth, the acting is great and the FX are nice and creepy, fitting with the overall mood of the film. If you can look past the absence of the Myers and the fact that this isn't a slasher movie, and instead view it as a stand alone horror movie, then I'm sure you'll find some enjoyment in it. I know I did.

4/5

Halloween IV: The Return of Michael Myers
Year – 1988
Director – Dwight H. Little
Tags – Slasher / Survival

The fourth Halloween movie obviously sees the return of Michael Myers, who is now on the hunt for his niece. The plot of this movie is forced, and the story really is sub par, but fortunately it is very well directed and the acting is good enough to keep my interest. It seems that whoever wrote this was really grasping at straws to find a way to bring back Myers and start a new storyline for him, and the end result is less than a savory one. While the story is always secondary in your typical slasher, the story in Halloween was so strong that maybe I just expected more out of it. But it is a good slasher, despite its lack of depth there is a lot of killing and that's at least something. I wish they had stuck with the original gameplan for this franchise, but at least here in the fourth installment we get a good slasher movie, even though through this movie I can definitely see the beginning of the downturn for the series.

3/5

Halloween V: The Revenge of Michael Myers
Year – 1989
Director – Dominique Othenin-Girard, Arthur Speer
Tags – Slasher / Survival

This movie takes place one year after the previous movie. Somehow the story is even worse in this movie, and this time they don't have the good direction to back it up. The pacing is pretty bad and the movie as a whole is just very boring, punctuated only slightly by some decent kills. This movie just breezed on by for me, leaving no memorable impression at all, the acting was weak and the new characters introduced were instantly forgettable. All I can really remember vividly is that I was pretty bored with the whole thing. But the movie is very much watchable, and I've seen a whole lot worse, but in the end this installment just isn't good at all and stands as the first nail into the coffin of this franchise.

2/5

Halloween VI: The Curse of Michael Myers
Year – 1995
Director – Joe Chappelle
Tags – Slasher / Survival

This movie takes place several years after the last movie. In this movie they try to explain the origins of Michael Myers and why he refuses to die. They should have just said that he refuses to die because he's a cash cow for the studio execs instead of coming up the batshit ridiculous reason on display in this, the worst Halloween movie yet. Pretty much the only positive thing I have to say about this movie is that there are some good FX and kills, but that's really it. The story is quite the stinker as it pretty much glosses over what happened in the previous films and makes me wonder if the writer even watched the other movies. Now, the direction in the last movie was terrible, but the direction actually manages to be worse here. The acting also left much to be desired as even Donald Pleasance had a look of boredom on his face. So in the sixth movie it seems as though the only people who really had any interest in making this movie were the FX people, and their work isn't in this movie enough to make it worthwhile.

1.5/5

Halloween VII: H20
Year – 1998
Director – Steve Miner
Tags – Slasher / Survival

This movie takes place twenty years after the original (hence the stupid H20 subtitle). The idea behind the movie is an interesting one, but once again the script isn't very good, but it is at least better than the last three movies, even with some glaring continuity errors. The acting varies from good (Jamie Lee Curtis), to very, very bad (LL Cool J). The direction is ok, and maybe the director could have done more if the movie had more substance. The kills are the low point of the movie as there are very few and they are incredibly uninspired and boring. In fact, they're all pretty much the same. Those expecting an epic battle in this movie will no doubt be sorely disappointed but it just doesn't work out that way, but it does end strong so I guess that's one positive point. This franchise is now officially stale and I don't think much of anything can pull it out of the trash now.

2/5

Halloween VIII: Resurrection
Year – 2002
Director – Rick Rosenthal
Tags – Slasher / Survival

This movie takes place three years after the last one. I was wondering how they were going to continue on with the franchise and the idea is decent enough, and then add to that the first ten minutes of the movie before the credits, and we're off to a good start. And then everything went to hell. Whoever cast this movie needs to have their head examined, because this group of "actors" are nothing but terrible. It was painful to watch them drag their sorry carcasses through different scenarios, all of which are equally terrible. The story is stupid and doesn't make any sense given the storyline of all the movies up to this point. And I can't believe the same person directed the second movie, which was great, here we have to sit through some truly awful pacing. I guess I do have to place the majority of the blame on the script though, which was obviously typed out by rabid baboons. This movie is horrible on every level, and if it weren't for the first ten minutes being very enjoyable, this would have easily been in the running for the worst slasher movie ever. R.I.P. Halloween franchise, I'll always have the first three movies.

1/5

Halloween [Remake]
Year – 2007
Director – Rob Zombie
Tags – Slasher / Survival

This remake follows the same storyline as the original but also explores more of the Michael Myers back story. When I began watching this movie, I was blown away, watching young Michael be a regular everyday kid and then seeing him kill and be thrown into an institution was a surreal experience. Then watching his interactions with Loomis and seeing his mind deteriorate was also pretty special. Clearly this has been the best work Rob Zombie has ever done. And then it gets into the remake, and all it ends up being is a sped up duplicate of the original but riddled with flaws. I have never seen Scout Taylor-Compton have a good performance and this movie is no different, she is terrible and annoying. The movie's pace also gets muddled and starts to become boring, then add some shaky cam and this movie went from awesome to bad in the blink of an eye. I hate the second half of this movie and for the life of me I can not figure out what happened. But I still have to give credit for the brilliant first half. I think the problem may be that Zombie is great with his own material, but can't cover someone else's work worth a shit. And that's ok, now we know he needs to stick to his own ideas. Enjoy the first half of the movie and then shut off your DVD player; it makes for a better viewing experience.

3/5

Hamiltons, The

Year – 2006
Director – Mitchell Altieri, Phil Flores
Tags – [Hidden to conceal spoilers]

After the death of their parents, four siblings try to cope with life, all while abducting and killing people. The Hamiltons is a well done, very dark movie with a slow pace, and that may not be for everyone. There's a great dynamic going on between the siblings as you have two that are just twisted, one trying to keep up appearances and keep the family together, and another one doubting his place in the family. The wonderful twist in the story is welcome and not easy to see coming. You can tell something is amiss, but you're not really sure what until the big reveal. This movie has its fair share of blood and sex as well. Even though the pace is deliberately slow it still felt too slow, which is a problem The Butcher Brothers tend to have, but at least a strong story and good acting propel this one forward, unlike other offerings. This is a good movie that is somewhat flawed, but still enjoyable.

3.5/5

Hammerhead
Year – 2005
Director – Michael Oblowitz
Tags – Monsters

A group of people are trapped on a mad scientist's island with his half man, half shark creation, and it's hungry for blood. Yeah, I know how this movie sounds and to be honest, I bought it for no other reason than it had Jeffrey Combs in it, because no matter how bad the movie, Combs always puts his all into it. Unfortunately, I wasn't expecting Combs to be literally the only good thing in this movie. The rest of the actors are pretty bad and the direction is just about as slow as you can get. Add some horrendous fight choreography and FX, and you definitely have yourself a terrible movie. When William Forsythe shot an assault rifle underwater at the shark, I just died laughing, but it was a pained laugh because right then and there I knew I had completely wasted my money. Don't make the same mistake I did.

1/5

Hand that Rocks the Cradle, The
Year – 1992
Director – Curtis Hanson
Tags – Suspense

A gynecologist is accused of sexual misconduct by a client, and after charges are filed against him, he commits suicide. Later on his wife has a miscarriage and then manipulates her way into the client's life as a nanny to try and get her revenge. The Hand that Rocks the Cradle is a very entertaining movie that shows the audience all of its cards from the get go and allows them to know how it's going to end before the opening credits even roll. There's no mystery here, you know who is doing what and what their plans are every inch of the way. Personally I like to be kept in the dark at times, or least be given some plot twists along the way. But here the movie is completely flat and transparent and I guess that would appeal to some people. Fortunately the movie is backed by good direction and excellent acting, and the story is good when viewed as a whole. Overall I liked this movie for what it gave me but could never say it was exceptional. Good entertainment value and nothing more.

3/5

Hannibal
Year – 2001
Director – Ridley Scott
Tags – Serial Killer (Fictional)

This is the sequel to The Silence of the Lamb and takes place several years after it. First I must mention that the acting here is great, and while Julianne Moore is a very good actress, she is miscast here and can not fill the shoes of Jodie Foster. The story is very good but definitely not up to snuff as far as the previous movies are concerned. It has its moments but I was a bit unfulfilled by the end. The direction is great though, and the only time it lags is when the story reaches one of its many dull spots. There are some nice, gruesome moments but they're cut short or obscured sometimes, which was kind of annoying. Overall this is still a very good movie and I enjoyed it quite a bit, but people expecting the same brilliance of its predecessor will probably be let down, so just enjoy it for what it is.

3.5/5

Hannibal Rising
Year – 2007
Director – Peter Webber
Tags – Serial Killer (Fictional)

This movie is a prequel to the Manhunter series of books and movies, focusing on the origins of Hannibal Lecter. Obviously this book was written just to become a movie right afterward because you can tell very little thought went into the story. It's sloppy and uninteresting for the most part, relying on gore shots over substantial storytelling. I did like the gore though, even though they didn't show nearly enough in detail. What they did show however were some very nice FX, too bad they weren't used to their full potential. The acting is ok, and I'm not sure if I can blame the actors or the characters for the lackluster performances on display. The direction was decent as well, while the movie hardly moves along quickly, it wasn't all bad. This painfully average cash-in is not a very entertaining movie, but at least it wasn't bad, and it definitely had the potential to be just that.

2.5/5

Happening, The
Year – 2008
Director – M. Night Shyamalan
Tags – Biological

Suddenly, and without explanation, people begin committing mass suicides in the Northeast section of America. At first it is believed to be a terrorist attack, until smaller towns also fall victim to the strange phenomenon. The idea is sound, but the execution is very poor. The acting is surprisingly bad here, and I say surprising because many of the actors here have shown good performances in the past. The direction is also sloppy and dull. The story itself also has little merit. What I did enjoy were the graphic death sequences peppered throughout the movie, those were quite nice and without them this would have been a complete waste. A lot of people say that Shyamalan has lost his ability to make good movies, that may be true, but every director with multiple movies under their belt has dropped at least a bomb or two. Time will tell for sure, but this movie is definitely far from greatness.

2/5

Hard Candy
Year – 2005
Director – David Slade
Tags – Suspense

A pedophile photographer and a fourteen year old girl engage in a serious cat and mouse game after meeting each other for the first time as she wishes to expose him for what he is. This is an interesting take on Red Riding Hood for the computer generation. Everyone knows there are tons of pedophiles trolling around on the internet, so to make a movie about it and flip it on its head is a great idea. The acting is great, but I do think that the lead actress tried to oversell her role too much. The direction was very good and the story played out in an unexpectedly graphic fashion. This is a very well done movie that came off a little overcooked, but was still a tasty treat.

4/5

Hatchet
Year – 2006
Director – Adam Green
Tags – Slasher / Survival

Hatchet is the story of Victor Crowley, who hunts the Louisiana swamps for victims. And thanks to a ghost tour boat stranding people in the swamps, he has many new victims to play with. The story of Hatchet is typical slasher fair, but I must add that the back story behind the killer is well thought out and particularly tragic. The movie plays out like so many before it, except for one thing and that is that this movie has pretty much the greatest kills in the history of the sub-genre. They're not trying to reinvent the wheel here, this really is old school American horror done in the startlingly brutal nature it should be done in. This is a prime example of how the movie should go, light on story (while still having one), heavy on gore, and even features some good laughs, an exceptional formula. I also like how they employed a trio of horror heavyweights to have cameos in the movie, just to let us fans know, "Hey, we did our homework." Excellent.

4.5/5

Haunted
Year – 1995
Director – Lewis Gilbert
Tags – Ghosts

A professor is invited to the home of a wealthy trio of siblings to calm their nanny, who fears that the house is haunted. The professor soon learns that her fears may have some truth behind them. The Haunted was visually appealing to say the least, unfortunately that was all I found to be appealing about this movie. I just thought the movie was very slow and predictable, as the "twist ending" could be seen practically from the opening credits. But maybe I've just watched too much horror to be surprised anymore. The ghost story takes a backseat to the love story, so if that's your thing, you may really enjoy this, but from a horror fan's perspective, I found the whole thing to be very blah.

2/5

Haunting, The
Year – 1963
Director – Robert Wise
Tags – Ghosts

A professor wishing to study the paranormal assembles a group of people to stay in the supposedly haunted mansion called Hill House. This movie is hardly a brilliant tale of the supernatural rather it is a very slow and non scary ghost tale that is only saved by a great story, nice acting and a wonderful locale. Nothing really happens in regards to the paranormal, there are some sounds and then… well, that's pretty much it. I'm all for leaving things to the imagination, but me give something here. The doors moving in and out as if they were breathing made for some pretty cool FX shots but overall the occurrences were dull and yawn inducing. At some points the movie did have a nice atmosphere to it but overall the movie is just dull. I really do find it hard to believe that anyone was scared by this. Don't get me wrong, I did like the movie, but if you're looking for the end all be all of ghost movies, you really do need to look elsewhere.

3.5/5

Haunting, The [Remake]
Year – 1999

Director – Jan de Bont
Tags – Ghosts

This remake follows the core of the original movie but moves the story along in a different manner. This movie could have topped the original but ended up not even coming close, and here's why. First off, while the occurrences in the original were just too subtle, here they are much too overt. They could have just stepped the paranormal experiences up, but they ended up going way over the top and overusing the CGI. At times the CGI looked very good, but then most of time it looked way too fake. The acting is fine, nothing great but definitely not bad. The direction was pretty bad though, as they movie seems to drag on for hours. The set design was just absolutely mind blowing though. The house was incredibly grandiose on every level, and that alone makes this movie worth watching, as everything else takes a backseat to it. In the end this is a decent movie but not good by any means.

2.5/5

Haunting of Molly Hartley, The
Year – 2008
Director – Mickey Liddell
Tags – Cults

Young Molly was almost killed by her mother prior to her eighteenth birthday, for she feared that her daughter would turn into something evil when her birthday came. Or something along those lines. I would like to explain more, but the story behind this crap made no sense and had no kind of direction. I'm going to list out even more reasons as to why this is one of the worst movies ever made. The acting was total crap, no talent needed for the young cast. Nothing of any consequence ever happens in the movie, the movie is just walked through like a man in the park who doesn't have a care in the world. The direction is horrendous, but I know it must be difficult to garner some good pacing in a story where nothing happens but still, awful. This movie is pointless and stupid and I have not one good thing to say about it. Makes House of the Dead look like The Godfather.

0.5/5

Headless Horseman
Year – 2007
Director – Anthony C. Ferrante
Tags – Slasher / Survival

This variation of the classic Sleepy Hollow tale finds a group of young adults trapped in a small town being stalked by a headless horseman. Yawn. Why even make this? This boring slasher movie really doesn't have much of anything going for it. A lack of good actors, paint by numbers direction, a dull story and some pretty bad CGI. The practical FX weren't bad though and there is a fair amount of blood, so if that's all you're looking for in a horror movie, you may be pleased, but I wasn't because blood isn't enough to make up for everything else that is really, really bad about this flick.

1.5/5

Hell of the Living Dead (Virus)
Year – 1980
Director – Bruno Mattei
Tags – Zombies

Since there is very little semblance of a story here, from what I can gather, a zombie virus is unleashed in a research facility / factory and then zombies pop up all over the surrounding jungles. This is so bad, seriously. One quarter of the movie is made up of stock nature footage, which is just weird. The acting is bad, and the dubbing is even worse. Like I said earlier, there is no kind of story here, it's like the filmmakers said, "Let's rip off Dawn of the Dead, and then just throw in a bunch of random occurrences that don't make a lick of sense". There is some good zombie action with FX that are decent for the time period (Think blue faced zombies and good usage of meat). This movie isn't so bad it's good, it's just pretty bad. Still, with random cross dressing and spur of the moment breast bearing, it is kind of funny.

2/5

Hellbent
Year – 2004
Director – Paul Etheredge
Tags – Slasher / Survival

On Halloween night a group of men are stalked by a hand scythe wielding maniac in a devil costume. I don't know if this is the first gay slasher movie, but if it is, that's freakin' brilliant. I get so sick of the "survivor girl" in all of these movies and it's nice to see a movie where there is no chance of that happening. But that's not just a gimmick because this is a well done movie. The story is fairly weak in terms of originality but it did have some good moments. The direction was very well done though and had good pacing for the most part. The acting is really good as well. There is some definite gore because the killer is really into decapitations, but he does switch it up and kill in different manners. And there's a clever use of a glass eye that I really dug. It's not the best slasher flick out there but it's really fun and I definitely enjoyed it.

3.5/5

Hellbound: Hellraiser II
Year – 1988
Director – Tony Randel
Tags – Demons

This movie picks up immediately after the first Hellraiser movie. Making a sequel so soon after the original, I figured it would just be a rush job, and those usually turn out to be less than desirable (just look at the Friday the 13th series), but fortunately this is a very well done sequel. The story is pretty similar to the original, which annoys me when people do that, but here it actually isn't much of a hindrance because the story is a natural progression of the first movie and it makes sense, similar or not. The acting is once again great and the direction is nearly as good as Barker's. There are more FX shots here and extra gore as well, and since the FX are great once again, that only adds to my enjoyment. I also liked that they showed the back story of Pinhead, leader of the Cenobites. If you love the original like me, then I imagine you'll love this as well.

4/5

Hellboy
Year – 2004
Director – Guillermo del Toro
Tags – Demons

A demon raised from infancy after being rescued from the clutches of Nazis grows up to be the defender of mankind against supernatural foes. First I have to say that the style and direction of this movie is absolutely superb. Del Toro uses Lovecraftian influence and his own unique style to create one of the more interesting superhero movies to come out in a long time. The story of Hellboy also helps in his creation of an original movie, as well as the great screenplay. The acting is very good for the most part, especially by Ron Perlman. The make-up and practical FX are absolutely top notch, and even the CGI looks good most of the time. There are a couple instances of some bad CGI, but for a movie that relied so heavily on it, its surprising great overall. So many movies nowadays that are CGI heavy look pretty pathetic, but obviously a lot of care went into this and helped to create some interesting creatures and dark, evil visuals. I'm not a big fan of action movies with horror themes because so many of them are disappointing, but this one has a great story and a wonderful director attached, and it shows.

4/5

Hellboy II: The Golden Army
Year – 2008
Director – Guillermo del Toro
Tags – Demons, Monsters

In this sequel we find Hellboy and his crew tangling with an Elven prince as he tries to wake up an unstoppable army of golden warriors. In this sequel we find damn near everyone involved in the first movie returning for the sequel. Some cast members return, the director, etc. So everything in that respect is just as good as the first movie, so this one really depends on the strength of the story. Fortunately the story is once again very good. I did feel that a large chunk of the story was nothing more than a set-up for the third movie, which was a little too obvious, but overall it was very enjoyable. They certainly upped the creature factor as well in this movie with literally dozens of well detailed and diverse beasts, many of which were once again Lovecraftian in nature. I would say this movie is damn near as good as the original if not as good, and I can't wait to see this series come to its conclusion in a third movie.

4/5

Hello Mary Lou: Prom Night II
Year – 1987
Director – Bruce Pittman
Tags – Ghosts

This movie has nothing to do with the original Prom Night. Here we see a popular girl die after winning prom queen honors and later coming back as a vengeful ghost thirty years later to kill off the competition for the new prom queen, and possessing one of the contestants along the way. This movie is much better than the original because it gave me what I wanted, nudity and blood. There are some awesome kills in this movie, and also some nice, weird dream sequences that both utilize great FX. The story is pretty solid too, no complaints there. The acting and direction could have been a bit better though. Some people may be jaded that this movie doesn't have any kind of continuity with the original, but get over it. This is a good horror flick that just happens on some other prom night in some other town. Good mindless fun.

3.5/5

Hellraiser
Year – 1987
Director – Clive Barker
Tags – Demons

A man comes into possession of an unholy puzzle box and upon opening it, is promptly ripped apart. Later on he manages to escape from Hell and enlists the help of his brother's wife to bring him men that he may sacrifice so that he can regain his human form. But while he is trying to become what he once was, Hell has sent a group of Cenobites to reclaim his soul. I have to say that the story behind the movie is probably the most original horror tale to come along in a very long time, and still is actually. But a well crafted story isn't all a movie needs to be successful, and fortunately for the horror community, the creator of the story jumped into the director's seat and did a masterful job. Aiding him even further was a wonderful cast and incredible FX. There's a reason this movie spawned so many sequels and become a genre phenomenon, it's just that good, and if you're in the mood for something different, look no further because this sexually charged, gore drenched movie is truly one of a kind.

5/5

*Hellraiser II can be found under Hellbound: Hellraiser II.

Hellraiser III: Hell on Earth
Year – 1992
Director – Anthony Hickox
Tags – Demons

This movie continues on a few years after the last one. I've always heard a lot of mixed opinions about this installment but I've always found it to be rather good. The tight direction, loads of gore and massive body count really made this movie great in my opinion. The acting is good but certainly not great and while the story is a good progression forward once again, I did miss the old Cenobites because the new ones, while cool in their own way, they really do lack the personality of the others. But Pinhead does of course return. The FX are very good but there is some use of shoddy CGI. Not too detracting though. I think this is a great addition to the series and it played out very well.

4/5

Hellraiser IV: Bloodline
Year – 1996
Director – Kevin Yagher, Alan Smithee
Tags – Demons

This fourth installment is actually told in three parts. First there is a prequel, and then a modern day sequel, and then finally a story set far into the future. This is an interesting attempt we have here, and while I don't think it worked out well exactly, it was still a somewhat entertaining flick. I liked the prequel portion of the movie the best. The origin of the puzzle box was a nice touch. The acting is ok and the direction sloppy and uneven, but the gore factor is certainly there, and we get to see the creation of a new Cenobite, which is pretty cool. The series definitely takes a downturn with this movie, but it's not a bad effort, it just doesn't match up with its predecessors.

3/5

Hellraiser V: Inferno
Year – 2000
Director – Scott Derrickson
Tags – Demons

This movie does not follow the rest of the series per se and is instead meant to be a more stand alone installment. Here an unscrupulous detective finds the box and soon after a visit from some sensual Cenobites, the people in his life start dying around him and his life descends into shambles. I really liked this one because instead of stretching an already thin story even further, the filmmakers instead tried to go in a different direction and I feel that it worked. The movie has a sort of noir feel to it and while this one may not be as graphic as previous installments, it still has its fair share of blood and some excellent atmosphere all wrapped up in a rather good mystery. The acting is very good but the direction does have some minor pacing issues. Overall I think this is good movie and while fans may feel a bit jaded by the story straying from the core story, I say get over it and enjoy.

3.5/5

Hellraiser VI: Hellseeker
Year – 2002
Director – Rick Bota
Tags – Demons

This movie continues on several years after the middle of the fourth movie. Don't worry, it's not as complicated as it sounds, when you watch the series it's all somewhat cohesive. I really disliked this entry and this is the first one in the franchise that I would call a bad movie. The acting is really good and is pretty much wasted on the boring story. The way the movie plays out is predictable and boring and with pacing issues galore. There's some decent FX that are underused and to top things off, there's hardly any blood. It's unfortunate to see an otherwise good franchise take such a massive downturn but that's what happens when you run out if ideas but still force out some more sequels.

1.5/5

Hellraiser VII: Deader
Year – 2005
Director – Rick Bota
Tags – Demons

This movie has hardly anything to do with the Hellraiser series. Here a reporter goes deep undercover to unveil the story of a group of people who seemingly kill themselves and then the leader of the group manages to bring them back to life. So I'm guessing that this script was not meant to be the seventh Hellraiser movie and instead just wasn't very good so they decided to change it and add Pinhead, who was clearly an afterthought. The story here is only slightly more interesting than the story in the last movie. The direction is about as worthwhile, or not worthwhile for that matter. They appear to have only had the money to hire one real actor, as everyone besides the lead isn't very good. Apparently this franchise has now been stretched so thin that they rely on non-Hellraiser stories to be the next Hellraiser movie. Bizarre.

2/5

Hellraiser VIII: Hellworld
Year – 2005
Director – Rick Bota
Tags – Demons

Here in this eighth and fortunately last Hellraiser movie (as of yet), some people playing a game called Hellworld are invited to an exclusive party where Pinhead is the real host. I do have to say that at least this story has more to do with the Hellraiser series than the last one, but that doesn't excuse the fact that the script is beyond terrible. The story is horrible. And to make matters worse, the same hack director that handled the last two movies returns for this one and does his worst job yet. The acting is also really bad. At least Pinhead plays a larger role in this movie, and it features Lance Henriksen, but that is nowhere near enough to make this good, hell it doesn't even make it passable. Please stop employing this director and writer because they really don't have any talent. A horrible end to a promising franchise.

1/5

Helter Skelter
Year – 1976
Director – Tom Gries
Tags – Serial Killer, Cults

This movie chronicles the real life exploits of Charles Manson and his "family", who killed an estimated 35 people. This movie follows the court case placed against him and his followers. While the movie doesn't show too much of the actual crimes, the deep look into the investigation and the prosecution of Manson was fascinating to say the least. The eccentricities of Manson were really showed off to full effect here and the great performances from everybody added a lot to the movie. While not a perfect movie, it is a spellbinding look into the Manson Family exploits and their eventual demise. If you follow serial killers at all, this is definitely a must see.

4/5

Helter Skelter [Remake]
Year – 2004
Director – John Gray
Tags – Serial Killer, Cults

I guess this is a remake even though it is pretty different from the original, but it still chronicles the same events after all. I like this movie because it managed to blend artistic filmmaking with graphic violence very well. Of course things could have been more violent, as some of the murders were especially brutal in real life, but it is still a commendable job. The acting is very good, especially by Jeremy Davies who not only looked to the part of Manson, but played him incredibly well. The direction is awesome as the movie moves along very smoothly with great pacing. This is a great look at the world's most notorious serial killer (who didn't actually kill anyone), and his followers. Recommended viewing.

4/5

Henry – Portrait of a Serial Killer

Year – 1986
Director – John McNaughton
Tags – Serial Killer

This movie is loosely based on serial killer Henry Lee Lucas who claimed to have killed hundreds of people, mostly women. This movie focuses on a certain time in his life instead the full body of his crimes. This movie is pretty brutal, but people saying it's one of the most graphic movies ever made haven't seen very many movies, or maybe I'm just numb to it all now. A lot of the bodies you see are just that, bodies, you don't get to see Henry killing them, but rather you are forced to look at the corpse while you hear them die in past tense. That's interesting, and I like it, even if I would have liked to have seen him in action more. But don't get me wrong, you do get to see him and his friend Otis killing people, sometimes in a rather violent fashion. And then they also begin to videotape their kills, allowing them to relive that moment over and over. The acting is superb, and I'm surprised Michael Rooker wasn't completely typecast after this movie. The direction is also excellent, the movie is a slow burn, but it feels good, it doesn't feel dull. This is definitely one of the better serial killer movies out there, even if it isn't a true portrayal in every sense of the word. The ending left me wanting more, but I guess that was the idea. I like this movie a lot but I did want more out of it as it kind of left me with cinematic blueballs, but I still highly recommend it.

4/5

Henry II – Portrait of a Serial Killer

Year – 1996
Director – Chuck Parello
Tags – Suspense

This sequel is uh, a sequel and takes place an indeterminate time after the last movie. I'm wondering if the people who made this movie realized that the original was based on an actual serial killer. This movie is more of the same sans the grittiness. The overall shell of the way the movie plays out is nearly identical to the original with only modifications on what situations occur. While I felt this movie was unnecessary and in essence strayed too far from what the original had intended, I still kind of enjoyed it. The stories, while undeniably similar, at least made enough of a change to keep from being outright plagiarism. The acting from the leads was pretty good, not so much from the supporting cast and overall I would have to say this was a good movie, which kind of surprised me, but it was a pleasant surprise for sure.

3/5

Hidden, The

Year – 1987
Director – Jack Sholder
Tags – Aliens

An alien parasite takes over human bodies and indulges in robberies, murders, sex, fast cars and heavy metal, changing bodies whenever the original takes too much damage. But an FBI agent is hot on its trail and enlists the help of a local cop to help kill it. Well this is a fun movie. The direction is good, the acting is good, the story is solid and the FX are great. It would have been pretty cool if they had explored the sexual addiction side of the alien more, and had Claudia Christian get naked (ha ha), but it did have a fair amount of violence to up the entertainment factor. No masterpiece here, just a very enjoyable movie.

3.5/5

Hidden 2, The
Year – 1993
Director – Seth Pinsker
Tags – Aliens

This movie takes place fifteen years after the original. Ah, the obligatory sequel, even mildly successful films are not immune to having a forced sequel thrown together. The first fifteen minutes of the movie are actually the last fifteen minutes of the original, what the hell? I'm not even exaggerating as the entire end of the first movie is replayed here. Who in their right mind would think that was a good idea? The story is a good direction to move into, but the time frame doesn't make any sense, and then eventually the story devolves into total and utter crap. The acting and direction are pretty bad too. But the movie does have some great FX, so it's not a total waste. This is just a pointless sequel with very little entertainment value.

1.5/5

Hideaway
Year – 1995
Director – Brett Leonard
Tags – Serial Killer (Fictional)

After a near death experience, a man begins to see through the eyes of serial killer. But the visions go both ways as the killer sees through his eyes as well and chooses the man's daughter as his next victim. I'm not a fan of Dean Koontz, as I don't find his books to be very entertaining, and this one isn't a very good adaptation of his book, which is probably why I like it so much. It improves upon his story a great deal, thus making it more interesting that is was initially. The acting is great, especially by Jeremy Sisto, who would go on to be quite the genre vet. The direction is very good too, allowing the movie to move smoothly with very few lags. I love the soundtrack too. The FX though, are pretty bad and are almost identical to those in The Lawnmower Man. This is just a very well done movie, and if you're one of those people who need to see an exact adaptation, just go read the book, but if you want to watch a good movie, then check this one out.

High Tension (Haute Tension)
Year – 2003
Director – Alexandre Aja
Tags – Slasher / Survival

A woman and her friend go to her family's house to try and study for school, but when a man shows up at their door with murder on his mind, their weekend of cramming turns into a fight for survival. I really liked this movie for the simple fact that it was extremely violent and paced very well. See? I'm easy to please. The gore shots were very impressive and unflinching, which I just had to appreciate on many levels. The acting was good and effective even though it wasn't particularly great. I really loved the whole movie until the batshit ridiculous ending, which I felt was interesting but didn't really work. Still, a bad ending didn't kill the rest of the movie for me and this is definitely a great blood drenched time.

4/5

Hills Have Eyes, The
Year – 1977
Director – Wes Craven
Tags – Slasher / Survival

A family's car breaks down in the desert, leaving them stranded. Later on they find out they are not alone, as there are a group of people living in the hills, a murderous group who have set their sights on the family. This is like The Texas Chainsaw Massacre, desert style, and that led me to want great things from it, unfortunately it came up pretty short. The violence is more insinuated than anything, as there wasn't very much blood and a few off-camera kills. In my personal preference, I want to see everything, I don't want it censored. The acting is good though, especially by the desert dwelling folk. The direction is ok but the movie does get kind of slow at times. This is a good movie and nothing more, but I must say that if it wasn't so watered down and slow, this could have easily been a classic given the idea behind it.

3/5

Hills Have Eyes Part II, The
Year – 1985
Director – Wes Craven
Tags – Slasher / Survival

This movie takes place years after the original. Now, the original may not have been brilliant, but it is when compared to this turd. This movie is just plain stupid, and the set-up for it happening is way too improbable. Not only that, this movie actually manages to be even more boring than the first. Also, a good chunk of the movie is actually footage from the last movie, which is always annoying to see. The acting is a mix of good and bad, mostly bad. The kills are very blah and the story is lame. There's very little entertainment value here and you're better off skipping it altogether and watching something more competent.

1.5/5

Hills Have Eyes, The [Remake]
Year – 2006
Director – Alexandre Aja
Tags – Slasher / Survival

This movie essentially follows the original plot to a tee with some minor tweaks along the way. I'm not a huge fan of the original, so remaking this was a good idea because while it was a great concept, it could use some more substance, and here they added it, with about a ton a of gore as well. I like this movie a lot, and I feel the people involved have made a much more engrossing picture than the original, probably partially due to a better budget. First off, there are more mutants and they actually look like mutants, not just unorthodox looking people. As I mentioned earlier, the gore is ramped up considerably. Gruesome kills, loads of blood and a fairly graphic rape scene are all here. The movie does run a bit long though in my opinion, which causes some lagging, but it's nothing too major. This is a great flick that tops the original.

4/5

Hills Have Eyes 2, The
Year – 2007
Director – Michael Weisz
Tags – Slasher / Survival

This is not the least bit related to the original sequel of the original movie and instead we have a storyline that follows the events after the remake. Here a group of National Guard trainees are dispatched to a familiar desert location for a routine assignment, but what happens after that is anything but. Here we see the gore, number of mutants, number of victims and the sexual sadism all increased, which should be appropriate for a sequel of this nature. However, this movie also suffers from a poor script, average actors, throwaway characters and a less competent director. Yeah, not very good. I didn't believe the actors as military soldiers, even as trainees, but it's not completely their fault because the characters themselves were rubbish. And like I said, the story just isn't very good. The one saving grace is the gore, because they certainly had some great kills and a lot of blood, but you really do need at least something behind that to make a movie worthwhile.

2/5

Hillside Strangler, The
Year – 2004

Director – Chuck Parello
Tags – Serial Killer

This chronicles the real life exploits of The Hillside Strangler, which was actually two men, who killed multiple women in 1970's Los Angeles. Serial killer movies really depend on the abilities of the actor more than anything, because we all know the story going into it, and here we have two great performances representing the two killers. The murders shown are fairly graphic and well done, but we are dealing with stranglers here, so they are bloodless. Lots of nudity, lots of violence, some truly great acting, especially by Turturro, who plays the outspoken Buono to Howell's quiet and reserved Bianchi quite well. This is an excellent portrayal of a pair of serial killers, and even though I feel they could have dug deeper into their actions, the people behind this film have created one of the more memorable true life serial killer films to date.

4/5

His Name Was Jason
Year – 2009
Director – Daniel Farrands
Tags – Horror Related

This documentary explores the aspects of the Friday the 13th franchise and its influence on horror. Undoubtedly this was made as a promotional tool for the 2009 remake, but it does have a lot of material in it that appeal to fans of the series. Hosted by Tom Savini, this doc goes through the entire series while having some behind the scenes shots and interviews with the cast and crew of the series, as well as some random people. One thing that irked me about this movie was that there were hardly any objective views on the series and instead people spent most the time performing verbal fellatio on Jason and his creators. There was some mention of some rather idiotic sequences that could be found in the franchise, but those lasted about two minutes total and the rest of time was spent gushing about this supposed groundbreaking series. Any real horror fan would tell you that the ground was broken by John Carpenter's Halloween and this franchise just followed in its footsteps, so all the pandering was definitely studio influenced and a bit overdone in the editing room. Still, this is a good documentary for a mostly decent horror franchise, and gives a lot of information that will undoubtedly satisfy the fans who crave to know more about their favorite masked killer.

3.5/5

Hitcher, The
Year – 1986
Director – Robert Harmon
Tags – Slasher / Survival

A young man driving cross country picks up a hitchhiker and it turns out to be the biggest mistake of his life as he finds out that the man is a murderer, and has set his sights on him. Things only compound from there as the hitcher tries to pin his murders on him and seems to stay one step ahead of him. I like that this movie takes no time to set things up and just gets right to the meat of the story. I also like that the movie never really explains what's going on and that there seems to be maybe a supernatural element to the hitcher, although that is never fully confirmed. The acting is really well done here, especially by Rutger Hauer who plays a creepy intensity very well. The direction is excellent as well, with all of the tense moments and action sequences, I was never given the chance to get bored. This is definitely a new breed a survival horror on display here and I can really appreciate the effort that went into setting this movie apart from all the others that litter the sub genre. Good times.

4/5

Hitcher II: I've Been Waiting, The
Year – 2003
Director – Louis Morneau
Tags – Slasher / Survival

This movie takes place about fifteen years after the original. This movie is very similar to the original, but it ultimately plays out much differently. The supernatural element I spoke of in the first movie seems to drive this one, but not overtly, still nothing is fully explained. The cast is good, Jake Busey took over for Rutger Hauer, and while not as good as him, he does play the character of The Hitcher differently, which I appreciated. The story as a whole is ok, but doesn't seem to have been thought out as thoroughly and has too many similar occurrences built into it. The direction is average as well, the movie held my interest but not all the time, allowing for too many lags in the pacing. While I don't think making this movie was necessary, I liked what they did with it at certain points, but this is still no better than average. At least they didn't soil the original though, which is always a plus.

2.5/5

Hitcher, The [Remake]
Year – 2007
Director – Dave Meyers
Tags – Slasher / Survival

This movie follows the same general storyline as the original, but has a couple involved instead of just a young man. And that's the first major issue I had with this remake. They took out the main unique element of the original and turned it into every other movie out there by forcing a female character into the mix too early. An annoying female character might I add. Then they tried to give a reason as to why the hitcher was chasing them down, which made me feel very disillusioned. By the time the movie got to the pathetic end scene, I was just constantly rolling my eyes. The acting isn't good at all, the direction leaves a lot to be desired and the story is devoid of many of the elements that made the original work so well. But after all of these complaints, I did find some good stuff to be had here. First off, they added a ton of gore and showed more detail in one certain scene, which was lacking in the original. Well, I guess that was really the only good addition to the movie, but it was really good. In all, this remake is undoubtedly ruined by studio interference, and while it's not completely worthless, it doesn't even come as close to the intensity of the original.

2/5

Hole, The
Year – 2001
Director – Nick Hamm
Tags – Suspense

Four private school kids decide to have a party in an abandoned bomb shelter. But after the fun is over, they find that someone has locked them in. This is such a great thriller all around, well acted, a nice story complimented by a good location, and fairly well paced to boot. But the direction was not very good at all. The movie jumped around so much it became annoying. The story demanded a non linear telling of the tale, but the way it was done was much to the movie's detriment. Don't get me wrong, I still like this movie, but it probably would have been better with someone else at the helm. Oh, and Thora Birch's accent was kind of annoying too.

3/5

Hollow Man
Year – 2000
Director – Paul Verhoeven
Tags – Suspense

A research team is charged with developing an invisibility serum, which was easy for them to craft, bringing the subject back however, proved more difficult. When they manage to bring back an ape, they overanxiously jump into human testing, and fail to bring their subject back. After a time, their subject begins to go mad and things only spiral downward from there. This is an excellent study in perversion, that's for sure. It makes sense though, I'm sure a lot of people given this situation would probably be doing some pervy things. I have to say the CGI in this movie for the most part is actually very good, which is hard to find. The story though, I don't know, I just don't care for it. Here we have another situation of things happening too conveniently for my tastes. I have to admit that this movie is an entertaining watch and features some good acting, but there's no depth here to extend it beyond that.

3.5/5

Hollow Man 2
Year – 2006
Director – Claudio Fah

In this sequel we see the invisibility serum developed in the first movie being used to full effect by government, but one agent has gone rogue and now hunts for the antidote, killing whoever he must to get it. I feel this is a justified sequel and a good progression for the storyline, but the second and third string actors mixed with the below average direction just couldn't hold my attention like the original. The FX are still fairly good here, but very much underused. The story is good but failed in its execution. This movie isn't anything terrible, in fact it's very much watchable, but it's certainly lacking enough punch to keep it from being anything but a below average movie.

2/5

Horror Business
Year – 2005
Director – Christopher P. Garetano
Tags – Horror Related

This movie is a documentary focusing on some very independent filmmakers who focus on the horror genre. After a shaky start, this documentary becomes quite compelling. It's interesting to see just how many people have a love for the genre and how they share similar ideals. There is some blatant bitching about Hollywood horror, and while I'll be the first to admit that Hollywood doesn't have the best track record in horror there have been several good movies to come out of them just as there have been several bad movies to come out of independent filmmakers. The people making the movies on display here are truly doing it for little cash and simply for the love of the genre, which I can always appreciate, and I also appreciate their enthusiasm and creativity, even if the end product leaves much to be desired. These are microbudget movies with no wide distribution, but the funny thing is that I actually already owned a couple of them and it was fun to see some behind the scenes action and get some insight from the directors. This documentary on guerilla filmmaking is a really entertaining watch and an excellent look into the minds of people who don't just make movies, but they have to make movies because the genre calls to them.

4/5

Host, The (Gwoemul)
Year – 2006
Director – Joon-ho Bong
Tags – Monsters

People relaxing by the Han River in Seoul are suddenly attacked by a giant monster. A man's daughter is taken by the beast but knowing in his heart that she is still alive, he sets off to find her. I wish all giant monster movies had the depth behind it that The Host does. This movie goes beyond the typical monster and delves deeper into family relations and the human side of such a sudden disaster. The script could have been just flat but adding that element really gave it a meatier subtext. The acting is really good, and there's quite a bit of comedy that really works out well. One problem I had with the movie is that it either wasn't paced well, or is too long, I can't decide which. But even then it didn't ruin my experience and it just hindered it a bit. The monster itself is pretty cool looking and it also looks great, about the half the time. Sometimes the CGI just doesn't look appealing. But in the end this is a great monster movie and I recommend it.

4/5

Hostel
Year – 2005
Director – Eli Roth
Tags – Suspense

Three guys traveling through Europe looking for sex and fun happen upon a club where people are sold to the highest bidder, and anything goes. I love the idea of what is essentially a torture and murder club. The first half of the movie comprises of sex and nudity, while the second half is composed of blood and gore. And really that's all we get, which is fine, but I was hoping for a bit more meat in the story. I felt that the idea could have a lot behind it and that this could be more of a movie than just your typical boobs and blood affair. But for what it is, it definitely has its entertainment value. The violence wasn't as graphic as I expected it to be either, and while it certainly has its moments, it's actually pretty tame. This is a very good movie with some missed potential, but a fun ride nonetheless.

3.5/5

Hostel Part II
Year – 2007
Director – Eli Roth
Tags – Suspense

Now we find three ladies exploring Europe and getting caught up in the same twisted games of the Elite Hunting Club. It's rare that a sequel surpasses the original, but such a thing has been done here. This movie gave me exactly what I wanted, delving deeper into the club, much better character development and much more graphic scenes of violence. I also like the women of this movie more than the men in the first, I just think they have better personalities and they are fleshed out to a greater degree. I also like the behind the scenes look at the club and how everything is arranged. And the violence, sweet violence, so much better in this go around. The Elizabeth Bathory sequence alone is worth the admission price. Everything about the sequel is amplified from the original. I love this movie, and I hope for a third to come out and continue the trend of great filmmaking.

4/5

House

Year – 1986
Director – Steve Miner
Tags – Ghosts

After his aunt commits suicide, a man moves back into the house he grew up in, which happens to be the same house where his son mysteriously disappeared. It doesn't take long before strange things begin to happen, which all leads into the house trying to kill its new resident. I absolutely love the story of this movie, as it is much more than your standard ghost tale. The many occurrences in the house are not only unique and fun to watch, but very cohesive and integral to the storyline. The acting is good, but I think the one major downfall of this movie is the direction. It's just too slow when there should have been a rapid hummingbird pace from one occurrence to the next. Don't get me wrong, the direction isn't terrible, but it could have been a lot tighter. Now, with such a great story packed with so much eye candy, you need great FX to pull it off, and this movie definitely has that. The things that were created looked amazing, and the bizarre happenings were really brought to life. This is a very fun and different ghost flick that I have enjoyed for years and I recommend every check it out.

3.5/5

House II: The Second Story
Year – 1987
Director – Ethan Wiley
Tags – Zombies, Monsters

This second House movie has nothing to do with the first, and it isn't even the same house, just a different set of adventures. This time a man must protect a crystal skull said to hold infinite power to those who possess it from some evil individuals who covet it. This one is more about comedy than horror, but the horror elements are definitely still there. The movie is kind of funny, but not enough. This one does feature even wilder occurrences than the last one, but once again they exist more for comic appeal than horror. The acting is fun, but the direction is very similar to the last one in that it can just get a little slow at times. This movie is almost as good as the last one, and while what happens in the movie is entertaining, it's just not as interesting as the original. Still good though.

3/5

House III: The Horror Show
Year – 1989
Director – James Isaac
Tags – Slasher / Survival

This movie keeps with the tradition that each House movie has nothing to do with the other ones. Here a serial killer is apprehended and sentenced to death and the officer who captured him attends his execution, where the killer vows his revenge against him. After he is executed he comes back to settle the score. I'm not sure which movie came out first, this one or Shocker, but they do have pretty similar plots, but that's probably just a coincidence. This movie does blow its proverbial load in the first fifteen minutes though, showing a lot of gore and great visuals, but afterward not so much. The acting is good, but the direction is pretty slow at times. This isn't a bad movie but it does tread dangerously close.

2.5/5

House by the Cemetery (Quella Villa Accanto al Cimitero)
Year – 1981
Director – Lucio Fulci
Tags – Zombies

A family moves into a new home but unbeknownst to them there is a zombie living in the cellar who requires human flesh and blood to survive. I have to honest here that I was bored to tears by this movie. At least until about the last half hour, when things really picked up. During the journey to the film's sweet spot, there were some punctuations of graphic violence but for the most part the story is dull and just not that interesting, and thus, the direction is also quite slow. But like I said, the last half hour contains a fair amount of brutality and the movie ends strong, which pulls it out of bad movie oblivion. Hardly Fulci's finest work, but it does have some good points.

3/5

House of 9
Year – 2005
Director – Steven R. Monroe
Tags – Suspense

Nine strangers awaken in a house together and are told that the one who walks out of the house alive will take home five million dollars. It doesn't take long for them to find out that their captor's intention is for them to kill each other for his amusement. At first they refuse to participate, but as he sends them less food and begins to raise the temperature in the house, people start to die. In a post-Saw world, you can expect a lot of imitators, and this definitely has the feel of one. What separates it from the rest, however, is that it stands on its own two feet and is done quite well. The death scenes are surprisingly brutal, which I did not expect, and the acting by this hodgepodge of mostly unknowns was mostly very good. I do have to say I was pretty annoyed by Dennis Hopper's faux accent. The movie moves along quite well and then treats the viewer to a great ending, if you can suspend disbelief and accept the miraculous timing of it all. But all told, this is a great thriller I have enjoyed on more than one occasion.

4/5

House of 1000 Corpses

Year – 2003
Director – Rob Zombie
Tags – Slasher / Survival

Two couples traveling around and writing a book on roadside attractions fall prey to vicious family of killers. So the similarities between this movie and The Texas Chainsaw Massacre are obvious because they both dealt with killer families, but that really is where the similarities end. The stories are completely different as well as the way they unfold. This is Rob Zombie's directorial debut and I must say I am impressed. You can tell the man is a lifelong horror fan and living his dream in finally making his own movie. House of 1000 Corpses has a very unique style to it, and I liked it very much, but I can see how some people wouldn't. The funny thing is that I've noticed that most people who are fans of his music like his movies and vice versa. The characters are the high point of this movie for me because they are all very different and well thought out. The story is good and the direction is great. The acting is also excellent, featuring multiple genre actors and vets. I do think this movie is fairly tame, and from what I understand the director's cut of this movie has been forever lost, how that could happen nowadays I'll never know. Maybe the director's cut featured more gore and graphic content, but I guess we'll never know. Still, I like this movie a lot.

4/5

*House of 1000 Corpses 2 can be found under Devil's Rejects, The.

House of the Dead
Year – 2003
Director – Uwe Boll
Tags – Zombies

Based on the popular arcade game, House of the Dead tells the story of a group of people who go an island for a rave, only to find an island full of zombies. The making of this movie is dubious from the start, as it is based on an arcade game, which does not even have a story because it's just meant to munch your quarters. And that's what this movie does as it has no story and eats your money and time. The direction in this movie is especially terrible, so poorly shot its ridiculous. The acting is really bad but all but two people (you know who), the script is horrible, the action sequences are boring and inane, and the list goes on and on. And the zombies, first off, they just don't look that good, and second, one minute they're running around, swimming and flying through the air, the next they're all suddenly slow and doing the Thorazine shuffle all over the place. And the splicing of video game footage into the movie? Whoever had that idea should be put to sleep. By far one of the worst movies ever made in this genre or any other.

0.5/5

House of the Dead II
Year – 2005

Director – Michael Hurst
Tags – Zombies

In this sequel we find a government group attempting to find a cure for the zombie virus. When a college campus is overrun with the undead, they go in to the college in the hopes of finding a cure. How do you make a sequel to one of the worst movies ever? Well, you can aim real low and still outdo the original. And that's what this one did, but unfortunately they aimed too low and only barely outdid the original. I honestly think this one had worse acting, as if that was even possible. And the characters here are even more unlikeable. But on the upside, the zombie action is better and well, that's about it. Everything else is just as bad as that unflushable turd known as the original House of the Dead.

1/5

House of Wax
Year – 1953
Director – Andre De Toth
Tags – Suspense

This is a remake of Mystery of the House of Wax and follows the original very closely. I liked the original and didn't love it, but even though this version follows the original so closely, it is still leagues better, definitely due in part to Vincent Price, who was nothing short of brilliant. This movie would also jump start his career in horror. But more than Price, this movie had everything about it done just a little bit better than its predecessor and features some excellent violence, even though it is very tame by today's standards. But sometimes suspense trumps gore, and that is very true with House of Wax. I especially loved the fire scene here, which was good in the original but it just looked amazing here. This remake is what remakes are all about, taking a great idea and improving upon over the original. Definitely recommended.

4/5

House of Wax [Remake]
Year – 2005
Director – Jaume Collet-Serra
Tags – Slasher / Survival

This remake of the remake follows the core plot of the original but is vastly different in how the movie plays out. I must admit that my expectations for this movie were beyond low and I actually avoided this movie for a long time. The company doesn't exactly have a good track record when it comes to genre films, and that fact that this was a remake starring Paris Hilton of all people, it was just destined to fail. So imagine my shock when this movie was actually pretty good. The story is well made and the movie is well directed. The acting is ok, some doing a much better job than others, but it's the FX that really made the movie shine. There's some awesome kills and blood, and the fire scene here, which actually takes place near the end of the movie, is nothing short of amazing. It's not perfect but this is a very worthwhile slasher flick and a very well done remake.

3.5/5

House on Haunted Hill
Year – 1959
Director – William Castle
Tags – Ghosts

A man invites a group of people to stay the night in a supposedly haunted house for his wife's birthday party. If they should survive the night, each will be paid $10,000. This highly entertaining film is much more than the gimmicky Castle movie it was viewed to be. Instead it is a rather well done ghost story with a mystery twist, making it much more than just a horror movie. The direction really flows nicely through its short run time. The acting is great, especially by Vincent Price who is really in his element here. There are some great, creepy moments, some of which may look a little cheesy by today's standards but some have held up very well. This may not be the typical ghost movie that you expect, but that's what I like about it. Definitely required viewing.

4/5

House on Haunted Hill [Remake]
Year – 1999
Director – William Malone
Tags – Ghosts

This remake of the original keeps the core story intact but goes about telling it in a very different manner, and now the people involved get one million dollars each (That's some massive inflation). And that really is how a remake should be done. You can't keep it exactly the same because what's the point? It's just too bad the new story isn't that great. Geoffrey Rush and Famke Janssen taking the reigns as the couple throwing the party were a great choice, and it was also nice to see Jeffrey Combs. Everyone else however, not so good. It was also strange that the two blonde women in the movie look so much like each other. The direction is ok, but nothing to write home about. It's the FX that really save this movie from complete crapdom however. The movie opted for a more straight horror approach and the loads of gore were accomplished wonderfully by the boys at KNB. The set design itself was also exceptional. The movie may have missed its mark but it's definitely not a bad remake, it's just not done as well as it could have been.

2.5/5

*House on Haunted Hill 2 can be found under Return to House on Haunted Hill.

Howling, The
Year – 1981

Director – Joe Dante
Tags – Werewolves

A newswoman has a strange encounter with a serial killer, and having difficulty trying to cope, she and her husband visit a rehabilitation center in the woods. The problem is that the residents are not what they seem. The Howling is often regarded as a classic in the werewolf genre, and while I do find it to be really good, I would hardly call it a classic. It takes too long to get into the real meat of the werewolf action, and that's always kind of turned me off toward this movie. Don't get me wrong, this movie is great, with an interesting set-up, the movie plays out nicely and I must say that the werewolves are some of the best looking ever. The make-up and transformation FX are incredible, rivaled only by the FX in An American Werewolf in London. So while I enjoy The Howling for multiple reasons, I just wish things would have moved along a bit more briskly and we could have had more screen time for those great looking werewolves.

4/5

Howling II: Your Sister is a Werewolf, The
Year – 1985
Director – Philippe Mora
Tags – Werewolves

So in the second Howling movie we find a group of people trying to kill a powerful werewolf witch, or something. This movie is so incredibly bad, it kind of hurts. The acting is laughably bad, the FX are horrible, the story is stupid, and everything is just horrible, except for Christopher Lee. Why is he even in this? The score consists of pretty much one song played about thirty times throughout the movie, and I'm getting a headache right now just thinking about it. I do have to admit that this movie made me laugh a lot for all the wrong reasons, which is why I am rating it higher than I should. The end credit sequence is hilarious, which consists of that same damn song played again while Sybil Danning rips her shirt off over and over. This movie is so horrible it made me laugh, and it's worth one watch for that alone, but be sure to avoid that second viewing like the plague.

2/5

Howling III: The Marsupials, The
Year – 1987
Director – Philippe Mora
Tags – Werewolves

Now we have a clan of werewolf marsupials living in the Australian Outback, and one breaks away to become an actress, and then the plot devolves even further from there. You know, it usually takes more movies than this to completely destroy a franchise, but after two terrible sequels, The Howling will now be known in infamy rather than anything else. At least the second movie made me laugh this one is just an abomination.

For some reason, the werewolves' just die from regular bullets, yep, no silver bullets needed here. And the werewolves, my god they look like poorly constructed Muppets. The story is senseless, the direction is atrocious, the acting is useless and this movie is worthless. Thanks for completely ruining what could have been a good franchise.

0.5/5

Howling IV: The Original Nightmare, The
Year – 1988
Director – John Hough
Tags – Werewolves

This movie is actually a quasi remake of the original, which is really strange. I guess maybe they were trying to restart the franchise after the last two disastrous sequels, and that does make sense in a way, but this piece of crap is definitely not going to cut the mustard, and instead this sucker cuts the cheese. The acting is ok, and there's a little bit of blood and nudity, but that is just not enough to redeem this complete waste. The direction is just plain bad. The movie is very boring and uneventful, and we don't even get to see much werewolf action until near the end. While this may be a more faithful adaptation of the book, who gives a rat's ass when the movie is this bad? Well, at least it's not as bad as the third movie, but the scary part is that it's close.

1.5/5

Howling V: The Rebirth, The
Year – 1989
Director – Neal Sundstrom
Tags – Werewolves

I think The Howling would have been a much more respected movie had there not been awful sequel after awful sequel churned out after its release. That being said, here in the 5th installment, we show a little back story to the werewolf curse, and how a man tried to end it, only to fail (Of course, wouldn't be much prospect for a new movie if he didn't). Fast forward a few hundred years to 1989 and we find a group of seemingly random people coming together at this werewolf castle, unaware that they all have something in common. Sounds familiar, doesn't it? Well, despite the unoriginality in the setup, what we have here is by far the best of The Howling sequels. And while I realize that might not be saying much, I found this movie to be fairly tense and well paced. It's mostly off screen kills, but the few on screen ones are pretty intense. Add to that a bit of nudity, acting that ranges from horrendous to noteworthy, and a story that keeps you guessing for the most part. That is the recipe for a pretty solid B movie. Let's just say I received much more entertainment value out of this installment than I ever expected. Surprising good.

3.5/5

Howling VI: The Freaks, The

Year – 1991
Director – Hope Perello
Tags – Werewolves

I actually had some hope for this one since the last one was actually pretty good. Here we follow a travelling carnival run by a mysterious man, and another man following said carnival for reasons not revealed until later. That's all you really need to know, because this senseless drivel is just bad, really bad. The story is lame, the acting is awful, the FX work is ok, but the werewolf himself looks horrible. The movie is also incredibly slow and often times straight out boring. Someone needs to put a silver bullet into this franchise after this horrendous turd.

1/5

Hunger, The
Year – 1983
Director – Tony Scott
Tags – Vampires

Two vampires swear to be together forever, but when the man begins to age inexplicably, the woman looks for a new companion and finds her in a doctor that researches premature aging. This is a vampire tale unlike any other. It is very erotic in nature and artfully done. The result is a unique tale that unfolds fairly slowly and ends incredibly strong. I just love the style of this movie, the way it was shot was beautiful, and the way it was acted lends it an even more unique flair. I knew from the beginning when Bauhaus was performing live during the opening credits that I would be in for something special, and what I received was a hazy, dreamlike gothic opus that would not soon be forgotten. I highly recommend this to vampire fans because even though the movie can be slow, it's still a very enjoyable watch.

4/5

I Am Legend
Year – 2007
Director – Francis Lawrence
Tags – Vampires

This movie is the latest adaptation of the Richard Matheson book / remake of The Last Man on Earth. In this movie we find that a virus has turned the vast majority of people into vampires, and one scientist, alone in New York City, struggles to create a cure. First problem with this movie is Will Smith, as he can not carry a movie by himself. If you're a fan of his, you'll probably love it, but not being a fan of his, I have to say he seriously lacks the chops to pull this off. Second massive issue is the horrendously awful CGI. The wide shots of the city look fine, but the lions in the beginning are just unbearably bad, and then when they finally show the vampires, that was just the final nail in the coffin for me. No pun intended. They just looked horrid, very poorly done. And while I have to say that the movie is very much watchable and not the worst thing to ever grace the silver screen, it needed a lot of improvement and a new lead actor to make it a worthwhile film. And maybe with a new lead actor who would demand less money, they could have had someone more competent in charge of the FX.

2/5

I Know What You Did Last Summer
Year – 1997
Director – Jim Gillespie
Tags – Slasher / Survival

Four friends accidently kill a man one night after partying and dispose of the body. One year later they begin receiving notes that someone knows, and then bad things start to happen to them. Teen slasher movies are hardly rocket science, and this may be one of the most dumbed down ones of all. Sure it's virtually bloodless, predictable and not in the least bit scary, but that's not to say I didn't like it. In fact I did like it, to a degree. This is the kind of movie I like to watch when I don't feel like being challenged, when I just want something simple and entertaining, and in that respect, this movie is a winner. But at the same time this movie is barely better than average and nothing special at all, so it really doesn't get a full recommendation from me. Mindless, but fun.

3/5

*I Know What You Did Last Summer 2 can be found under I Still Know What You Did Last Summer.

*I Know What You Did Last Summer 3 can be found under I'll Always Know What You Did Last Summer.

I Know Who Killed Me
Year – 2007
Director – Chris Sivertson
Tags – Suspense

A college student is kidnapped by a serial killer and found half dead in a ditch. When she awakens, she insists she's not who everyone thinks she is and meanwhile the killer is out looking to tie up loose ends. So I expected absolutely nothing out of this and was somewhat pleasantly surprised. The story is fairly interesting in how it plays out, hardly the most unique and engaging thriller but a decent time killer nonetheless. The acting is ok and the direction is average, pretty plain really. This is a marginally good movie that didn't knock my socks off but entertained me much more than I thought it would.

3/5

I Still Know What You Did Last Summer

Year – 1998
Director – Danny Cannon
Tags – Slasher / Survival

After the events of the first movie, the survivors move on with their lives. After winning a trip to an island resort, they find that the killer has returned, and is stalking them on their tropical vacation. Ok, the fact that the killer would set up a fake contest for a remote resort vacation, and then crash the party and start killing is probably the stupidest premise for a sequel ever (hence why I actually gave a synopsis). Why would he just not use the element of surprise and kill them while they slept in their beds? Why go through this elaborate ordeal of getting them to an island? Whoever wrote this junk should be beaten with a rubber hose. That aside, we once again have a brainless teen slasher movie that has less entertainment value and is thus less worthwhile. They may have tried to amp up the blood but again we have people involved in a genre movie that have no idea how to make a genre movie. It has some value, but not much, and surprisingly they even made another one after this train wreck.

2/5

Ice Queen
Year – 2005
Director – Neil Kinsella
Tags – Monsters

A prehistoric human is discovered and the only way to keep it in check is to keep its body temperature high, but when the heat system malfunctions, she comes back to life, killing the pilot of the plane she was on. Then the plane crashes and creates and avalanche, trapping the people in the resort below with her. Really, is that the best the writers could come up with? A prehistoric woman that for some reason needs cold to stay alive, that's stupid. Why not just make it some kind of monster? Anyway, despite the absolutely dumb premise, this movie does have a couple of good things going it. It's not the acting, that's fairly bad, and the mannerisms of the ice queen were just ridiculous. It's not the direction either because this movie is slow and boring. We've already established that the story is rubbish, so the good points aren't there either. So what is it? Well, the avalanche was actually pretty cool with a good use of miniatures it was actually kind of impressive. There was some gore and decent FX as well, but honestly that's pretty much it. This is definitely a bad movie.

1.5/5

Identity
Year – 2003
Director – James Mangold
Tags – Slasher / Survival

Ten strangers assemble at a Nevada motel during a particularly nasty thunderstorm that has washed out the roads. But that's the least of their worries as they realize that someone there is killing them off one by one. This is a pretty slick merge of a slasher movie and a psychological horror flick, so I've got to give it points there. The acting is very good from most everyone involved as well. The story is great but it's just too easy to figure out and I think it could have been much better if more things were shrouded in secrecy. The direction was very good as well, with few slow spots to speak of. While you don't really get to see many death scenes, the aftermath almost makes up for it, making this a very good thriller with only a couple flaws hindering it from greatness.

3.5/5

Idle Hands
Year – 1999
Director – Rodman Flender
Tags – Demonic Possession

A teenage boy discovers that his hand is possessed and forces him to kill those around him. This movie is billed as a horror/comedy but unfortunately it's pretty light on horror and very light on comedy. The movie just isn't funny and it's made even sadder by the fact that you can tell the movie is really trying to be. On the horror side, it's not bad but there isn't enough gore or good moments to keep it very interesting. I think it's a combination of less than great direction with a half assed script. The acting is also not very good but at least the FX are pretty cool. As far as possession flicks go, this movie is hardly one of the best and as far as horror/comedies go, it's easily one of the least effective. Bad, but not the worst.

2/5

I'll Always Know What You Did Last Summer
Year – 2006
Director – Sylvain White
Tags – Slasher / Survival

So some kids cover up a friend's death and then a year later they're stalked by a killer with a hook, blah, blah, blah. Seriously, who green lit this? Did we really need a third? Not even the actors from the original would return in this horrid tripe. Instead we have to be subjected to some bottom barrel "actors" and sit through some poor direction derived from a terrible script. I don't want to go on too much because this movie doesn't deserve it. I struggle to find a good thing to say about this movie, everything is just so bad, it's just that some aspects of it are less bad, if you catch my drift. A terrible end to a pretty terrible franchise.

1/5

In the Mouth of Madness

Year – 1994
Director – John Carpenter
Tags – Monsters

An insurance investigator searches for an acclaimed horror author who has mysteriously disappeared. His investigation leads him to the town of Hobb's End, which is supposedly a fictional place created by the author. And this town harbors innumerable terrors that drive him to madness. This movie is probably the best showcase of Lovecraftian filmmaking I've ever seen. While it isn't a direct adaptation of a Lovecraft story, there are many elements of his stories present in the movie which will most assuredly appease fans. There are so many creepy and strange occurrences in the movie that I found myself to be completely spellbound by them. The FX work really brings this movie alive with some amazing creature creation and make-up. I don't want to go into too much detail but suffice to say that I was blown away by the sights and sounds of this movie. Great acting, excellent direction, and a truly unique and well imagined story make for one of the more memorable movie watching experiences I've had.

4.5/5

Infection (Kansen)
Year – 2004
Director – Masayuki Ochiai
Tags – Infection

A financially unstable hospital gets a highly infectious patient dropped at their doorstep. This never before seen illness inspires one of the doctors there to begin research on it, but when the infected person liquefies and then other staff members begin exhibiting symptoms of the illness, things quickly spiral out of control. This movie was pretty awesome. There were some excellent gooey moments that I wish they had shown more in detail, and the first stage of infection, which was apparently complete madness, offered up some nice disturbing imagery. The movie was rather suspenseful at times but did have its moments of lagging. The acting was good but some of the characters were a little annoying. This is well done addition to the sub genre of infection, which has loads of possibilities that still need to be explored, and I'm glad this movie did so in a very unique manner.

3.5/5

Inferno
Year – 1980
Director – Dario Argento
Tags – Witchcraft

This is a pseudo sequel to Suspiria and while it doesn't exactly follow directly from that movie it exists in the same universe. Here a woman is trying to uncover the secrets of The Three Mothers, powerful witches who each control some of largest cities in the world.

While Suspiria focused on one witch, Inferno focuses on a new one, rumored to be the most evil of all. I could never get into this one like I could with Suspiria mainly because the story just isn't as exciting. The story kind of plods around with no distinct direction and doesn't really culminate into a satisfactory ending. But it still had plenty of good things going on. Namely the locations and gore. The direction is beautifully done as usual but this time around it seems kind of slow. While not fully in love with this pseudo sequel to the timeless classic, I still found enough good things going on to enjoy it.

3.5/5

Innocent Blood
Year – 1992
Director – John Landis
Tags – Vampires

A vampire feeds upon the leader of a New York City mafia ring but fails to kill him, thus turning him into a vampire as well. And now with his new found power he seeks to create a mob of vampires and rule New York. It's up to a cop and the vampire who turned the mob boss to put a stop to him. This horror/comedy by Landis is a bit light on both comedy and horror. I do like the mob angle however, as I feel that organized crime has not been used in the horror genre as much as it could be. The acting is very good and the direction is mostly good, but the story just doesn't have the bite that it should. Yes, that was a pun, sorry. Innocent Blood isn't a bad movie I just don't think the vampire / mob melding of genres was pulled off as well as it could have been.

3/5

Insanitarium
Year – 2008
Director – Jeff Buhler
Tags – Infection

A man, unable to see his sister after she is committed for attempting suicide, feigns mental illness to gain access to the hospital and her. Unfortunately the doctor uses the mental patients to experiment his new drug on. Their lust for blood and meat goes out of control and all hell breaks loose. This movie surprised me. My first thought was, "Why is Peter Stormare is this?" Because it's awesome, that's why. The build up to the final act is slow but the movie does not plod along, things are kept interesting with character development and an unfolding mystery. And then the final act comes, and the movie explodes into an insane gorefest. The movie resembles a zombie movie, as the infected patients crave warm flesh and blood, so zombie fans will want to take note. There is so much arterial spray, mangled remains and blood on the walls that you just can't help but smile. This is just a fun movie that takes a little while to get to the payoff, but when it does, you'll find yourself very pleased with the result.

4/5

Inside (A l'interieur)
Year – 2007
Director – Alexandre Bustillo, Julien Maury
Tags – Slasher / Survival

After a tragic car accident leaves a woman widowed, she must give birth to her child alone. But on the night before she is to give birth, she gets a visitor at her house, and the only thing this visitor wants, is the woman's baby… by any means necessary. There was a lot of hype behind this movie and honestly, when there is so much behind a film it usually doesn't live up to it. Well, I am happy to say that here it does. I have seen a multitude of horror movies in my life (obviously) and this is by far one of the most brutal films I have ever watched. The gore is off the charts, and while the movie is bloody as hell, it's realistic and not overdone. And the movie isn't just a one trick pony of amazing gore, it is also very tight and tense thriller aided by a well written script and excellent acting. The movie was pulled off quite well and I look forward to seeing more from these directors.

4.5/5

Interview with the Vampire
Year – 1994
Director – Neil Jordan
Tags – Vampires

Based upon the Anne Rice novel, this movie explores the life of a vampire throughout his many years of existence. I like the works of Anne Rice because she really knows how to make great characters, and that is ever present in this movie. All of the main vampires present here are fleshed out extremely well, and the actors who played them did wonderful jobs for the most part. I think Tom Cruise was miscast as Lestat, and while he did do a good job, I've always pictured Peter Murphy in that role. The story is wonderful, chronicling the life and times of vampires throughout a couple of centuries. And in that respect the set designs and costumes are really well done as well. The direction is very tight and never allows for dull moments. In the realm of vampire movies, this stands out as one of the best, and if you are a fan of the sub genre, no collection is complete without this excellent film.

4.5/5

Invasion, The
Year – 2007
Director – Oliver Hirschbiegel
Tags – Biological

In this third remake of Invasion of the Body Snatchers, it follows the same essential story with minor changes. This movie was obviously killed by studio execs, as no director in their right mind would produce garbage like this. The direction is slow, much too slow, and the acting is fairly bad too. Well, Nicole Kidman had a couple of good moments, but I just wish she would have picked an accent and stuck with it. Sure the pod people have no emotions, but seriously, the pod people in this movie are tremendously overdone. The story is fine as it keeps the core elements there but also introduces new things. Well I was fine with the story until the abrupt and asinine end. This is just not a good movie, and after a solid run of great movies, the "series" jumps the shark here and ends on a sour note.

2/5

Invasion of the Body Snatchers
Year – 1956
Director – Don Siegel
Tags – Biological

A small group of people uncover a plot where seed pods from outer space create physical copies of human beings and then steal their minds while they sleep, creating a race of emotionless copies that destroy the originals. This is such a classic movie. The idea behind it is really great, creating a sense of fear and paranoia because you never know who you can trust, all while being very tense and quickly paced. As the town starts to be taken over, the pod people expand their operation, all while the few remaining humans try to stay awake and escape. The acting is superb and the direction just as good. The FX for the movie are also very good. When we get to see the clones coming out the pods, it really is a cool experience. I think the most intriguing thing about the story is that being a pod person really isn't that bad. There would be no crime, no war, just a perfectly peaceful world where everyone gets along, but you would have to sacrifice your humanity for it, and everyone would be the same. This actually isn't much a stretch if you think about it. With all the fashion and technology trends out there today, people feel like they need to belong and be like everyone else, so even today this movie carries quite the social commentary with it. Who knows, maybe there are pod people out there, just trying to get everyone to conform. But seriously, this is an incredibly well done movie.

4.5/5

Invasion of the Body Snatchers [Remake]
Year – 1978
Director – Philip Kaufman
Tags – Biological

This remake follows the same story as the original and just goes about the unfolding of the story differently. I love the first movie, and this one does something incredibly rare, it actually surpasses a classic original. I think that is due mainly to the increase of atmosphere and the overall bleakness of the story. Speaking of the story, it is very much enhanced both in scale and grandeur. The cast is a great mix of genre actors and vets who put on amazing performances. I also enjoyed seeing Kevin McCarthy make a nice cameo.

The direction is also incredibly well done as the movie is kept very suspenseful throughout its entire run time, which is quite the feat. While I liked the FX of the original they look even better here, with the formation of the pod people being even more detailed. While staying true to the original at its core, this movie expands upon nearly every aspect of it to great results, and this is one movie that should never be missed.

5/5

Island of Dr. Moreau, The
Year – 1977
Director – Don Taylor
Tags – Monsters

A man lost at sea comes across an island where a doctor has been experimenting with genetically splicing humans and animals. Now he's trapped between a mad scientist and his inhuman creations. I think probably the highlight of this movie for me is the animal fight scenes, especially the tiger fight, because you'll never see anything like them again. At least not a real one, but you'll probably see it with CGI (oh boy). The acting is good, if not somewhat hammy and the direction is respectable but far from perfect. I liked how the creatures looked as well and felt they were constructed very nicely. I really like the story but I don't think the movie really unveiled to its full majesty. This is a nice tale of experimentation gone wrong and a fun ride.

3/5

Island of Dr. Moreau, The [Remake]
Year – 1996
Director – John Frankenheimer
Tags – Monsters

This remake follows the same core plot as the original but switches the story up considerably. I think this movie gets a bad rap because I found it to be very entertaining and a little bit better than the previous effort. Sure it's kind of a mess and overly silly, but I thought the acting was good (hammy once again) and the direction was fairly smooth, even though the director was actually the second one to take the helm. The original director was also the writer who probably could have done a better job, but I like it nonetheless. There are also a great deal more creatures in this one and they look incredible due to Stan Winston's FX wizardry. The story also feels better here as well. I found this remake to be enjoyable and fun, despite its flaws.

3.5/5

Island of the Dead
Year – 2000
Director – Tim Southam
Tags – Infection

A missing person investigator goes to New York's Hart Island, a place where the unknown dead have been buried for decades. A group of inmates on work detail accompany her, as well as the owner of the island who has plans for it, but ulterior motives lie behind what he is presenting. It was hard to tag this movie because it's just such an incoherent mess. There are swarms of supernatural flies on the island which seem to have some tie to the dead who are about to be wronged by this millionaire, and when they infect a person they decompose rapidly. So there's flies, which may be ghosts, but whatever. The acting is surprisingly good given the content, or lack there of. And there's some good FX also. The direction is incredibly disjointed as well, which makes sense since the same guy wrote the script. This would have been better off as a straight-up zombie movie or ghost story, but instead there's this, a movie that had promising attributes but a terrible script and director.

2/5

Isolation
Year – 2005
Director – Billy O'Brien
Tags – Animals

On an isolated farm, genetic testing has gone wrong and created a mutant, bloodthirsty calf. But there is more danger than just the calf itself, because it carries something even more deadly inside of it. This rather grim tale may just be a peek into the future due to all the genetic tampering humanity is committing nowadays, well, this is probably to the extreme, but it's still damn good. The birth sequence alone is incredibly intense and just a precursor to the great FX work. The acting is also really good and the direction is well done. The story is good and features some nice elements but I did feel that more could have been with the subject matter. Not perfect and a little rough around the edges, but very good nonetheless.

3.5/5

It
Year – 1990
Director – Tommy Lee Wallace
Tags – Monsters

This Stephen King adaptation is based on the lives of some children in a small Maine town. Children have been going missing at an alarming rate, and a band of outcasts join together to stop the heart of the problem, a creature simply referred to as It. A made for TV movie is always shaky ground, mainly because it has to be edited down even more than a theatrical release for very general audiences. No swearing, nudity and very little blood will be permitted. And It, as a novel, was fairly graphic, but I feel it faired well despite this. Now another problem with a TV movie is length. You can either have the movie, or something more akin to a miniseries. While It was a lengthy book, I feel it fell in-between the TV movie and TV miniseries and would have benefited more from being a two to two and a half hour long feature. The director could not have got the job done in a single hour and a half airing, but it's nearly three hour, two part runtime is loaded with filler that could have easily been left on the cutting room floor. Despite my feelings that it should have been shorter and unedited for TV, this is a very good movie told in two parts, once with children, and again when the children are all grown up. It can get pretty creepy, and for those people with a fear of clowns, it's best to avoid this movie. Tim Curry is perfect as Pennywise the Dancing Clown, and pulls off a perfectly frightening performance. A shorter and bloodier version would have been mind blowing, but we still have this, which is proof you can make a genuinely scary TV movie… just as long as you cast Tim Curry.

3.5/5

It's Alive
Year – 1974
Director – Larry Cohen
Tags – Monsters

A woman gives birth to a child that murders all the doctors and nurses in the delivery room and then escapes, only to continue its murder spree. Now the father attempts to find it before the police can destroy it. The idea is pretty cool. A monster baby that goes on a killer rampage has a good ring to it, but damn, this movie is boring. The kid, when you really get to see it, does look pretty awesome. The kills are decent enough but not very bloody. The acting is good, nothing outstanding. I was left wanting more from this movie, I think it had more potential but didn't really live up to it. It's not bad, it's not good, and it ends up being just kind of in-between. I liked it for what it was, but I just wish it was something more. Good, but far from greatness.

2.5/5

It's Alive 2: It Lives Again
Year – 1978
Director – Larry Cohen
Tags – Monsters

This sequel continues on the original storyline and here we have a government group systematically eliminating the creatures before they can be born, and at the same time there is another group of people who take the pregnant women and allow them to give birth to the creatures before the abortion squads can get to them. I liked this better than original because while I feel the original movie was just a concept, this movie actually has a story behind it. There are more babies this time around, and we get to see them a little better, and yeah, they're pretty cool looking. The acting is good and the direction is better, because now Cohen has a bit more to actually work with in terms of story. And the abortion squad deal is brilliant because I could actually see that happening. This is a pretty enjoyable movie even though I was hoping for more blood (again). Definitely a step in the right direction for this franchise however.

3/5

It's Alive 3: Island of the Alive
Year – 1987
Director – Larry Cohen
Tags – Monsters

There is a court order put in place that would confine all of the monster babies born to a deserted island. An expedition heads to the island years afterward to try and learn more about them. I'd say this movie is pretty much on par with the second one. We also learn here what might be the cause for the monster babies, and it was interesting, but also had me thinking: "Is that it?" We are also treated to seeing what the babies look like after a couple of years, and to be honest, it's a bit too cartoonish. There's more blood this time around, which is nice but doesn't feel like enough, still. It's good to see a franchise keep evolving through the sequels and not sound like a broken record. While I can appreciate that the people involved made strides to see that each movie was very different from one another, this is still hardly my favorite series. But it has been good enough throughout, and this one is no different.

3/5

J-Horror Anthology: Legends
Year – 2003
Director – Multiple
Tags – Short Film Compilation

This DVD is comprised of six stories having to do with dark Japanese legends. I think this may have been a TV show in Japan given the somewhat low production values on display here. The acting is ok in each segment, nothing great. The stories are all fairly good, and none that I would say were bad per se. She-Bear is the best of the bunch, which happens to be a pretty awesome short and the rest range from decent to good. The direction is good throughout, and each short is only between ten and twenty minutes long, so each run briskly. This is a very nice collection of Japanese short horror films and I definitely recommend you check it out if you're a fan of J-Horror.

3.5/5

J-Horror Anthology: Underworld
Year – 2005
Director – Multiple
Tags – Short Film Compilation

This DVD, much like the one that came before it, contains six short horror films, but this time they are based on stories from the Japanese underworld. This one definitely isn't as good as the last one, but it's still not a bad collection. I know these two volumes are related (aside from the name) because the same guy hosts all the episodes and well, they just look similar. Everything here is about the same as the previous volume in terms of acting and direction, but here the stories just aren't as interesting. They are all just across the board average, and nothing really stood out to me. Maybe I'm just more into the legends and folklore of other countries. But like I said, it's still not bad.

2.5/5

Jack Brooks: Monster Slayer
Year – 2007
Director – Jon Knautz
Tags – Monsters

Jack Brooks has anger issues, and finds it difficult to keep his rage inside. But when his night school teacher turns into a flesh hungry beast, he finds an outlet for his rage and becomes a monster slayer. I like this movie a lot, but I did expect more from it. It has a very Evil Dead feel to it, not a rip off though, the storylines are very different, but it just has the feel of that movie. Just like Jack Brooks kind of feels like Ash, even though they are also quite different. The monster action is fairly sparse, and this movie instead focuses more on character development and back story, proving that this is just the starting ground for a new franchise. I imagine the sequel will focus more on monsters, but I wish they would have spread the back story out more so there were fewer lulls in the production. The FX is a throwback to the 80's, a bit cheesy, but very fun. Good acting, especially by Robert Englund, and just an overall good movie. Makes me anticipate the sequels because there is much more that can be had here.

3.5/5

Jacket, The
Year – 2005
Director – John Maybury
Tags – Suspense

A Gulf War veteran is sent to an asylum for the criminally insane where he is the subject to a doctor's cruel experiments of drug use and sensory deprivation. During these experiments he believes he can travel ahead in time where he tries to solve the mystery of his own death. If the movie sounds complicated, it's really not, in fact it is a very well crafted thriller that does have some flaws but is an overall well thought out experience. The acting is very good and the direction is well done as well, with only minor issues to speak of. I really liked how the story unfolded and it really lent a fair amount of originality to the production. This is a well made thriller that may not amaze, but it definitely satisfies.

3.5/5

Jacob's Ladder
Year – 1990
Director – Adrian Lyne
Tags – Suspense

A Vietnam veteran begins having much more than flashbacks when he begins to see otherworldly creatures and other things that just can not be. This movie really does transcend beyond a form of entertainment because it really is an experience to watch. The acting is great, especially by Tim Robbins as the title character who puts a lot of passion into his performance. The direction is great too as there is rarely a dull moment. The movie is almost Lovecraftian in a way the way it unfolds, which I always appreciated since I really dig that style of filmmaking. And while the story is well crafted, I think there could have been more done. I was just left craving more incredible visuals and all the time spent talking about them could have been better put to use by completely frying my brain. This is a trippy movie that is as dark as it is beautiful.

4/5

Jason Goes to Hell: The Final Friday
Year – 1993
Director – Adam Marcus
Tags – Slasher / Survival

This ninth Friday the 13th movie happens sometime after the eighth, who knows at this point? So I think New Line bought the rights to this franchise just so they could (almost) kill Jason, and that amuses me. It starts out as just another Friday the 13th movie, but then quickly becomes something entirely new for the series, and already I was impressed. Too bad it didn't get any better from there. The story is pretty lame, just making up things as it goes along, but there are some cool death scenes and amazing FX, so that kept my interest. The direction and acting are fairly average, nothing special to speak of, but nothing terrible either. I like this movie, it's definitely better than most of the previous ones, but they could have done a while lot more with the concept presented here. Entertaining, but in the end it's only a barely above average movie.

3/5

Jason X
Year – 2001
Director – James Isaac
Tags – Slasher / Survival

This tenth Friday the 13th movie takes place, oh, about a few centuries after the last one. And this time we are treated to Jason in space. Hey, don't laugh too hard. It is a fresh idea for a very stale series, and while I was really into this movie at first, it quickly devolved into some pretty stupid material. There are some awesome kills in this movie, but most are boring. The practical FX look good, but the CGI is just awful. The acting is uniformly bad with people cast that don't act or even look their parts. And apparently in the future all women dress like dime store whores as well. The direction is decent, could have been better but it wasn't bad. The story started out interesting enough, but by the time it hit the Jason vs. android battle, it became so incredibly lame that I could barely stand it. There was enough good stuff in this movie to make it watchable, but in the end this is just another silly slasher movie with no real merit.

2.5/5

Jaws
Year – 1975
Director – Stephen Spielberg
Tags – Animals

A giant great white shark terrorizes the small island community of Amity and the local sheriff, a grizzled fisherman and a marine biologist set out to stop it. One of the all time greats right here. This movie, based on the Peter Benchley novel, who thankfully also wrote the screenplay, is just a masterpiece. The characters are so well written and subsequently performed, and that really is the strongest point in this movie for me, the shark is just an afterthought, it's the people and the actors who played them that made this movie so incredible. But the shark itself is also so large and menacing that it really does complete the puzzle. The direction is perfect, never a dull moment and every single frame shot just as it should be. The score adds to the tension as well, as simple as it was, it is now the iconic series of notes signaling danger. I could go on and on gushing about how wonderful this movie is, but instead of reading more, those few of you out there who haven't seen this movie owe it to yourselves to begin watching it now.

5/5

Jaws 2
Year – 1978
Director – Jeannot Szwarc
Tags   Animals

This movie seems to take place a few years after the original. So this movie is pretty much just a copy of the first one with minor differences sprinkled throughout and then a different ending. And for that I don't like the movie because they really didn't even try it seems. Instead they just went for the quick cash-in on a hugely successful film (I think the original was the first to break the one hundred million dollar barrier at the box office). The reasons I do like the movie are as follows: It was nice to see a lot of familiar faces in this sequel and the acting was good. The direction was also good as there were not many instances of poor pacing. The shark however, just didn't look as good this time around, or maybe they just used it too much. Of course this is nowhere near as good as the original but just watching it as a movie, it's not bad, and ends up being just slightly better than average.

3/5

Jaws 3
Year – 1983
Director – Joe Alves
Tags – Animals

This time around we find a great white shark trapped inside a man made lagoon inside Sea World. You know, I actually love the concept because there is a great opportunity for a massive body count, but unfortunately the filmmakers decided to not take advantage of that fact and instead had a very low body count. The portions of the movie shot in 3-D look absolutely terrible, like cardboard cutouts. There's a part of the movie where Jaws attacks a window as it is busting through, the shark stays completely stationary, not even moving its tail as it approaches the window, it's pretty pathetic. It definitely has some cool ideas, it just doesn't follow through with them and the whole movie feels just too sugary for my taste. It is paced and acted fairly well though, so it's not a complete loss, but in the end, I'm more disappointed with what they didn't do than with what they did.

2/5

Jaws: The Revenge
Year – 1987
Director – Joseph Sargent
Tags – Animals

A killer shark goes on the warpath to hunt down the Brody family and wipe them out of existence. Are you kidding me? Is this seriously the best someone could come up with? This is the end to this franchise? Wow, that is one of the worst plots I've ever heard in my life. To think that a regular old shark could possibly set traps and lure certain people in, let alone find these people, or even know who the hell they are, is completely ludicrous. Add to that the poor direction, the actors forced to choke out terrible dialogue and just the completely stupid way the movie unfolds, and you have this piece of crap. I can't even go on, it's just too bad. At least the fake water was pretty, and at least there was some blood, too bad it didn't belong to the creator of this mess, hehe.

1.5/5

Jeepers Creepers
Year – 2001
Director – Victor Salva
Tags – Monsters

On a long stretch of highway, a brother and sister are driving home for Spring Break when they are harassed by a local in his old truck. A short while later they see the truck again, parked next an old church while a man in a trenchcoat is throwing what appears to be wrapped up bodies down a large pipe. But it is no man and now the siblings are in the fight for their lives. I like this movie a lot because it took the time to not only create a great new monster, but to really flesh it out and make it unique. The Creeper is the kind of monster that years down the road will be seen beyond this franchise and will become another horror staple like vampires or werewolves. The Creeper looks awesome too, and has quite a personality as well as many abilities that I won't go into but allow you to see for yourself. There's some fun kills and decent blood but I did want a bit more. The acting is great, the direction is really good and the FX work is pretty nice as well. This is a great new creature feature with a couple of minor flaws that did not ruin the experience for me. Recommended.

4/5

Jeepers Creepers 2
Year – 2003
Director – Victor Salva
Tags – Monsters

This sequel takes place shortly after the original. I like this movie, but not a whole lot. What I liked so much about the original is that the brother and sister team were great characters, here we have a lot more people but no stand out characters, most are just throwaways and the rest just aren't fleshed out very much at all. Aside from that, the movie is still pretty entertaining, but I just don't think that as much effort went into the sequel. The acting is fine but there really are no stand-out performances. We do get to see some more Creeper weapons, but we also get to see more Creeper, which kind of ruins the air of mystery that surrounded him in the first movie. It's a competent sequel, just not that great.

3/5

Jekyll + Hyde
Year – 2006
Director – Nick Stillwell
Tags – Suspense

This movie does not use the classic story of Jekyll and Hyde but rather uses to concept in a new way. Here a man is creating a new recreational drug that gives him strong sexual and murderous desires. I expected another low budget turd with this movie but instead I received a competent thriller that doubles as a slasher movie. The acting is fine, nothing grand but nothing bad. The story is pretty good and the direction is ok. There's some blood and nudity which work well in the movie, but overall there just could have been more. More of everything. Still, this is much better than I expected it to be and if you're a fan of the story you'll probably enjoy this alternate take like I did.

Joshua
Year – 2006
Director – Travis Betz
Tags – Slasher / Survival

The death of his father brings a man back home where secrets from past arise. Because when he was a child, he and two of his friends raised a baby in secret to make it evil. But if their "son" Joshua really did die in the fire they set, then what is in the basement? I honestly love the story here, but it's just too bad that it didn't reach its full potential. Most likely the flaws come from budgetary constraints, and not being able to find good actors or a real writer and director to adapt it. The movie is very slow and mostly uninteresting, which is sad because I see where it could have gone right. This is a disappointment because in some more capable hands, this could have been a classic, but it ends up coming off as a poorly executed horror flick that's too rough around the edges to be called good.

Joshua
Year – 2007
Director – George Ratliff
Tags – Suspense

After a new baby is born, the older child in this family of four begins acting strange and takes on some rather morbid interests. Now this refined boy becomes a twisted shadow of his former proper upbringing. There have been several evil child movies made throughout the years, some with supernatural elements, and some without, this is one without. Joshua is a normal boy from the outset but his taste for the darker things in life, including cruelty toward his new sister, animals and other people, overtakes him. And yet he maintains his composure throughout, skillfully manipulating people into thinking that other people are the problem and he's just a little angel. As far as child actors go, this kid has limitless potential, and I'm not sure if I've ever seen a performance by a child come off this good. The other actors in the movie are also excellent, but Jacob Kogan is especially gifted. The direction is very good, with only a few lags in the pacing department. This is a brilliantly twisted movie and in the realm of child horror, this stands at the forefront as one of the most well made and subtle films of its kind.

Joy Ride
Year – 2001
Director – John Dahl
Tags – Slasher / Survival

Some college kids driving cross country decide to play a game with a trucker at his expense, but afterward they realize that the trucker is a psychotic killer who doesn't appreciate being the butt of their joke. I'm surprised that this movie wasn't rated PG for how tame it was. A low body count and unseen, bloodless kills were all this movie was about. Now this would usually make me hate your typical slasher film, but this isn't your typical slasher film. No, this one actually has a good story, good acting and some really good direction, so I can forgive the lack of blood. This movie is a pretty great suspense tale just lopped in with the bulk of teen horror that came out around this time. Check it out, you be pleasantly surprised at how well this movie was pulled off.

3.5/5

Joy Ride 2: Dead Ahead
Year – 2008
Director – Louis Morneau
Tags – Slasher / Survival

This movie continues on some time after the last one. Now this one loads up much more blood and gore than the original and even a smidge of nudity, which is a great thing to see. But what's this? They gave away the good acting, direction and story for it? Rats. I guess I shouldn't have expected much. This movie is definitely below average, but I can't really say it's bad. Sure it has some really annoying characters played by really annoying actors, and the story is just about as one dimensional as they come, but least the direction was… passable I guess. Oh who am I kidding this is a bad movie but not the worst by any means.

2/5

Ju-On
Year – 2002
Director – Takashi Shimizu
Tags – Ghosts

A vengeful spirit marks and tracks down anyone who dares enter the house in which it resides. This movie kind of plays out like an anthology with different segments that end up colliding with one another. There are some great genuine scares here, the most effective being a clever use of sound effects. But in addition to the greats sounds there are also some excellent visual scares, utilizing good creepy moments instead of the cheap jump scares. I like the story a lot, and it is much more than your traditional ghost story. The direction is very good, as is the acting, and overall this is a great ghost story. I am a little confused about the whole Ju-On / Ju-On: The Grudge titling, and I'm not sure if they are different movies or the same ones with slightly different names. But anyway, yeah, great movie.

4/5

Ju-On 2

Year – 2003
Director – Takashi Shimizu
Tags – Ghosts

This movie takes place not long after the original. This is a good follow up to a very inventive ghost movie. I like this, it's good, but that's all it is. This movie has less scares and less creepiness to it, but it does end on a nice, twisted note. The acting is just as good as the original but this time the direction is noticeably slower. This time around the movie is told is more linear fashion, there are different segments, but they run together easier. Maybe that's the problem, I don't know, it's hard to say. There are some awesome kills and good visuals, but just not like before. Still, this is a good follow up and the story continues on in good fashion, just don't expect the same level of scares you witnessed in the original.

3/5

Kaidan

Year – 2007
Director – Hideo Nakata
Tags – Ghosts

A man neglects his wife and soon after doing so, she dies. In writing she swears that if he remarries, she will return to wreak vengeance upon his new bride. But he disregards the warning anyway. This is a really good movie that perhaps overstayed its welcome. The story is really good and I enjoyed that aspect of the movie the most. The acting and direction were both good, but nothing outstanding. I think that the movie would have maybe run a little better if it were shorter, because at two hours it became a chore at times and the pacing was affected to some degree. The ending was very beautiful though and I really enjoyed that. The back story intro also looked great, I just wish everything in the middle was as good as what bookended the movie. Though it was still a good watch to say the least.

3.5/5

Kalifornia

Year – 1993
Director – Dominic Sena
Tags – Serial Killer (Fictional)

A man writing a book on serial killers takes a cross country trip with his wife and two strangers, visiting the sites of famous killers and sharing expenses and stories along the way. But it doesn't take long for the husband and wife to find out that the man they're sharing so much with is a serial killer himself. I've always liked this movie for the simple reason that it is just acted and directed so well. The characters are well thought out and their diverse personalities make for some very interesting times. There is a fair amount of violence, but I think there was an unheeded call for more. The serial killer character was a particularly stone hearted and vile individual and I would have liked to have seen more of his dark side. The story could have been meatier, maybe a bit more graphic, but other than that this is a dark, well done thriller.

4/5

Killer Klowns from Outer Space
Year – 1988
Director – Stephen Chiodo
Tags – Aliens

A comet falls to Earth, but instead of finding a meteorite, the residents of a small town instead find a circus tent filled with killer clowns. This in undoubtedly the cheesiest movie ever made, but in that same respect, it has so much originality and is so much fun to watch that you just have to like it. A big top spaceship, cotton candy cocoons, popcorn guns, it's all here. The clowns look absolutely incredible, and they are so well done. The rest of the FX are really good as well, even when it looks cheesy, it fits the mood of the film and works perfectly. The story is good but the pacing could have definitely used some work. This is a unique movie that garners a lot of laughs and has a few iconic scenes that will never be forgotten. Not to be taken seriously, Killer Klowns from Outer Space is the quintessential meaning of the words Cult Classic.

3.5/5

Killer Pad
Year – 2008
Director – Robert Englund
Tags – Demons

Three guys move into a giant house with dirt cheap rent. The only problem is that there is a portal to Hell in the basement, and once they find it they do what anyone would do, throw a party. The horror/comedy is the first feature length movie Robert Englund has done is twenty years, and I think because of that it still carries that 80's vibe. I thought this movie was hilarious and it had me laughing on several occasions. It's the horror side of the story where I felt the movie came up a little light. This movie was rife for loads of gore and nudity but there was really none to be had, which is a shame because I feel that certainly would have enhanced my enjoyment of it a great deal. The direction is great and I really wish that Englund would direct more because he has a natural skill. The FX and make-up were very good with a little bit of bad CGI thrown in. The acting was interesting to say the least, very slapstick, which works most of the time. I really liked this movie and thought it was very fun. Should there have been a large amount of boobs and blood thrown in, then this would have easily been a classic.

3.5/5

Killing Gene, The (W Delta Z [WAZ])
Year – 2007
Director – Tom Shankland
Tags – Serial Killer (Fictional)

A serial killer forces his victims to choose between their lives and the lives of a loved one. Now it's up to two detectives to put a stop to the killing. While I think that the bulk of the story is pretty standard stuff, I do like the twist in how the killer kills. I also like the main actors playing the detectives, and while they are good in their own right, I do feel they were miscast here and miss their marks. The acting is still good but I think there were better choices to be made in casting. The direction is pretty good, despite the general lull in the story itself. This is good stuff, and if you're a fan of these types of movies I would say it's worth checking out. It's not bad by any stretch of the word, it's just lacking in multiple areas that prevent it from being great.

3/5

Kiss the Girls
Year – 1997
Director – Gary Fleder
Tags – Serial Killer (Fictional)

A man calling himself Casanova is kidnapping girls and holding them somewhere for his own pleasure before he kills them, but when one escapes, she helps the police to find him before he can kill anyone else. The story really is an underwhelming effort, as it plays out like your standard serial killer movie. Fortunately the acting and direction lend the movie a lot of much needed power. Don't get me wrong, the story isn't bad by any means, it just feels very mundane. I do like how the killer kept his victims awhile before dispatching them, as well as his affinity for more refined women, and the killer as a whole was unique, but the search for him and the other characters were fairly one dimensional. I like this but I wouldn't say I loved it, it is a good show and pretty entertaining, but doesn't leave a lasting impression.

3.5/5

Kolobos
Year – 1999
Director – Daniel Liatowitsch, David Todd Ocvirk
Tags – Slasher / Survival

A group of people gather at a house to conduct an experiment on human behavior. What they don't realize is that the house is rigged with traps and there is a killer inside. And now the house has been sealed to prevent escape. I figured upon another low budget slasher flick devoid of any talent and existing only to take up space here, but I was wrong. And it's movies like this that make me watch low budget dreck, because I know eventually, through all of the crap, something good will come along. This movie is not particularly well acted, but the direction is pretty good, and the story manages to have some original material to it. But it's the FX and kills that really make this movie stand out. Lots of blood and guts and a good variety to the murders made this movie what it is. And a guest appearance by immortal scream queen Linnea Quigley doesn't hurt either. Good fun.

3.5/5

Lady in the Water
Year – 2006
Director – M. Night Shyamalan
Tags – Monsters

An apartment complex maintenance man finds a woman in the swimming pool, and she tells him tales about mankind and her kind, and also of the monsters who want nothing more than to see her dead. This movie is built like a fairytale for adults, complete with monsters and fantastical creatures, and its all set in the modern day, and in a normal place. This could have been really cool but to be honest, the story just isn't that good. The characters are far from being stereotypical, which I really appreciate, but the problem is that they just aren't that good and often times they don't fit into the situation they are supposed to. The story also seems to just be made up as the movie goes along, there are way too many instances of convenience and oh, by the way, this happens so that makes this happen and now the problem is solved. The idea is sound but the way the story unfolds is just plain crap. The acting and direction are very good however, so this movie isn't a total loss. The creature design is also a little underwhelming as I feel a lot more thought could have gone into the final product. I really wanted to like this because it does sound cool, but a contrived story really shot this movie down for me.

2/5

Lady Vengeance (Chinjeolhan Geumjassi)
Year – 2005
Director – Chan-Wook Park
Tags – Suspense

A woman is forced into confessing to the kidnapping and murder of a five year old boy, and after thirteen years in prison, she is released whereupon she begins her very intricate revenge scheme. After seeing Oldboy I was expecting another good movie, but never did I think it would be this damn good. The man is just a genius. The story is nothing short of brilliant and later in the movie when the plot thickens, it manages to get even better. At first I didn't like the style of filmmaking where the timeline of the movie bounced around, but once I learned who all the players were the style really grew on me. The acting was incredible and the direction was near perfect. This isn't just your typical revenge flick, and this film is nothing short of remarkable.

4.5/5

Lake Dead
Year – 2007
Director – George Bessudo
Tags – Slasher / Survival

Three sisters are left a motel and some land by a grandfather they never knew, and when they go to see their new property, they find a twisted family waiting for them in the woods. If you have ever seen The Texas Chainsaw Massacre, The Hills Have Eyes, Wrong Turn, and similar movies, then you've seen this movie and you've seen it done better. This movie follows the same formula as those I mentioned and really doesn't offer up anything new. The acting is bad, the direction is ok, the FX are decent, but there aren't many on camera kills so it doesn't really matter. This is a completely watchable movie and does have a couple of cool scenes, but for the most part it's just another slasher flick and a time killer at best.

2/5

Lake Placid
Year – 1999
Director – Steve Miner
Tags – Animals

Residents of a small Maine town discover that a giant crocodile resides in their lake. Experts are then called in to deal with the problem. So the premise is pretty ridiculous, and sensing that, this movie was made into a horror/comedy. Betty White spewing out filthy expletives is priceless, and there are a few more funny moments that make this movie work for the most part. On the other hand, the movie also tends to get a bit too cornball at times. The animatronic croc looks great and the CGI one is ok. The movie can get a bit slow at times, relying too much on comedy that only works half the time. Still, the movie is entertaining and does have some great moments, but they are too spread out to make this movie really worthwhile.

2.5/5

Lake Placid 2
Year – 2007
Director – David Flores
Tags – Animals

This movie, while billed as a sequel, plays out more like a remake as the stories are nearly identical and there are only trace elements linking it to the first. Terrible doesn't even really begin to describe this movie, but let me get to the good stuff. Cloris Leachman takes over for Betty White and is kind of funny, and the only real actor in the movie. Now onto the bad. All of the other actors range from bad to some of the worst I have ever had the displeasure of watching. The FX are definitely some of the worst ever made as well, I'm serious. When the cartoon alligator comes toward people, the water doesn't even ripple, how lame is that? And the direction sucks to boot. As I stated earlier, this is just a rehash of the original sans good actors and funny moments. I'll give a point for Leachman but everything else is trash.

1/5

Lakeview Terrace
Year – 2008
Director – Neil LaBute
Tags – Suspense

A racist cop has issues with the interracial couple that moved next door to him which culminates in a war between the neighbors, but the couple has no one on their side and the cop has the entire LAPD. I think this movie came along a little too late to be anything poignant. Interracial couples just don't feel the social stigma like they used to nowadays. The story isn't bad but it's pretty weak and has a completely unrealistic ending, like painfully unrealistic. Fortunately the acting is very good and the direction moves along nicely which makes up for the glaring issues in the script. While hardly a mind blowing thriller or even a competent one, Lakeview Terrace is definitely a good watch and has its entertainment value.

3/5

Land of the Dead
Year – 2005
Director – George A. Romero
Tags – Zombies

In this fourth Romero zombie movie we find the dead have completely dominated the world and here in a city barricaded against them, a social order plays out crueler than the walking dead themselves. Romero's social commentary here is just a blatant slap in the face instead of subtle introduction we have seen from him previously, and that does make the movie come off a little overly preachy. But the zombie aspect of the movie is as good as ever. The zombies continue to outnumber the living by even more staggering numbers and they continue to evolve as well. There's great gore but there is also the use of CGI blood, and that never really looks good. Everything practical looks great, but the CGI? Yeah, not so much. This is still an awesome zombie movie and I enjoyed it a great deal. It sure is nice to see the master of the undead come back after a long absence to give his fans more zombie action.

3.5/5

Langoliers, The
Year – 1995

Director – Tom Holland
Tags – Monsters

A group of people awaken on an airplane to find that most everyone on board has disappeared. When they land they find an empty airport in an empty town and everything appears to have been deserted. But then they hear a noise from far away, but it's getting closer, and something is coming for them. This is probably one of the most accurate adaptations I've ever seen, it's just spot on with the Stephen King novella. I like the story and the idea behind it, but it is rather uneventful for the most part. When the monsters do finally arrive we are also subjected to some very bad CGI. It runs long but manages to stay interesting most of the time because at its heart the movie is really a mystery. The acting isn't the best either, but it's not bad. At the end of the day The Langoliers is an entertaining movie and something different that probably would have been much smoother as a two hour movie in a theatre than a three hour miniseries.

3/5

Last Broadcast, The
Year – 1998
Director – Stefan Avalos, Lance Weiler
Tags – Suspense

This faux documentary chronicles the last moments of a group of people traveling into the Pine Barrens to search for the Jersey Devil, who would later be found dead, all except for one, who would be accused of killing them. This is a well done movie with a fairly interesting story that comes together well in the cinema verite style. The acting is natural for the most part but not entirely well done, and the same goes for the direction. You can tell this is a microbudget effort but it doesn't hinder the movie that much at all. The movie is well constructed up until the last ten minutes or so when things get pretty silly. I can see what they were trying to go for but it didn't really work. Still, this is a very good movie and it really does feel like a documentary until the end hits and I enjoyed it quite a bit overall.

3.5/5

Last House in the Woods, The (Il Bosco Fuori)
Year – 2006
Director – Gabriele Albanesi
Tags – Slasher / Survival

A couple arguing through an already strained relationship are attacked by a trio of men on the side of a seldom used road. They are saved by another couple, only to be thrown into a more dangerous situation. This is meant to be an homage/throwback to the Italian horror of yesteryear, but what it ends up being instead is an affront to the genre. The story is rubbish and the direction is terrible. The movie is just plain boring and uninteresting. The acting sucks as well. The one thing this movie does have going for it is some gore, but the violence is badly choreographed and you really see more aftermath than actual killing. This is just a bad movie, plain and simple, and buckets of blood and entrails don't make it much better.

1.5/5

Last House on the Left, The
Year – 1972
Director – Wes Craven
Tags – Suspense

Two girls go into the city for a rock concert and instead get kidnapped by two escaped criminals and their cohorts. I'll leave the synopsis there for spoiler's sake. This movie does have some fairly graphic sequences of murder and rape so the viewer must prepare for that. I like this movie a great deal, but for some strange reason, Wes Craven seemed to back off and try to lighten the mood, which was stupid. If you're going to make a movie like this, you go all the way, you don't wimp out and put in sections of comedy and happy music, because they just don't fit and they take you out of the experience. Fortunately there aren't many occasions of that happening, but when they did, it certainly killed the dark ambiance that had been building. And FYI, this is a quasi remake of the movie The Virgin Spring, but adopts the concept more than the actual movie. This is a somber look at the darkness that is present in the human heart, but it's just too bad the movie flinched, because it could have been an all time masterpiece.

4/5

Last Man on Earth, The
Year – 1964
Director – Ubaldo Ragona
Tags – Vampires

Based on the Richard Matheson novel "I Am Legend", this movie follows one man in a world that has been destroyed by infection, killing most people and turning the rest into vampires. He spends his days gathering supplies and staking the undead creatures, all while dealing with his intense loneliness. It takes one hell of an actor to pull off a role like this, and Vincent Price is the right man for the job. The story though, could have been a lot better. I know that Richard Matheson was involved in writing the screenplay and disliked it so much that he refused to put his name on it, and I can tell why. The story just isn't up to snuff and could have been a whole lot better, and as a result, the direction suffers a bit as well. The vampires are also rather zombie like, which I have mixed feelings about. But I still liked the movie, even though I thought the filmmakers could have done more with it. It's worth watching for Price's tour de force performance alone.

3/5

Last Winter, The

Year – 2006
Director – Larry Fessenden
Tags – [Hidden to conceal spoilers]

An oil company is working in Alaska in the hopes of making America non-dependant of foreign oil. But while a small team resides there, some environmental changes appear to have unleashed something deadly. The movie sounded interesting to me, but it's not. It ends up coming off as one big environment PSA and that's pretty lame. The acting is great and completely wasted on fluff like this. The direction is a mix of beautiful shots and horrendous pacing, making for a pretty, but boring movie, or maybe it's just pretty boring. There is also some cool practical FX work, with less than spectacular CGI. This is a strange movie because it seems as though whenever it has something going for it, it has something bad to counterbalance it. I wish I had good things to say, but there just aren't enough to make this a good movie.

2/5

Lawnmower Man, The
Year – 1992
Director – Brett Leonard
Tags – Suspense

A scientist uses a simple minded man in a series of experiments involving a special drug and virtual reality. But as the tests go on and his intelligence increases, he starts to gain frightening powers. I think its funny how Stephen King's name was removed from the movie after a lawsuit because this story has literally nothing to do with the short story it was meant to be based on. I've seen people take a lot of liberties with an original story but to leave nothing left of the original story at all is pretty funny. Anyway, the new story here is ok but nothing special and the direction is about the same. It moves along nicely but doesn't wow me in the least. The acting is good though, especially by Jeff Fahey who puts on a very remarkable performance, too bad he never received the work he deserved to get after this. The FX in the movie are easily just some of the worst ever. I mean bad. But in a way they're also kind of fun because they are just so damn silly. This is a good movie, nothing I would call badly done per se, but it definitely doesn't go beyond being good either.

3/5

Lawnmower Man 2: Jobe's War, The
Year – 1996
Director – Farhad Mann
Tags – Suspense

This movie picks up right after the last one left off, sort of. If this isn't on the list of worst movies ever made, there is something wrong with this world. It isn't just a bad sequel, it's a bad movie. Everything about it is complete garbage. The acting is terrible, the story is absolute shit, and the direction is horrendous. The FX manage to be worse than the original as well. I think the biggest tragedy of all with this movie is that the people behind it were allowed to keep working. I have seen a lot of painful movies in my time but none in recent memory have sucked as hard as this one. If this isn't the worst movie ever made then it comes very close.

0.5/5

Leatherface: The Texas Chainsaw Massacre 3
Year – 1990
Director – Jeff Burr
Tags – Slasher / Survival

This movie kind of ignores the continuity of The Texas Chainsaw Massacre series and sets up a new family in Texas, even though Leatherface is still a part of a family. I don't know about this one, it's a good movie but doesn't fit with the first two movies. The family here is also a little too normal looking to really be the Sawyer family. But aside from the obvious continuity errors, the third movie is a lot of fun. Some good blood and violence, but not many victims this go around, which is kind of a shame. Ken Foree's presence as a survivalist is pretty cool though. The acting is really good, but like I said, the family is too normal, and even Leatherface just doesn't have quite the same qualities as he did in past movies. But the movie is entertaining for sure, and that's what matters the most, especially in the realm of sequels.

3.5/5

Legion of the Dead
Year – 2005
Director – Paul Bales
Tags – Mummies

Archaeologists unearth an Egyptian tomb in California (no double takes, you read that right), and now a 4000 year old priestess has risen to take over the world with her army of mummies. Whoa, what kind of psychedelics was this writer/director on to come up with some crap like this? And where can I get some? Besides the stupid premise we also have to sit through some really bad acting, terrible direction, poor FX work and scene after scene of moronic, nonsensical garbage. This movie is just so silly and awkward you would think a three year old put it together between naps and eating his boogers. If I had to say one positive thing about this movie it would be that I have seen worse, but that's the best I could come up with.

1/5

Leprechaun
Year – 1993
Director – Mark Jones

An Irishman steals a leprechaun's gold and hides it on his property. But the leprechaun does not appreciate the man's actions and seeks him out, killing his wife in the process. The man manages to trap the leprechaun in a crate however, where he stays for years until some hapless people come along and accidently set him free. And he still wants his gold and will get it back by any means necessary. This is a fun movie. I don't think there has been a slasher movie before or since that gave the killer magical powers, so that's pretty cool. The story is good but very much like a traditional slasher movie in how it unfolds so you can pretty much guess how it will play out. There's also a ton of problems with the fact that this leprechaun has all of these magical powers but is having trouble with some bumbling people. The direction is fine and the acting is typical B movie stuff, which means it isn't that great. But Warwick Davis completely owns the role of the leprechaun and gives the character so much personality that anyone else would be wrong for the role. This isn't anything brilliant but it sure is a fun time.

3.5/5

Leprechaun 2
Year – 1994
Director – Rodman Flender
Tags – Slasher / Survival

The Leprechaun returns and this time he's looking for a bride, and more gold of course. The first movie was so bad that it was entertaining, this one is just bad. From the bad actors, aside from Warwick Davis, to the incredibly slow direction, this movie kind of blows. It does have some good kills, but it's too bad most of them are off camera. And it does have a couple of laughs, so I guess it's not all bad. The story wasn't bad either but it wasn't nearly as fun as the original. It's not like Leprechaun was a classic genre defining film, but I think it deserved a better sequel than this.

2/5

Leprechaun 3
Year – 1995
Director – Brian Trenchard-Smith
Tags – Slasher / Slasher

Here the Leprechaun takes on Las Vegas and searches the strip for his missing gold. This one was actually pretty good. The acting is only minutely better in this one than the last one, but the direction is much better and the movie moves along smoother. The story has its good points but the leprechaun's rhyming was really bad this time around so whoever wrote the dialogue won't be writing any hit songs anytime soon. There was a little bit of nudity and some bloodier shows this time around, which really helped the movie out. This may not be anything great but at least it's better than the last one.

Leprechaun 4: In Space
Year – 1997
Director – Brian Trenchard-Smith
Tags – Slasher / Survival

Yep, he's in space this time. Set far into the future the leprechaun is attempting to wed an alien princess… eh, the rest doesn't matter. I liked the last movie and when I saw this was by the same director, I had good hopes for it, despite it sounding so stupid. But it was stupid, and worse than I ever could have imagined. The story is probably the worst I have ever come across, and that's really saying something. I'd rather watch a thousand generic slashers in a row then deal with this garbage again. Beyond the terrible story we have some incredibly terrible acting, I mean really bad. The practical FX have some interesting moments but the CGI is god awful. Even further issues include the fact the leprechaun doesn't even rhyme in this movie, all the dialogue is horrible, and when it comes time for some random breast bearing, you just want her to cover them back up. If it wasn't for some genuinely good FX work, I would have called this movie worthless. This is an occasion where I really do want my hour and a half back.

1/5

Leprechaun 5: In the Hood
Year – 2000
Director – Rob Spera
Tags – Slasher / Survival

Yep, he's in the hood this time and looking for his magic flute which was stolen by some rappers trying to make it big. The story is so stupid that it's pretty funny, and that's just part of what makes this the best Leprechaun sequel yet. And I know that's really not saying much, but this movie features some good acting, some genuinely hilarious bits and some pretty solid direction. Now, I hate rap music so I hated the rap aspect of the movie, but the Leprechaun's rap at the end was kind of amusing. Everything else is more of the same, but this is a movie in the series that I actually consider to be good.

3/5

Leprechaun 6: Back 2 tha Hood
Year – 2003
Director – Stephen Ayromlooi
Tags – Slasher / Survival

Now the Leprechaun goes back to the hood (Notice how I spelled that correctly?), and here some people have stolen his gold after he was imprisoned and now he's free and looking for his treasure. The last movie was pretty good and I was afraid they were just going to rehash it here, but I'm really glad they didn't. The story was much different but played out well, not as funny as the last one but more solid overall. The acting is pretty good again and the direction is equivalent to the last effort. In some ways I actually like this one better than the last one, or at least it's as good. It was good to the point that now I actually want a seventh Leprechaun movie. Maybe they'll go with Warwick Davis's idea of the Leprechaun versus pirates, which would be brilliant, or maybe a prequel in medieval times. In the Leprechaun series, the possibilities are endless.

3/5

Leviathan
Year – 1989
Director – George P. Cosmatos
Tags – Sea Monsters, Infection

An underwater mining team happens across a sunken Russian boat and brings something from it on board. That something alters people's genes, turning them into sea monsters. The infection is spreading through the station, and with the crew transforming into these beasts, they have more to worry about than just sickness. Leviathan is awesome for one main reason: Stan Winston created the monster FX. The creatures look cool as hell. The cast does a great job here, and the sets and props look great as well. It does take awhile for anything of significance to happen though, and the pacing could have definitely been better. This movie can easily be compared to others but I believe what sets it apart is that humans become the monsters instead just happening across some creature deep in the ocean. Worth a watch for the amazing creature FX alone.

3.5/5

Lifeforce
Year – 1985
Director – Tobe Hooper
Tags – Vampires

An American and British joint research venture travel into deep space to investigate Haley's Comet. What they find is a spaceship in the head of the comet, and inside are three people in stasis. They bring the people aboard the shuttle, and soon after they are never heard from again. But the government manages to retrieve the mysterious cargo and find that the people are not human at all, but a soul sucking vampire alien race. This movie is much cooler than it sounds. It sounds like absolute cheese but since it's handled in a serious manner, it actually makes the movie much more compelling than you would think. The story is pretty awesome, especially during the second half, but it's just too bad the movie is overly long and thus fairly dull. Fortunately it picks up the pace quite well after the first half. The FX are awesome and I especially enjoyed the puppetry of the vampire victims. The acting is very good as well and it was nice to see some people with talent. A surprisingly well done sci-fi/horror flick with a unique story. It has some flaws, but nothing to detract too much from my overall enjoyment.

3.5/5

Lightning Bug
Year – 2004
Director – Robert Hall
Tags – Horror Related

A boy wishes to become an FX artist in Hollywood, working on horror movies. This is a coming of age tale where he must overcome an alcoholic mother, abusive stepfather, religious fanatics and a fragile young love to reach his dreams. This movie is just absolutely perfect, and I think that's because the director is actually an FX artist, so he fully grasped the passion that drives the storyline. I can only image how tough it would be to have a dream that would not be so well received in a small town. Between his stepfather calling him a fag and the townspeople calling him a devil worshipper, it's a wonder he didn't just give up. This movie is about as dark as it comes, almost a horror movie itself. The relationship he has with the local video store clerk / Goth girl is really the most fascinating and at the same time, heartbreaking plot point in the whole movie. The acting is incredible, the direction is remarkable, and the story is perfection. This is one of the best movies I have ever seen, hands down.

5/5

Little Girl Who Lives Down the Lane, The
Year – 1976
Director – Nicholas Gessner
Tags – Suspense

A suspicious thirteen year old girl seems to do as she wishes in her young life without objection from her father, who is always conveniently busy or away when an adult wants to talk to him. But she is comfortable in her life and will do anything to keep it the way she wants. This is strange little film for many reasons. Maybe it was the underage girl nude scene or Martin Sheen playing a very brash pedophile but the whole movie is just plain weird and I like that. It shows that the filmmakers were going for something different, as to whether or not it worked is still up for debate in my mind. The story was good but lacked a truly cohesive nature to make it work. Sometimes things happen in the movie that are just senseless, and only happen for the sake of being weird, having little or no bearing on current events. But the acting is tremendous and the direction is great. This is a strange movie that will undoubtedly be disturbing for casual viewers but to me it's just a very good thriller.

3.5/5

Loch Ness Terror (Beyond Loch Ness)
Year – 2008
Director – Paul Ziller
Tags – Sea Monsters

A cryptozoologist, who as a boy witnessed his father being killed by the Loch Ness Monster, tracks the creature to a US lake (actually filmed in Canada) and teams up with local police in an attempt to kill it. The idea behind the movie isn't the greatest, diving blatantly into B movie waters and not having the humor or cheese factor to back it up, but that being said, it's not a bad movie at all. The problem is that it takes itself too seriously, much like Brian Krause as the cryptozoologist. The design of Nessie is cool looking, but the CGI in this movie is absolutely terrible. The kills are also surprisingly gory, but too many of them are that same terrible CGI. The pacing is good, but could've been better, and the acting is decent as well. What we're left with is a decent enough sea monster movie, much better than I expected, but not anything really special.

2.5/5

Lord of Illusions
Year – 1995
Director – Clive Barker
Tags – Cults

This is the story of a place where magic is real, and where people can wield it in wonderful and terrible ways. One such man began a cult, and deserters of the cult returned to stop him, bind him, and place him in the ground forever. But the leader still has faithful followers, and now they are trying to resurrect him. Clive Barker is a great writer, and when he steps behind the camera, something great usually becomes the end result. This is also the case here with a somewhat flawed but original and engaging movie. The movie, while a bit disjointed, is an interesting ride. The CGI is your typical cheesy 90's era stuff, and as usual the practical FX outshines it. The visuals are great and have that Barker touch. The story, also done by Barker is excellent, but as I said, it does have its flaws, and that does prevent it from reaching the legendary status of other Barker movies. Still pretty great, don't get me wrong, but could have benefitted from more polish.

3.5/5

Lost, The
Year – 2006
Director – Chris Sivertson
Tags – Suspense

Based on a Jack Ketchum novel that is based on a true life crime, The Lost is about a young man who decided to murder two young girls one day for fun. Having never been caught for the crime, he thinks himself something pretty special, but in reality his madness just grows every day, which culminates into one of the most shocking crimes in US history. Consider Ketchum adaptations to be two for two now. This is just an incredibly well performed movie. The movie is a slow burn and flows smoothly. The acting is incredible, especially by Marc Senter who plays the main character with such passion that I'm sure he'll either go on to great things or be forever typecast like so many that came before him. While The Girl Next Door was a very graphic and disturbing movie, this one is more so. The violence, while of a different nature, is even more graphic and bloody here, and I must say the ending really blew me away. Not your typical ending here, it is definitely more akin to what would happen in real life, which makes sense since this is based on a real crime. This is a remarkable indie film that shows a lot of talent from everyone involved.

4.5/5

Lost Boys, The
Year – 1987
Director – Joel Schumacher
Tags – Vampires

A mother and her two teenage sons move to the "Murder Capital of the World", Santa Carla, California after a divorce. The younger son gets together with a couple of self proclaimed vampire hunters, while the other unknowingly falls in league with the vampires themselves. Now to save his brother from the vampire curse, the younger one must team up with the Frog Brothers to eliminate the vampire clan. The Lost Boys is a teen horror flick, and really sets the tone for all teen horror movies that come after it, too bad none have really reached the mark that this movie has set. It's just perfectly done, it flows like blood, it stars a great young cast, the story is well written, it's well shot, the vampire make-up is subtle, which works wonders, and the seminal soundtrack just compliments every scene. One of, if not the greatest vampire movie ever. They did it right, too bad even twenty plus years later, there is still not a teen horror movie as competent as this.

5/5

Lost Boys II: The Tribe, The
Year – 2008
Director – P.J. Pesce
Tags – Vampires

This takes place many years after the original and doesn't have very much to do with that movie. If any movie didn't need a sequel it was The Lost Boys. Here's the formula for the sequel: Take the original Lost Boys, keep this one pretty much the same, but add more gore and sex. Next, take out the really cool soundtrack and replace it with a really bad one. Then replace the cool vampires with really lame TV show Buffy vampires who play too many video games and emulate Jackass. Sprinkle in some bad acting and a borderline annoying female lead, and you have Lost Boys II: The Tribe. All that being said, it really wasn't that bad, calling it an average movie may be a little generous but I will leave it as such. It's insulting to have this movie bear the Lost Boys name, because it does not have nearly the same heart or atmosphere. But as a vampire movie, you're looking at a mediocre horror version of Laguna Beach, or the OC or some other equally horrible show. I can not solidly recommend it, but I can say that it does have some nice gore and Corey Feldman does a nice job as Edgar Frog. Remember how he was in the original? Cheesy and fun? Same thing here, good job Corey. And revealing anything else would be a spoiler. It has its entertainment value, but not much beyond that.

2.5/5

Lost Highway
Year – 1997
Director – David Lynch
Tags – Suspense

A jazz musician and his wife, along with a young mechanic, a mob boss and his main squeeze have their lives intersect in a shroud of mystery and suspense. There's no concrete story here to give you a synopsis, rather this is a very surreal and nightmarish movie that doesn't make complete sense, but that's just part of its beauty. By this point in the book I'm sure you realize that I find dark things to be very lovely indeed, and this film is very dark indeed. This is aided by the well constructed soundtrack that is easily one of my favorites. I was disappointed not to see This Mortal Coil's "Song to the Siren" on the actual CD, as its usage was the high point in the movie and was played during some of the best cinematography I've ever seen. But oh well, I have it elsewhere. Anyway, off topic. The story is far from being straightforward, but it's just fascinating to watch. The acting is great and the direction is masterful, making for one of the most unique and darkly gorgeous movies I have ever had the pleasure to witness.

4.5/5

Love Object
Year – 2003
Director – Robert Parigi
Tags – Suspense

A lonely man orders a realistic sex doll for his own personal pleasure and ends up treating it like a real woman. It begins to consume his mind and causes him to do things he wouldn't normally do. When he finds a real woman he has trouble severing his ties to the doll. I love this movie because it's just so damn twisted. The way it plays out is so weird and at times so embarrassing that I couldn't turn away. And when the movie hits its climax, I was blown away. The direction is awesome and supported by some terrific acting. This is a great thriller that just oozes originality and has a terrific dark sense of humor. I wouldn't change much with this movie, it's just good stuff. And how can you not love that plot?

4/5

Lurking Fear
Year – 1994

Director – C. Courtney Joyner
Tags – Monsters

This H.P. Lovecraft adaptation showcases the town of Leffert's Corners and the Martense family, a group of otherworldly creatures who feed upon the townsfolk, and now there aren't many left. And on the night that the remaining few fight back, another group comes along looking for buried treasure. Lovecraft fanboys will no doubt take issue with this movie, as it is not exactly a true adaptation, but I found it to be a good movie that just happens to be riddled with flaws. The acting isn't very good, but a couple of genre vets do star here and pick up the slack. The direction is pretty good and keeps things moving along nicely. The Martense family really does look awesome though, like some twisted subterranean zombies. There is some blood but not enough in my opinion, had the movie been drenched with gore, it certainly would have made for a better flick. And the creatures do take a backseat to the crime aspect of the story, which is a shame because the creatures are much more interesting. I still liked it though, I just wish there had been more… of everything.

3/5

Machinist, The
Year – 2004
Director – Brad Anderson
Tags – Suspense

A man who hasn't slept in a year and continues to lose weight at a rapid rate begins to question his own sanity as strange occurrences in his life just don't add up. This is major achievement of a movie right here. Seriously, the story alone makes this movie worth watching, but when you add the incredible skills of the director and the amazing cast, you have solid gold. Christian Bale in particular is astounding in his role, not just for his acting ability but for his physical transformation into the emaciated machinist. I don't want to say too much for fear of giving away any key points in the story that could reveal the remarkable plot twist, so I'll just say that this is a top notch thriller and if you're a fan of suspense films then you should never miss this.

4.5/5

Malevolence
Year – 2004
Director – Stevan Mena
Tags – Slasher / Survival

After a robbery doesn't go quite as planned, a quartet of thieves head off to the countryside with two hostages, but instead of getting away with their crime, they come across a crazed local with murder on his mind. This low budget movie isn't like most of the slashers I've seen, as this one actually has a story and some drama behind it. The actors weren't the best I've seen but they were pretty damn good, especially for a low budget movie. The direction was great and well paced as well. One problem I had with this movie was the overly loud score and attempts at jump scares because this movie is better than that and it was kind of annoying. I would have also liked to see more gore but it was still good the way it was. This is a very good slasher movie and I'd like to see what this guy can do with an actual budget.

3.5/5

Man-Thing
Year – 2005
Director – Brett Leonard
Tags – Monsters

Based on the Marvel comic book, this movie focuses on a wealthy land owner who drills for oil in the sacred area of an ancient swamp, unleashing a killer beast of lore. People may be interested to know that the Man-Thing character was created before the much more popular Swamp Thing in comic form. This movie definitely got the low budget treatment with bottom barrel actors and an under the barrel script. Seriously, the story in this movie is just plain terrible and includes one of those obligatory love interest side stories, which serves no purpose whatsoever. The movie is also pretty damn slow as well. There are some good aspects though, like the Man-Thing does look pretty freakin' awesome, and there's a fair amount of blood as well. This could have been a whole lot better, but to be honest, I'm surprised to see a Man-Thing movie at all.

2/5

Mangler, The
Year – 1995
Director – Tobe Hooper
Tags – Mechanical

After a grisly death at the local laundry, a local cop does not like it being called an accident and decides to investigate further. What he finds is that the giant laundry folder may be possessed by a demonic force and is killing people on purpose. Wow, what an idea. Whatever Stephen King was smoking when he wrote this story must have been awesome, and I want two cases of it. But seriously, I liked the short story but the screenplay stretched it so wafer thin that it just gets ridiculous. And to stretch it to an hour and half run time would be difficult, but this movie is even longer. The acting ranges from very good to really bad but fortunately the good performances are in the lead roles. The direction is good but the script really kills the pacing. At least there are a few awesome gore shots. This movie is just silly but I did find it to be somewhat appealing and not really that bad. Maybe this should have been an anthology piece instead of a feature length movie, as it would have made for a more entertaining time.

2.5/5

Mangler 2, The
Year – 2001
Director – Michael Hamilton-Wright
Tags – Mechanical

This one has nothing to do with the previous movie and instead focuses on a computer virus that infects a private school's computer system and turns it against the students and faculty that remained on campus after everyone else had gone. So The Mangler wasn't exactly a brilliant movie, but it was fun, this on the other hand definitely makes my list of worst horror movies ever. There are no actors here except for Lance Henriksen, and they even spelled his name wrong in the credits. Probably the most glaring issue with the movie is the infamous missing scene. Some kids are running through the school and then the next thing you know, they're outside and crying about the kid who just died. What?! How could they release this movie with a missing scene like that? The acting sucks, the direction is terrible, the story is rubbish and there is a severe lack of blood and nudity. Those issues alone would make this movie worthless, but when there's even more wrong with it beyond those issues, that takes this movie to whole new level of crap.

0.5/5

Mangler Reborn, The
Year – 2005
Director – Matt Cunningham, Erik Gardner
Tags – Mechanical

A man becomes obsessed with building a machine and then begins kidnapping people to feed to it. What is it with people making a sequel when the previous movie is so wretched, and then aiming so low it only ends up being marginally better than the previous piece of trash? That statement was never truer than with this unbelievable sore that is The Mangler Reborn. Reggie Bannister is the only actor here and everyone else is really bad. The story is just plain stupid and the direction is painfully slow and boring. Forty-five minutes could have easily been cut out of the movie. There is some good gore but not enough to make this anything worthwhile.

1/5

Manhunter
Year – 1986
Director – Michael Mann
Tags – Serial Killer (Fictional)

An FBI specialist tracks down a serial killer who viciously murders entire families at random. I like this movie mainly because it does something different, and that is that it gives the killer a face and follows him throughout his daily life, instead of just showing him at the end of the movie after all of the clues have been solved. And speaking of the killer, Tom Noonan does a wonderful job at making him not only cold and calculated, but actually human as well. Don't worry, that's not a spoiler, the movie lays out who everyone is. The acting is excellent all round, but Noonan especially deserves credit. The direction is good but the movie does lag at times which makes me believe that it could have been shorter to make it run smoother. The story is great, no complaint there. This is just a great movie all over that could have been a bit better, but as it is this is still a very good watch.

3.5/5

Maniac Cop
Year – 1988
Director – William Lustig
Tags – Slasher / Survival

A cop, or someone dressed up as one, is loose in New York City, killing innocent people. Another cop is framed for his crimes and now he must find a way to expose the truth before the Maniac Cop can kill again. This is a good time, mainly because I think a cop killing random people is a fun idea. I especially liked that at the height of panic created by the killer, people turn on the police because they are so afraid of whom the Maniac Cop might be. The acting ranges from good to bad but the cast does have a couple of genre vets in it, so it kind of balances itself out. The direction is pretty good but the movie definitely has some pacing issues. The kills are alright but they do lack variety. This is a very good slasher flick from an era that was so chock full of them it was ridiculous, and the great story really sets it apart from all the others. Recommended for fans of the sub genre.

3.5/5

Maniac Cop 2
Year – 1990
Director – William Lustig
Tags – Slasher / Survival

This movie picks up right after the last one. The original was a cool movie, but I never expect too much from sequels, so imagine my surprise when this one surpassed the original. The story is a brilliant progression from the first and it plays out in a multitude of great ways, some rather unexpected as well. The acting is overall a bit better as well. The direction is still about the same, so nothing wrong there. Add a much higher body count, more blood and some nudity and you have yourself a pretty damn good movie. Maniac Cop 2 actually tops the original and makes me appreciate the first that much more.

4/5

Maniac Cop 3: Badge of Silence
Year – 1993

Director – William Lustig, Joel Soisson
Tags – Slasher / Survival

This movie picks up where the last one left off. The first Maniac Cop was good fun, the second was even better, and this one, well, it's actually good too. I really expected this franchise to fail at some point but it never ceased to entertain me. This is definitely the weakest entry though, and I'll tell you why. The acting is on par with the previous movie but the direction isn't as good, still not bad, but it's missing something. There are two directors credited, one with a good track record and one with a bad track record, so that could be the culprit. The story isn't as strong either but that's almost more than made up for by the end sequence, which is pretty awesome. This time around the Maniac Cop is almost a good guy because he is disposing of some scummy people, but I say almost because some innocents do get caught in the crossfire. This is a pleasing movie and while not great, I really dug it nonetheless.

3/5

Manticore
Year – 2005
Director – Tripp Reed
Tags – Monsters

Some US soldiers in Iraq are sent to a far off village to rescue a reporter and her cameraman and instead find a mythological creature with an insatiable hunger for human flesh. Ah, the Sci-Fi Channel original movie, almost guaranteed not to be good from the get-go. The FX are so terrible and I can not fathom why they continuously use these bottom barrel FX companies. The acting is fairly bad but there are a couple of good performances, and that actually hurts the movie because the two best actors survive the longest and that's not a spoiler because it's made way too obvious from the start. The story is actually good to a degree but I can see where it could have been made even better. The direction is pretty bad as well. In addition to the FX being horrible, the design of the Manticore is also really bad and I just don't understand how they could have screwed it up so bad. A Manticore is a lion with wings and a spiny tail, so why does it look like a lame dinosaur? Why didn't it just look like a lion? Stupid. But I shouldn't expect more. It's not all bad but I have a suggestion for the people at the Sci-Fi Channel. Instead of making ten crappy movies, how about you pool your money together and just make one good one?

2/5

Man's Best Friend
Year – 1993
Director – John Lafia
Tags – Animals

When a reporter breaks into an animal research lab trying to get a story that's more than a fluff piece, she unwittingly releases a dog from captivity that has been experimented on with gene splicing, and without its medication, it will be subjected to a psychotic break and begin killing everyone around him. This movie is yet another guilty pleasure for me because even though everything about this movie is so preposterous and stupid, it's just so much fun too. The idea that you could give a dog the strength of a bear, the speed of a cheetah, eyesight of an eagle and more, just has to make you laugh. And when they revealed that it could also act like a chameleon, I just lost it. I need to find a dog that can look like a pile of rags, because that would just be the ultimate. The direction is great, as the movie moves along nicely and kept me interested. The acting isn't bad, just a little overdone. This movie is just stupid entertainment.

3/5

Marebito
Year – 2004
Director – Takashi Shimizu
Tags – [Hidden to conceal spoilers]

A freelance cameraman travels into the tunnels under the city after witnessing a grisly suicide and eventually comes to a place that no human could have built. There he finds a nude girl chained to the wall, and he frees her, taking her with him to his apartment. But that is where is his strange journey only begins. This is a very well made and original film, which is pretty rare to see in the bulk of Asian horror. Finally, something without ghosts and long black hair. The story is such an incredible and multi-faceted construction. There's a lot going that always leads into something else completely different. It's also pretty twisted, making it even more enjoyable. Great direction and acting only add to the entertainment factor. This is easily one of my favorite Asian horror movies for its originality alone, and while not perfect, it still makes for a great time.

4/5

Martin
Year – 1977
Director – George A. Romero
Tags – Vampires

This movie chronicles the life of a young man named Martin, who believes that he is a vampire. He goes around killing young women and drinking their blood, then making their deaths look like suicides. But is he really a vampire or is his mind just twisted? This classic tale from Romero showed that he really is capable of making more than just epic zombie flicks. This modern day gothic story is very engrossing and just fascinating to watch. The way he kills and what he does with his victims is twisted but brilliant. The acting is great and the direction is smooth, although I felt it was pretty slow the first time I watched it, on my second viewing I was completely enthralled. The story is just that good and it leads into a very remarkable ending. This is a vampire/serial killer movie unlike any other and is just a compelling film, period.

4.5/5

Mary Reilly
Year – 1996
Director – Stephen Frears
Tags – Suspense

The classic tale of Dr. Jekyll and Mr. Hyde is told here through the eyes of the doctor's maid, Mary Reilly. I like the idea of pulling background characters to the forefront of stories that have been told multiple times to give it a new perspective, but it didn't quite work here. The way the story has changed and is told differently isn't that good, and it matches the direction, which is fairly slow and plodding. The acting on the other hand is nothing short of exceptional and John Malkovich is the perfect choice to play Dr. Jekyll and Mr. Hyde, it's just a pity that you could barely distinguish the difference between Jekyll and Hyde physically. This is still a good movie, but it's a very underwhelming effort in the end.

3/5

Mary Shelley's Frankenstein
Year – 1994
Director – Kenneth Branagh
Tags – Monsters

This traditional tale tells the story of a man obsessed with cheating death and through his experiments ends up reanimating the dead tissue from several bodies into one hideous beast. He tries to destroy the creature but ends up being stalked by it instead. This movie and Bram Stoker's Dracula hit movie theatres like a one two punch, I just wish this movie would have hit as hard as the aforementioned Dracula. This is a very good movie but with the budget and acting power behind it, it could have been a lot more. The story just doesn't unfold as well here as it did in previous efforts and I think that is the movie's main shortcoming. The acting is very good and the direction is well done, but I really didn't care for the way the monster looked. His stitching just didn't make sense in my opinion. But anyway, I do have some complaints but this is still a very good movie, I'm just a little disappointed by it.

3.5/5

Maximum Overdrive
Year – 1986
Director – Stephen King
Tags – Mechanical

A comet passes by Earth and then suddenly all of the machines in the world gain a mind of their own and attack every human they come across. This movie focuses on a group of people trapped inside a diner by a marauding fleet of trucks. This movie is so campy you can't help but appreciate it. The story is silly and recognizing that, King makes a very entertaining and mindless joy ride. This is the only movie Stephen King has directed to date, and I wish he would do more because he did a damn fine job with this. The movie is paced well and has loads of action. While I am not a big fan of AC/DC, their music does fit the movie very well. The acting is cheesy and overdone, which also fits the movie. And some very nice FX and gore round out a damn fine movie. This is no brilliant masterpiece of the genre but I like it a lot. This movie is good fun and doesn't disappoint in the least.

3.5/5

May
Year – 2002
Director – Lucky McKee
Tags – Suspense

May tells the story of an awkward young woman and her desperate searches to make meaningful connections with people in her life. Never have I felt so uncomfortable watching a movie in my life, and that is the result of unparalleled acting from the lead, Angela Bettis. Her outstanding performance actually made me feel embarrassed for her, and to illicit such emotions in a fictional role is quite astounding. Her performance is helped even more by the masterful direction of McKee, who also wrote the powerful script. The situations May gets into made me yell out loud and squirm in my seat, which very rarely ever happens. The movie is just so masterfully crafted in every way that I just felt like I was there and damn it, I just wanted to give May a hug. There's not a lot I can go into without revealing key aspects of the movie, just suffice to say that this is one of the finest movies I have ever seen, and probably the best performance by anyone that I have ever witnessed. May is a masterpiece, and I can tell you for sure that this is even more than a story of a traumatized woman, when the horror aspect kicks in, it bites down hard and never manages to let go.

5/5

Meat Market
Year – 2000
Director – Brian Clement
Tags – Zombies, Vampires

Two people team up with a trio of vampires and a Mexican wrestler to fight an ever growing army of zombies. This is microbudget horror not quite at its best, but close. The unlikely group of survivors is definitely a new twist and a lot of fun. The FX work here is really pretty good, with lots of gore and the zombies are nice as well. There's a fair amount of nudity here too. The direction tells the story not only from the viewpoint of the rag tag group of survivors but also from multiple other areas as well, which is interesting but it does damage the pacing a bit. The acting isn't the greatest, but we are talking a budget of a couple thousand dollars. This movie shows a lot of creativity and for a microbudget flick, it's a fairly professional job. One of the better zombie movies in an oversaturated market, if you can deal with the budget shortcomings of course.

3/5

Meat Market 2
Year – 2001
Director – Brian Clement
Tags – Zombies, Vampires

This movie continues right after the last one and then progresses further into the zombie apocalypse. I think this is a good progression to the story and pretty sensible if you thin k about it. This movie has pretty much all of the same people behind it as the previous one, so everything is about the same as far as the acting and FX departments. The direction is better here though, and I think the movie benefitted from a more linear and cohesive direction style, rather than the mish mash storytelling of the original. There is also a lot more gore, nudity and just random moments of weirdness, making this movie a bit better than the last one. This is still microbudget horror with budget related shortfalls, but as a movie, I dig it.

3.5/5

Memory
Year – 2006
Director – Bennet Davlin
Tags – Serial Killer (Fictional)

A doctor begins to have flashbacks from before he is born of a masked figure killing little girls. As he tries to unravel the mystery of not only the identity of the killer, but why he is having these visions, he learns far more than he expected. While on some level the subject matter in this movie is way out there, it still makes for a rather entertaining movie. The acting is excellent and the direction is very good with few pacing issues. The story, as I said, is way out there and pretty predictable at times but it makes for an overall enjoyable time. I'll give the movie points for being different and take away just as many for being ridiculous, but I have to say it was a pleasure watching it.

3.5/5

Messengers, The
Year – 2007
Director – Oxide Pang Chun, Danny Pang
Tags – Ghosts

A family moves from the city to the countryside to try their hand at farming, but the land they buy has a checkered past. Wow, that doesn't sound familiar. The main idea behind this movie is that children can see ghosts and believe in them, while adults dismiss their claims. That's what the whole movie is based on, and it's stupid, and not only is it stupid, but it's been explored in other movies. The story just has no power behind it and comes off boring and shallow. The direction and acting also reflect this and are especially stale. The FX work is terrible too, as everything is done with very bad CGI. I wish Sam Raimi would avoid producing generic crap like this and do something good with his fame and wealth, because movies like this are really dragging the Ghost House name through the mud. The movie is not scary, not fun and not interesting.

1/5

Mimic
Year – 1997
Director – Guillermo del Toro
Tags – Monsters

A deadly disease is killing the children of New York, carried by the common cockroach. A bug expert creates a new kind of insect to deal with the cockroaches, one that could kill all of them and then die itself due to infertility. But three years later they find out that the insects did not die, instead they evolved rapidly and became something they never could have imagined. I really like this movie but it does have its share of flaws. The acting is very good but there is just something lacking. No complaints about the story or direction, but the movie did feel a tad long. The FX were good but the CGI was just awful. This is a very nice giant bug / monster movie with great locations but it just came up short of greatness.

3.5/5

Mimic 2
Year – 2001
Director – Jean de Segonzac
Tags – Monsters

This movie continues on an indeterminate amount of time after the last one. The story element of the movie is fairly non-existent, as everything is seemingly thrown together, over explained and just not thought out to its full potential. The clear indications of a rush job. The acting is good though, and the direction isn't too terrible, but there are several pacing issues, especially during the first half of the movie. The FX are definitely a highlight though, because the creatures look pretty cool and there are some nice visuals. This had some potential to be worthwhile if some actual thought had been put into the script, but all we're left with is a below average attempt at a sequel.

2/5

Mimic 3: The Sentinel
Year – 2003
Director – J.T. Petty
Tags – Monsters

Once again, this movie continues on an indeterminate amount of time after the last one. This is only related to the other Mimic movies in a small way, which I guess works for it in a way, seeing as the story was really only good for one movie and it had nowhere to go after that. The story here is better than the last one even though it does tend to borrow heavily from other movies, it's still pretty interesting. The acting is ok and the direction is fairly good, but the FX are pretty bad in this movie. I probably could have done just fine without there having been any sequels to Mimic, but at least this one is better than the last one.

2.5/5

Miner's Massacre (Curse of the Forty-Niner)
Year – 2002
Director – John Carl Buechler
Tags – Slasher / Survival

A group of friends head to a gold mine hoping to strike it rich but instead find a resurrected miner who was awakened by another friend and is now trying to kill everyone who gets too close to his gold. Who does this guy think he is, Leprechaun? Here we have yet another low budget slasher flick that shows little promise and still doesn't manage to deliver to low expectations. Bad acting, slow direction, unimpressive kills and not much blood either. This movie somehow does everything wrong. This is a bad movie but I do have to say that it is at least watchable, and when I have seen movies that were literally painful to sit through, this one at least was at least an easy watch to the end.

1.5/5

Misery
Year – 1990
Director – Rob Reiner
Tags – Suspense

In this Stephen King adaptation we find a writer forced off the road by a blizzard and staring into the eyes of certain death. But he ends up being saved from his mangled car by none other than his self proclaimed number one fan. As she takes him to her secluded farmhouse and begins to nurse him back to health, it quickly becomes apparent that she may not be quite right in the head. This is a King adaptation that works, and it works in large part to the brilliance that is Kathy Bates. I mean she didn't win a Golden Globe AND an Oscar for nothing. She is absolutely perfect in this role, and she had to be because the story depends so much upon her mania. Everyone else does a terrific job as well, but she simply steals the show. This movie is so chock full of tension you just can't wait to see what happens next. I really can not say anything bad about Misery, as it is definitely an accomplishment in suspenseful cinema.

4.5/5

Mist, The
Year – 2007
Director – Frank Darabont
Tags – Monsters

After an intense storm in a small New England town, a man and his son travel with their neighbor into town for supplies. A strange mist is crawling across the lake from the mountains, and by the time it reaches town, all hell breaks loose, and our main characters find themselves trapped in a grocery store. Inside the mist are Lovecraftian type creatures from another world, hungry for flesh and blood. With the modern world as they know it dissolving, order gives way to chaos as religious mania and a loss of rationality become the standard. The Mist is a novella by Stephen King, and it has always been one of my favorite written works. And in a truly rare event, Frank Darabont has not only done it justice, but managed to actually improve upon it. There was one part of the story I never liked and he took it out, he fleshed out smaller sequences, and he added just one of the most mind blowing endings I have ever seen. The cast does an extraordinary job, Thomas Jane especially eats up the screen, but everyone is exceptional. So the CGI may be a little lacking when you can fully see the monsters in the light, but this is a fairly low budget film for Hollywood. Really that is my only complaint, and it is very minor. This is one of the best adaptations I have ever seen, if not the best, and just one of the best movies ever as well. The mixture of a terrifying scenario with absolutely horrifying beasts, and add to that the human drama as well, and you have an absolute masterpiece. A must see.

5/5

Monster
Year – 2003
Director – Patty Jenkins
Tags – Serial Killer

Monster chronicles the life an exploits of prostitute turned serial killer, Aileen Wuornos, who would kill her johns and rob them. Charlize Theron is perfection in this movie, the physical transformation alone is noteworthy, but she really pulls out one hell of a performance here. The movie itself is pretty good, but I do think that their portrayal of Wuornos is a bit one-sided. While she was undoubtedly a victim herself, her crimes are almost glorified here, which just doesn't work in the context of the movie. I just think the director tried too hard to get people to care about her, and show the audience that she tried to mend her ways, to no avail. This was overdone to some degree, and there are just so many instances of her being human that I started to feel she wasn't even real. Still, it's well done besides the obligatory push for concern toward Wuornos, and an excellent portrayal of a rare female serial killer.

3.5/5

Monster Squad, The
Year – 1987
Director – Fred Dekker
Tags – Vampires, Werewolves, Mummies, Monsters

A group of kids obsessed with monster movies find out that Dracula and the rest of the Universal monsters have joined together to destroy an ancient amulet that holds back the powers of darkness. I watched this movie about a hundred times as a kid and never got tired of it. Now as an adult I can watch it again and it makes even more sense to me. This is a children's movie at heart but has a distinct edge to it that really will appeal to adults. The concept is great because it's essentially a horror version of The Goonies. The script and direction are great, and the movie flows with an ease that is pretty damn remarkable. The creature FX created by Stan Winston himself are the real highlight as he had a ton of work put ahead of him and he really gave each monster a great deal of care and personality all their own. The acting is also incredibly good, which is especially poignant seeing as how most of the main cast is comprised of children. This is a near perfect movie that shows a lot of talent and just a love for the genre by everyone involved. Sweet, funny, infinitely quotable and full of monsters. I couldn't ask for much more, except maybe a sequel.

4.5/5

Mortuary
Year – 2005
Director – Tobe Hooper
Tags – Zombies

A single mother and her two children pick up and move to a new town. The house they move into is a funeral parlor with dark secrets buried underneath it. This movie would have been complete trash if not for Tobe Hooper's involvement. The story is kind of crappy and doesn't make much sense, which is a very bad thing. The CGI is total garbage while the practical FX are passable at best. The acting is fair and the pacing is ok. Hooper did a good job at direction, but there just wasn't much here for him to work on. The added Lovecraft angle was small but helpful. Mortuary is a mild form of entertainment and should really only be acceptable to hardcore zombie fans.

2/5

Mother of Tears, The (La Terza Madre)
Year – 2007
Director – Dario Argento
Tags – Witchcraft

The third and final chapter of the Suspiria saga involves the wickedest mother yet as she causes madness in the streets while she calls upon all the witches of the world to converge upon Rome for the final battle of good versus evil. First it must be said that gorehounds should take note of this movie for its massive gore sequences and general crazy shit happening in this movie. And while that works exceedingly well it is unfortunately underused. The bulk of the story is actually kind of boring and if they had focused more on the madness caused by the witches it would have been an even more rewarding experience. The acting is good from the main cast but honestly I've seen each of them do a better job elsewhere. The pacing also suffers from the slow points in the story but honestly I found this to be very enjoyable if for nothing more than the great FX and gore.

3.5/5

Mr. Brooks
Year – 2007
Director – Bruce A. Evans
Tags – Serial Killer (Fictional)

A wealthy business executive moonlights as a serial killer, and during his latest crime, he is photographed by a man who wants the killer to help him commit his own murder. I wasn't expecting much here because it really just looked like some geriatric thriller, but it turned out to be a superbly crafted serial killer movie. The acting is excellent, and I especially enjoyed the interactions between Kevin Costner and his alter ego played by William Hurt. That was a great addition to the story. The story is well thought out and there are multiple characters and multiple angles that keep things very interesting. The story is very human and I like that. There were some parts of the movie that didn't quite fit however. This is an intelligent thriller but then all of sudden there's a slow motion shootout with blaring techno music like something out The Matrix. What the hell? That just didn't fit at all. And there was more than one occasion of off putting moments. But for the most part this is great movie and even has some very bloody moments. Definitely worth checking out.

3.5/5

Mulberry Street
Year – 2006
Director – Jim Mickle
Tags – Infection

The streets underneath New York City are infested with rats, but the rats under Mulberry Street are different. Here they carry a virus that can transform humans into rat people with a single bite. With quarantine under effect, the residents try to survive and fend off the bloodthirsty beasts. The plot makes this movie sound like a lame B movie, but this one is actually pretty good. I like the realistic feel of the movie for starters. It almost feels like a documentary and the actors they used look and act in a very natural manner. The only problem with this is that the director employed the use of some shaky cam, which is always annoying, but here it's really not that bad because it tends to jerk around with the movements of the actors, giving it a more natural feel and only being mildly irritating. The rat people look awesome, like you would expect humans who took on the traits of vermin to look like. It's fairly bloody, could have used some more gore, but that's a mild complaint. And the CGI they use is pretty much the worst I've ever seen but fortunately it's only used a couple of times for fire effects and whatnot. Mulberry Street plays out like a zombie movie but with much quicker and more agile opponents and I feel that this movie is a very welcome and different entry into the genre.

4/5

Mulholland Dr.
Year – 2001
Director – David Lynch
Tags – Suspense

A bright eyed aspiring actress gets mixed up with an amnesiac woman and together they try to solve the mystery of who she is. Meanwhile a director is forced into recasting the lead role of his movie with a woman he doesn't want. David Lynch is definitely a master filmmaker because even though his movies hardly ever culminate into a direct resolution and at times just don't make sense, they're incredibly compelling to watch, and this movie is no different. It's incredibly suspenseful, sexual, dark and weird, which makes for a rather unique viewing experience. The acting is great and the direction is constantly engrossing. The story never goes anywhere definitive, which is to be expected, but the journey to the end credits is such an interesting one that I couldn't help but love this movie.

4/5

Murder Party
Year – 2007
Director – Jeremy Saulnier
Tags – Slasher / Survival

Murder Party is a story about a lonely man, who finds an invitation to a mysterious party, and upon his arrival, is kidnapped by a group of art students looking to create the ultimate masterpiece of art though murder. This movie is brilliant. For the most part, the movie is a comedy, and a very well done one at that, but then it masterfully switched gears and turned into an over the top gorefest that should please even the most uptight gorehound. This movie is a prime example on what dedicated people can pull off with a very meager budget, a gem in the independent film world. I suppose that given the fact that the core group of actors and crew were longtime friends enabled them to make such a smoothly acted and directed movie. This is just top notch and a perfect example of originality and a well crafted script, highly recommended.

Mutant (Night Shadows)
Year – 1984
Director – John 'Bud' Cardos
Tags – Infection

Two brothers are run off the road by a truck full of rednecks, trapping them in a small town. But unfortunately for them things only get worse as the people in the town get sick and begin to change into crazed mutants that excrete acid from their hands. The idea behind the movie is a cool one, but it takes way too long to get to the meat of the story. The acting and direction are ok but nothing really noteworthy, it's just not bad. The creatures are simple but they look good. This is prime remake material because the ideas behind it are sound, but they just aren't executed as well as they could have been. Good, but could have been more.

3.5/5

My Bloody Valentine
Year – 1981
Director – George Mihalka
Tags – Slasher / Survival

Twenty years ago a man went on a killing rampage in a small mining town on February 14th. After that, Valentine's Day was never celebrated, but now the townsfolk have decided to celebrate it after all, and when they do, the killer returns. I really like this movie because for once the victims aren't teenagers, they're blue collar workers, and that's refreshing. What's also refreshing is the location. Not a camp, not the suburbs, but a mine, which already carries a certain amount of creepiness. Add some pretty good acting, very good direction and FX, and you have a recipe for a damn good slasher movie. Too bad a sequel was never made, but it always seems that some of the best slashers never get them. Maybe it's for the best, because we've seen how bad things can turn out in sequels.

4/5

My Bloody Valentine [Remake]
Year – 2009
Director – Patrick Lussier
Tags – Slasher / Survival

This essentially follows the same plot as the original. Let's be honest here, 3-D was lame in the 80's and it's still lame now. In my opinion, nothing detracts from the movie experience quite like wearing uncomfortable cardboard glasses on your face to watch a movie that ultimately looks kind of blurry. But now that that is out of the way, let's get to the movie. My Bloody Valentine was an overlooked slasher flick from the 80's that was pretty good, and to remake this underappreciated gem is a nice idea. It didn't fully pan out though. They had the right game plan by just giving the audience what they expect from this kind of movie, loads of kills and gore sprinkled with sex. And even though they achieved that, the movie was still ultimately very dull. The kills did not really look that great because they were mostly made up of poorly constructed CGI shots, and I still firmly believe that practical FX will always work better in these kinds of movies. And the story is just too loose, as it strays from what made the original work. So this remake is shelved with so many others, inferior to the original. But it's not horrible, and it does have its entertainment value, just not enough to truly make it memorable.

2.5/5

My Boyfriend's Back
Year – 1993
Director – Bob Balaban
Tags – Zombies

Johnny loves Missy, but has never had the guts to tell her how he feels. One day he makes a split second decision to dive in front of a bullet and save her life, costing him his own life. With his last breath he asks her to the prom, she accepts, and then dies, only to come back as a zombie. This is a very light hearted horror/comedy. This movie is great because it's just so damn funny. It's high on laughs and low on blood, but that definitely works for this flick. The acting is good, and you'll see a lot of familiar faces here. The story is nice and this kind of movie is great when you need a break from all the graphic ultraviolence. It's also the perfect date movie, a love story for your date and some zombie action for yourself. Fun times.

4/5

My Name is Bruce
Year – 2007
Director – Bruce Campbell
Tags – Monsters

B-movie legend Bruce Campbell is kidnapped and taken to a small town that is under attack by the ancient Chinese god of bean curd. Now it's up to him to put a stop to the monster, even though he insists he's just an actor. I love the concept but the execution leaves a lot to be desired. The truth is that this movie just isn't funny even though it tries really hard, and in fact it tries way too hard. The monster is also pretty stupid looking, also not funny. The acting is typical B-movie stuff, but the direction is good. The story could have been better, but it's ok and not necessarily bad. I really wanted to like this movie but I just couldn't get into it all the way. This movie is simply average at best. Maybe next time the filmmakers can get better joke writers and FX people.

2.5/5

Mystery of the House of Wax
Year – 1933
Director – Michael Curtiz
Tags – Suspense

A man who survived a fiery blaze at his last wax museum opens up a new one in New York City, but uses the bodies of real people in the display. Maybe it's just me but I was kind of annoyed at how people talked in this movie, but it didn't bother me too much and I just chalked it up to the time period. The movie, while entertaining for the most part, was fairly dull in terms of direction and the acting wasn't exactly the best. But the way the story unfolded was great and I really liked the various FX that were in use, especially during the fire scene of the original House of Wax. A great story performed in a somewhat mediocre way is what this movie ended up being. A good movie, but it could have been much better.

3/5

National Lampoon's Class Reunion
Year – 1982
Director – Michael Miller
Tags – Slasher / Survival

This horror/comedy centers on a group of people attending their high school reunion and being stalked by a killer who they wronged ten years before. The plot has been done before, but this is National Lampoon and I guess that's kind of the point. The characters are all stereotypical to the point that they are overdone, which is also the point. For example the token Goth guy is so Goth that he's a vampire. I found this to be pretty clever, but unfortunately the rest of the movie isn't so much. The acting is also overdone, but it gets to be too much, and on top of that, the movie just isn't that funny. There's also no blood and very little nudity so this movie doesn't have much to offer. I did think the killer's mask was pretty funny though. This movie just tries too hard to be over the top and it really drags it down. It has some good moments, but not nearly enough.

2/5

Natural Born Killers
Year – 1994
Director – Oliver Stone
Tags – Serial Killer (Fictional)

A man meets a young woman and instantly falls in love, soon sweeping her away into a life of murder and mayhem that would soon become legendary. I think that this is just a brilliantly fun and entertaining movie shot and edited in such a unique way that it really brings everything to life. It's almost as if this movie was shot to appeal to people with ADD because it's constantly shifting perspectives and styles to the point where it makes you feel like you might have epilepsy, which is impressive. I can only imagine the time it took to edit this movie into the final product. The acting and violence are so greatly over the top that it really adds a lot to the unusual production. The soundtrack was also beautifully constructed. This is just a perfect movie in my eyes with flawless pacing and a wonderfully unique execution. I never cease to have fun when I watch Natural Born Killers.

5/5

Near Dark
Year – 1987
Director – Kathryn Bigelow
Tags – Vampires

A man comes across an insanely gorgeous woman in his town and can not resist the urge to take her out. But as dawn approaches and their night together draws to a close, she bites him and runs off, and then he begins to change. Soon afterward he finds himself kidnapped by her clan and taken away from his family. This movie is an incredible achievement, adding such luster to the tired vampire sub genre. The beauty part is that no one even says the word vampire throughout the entire movie, you know what they are, and that's just enough. If vampires were real, this is exactly what they would be like, just average people, some good, and some evil. The movie is really helped out further by the music of Tangerine Dream, as it adds so much atmosphere and drama, and manages to make a great film even better. Everything about the production is top notch, and it's a wonderful one-off movie that needs nothing else. I'm really glad they have not ruined the legacy of the movie with an unneeded and pointless sequel, yet. This movie is a masterwork of the genre and should be seen by everyone.

5/5

Needful Things
Year – 1993
Director – Fraser Clarke Heston
Tags – Devil

A mysterious man sets up shop in a small Maine town, and he has just what everyone desires, and payment is negotiable. His products go beyond material items however, and he can grant even the most far fetched wish, if you grant him your soul. Needful Things, much like the book it is based on, runs long. I was always fascinated by the fact that if the devil could run around and do anything, his favorite thing to do would just be going to small towns and start kicking up some shit. In exchange for his priceless goods, the shopkeeper has his patrons perform pranks on one another, which leads to fingers being pointed in wrong directions and ultimately, total chaos. If there had been more focus put on the items "sold" and the pranks that ensued, I think this movie would have been a lot more interesting, it's still good, it just drags in places and the potential for more was lost.

3/5

Neon Maniacs

Year – 1986
Director – Joseph Mangine
Tags – Slasher / Survival

Some teenagers find a group of homicidal humanoid creatures living under the Golden Gate Bridge but no one will believe them, so now it's up to them to put their killing spree to an end. This is a fun 80's flick that had a lot going for it but it just really failed to pull anything off with greatness. The humanoids looked great, but weren't used enough. The FX were awesome, but there just wasn't enough blood and gore. The acting is typical of low budget horror, crap, but not too bad. The direction was good but like I said, there just should have been more done with the subject matter. Even without reaching its full potential, it's a fun movie and I enjoyed it. This would be prime remake material because someone could take the original story and do more with it.

3/5

Netherworld

Year – 1992
Director – David Schmoeller
Tags – Witchcraft

A man is summoned to his late father's estate and discovers that his father wishes for him to get involved with a witch who has the power to bring him back from the dead. The plot is nice and fresh but may be a bit too ambitious for a B-movie. The acting is ok and the direction is good. The movie features a fair amount of blood and nudity as well, but it just never really goes anywhere concrete. Everything is seemingly thrown together and that makes the good plot turn into a predictable and somewhat dull story. But it's not all bad, as it's just another average offering from Full Moon.

2.5/5

New Nightmare

Year – 1994
Director – Wes Craven
Tags – Slasher / Survival

This epilogue to the nightmare series follows the director, part of the cast and some studio execs from the original movie as they are haunted by Freddy in their dreams. But it is not really Freddy, rather an ancient demon who is using the character to wreak havoc. Now Heather Langenkamp must reprise the role of Nancy one last time in order to stop it. This is a very interesting idea for a movie, and it does end up being a pretty good movie even with a couple flaws. First off, it runs long. It would have run much smoother and lagged so much had it been shorter. Second, the CGI is pretty bad, which blows because the practical FX are awesome, so they should have just stuck with that. The acting is great, which is funny since a few of the actors aren't even actors. The story is great and the whole movie is pulled off well, especially since Freddy is back to his old, dark self. And speaking of Freddy, he has a new appearance here which is nice. He looks more demonic, has some better clothes and new a glove with five razors on it instead of four, and is just cooler looking overall. A nice closing point to the franchise before the inevitable remake comes along.

3.5/5

New York Ripper, The (Lo Squartatore di New York)
Year – 1982
Director – Lucio Fulci
Tags – Serial Killer (Fictional)

A serial killer who brutalizes women in New York City taunts the detective who is trying to catch him. This is another one of those movies that was supposedly too controversial for the US, and after viewing it, I can see why. This just may be Fulci's most brutal movie. It features multiple cringe worthy moments, for women in particular. The movie moves from graphic murder to graphic sex and back again over and over, and it only seems to get more and more graphic each time. And the killer talking like a duck is kind of creepy as well. But the movie isn't all about sex and violence, it has a very good story behind it as well. The movie has a couple of pacing issues, but nothing too bad. This must be seen in its uncut format for the full effect because if you have only seen the censored version, then you haven't seen this giallo.

4/5

Night Flier, The
Year – 1997
Director – Mark Pavia
Tags – Vampires

A tabloid journalist follows around a serial killer who flies into small airports and slaughters everyone in a manner to suggest he may be a vampire. I love the story here because it's a very unique take on the vampire sub genre. This vampire is very different from others you may see as well as his actions. This movie is also gory as hell which is a nice change of pace from the milder flicks out there and it has good FX to back it up. The acting is also good, especially by Miguel Ferrer who plays a prick better than anyone else in my opinion. The direction is also very good and tightly paced, which is always nice to see. I also rather enjoyed the end of the movie. This is one of the few Stephen King short story adaptations that actually worked as a feature length movie without feeling too drawn out. It's not a perfect movie but it's a damn entertaining one.

3.5/5

Night of the Comet

Year – 1984
Director – Thom Eberhardt
Tags – Zombies

A comet passes over Earth one night and turns everyone who sees it into dust. Those who survived are divided however, some coming through the experience just fine while most of the rest turn into zombies. This movie was touted as Valley Girl meets Dawn of the Dead, and that's a fair assessment, but for my taste, it's way too much Valley Girl and not enough Dawn of the Dead. There are hardly any zombies in the movie and its way too dialogue heavy. The movie is pretty slow but the acting is entertaining. The zombies look good but they don't seem to have any interest in eating flesh so where's the fear factor? Still, the movie is fun, even if it is light on zombies, so for those of you only looking for small amounts of horror in your movies, this is definitely the flick for you.

3/5

Night of the Dead
Year – 2006
Director – Eric Forsberg
Tags – Zombies

A doctor is working on a reanimation serum when his test subjects escape and prowl the hospital for fresh meat. If this movie sounds like a cheap rip-off of Re-Animator, that's because it is. They just basically copied the idea of the movie and tried to go more extreme with the violence, which doesn't really work. The acting is god awful and the direction is about as stagnant as I've ever seen. There are some random breasts and buckets of gore though, so it does have something going for it, kind of. The FX really are not too bad and there are just gallons of blood in use that makes things almost interesting. This ends up being an uninspired, derivative zombie movie that's only mildly satisfying.

1.5/5

Night of the Demons
Year – 1988
Director – Kevin Tenney
Tags – Demonic Possession

A Halloween party at an abandoned funeral home goes terribly wrong when a dark, demonic force begins possessing the partygoers. Those possessed by demons begin to stalk and kill the other partygoers, adding them to their ranks. This is a classic horror movie, not just a classic 80's horror movie. I love it when a movie transcends an era, and this movie is still effective today. The make-up and FX are some of the best I have ever seen. Those possessed look very creepy and distinct, and the kills are very well done. Also, there is an infamous "lipstick" scene involving Linnea Quigley that is just freakin' awesome. And when Angela dances to Bauhaus, it makes for one of my favorite scenes ever. The feeling of sheer claustrophobia and dread is very well done. Also, the mini story about an old man who hates Halloween that happens to bookend the movie is pretty cool. This movie is great on pretty much every level and genuinely scary to boot. No fan of horror should be without this gem.

4.5/5

Night of the Demons 2
Year – 1994
Director – Brian Trenchard-Smith
Tags – Demonic Possession

This sequel finds a group of kids having another party at Hull House, but when they decide to cut out early, they unknowingly bring a demon back with them to their school. The way this movie started out I thought they just may end up copying the first one in its entirety, but fortunately, they only used the party as a set-up and quickly moved the story back to the school. I did think it was funny that they used some stock footage from the first movie here, and that's kind of lame. The FX work here is very good for the most part, and this is where I stop with the positive aspects. The acting is ok, the direction is sloppy, the story isn't very good, and it has an absolutely terrible end scene as well. This movie is watchable and not all bad, but it definitely isn't great either. Shame to see such a promising franchise start out its sequels on a bad note, but hey, it could have been a lot worse.

2.5/5

Night of the Demons 3
Year – 1997
Director – Jim Kaufman
Tags – Demonic Possession

After a violent incident at a convenience store, a van full of youths take sanctuary from the cops at Hull House. Of course Angela will be there to show them a bloody good time. This third installment in the Night of the Demons franchise is just dismal. The story and acting are just very blah, the direction is bad and the FX are just not very good. This movie is incredibly boring because the pacing is horrible, as most of the kills are off camera, and there's very little blood. At least there's some good nudity, but that's really all this movie has going on. It's a shame that such a great movie had two bad sequels, but that's ok, because I'll always have the original, and this third movie is easy enough to forget.

1.5/5

Night of the Lepus
Year – 1972
Director – William F. Claxton
Tags – Animals

An overpopulation of rabbits in the southern Arizona desert brings about a unique way to dispose of them. But when the injections given out to quell the population growth instead make the rabbits grow to enormous sizes, a relatively small problem has become a very large one. Yes, the movie is about as stupid as it sounds. I can really get into giant animals killing people, but we're talking about bunnies here. And no matter how big they get, they're still just too damn cute. There are actual actors in this movie, but they appear to be confused as to why they're there. The direction is pretty bad in terms of pacing but I love how they made the rabbits huge. The use of miniatures and real rabbits looked great and as silly as the movie came across I still have to admire how it looked. There's also a lot of blood but no wounds on people, which was pretty hilarious. Yeah, that's right, people covered in blood and tattered clothes but not having a single scratch on them. Even for all of its massive faults, I still found reason to laugh at it and if nothing else, this movie made me want a bunny of my very own.

2.5/5

Night of the Living Dead
Year – 1968
Director – George A. Romero
Tags – Zombies

A group of people happen upon each other and gather at a farmhouse. Outside an ever growing mob of flesh eating zombies attempt to gain entrance and the people inside barricade themselves in and pray that help may come for them. This movie has been the basis for most zombie movies ever made after it, and horror in general in that case. Night of the Living Dead ushered in a new era of horror, never before had a film like this ever been made, and it continues to shape horror today. The idea is certainly a fresh and terrifying one, what if everyone you knew was suddenly clamoring to eat your flesh? Your friends, neighbors and family were all dying and coming back as these creatures. Quite a thought. Sure there had been zombie movies in the past, but never like this, and never on this scale. Such a massive amount of killers coming together for one purpose. Add to that the human horror inside of the house, the clashing of egos and the underlying current of racism. This was much more than just a movie. I actually do consider it to be a flawed low budget movie, but it just persevered on so many levels that it became a masterpiece of the genre. It's legendary for reason, and I could talk all day about why, but I think it would be just better for everyone out there to just watch this movie and see how it shaped the world of horror first hand.

5/5

Night of the Living Dead [Remake]
Year – 1990
Director – Tom Savini
Tags – Zombies

This remake follows the original very closely while giving it some new angles as well. Remaking a legendary film is almost like sacrilege, but George A. Romero himself approached Tom Savini to do this, so it couldn't be all bad, right? Not only is it not bad, it's freakin' incredible. This may be some sort of blasphemy to say it, but I think this tops the original in some ways. I like the new story elements better here than what were in the original. Of course the writer was none other than Romero himself. This more than worthy film is an exceptional update for a masterpiece. Tony Todd is just simply incredible in his role as Ben, and no one else could have done this, as he was perfection. And Patricia Tallman was also excellent as the new and improved Barbara. The whole cast was great, but those two in particular deserve extra praise. So much care went into this production that you can tell it was a labor of love. Romero had a great idea here, update the classic with a more modern feel but keep the core story intact. Brilliant on every level.

5/5

Night of the Living Dead 3-D
Year – 2006
Director – Jeff Broadstreet
Tags – Zombies

This latest remake has a similar story to the original and offers some 3-D sequences. This movie is terrible in every possible way. How could this movie go so wrong where a previous attempt went so right? The changes to the script of the original are just plain stupid, the direction is some of the worst I've seen, and the acting is painful for starters. And the human element that made the other two work out so well is completely missing here. The FX and CGI are also just plain ugly. One good thing I will say is that some of the zombies did look pretty awesome, but that is hardly enough to make this movie worthwhile. It's a shame that any idiot is allowed to call his movie Night of the Living Dead due to the fact that the movie is public domain, and it tends to sully the reputation of the original and the remake that both had heart, where this has none. Don't be fooled by the title, avoid this steaming pile at all costs.

1/5

Night of the Living Dorks (Die Nacht der Lebenden Loser)
Year – 2004
Director – Mathias Dinter
Tags – Zombies

Three losers die in a car crash and are brought back from the dead as zombies in a voodoo ritual. Now with their new powers they try to get back at the people who bullied them and rule the school. This German horror/comedy was one that I wanted to see for awhile, the problem is that the movie just isn't very funny. I laughed a couple of times but there was nothing really that special. The movie also lacked the gore factor, sure there was some blood but not as much as there should have been. The acting and direction were good and the overall story wasn't bad. I would have liked more from this movie, and it's not a bad watch but I can see where it could have been a lot better. Hopefully the eventual American remake will do it well (yeah right).

3/5

Night Watch (Nochnoy Dozor)
Year – 2004
Director – Timur Bekmambetov
Tags – Vampires

The powers of light and the powers of dark have an uneasy alliance, each setting up organizations to watch over each other and make sure everyone follows the rules. But there is a prophecy that one will come along and tip the balance in favor of one side or the other. This is high fantasy set in the horror universe and I can't help but respect how it was pulled off. This does for horror what The Matrix did for Sci-Fi, only much better. The style is something so fantastical in nature that I don't even think it could work outside of the Night Watch universe, so imitators will likely fail at copying it. The FX are just mind meltingly intense, with both practical and CGI melding together with near perfection. The acting and direction are also pretty great. And while the movie is very much visually appealing, I think the story itself is much too epic in scale to be captured properly on screen, and I also believe a little something gets lost in the translation. Still, the eye candy factor alone makes this movie worthwhile, and for something very different than what you're used to seeing, you need to check this movie out.

4/5

*Night Watch 2 can be found under Day Watch.

Nightbreed
Year – 1990
Director – Clive Barker
Tags – Monsters

A man searches for a place called Midian, a magical place where monsters live, because he fears that he may be a serial killer and thinks he belongs there. The make-up and creature FX in this movie are without a doubt some of the best looking and most original I have ever seen. And that's the big plus for me, that and set design. The story is very good, but not one of Barker's best. The direction is great, the movie rarely slows down, and the big battle at the end between the humans and monsters is just really cool looking. I love how unique this movie is even if the story is not a favorite of mine. I found it worth watching for the creatures alone, and the Boston Terrier that has a few great scenes (I have one). Nice movie.

3.5/5

Nightmare City (Incubo Sulla Citta Contaminata)
Year – 1980
Director – Umberto Lenzi
Tags – Infection

A plane makes an emergency landing, and when greeted on the runway by airport police, a horde of insane people, infected by some sort of radiation, come spilling out and killing everyone. Now their killing spree moves into the city, where they infect more people and drink their blood to sustain their murderous rage. This movie is often regarded as a zombie movie, and while the attackers do have zombie like tendencies, they are still very much alive. With these infected people running around using weapons, it makes for some pretty terrifying adversaries, add the fact they are very hard to kill, and you can just kiss your ass goodbye. The acting and direction are pretty good, but the movie is really all about the FX. The infected people may look a little silly, but they also appear very feral, which is cool. There are tons of gore and some of the infected rip open women's shirts before they kill them for a little breast bearing. That always makes me laugh when they do that in movies. Lots of action, killing, blood, random nudity, headshots, explosions, stabbings and more. Great stuff.

4/5

Nightmare Detective (Akumi Tantai)
Year – 2006
Director – Shinya Tsukamoto
Tags – Slasher / Survival

Something is making people commit suicide in their sleep and a detective teams up with a man who can enter people's dreams to try and stop the killing. No, this isn't the Asian version of A Nightmare on Elm Street, it's quite different. The story is in fact very inventive and well made with a pretty creepy looking killer. The first hour of the movie can be pretty slow at times, but it does pick up once a certain plot point in the movie is revealed. All throughout though there are very bloody kills and before the dream killer is shown on screen, there are some great sound effects of it stomping around, but also some use of shaky cam, which sucks. This is still a very good movie with its flaws and I definitely look forward to the sequel.

3.5/5

Nightmare Man
Year – 2006
Director – Rolfe Kanefsky
Tags – Slasher / Survival

A woman believes herself to be stalked by a masked devil man. On her way to being committed to a mental hospital, the car runs out of gas, and as her husband walks to a gas station, the Nightmare Man strikes. This movie is so terrible, but it does have a charm to it. The acting is fairly bad, with Tiffany Shepis being forced to carry the entire group as she is the only one with talent. The story doesn't work because it's supposed to be a slasher flick with a supernatural element, but it just comes off kind of stupid. Some of the kills are really good though. Gratuitous nudity is just that, it was completely unnecessary and felt forced, lame. Still kind of entertaining though, but I must say that without Shepis this movie would have been a complete failure instead of just a moderate one.

2.5/5

Nightmare on Elm Street, A
Year – 1984
Director – Wes Craven
Tags – Slasher / Survival

A group of teenage friends find themselves having similar dreams about a man, horribly burned and wearing a glove of razors on one hand. It doesn't take long for them to realize that if this man visits you in your dreams, and manages to kill you, you die for real. A Nightmare on Elm Street is such a cool concept, your death in a dream equals death for real, that's pretty cool. This movie owes its longevity in the horror community to Robert Englund, who played Freddy Krueger, the villain. Although Wes Craven created the character, it was Robert Englund who made it what it is and was able to carry Freddy into being an icon. Don't get me wrong, the rest of the cast is great, but Robert shines. I would like to have seen them delve more into the dreams, because there is a ton of potential there, but I imagine they could not have done as much due to budget constraints, as this is a fairly low budget movie in the grand scheme of things. The FX are great, both in Krueger's make-up as well as the great, bloody kills. Sometimes incredibly bloody. There is a reason A Nightmare on Elm Street has achieved legendary status and a slew of sequels, it is just that good. A definite high point in the slasher sub genre, as it took your typical scenario and just added completely unique elements. Very much a classic.

4.5/5

Nightmare on Elm Street 2: Freddy's Revenge, A
Year – 1985
Director – Jack Sholder
Tags – Slasher / Survival

The first sequel in a series, and always considered the bastard of the group. In this one we find Freddy attempting to enter the real world through a teenage boy named Jesse. He forces Jesse to commit murders in an attempt to fully take control over him. I guess that's what he was trying to do anyway, I'm not really sure. This one breaks the rules set by the first movie, which is strange because usually rules are not tampered with until well down the line and they run out of ideas. I don't know why Freddy would try to take over a kid to enter the real world when he has absolute power in the dream world. And the plot just always bothered me about the movie. Now, as a stand alone movie, this is pretty good, not great, but pretty good, but it just doesn't fit in the Freddy universe. An entertaining watch from a direction, acting and FX standpoint, but the horrible plot makes it a bit unappealing at the same time. There is a plus though as Freddy was very dark and it marks a time before Freddy Krueger turned into the greatest pun spinner this side of the Cryptkeeper.

2.5/5

Nightmare on Elm Street 3: Dream Warriors, A
Year – 1987
Director – Chuck Russell
Tags – Slasher / Survival

Now we're back on track with the series. In the third installment we see a more direct sequel to the original, taking place years after it. I like this sequel a lot because they really delved into the dreams this go around, and furthermore gave the kids powers to fight Freddy, because come on, don't you have special powers in your dreams? In a lot of ways this movie is actually better than the original, mainly due to the bigger budget allowing them to delve deeper into the dream world. The FX are some the best of the series, and with a little bit tighter script, it may have actually surpassed the original. This also marks the beginning of Freddy Krueger being a little less of a dark and ominous figure and bit more of a comedian. The balance works here though, as opposed to the more cartoonish sequels down the road. A very solid movie.

4/5

Nightmare on Elm Street 4: The Dream Master, A
Year – 1988
Director – Renny Harlin
Tags – Slasher / Survival

In the fourth entry, Freddy returns by a fiery stream of dog urine (No, I'm not kidding), and continues on a couple of years after the last movie. So in previous installments, Freddy just kind of came back to kill again, so why the grand spectacle this time around? It's weird, but I do have to appreciate the originality. Freddy continues on with his comic routine rife with puns and all. There is also some good exploration into the dreams of the kids, but it's just not quite as clever this time around. I also found some of the kills to be kind of boring for Freddy, as he is usually more inventive than just stabbing someone in the guts. The practical FX look really good here and the story arc is a very good place for the series to go. So despite some weak moments, number four is still a very strong sequel and I enjoyed it.

3.5/5

Nightmare on Elm Street 5: The Dream Child, A
Year – 1989
Director – Stephen Hopkins

The fifth movie picks up not long from where the fourth movie left off. I consider this movie and the fourth movie to be polar opposites. Here we have some excellent dream sequences with some of the more inventive kills in the series. But the story is just not up to par. The FX work is slightly uneven, but the good is good and the bad isn't too terrible. It can also get a little slow at times, which is unfortunate. Still, the poor story and plot behind the fifth movie really does drag it down, fortunately the excellent kills keep it from being the worst in the series.

3/5

*A Nightmare on Elm Street 6 can be found under Freddy's Dead: The Final Nightmare.

*A Nightmare on Elm Street 7 can be found under New Nightmare.

Nightmare Sisters
Year – 1987
Director – David DeCoteau
Tags – Demonic Possession

Three sorority sisters find it difficult to get men interested in them. That is until they are all possessed by the spirit of a succubus, whose only desire is to eat the souls of men. With the power of three scream queens and a silly story backing it, I was expecting a cheesy 80's flick soaked with blood and T&A. What I wasn't expecting was this movie to be so terribly directed is was almost painful to watch. Also, there was no blood at all, instead, we get steam. Yes, steam. That's just ridiculous. But as for the T&A portion, yes, loaded to the gills with nudity, that is, after the incredibly long introduction. I think that with a more competent director, this movie could have been a lot of fun and a great 80's horror movie, but we didn't get a very good director and instead received this dreck saved only by the three succubi dancing naked in front of the camera.

2/5

Nightstalker
Year – 2002
Director – Chris Fisher
Tags – Serial Killer

This movie is based upon real life serial killer Richard Ramirez, who killed 14 people over the course of about a year. He was a known drug addict and Satanist with more than his fair share of mental issues. One major problem I had with this movie is that it focused upon the female detective chasing Ramirez rather than Ramirez himself, and I did not like this for the simple fact that she just wasn't very interesting. It did show some of the Nightstalker's exploits, but they were shot in a very annoying drug haze / insanity way with a lot of death metal and shaky cam, which was pretty annoying. And also the kills weren't very graphic at all. The acting was fairly bad with only Danny Trejo standing out as being any good in his role and the direction was ok, but needed some improvement. Overall this movie is a disappointment and could have been a lot better. It's not all terrible, but I didn't really like it. I hope someone else comes along in the future to make a better movie about Richard Ramirez, because this one just doesn't have much to it.

2/5

Ninth Gate, The
Year – 1999
Director – Roman Polanski
Tags – Devil

A book collector possesses a book supposedly written by Satan, and hires a book expert to hunt down the other two copies in existence to find out if his copy is real or a forgery. The expert runs into quite a bit of trouble along the way. This movie is just so dry and predictable that I could barely stand it. It's so easy to figure out what's going on that it's ridiculous. Who's behind this incident? Who's this person? Who did that? It's all so easy to figure out that it just left me disillusioned with the project. And then to add insult to injury, the movie creeps along at a snails pace, dragging you from one obvious revelation to the next. The locales were very nice though, and I wish I had more positive things to say about this movie, but I just don't. Such a letdown.

1.5/5

No Man's Land: The Rise of Reeker
Year – 2008
Director – Dave Payne
Tags – Slasher / Survival

After a short prequel as to the origins of the Reeker the movie follows a group of random people as they become the next targets of it. I liked the original but this doesn't have a lot going for it. The actors aren't nearly as good as the last cast and despite the prequel being pretty cool, the bulk of the movie plays out like the last one. I wasn't a fan of the original's ending and now armed with the knowledge as to what's going on, the writer tries to backtrack and explain things, with little success. The Reeker does get a few new toys to play with and once again there are some good kills, but the entire movie is just not that interesting. Maybe this sequel was made too soon or maybe they're just aren't any good ideas left for it. Painfully average.

2.5/5

Nosferatu [Silent]
Year – 1922
Director – F.W. Murnau

This is sort of an adaptation of the novel of Dracula but since the director could not obtain rights, he just used the story and changed all of the character's names. Here a young man attempts to sell property to a Count Orlok, who happens to be a vampire with a fondness for the young man's wife. I'm going to honest here, this movie is very impressive for its time period but it's hardly a classic. The vampire is one of the most memorable ever committed to film because he just does look that creepy. At times the film looks great with wonderful cinematography but there where occasions where it just became much too slow for my liking. I like the changes made to the story as they do go a bit beyond just name changing and overall this is a good time. I did really enjoy Nosferatu but I just don't think it's perfect. Still, it is one of the most iconic vampire movies ever made and for good reason.

4/5

Number 23, The
Year – 2007
Director – Joel Schumacher
Tags – Suspense

A man's wife buys him a book for his birthday, and as he reads it he realizes that the book is mirroring his life, and the book's topic of the number twenty-three becomes an obsession for him, as he finds the number in every aspect of his life. I can appreciate the time and effort that went into creating all of the ways things could be boiling down to the number 23, I just wish more time and effort was put into the actual story, which is sorely lacking. The acting by Jim Carrey and Virginia Madsen in their dual roles is excellent, but most everyone else is pretty forgettable. The direction is good, and I especially liked the clear designation between what is reality and what are scenes from the book. This is a good movie and it's always nice to see Carrey in a serious role because I think he has more skill in that respect than as a comedian, but this movie just wasn't anything great.

3/5

Oldboy
Year – 2003
Director – Chan-Wook Park
Tags – Suspense

An average businessman is kidnapped and imprisoned for seemingly no reason. After fifteen long years he is released with a new suit, money and a cell phone. Then he begins his hunt for the man who did this to him so that he can finally taste the revenge he had been dreaming of. Wow, now this is one hell of a movie. This is yet another kind of movie that you would never see in the states, well, you will in the eventual remake with everything that made this movie great cut out. It's just so unconventional but at the same time, realistic. Like with the fight scenes, they're not extravagant with high flying wire work and bold moves, they play out like actual fights. They look and sound real. The story is remarkable and has a lot of cool and unique elements to it, and toward the end, it only manages to get better. With fabulous acting and an incredible execution, Oldboy is one of the most pleasurable movie going experiences I have ever seen.

5/5

Omega Man, The
Year – 1971
Director – Boris Sagal
Tags – Vampires

This is a remake of The Last Man on Earth, and follows essentially the same storyline where a man is seemingly the last one alive after a plague either killed everyone else or turned them into light phobic vampire-like creatures. So this second adaptation misses the mark again, not truly living up to its potential, but I must say I did like it the best out of all three adaptations thus far. The story is better here but Charlton Heston could hardly carry the movie. If Vincent Price had been paired with this story, we would have finally received a great movie. The vampires here aren't really vampires at all, which is kind of disappointing, but they are better than the zombie-like creatures of the last adaptation. All of the acting is pretty hammy here, but at least we get some solid direction in return. This is my favorite adaptation of I Am Legend, and even though I didn't think it was great, it was still pretty damn good.

3.5/5

Omen, The
Year – 1976
Director – Richard Donner
Tags – Devil

A man's baby dies at birth and he is given a chance to immediately adopt another baby without anyone else knowing, and he accepts. Years later however, he learns that his son may be the Antichrist, and he struggles with the concept. This is a brilliant movie and I feel it tops the other well known religion / devil movie of the 70's, The Exorcist. The acting is great, and Gregory Peck in particular is astounding. The kid is creepy without even saying a word, which is also pretty astounding. The direction is great and the death scenes in the movie are nothing short of amazing. And rightfully so, we are dealing with the son of the devil and mundane deaths just won't cut it. This movie is very tense and deals with the always taboo subject of killing a child, which really makes it stand out to me. The incredible ending and immaculate score are also icing on the cake. This is easily one of the most iconic horror movies of the 70's or any other decade and essential viewing for anyone interested in the genre.

5/5

*The Omen II can be found under Damian: The Omen II.

Omen III: The Final Conflict, The
Year – 1981
Director – Graham Baker
Tags – Devil

This movie continues on several years after the last one. This series works as a trilogy very well in my opinion (let's just forget about the fourth movie and the remake). While this one is definitely the weakest entry thus far, I still enjoyed it quite a bit. The story progresses well again and the ending is interesting because I was nonplussed and yet intrigued at the same time. Sam Neill as the antichrist was a great casting choice and the rest of the actors are very good as well. The direction is good but the movie was a little slow at times, still satisfying overall though. This is a well done movie and enjoyed it, not much I can say beyond that.

3.5/5

Omen IV: The Awakening, The
Year – 1991
Direction – Jorge Montesi, Dominique Othenin-Girard
Tags – Devil

This movie picks up right after the last one in a way. While I felt that The Omen series would have been better off just as a trilogy, this movie's plot is a sensible progression. I just wish it would have reached its full potential. Maybe if it hadn't been a TV movie it could have better, who knows? The story starts out in a good way but then devolves into a rehash of the original and just transposing the father/son relationship with a mother/daughter one. The acting isn't very good and I just didn't like the kid in the movie either. The direction is ok I suppose, the movie can get pretty boring at times but it isn't all bad. The score however, was terrible and didn't fit the movie at all. The series is known for its great death sequences, and here, since it's a TV movie they try but are forced to cut away before the money shot. This is far from being even as remotely good as the original trilogy but I guess it's not all bad.

2/5

Omen, The [Remake]
Year – 2006
Director – John Moore
Tags – Devil

This movie is nearly a shot for shot remake of the original. And that's where the main flaw of the movie comes into place. This remake is obviously just a gimmick because it came out on 6-6-06 and offered little to no originality on the original tale. Another problem is with the casting. The kid had no personality and Julia Stiles as his mother, are you kidding me? She couldn't act if her life depended on it. And while Gregory Peck could never be topped, Liev Schrieber did do a very good job. The death scenes were also toned down a bit and there was CGI usage, which was very disappointing. This movie is more less an act of plagiarism and offers too little variation on the original to be worthwhile. I'll award points for Liev Schrieber and Mia Farrow but everything else is just garbage.

1/5

One Hour Photo
Year – 2002
Director – Mark Romanek
Tags – Suspense

A photo developer gets an unhealthy obsession with one of his customers and dreams of being part of their family. But then something happens that ruins his perception of this perfect family, which sends him off the deep end. I have to state for the record right now that I am not a fan of Robin Williams, but he is just brilliant in this movie. I think of him like Leslie Nielsen, I don't care for the comedy aspect of his work at all, but when gets into a dramatic role, particularly a genre one, he just shines. The rest of the cast is good as well, but nothing overly terrific. The direction is very good and I liked the sterile feeling of the movie. I also liked the story for the most part but was a little put off by how it unfolded, especially toward the end. Still, I really did like this movie and even if it didn't play out the way I would have liked it to, this is still a very solid thriller.

3.5/5

Open Water
Year – 2003
Director – Chris Kentis
Tags – Suspense

A couple goes scuba diving way out in the ocean with a group of people, only to surface and find their boat has left them behind after a miscount of people aboard. Now they struggle to survive as the current pulls them further away from land and sharks begin to gather. This is a true life tale and it's a pretty damn scary one in my opinion. Talk about a helpless situation. But even at a short 81 minutes, the movie feels too long and may have been better off as a part of a true life anthology or something. By forcing this story into a feature length movie, the script ends up feeling bloated. But I do understand what the filmmaker was doing here, trying to create a deep drama between the married couple, but the people playing the couple were bad actors and just couldn't pull it off. This is a low budget movie in every meaning of the word but if you're going to make a movie like this that depends so heavily on the actor's performance, then you need to get some good actors. There are some wonderful shots and definitely some tense moments, just not enough. The idea was there, but the final product just doesn't match up.

Open Water 2: Adrift
Year – 2006
Director – Hans Horn
Tags – Suspense

This "sequel" is actually just another similar situation where a group of friends go yachting and swimming far out into the ocean, only to realize they didn't lower the ladder on the yacht and now can not climb back on board. I actually like the premise because it's such a stupid thing to forget that it just seems so plausible. I have a sneaking suspicion that this movie was made and simply called Adrift, and then when the rights were bought the studio slapped on the Open Water 2 part for more marketability. I may be wrong, but that's my theory. I like this better than the original mainly because the performances are much better and the addition of more people makes the runtime feel more appropriate. It still gets boring at times, and all of the acting isn't the best, but it's an improvement. This is a good movie that I enjoyed but didn't love.

Orca: The Killer Whale
Year – 1977
Director – Michael Anderson
Tags – Animals

A boat captain is stalked by a killer whale after he kills the whale's mate which leads into a dramatic confrontation of man versus beast. Overly dramatic actually. So this movie was an obvious attempt at a cash-in after the success of Jaws, but fortunately it's not just a copy of the more popular movie. For instance, the people attacked in Jaws were innocents and here the creature stalks a genuine piece of shit, which I appreciated. The story is ok but offers up too many ludicrous ideas just make the clash occur. The acting and direction are fine but doesn't offer anything noteworthy. There are a couple of gory scenes that are brief but effective. This isn't a bad movie and it does offer up some interesting tidbits for the animal attack sub genre but it's still an underwhelming effort.

Organizm (Living Hell)
Year – 2008
Director – Richard Jefferies
Tags – Biological

A man carries information about a military facility due to a traumatic childhood incident. Now they are decommissioning the facility and he rushes to warn them of a secret buried deep within, but he was too late and now an uncontrollable viral organism is loose and devouring everything in its path. Organizm is a pretty solid movie that suffers from two problems. The movie contradicts itself at times, and some of the most atrocious CGI and green screen work I have ever seen. Bad CGI usually doesn't bother me because its par for the course in low budget movies, but it is just so bad that it deterred me from fully enjoying the movie. And another problem is that the movie seemed to have some sort of budget because everything else about it was pretty good, so the CGI issue really is unforgivable. Now thus far it may seem as though I'm bashing the movie, but I did enjoy it. In fact, if the CGI had been in the hands of more competent individuals, then this would have received a four star rating easily. But as it stands, we are left with a nice sci-fi/horror time killer worthy of watching, but just don't expect the next classic here.

2.5/5

Orphanage, The (El Orfanato)
Year – 2007
Director – Juan Antonio Bayona
Tags – Ghosts

A woman returns to the orphanage where she grew up to turn it into a home for special children when her own child disappears, forcing her to uncover the secrets of the orphanage. When people say to me that movies are not art, I point them toward this movie and say: "Look, art." This dark, haunting, and gorgeous movie is easily one of the best ghost stories ever crafted. Like much modern Spanish horror, the best ones anyway, this isn't just a straightforward horror tale, instead we get a deeper human story, and here it is about an undying mother's love. The acting is great, and the direction is well paced and beautifully shot in a gloomy sense. The story is remarkable on every level and not only does it have creepy moments and a good atmosphere, but it's just solid even when creepy things aren't happening. And the ending, wow, the ending just gives me chills. Some people will say it's sad, some will say it's happy, and well, I like to think it's both, and the ending much like the movie in and of itself is just brilliant.

4.5/5

Other Side, The
Year – 2006
Director – Gregg Bishop
Tags – Demons

A young man waiting for his girlfriend to arrive for a romantic evening is killed and sent to Hell. But he escapes with a group of other people back to the land of the living. There he finds out that Hell has sent demonic bounty hunters called Reapers to reclaim all the escaped souls. Now he tries to elude them while searching for his girlfriend, who has gone missing. I'm going to say it, this is the most impressive low budget movie ever made. For something like $15,000, Bishop made this movie look like a multi-million dollar production. Great acting, a magnificent score, tight direction and an incredible story, definitely one of the best movies I've ever seen. Add the fact that this movie has a fair amount of gore and a stellar ending, and you have yourself one creative and well done genre flick. Even the CGI isn't bad looking for the type of budget they had. This movie is quite simply a remarkable accomplishment in filmmaking and marks Bishop as one of the best directors to watch out for.

4.5/5

Others, The
Year – 2001
Director – Alejandro Amenabar
Tags – Ghosts

A woman and her two children experience strange events in their home that might just be the work of ghosts. This is one of many Sixth Sense clones to come out in the years after that movie's release, what separates it from the pack is that this one actually has some merit. The movie is high on atmosphere but perhaps to a fault, because the movie relies so much upon that, it often times drags unbearably through the transparent storyline. Ghost movies became the big sell after 1999, and this one doesn't try to reinvent the wheel, it plods through your typical occurrences and then tries to cover the obvious plot twists to no avail. But it is very well shot and the constant darkness casts an eerie and ominous tone across the entire film. This movie could have benefited from a couple of rewrites and some fat trimming in the editing room, but it's still enjoyable to some degree, which is more than I can say for many of the other ghost movies released around this time.

2.5/5

Otis
Year – 2008
Director – Tony Krantz
Tags – Serial Killer (Fictional)

Otis is the tale of oafish man who has resorted to kidnapping teenage girls to live out his fantasies. After the untimely death of girl #5, he kidnaps a sixth, but rather than the parents being your typical helpless, grief stricken people, they seek revenge. Otis is very entertaining for nothing more than its unusual plot mechanisms and dark brand of humor. The title character is just a pathetic individual with a childlike mind in a way. Don't get me wrong, he's a total pervert, but his desires are not to kidnap girls and rape and murder them, he wants to pretend he's still in high school and then take them on dates and to the prom. After awhile you kind of feel sorry for him because he's just so lame and can't even talk to people unless it's in his own creepy scenarios. His brother degrades him and beats him, and ultimately he just wants to be loved. So you want to like him and yet he is just too messed up to endure at the same time. I also like how the police are portrayed as pretty useless, which they are in situations like these, and as I mentioned earlier, how the parents and brother of the sixth girl are vengeance seeking vigilantes and refuse to stand by and let the police handle things. I would like to say more, but I would hate to give away anything. Good times.

Outbreak
Year – 1995
Director – Wolfgang Petersen
Tags – Infection

A deadly virus first found in Zaire has made its way to the US and is spreading through a small town like wildfire. Now the race for a cure has begun before extreme measures can be taken by the government. This moderately entertaining thriller has a strong plot but a fairly weak story attached to it. The attempt at drama behind the main infection is very loose and doesn't completely work. The acting is really good but given the caliber of actors involved, I did expect more and they really didn't put their all into it. The direction is pretty good but it's just so linear and lacks any real flair, which isn't necessarily a bad thing, because sometimes I just want to watch a movie and not think, but here it makes for some very uneven pacing. This is good stuff and for what it is, it's a pretty good movie, but there really is nothing outstanding here.

3/5

Outpost
Year – 2008
Director – Steve Barker
Tags – Zombies

A group of mercenaries are hired to escort a man to a disused outpost deep in the woods. But once there they find out that it is former Nazi bunker and that it is anything but abandoned, as the former occupants are still around, only now they're ghost-like zombies. This is a really good movie but I just can't help but feel that it could have been so much more. The acting is great, and the location used is excellent. The direction is a little uneven however. There are some great firefights and atmospheric moments but there are also few definite lags, overall however, it was pretty good. The story also had a few points that I would have liked to have seen fleshed out a bit more, while others dropped altogether. I did like the way the zombies looked, or ghosts, the movie can't seem to decide which they are. This is still a good movie even with its flaws and while I had hoped for more, I still left satisfied.

3.5/5

P2
Year – 2007
Director – Franck Khalfoun
Tags – Suspense

A workaholic woman finds herself trapped in her office building on Christmas Eve with a mentally unstable security guard who wants nothing more than to declare his love for her. This movie really has no tension or suspense to speak of, which is sad since it had the potential for just that, but in that regard the movie is a failure. The movie does have one spectacularly bloody kill, and then that's pretty much it. The minimal cast hurt this movie in my opinion, because the one constant victim, played by Rachel Nichols, couldn't really carry the movie. The director did get one thing right however, he kept the movie constantly moving from one situation to the next, trying not to let it get too dull. But it was dull, a particle board thriller, but I'll give it an average rating for the nice pacing and that one great kill. Nothing special here.

2.5/5

Pacific Heights
Year – 1990
Director – John Schlesinger
Tags – Suspense

A couple renovates their dream home and become landlords to help pay their large mortgage, but one of their tenants has other ideas. First I have to say that I love the direction here, I found this movie to be very well paced and it ran smooth from start to finish. I also liked the performances by Matthew Modine and Michael Keaton, but Melanie Griffith's acting left a lot to be desired for me. I liked the story as well, but can't say I loved it. This movie has its moments of tension and violence, but not quite enough. I liked this movie even if I found it to be too tame, actually that kind of worked for it and allowed to be a little different. Good stuff.

3.5/5

Panic in Year Zero!
Year – 1962
Director – Ray Milland
Tags – Suspense

A nuclear attack rocks the US, causing massive turmoil amongst the survivors. This movie focuses on a family of four and their struggle to survive against a world gone mad. I really liked this movie because even though it was made so long ago, it's incredibly poignant even today. We've seen how fast civilization degrades when faced with disaster, just look at what happened after Hurricane Katrina, rape, looting and murder became part of everyday life, and those subjects are explored in this movie to great effect. The acting is very good and the direction is great. One problem I had is that when the family escaped and found a secluded spot to lay low, the movie lost some of its charm. What made it work so well were the interactions between the family and the people they encountered. Still an awesome movie though, loaded with tension and social commentary that still makes sense today.

3.5/5

Pan's Labyrinth (El Laberinto del Fauno)
Year – 2006
Director – Guillermo del Toro
Tags – Monsters

Set in 1944 during a civil war in Spain, the stepdaughter of a sadistic military captain becomes entangled in a fantastical world of fairies and loathsome creatures. Yeah, so I'll have to say that this easily one of the most creative and well made movies ever made. Ever. Much like in The Devil's Backbone, war is the backdrop for a story of supernatural means and here the war aspect is very much in the forefront and features quite a lot of brutality. The story is a fairytale but this is hardly a children's movie because it is very dark and features some truly creepy creatures, especially the dining hall beast that has self portraits, with him killing children, engraved into the walls. The design of said creatures is amazing and fortunately the FX work if also great and really brings them to life. The acting is brilliant and the direction is absolutely flawless. A little bit war epic, a little bit family drama, a lot a bit of fantasy and many horror elements all come together to make one of the best movies ever made. This is quite simply a work of art and finally gave del Toro the notoriety he deserves.

5/5

Parents
Year – 1989
Director – Bob Balaban
Tags – [Hidden to conceal spoilers]

This movie follows a young boy through his nightmares and everyday life, which turns out to be quite the nightmare as well. His parents are harboring a secret, and they will do anything to preserve it. I watched this movie about a hundred times as a kid, even though I couldn't fully comprehend it. It is so surreal and dream-like that it was hard to follow with my fragile young mind, yet I was still compelled by it. And now that I understand what's going on, the movie works its magic to even greater effect. Fans of David Lynch would probably eat this up, as this is the closest to his style I have ever seen. The haunting and often times harsh score melds mercilessly with the whimsical soundtrack and really adds a lot to the movie. The acting is exceptional, especially by Randy Quaid, who puts on probably his best performance ever here. With a solid story, great direction, wonderful acting and a truly dark and bizarre style all its' own, Parents is a classic movie that needs to be seen by everyone at least once.

4.5/5

Pathology
Year – 2008
Director – Marc Scholermann

A doctor falls in with a group of pathologists who play a very deadly game. They will murder people by inventive means and challenge the others to try and guess how they died. That's a pretty cool concept for a movie even if it is quite a stretch that five or six people would have that frame of mind all in the same place. The movie itself is a very good thriller with decent pacing and a ton of gore. The gore part I was not expecting, but there are some pretty graphic autopsy scenes. And that's where the real beauty of the movie lies, in the FX. For example, there was a full body model of an actress cast and filled with blood and organs for a particularly realistic and grisly scene. Very impressive. While I do feel this movie could have been tightened up and tweaked a bit, you still have a strong plot, great acting, stupendous gore and finally just a well done movie.

3.5/5

Penny Dreadful
Year – 2006
Director – Richard Brandes
Tags – Slasher / Survival

A young woman has an extreme phobia of cars and goes with her psychiatrist to a retreat in hopes of getting past her fears. On the way there they encounter a hitchhiker and now Penny has even more to be afraid of. Penny Dreadful is a cool concept, but would have been pulled off much better as part of an anthology. It was a great idea, something new, but it didn't deserve the full length movie treatment. An hour and a half was just too long and the movie felt really drawn out and forced. Thirty minutes could have been trimmed off of this and it would have been a much tighter thriller. Other than that it was great, but the overly long run time and poor pacing reduced Penny Dreadful to an average horror film at best.

2.5/5

People Under the Stairs, The
Year – 1991
Director – Wes Craven
Tags – Slasher / Survival

Two adults and a young boy break into someone's house in the hopes of finding a rare coin collection, but instead find themselves trapped inside with a couple, their killer dog, and a group of stolen children that they keep in the cellar. The idea behind this movie is very fresh and interesting, but the story itself could have used some more work. The acting is ok, the direction is great and the make-up and FX are also good. The real star of this movie is the house, which is pretty badass to behold and I especially liked how it really felt like a prison. When the burglars get trapped inside, you really do get the feeling that they're trapped. This is human horror that plays out like a slasher movie, and while I didn't find the story to be entirely compelling, I did find this movie to be very entertaining and somewhat original.

3.5/5

Perkin's 14
Year – 2009
Director – Craig Singer
Tags – Slasher / Survival

Fourteen children were kidnapped in a small town several years ago, now a local sheriff, whose son was one of the fourteen, finds that the possible kidnapper may just be in his jail cell for other reasons. But this man has been brainwashing and training the kids for years, and now they're out, ready to kill. This plot won an online vote to be made into a movie, and I have to admit the plot was great, unfortunately, after it won, the first god awful script they found in the trash was slapped onto it, and this movie was born. Seriously, the writing is awful, then couple that with poor direction, half assed camera work, and uneven acting, and you have this monstrosity. Now, I will say that the 14 looked pretty good, just how you would imagine that people locked up and treated inhumanely would look. The kills could have been better, but there are a couple instances of good ones. That's the most I have to say in favor of this movie, it's just a shame no care went into this movie, it could have been something great.

1.5/5

Perfect Creature
Year – 2006
Director – Glenn Standring
Tags – Vampires

Vampires and humans coexist peacefully until a rogue vampire begins killing innocent humans. Now it's up to the rogue vampire's brother to stop him by any means necessary. This movie definitely has the potential to become to the next Night Watch or Brotherhood of the Wolf, but it just didn't have the budget behind it to pull it off. The story, while good, could have also used some more tweaking. This movie definitely has a style akin to the aforementioned films but is not a copy, and rather it is its own monster. The acting and direction are very good but just not enough. Everything about this movie is just not enough. I would like to see this guy get some great funding for the inevitable sequel to see the series reach its goals.

3/5

Pet Sematary
Year – 1989
Director – Mary Lambert
Tags – Zombies

Beyond the property of the Creed family there is a pet cemetery built by broken hearted children, but beyond that is an ancient Indian burial ground that is said to resurrect the dead buried there. But the ground is sour and things sometimes don't come back as they are supposed to. I've always loved this story. I remember reading the novel back in 1st grade and just being fascinated by the story. I had wondered how it would be translated to the silver screen and I must admit that the filmmakers were not afraid to show all of the gory details. There are taboos in the story that are traditionally hidden in movies but not only is it shown here, it's fairly graphic as well. The acting is smooth and the direction is very good. The movie features probably the creepiest performance by a child ever, and the most impressive thing is that the kid is what, two or three? This is a great horror movie wrapped together neatly with a wonderful family drama. Recommended.

4/5

Pet Sematary Two
Year – 1992
Director – Mary Lambert
Tags – Zombies

This movie continues on years after the original. Though creating the movie was totally unnecessary, as the original ended so nicely, at least here we don't have a carbon copy of the first. The director returns and does an admirable job once again, even though the story just isn't as strong. Don't get me wrong, the story is good, albeit predictable, but it's not a match at all for the original. The acting however, is very good, which is surprising for a sequel like this. Clancy Brown is especially good and I'm surprised he doesn't get more roles because the guy is very skilled, especially when it comes to playing an asshole, no offense Clancy. The movie has its bloody moments but lacks the punch of its predecessor. Still, it's a well done sequel and just because it isn't as good as the original doesn't mean it isn't good at all.

3/5

Phantom of the Opera, The [Silent]
Year – 1925
Director – Rupert Julian
Tags – Suspense

This is the classic tale of a woman who is trying to make it big in the opera and the man who will do anything to fulfill her dreams and win her heart, by murder if necessary. So I'm not a huge fan of silent movies but this one is undeniably brilliant. Chaney alone makes this movie worth watching and I can see how his facial appearance terrified people when this was released because it's still pretty creepy today. The movie moves along nicely and has a good bit of humor to it, and I especially liked the ballet dancers running about, as it was pretty hilarious. Overall the movie is pleasure to watch, I just wish I could find a really good restoration of the print because even "The Ultimate Edition" that

I own is really whitewashed at times. There was also a 1929 restored version that gave this movie sound but I'll stick with the original because I feel it works better.

4.5/5

Phantom of the Opera, The [Remake]
Year – 1989
Director – Dwight H. Little
Tags – Suspense

This remake follows the same story as the original but offers an interesting bookend to the movie in the modern day. People get down on this remake mainly because it's gory but that's actually closer to the source material than the pure romance versions. Robert Englund makes for a brilliant Phantom and his make-up work is great. There are also a couple of other good actors but the rest, eh, not so much. I really liked the practical FX and the direction was pretty damn good overall. This isn't the best Phantom adaptation but its straight horror elements really appealed to me and I enjoyed it quite a bit.

3.5/5

Phantom of the Opera, The [Remake]
Year – 1998
Director – Dario Argento
Tags – Suspense

This remake, well, let's just say it uses many of the same elements, but let's also say that it's pretty different. Here the Phantom is not disfigured and he was raised by rats. Uh, ok. Well hell, I'm not sure what to say here. This ultra gory and absurdly sexual adaptation is definitely not Argento's finest hour. Asia Argento and Julian Sands are good in their roles but I must say that I didn't care much for the supporting cast. The story is pretty ludicrous, but I do have to admit that it has its interesting moments. But when Sands put the rat down his pants for some kind of sexual pleasure, what the hell? The direction wasn't very good and the movie got pretty slow at times. The practical FX were nice but the CGI was simply atrocious. If you're a fan of the original, you owe it to yourself to see this bizarre mess, but audiences will surely be split on whether or not they like it. Me... not really.

2/5

Phantoms
Year – 1998
Director – Joe Chapelle
Tags – [Hidden to conceal spoilers]

Two sisters visit a small Colorado town and find the entire population either dead or missing. And something is still out there. This Dean Koontz adaptation is interesting but very thin. Something cool will happen and then nothing for about twenty minutes until something else happens. And then by the time the movie reaches its conclusion you can't help but say, "That's it?" So the story is ok but still lacking any punch to help resonate with the viewers. The acting is ok but nothing special there either. The direction is solid, even if there wasn't a whole lot to work with it still manages to move along nicely. The FX are really cool for the most part though and offer up some nice imagery. This is a good movie but I think more could have been done with the material and it could have been a whole lot more interesting.

3/5

Pitch Black
Year – 2000
Director – David Twohy
Tags – Monsters

A spaceship carrying a random assortment of people, as well as a deadly convicted murderer, crash land on a desert planet. Soon they find out that they have more to worry about than just the convict among their ranks as they come across a massive nest of creatures dwelling in the caverns underneath their feet. I really like the style of this movie and how everything eventually plays out, even if the movie does feel a little long. The characters are very stereotypical and die off pretty much how I would have expected them to, which took me out of the experience a bit. But on the plus side is everything else about the movie. The direction was very good, great acting, awesome monsters, and for the most part it had good CGI and FX. This is just a very fun movie with a lot of cool things happening for it. And by the way, there are a couple of sequels but they are just straight sci-fi (Dark Fury and The Chronicles of Riddick) and I'm not going to put them in the book.

3.5/5

Plaga Zombie
Year – 1997
Director – Pablo Pares, Hernan Saez
Tags – Zombies

Aliens bring a zombie plague to Argentina for scientific reasons and a trio of unlikely heroes tries to put a stop to it before everyone they know is dead. This microbudget effort is much like the many that had come before it and would come after it, showing that lack of talent really has no borders and anyone with a camcorder wants to make a movie. This movie is supposed to be a horror/comedy, but it's just not funny and it tries too hard to be, making it pretty lame instead. The acting isn't bad but the guy in the unitard was disturbing, and not in a good way. I do admire what they did with very little money in terms of FX and clever editing but the silly story and unfunny nature of the film just leaves me nonplussed about my entire viewing experience.

Plaga Zombie: Mutant Zone
Year – 2001
Director – Pablo Pares, Hernan Saez
Tags – Zombies

This movie picks up right where the last one left off. After I watched the first movie I wasn't really looking forward to the second one and put off watching it for awhile. But I do have to say that this one is at least a little bit better than the last one. The sequel is actually funny, at least I laughed a few times, and the FX are a bit better (They probably had a bigger budget than the paltry $120 of the last movie). The direction and acting are about the same, which means it's not very good. The movie is also much longer this time around, which is very much to its detriment. The story is a decent enough progression from the last non-story, but eventually devolves into being more of the same. This movie isn't good but at least it improved upon the last one.

2.5/5

Plague, The
Year – 2006
Director – Hal Masonberg
Tags – Infection

The children of the world have fallen into a catatonic state and there seems to be no cure in sight. Ten years pass and now people need to worry about the kids waking up. I had heard a lot of bad things about this movie and when I got around to watching this, I wasn't expecting much. What I got started out as a pretty damn good apocalyptic thriller / infection horror movie in the vein of 28 Days Later and I was really digging it. The acting was fine and the direction was good. The story was also very well done and there were some very bloody moments. Things were going great, until about the halfway point when everything gradually got worse and eventually culminated in a rather nonsensical and dumb ending. So the movie started out great but didn't end up going anywhere good, so while it had its moments, there just weren't enough overall.

2/5

Planet Terror
Year – 2007
Director – Robert Rodriguez
Tags – Zombies

This is part one of the theatrical experience called Grindhouse. A group of rogue army soldiers carry a deadly infection that spreads into a small town, turning the locals into zombies. Meant to be a throwback to the 70's era grindhouse movies, Planet Terror definitely delivers the feel of the whole guns, girls and gore schematic. The gore is amazing, definitely one of the bloodiest movies I've ever seen. Speaking of which, the FX work is spellbinding, a mix of modern day work and the cheesy stuff from back in the day. The way they manipulated the film post production to give it the feel of a flawed, cheap production, complete with missing reels is just a great. The whole movie is over the top, which is just the way it should be. This is just a great time, loads of fun, and I highly recommend this movie.

4.5/5

Plasterhead
Year – 2006
Director – Kevin Higgins
Tags – Slasher / Survival

A group of young adults on Spring Break find a purse full of money and take a detour to try and find the owner. What they find instead is a town with a secret and a killer with no face. This low budget effort is just across the board average. There is nothing bad to say about it or good, it is completely average. And I guess there's really nothing wrong with that per se. While I would have liked to have seen more effort of course, this is a low budget slasher movie and it delivers in that respect. It is a slasher movie riddled with flaws but is not a bad experience. I've seen worse and I've seen better, nothing much more I can say about it.

2.5/5

Poker Club, The
Year – 2008
Director – Tim McCann
Tags – Suspense

This movie offers up an interesting premise. What would you do if you were playing poker with your buddies and came across someone robbing your house, and then in the course of confronting him, you accidently killed him? If you answered, call the police… then enjoy your prison sentence, because that probably what's going to happen. You just can't have faith in the justice system these days. So they decide to cover it up, and then people start dying around them, thus making them wonder if maybe there was more than one person there on that night. Add to that a police detective who is figuring things out a bit too well for their tastes and adding to the tension. I have to say I really enjoyed this movie, it has a tight script, its very well acted and is just all around well done. I do have to say that it is pretty slow, but not from bad pacing, it's just a slow burn to the finale kind of film. I did feel it detracted from the overall experience however. Nowadays it's hard to keep twists and turns in the shadows before the reveal, but The Poker Club pulls it off splendidly. Once it got to the end, and the final reveal came about, I found myself saying: "Wow, didn't see that one coming." Excellent movie.

4/5

Poltergeist

Year – 1982
Director – Tobe Hooper
Tags – Ghosts

A family nestled comfortably in the suburbs begins to have strange occurrences in their house. They start off harmless enough, but quickly evolve into something much more dangerous as their youngest daughter disappears and is now the prisoner of a malevolent force. Poltergeist is a really great ghost movie because it takes the paranormal out of the spooky old house on the hill and thrusts it into your living room. The story is very well done with a good deal of character development in the hopes that you'll care about the family. So many filmmakers forget such details when they're making a movie it seems. The direction is also very good but I felt the movie could have been shorter and that would have made the whole thing run smoother. The cast is excellent and they do well in their roles. There's a lot of visual eye candy too, much of which is very creative, and the FX are impressive, especially for the time period. It may not be a perfect ghost tale but it sure is an entertaining one and I definitely recommend it.

4/5

Poltergeist II: The Other Side

Year – 1986
Director – Brian Gibson
Tags – Ghosts

This movie takes place about a year after the original. While overall I liked this movie, it is definitely inferior to the original. This movie has a great progression of the original storyline and reveals that there was more at play than alluded to in the first movie, and I really appreciate the effort put into that. There are many actors returning to this one from the first, so the acting is definitely on par. The direction is ok but the movie does feel fairly slow at times. I also found the ending to be kind of stupid and rushed. The FX were still good here, but definitely underused. This is a good sequel that had some thought put into it, which is nice, but I can't say I loved it.

3/5

Poltergeist III

Year – 1988
Director – Gary Sherman
Tags – Ghosts

This movie takes place not long after the last one. While I felt the second Poltergeist movie had a good story and was worth making, this one seems a bit forced with regards to how the story progresses. There are only a couple of returning actors this time, but the acting is still above average. The direction here is on par with the last movie, decent but slow. The FX are still good and I do think they were utilized better here than the last one with some interesting and creepy occurrences. But despite the good things, I still can't get over the poorly made script. While this may not be the best horror series around, as least it didn't deliver any terrible movies. Of course we haven't seen the remake yet.

2.5/5

Pool, The (Swimming Pool – Der Tod Feiert Mit)
Year – 2001
Director – Boris Von Sychowski
Tags – Slasher / Survival

A group of soon to be graduates break into an indoor swimming pool for a party, but what they didn't expect was a masked killer to ruin their fun. What sounds like a throwaway slasher actually had some good stuff going for it. I liked how in the beginning when the killer was stalking a young woman, she didn't run and hide, she grabbed a double barreled shotgun AND a bandolier of shotgun shells. Finally, someone does something sensible. The acting and direction were fine, nothing too special. There a couple of great kills mixed with standard stuff. The killer had a cool get-up as well. The story is good and throws up a lot of red herrings as to who the killer might be, but as people die it gets pretty easy to figure out what is going on. This is a good slasher, nothing over the top extraordinary, just plain good.

3/5

Population 436
Year – 2006
Director – Michelle Maxwell MacLaren
Tags – Suspense

A census taker travels to the small town of Rockwell Falls and after only a few short days he realizes that the town is not as perfect as it seems and in fact hides a very dark secret tied to the population. It's refreshing to see a movie attempt a different kind of plot, but I do have to say attempt because I don't feel it was a complete success. The acting is good which was a surprise considering that Fred Durst starred, but I must say, he can actually act to some degree. The direction isn't very good however, as it feels very amateur and the movie ends up being poorly paced. The story is good but lacking any real substance until the third act. This is still a good movie however, despite it being fairly predictable, and I must say I enjoyed it.

3/5

Predator
Year – 1987
Director – John McTierman
Tags – Aliens

When a group of commandos complete a mission in the South American jungle, they then find themselves hunted by an extraterrestrial warrior. Predator is such an awesome movie. There are lots of guns, lots of blood, explosions and one badass alien. First I'll start with the alien, which Stan Winston did an incredible job with. It has the coolest weapons and gizmos, making it quite the opponent. The soldiers fighting it however, that's where I see the movie's major flaw. They have no personality, except for maybe Jesse Ventura's character, as they have no voice of their own and are easily interchangeable. And the filmmakers felt the need to add a female character where there didn't need to be one, and that's always annoying. The direction is great though, and the movie runs along at a quick clip and never gets dull. This is a great sci-fi/horror movie filled with bullets and blood, and even with disposable characters, it ranks high on my list of favorite alien movies.

4/5

Predator 2
Year – 1990
Director – Stephen Hopkins
Tags – Aliens

This time the Predator is in Los Angeles and it's up to a grizzled cop to stop him. This movie really sucks. I know a lot of people like it but for the life of me I can't figure out why. The story is terrible and pointless for starters. The characters in the original weren't very good at all, but here they are absolutely pathetic. Even with some big name actors, the acting for the most part is pretty bad. There's some good blood and decent FX, even a little nudity, but if that's the best the movie has to offer than I would just as soon not watch it at all. The direction is also pretty bad, as the movie moves along very slowly and overstays its welcome. It starts off violent but quickly moves into being pretty stupid and then finally drags its dead carcass into the end credits. Very little entertainment in this movie for me.

1.5/5

Premonition (Yogen)
Year – 2004
Director – Noria Tsuruta
Tags – Suspense

A man foresees the death of his child through a mystical newspaper but acts too late to save her. Now the newspaper tells of other tragedies and he finds himself torn as to whether to help these strangers at the cost of himself or to not act at all. A "Newspaper of Terror" isn't very terrifying at all, but the movie does have some good moments. Nothing concretely brilliant, but passable at least. The direction is good but not terribly well done, I did enjoy the acting however, especially by the male lead. The story is ok but nothing too tremendous. The CGI is pretty bad at times but fortunately not used too much. This is an ok movie, nothing great, but nothing really bad either.

2.5/5

Primeval
Year – 2007
Director – Michael Katleman
Tags – Animals

A group of people go into the African bush in search of a killer crocodile and find much more than they bargain for. This movie reminds me of Congo in the sense that the characters have animals to deal with, as well as a country caught up in civil war, but that really is where the similarities end. I find it ironic that the kills performed by the humans in the movie are much more cold and heartless than that of the crocodile, and that was probably intentional. The giant killer croc story actually takes a backseat to human horror for the most part, which works most of the time. The acting is good, but I do hate the obligatory comic relief character shoved into the mix, as I feel this movie would have better if it was taken seriously. The pacing is good and the movie rarely slows down, but when it does you'll find yourself staring at the wall. The FX work is good for the most part but there's really nothing here to write home about. Overall this is a pretty good flick and while it has its share of problems, it's nothing too major. A good time.

3.5/5

Prince of Darkness
Year – 1987
Director – John Carpenter
Tags – Demonic Possession

An odd canister of liquid is found in an abandoned church along with various other artifacts. A group of college people are assembled to make sense of it all, but what they discover may just be the devil himself. Prince of Darkness is a pretty unique movie as it really defies a proper category, which makes sense, since it is a John Carpenter flick. It carries a great atmosphere to it, due in part to the great location in which the movie was shot (which isn't actually a church if I remember correctly, because I believe they just slapped a cross on top of the building). The movie is full of those great Carpenter nuances and original touches, but unfortunately it can also be rather slow. I guess a movie like this couldn't exactly be a mile a minute kind of movie, because there is a lot of technical and theological discussion that must be made, but it still shows through. Still a great movie if you have the patience for it. Think of it as thinking man's horror. Yeah, that'll work.

3.5/5

Progeny

Year – 1998
Director – Brian Yuzna
Tags – Aliens

The wife of a doctor finds out that she is pregnant after a strange event, and as the fetus grows, so grows the parent's suspicions that their child may be of alien origin. I really wasn't into this movie for the first hour or so. There were some good actors in the movie but not particularly great performances. The direction was kind of slow and the story was fairly weak. Needless to say I was quickly becoming disinterested. But when Brad Dourif took a larger role in the film and the last half hour came, the movie took a major upswing and almost managed to redeem the previous hour. That's when the gore and gooey moments came into play to full effect. This is far from being a great movie, in fact it's just barely better than average, but at least it wasn't all bad.

3/5

Prom Night
Year – 1980
Director – Paul Lynch
Tags – Slasher / Survival

Years after the tragic death of a child, the kids that were involved with the death receive mysterious phone calls and messages on the day of the prom. Then a killer begins to kill them one by one. This movie is about as vanilla as a slasher can be. The story is very plain and it takes forever for anything to actually happen. I don't even think the first kill comes along until about an hour into the movie, and then when they do start coming, they also end up being plain and not very bloody. I think more time is spent disco dancing in this movie than killing. Still, it moves along nicely enough, and the acting isn't bad, so I guess that counts for something. Quite simply put, there are far better movies than this that have similar content, but at the same time, this one isn't bad and at least I got some enjoyment out of it.

2.5/5

*Prom Night II can be found under Hello Mary Lou: Prom Night II.

Prom Night III: The Last Kiss
Year – 1990
Director – Ron Oliver, Peter R. Simpson
Tags – Demons

This movie is a continuation of the second Prom Night, which seems to take place around the same time. This time Mary Lou is some kind of demon instead of a ghost. This one is more comical than horrific, which some actual funny moments. Of course the movie ends up trying too hard and the attempted comedy gets old quick. The horror aspect is lacking, but it did have some interesting kills, even if the blood was lacking as well. The acting is just terrible and the direction could have used a lot polish. This movie is barely passable but it did manage to get me to laugh a few times, and I did enjoy some of the kills, making it a worthwhile watch for fans of the second movie.

2.5/5

Prom Night IV: Deliver Us from Evil
Year – 1992
Director – Clay Borris
Tags – Slasher / Survival

After having some continuity between the second and third movies, for the fourth entry into the series it moves off into other territories again. This time a psychotic priest stalks two couples who he feels are unclean and blights against God. Well hell, I guess there had to be a downright stinker in this franchise eventually. This movie is incredibly boring, taking way too long to get to the meat of the story. And when you have actors as bad as these and you know they can't carry the storyline, it's best to just get on with the sex and violence. When will people realize that? The kills are all fairly standard and not extravagant in the least, which only displeased me more. Easily the worst of the series, but still better than the remake, which is really sad.

1.5/5

Prom Night [Remake]
Year – 2008
Director – Nelson McCormick
Tags – Slasher / Survival

This is really a remake in name only, as this movie doesn't follow the original storyline at all. In this movie a girl is stalked by an obsessed man and he ends up killing her parents, Years later he escapes from the mental home he is housed and hunts her down on the night of her prom. This movie just sucks. There's really no ifs ands or buts about it. This movie blows. One good thing I will say is that Jonathon Schaech plays a good killer, but the rest of the acting is terrible. The unattractive cast bumbles through their lines like a group of mental cases overdosing on Thorazine. This movie also falls into several clichés and it gets tired quickly. A terrible story and sloppy direction just drag this movie down further. I don't know what rock they overturned to find this cast, or what color crayon was used to write the script, but I can tell you that this is definitely one of the worst movies to hit theatres in a long time.

1/5

Prophecy, The
Year – 1995
Director – Gregory Widen
Tags – Suspense

There is a war raging in Heaven that is at a stalemate, so the angel Gabriel goes to Earth to search for the blackest soul to help tip the odds in the favor of some rogue angels. Now it's up to an ex-priest to stop Gabriel from retrieving the soul that has been hidden inside a little girl. In the realm of religious thrillers, this has always been one of my favorites. And the main reason it is one of my favorites is because of the extraordinary cast performing so perfectly. Don't get me wrong, the story is an excellent one, and the direction is great, but the acting is otherworldly. And no, that wasn't meant to be a pun. Christopher Walken, Eric Stoltz and Viggo Mortensen are especially good, but everyone puts on a great show. There is a lot of great eye candy as well with multiple twisted visuals sure to upset religious folk, I love it. This is a very unique and well done thriller and worth viewing more than once.

4.5/5

Prophecy II, The
Year – 1998
Director – Greg Spence
Tags – Suspense

This movie continues on years after the original. While The Prophecy hardly needed a sequel, let alone so many sequels, this movie isn't all bad I guess. The story is much weaker than its predecessor and is really only mildly interesting. There are also far too many instances of reusing moments of the original that made it so iconic. The acting is great once again though, with Christopher Walken putting on yet another memorable performance. The direction isn't so bad but could have used some tweaking because the movie did get pretty slow at times. Not bad, not good, just an average sequel where they're needn't even be one.

2.5/5

Prophecy III: The Ascent, The
Year – 2000
Director – Patrick Lussier
Tags – Suspense

I guess this movie continues on several years after the last one even though no one seems to age properly from the previous movies. The story progresses here to some degree and has its fair share of continuity errors and a pretty big cheese factor, which doesn't fit in the series. My eyes were rolling on many occasions at the spectacle before them. The acting is definitely a downgrade here and even though Christopher Walken returns yet again for some reason, his role is rather small. The direction is average at best and the story is downright silly at times. I really wish I had good things to say about this movie and series in general but it appears as though all the good ideas were done in the first movie. This one isn't all bad, but it's close.

Prophecy IV: Uprising, The
Year – 2005
Director – Joel Soisson
Tags – Suspense

After the initial trilogy the series continues with a new storyline. Here the saga of angels versus mankind continues in Eastern Europe and focuses on an unlikely hero and a holy book that contains information that the angels will do anything to possess. I wasn't impressed with the last two movies and this one is nothing different. The acting is good and the movie starts out with a bang and had the potential to be a very engaging thriller but then the story begins to get boring and the whole movie begins to lag. I'll give this movie points for the great cast and the good start, but after the first act this movie became somewhat of a chore to sit through.

2/5

Prophecy V: Forsaken, The
Year – 2005
Director – Joel Soisson
Tags – Suspense

This movie picks up where the last one left off. I really wasn't looking forward to this movie after the last one, but surprisingly this is definitely the best sequel in The Prophecy series. The cast is great once again and the addition of Tony Todd really gave some life to the movie. The story progresses nicely from the last one, which I guess makes sense because it really had nowhere to go but up. The direction is better as well and the movie is not nearly as boring as the last one. Of course it probably also helps that this movie is only about 75 minutes long so there isn't much in the way of unnecessary elements. This is definitely a step up and if there should be a sixth movie down the road, I'll look forward to seeing it.

3.5/5

Psycho
Year – 1960
Director – Alfred Hitchcock
Tags – Slasher / Survival

This is the story of a young woman who steals a sizable amount of money from her employer and then goes on the run. While running she comes into contact with a young man who runs a motel. But she soon finds out that the young man is not well at all after being under the thumb of his domineering mother his entire life. Psycho really is the first full blown slasher movie ever made, and that's not a slight against it at all, because it created an entire sub genre. Even though that sub genre is now overflowing with watered down crap, Psycho remains the best that ever was, for many reasons. First off, the direction is immaculate with every shot just so well crafted that it could only come from a master. Second, a twist in the middle of the movie with the lead actress was pretty much unheard of and really made it stand out above all others. Beyond that, the acting is great, the story is one of a kind and this is just a beautiful movie. An absolute masterpiece.

5/5

Psycho II
Year – 1983
Director – Richard Franklin
Tags – Slasher / Survival

This movie takes place many years after the original. Now I'll be the first to admit that a sequel to Psycho seems like a pretty useless idea as the original ended so well I would have preferred if it was just left alone. But I'll also be the first to admit that this movie is pretty damn good. The story is wonderful and is a great progression on the original, and some definite thought went into it to ensure that it wouldn't appear as just some cash-in attempt (even though ultimately it was). The acting is really good as is the direction. It may not be a stand out movie that blew me away, it's just very well done and I have no complaints about it.

3.5/5

Psycho III
Year – 1988
Director – Anthony Perkins
Tags – Slasher / Survival

This second sequel takes place not too long after the last movie. So here we see Anthony Perkins step behind the lens for this third Psycho movie, and I must say he did a good job. I wonder how much better he would have done with a more polished story though. The progression of this movie is somewhat mundane and this movie is definitely just a slasher flick without much depth behind it. The acting is good though for the most part. I liked this movie for what it was, even though it was not anything that great, but I did find it to be entertaining nonetheless.

3/5

Psycho IV: The Beginning
Year – 1990
Director – Mick Garris
Tags – Slasher / Survival

Here we have a bit of sequel mixed in with a big chunk of prequel. And this is the first time I get to say that a Psycho movie isn't good. First off there's a load of continuity errors in this movie, and if you're going to make a prequel you better check out your source material thoroughly to avoid errors the likes of which we see here. And seriously, since when was Norman Bates' mother a young woman with an English accent? There are good actors here that don't put on very good performances, but for the most part they are passable. The direction is ok but nothing really special to write home about. Overall though the movie isn't good at all, in fact it's bad, but at least is has a mild entertainment value to it.

2/5

Psycho [Remake]
Year – 1998
Director – Gus Van Zant
Tags – Slasher / Survival

This is actually a complete shot for shot remake of the original, exactly the same. And that's why I hate this movie, it is absolutely pointless. Making a shot for shot remake of an American movie is just plain stupid. I can understand it for a foreign movie in a language other than English, but for an American movie? Come on. To make matters worse, the cast lacks the charisma of the original cast. They are good in their own rights but I felt all of them were miscast here. The movie was watchable, after all, it is an exact copy of a masterpiece, but I just can't get past how useless it is. This is just blatant plagiarism masked as an update. There really is no reason to ever watch this movie.

0.5/5

Pulse (Kairo)
Year – 2001
Director – Kiyoshi Kurosawa
Tags – Ghosts

University students investigate a rash of suicides that all seem to be connected to a website where people can supposedly commune with the dead. This movie shows what I love about foreign horror, and here we have a ghost movie that actually tries to be scary and doesn't rely on stupid jump scares, instead opting for the respectable atmospheric scares. And there's another thing about the scares that make them work so well, they're slow. Most people try to rush into a scare by having a ghost lunge at a person, here, they creep up so slowly that it really heightens the tension and allows for some skin crawling moments. I have to be honest here and say that I thought the story sounded lame, but it actually worked, which is a rarity for "internet horror". I do think the movie was too long and it really slowed things down quite a bit, but overall there was good acting, FX and wonderful aural and visual scares.

4/5

Pulse [Remake]

Year – 2006
Director – Jim Sonzero
Tags – Ghosts

This remake follows the same plot as the original. Well, here's yet another movie that was swept up into the madness of remaking every Asian horror film ever made, but at least this one isn't all bad. The first mistake though, is taking a genuinely scary movie and removing all of the scares, opting instead for very poor jump scares that failed to get a rise out of me. The next is the addition of one dimensional characters played by some good actors and some bad actors. You'll easily be able to tell which is which. They also failed to use the aural scares that worked so well in the original, which includes the creepy score. But fortunately they did do some things right. This movie is shorter and runs smoother, and I also liked the scale of the movie, which was much bigger and apocalyptic. This one isn't too bad but it certainly missed the high mark of the original.

2.5/5

Pulse 2: Afterlife
Year – 2008
Director – Joel Soisson
Tags – Ghosts

This sequel to the remake picks up right after the last one left off but with mostly different people. This movie is so poorly done it's disgusting. For some reason there is an obscene amount of green screen work, and it's easily some of the worst I've ever seen. They use a green screen for everything. Woman walks down the street. Green screen. Woman stands in front of a cabin. Green screen. Woman walks into cabin. Green screen. Seriously, every other scene is shot with a green screen and it's ugly. The story is also really bad and is only even barely related to the original story. The acting is atrocious by the female lead and some others, and at best the rest of the acting is passable and not good at all. To top things off the direction is poor and the pacing is pretty bad. This movie is just plain hideous and it hurts my eyes to look at it. But I do suggest people watch it if they are into sadomasochism because it will certainly be a painful experience. Worthless in every way it could be and more.

0.5/5

Pulse 3: Invasion
Year – 2008
Director – Joel Soisson
Tags – Ghosts

This movie continues on seven years after the last one. Well I wasn't looking forward to this movie because the last one was an utter abomination and the same guy who did that one is behind this one. So is this a completely worthless, steaming pile of dog shit like the last one? Well yes it is, although I do have to say it is minutely better than the previous garbage pile. It's a shame Rider Strong wasted his time with this junk because he's a pretty good actor. As for everyone else… they're pretty bad. And the lead character was very much unlikeable and I couldn't wait for her to die. The same baffling use of green screen with horribly drawn backgrounds is on display here and the story is crap once again. I really enjoyed the original and the remake wasn't half bad, but these sequels should have never been made and I recommend no one ever watch them, even for free.

1/5

Puppet Master
Year – 1989
Director – David Schmoeller
Tags – Slasher / Survival

A group of psychics visit an old hotel to pay their respects to an old friend when they come across a group of animated puppets that had been stashed there years before. But they are anything but hospitable. I think the main thing I liked about this movie was the fact that there are several puppets trolling around the hotel killing people, not just one. And I liked the fact that they are all very different as well. No two are alike. The kills are also pretty good for the most part, because a variety of puppets equals a variety of ways to die. Now I do think that the movie took too long to get to the meat of the story, but once the puppets start killing, the pacing gets a lot better from there. The acting is typical low budget stuff, nothing all that grandiose. The puppets look great, the FX are good, and I especially liked the puppet cam where you get to see things from their point of view. It's got blood, it's got nudity and it's got puppets, you can't ask for much more than that.

3.5/5

Puppet Master II
Year – 1991
Director – Dave Allen
Tags – Slasher / Survival

In this sequel we find the puppets resurrecting their master, Toulon, and then they begin killing off some paranormal researchers so that Toulon can get the brain fluid he needs to fully reanimate himself. The story is an interesting direction for the franchise to go, but it kind of ends up being sour. The movie is very slow and most of the kills are bland. The acting is about the same, but it was nice to see Buck Flower in a small role. There's also a disturbing lack of blood and nudity in this one. At least we get a new puppet here, so that part is cool, but overall this movie is just dull and unappealing. Not a good first step into being a franchise if you ask me, but we'll just see how the story goes from here.

2/5

Puppet Master III: Toulon's Revenge
Year – 1991

Director – David DeCoteau
Tags – Slasher / Survival

This movie is actually a prequel to Puppet Master and shows Toulon and his puppets taking revenge in Nazi Germany after the death of his wife. Meanwhile, the Nazis are searching for him in order to get their hands on his serum that gives the puppets life, and to aid them in their program for reanimating the dead. Now this is a very good addition to the series. The movie really does look like it takes place in war torn Berlin. This movie also shows the origins of the puppets and the creation of Leech Woman and Blade, which is pretty damn cool. The acting is definitely a step above the last two movies and the direction is good as well. I would actually say this one tops the original to some degree, and despite some flaws is easily the best movie in the franchise.

3.5/5

Puppet Master IV: When Bad Puppets Turn Good
Year – 1993
Director – Jeff Burr
Tags – Demons

This movie happens sometime during the franchise's timeline, it's not a direct sequel to any of the other movies. Given that the last movie, even though a prequel, showed the puppets killing Nazis, it was a natural progression for them to become good, because it was just what the fans wanted. We love the puppets and found we could love them even more if they killing off bad people. Here a demon sends some conveniently puppet sized demons to Earth to try and reclaim the secrets of animation that Toulon "stole" from him. So right of the bat there's continuity errors, but they made me laugh more than anything. The acting is ok, and the direction isn't bad, but the story does feel a bit hokey. We get another new puppet but this one is kind of lame, like someone was trying too hard. The fourth movie in the series is completely watchable but it's not what I would call good per se, so it's pretty much just for hardcore fans of the series.

2.5/5

Puppet Master V: The Final Chapter
Year – 1994
Director – Jeff Burr
Tags – Slasher / Survival

This movie takes place immediately after the last one. Final chapter my ass, I'm not falling for that again. With the same director and some actors returning from the last movie, we are given some good continuity, but who really cares at this point? The series isn't exactly riddled with masterpieces and this one is no different. Acting and direction are pretty much on par with the last movie but this one's story really isn't much of anything at all, it's more like a hurry up and release a sequel kind of movie. No thought put into this it seems. Not the worst of the series but definitely not good either, once again this is just for hardcore fans.

2/5

* **Puppet Master VI can be found under Curse of the Puppet Master.**

* **Puppet Master VII can be found under Retro Puppet Master.**

Puppet Masters, The
Year – 1994
Director – Stuart Orme
Tags – Aliens

Based on the novel by Robert A. Heinlein, this movie is about a parasitic alien that attaches itself to a human host and works it like a puppet (hence the name). Now an elite government agency must stop them before they can multiply and further and take over the world. This is a very good movie that displays nothing exceptional but is a very rewarding and entertaining movie nonetheless. The acting is great, and the direction is very good, allowing the movie to move along fluidly. The alien FX are also very good looking but underused. The story is good but not particularly engaging. You know how it's going to play out from the get go, but it's still fun.

3.5/5

Q: The Winged Serpent
Year – 1982
Director – Larry Cohen
Tags – Monsters

A winged beast from South American lore begins terrorizing New York City, plucking citizens from the rooftops and eating them. Now it's up to a small time crook and the police force to find the creature's nest before it can kill again. I firmly believe that if this movie had a major budget behind it, it could have been one hell of monster movie. Instead we get a Claymation bird that really does look like crap. The story is pretty good, even if it is completely far fetched. The direction is typical Cohen, slow, but ultimately good. The acting is pretty good as well. And that really does sum up the movie, as its good all around, just nothing great. This is a fun movie with a few good, bloody moments and a really cheesy villain. Definitely a must see if you're a fan of 80's horror, for everyone else, go into it expecting very little, and you might actually get something in return.

3/5

Queen of the Damned
Year – 2002

Director – Michael Rymer
Tags – Vampires

In this Anne Rice adaptation, we find Lestat in modern times making a name for himself as a rock star while simultaneously angering his fellow vampires and waking the queen of the vampires. There are major flaws with this movie, the first being that they forced two novels (Queen of the Damned & The Vampire Lestat) into one movie, making it feel like too much in a too short run time. The second is that Anne Rice did not write the screenplay, and with complicated works such as hers, it really is best to have her do it herself. The acting is ok, but there are really no great performances here. The soundtrack is pretty awesome though. In all this is an unworthy adaptation that suffered from trying to force too much into a bloated script, and while it is still entertaining, it's also barely average.

2.5/5

Quick and the Undead, The
Year – 2006
Director – Gerald Nott
Tags – Zombies

Eighty-two years ago a viral outbreak turned most of the world's population into zombies. Now zombie bounty hunters are the only chance the last vestiges of humanity have left for survival. I love the Z-Grade zombie movies, the DIY microbudget gore fests, so I picked this one up for cheap not expecting much, and I actually found myself enjoying it. The plot is pretty good, and it is pulled off decently. The acting is so-so, not bad, and I've definitely seen worse. The zombies look pretty good, and the gore is above average as well. It has all of the elements a watchable zombie movie needs, and while the pacing could be tightened up, and maybe some more zombie action could have been included I was never really bored by the movie. It also had some pretty good production value as well, this is no camcorder movie. It may not be the next zombie epic, but it is still better than a lot of crap out there. I would call this an above average zombie movie, not great by any means, but still a solid addition to anyone's zombie collection.

3/5

Quicksilver Highway
Year – 1997
Director – Mick Garris
Tags – Anthology, Suspense

This anthology features two stories and a wraparound. The wraparound is just lame as hell and it doesn't really matter what it's about, it's just some weird guy introducing the stories more or less. The first story is about a traveling salesman, a hitchhiker and a curious pair of chattery teeth. The second is about a doctor whose hands gain a mind of their own. This movie is pretty bad. The first story, a Stephen King adaptation, is a pretty weak story, but decently adapted. The second is Clive Barker tale, but very horribly done. The movies feature some good actors who put on some fairly poor performances. While I liked the first story, everything else about the movie was pretty much crap, and the direction was fairly bad. The movie is saved from doom by a somewhat entertaining King story, but that's all this has going for it.

2/5

Rage, The
Year – 2007
Director – Robert Kurtzman
Tags – Infection

A mad scientist is testing a deadly virus when his subject escapes into the woods. The virus is then transmitted into a pack of vultures and they begin to attack humans, spreading the infection even more. Unfortunately this movie is nothing more than a showcase of FX. The acting is mostly terrible aside from the genre vets, the CGI and green screen work is atrocious, and to make matters worse, there's just a throwaway story slapped onto it. But as I said, the FX work is top notch, loads of gore and lots of cool kills, dead bodies and make-up. Not to mention the infected vultures. So while the FX are the main draw here, as everything else is pretty much crap, it does make the movie entertaining at least. Oh, and there's a small live performance from the band Mushroomhead, which is awesome. But other than that, this one's a stinker.

2.5/5

Rage: Carrie 2, The
Year – 1999
Director – Katt Shea
Tags – Suspense

This sequel to Carrie takes place twenty years after the original. I was pretty leery about a sequel, but I do like how they made this one. It does bear too many similarities to the original for my tastes, but does have enough original material to hold my interest. The direction was really good and I found that the movie was paced well. The acting was also good, even if there wasn't anything outstanding. The final showdown at the end is pretty similar to the original but features some pretty gory moments which were good fun. Overall I would have to say I liked this movie even though I don't think a sequel should have been made, it was still really entertaining.

3/5

Raising Cain
Year – 1992
Director – Brian de Palma
Tags – Suspense

An adulterous mother suspects her husband of attempting to recreate the failed experiments of his father and believes he may be responsible for the recent rash of kidnappings. I wish that I had a massive amount to praise to bestow upon this film but the fact of the matter is that it is a flawed movie, without question. John Lithgow puts on a very well done performance in many parts and everyone else is adequate but the movie is just too slow and at times uninteresting. It definitely has its good moments but there are not enough of them to truly make this anything remarkable. Raising Cain is a good movie but not anything that really stands out above other thrillers on the market.

3/5

Rasen

Year – 1998
Director – Joji Iida
Tags – Ghosts

This is an alternate sequel to the movie Ringu, while there is a Ringu 2 this movie shows other events that were a result of the first Ringu movie. I really like the idea of showing another angle on Ringu 2 and this is like what happened behind the scenes, and thus, it is a pretty slow and uneventful movie. The acting is fine but the story and direction just weren't very interesting. I really wish this would have panned out because I would have liked to have seen more intersecting and alternate sequels of horror movies in the future, but if this is any indication as to how they will be, I guess it's best to skip the idea.

2/5

Ravenous

Year – 1999
Director – Antonia Bird
Tags – Cannibals

Set during the Civil War, Ravenous is about a man who is assigned to a remote fort in California. During his stay, a man comes out of the wilderness with a disturbing tale of cannibalism. For some reason, this movie had a string of humor in it, especially during the beginning that just didn't fit with the theme of the movie. It was still pretty funny, but it doesn't work to the full luster that I expect the filmmakers wanted it to. The pacing can be a little off at times as well. But other than that, this is a well shot and well acted film with an interesting story and a plot that conceals a few twists and turns along the way. This may not be the best way to get you cannibal fix, but this is by no means a bad movie.

3/5

Raw Meat (Death Line)

Year – 1972

Director – Gary Sherman
Tags – Cannibals

Many years ago a cave-in underneath London trapped a group of people underground, and no attempts were made to save them. But what they don't realize is that the people survived by eating one another. Now years later there is only one left and he's searching the subway for more than just meat, he wants a mate. So much potential here completely squandered. The great locale is not put to good use and much like the cannibal, we hardly ever see it. Most of the movie is spent above ground and with the police instead of in the tunnels where it should have been. The acting is very good but the direction is quite slow, probably due to all of the non-action sequences in the movie. It's very droll, like dry English humor. When the cannibal does attack, it's pretty bloody and feral, very exciting. The rest of the time, I'm fighting to stay awake. This is a good movie but it could have been so much more. Maybe someday someone will remake this diamond in the rough and shine it to its full luster.

3/5

Razor Eaters
Year – 2003
Director – Shannon Young
Tags – Serial Killer (Fictional)

Loosely based on a true story, this movie chronicles the actions of a gang of men as they terrorized Melbourne, Australia by assaulting and killing people that they felt deserved to die. I had heard some good things about Razor Eaters, and I feel those good things are very justified. The film is very gritty, and in a documentary style, which cleverly hides the low budget. But it works, it definitely works. And even though this is a low budget movie, it's well acted, well shot (even though most of it is shot on handheld), and well written. This gang committed loathsome acts, but gained a cult following, why? Because you had to kind of admire what they were doing. Killing a guy who ran a dog fighting ring (my favorite part), drug dealers, an arms dealer and more. But the movie isn't all about random violence, there's some depth behind everything, and I'll leave it at that, I don't want to ruin things for you. This movie is compared to Natural Born Killers, and while it doesn't quite reach that caliber, it is still a very entertaining ride.

4/5

Re-Animator
Year – 1985
Director – Stuart Gordon
Tags – Zombies

Loosely based on a written work by H.P. Lovecraft, Re-Animator tells the tale of Herbert West, a medical student who is hard at work developing a serum that will reanimate the dead. He gains the assistance of another medical student for his studies, but their experiments get out of control. This movie is classic not just because it is gory as hell or because of the humor in it, or even because Barbara Crampton gets naked, no, it is a classic because it's pretty damn unique. The zombies of Re-Animator are different here than in other zombie movies because depending on how long after death they were brought back, they have different personalities. Sure, a lot of liberties were taken from the original written work, but that was just to make a more entertaining film, which was accomplished. Those expecting a zombie apocalypse type movie may be disappointed, there are no Romero zombies here, what we have here is a very different, very fun take on the zombie sub genre, and it's a success.

4.5/5

*Re-Animator 2 can be found under Bride of Re-Animator.

*Re-Animator 3 can be found under Beyond Re-Animator.

Real Friend, A (Adivina Quien Soy)
Year – 2006
Director – Enrique Urbizu
Tags – Suspense

This is part of the DVD box set "6 Films to Keep you Awake". A young girl is an outcast at school and has imaginary friends over real ones. But they are not your typical imaginary friends. Her friends are the vampire from Nosferatu and Leatherface from The Texas Chainsaw Massacre, and they will do anything to protect her. To me this is a cute movie. I'm sure a lot of people would think this girl was twisted for having such friends but I think that it's pretty cool and a nice new concept to boot. It plays out like a mystery and you're left wondering just what is going on, and when the story progresses, it makes sense, and then the friends really get to play. I know that's vague but I don't want to reveal too much. This is a fun and inventive story with a very strong ending and I greatly enjoyed it.

4/5

Reaping, The
Year – 2007
Director – Stephen Hopkins
Tags – Suspense

An investigator who specializes in debunking religious miracles travels to a small Southern town that seems to be suffering from the biblical ten plagues. The ten plagues, while easily explained by science, were all rather fascinating so this movie had the potential to be awesome, so why wasn't it? Well, let's begin. Each plague is very poorly represented and each graced the screen for at most only a couple of minutes and in some places, mere seconds, and I'm sorry, but if that is the basis for your story, maybe you should pay some more attention to it. The CGI was also really bad at times, which was strange because a good deal of it actually looked pretty good. The acting was good but the direction was very haphazard and unappealing. The story starts out good enough but tends to get pretty weak as the movie progresses and culminates into a bad plot twist and even worse ending. It's not all bad but it's also far from good, The Reaping is just very disappointing.

2/5

Rear Window
Year – 1954
Director – Alfred Hitchcock
Tags – Suspense

A wheelchair bound man who passes the time spying on his neighbors observes what he believes to be a man murdering his wife. Now he must find a way to convince his friend in the police department that the man is a killer before he disposes of all of the evidence. A true classic in every sense of the word, Rear Window is an incredibly suspenseful movie that trains its main focus on the voyeuristic tendencies that every person possesses, whether they'll admit it or not. The story is nothing short of brilliant, the direction is remarkable and the acting is great, I found absolutely nothing to dislike about the movie. An enjoyable film from start to finish, while watching this it's easy to see why Hitchcock has been and always will be considered as one of the greatest directors to have ever lived. A must see.

4.5/5

Red
Year – 2008
Director – Trygve Allister Diesen, Lucky McKee
Tags – Suspense

One day a man is fishing when accosted by some youths, and for no reason whatsoever, one of them shoots his faithful dog Red, a gift from his late wife. The man seeks justice for what has happened to his beloved pet, but when none can found through normal channels, he takes matters into his own hands. I found this movie to be nothing short of astounding. I'm sure it will relate better to dog owners, because as one myself, if anyone had done this to one of my dogs, I would not have been nearly as restrained as the main character. To those who aren't animal lovers, you'll probably just say, "Who cares? It's a dog", and I will say that this is not the movie for you. The story is amazing and the resolution of the matter at hand will undoubtedly divide audiences but I loved the unique approach. I was worried about the direction since McKee had to drop off the project for reasons unknown to me and Diesen had to take over, but the direction is seamless and perfect nonetheless. The acting is also extremely well done with Brian Cox in particular putting on an absolutely tour de force performance. This movie blew my mind with just how amazing it is. A must see.

Red Dragon
Year – 2002
Director – Brett Ratner
Tags – Serial Killer (Fictional)

This is a remake of the movie Manhunter and follows the same story. This movie is very close to being as good as Manhunter. The acting is great here as well, some being better here and some not, but all very well done at least. The direction is about the same. There are additional segments in this movie that were only spoken of in Manhunter, which I have mixed feeling about because I know they were only added to this movie to help show the relationship between this movie and The Silence of the Lambs, especially that final sequence, which was completely tacked on and lame. I also didn't like the end of this movie as I felt it was cheap. Still, it's a very good movie and a definitely worthy remake, but I just can't get over the ending because it's really not very good at all.

3.5/5

Red Eye
Year – 2005
Director – Wes Craven
Tags – Suspense

While a woman is taking a flight to visit her father, she meets a seemingly nice man, but once the flight begins, she finds out he is anything but. This movie is terrible. I can list everything right about this movie in two words: Cillian Murphy. The guy is great, and even with a terrible character and poorly written story, he somehow manages to shine, and that takes talent. Now onto the bad. The biggest problem is Rachel McAdams, as she gives an absolutely horrid performance. And I'm sure that part of the blame must be placed again on the writer, but she just has no excuse for being this bad. Usually in a situation like this, you feel bad for the character and want her to persevere through this adversity of dealing with a madman. Here, I wanted her to die. I did not want a happy ending for her, I did not want her to find her inner strength, I wanted her to die a slow and painful death in the hopes that she would shut up and the movie would become interesting. The story is garbage, the direction is shoddy, and this movie is just awful. Case closed, move on.

1/5

Red Riding Hood
Year – 2003
Director – Giacomo Cimini
Tags – Slasher / Survival

An orphaned girl living in Rome is urged to move back to the states with her grandmother. But she has unfinished business with the sinners of Rome, and she and her friend George, a massive man dressed as a wolf still need to teach them a lesson. Never have I really had such mixed feelings about a movie. While I am intrigued by the story and the general weirdness of the movie, and somewhat impressed by the gory kill scenes, it also features easily one of the most annoying performances by a child actor in history. This kid was so grating I wanted to gouge my eyes out. The rest of the cast wasn't very good either, but in comparison to the lead, they were brilliant. The direction also leaves much to be desired as it could get dull in places. So while I don't really recommend this movie, there were some things I liked about it, but a painful performance by the orphaned kid really killed it.

2/5

Reeker
Year – 2005
Director – David Payne
Tags – Slasher / Survival

A group of college kids on their way to a rave in the desert break down at a gas station that is mysteriously deserted. Soon they begin to be killed off by a spectral creature that reeks of death. I like the killer here because it's so different from all the other killers out there, and the kills themselves are pretty good, which are the most important elements of a slasher flick. The good acting and direction are just icing on the cake. But I'm not going to say that this movie is a classic because while things about the movie are good, there's really nothing great about it. The story is good but lacks any real punch and I really disliked the ending because I found it to be kind of stupid. Still, the movie has some good gore and it's just a fun time, so that makes it worth checking out in my book.

3.5/5

*Reeker 2 can be found under No Man's Land: The Rise of Reeker.

Reincarnation (Rinne)
Year – 2005
Director – Takashi Shimizu
Tags – Ghosts

An actress begins having visions after landing a role in a movie that chronicles a real life murder spree. I'm not quite sure how to feel about this movie. It wasn't bad, but I just found it to be an hour of boredom before things finally picked up. The events surrounding the actress were too spaced out, and that made me tune out. The first hour of set-up is very slow, but then in the final act, things definitely got interesting. I really like how the movie played out from there, everything came together quite nicely and the tension was top notch. Asian horror is always a tough sell for me, because more often than not their pacing is really bad, and this movie is no exception. But a strong close to the movie saved it in my opinion, it didn't make it a great flick, but it did save it from being labeled as worthless.

2.5/5

Relic, The
Year – 1997
Director – Peter Hyams
Tags – Monsters

A museum receives a shipment including a strange artifact and some leaves from a scientist in the field, but they also get a strange beast that requires a certain part of the human brain for nourishment. I like this movie, it's very well done. The creature looks awesome, something that has a lot of character to it. The movie runs smooth with very little hiccups and the story is moved along well with not only good direction, but with great acting as well. There are several decapitations here, which makes sense since the creature requires human brains, and a good deal of other kills and blood. This is a nice entry into the genre and just an all around good monster movie. I like the museum setting and I like the way it plays out, nothing terribly amazing about it, it's just good.

3.5/5

Resident Evil
Year – 2002
Director – Paul W.S. Anderson
Tags – Zombies, Monsters

An elite team of special agents infiltrate an underground base after a deadly virus is unleashed within. Based on the popular video game series, fans of the series will no doubt be disappointed that the movie has hardly anything to do with any of the games, which in a way is sad since the first game had so much movie potential, but anyway. The film is shot in a very stylish way that will appeal to those who suffer from ADD, and in this respect, the movie is always moving forward and never gets a chance to lag. I do wish Michelle Rodriguez was not cast here as her "Badass Woman" role is very stale and overplayed. The zombies look great, and as for the other mutations, well, they are CGI, and not that well done. The film is undeniably entertaining, despite its lack of brains, and I like it, 'nuff said!

3.5/5

Resident Evil: Apocalypse
Year – 2004
Director – Alexander Witt
Tags – Zombies, Monsters

This is the first sequel to the Resident Evil franchise and picks up directly after the events of the first movie. I actually like this movie better than the first one, mainly due to the larger scale and the greater level of action. It's just about as mindless as the first, but also just as entertaining. The characters are a bit better here, despite the presence of the obligatory humor character. Fans will find that this movie more closely follows the video games and incorporates elements from the second and third games to pretty good effect. Everything I liked about the first one is here, but enhanced, and everything I didn't like about the first one is here to a lesser degree.

4/5

Resident Evil: Degeneration
Year – 2008
Director – Makoto Kamiya
Tags – Animated, Zombies, Monsters

A terrorist attack at an airport lets loose a virus that turns people into flesh eating zombies, but that is only the tip of the iceberg. I have to say right off the bat that this movie is not related at all to the live action movie franchise and is related instead to the video game series. I best as I can figure, I think this movie takes place between the events of Code: Veronica and #4. The animation is incredible, there were times I couldn't even tell it was a CG movie. The story is typical RE stuff, but I think the over the top plot is better played out in a game than an hour and a half movie, because here it just feels too condensed. For fans of the video game series, there's a lot of good stuff here for you, for those of you who did not play the games, you may feel a little lost.

3.5/5

Resident Evil: Extinction
Year – 2007
Director – Russell Mulcahy
Tags – Zombies, Monsters

The third RE movie takes place years after the second installment. I just have to say that this movie did not have enough zombie action for me, it's like this time around, they want to remove the formula that made the first two acceptable. I have to say that the writer obviously ripped off Day of the Dead, and I don't think it's a coincidence that the third RE movie mirrors the third Romero zombie epic. This one is more about talk and less about action, but it just doesn't work very well here as opposed to when Romero did it. There is still some great action, don't get me wrong, but it's just too far apart, and the non-action sequences are punctuated with lame and forgettable characters. For example, Ali Larter plays a horrible Claire Redfield. This movie is still entertaining, but it's theft of another movie and poor characters regale it to being no better than average.

2.5/5

Rest Stop: Dead Ahead

Year – 2006
Director – John Shiban
Tags – Slasher / Survival

A woman and her boyfriend pull over at a rest stop and when she comes out, he's gone. And in his place is a madman in a truck who begins to play a deadly game with her. What the hell is this? The story is just an incoherent mess. It doesn't make any sense. And being weird for weirdness sake never works. Being bizarre is what made The Texas Chainsaw Massacre work so well, but it made sense, here it's just weird and doesn't go anywhere. On top of that, the acting and direction is not very good. There are some nice gore shots but the entire movie is just an underachieving mess. Strange and ultimately pointless, Rest Stop: Dead Ahead is an instantly forgettable stinker in the slasher sub genre.

1.5/5

Rest Stop: Don't Look Back

Year – 2008
Director – Shawn Papazian
Tags – Slasher / Survival

After a bit of a back story, this movie takes place one year after the original. Really, did we need a sequel to Rest Stop? The short answer is no. But we have one anyway, and since I'm a glutton for punishment, I decided to check it out. I didn't think things could get much worse, silly me. The acting and characters manage to get worse this time around, which is astonishing. Well, Steve Railsback is in the movie and he's just a good actor, so there is one good thing to say I suppose. The direction is actually worse here as well. The story, even when it gives some history, still proves to be an incoherent abomination and only adds to the stupidity witnessed in the original. If there is to be a third Rest Stop movie, the apocalypse will be well on its way.

1/5

Resurrected, The

Year – 1992
Director – Dan O'Bannon
Tags – Zombies

A woman hires a private detective to find out what her husband is up to. What he finds is a man gone mad with scientific research involving the reanimation of the dead. This is easily one of the best Lovecraft adaptations I have ever seen, and I've seen most of them up to this point, so that's really saying something. Based on the novella The Case of Charles Dexter Ward, this movie stays pretty true to the source material and ends up creating an adaptation that really captures the essence of Lovecraft's writing. The acting is good and the direction is exceptional. The FX work is quite simply amazing. The abominations created by Ward's scientific research are brought to life here in all of their grotesque glory. They just look astounding. They are not your typical zombies even though they do sustain themselves on the flesh and blood of the living, as these are actually constructed of many rotten pieces that form something only remotely humanoid in appearance. The set design is also incredible, or maybe they did use actual catacombs, I'm not sure, either way the scenes in the catacombs alone make this movie worthwhile. Genuinely frightening and riddled with gore, you're not going to get much of a better Lovecraft tale than this. And as a side note, Dan O'Bannon really needs to get behind the camera more often because he really is a remarkable director.

4.5/5

Retribution (Sakebi)
Year – 2006
Director – Kiyoshi Kurosawa
Tags – Ghosts

A detective begins an investigation into the death of woman when more murders arise and point toward fact that the murder may be the work of a serial killer. As the investigation progresses, the facts start to point toward him as being the killer, and meanwhile he is being pursued by the ghost of a woman in red. At first I didn't like this movie, but as it progressed I started to enjoy it more and by the time it reached its climax, I rather enjoyed it. But getting there was tough at times because the movie was pretty slow. But the acting was really good and the story is somewhat solid throughout. If it wasn't for the pacing issues and the occasionally muddled storyline, this could have been great, but as it stands it's still a pretty good ghost tale that manages to be different.

3/5

Retro Puppet Master
Year – 1999
Director – David DeCoteau
Tags – Slasher / Survival

This seventh Puppet Master movie is a prequel to the prequel (that's got to be a first), showing how Toulon came across the magic of his puppets. And it doesn't coincide with what was told earlier in the series, but no surprise there, massive continuity errors are commonplace in this franchise. The acting is fairly bad, the direction is dull and unappealing, and the story just isn't very well told, or even good for that matter. This movie may not be the worst of the bunch as yet, but it's still pretty damn bad. I find it funny that this series is the bread and butter of Full Moon because it really isn't very good. Sure, there have been a couple of good movies in the series, but nothing extraordinary. This is just another sad attempt at trying to keep the series going when it should have died with at least some dignity long ago.

1.5/5

Return, The
Year – 2006
Director – Asif Kapadia
Tags – Suspense

A woman returns to her hometown for a work assignment and begins having nightmares about real places and becomes drawn in to the locales. Sorry, that's the best I can do with a synopsis because the story behind this movie is just worthless. It's so drawn out and poorly designed that I couldn't help but become completely nonplussed about it. I didn't know what was happening, nor did I care in the least. It's like a supernatural murder mystery written by a child. The direction and acting also reflect this, as they had nowhere to go, nothing to do. I do have to commend the people involved for trying their best with no worthwhile content but the truth of the matter is that this movie should have never been made.

1/5

Return of the Living Dead, The
Year – 1985
Director – Dan O'Bannon
Tags – Zombies

A pair of employees at a medical supply warehouse accidently let a toxic gas loose in the air that revives the dead. This movie is such a horror/comedy classic. Meant to be a parody, this movie is not only hilarious, but features by far the most terrifying zombies ever to be seen in a movie. The zombies here are smart, they think and plan accordingly. They also run (one of the first movies to feature running zombies, if not the first), and to top things off, you can't kill them. Chop off some parts and the parts will still come after you. Then add some great overacting, lots of blood, wonderful FX and a lot of cheese and this is the result, a quintessential 80's horror flick. And it doesn't hurt that Linnea Quigley is completely naked most of the time either.

4.5/5

Return of the Living Dead 2
Year – 1988
Director – Ken Wiederhorn
Tags – Zombies

This movie, as well as the rest of series, is more or less a stand alone movie with little relation to the one before it. This one has some kids finding one of the Trioxin barrels, which happens to have fallen out of a truck near a graveyard, and letting loose the gas to make the undead rise again. This is a terrible follow up here. The script is pretty bad, trying to be as clever as the first movie, but failing hard. There's hardly any amusing moments and instead the attempted humor is dry and just not funny. The direction is also very bad, as poor pacing makes for a rather boring movie. The acting is of the same class here but without the humor the overacting doesn't work. The zombies however look cool and there's some nice action. These are the same type of zombies as the first, but in this movie there is a way to kill them, which completely ruins them. This is a bad movie, and not in a good way, but I have seen worse zombie movies.

2/5

Return of the Living Dead 3
Year – 1993
Director – Brian Yuzna
Tags – Zombies

For the third installment of the series we find the Army testing the Trioxin gas in a very controlled environment. But when the son of a Colonel watches his girlfriend die in a motorcycle accident, he sneaks into the base to reanimate her and unwittingly sets loose the zombies. Leave it to Yuzna to bring this series back from the dead… so to speak. After a dismal sequel, the third movie sends the series into a more serious direction and avoids the comedy all together, which works really well. Here we are treated to a story with more drama, gore, and at the heart of it all, love. There are some great FX sequences and the zombie design is some of the best I've seen. The acting is ok, nothing exceptional, but the direction is probably some of Yuzna's best. In all this is a great zombie movie with a wonderful multi-faceted story. It may have a few flaws here and there but nothing too bad, and definitely nothing to ruin my overall opinion.

4/5

Return of the Living Dead 4: Necropolis
Year – 2005
Director – Ellory Elkayem
Tags – Zombies

A large corporation is experimenting with the Trioxin gas, creating a legion of zombies, but when a group of kids break into the labs to rescue a friend, they unwittingly set the zombies free. Where do I even begin with this movie? I suspect the Return of the Living Dead name was slapped onto this so they could try and pawn this crap off as part of the series, but the truth is that it doesn't have much to do with the franchise. First off, the zombies here don't run, and they can be killed, sometimes just by shooting them in the chest, and that's pretty lame. Next we have a terrible director at the helm. Then we have a group of non-actors hamming it up on screen (I found the frog faced, constantly frowning kid to be particularly annoying). Finally, the story just plain sucks, even though they tried to rip off Resident Evil. I do have one good thing to say though. There are some very nice FX in the movie and a fair amount of gore. But that doesn't make a good movie. Kudos to the FX group but as for everything else, this is boring pile of garbage even the hardcore zombie fan should ignore.

1.5/5

Return of the Living Dead 5: Rave to the Grave
Year – 2005
Director – Ellory Elkayem
Tags – Zombies

This movie continues on a couple of years after the last one I think. I can't tell because there are returning actors but they seem to have forgotten about the zombies. I don't know as this is just a dumb movie. This movie and the last one were shot back to back I guess, which made me groan. The director and actors are still incredibly shitty, maybe even more so this time around. The story is a little better this time, as I liked that some college kids were making a hallucinogenic drug out of the Trioxin. That's a pretty cool idea, but the movie plays out like crap, no shock there. The FX are once again pretty great though, which seems like a waste on a movie like this. Only slightly better than the last movie, the director behind these two crapfests needs to be banned from making zombie movies or something, seriously, no talent at all.

2/5

Return of Swamp Thing, The
Year – 1989
Director – Jim Wynorski
Tags – Monsters

This movie continues on years after the original. Well hell, what exactly is this? This movie is much too campy for its own good and the cheese factor is massive. But I will say that the movie had much better FX and the monsters were pretty cool looking, too bad they were so underused. The story is about as weak as the first but is so much more frustrating because it could have been so much more. The acting is uh, well its acting I guess, not necessarily bad but the whole movie is campy so it kind of fits. But the fat kid was ungodly annoying. The direction is ok but the movie is slow at times. I don't know what else to say really. The movie is not much more than a big hunk of swiss, but it does have some charm.

2.5/5

Return to House on Haunted Hill
Year – 2007
Director – Victor Garcia
Tags – Ghosts

This sequel to the remake of House on Haunted Hill takes place years after that movie. While the story in the remake wasn't very good, the story here is just downright dumb. This movie was meant to be a choose-your-own-adventure kind of gimmick, and as we know, unless you're William Castle, if your movie is gimmicky, it's probably that way to hide the fact that it sucks. It was nice to see Jeffrey Combs return, but most of the other actors are terrible. It's kind of sad when the guy with hardly any lines outshines the rest of the cast. The gore factor is amped up greatly here, too bad a lot of it is terrible CGI, but when they do use practical FX, things look great. This movie does have some entertainment value, but not much.

2/5

Return to Sleepaway Camp
Year – 2008
Director – Robert Hiltzik
Tags – Slasher / Survival

This is actually the fourth movie in the Sleepaway Camp franchise, not the fifth. The fourth was only partially made and never finished, only consisting of a few scenes, so in my opinion this is the fourth movie because it's an actual movie, not just a bunch of scenes that don't even tie together. This movie continues many years after the third movie. I expected nothing here, and maybe that's why I enjoyed it so much. This one is a lot like the original, complete with cheesy acting, but I don't consider it a rip-off because nothing is specifically taken from the original, it just has a similar chain of events. The movie is pretty funny at times with the kids at the camp picking on the fat kid non-stop. The difference between the kid here and Angela of the original is that the kid here is gross and a prick so he kind of deserves to be picked on, but here the identity of the killer is way too obvious. The kills are awesome, and there are a couple in particular that really made me chuckle. The practical FX are great but the CGI is terrible, fortunately it isn't used very much. The direction is good with some generally decent pacing. I really liked this movie because it was funny and had some excellent gore, and I don't need much beyond that to enjoy a slasher movie.

3.5/5

Riding the Bullet
Year – 2004
Director – Mick Garris
Tags – Suspense

A college student finds out his mother has suffered from a stroke and decides to hitchhike back to his home town. What he experiences along the way is a variety of strange occurrences culminating in a painful decision. I could not wait for this movie to end. I kept expecting it to get good but it just never did. Stephen King's work did not translate well here and to add insult to injury, the direction was terrible. This movie was a convoluted mess and so completely disjointed that it was almost unwatchable. Really the only saving grace here is some good acting and sparse but effective FX. This is just a bad movie.

1.5/5

Right at Your Door
Year – 2006
Director – Chris Gorak
Tags – Suspense

Los Angeles is hit with a biological terrorist attack and one man sets out to find his wife. Blocked from leaving his neighborhood, he waits as long as he can and then seals the house with plastic sheeting and duct tape. But his wife arrives shortly thereafter, and when he refuses to let her in because she is contaminated, the drama really begins. This is an interesting movie. The acting is great, and when the drama unfolds between the husband and wife, dark things come to light and are very well done. The movie is really slow though, and while the story is finely crafted, I think this could have been shortened to run smoother. The end is nice even though it was kind of obvious, and this is just a good movie that I wish had a bit more substance.

3/5

Ring, The
Year – 2002
Director – Gore Verbinski
Tags – Ghosts

This is a remake of the movie Ringu and follows the same essential plot. This is definitely one of the better Asian horror remakes, making improvements on the original and then equally failing in other regards. First off there's the tape. It's longer and has a lot more going on, but it's pretty easy to tell that most of which is going on is not so random and instead very much tied together, which felt pretty cheap to me, like the filmmakers were dumbing things down for the American audience. While most of the movie was taken directly from the original, they added a lot to the story, most of which worked and added a little something which each new stride. The acting is really good, but I did strongly dislike the kid in this movie. The direction is also very well done with few lags in the pacing. It's nice to see a remake that some actual thought went into, and while this one isn't quite as creepy or as good as the original, it does come damn close.

4/5

Ring 2, The
Year – 2005
Director – Hideo Nakata
Tags – Ghosts

This movie continues on about six months after the original remake. Wow, this movie is just unbearably bad. This movie is so incredibly boring and I think the main problem is that they did not continue this movie on like they did with the Ringu series. Ringu 2 was hardly brilliant but it was much better than this trash. And while this movie does use elements of Ringu 2, it almost completely abandons everything good about it and instead creates this new story that's so painfully dull and pointless that it really kills the entire experience. And it's not the least bit creepy or scary to boot. Some actors return from the original but they look bored just being in it, not a good sign. The direction is also completely uninteresting. Perhaps The Ring 2 was created for no other purpose than to act as a sedative, and in that regards this is a success, but for those of us who wanted to watch a good movie, we need to look elsewhere.

1/5

Ring of Darkness
Year – 2004
Director – David DeCoteau
Tags – [Hidden to conceal spoilers]

The lead singer of a boy band disappears, so they decide to hold auditions for a replacement, and then the final contestants are flown to an exotic island where they begin to get killed off. Watching this movie was the equivalent of having the worst diarrhea a person could ever have. Everything about this movie is just beyond terrible, the script, the acting, the direction, the FX, the supposed twist ending that tells you what's really going on, everything about it, just horrible. I have to wonder why Adrienne Barbeau is in this, the only real actor in the bunch, they must have blackmailed her to participate or something. This is by far one of the worst movies I have ever seen in my life, and it doesn't even have any boobs or blood to make it the least bit entertaining. Avoid!

0.5/5

Ring Virus, The
Year – 1999
Director – Dong-Bin Kim
Tags – Ghosts

This is a Korean remake of the movie Ringu and follows the same essential plot as the original. This is an interesting remake, because even though this isn't as good as the original, I still enjoyed it. The acting is fine and the direction is ok. The movie follows the original fairly closely but does offer up some new ideas and occurrences, not all of which I was pleased with. Also, here the video isn't very interesting and tries to explain what it is, which is kind of dumb. The movie isn't very creepy either, which is something the original and the American remake were able to accomplish. I guess I liked this remake even though I wasn't particularly impressed by it. An adequate telling of a now familiar tale, just not everything it could have been.

3/5

Ringu
Year – 1998

Director – Hideo Nakata
Tags – Ghosts

A reporter investigates a mysterious video tape that is said to kill the watcher seven days after viewing it. Now after watching it, her clock is ticking to try and solve the mystery of the tape before her time is up as well. What a very unique approach for a ghost movie, but it does have the potential for being pretty lame, fortunately things weren't done comically and instead the very serious approach worked wonders. The story is merely a mystery with a supernatural twist, which works very well. The images on the tape are very random and have a creepy vibe, but the tape if just too short and I wanted to see more. The acting is very good and the direction is about the same, but the movie is a little slow at times. This is a great horror movie with a nice amount of originality and ends up being a fun ride.

4/5

Ringu 0
Year – 2000
Director – Norio Tsuruta
Tags – Ghosts

This is a prequel to the movie Ringu and explores the origins of Sadako as she tries to escape her past by becoming an actress, but visions of the dead and her dark powers manifesting to their full luster prevent her from having a normal life. This just isn't a very good movie. The direction was incredibly slow and uninteresting for the most part. At least up until the last thirty minutes or so, once the movie reaches the third act, it really picks up and the story gets much more interesting, featuring some really creepy and awesome sequences. The acting is good throughout but the first hour is just so slow I couldn't fully get into this movie. It is worth watching for the final act though, that's great stuff.

2.5/5

Ringu 2
Year – 1999
Director – Hideo Nakata
Tags – Ghosts

This sequel picks up right after where the original left off. I like the story here, but only in certain places. It's real patchy because there are moments where I am wowed and love what I'm seeing and then there are times when I'm downright bored and waiting for something interesting to happen. The acting and direction are on par with the original, so no big complaints there. I don't know what else to say because it's a pretty bland sequel for the most part, it has its good moments, but there are just not a whole lot of them. Still a good movie, but just barely above average.

Rise: Blood Hunter
Year – 2007
Director – Sebastian Gutierrez
Tags – Vampires

A journalist is kidnapped and nearly killed by vampires, but instead of dying she becomes one of them and sets out for revenge against those who took her mortal life. This is definitely a well executed vampire movie that really only suffers from one issue: it is way too long. It clocks in at just over two hours and to be honest, that's too much. Each scene seems to be drawn out to meet the run time when easily each scene could have been chopped up a bit to make it run smoother. But other than that, the acting is great, there's lots of blood and nudity, good action, good story, just a damn good movie. And as a side note, Marilyn Manson has a small role in the movie and does a great job, so I hope to see him in more acting roles in the future. Good times.

3.5/5

Rise of the Dead
Year – 2007
Director – William Wedig
Tags – Ghosts

A woman is suddenly attacked over and over again by otherwise law abiding citizens. Soon she realizes that these people who are attacking her are possessed by the son she gave up for adoption, and who died under the care of other people. This was billed as a zombie movie, but it's not even close to one. The story is intriguing and it culminates into a very Bava-esque ending, but everything else about the movie is just so blah. The acting is ok, the direction is ok, the FX are fine, but there's nothing about it that I would necessarily call good. There is plenty of blood and nudity if that's your thing though. This is an average movie but at least it's not a total waste.

2.5/5

Rise of the Undead
Year – 2005
Director – Jason Horton, Shannon Hubbell
Tags – Zombies

A fiery cataclysm engulfs a city and seven strangers escape into a building. Unfortunately for them, they are also trapped inside with a horde of zombies, but that may not be all. As far as microbudget horror goes, this movie is pretty ambitious. Sure the CGI is horrid and the acting for the most part is crap, but that's just to be expected. The way the movie is shot is interesting. The use of color and angles is different, and it gives the movie an artistic feel. The way the story is presented feels a bit disjointed, it is a nice attempt, but doesn't completely work, though it doesn't completely fail either. You expect one thing from this movie as you watch it, and you get it, but then you get something else too and it's a nice surprise. I know that sounds vague but I don't want to ruin anything. The directors need to work on their pacing, but given a good enough budget, I think they will have the ability to make something worthwhile in the genre. There is definitely a good style here, but the end product just needed some work.

2.5/5

Rogue
Year – 2007
Director – Greg McLean
Tags – Animals

A river boat tour is suddenly attacked by a giant crocodile, and with their boat crippled, they are forced to drive it to a small patch of land before it sinks. Only after this do they realize it is a tidal river and the land they are standing on is slowly being eaten away by the water. This movie really is great, after the attack, the tension surrounding the people hardly ever lets up. The croc attacks come in two varieties, quiet, stealthy kills and violent, straight out kills. The mixture is extremely effective. Also, you never know who will live and who will die, which is always pleasant. The croc is CGI, and fortunately they don't show it much, and when they do, it's usually cloaked in shadows, which help to cover up the fact that it just doesn't look that great. This is a solid movie with a real feel of dread permeating it. If only they had the budget to make a better crocodile with practical FX, then the scenes where it is shown would have been more effective. This is still definitely one to check out though.

4/5

Roman
Year – 2006
Director – Angela Bettis
Tags – Suspense

A man's obsession with his neighbor leads to murder and then him keeping the body in his bathtub in order to always have her around. But when a new woman enters his life, he finds himself torn between his obsession and this new romance. The immaculate duo from May return, and this time they switch roles. Lucky McKee really surprised me as he was excellent in his role as Roman. I already know he's an incredible director but I never imagined he could be such a great actor as well. Or maybe he is just that creepy, either way, it works. The acting by all three leads is great, everyone else though, not so much. But the movie focuses mainly on the three, so they're all that really matters. The direction is great and has a very artistic flair to it. The story is a very powerful one and culminates into one of my favorite endings. It is as beautiful as it is dark. There are some budget related flaws, as obviously this is a very low budget movie, but it still manages to shine and be a movie that I can honestly say I loved.

Room 205 (Kollegiet)

Year – 2007
Director – Martin Barnewitz
Tags – Ghosts

Looking for a fresh start, a woman enrolls in a University and moves into the dorms, where she discovers a ghostly presence with murderous intentions. Just when I think foreign horror is where it's at, stuff like this comes out and reminds me that there are crappy movies being made everywhere. I can't say this movie is completely awful though, but it's just pointless in the grand scheme of ghost movies. The acting and direction are very blah, the story and FX are ok but nothing amazing. It's not something I would bash as being terrible but it doesn't get my recommendation either. This is simply a dull ghost story and doesn't do much of anything for the sub genre.

2/5

Roost, The

Year – 2005
Director – Ti West
Tags – Animals, Zombies

Some friends on a trip to another friend's wedding have some car trouble and end up getting stranded in the middle of nowhere. When they find a distant farmhouse they come across a roost of bats in a barn whose bite turns people into flesh eating zombies. If that sounds like the plot for an old cheesy B movie to you, then you're already ahead of the curve. That's exactly what the movie is meant to be. This is hinted at further by the intro and outro portions of the movie, which are awesome. The acting is more than passable and the story is good fun, but it's the direction that gets me. West definitely has a distinct style to his movies that will not appeal to everyone as this movie gets pretty slow at times, but I really love the way he shot it, so I really do have a love/hate relationship with his style. The FX are good, mainly because they are masked by the graininess of the movie, but the practical FX are just plain good with some nice blood work. This movie is definitely not for everyone, and I can see how people would dislike it, but if this is your type of film, then expect a slow but entertaining ride.

3.5/5

Rose Red

Year – 2002
Director – Craig R. Baxley
Tags – Ghosts

A college professor gathers a group of psychics to enter a house that's not just haunted, it's alive. I'll tell you what, this is a really great made for TV miniseries, but it really should have been done in two parts, not three. Having this movie run over four hours long made it feel overextended. Besides that, the story is great and with a bit more substance than most ghost stories, and even has some great atmospheric moments. The ghosts look pretty cool too. The acting is good all around, nothing really remarkable though. The pacing is also good but as I stated earlier, this movie is definitely too long. I liked this movie and it's definitely one of the better TV adaptations for King's work, so if you're into ghosts I can wholeheartedly recommend this.

3.5/5

*Rose Red 2 can be found under Diary of Ellen Rimbauer, The.

Rosemary's Baby
Year – 1968
Director – Roman Polanski
Tags – [Hidden to conceal spoilers]

A woman and her husband move into a new apartment building filled with peculiar neighbors. When she becomes pregnant under mysterious circumstances she becomes obsessed with the welfare of her child, to the point of madness. So I assume that everyone out there knows what's really going on with Rosemary's Baby, but for that one person out there that hasn't seen it yet and doesn't know, I'll keep this spoiler free. I consider this to be the best movie ever made where absolutely nothing happens. And really, not much of anything happens in this movie, save for the surreal impregnation scene. But the movie is still rather interesting. The acting is great but I've always had a hard time believing that anyone could be so naïve as Rosemary. The direction is very good with only a few lags but it's pretty impressive given the fact that there isn't much occurring besides dialogue heavy scenes. This is hardly a horror movie that all other horror movies should live up to, but it's still a great job and a worthwhile watch any day.

4/5

Ruins, The
Year – 2008
Director – Carter Smith
Tags – Biological

The Ruins tells the tale of some friends on vacation who travel off the beaten path to see some ruins from an ancient civilization. Once there they are not allowed to leave as some locals force them onto the ruins and camp out to make sure they don't escape. But that's the least of their worries as they discover that the plants covering the ruins are not normal in the least. This is a slow but rewarding movie. There are some incredibly gruesome moments in the movie that are very welcome but the most part the movie is uneventful. There is an air of tension set throughout, but just enough to keep it immensely interesting.

The cast is very good and they allow you to really like the characters, which is important. The great moments in this movie really are something amazing, there's just too few of them in my opinion. But still, this is some excellent, original, risk taking horror, and it pays off for the most part. An entertaining movie.

3.5/5

Running Man, The
Year – 1987
Director – Paul Michael Glaser
Tags – Slasher / Survival

Set in the future, this movie chronicles the events of America's #1 rated show, The Running Man. In this TV show, convicted felons are forced into a walled-in wasteland where they must deal with "stalkers", people whose only duty is to kill the competitors. If TV was really like this, I would start watching TV again. This large scale sci-fi/action flick is really nothing more than a slasher movie in disguise, albeit a very clever and entertaining slasher movie. I love the game aspect of it but everything else is pretty much forgettable, they should have just focused on the game and there could have been a franchise here. Anyway, I still dig the story, a lot, and the direction is very well done as well. There could have been some more blood in my opinion, but this isn't bad. The acting is fine, but nothing extraordinary. This is flashy fun that still entertains me now as it did in my childhood. Good times.

3.5/5

S. Darko
Year – 2009
Director – Chris Fisher
Tags – Suspense

This sequel to Donnie Darko continues on seven years after the previous movie. When there was word of a Donnie Darko sequel in the works, I was able to take the news without uttering the words "epic" and "fail", because I am not a fanboy. The original was a great movie but hardly the end all be all of modern cinema. So I went into this movie with an open mind. The first problem here is the budget, because without a good budget they weren't able to have the good things life like good actors, a good director, a good screenwriter, a good soundtrack and a good FX company. I kid, it's really not that bad, but you can definitely tell that this is a massive step below the original. Everything is about half as good, not all bad, but close, and thus I will give this sequel half the score I gave the original.

2/5

Salem's Lot
Year – 1979

Director – Tobe Hooper
Tags – Vampires

This Stephen King made for TV adaptation focuses on a writer's return to the town he grew up in. His return also marks the arrival of two strangers who open an antique shop and purchase an ominous house with a sordid past. Now people are dying and disappearing, and then sometimes, they come back. This is a great vampire story and a pretty damn good adaptation as well. It is pretty slow and overly long, but the story is great. And I must mention that the vampires are very well done, and the head vampire is especially creepy. If you have the patience to deal with the bloated three hour run time, then you will be rewarded with a great vampire movie directed by none other than Tobe Hooper.

3.5/5

Salem's Lot [Remake]
Year – 2004
Director – Mikael Saloman
Tags – Vampires

This remake follows the events and storyline almost exactly the same as the original. I was looking forward to this remake because even though I enjoyed the original, I felt that it was a bit dated and could benefit from a fresh take. This adaptation really is more of the same with a few exceptions. First, I feel the pacing is better here than the original, even though it still feels bloated with its standard mini series three hour run time. The vampires here however, as much less effective, as they look like pale people with two long teeth and are not nearly as creepy as the ones in the original. Other than that, this one is on par with the original, which kind of makes it seem fruitless in my opinion. Oh well, still got my entertainment value out of it.

3/5

Salvage
Year – 2006
Director – Jeff Crook, Josh Crook
Tags – Suspense

A woman keeps having reoccurring dreams about a man, a man who does nothing but kill her over and over again. This is a very well made low budget horror movie. The story is very good and the ending, while I could see part of it coming, was excellent. The acting was pretty good overall, especially for a low budget movie, and the direction throughout the short run time was also good with only a few pacing issues. This is a well made tale that I found to be rather enjoyable, even with some minor issues. If you're in the mood for a good, fairly original movie, you should definitely check this out.

3.5/5

Satan's Little Helper

Year – 2004
Director – Jeff Lieberman
Tags – Slasher / Survival

On Halloween night we find a little boy obsessed with Satan because of the video game he's currently playing, and decides that his costume shall be that of, you guessed it, Satan's Little Helper. The plot thickens as the boy comes across a killer dressed up in a Satan costume, and befriends him, ultimately aiding him his nefarious misdeeds. All the while he thinks everything is a game. The plot of this movie is pretty silly, but you have to admit that it is also fairly interesting. A killer preying on the naivety of a child? Sounds interesting to me. The movie plays out in a pretty over the top fashion, as well as it should, if this movie tried to be serious, it would be a complete failure. As it stands, we are left with a rather fun little film. The acting is good for the most part, the gore is good, but I was hoping for a bit more, and the humor is so cheesy is manages to be entertaining. Definitely no groundbreaking classic here, but by and large, this is B movie fun and you could do a lot worse. Enjoyable.

3/5

Savage Harvest

Year – 1994
Director – Eric Stanze
Tags – Demonic Possession

A woman gathers some friends together to help her uncle with some work at his cabin. There he tells them a tale of a Cherokee chief who was exiled when he tampered with demons. Now the land is cursed, turning people into animal demons when they touch certain rocks carved with symbols. Supposedly the demons are asleep, but these new visitors have woken them up, and a leisurely weekend has turned into a massacre. That synopsis doesn't really do the story justice, but you get the idea. And while the inspiration for this movie is clearly The Evil Dead, there is very fortunately a great story behind it that sets it apart from that movie. This microbudget movie is certainly impressive because it has that great story, the direction shows a lot of talent, the acting actually isn't that bad, and the FX work is quite simply remarkable. The make-up is simple but very effective for the different demons, and the loads of gore are realistic and just look great. I did hate the harshness of the score during action sequences though. If you can appreciate a lot done with a little, then Savage Harvest is your ideal movie, because this is definitely impressive seeing as how there was no money here.

4/5

Savage Harvest 2: October Blood

Year – 2006
Director – Jason Christ

This movie takes place about ten years after the last one. I really enjoyed the progression from the original story here and how the first half of the movie played out like a mystery as the friends and family of the original protagonists try to figure out what happened. And then not to disappoint the fans of the original, the second half is pure horror and laden with loads of gore. The acting is pretty good once again and the direction is good, just not as good as the original. Probably the one thing I didn't like about this movie was the run time. The original worked so well because it was so short and concise while this one pushes two hours long and I feel it easily could have been trimmed down to run smoother. Still, it's a well done sequel and very worthy of the great original. While I didn't enjoy it quite as much as the first, it was still a very good time.

3.5/5

Saw
Year – 2004
Director – James Wan
Tags – Suspense

Two men awaken in a room, chained to pipes, having no idea how they got there. After they awaken, the game begins. Saw is an extremely solid thriller with only one major flaw, a bloated script. It just strikes me as too much that didn't need to be there. But I must say that that is a very small gripe in an otherwise superbly crafted movie. The end is one of the most memorable parts, as I just did not see it coming and really was one of a kind. Also the thought of creating a serial killer that doesn't actually kill anyone is brilliant. He actually puts people into situations where they end up killing themselves. The success of this movie did create a craze to copy its formula, but none of the rip-off movies have quite done this movie justice. Great job.

4/5

Saw II
Year – 2005
Director – Darren Lynn Bousman
Tags   Suspense

In the second installment of the Saw series, the games continue, but with more people and even more traps. I actually like this movie better than the original, probably because there are more people and a better storyline. And I think with those two elements in place, it led to better pacing and a higher blood allowance, which always enhances my Saw viewing pleasure. Everything about the movie just seemed to be ramped up, but not too much, it was just right. You definitely don't want to try and go overboard on your second outing. As much as I like the first, I think the second did it better, but either way, it's still a great start to a new franchise.

4.5/5

Saw III
Year – 2006
Director – Darren Lynn Bousman
Tags – Suspense

The third movie picks up directly where the last movie left off. In the third edition we find the gore factor ramped up, and also the addition of some new particularly nasty traps manages to keep it interesting. The story is great once again, and we get some nice flashbacks to fill in some of the story. I would say the third movie is on par with the original in terms of entertainment value. This is a smart step in the series because even though you can feel that the story isn't as strong here as in previous entries, they added new elements to help carry the movie and make it a joy to watch. The series is still good in my book, which is kind of rare because most franchises tend to begin to crash by the third movie, but I feel that the Saw series is still going strong.

4/5

Saw IV
Year – 2007
Director – Darren Lynn Bousman
Tags – Suspense

The fourth movie continues on some indeterminate time after the third movie (You'll find out when by the end of this movie). Bousman closes out his Saw directing days quite well here. While I do think this is the weakest entry in the series up to this point, it's still pretty damn good. The story is now stretched fairly thin, but we are treated to some Jigsaw back story for a good quarter of the movie, which I feel was very smart, because it allowed for less to be told about the current story, which as I said, was thin. The gore factor is ramped up again, and the new traps are on par with the old ones for the most part. The story is still good here, but there really isn't much left to go on beyond this, which means for a fifth, they'll probably have to go out into left field and start something new, which will probably cause all kinds of continuity issues, but only time will tell. The series is still good after four entries, but I can also feel it starting to wane.

3.5/5

Saw V
Year – 2008
Director – David Hackl
Tags – Suspense

The fifth movie picks up immediately after the fourth movie. Here we see the story really start to take a nosedive. It began with the last movie, but now it's even more apparent. We are also subjected to some fairly bad direction as well, as this was the first Saw movie that bored me. It was also far too predictable and seemed to be not much more than a set-up for the sixth movie. The story bounces back and forth between the newest game and an investigation into the identity of the killer, which eventually will collide. The acting is still very good though. This movie does treat us to new traps and loads more gore. I like the gore, but some of the traps are severely lacking from previous ones. This movie isn't bad, but it's definitely the worst in the series. I hope they shape things up better for the sixth movie and beyond, because as it stands now, this franchise is on the fast track to failing big time.

2.5/5

Scanners
Year – 1981
Director – David Cronenberg
Tags – Suspense

There is a new race of people in the world known as Scanners, and they have great telepathic abilities. One corporation seeks to medicate these new people and keep their powers in check, while another seeks to bring all of the Scanners together and dominate the human race by creating more of their own. I really like the story here, because once again Cronenberg manages to bring another very original and engaging tale to life that transcends your typical horror tale. The acting is really great, especially by Michael Ironside, who plays a villain better than most and his role here is no exception. The direction is very good but there are some lags in the pacing. The FX though, the FX are mind blowing, and that's not a pun. You'll understand when you see the movie. This is a great film with only a few minor issues that didn't keep me from loving it.

4/5

Scarecrows
Year – 1988
Director – William Wesley
Tags – Slasher / Survival

A group of people who robbed a military base have made their way to a remote farmhouse after being double crossed by one of their own. What they don't realize is that the scarecrows around the farmland have minds of their own and will kill anyone they come across. Up until this point I don't think there have been any movies based on scarecrows, which is strange since they are inherently creepy figures, and this movie really manages to make them even creepier, and that's before they're even animated. The story is solid and the direction is pretty good. The acting is well done and the FX work is great. There's plenty of blood and even a really cute old dog. What? I like dogs. It may not be a shining example of horror that breaks all the boundaries and redefines the way we think about movies, but it's damn entertaining, just like it was meant to be.

3.5/5

Scream

Year – 1996
Director – Wes Craven
Tags – Slasher / Survival

Students in a small town are targeted by a masked killer who is obsessed with horror movies. I love this movie for what it is but hate it for what it created, which was a slew of crappy teen slashers that flooded the theaters for years afterward. But as for Scream itself, it is a wonderfully crafted horror movie that exudes a lot of fun and originality. It also plays on the clichés of horror movies past, showing people the "rules" of the movies, and then defying them, well some of them anyway. It falls into its own clichés at times, which would have been funny if only done once or twice, but it does it multiple times which had me scratching my head wondering what the point was in revealing the rules if all they had planned on doing was following them. Watch the movie Feast to see a similar style, but done correctly. Still, the movie is well directed, well acted, highly entertaining and ends very strong, making for one very good time at the movies.

4/5

Scream 2

Year – 1997
Director – Wes Craven
Tags – Slasher / Survival

It appears as though this movie takes place within a year or two of the original. The first thing I noticed about this movie is that the story is definitely lacking. The acting and direction are on par with the original, but the script is almost completely without the clever feel that made the first movie so much fun. This one instead feels like more of the same and offers little in the way of distinguishing itself from the original. It does seem a little bloodier this time around, but that hardly makes up for the shortcomings in the story. But this movie is still good and I liked it to a small degree, but it's obvious that this franchise has nowhere to go but down from here.

3/5

Scream 3

Year – 2000
Director – Wes Craven
Tags – Slasher / Survival

This movie seems to take place a couple of years after the last one. What was clever in the first movie was still passable in the second, but here the story is truly dried up and unappealing. The acting and direction are good, but without any really good content in the story, this movie isn't very worthwhile. It appears as though this franchise has now overstayed its welcome as this movie is very contrived and almost forced in a way into becoming a trilogy. It's movies like this that actually damage the reputation of the series as a whole, and this movie is not just bad, it makes the other movies be looked down upon in comparison. It never needed to be made and the script showed that.

2/5

Screamers
Year – 1995
Director – Christian Duguay
Tags – Mechanical

Set far into the future on a distant mining planet ravaged by years of war, scientists have perfected a weapon to eliminate ground fighting: blade wielding machines that attack anything that moves. But as a new mission presents itself, the people there discover that the machines are creating themselves, and to make matters worse, they're evolving. This movie is so much fun. It may not be perfect but its one of those movies I can pop in anytime and I know I'll enjoy it. The story is good and complimented by very good acting and direction. The Screamers look cool and there's some good gore, which makes sense since we're essentially dealing with intelligent buzz saws. I just wish there was more interaction with them. I also like the FX even though the green screen work and CGI left a bit to be desired. This is just a very well done mix of horror and sci-fi and I like it.

3.5/5

Secret Window
Year – 2004
Director – David Koepp
Tags – Suspense

A writer is stalked by a man who claims that he has stolen his story and demands reparations are made. But every time the writer tries to prove that the story is his, the mysterious man is on step ahead of him and foils his attempts. This Stephen King adaptation is a very solid tale of suspense. Johnny Depp plays an eccentric writer very well, which is good since the story depends so much on his performance. The direction is very good, and the movie travels through the story at a nice pace. This is just a good movie, not great, but a very solid thriller that held my attention and ended well. Not much more I can say beyond that.

3.5/5

See No Evil
Year – 2006
Director – Gregory Dark
Year – Slasher / Survival

A group of inmates strike a deal to get time knocked off their sentence by cleaning an old hotel that will be made into a homeless shelter. But there is a man inside the hotel that does not like them being there. I wasn't expecting much here, maybe just a boring slasher that would appeal to wrestling fans, since this is a WWE film starring a wrestler, but I was pleasantly surprised. First off, the plot is ridiculous, a group of inmates getting time off for community service, and the fact that it is a coed team, and the fact that they are pretty much unsupervised, is lame. But this is a slasher movie, not rocket science. The movie starts off quick and the pacing is excellent, kills come along quickly and they are very bloody. The killer has an eye fetish that would make Lucio Fulci proud, which is a nice bonus. Another great part about this movie is that you never know who is going to die next, as this movie doesn't follow the typical slasher formula. I think that's the most impressive part about this movie, certain characters should have died quick and others lived longer, but it really mixes things up. The movie unfortunately slows down in the third act and the kills get a little more uninspired, but it does end very strong. Color me shocked, this is actually a pretty damn good slasher movie, even with its flaws.

3.5/5

Seed of Chucky
Year – 2004
Director – Don Mancini
Tags – Slasher / Survival

This movie continues on a couple of years after Bride of Chucky. I have to say that first time I saw this movie, I hated it, but I watched it a second time and once I had told myself this was a comedy more than a horror movie, then I was able to enjoy it, quite a bit actually. The movie gets off to a shaky start and the story is pretty ludicrous, but it only adds to the comedy. The acting was very good, which surprised me seeing as how rappers generally can not act but Redman was actually pretty good. And Jennifer Tilly in her dual role was great. The movie has some hilarious moments as well as awesome kills. And the kills are just so bloody and over the top it only adds to the comedy more. If you were like me and hated the movie, watch it again as a comedy and you might just like it as much as I did.

3.5/5

Seedpeople
Year – 1992
Director – Peter Manoogian
Tags – Biological

Residents of a small town are besieged by the Seedpeople, small plant creatures that turn humans into drones. So this movie is all over a pretty blatant rip off of Invasion of the Body Snatchers with the small exception of the Seedpeople themselves, which look pretty cool in a cheesy sort of way. The acting sucks, the movie is boring and the story bears too much of a resemblance to the aforementioned classic. But it is so lame that it might be fun for some people to gather up some friends and mock it for its eighty minute run time.

1.5/5

Session 9
Year – 2001
Director – Brad Anderson
Tags – Suspense

A hazardous material cleaning crew begins work on cleaning an old mental hospital when the hospital's checkered past comes back to haunt them. This movie is strange to me because it's really well done but at the same time it's extremely slow as well. The story and characters are well thought out and well executed, but the pacing is just atrocious. I think the director did an excellent job on hiding just exactly what was going on in that mental hospital because multiple scenarios played out in my head as to what was going on. Everything from the conventional to the supernatural. Those with the patience to watch this to the end will be treated to a great final act, but the journey to get there is an arduous one. I did love the location however, it was so awesome, but unfortunately I think it's been torn down for condos now. Bastards.

3/5

Sentinel, The
Year – 1977
Director – Michael Winner
Tags – [Hidden to conceal spoilers]

A young model moves into a plush Brooklyn Heights apartment. Strange things start to happen while she is living there all seeming to tie in with a blind priest who lives on the top floor. I apologize about the vague synopsis but to give much detail would certainly ruin the story, which is a supernatural religious mystery unlike any other. This movie certainly gets a prize for having the most bizarre occurrences to ever fill an hour and a half. The movie feels like an Italian movie by the strangeness of it all and the graphic gore thrown in. Don't get me wrong, this isn't a straight gory movie rather it is an atmospheric piece more than anything, but it definitely has moments that would make Fulci, Argento and the rest proud. There is a great cast involved that do a remarkable job. The first time I watched this movie I found it be very slow, but on the second viewing I really found it to move along quite nicely from one strange bit to the next. If you're in the mood for a taste of the creepy and bizarre, look no further than The Sentinel.

4.5/5

Seven (Se7en)
Year – 1995
Director – David Fincher

Two detectives hunt down a serial killer who patterns his crimes upon the seven deadly sins. This is a perfect thriller, and it really doesn't get much better than this. Great casting, an excellent story, immaculate pacing, twists and turns, everything is great. This movie is incredibly dark as well and pulls no punches, which I can really appreciate, because as a watered down version of itself, it wouldn't have even been half as effective. The manner in which each victim is killed is incredibly inventive and unique. And the end, well, let's just say it's one of the more memorable endings in cinema history. Brilliant all around, you would have to look hard for a more competent tale of crime and suspense.

5/5

Seventh Sign, The
Year – 1988
Director – Carl Schultz
Tags – Suspense

The signs of the apocalypse are showing up all over the world and it's up to one woman to put a stop to it. The premise here is extremely silly, seriously, one person can stop the apocalypse? If the apocalypse is going to happen, it's going to happen. Still, the movie was fairly entertaining. The acting is great, no issues there. The story isn't that good, but the direction almost makes up for it by being pretty smooth with only a few lags in the pace. I don't know, I just can't get past the dumb premise and it just seems like a waste of a movie. But still, it's entertaining even if it is unintelligent.

3/5

Severed: Forest of the Dead
Year – 2005
Director – Carl Bessai
Tags – Zombies

Loggers and tree huggers clash with one another, and when a tree hugger spikes one of the trees, a loggers' chainsaw blade snaps and injures him severely. The problem is that the logging company has been using an experimental chemical on the trees to help them grow, and the infected sap gets into the man's bloodstream, turning him into a zombie. Shenanigans ensue. Big props to someone for creating a new kind of zombie movie. The secluded forest setting and tree sap infection deal are very original, and the setting in particular is great for zombie action. This movie is pretty solid, but does have a couple of flaws. First off, the use of shaky cam, while not frequent, is pretty annoying, and second, the characters are pretty much your typical zombie movie fare. You have your cool and collected guy, your scared guy who seems to get everyone in trouble, etc. With steadier camera shots and maybe some characters as unique as the storyline, this could have been in my top ten of zombie movies, but it's still a very good zombie experience.

3.5/5

Severed Head Network, The
Year – 2000
Director – Multiple
Tags – Short Film Compilation

This collection of short films ranges from experimental stuff and music videos to horror and a dark comedy musical. Some of this stuff is pretentious but most is genuinely interesting. My favorite segment is Sedgewick, which is a very fascinating look at the mind of an old man. The music videos are well shot but I didn't enjoy all of the music. There's eight shorts in all, I really did enjoy five of them a lot, two were ok and one (Vomire), was that pretentious stuff I was talking about, which makes for an overall good time, but not a great one. This compilation is made by Wicked Pixel, who have made some stellar low budget horror and it's nice to see their artsy and more creative side in addition to the heavy gore side.

3.5/5

Severance
Year – 2006
Director – Christopher Smith
Tags – Slasher / Survival

This horror/comedy follows a band of defense contractor employees on a week long getaway in the woods for team building exercises. What they don't know is that there is a murderer on the loose. This movie is hilarious and bloody, which is always a lovely combination in my book. The kills are very nice I must say, not particularly inventive, but violent and gory nonetheless. All the blood is interspersed with some truly funny dialogue and occurrences. Leave it to the Brits to really nail down the horror to comedy ratio perfectly. The movie has its share of minor flaws, as I would have liked to have seen some more original kills for example, but they didn't take away from my overall experience. This is a fine movie and just what the doctor called for when you're in the mood for blood, guts, and laughs.

4/5

Shadow of the Vampire
Year – 2000
Director – E. Elias Merhige
Tags – Vampires

This is a dramatization of the making of the movie Nosferatu. Here the filmmakers offer up an idea that Max Shreck, who played the classic character, was in fact a real vampire. That's a pretty cool idea I must say, and a pretty well done one at that. Not as well done as it could have been, but respectable nonetheless. The casting choices are great and they each put on great performances. The story is very good and the direction is fine but the movie does get slow at times and I wished some of the scenarios played out better. An entertaining and inventive movie for sure, Shadow of the Vampire is a must see for all fans of vampire movies and especially for fans of Nosferatu, because I can guarantee you'll never see that movie the same way again.

3.5/5

Shadowzone
Year – 1990
Director – J.S. Cardone
Tags – Monsters

A research team unwittingly unleashes a shapeshifting creature from another dimension. And now with the bunker on lockdown, they are trapped inside with it. While I liked this in all of its B-movie glory, I see how it could have been so much better. The story is really good but never quite reached its full potential, same goes for the direction. The acting is surprising because there were some really good actors involved. There were some gore sequences and plenty of blood, but what was lost on me is why they showed such great gore to start out with and then it was nothing but off camera kills from there. That was kind of annoying. The FX were great though, and when the creature shows its true form, it looks pretty damn cool. While there was definitely some missed potential here, because I feel this movie could have been so much more, it was still pretty damn good.

3.5/5

Shaft, The (Down)
Year – 2001
Director – Dick Maas
Tags – Mechanical

In the Millennium Building in New York City, the elevators gain a mind of their own and begin killing people. Are we so desperate for stories nowadays that we make a killer elevator movie? Yeah, it's about as good as it sounds. The first thing I wondered is how they got a handful of good actors to be this dreck. And while there are a couple of good performances, most of the actors involved are pretty bad. The story is just absolutely pathetic and the direction is laughable. There is some blood in the movie, and even a bit of nudity, but that doesn't save this otherwise disastrous movie. I fail to see how this could be scary. Hmmm, a killer elevator eh? I'll just take the stairs, crisis averted.

1.5/5

Shallow Ground
Year – 2004

Director – Sheldon Winston
Tags – [Hidden to conceal spoilers]

A naked boy, covered in blood enters a sheriff's office one year after a gruesome murder had shocked a small town and eventually ruined it. And as the day progresses, they find out there is much more to the boy than they ever could have imagined. This is an ambitious movie and can see where the filmmakers were trying to go with it, but unfortunately it just didn't quite pan out and at times becomes downright convoluted. The acting is pretty good but the direction is awfully slow. The story had merit that didn't quite see its full potential, but still managed to have some rather interesting ideas. Maybe it was budget thing, or maybe the director couldn't quite pull it off, but this movie missed its mark. While not completely bad, it didn't really work for me. I would like to see what this guy could do with a budget though.

2/5

Shatter Dead
Year – 1994
Director – Scooter McCrae
Tags – Zombies

This movie is set in a world where people just stop dying, and instead they walk around and panhandle, shunned by society. But one man is gathering the undead together for one reason, to kill the living and make everyone the same. I do have to give some major props here for this guy making a rather unique movie, even with all of its soft core porn moments that were completely unnecessary. But wait, what's this? A hardcore moment as well? Yep, this movie has a close up of a woman being penetrated with a handgun, yes, you read that right. But I actually kind of have to respect it because this movie did something right that so many other movies have done wrong. You see, if someone was to die and be undead, then their blood wouldn't flow, which means they would be unable to achieve an erection, and this movie explores that by offering up a different means of fornication. And while it is really off the wall, I still have to respect it because creatures like vampires and zombies just couldn't have sex (I'm talking to you True Blood). Anyway, this is microbudget movie and the acting is definitely bad. The direction is pretty good however, and the movie flows smoothly. With an interesting and somewhat flawed script, this definitely amounts to an above average movie. You'll definitely feel like a pervert when you watch this, but I do have a certain amount of respect for someone who makes a movie with not only original ideas, but some original execution. Heavily flawed but respectable.

3.5/5

Shaun of the Dead
Year – 2004
Director – Edgar Wright
Tags – Zombies

A man tries to sort his life out, win back his ex-girlfriend and get ahead in general, all while trying to avoid a horde of the living dead. Not only is this one of the best zombie movies I've ever seen, but it's also one of the funniest comedies, talk about an accomplishment! This movie is seriously hilarious, and not even in that dry, British way, it's just funny. And zombie fans will be pleased with all the small references to the iconic zombie and zombie related movies of yesteryear. Gorehounds will also find plenty of blood here, and a nice amount of kills to satisfy their needs. This is an exceptional movie all around, with obvious dedication to the script and direction, the people involved accomplished just what they were trying to do. They made a romantic comedy with zombies, and it works.

5/5

Shining, The
Year – 1980
Director – Stanley Kubrick
Tags – Suspense

A man lands a job as the winter caretaker for a large resort set far away from civilization. He and his wife and son set off to spend the season there alone, but there is a presence there that slowly turns the father mad whilst giving his psychic son visions of the past and future. I can see why Stephen King hates this movie, as it deviates greatly from his masterful novel, but the fact of the matter is that this is one of the greatest movies ever made. Sorry Stephen. Kubrick is at the top of his game here. The acting, especially from Nicholson, is timeless. No one has ever displayed the slow onset of murderous insanity quite like him. The tension is ever present in this movie, and it is only amplified magnanimously during certain times. The creepy and bizarre imagery used throughout the movie is incredible and the hotel itself has the feel of a cold, dank tomb. This is one that will stick with the viewer for a long time after seeing it.

5/5

Shining, The [Remake]
Year – 1997
Director – Mick Garris
Tags – Ghosts

This remake follows the same general story but goes about things differently. Many people would say that this movie should have never been made and I would have to disagree. The novel that this and the original are based on is a very personal book for Stephen King and he just wasn't pleased with how Kubrick strayed from it. So here we have King's lackey, Mick Garris make the movie to his specifications. And elitist readers will undoubtedly be pleased that this one follows the novel better, and it should have considering that King wrote both. But a faithful adaptation does not a good film make. And this movie is absolutely wretched. Kubrick's original took many liberties but that's what made it such a great experience. It had heart and originality, and its bizarre nature made for nothing short of an amazing time. Here the story is so rigid and by the numbers that it comes off very dry and dull. And since the movie is so long at over four hours, it really is painful to sit through. The pacing is really off too. Onto the acting. So many say it was overdone in the original, but it was entertaining to watch, here everyone is flat and delivers fairly weak performances. Well, not everyone, there is the matter of the kid. I don't know where they found this inept little runt but he is by far the worst child actor I have ever seen. His acting was terrible beyond belief and he was so incredibly annoying that I actually had thoughts of smashing his face in with a hammer because even looking at him was an annoyance. Oh, the CGI usage was ridiculously bad. Yes I hated this movie but honestly I may not have hated it as much if there was a different kid cast, he was seriously that awful. This movie is worthless and bad in every way it could be. And for those of you who love it because it follows the book better, who gives a shit? If you want something so close to the source material then just read the damn source material because this is garbage.

0.5/5

Shocker
Year – 1989
Director – Wes Craven
Tags – Slasher / Survival

A serial killer is caught through the dreams of a young man, but even after he is executed, he continues to kill by possessing people through electricity. I had never seen this movie until I started writing this book and that is mainly because I heard it wasn't very good. But when I started watching it, I was digging it. The acting wasn't the best but it had some good gore and it moved along nicely. Then when the killer gets caught, the movie takes a major downswing and not only becomes pretty boring, but it also gets pretty stupid as well. And another problem is that the movie is way too long and filled with pointless scenarios. Now I see why it took me so long to finally get around to watching this.

2/5

Shrieker
Year – 1998
Director – David DeCoteau
Tags – Monsters

A group of students secretly live in an abandoned hospital to avoid paying rent, but soon wish they had as a demonic creature begins killing them off one by one. I like this movie because it's just a fun low budget romp into familiar territory and has a fair amount of entertainment value. The acting is decent, the direction is slow, but the story and FX definitely help pick up the slack. The monster is a pretty slick looking beast with good originality to it. There are some bloody kills, but they could have done more with it, and a little nudity wouldn't have hurt either. But this is still good stuff for the most part, nothing brilliant but a solid low budget monster movie.

3/5

Shrooms
Year – 2007
Director – Paddy Breathnach
Tags – Slasher / Survival

A group of friends go into the Irish woods to pick mushrooms and trip out. When someone or something begins to come after them, is it real, or just another hallucination? I have to commend the attempt to make a different kind of slasher movie, but the end result just isn't quite right. The ending is pretty predictable, but even knowing how things are going to play out didn't take the enjoyment out of the movie for me. The direction is great and the movie moved along well. The acting was good, no real complaints there. The story has that great psychedelic angle to it, and the back story of the troubled woods is nice. The kills aren't bad but there could have been more done with them. This is still a very good slasher that made strides not to be lumped in with the rest, and I respect that.

3.5/5

Shuttle
Year – 2008
Director – Edward Anderson
Tags – Slasher / Survival

Two women back from vacation take a shuttle from the airport to a downtown location, but the driver has other ideas for them and intends for them to not reach their destination. I know that sounds like a hundred other movies, but this one has something that the others don't, and that's talent. The writer/director has crafted a story that is not only interesting but features multiple twists and turns, not all of which are easily seen coming. The movie also has some very cringe worthy moments and a fair amount of blood and violence. The direction is exceptionally smooth with really no pacing issues whatsoever, I was interested the entire way through and then was treated to a great ending. The acting is fine, not bad, with the only great performance coming from the driver. This is an awesome movie and not your standard fare, and I firmly believe this is worth everyone's time.

4/5

Sick House, The
Year – 2007
Director – Curtis Radcliffe
Tags – Slasher / Survival

An archeologist is performing a dig at an old orphanage when she unleashed the black plague. Now her and a group of kids who stumbled upon the orphanage are trapped inside with not only a sickness, but a being hell bent on killing them. On the outside this is a genuinely interesting concept but it never pans out to anything worthwhile. The story isn't well made and features many chances to become interesting, it just never does and the viewer is forced to sit through it up until the dumb ending. Gina Phillips is the only good actor here and I really wish someone would give her good roles besides ones in crappy low budget horror like this. The direction is also boring and doesn't have much appeal. It's a shame that a good plot was wasted but it wasn't the first time and it certainly won't be the last.

1.5/5

Sick Nurses (Suay Laak Sai)
Year – 2007
Director – Piraphan Laoyont, Thodsapol Siriwiwat
Tags – Ghosts

A doctor and a group of nurses begin selling dead bodies, but when one of the nurses threatens to tell on them, they kill her, and then her ghost comes back for revenge. I like this movie but I have to admit that this is very familiar ground. The story may be different but the concept has been seen multiple times before, especially in Asian horror. So while there is a definite lack of originality in the plot, the execution shows such flair that it really does stand out among the others. The visuals and gore are really something to behold, as there are a lot of insane things happening at various points of the movie, which I liked a lot. In between these times however there is a definite lull in the pacing that occasionally made me tune out. The FX are great and that alone makes this movie worthwhile. I didn't love this film but I really did appreciate the effort that went into it.

3/5

Signal, The
Year – 2007
Director – David Bruckner, Dan Bush, Jacob Gentry
Tags – Infection

Over the TV, radio and phone lines comes a strange signal in Terminus City. And all who listen to it and watch it are infected with a mania that drives them to kill everyone in sight. This is a different kind of infection, as it affects the brain and not transmitted by normal means, it is transmitted by technology, nice. This movie plays out like an anthology as it is cut up into three sections, or transmissions. Each transmission follows one of the three main leads, and even though they were each directed by a different person, they blend together seamlessly and it just works. There is a very dark brand of humor in this movie that I really appreciated, given the circumstances of the plot, you would think that the movie would be very dark and serious, but it is actually very lighthearted. A bold move that works wonders. The murders, and there are a lot of them, are very graphic and bloody, some of the best I've seen in awhile. The actors do a wonderful job in portraying lunacy, which is no easy feat, and they should definitely be commended for pulling off such challenging roles. The movie is ambitious and the directors pull it off in pretty much every regard. A fine addition to the genre.

4.5/5

Signs
Year – 2002
Director – M. Night Shyamalan
Tags – Aliens

Crop circles begin appearing all over the world, and this movie focuses on a family that has one right on their own farm. But they are only a sign of much more frightening things to come. I like this movie a lot as it has some great creepy moments and good scares, but at the same time it gets much too dialogue heavy and slow. The acting is great, except by the children in the movie, who I didn't really care for. The direction is excellent as well, even with a few slow areas. I like the story as well but I didn't really care about the family that the movie focused on, maybe because the kids were so annoying. The CGI was pretty terrible too and I can not figure out why they didn't just use practical FX for the aliens. But this movie overcomes most of its shortcomings with atmosphere and funny moments, making for a very good movie overall.

3.5/5

Silence of the Lambs, The
Year – 1991
Director – Jonathan Demme
Tags – Serial Killer (Fictional)

A budding FBI agent must trust and confide in Hannibal Lecter, a convicted killer, cannibal, and brilliant doctor if she is to find the serial killer known as Buffalo Bill. This is one of the only horror movies to ever be recognized by The Academy and to have won several Oscars and for good reason since it just happens to be one of the best movies ever made. The acting is absolutely amazing, Anthony Hopkins as the intelligent sociopath plays off Jodie Foster's naïve innocence to perfection. The story is also remarkable, and how it plays out is even better. This is another one of those rare movies that is not only atmospheric and tense, but pretty graphic and gory as well. The direction is quite simply some of the best I have ever seen as well. All this makes for the recipe to an absolute masterpiece that everyone, horror fan or not, simply must see in their lifetime.

5/5

Silent Hill
Year – 2006
Director – Christophe Gans

Based on the video game series, this story is about a woman and her adoptive daughter who go to the town of Silent Hill and once there, they find it deserted, with ashes falling from the sky like snow. But when an unnatural darkness falls upon the town, all manner of creatures rise and assault all those who dare tread on the streets and in the buildings, and now they're trapped there with them, desperate for a way out. Video game adaptations have a poor track record, mainly because Uwe Boll directed so many of them, but fortunately he didn't get his filthy mitts on this one and some people with talent constructed this beautifully dark instant classic. This movie, while having a separate storyline, is still very much a great fit into the Silent Hill universe. The creatures are so varied and just look so wonderful. The FX are great and even the CGI is impressive. There are many death scenes and they just look great, including lots of blood and there's even a very well done burning scene. The acting is phenomenal by the mostly female cast, and I'm glad to see mainly women in action since a large part of the story is about a mother's love. The direction is smooth and beautifully shot and this is just quite simply eye candy for the dark minded folk like me. Gorgeous and undeniably well done, Silent Hill is damn near perfect in every way it could be.

4.5/5

Silent Venom
Year – 2009
Director – Fred Olen Ray
Tags – Animals

A submarine crew is ordered to pick up a doctor and her assistant from an island where they are performing experiments on snakes. Once their cargo is brought aboard, it escapes (of course) and begins to take down the crew one by one. I expected nothing from this movie but it turned out to be a rather pleasant surprise. First off I have to say that the CGI is easily some of the worst ever and when I saw it, my expectations managed to drop even lower. Fortunately, once aboard the sub they use real snakes and some models more than the CGI, which was a nice sight to see because people are so lazy nowadays they do everything with CGI. The acting and direction were also surprisingly good, the movie moved along well despite the lack of story. I expected "Snakes on a Submarine", what I got was a good movie that had some snakes in it. Color me shocked, I actually liked this movie.

3/5

Silver Bullet
Year – 1985
Director – Daniel Attias
Tags – Werewolves

A killer is stalking the town of Tarker's Mills and chooses a young wheelchair bound boy as his next victim. But the boy escapes and now knows the killer's secret, he's a werewolf. I always loved Cycle of the Werewolf as a kid, which this is adapted from, probably because of all the cool pictures. I was really happy to see that Stephen King wrote the screenplay too, because that really helped this movie become what it is. It's a more traditional werewolf tale, nothing new added to the genre, but that's just fine because the story is so well done. The direction is very good with hardly a lull in the pacing. The acting is a very strong point here, excellent acting all around. The werewolf is pretty cool looking, I've seen better, but it's still very nice. A fair amount of blood and good kills are also present here. This is one of the better werewolf movies out on the market, it's not perfect but it's still very entertaining.

4/5

Single White Female
Year – 1992
Director – Barbet Schroeder
Tags – Suspense

When a woman places an ad for a roommate, she found a shy and sweet girl that fit the bill. But soon an obsession starts brewing and her new roommate starts borrowing not only her clothes, but her entire life. While Single White Female isn't anything particularly new or inventive, I do like how it plays out and that is really what sets it apart from similar movies. There's a lot of sex, nudity and eventually violence, which only helps the movie achieve more of its potential over the watered down rivals. The acting is excellent and the direction and pacing are also well done. I don't want to reveal too much of the movie but suffice to say that the roommate does get into some very creepy moments that really stood out for me. Not the best tale of suspense on the market but a very comparable one.

3.5/5

Single White Female 2: The Psycho
Year – 2005
Director – Keith Samples
Tags – Suspense

I'm not even going to bother with a synopsis since this sequel, which has nothing to do with the original, is essentially just a carbon copy of it instead. Sure they changed a few things here and there, but it is basically exactly the same. So that's never a good sign, but that's not all that's wrong with this movie, not by a long shot. Next you are subjected to an unattractive cast of non-actors whoring it up on screen and looking like lost animals in the process. The direction is just painful, and this whole movie is painful to be honest. I'll never understand how shit like this gets made, and the fact that this movie has a budget only enrages me more.

0.5/5

Sixth Sense, The
Year – 1999
Director – M. Night Shyamalan
Tags – Ghosts

A child psychologist with his personal life in turmoil attempts to help a young boy who claims that he can see dead people. Directorial debuts in horror usually leave something to be desired, but right out of the gate Shyamalan delivers an exceptional ghost movie with multiple psychological horror elements. The story is superbly crafted and is obviously a labor of love. The direction is excellent and immaculately paced which is supported by some tremendous acting talent. The ending of this movie was spoiled for me and it is one of the main reasons I try to conceal spoilers to the best of my ability in this book. This is dark and atmospheric thriller that is not only highly original, but also very entertaining and easily one of the best ghost movies ever made.

4.5/5

Skinned Deep
Year – 2004
Director – Gabriel Bartalos
Tags – Slasher / Survival

A family on vacation is accosted by a family of psychotics, one of whom has his eye on the young daughter. Yep, just another cheap rip-off of The Texas Chainsaw Massacre. I will give credit for the just plain weird members of the family, because they are pretty unique, but that's where the compliments end. The story is absolute crap and pretty much worthless, offering nothing new or interesting. The acting is really bad and the direction is slow and boring. The FX aren't terrible but there's nothing noteworthy here either. The kills are ok though. This is just another low budget slasher movie is a long line and another one that can easily be skipped.

1.5/5

Slashers
Year – 2001
Director – Maurice Devereaux
Tags – Slasher / Survival

Six contestants try to survive in a maze against a trio of killers in Japan's #1 TV show. Well, that's the whole synopsis, pretty awesome idea I'd say. Reminds me of The Running Man, except without the technology, just edged weapons. I have to say that the way this was shot really makes it feel like a TV show, which is a nice accomplishment. Now I also have to say that the acting is so incredibly bad that it actually hinders the movie. The woman who gets the most screen time is actually the worst actor of the bunch, and just downright annoying. The FX work is obviously done on a tight budget, but I like it, I actually like everything about this movie, but the acting just damn near killed it for me. If there had been different people cast in about half of the roles that could actually act, this movie would have been incredible, as it stands, it's just above average.

3/5

Slaughter
Year – 2009
Director – Stewart Hopewell
Tags – Suspense

A young woman moves far away to escape an abusive relationship and ends up befriending and living with a young farm girl. But the family that lives at the farm turn out to be anything but normal. This movie has a bad, derivative script, and thus has bad direction, and thus has bad acting. See how things trickle down? The story is unoriginal and tired, very predictable, and just about as plain as you can get. It's boring and features very little blood and no nudity. I'm sorry, but if you're going to deliver a poor script, you at least need to throw tons of gore and nudity at the viewer to keep them interested. The torture aspect of the movie is very weak, and the supposed twists and turns of the storyline can be seen coming from a mile away. Word to the wise, if you're going to try and cash in on the torture movie craze, or any other craze for that matter that may come along, then do something worthwhile and stop giving us this bullshit, we've had enough already.

1/5

Sleepaway Camp
Year – 1983
Director – Robert Hiltzik
Tags – Slasher / Survival

Years after a tragic boating accident, a girl is sent to a camp with her cousin but does not manage to be socially active and quickly becomes an outcast. She gets picked on regularly and is saved only by her cousin, and then the people who wronged her begin to have fatal accidents. So given the camp location I could only assume that someone is trying to cash in on the success of Friday the 13th, but the thing is, this movie is actually better. It is cheesy as cheesy can be, with some terrible acting, but that actually adds to the humor of the movie, for which there is quite a bit. But on top of the humor there are some rather grisly kills that lead into one of the most shocking endings in horror history. I kid you not, when I saw it the first time my jaw literally dropped. That was the moment that the movie ceased to be humorous and became downright serious. The FX work is also pretty damn good with some excellent shots of post kill bodies. This is definitely a slasher movie to watch with only some budget related flaws, and is by far one of the more bizarre movies I have seen to boot.

Sleepaway Camp 2: Unhappy Campers
Year – 1988
Director – Michael A. Simpson
Tags – Slasher / Survival

This movie takes place many years after the original. I loved the original but this one is completely lacking. The kills come along at a quick rate, but for the most part they're all pretty standard and not graphic at all. There is a lot of sex and nudity though, so that's a plus. The acting is still bad here, but the movie doesn't have the campiness of the original to make it forgivable. The story is very clichéd and tired as well. This movie just flat out isn't good, hell it isn't even average, and while it is watchable, I can't say I recommend it. Just stick with the original.

2/5

Sleepaway Camp 3: Teenage Wasteland
Year – 1989
Director – Michael A. Simpson
Tags – Slasher / Survival

This movie takes place a year after the last one. Being thoroughly unimpressed with the last movie I was expecting more of the same here, but I'm happy to say that the franchise bounced back a bit here. Right off the bat the direction is better, and while not perfect, the pacing is definitely a large improvement. There is also a pretty big body count, a variety of kills and some nudity for good measure. The acting is just as terrible and the FX work is very cheap, but sometimes still effective. Here we have a decent enough slasher to be called good, but it's still far from being great. It was nice to see them bring some humor back into this series as well as blood.

3/5

*Sleepaway Camp 4 can be found under Return to Sleepaway Camp.

Sleepstalker
Year – 1995
Director – Turi Meyer
Tags – Slasher / Survival

A serial killer nicknamed The Sandman is finally caught after slaughtering numerous families and is then sentenced to death. Seventeen years later when he is finally put to death in the gas chamber, he returns, but his body now composed of sand, and he sets out to kill the one person who got away from him. This is a pretty damn interesting concept for a killer that opens up a lot of opportunities. And while they did capitalize on some cool kills and sequences, I think the filmmakers could have done more with the character.

The acting is just ok, and the direction is pretty much the same. I think quite a bit could have been left on the cutting room floor. The FX were nice but I would have liked to have seen more of the kills in detail as some of them were primarily off camera. The story plays out like a typical slasher movie but the abilities of the killer are definitely its high point. Good stuff if you can stand the overly long run time.

3/5

Sleepwalkers
Year – 1992
Director – Mick Garris
Tags – Monsters

A mother and son, who happen to be supernatural cat creatures, move from small town to small town feeding off the life force of virgins. This is a completely new creature for the horror genre, something akin to vampires but still incredibly different. Stephen King puts together yet again another great story that just oozes with originality. The Sleepwalkers are pretty cool looking, and a lot of the FX work is really good, even with some obvious green screen work. The acting is good with a pretty diverse cast of familiar faces, and there's also a ton of cameos by famed horror directors and King himself. The pacing is good, the direction is good, the soundtrack really fits the mood, and this is just an overlooked gem from the early nineties. Not the greatest horror movie, but still a nice original tale with a lot of entertainment value.

3.5/5

Sleepy Hollow
Year – 1999
Director – Tim Burton
Tags – Ghosts

Burton puts his own spin on the classic tale of a small New York town under siege from the Headless Horseman, which is the ghost of a sadistic soldier killed many years ago. Now it's up to a constable to solve the mystery of the horseman before there is no one left in the town. While I can appreciate the dark style Burton attempts to place on timeless stories, it doesn't always work for me, and that is very true here as well. I liked Johnny Depp's portrayal of the aloof Ichabod Crane, and other people in the movie did well in their roles, but I feel that Christina Ricci was not a good fit for her role. The movie was certainly gory with multiple decapitations, but much of gore came from CGI, and as I've stated before, CGI blood just doesn't look right. The direction is ok but the movie definitely lags at times. This was an enjoyable experience but I can't say it was one I liked a lot.

3/5

Slither

Year – 2006
Director – James Gunn
Tags – Aliens, Zombies

A comet crashes to earth carrying an alien parasite. One man becomes infected and soon he begins spreading it to others by way of brain eating slugs. The slugs turn their hosts into flesh hungry zombies, while the original man turns into something far worse. This movie is obviously inspired by Night of the Creeps, but James Gunn takes the idea presented by that movie and moves beyond the simple storyline and creates new angles for this movie. The movie never takes itself too seriously, and big applause goes to Nathan Fillion for delivering hilarious lines with expert precision. The pacing is great, the acting is great, and the mixture of practical FX and CGI really works most of the time, but then sometimes the CGI is just really bad when it's on its own. There are some truly off the wall moments that just make you say "What the hell?" out loud, a mark of true creativity. Any issues with this movie are pretty small and most likely budget related, and the end product is just a ton of fun and a throwback to 80's horror/sci-fi.

4/5

Slugs
Year – 1988
Director – Juan Piquer Simon
Tags – Animals

Residents of a small town must deal with carnivorous slugs that have been mutated to large sizes from toxic waste. And now they're breeding. When I saw this movie I just could not resist buying it. Killer slugs? Yes, I have to see it. Too bad the movie was so poorly directed that it was just unconscionably boring. And the acting is pretty bad, but it is a Spanish movie dubbed into English so I can't really place any fault there. What I did like were the slugs, which looked awesome, especially when there were thousands of them at once. The gore was the highlight of the movie, as there were some incredible FX shots and loads of blood. I also liked the aftermath shots of people being stripped to the bone, those looked cool. This is a fun 80's movie that was just poorly shot, but I'd love to see this movie remade with a more competent director in the same 80's style because this movie has the potential, now it just needs to be done properly.

2.5/5

Snakes on a Plane
Year – 2006
Director – David R. Ellis, Lex Halaby
Tags – Animals

A man is a witness to the crimes of a reputed crime lord, and when he is flying from Hawaii back to the mainland to testify, a group of poisonous snakes are unleashed on the crew and passengers. So I like that this movie is just pure cheese and a throwback to the silly horror flicks of yesteryear, but its execution leaves much to be desired. First off there are so many errors in the movie. Second, it takes a rather long time to actually get to the snakes on the plane. Third, the snakes look so fake that the filmmakers would have been better off just using rubber ones because they would have looked better than the awful CGI ones. The acting is fine and the direction is ok, but the movie could have had much better pacing. Still, with all these issues, the movie does have good entertainment value, but this is hardly a brilliant exercise in filmmaking.

2.5/5

Snow White: A Tale of Terror
Year – 1997
Director – Michael Cohn
Tags – Witchcraft

This adaptation of the original story of Snow White (forget about all those kid friendly, commercialized fairy tales), this story follows a young girl as she comes under the dark powers of her stepmother, who is trying to kill her. While I love the idea of making a true adaptation of Snow White, this one doesn't quite work for me. There are some great actors involved, genre vets no less, but the rest of the cast are just passable and tend to force their lines in medieval tongue. The story is as it should be but the direction is awfully slow and it really took me out of the movie. And that's sad because it's really a beautiful movie with great locales. I don't hate this movie by any means, as I was just terribly unimpressed by it.

2.5/5

Soho Square
Year – 2000
Director – Jeremy Rafn
Tags – Serial Killer (Fictional)

A troubled detective searches for a serial killer who burns his victims to death. The story isn't exactly original, the burning aspect is cool but that's really all it has going for it, everything else is either a rehash of other serial killer movies or just predictable and somewhat pointless. The direction is an interesting beast because I love the way the movie was shot but the pacing was pretty bad, so I think the guy behind the movie has talent but really needs to work on his craft. The acting was surprisingly good and the real highlight was in the post burn FX. One particular survivor had some rather well done make-up applied to her body. While not completely unsatisfying, this movie really isn't very good.

2/5

Solstice
Year – 2008

Director – Daniel Myrick
Tags – Ghosts

After the suicide of a young woman's twin sister, she and a group of friends take their annual trip deep into the bayou, and while there they decide to perform a pagan solstice ritual to commune with the dead. Ever since The Blair Witch Project, the two directors involved have gone their separate ways to make their own movies, and each of them was pretty bad, but I still hold out that they can create another good movie, but this definitely isn't it. The story here is nothing short of atrocious. The solstice ritual doesn't even come into play until after about an hour of the movie has passed, and up until that point there is nothing but painfully boring dialogue and a useless back story. And then after the ritual, well, things actually don't get any better. It just continues on the boring trail of nothingness until it reaches the yawn inducing climax and then finally ends. The acting is fairly good from most of the cast but the lead actress isn't very good, nor is her character likeable. The movie is boring from start to finish and even the good actors involved can't make it interesting. This is just a terrible movie.

1/5

Someone's Watching Me!
Year – 1978
Director – John Carpenter
Tags – Suspense

A woman moves into a new apartment and into a new job, but before long she starts to receive obscene phone calls and learns that there is a peeping tom in the vicinity. When you get a movie like this that treads familiar ground, it really comes down to well the movie is made, and fortunately with John Carpenter both writing and directing this made for TV movie, it was pulled off quite well. While the movie does feel very familiar, it doesn't copy any formulas and instead goes out on its own to make a rather tense thriller. The acting is very good and the characters are well thought out. It is extremely tame, which is to be expected from a TV movie made in the seventies, but it could have been a lot better as a feature with some violence and nudity, or maybe not, who knows for sure? What I do know is that this is a very good tale of suspense from a master filmmaker and really has shades of what was to come from him in the future.

3.5/5

Sorority Babes in the Slime Ball Bowl-A-Rama
Year – 1988
Director – David DeCoteau
Tags – Monsters, Demonic Possession

Such an awesome movie name, what an attention grabber! A trio of college guys caught peeping on a sorority house initiation are forced to aid the women on their quest of stealing a bowling trophy. Unfortunately, the trophy they choose contains an imp with the power to grant wishes, wishes that end up turning very bad. One by one they become possessed and hunt down the rest. This movie is ridiculous fun. If the title doesn't give it away, then I will tell you that this is cheesy 80's horror cinema at its peak. The acting is goofy, the imp is a crappy rubber puppet, the FX work is of the dime store variety and the story is full of holes and really lame. So why do I like this movie? How can you not? It's obvious that everyone involved in this movie is just having fun with it, and that allows me to have fun watching it. They had no money, no good talent (Other than Buck Flowers and the bevy of scream queens), but they just went out to make this cheesy crap for fun, and I enjoyed it. Lots of nudity, lots of violence, and an imp that sound like a black pimp. Why are you not watching this yet?

3.5/5

Species
Year – 1995
Director – Roger Donaldson
Tags – Aliens

Alien organisms are mixed with human DNA in a lab to create a rapidly growing test subject. But when the subject is ordered to be destroyed, she escapes into the world and continues to grow, now reaching maturity and seeking a mate. A group of specialists are assembled to find her before she can procreate. Species is a fun movie that isn't anything great but certainly has a good entertainment factor to it. The acting is good, the direction is good, and the story is good, nothing wrong there but also nothing to give it that boost it needed to make it something extraordinary. The movie does have its fair share of nudity and gore, which was a nice touch. The practical FX are excellent but there is some terrible CGI as well. The design of the alien form was created by H.R. Giger, who also created the creatures in the Alien series, so you know it looks great. This is a B movie disguised as a high budget film, and while I like it, I can't say it's anything too special.

3.5/5

Species II
Year – 1998
Director – Peter Medak
Tags – Aliens

This movie continues on not too long after the last one. So this sequel is obviously a thrown together mess of bad ideas, but there's still something about it that I just don't hate. Even the returning actors look like they know this movie is crap and I could swear that I saw a couple of them checking their watches to find out when they would be done so they could get paid. The CGI is just as awful as the first movie and there aren't many practical FX. The direction isn't bad, as the movie is actually paced fairly well, and given the complete lack of worthwhile material, that's kind of impressive. This is a rush job sequel that feels every bit like a rush job sequel, but I do have to say it is watchable and even worth a couple of laughs, at the plot's expense of course.

Species III
Year – 2004
Director – Brad Turner
Tags – Aliens

This movie picks up where the last one left off. Sitting through this was actually a bit of a chore. The story was extremely mundane and the direction was ungodly boring. The whole movie played out so completely one dimensional that it was difficult to find anything good to say. There were some cool practical FX but the terrible CGI just about waxes out any positive aspects there. The acting ranges from passable to terrible so there's nothing special to speak about there. There's some nudity and some blood, but nothing remarkable. This is just a plain, dull, boring mess with very little going for it and I can't help but ask myself, why do they keep making sequels?

1.5/5

Species IV: The Awakening
Year – 2007
Director – Nick Lyon
Tags – Aliens

This movie happens some indeterminate time after the last one. I told myself going this that this time they were going to get the sequel right and this would be a good movie, but really, who am I kidding? I really wish they would hire women with acting talent instead of just women who are conventionally attractive and willing to get naked. Natasha Henstridge may not be the greatest actor but she was still pretty good. So the acting sucks for the most part, the direction is so slow I swear I could feel my beard growing and the FX were downright awful. But that really isn't anything new by this point in the series. The story is also disturbingly inadequate and all of that put together ensure that this would be a terrible movie, and it is. I just pray that there will never be a fifth.

1/5

Speck
Year – 2002
Director – Keith Walley
Tags – Serial Killer

This movie is about Richard Speck, a serial killer best known for the night he broke into the house of eight nursing students and systematically raped and killed them one by one. And this movie focuses mainly on that night. There was a lot of potential here to make a very gruesome and disturbing movie, but the end result is a fairly tame and poorly acted thriller with only a few redeeming qualities. The direction is interesting and I liked it.

There are some good shots and the pacing is pretty good, I would really like to see what this guy could do with a more competent script and a decent budget. I think this movie missed its mark and didn't capture the brutality of this individual so I can't really recommend it.

2/5

Spectre (Regreso A Moria)
Year – 2006
Director – Mateo Gil
Tags – Suspense

This is part of the DVD box set "6 Films to Keep You Awake". This movie follows a man as he recollects a past love with a woman whom everyone in the village referred to a witch and whore. And now in the present day he is haunted by his past and seeks a way to end his waking nightmare. This is a little bit thriller, little bit coming of age drama, and a little bit supernatural horror that ends up making a very tasty soup of genres. The movie is fascinating to watch, aided greatly by the well conceived story and the great direction. It is aided ever further by the wonderful performances. This is a very unique movie that talking about in detail would damage the initial viewing for people, so I'll just say that this is a great film.

4/5

Sphere
Year – 1998
Director – Barry Levinson
Tags – Suspense

The US finds a crashed space ship in the Pacific Ocean and assembles a team of scientists to explore it. Once inside they discover a sphere of what seems to be of alien origin and after one of the scientists goes inside the sphere, strange things begin to happen and people start to die. I really like this movie because it manages to keep you guessing as to what exactly is going on. The FX are great, you get to see multiple sea creatures in great detail and they all look really good. There are also some awesome death scenes, which surprised me. The acting is well done from the leads but everyone else is forgettable. The direction is good, but I was kind of annoyed with the "chapter markers" that came across the screen, as the viewer is treated like a complete moron. Yes, we realize they are on the surface, yes, now we understand that they entering the ship. You don't have to tell us with words emblazoned across the screen. But other than that the pacing was pretty good and it was well shot. Overall this is a fun flick that's pretty different from everything else, it has some flaws, but it's still a good show.

3.5/5

Spider

Year – 2002
Director – David Cronenberg
Tags – Suspense

A mentally ill man takes up residence at a halfway house and slowly begins to recall his past and the events during his childhood that led to his illness. I always appreciate films that deal with dark subject matter so candidly. The acting and direction are very good, but it's the story that's so compelling. The way it's told during the present day through flashbacks is very slick and works well where other similar storytelling methods have failed. The story does unfold slowly at first but then the pace picks up and some unexpected things begin to happen, making for some interesting times. The movie has some minor flaws that hold it back from greatness, namely the slow start, but it did not hinder the overall experience and Spider makes for a very good movie.

3.5/5

Spiral
Year – 2007
Director – Adam Green, Joel Moore
Tags – Suspense

A woman wriggles her way into the life of a troubled artist and finds a certain quality in him she has not experienced before, but there is also a dark side to him. Every once in awhile a movie comes along that just amazes me and when the credits start to roll, I just can't help but say wow, and this is that movie. The story is just so brilliantly crafted that I appreciated it on every possible level. This was enhanced further by the great acting on display and enhanced even further by the incredibly smooth direction. I was nothing short of enthralled by this movie and watched it with such amazement that I knew this would be one of those movies that I could never watch again for the first time, and that hurt. But even on repeated viewings the movie is remarkable. Definitely one of the best thrillers ever constructed in my eyes.

5/5

Splinter
Year – 2008
Director – Toby Wilkins
Tags – Monsters, Infection

A couple, merely wanting to go camping, instead find themselves kidnapped by a wanted murderer and his junkie girlfriend. They end up hitting some bizarre animal on the road and are forced to stop at a nearby gas station. Little do they know, an unknown infection has taken over the attendant, and now they are under attack from the creature he has become. Wow, this movie is just so well done. The concept is fresh and it's pulled off with great skill. The acting is superb, the FX work is excellent, and the script and direction are just A-list stuff. The monster is very unique and there just hasn't been anything quite like it, same goes for the way it infects, which is from these black barbs that push their way out of the skin and blood of the host. Very cool. I guess my only complaint in this stellar production would be the use of shaky cam. I hate it, but they fortunately don't use it too much, so it's not a big deal. Very suspenseful, nice and bloody, one hell of a ride.

4.5/5

Starkweather
Year – 2004
Director – Byron Werner
Tags – Serial Killer

This is the story of Charles Starkweather, a 19 year old man who in 1958 went on a two state killing spree with his 14 year old girlfriend. This movie, much like Ed Gein is a very accurate telling of a serial killer's exploits, but ultimately somewhat boring. The acting is a mixed bag, some done very well, others not so much. The direction could have used some improving, especially in the area of pacing. This is an informative watch and while as I said before, it can be a bit slow and sometimes uneventful, it is still entertaining and if you are into true life serial killer cinema, you can do better, but you can also do a lot worse.

3/5

Steel Trap
Year – 2007
Director – Luis Camara
Tags – Slasher / Survival

A group of people are summoned away from a party to another floor of the building they are in. Now they are being hunted by a killer who has laid traps out in the building to stop their escape. This movie is an abhorrent mess. I can look past the bad acting, its par for the course, but let me tell you something, I don't think Steel Trap has any excuse in being the abomination that it is. This movie obviously had some kind of budget, and apparently blew it on the most annoying "actors" they could find. Take drag queen Nicole for instance, never have I been so annoyed by someone in my entire life, her voice alone killed this movie. But I can not place all the blame on the disturbingly wooden cast, because let me tell you, whoever wrote this trash has penned quite possibly the worst dialogue I have ever heard in a movie. So maybe the bad acting wasn't their fault, maybe they were just flabbergasted at the lines they had to spew out. No, it was both. There is nothing original here either, it kind of sounded like it would be a cross between Cube and Saw, nice. But no, it wasn't. It was just a slasher movie with sparsely laid traps. Ooo, the elevator doors have teeth now! Lame. But why would we watch a movie like this? Gore, death, and all that good stuff. Well, the violence is very tame, minimal gore, off camera kills, just done to annoy us further. And then comes the extremely predictable outcome, I will not spoil things for you, heh. I actually found nothing redeeming in this movie, nothing. That's really hard for me to say. I can usually find something worthwhile in anything I watch, but here I draw a blank. This poorly constructed piece of garbage is one of the worst horror movies I have ever seen.

0.5/5

Stay Alive
Year – 2006
Director – William Brent Bell
Tags – Ghosts

Some people playing an underground video game realize that when you die in the game, you die for real outside the game. Yeah, this is essentially just The Ring with a video game instead of a video tape, but not at all clever. The "graphics" of the game a.k.a. the CGI, is pretty bad. The story is fairly dumb and uninteresting to boot. There are some decent performances and the direction isn't all bad, so I guess there are some things keeping this movie from being a complete waste, but in all honesty I'm not going to recommend it because it's just not scary, bloody, or good.

2/5

Stir of Echoes
Year – 1999
Director – David Koepp
Tags – Ghosts

After being hypnotized, a blue collar man becomes haunted by the ghost of a girl and he becomes obsessed with solving the mystery of her death. This movie came out around the same time as The Sixth Sense and got lost in the shuffle. While they do have similar plots they are in fact very different. While I do think that The Sixth Sense is a slightly better film, this one definitely does not deserve to be dismissed. The acting is great, as is the direction. The story is excellent and I love how it progresses and eventually culminates. The cast really adds a lot to this movie and makes it feel very personal. This is a great ghost movie that deserves the attention it lacked due to an unfortunate release date.

4/5

Stir of Echoes 2: The Homecoming
Year – 2007
Director – Ernie Barbarash
Tags – Ghosts

This sequel has nothing to do with the original but rather this one is about a man coming back from a war in the Middle East and having the ability to see the dead. I don't know why companies tack on a title to certain movies hoping for more commercial appeal because it never seems to work. Had this just been a ghost movie I may have had more respect for it but the fact of the matter is, this movie is just across the board second rate from the original. The acting, direction, story, everything is just half as good. Well, a title doesn't make me enjoy a movie less actually, because this just isn't a good movie, and turd by any other name would still smell like shit.

2/5

Storm of the Century
Year – 1999
Director – Craig R. Baxley
Tags – Suspense

A massive storm begins to roll in on a small island off the coast of Maine. At the same time, a stranger comes to town and commits a heinous murder. Once captured the people of the island slowly begin to realize that this stranger is no ordinary man and seems to know all of their darkest secrets. First I must say that this movie is ungodly long and thus becomes incredibly slow on more than one occasion. The story starts off slow but progresses better as the movie goes on, up until about the final hour when it becomes a gripping and compelling piece of fiction. I liked many of the story's aspects, but it was very bloated and easily could have been trimmed down into a smoother presentation. The acting is good from most of the cast, but some of the actors, especially the child actors, are downright terrible. This movie would have been exceptional had it been shorter, but as it stands the movie is painfully long and the story stretched about as thin as it can get. Great idea, not so great execution.

2.5/5

Storm Warning
Year – 2007
Director – Jamie Blanks
Tags – Slasher / Survival

A couple becomes lost while boating and happened upon a house in the middle of nowhere. Finding no one there, they enter the house, but when the owners come home, they don't quite get the help they were looking for. This movie definitely has a good deal of brutality to it, including a particularly cringe worthy moment for men. There's some excellent gore and each kill is very much thought out and executed in a very special way. The acting is good and the direction is also good, the movie doesn't slow down often. This is an excellent addition to the survival sub genre that I feel will please most people looking for a bloody good time. It could have been improved on a bit, but I still like this movie a great deal.

4/5

Strangeland
Year – 1998

Director – John Pieplow
Tags – Suspense

A man is luring people to his house of pain through the internet and committing acts of torture against them through body piercing and other means that are normal in his alternative lifestyle. I like this movie because it's so very different. You can't call the guy a serial killer or a slasher because he just doesn't kill anyone, and instead he kidnaps them to modify their bodies and perhaps to show his power over them. And while I was a little disappointed that I didn't get to see any graphic deaths, I enjoyed it for other reasons. I liked the filmmaker's delving into the alternative lifestyle (tattoos, piercings, scarification, industrial music, suspension, etc.), because hardly anyone goes there and that really is a shame because there a large group of interesting people living that lifestyle. I also liked the soundtrack and the fact that the band Bile had a live performance in the movie. This is definitely something different with solid acting (especially by Dee Snider and Robert Englund). The direction is good as well, but it could have been better. Overall this is a fun movie with some nice originality, a good story that evolves and unfurls in unexpected ways, and some really good content and visuals.

3.5/5

Strangers, The
Year – 2008
Director – Bryan Bertino
Tags – Suspense

A young couple with a troubled relationship are besieged by three masked assailants at a vacation home nestled far out into the woods. I have to admit I wasn't expecting much from this movie because it seems like just another studio picture that would just be as bland as the hundreds that came before it. But this is actually a well crafted, atmospheric thriller that may not be among the best created, but still ends up being a damn good time. The acting is very good and carried mainly by Liv Tyler, even though I preferred the strangers themselves. The direction is also great. The movie runs smoothly and has great tension throughout. And that's the key here, the movie is tense and doesn't rely heavily on jump scares, always a plus. I also loved the masks the strangers wore. This may not be intensely original or thought provoking but I know a good time when I see it and The Strangers is definitely a good time.

4/5

Stuck
Year – 2007
Director – Stuart Gordon
Tags – Suspense

Stuart Gordon takes a break from Lovecraft to direct this incredibly strange but true story. On the way home from a club one night, a nurse hits a homeless man with her car, and instead of taking him to a hospital, she instead takes him to her house, while he is still stuck in the windshield, and waits for him to bleed to death. Truth really is stranger than fiction. I mean, who would think of a concept like this, it had to be a true story. Now the movie doesn't play out exactly how it did in real life, tweaks had to be made to make this into a feature length movie. In the hands of a less competent director, this would be incredibly boring, as it does focus on a man stuck in a windshield after all. But Gordon manages to make a rather suspenseful movie out of a fairly one dimensional premise. I also like that a nurse, who is supposed to help people, is the one person who will not help him. Now there does seem to be some filler in the movie to pad the run time, but it's not too much of a nuisance in this otherwise great flick.

4/5

Stuff, The
Year – 1985
Director – Larry Cohen
Tags – Biological

A new product is on the market that's better than ice cream and has no calories, but are you eating it or is it eating you? The Stuff is a very fun and cheesy movie from the 80's that has a respectable amount of originality to it. I'm sure a lot of people compare it to The Blob, but I don't remember people eating The Blob as a tasty and nutritious part of their diet, do you? The practical FX work here is pretty awesome, especially since when people ingest large amounts of The Stuff, they tend to bleed The Stuff. Bleeding what looks like marshmallow paste? Awesome. The movie can be a little slow at times and has some what I assume are budget related flaws, but this is still a pretty cool movie. But that damn theme song for The Stuff is forever stuck in my head, so prepare yourself for that.

3.5/5

Subject Two
Year – 2006
Director – Philip Chidel
Tags – Suspense

A doctor invents a resurrection serum and tests it on his assistant by killing him over and over again. You got to love that synopsis, and that's what really had drawn me to the movie. Too bad the story is an overall dull affair and the direction is practically coma inducing. This really is one of the slowest movies I have ever seen and it's not that nice slow burn kind of pacing, because there really is no big pay off for all of your patience. The end comes and you say to yourself that you figured as much and move on with your life. The acting is really good and natural though, and there are some nice FX, so it's not a complete waste, but it definitely is a prime example of wasted potential.

2/5

Sublime
Year – 2007
Director – Tony Krantz
Tags – Suspense

A man heads into the hospital for a routine colonoscopy when he receives and unnecessary surgery by mistake. The results of this surgery only complicate his health further and plunges him into madness and worse. This movie really frustrates me. The concept is a good one, but the opening scene gives away the ending and from there the entire way the movie plays out becomes transparent when it should have been hidden. The pacing is also terrible and this nearly two hour long film drags on endlessly through multiple pointless flashback sequences. The movie also had a chance to be completely surreal but missed the mark there as well. But on the plus side the story did have some great moments and at times was interesting, and the acting was really good by most of the cast. Had someone else been behind the helm, maybe it would have been great, or maybe it just wasn't good enough from the beginning. I guess we'll never know and all we're left with is a disappointing movie.

2/5

Subspecies
Year – 1991
Director – Ted Nicolaou
Tags – Vampires

Some students set out to a small Romanian village to further their studies when they come across Radu, an evil vampire who wishes to usurp the power of his father and will let nothing stand in his way. This was one of my favorite movies as a kid and now into adulthood it still holds up as one of the best vampire movies ever. The location is so ridiculously perfect and it so much atmosphere the modernly Gothic tale. Radu is easily one of the creepiest and well constructed vampire characters ever made with powers that are rather unique to him. The story is very well made and the direction is nearly flawless. The acting is also rather good, especially for a low budget movie but Anders Hove as Radu really steals the show. This is a must see for vampire fans and even the string of sequels that came after it were impressive.

4.5/5

Subspecies II: Bloodstone
Year – 1993
Director – Ted Nicolaou
Tags – Vampires

This movie picks up immediately after the first. And it starts off with quite a bang and moves the story into a great direction, pretty straightforward, but more than adequate. This movie features everything that made the original so great. Awesome score, great FX (even though some are dated), solid acting, well done direction and an engaging story. Fans of the original can not help but love this sequel and I'm really glad to see that some great care went into creating it. While it doesn't quite reach the mark set by the original, this is a more than worthy follow up and a highly enjoyable vampire tale.

4/5

Subspecies III: Bloodlust
Year – 1994
Director – Ted Nicolaou
Tags – Vampires

This movie picks up immediately after the last one. This and the last one were shot back to back and it shows considering that this one is just as good. The progression here is once again very natural and well done, and to be honest I'm surprised the franchise has held up this well. Everything is the same as the last one as far as actors and the director go since there are many returning cast and crew. I guess there isn't much more to say here other than if you're a fan of the series up to this point, odds are you won't be disappointed with this one either.

4/5

Subspecies IV: Bloodstorm
Year – 1998
Director – Ted Nicolaou
Tags – Vampires

This movie picks up right after the last one. Well, they all do and that's why the continuity is so great in this franchise. Should this have just been a trilogy and ended on a high note? Nah, I really like this one too, and I wasn't expecting to. The story is made up of two separate halves that eventually come together. One deals with Radu and his past made present, and the other deals with another character and the introduction of new characters. I really like Radu's part, but the other is just ok. The acting, direction and everything else are on par with previous efforts, I just didn't like the story quite as much. Still, a very fine close to a consistently great franchise.

3.5/5

Substitute, The (Vikaren)
Year – 2007
Director – Ole Bornedal
Tags – Aliens

An elementary school class gets a new substitute teacher who happens to be an alien searching Earth for the emotion of love, as her race only knows how to create war. This movie has a nice concept behind it that carries quite a bit of whimsy, which is different and welcome. I like how the teacher doesn't bother putting on a facade and instead allows the children to know right away that something is amiss with her, I mean after all, what adult would believe a child about their teacher being an alien? The acting is good as well as the direction, the movie moves along nicely with few slow parts. The FX are a mix of really bad CGI and then some good CGI and practical stuff. The story is good but not great as I found it to be predictable and too dull at times. But in the end this is a fun and somewhat light hearted movie that I enjoyed.

3.5/5

Summer of Fear (Stranger in Our House)
Year – 1978
Director – Wes Craven
Tags – Witchcraft

After loosing her parents to a car accident, a young girl moves in with her aunt and her family. But when things out of the ordinary begin to occur, the girl's cousin begins to suspect that she may be a witch. This movie should have been called Summer of Boredom, because that's how I felt while watching it. This movie is fairly painful to sit through because it is just so uneventful, and it's the kind of movie that ends and you just say to yourself: "That's it?" The acting is fine, but Linda Blair's hair was way too distracting. Seriously, her hair was hypnotic and completely took me out of the movie. You'll know what I'm talking about when you see it. A weak story is all this movie has to show for it, and I would just have to say skip it.

2/5

Sunshine
Year – 2007
Director – Danny Boyle
Tags – [Hidden to conceal spoilers]

The sun is dying, and a team of scientists and astronauts have been deployed to reenergize it by dropping a nuclear payload the size of Manhattan into the star. The story is really cool, and I know it doesn't sound much like horror, but there is a plot point that completely turns everything on its head and introduces a big horror element. Just trust me, as I don't want to spoil anything. This movie is a visual feast, easily some of the best CGI I have ever seen, whoever performed the FX on this movie should have people beating their doors with work. The story feels a bit disjointed to me, which was partially alleviated after a second viewing, but I still get that disjointed feel from it, which sucks because that is the only issue I had with this movie. It is very well acted and the set design matches the incredible look of the other FX work. This movie is eye candy with a good story that loses me at times, but that still didn't detract too much from this beautiful film.

4/5

Suspiria

Year – 1977
Director – Dario Argento
Tags – Witchcraft

A woman attending a prestigious ballet school abroad becomes suspicious that the school is actually run by a coven of witches after people start to disappear and die mysteriously. This classic tale by Argento didn't grow on me until after the second viewing. Once I had watched it again, I really appreciated how unique and engrossing the story really was. The death sequences are incredible and go far beyond your typical "creature kills person". They are long and suspenseful and end with a rather gory climax. The direction is great and the acting is also very well done. I especially enjoyed the score by Goblin, as not only was it a unique blend of chamber music and neofolk, but it also fit really, really well. This really is a classic, and even though I didn't love it the first time I watched it, it grew on me heavily and now I absolutely adore it. Quite simply an accomplishment in horror cinema.

4.5/5

Swamp Thing

Year – 1982
Director – Wes Craven
Tags – Monsters

A scientist developing ways to prevent world hunger has his lab deep within the swamp ransacked by a group of thugs, who nearly kill him but instead end up transforming him into a plant monster. Now the leader of the gang wants his secrets for himself and only the newly transformed scientist can stop him. Yep, the movie is about as cheesy as it sounds, nope, even more actually. This is a total B movie but has some great acting in it and also some very good direction. It's the story and FX that make it cheesy. But I have to be honest because the story is pretty weak and missed out on some golden opportunities. But it's not all bad and did manage to entertain. But the FX are so bad they're good in the realm of the B movie. The monster suits are so bad and pyrotechnics are nothing more than blown air and sparkles, hilarious. This is good fun but no classic and if you realize that going into it, then you'll probably have a good time.

3.5/5

*Swamp Thing 2 can be found under Return of the Swamp Thing, The.

Swimfan

Year – 2002
Director – John Polson
Tags – Suspense

The new girl in school becomes obsessed with another girl's boyfriend. That's pretty much it for a synopsis, as this is just an unoriginal and ultimately uninteresting movie. The acting isn't the greatest, seems like they're pretty much scraping the bottom of teen actor barrel here. This has all been done before and it has all been done better. It's very tame and that's where the movie really hits its low point as nothing really happens. Obsession tales are tricky business because it has been done to death and to make a worthwhile one nowadays, you have to do something pretty severe to make it a good movie, and Swimfan doesn't do it. It's not a terrible movie, but it's just a rehash that doesn't really do anything for me.

1.5/5

Sympathy for Mr. Vengeance (Boksuneun Naui Geot)
Year – 2002
Director – Chan-Wook Park
Tags – Suspense

A deaf and dumb man goes to the black market to find a kidney for his ailing sister, but when he ends up having his own kidney as well as his life savings stolen, he reaches a point of desperation. His girlfriend suggests kidnapping the daughter of his former boss for ransom, but when he does, things quickly spiral out of control. Wow, Park never ceases to amaze me with his well crafted revenge thrillers. The story here is amazing and plays out in a very intricate and compelling way. The direction is great and the acting is top notch. There is some wonderful violence here but I would have liked to have seen the revenge angles played out in even more brutal and intricate fashion, but still, it was very pleasing. Revenge thrillers just don't get much better than what Park can create, and that's one hell of a statement, but damned if it isn't true.

4/5

Tale of Two Sisters, A (Janghwa, Hongryeon)
Year – 2003
Director – Ji-Woon Kim
Tags – Suspense

Two sisters return home and are forced to deal with their occasionally cruel stepmother whose mania targets one of the sisters in particular. This leads to disastrous happenings and odd revelations. This is one of those movies I just couldn't get into the first time I watched it and by the second viewing I had to wonder what was wrong with me because this is a rather brilliant film. I guess I was turned off by the pacing at first because the movie is slow, but upon my second viewing I found it to be more of a build up instead of poor pacing. The story is great and while one plot twist was pretty easy to figure out, another made me go "Oh, that's what's going on." So I think they make one aspect of the movie transparent to throw the viewer off the trail of another, very clever. The acting is great as well and the movie has some nice, creepy moments and a killer atmosphere. While not my favorite Asian horror offering, it is a very respectable one nonetheless.

Tales from the Crypt
Year – 1972
Director – Freddie Francis
Tags – Anthology, Suspense

This anthology features five stories and a wraparound. The wraparound is about a group of people who become lost during a tour of an old crypt and come into contact with the strange crypt keeper. The first story is about a woman who kills her husband on the same night a maniac is on the loose. The second is about a man who tries to leave his family with disastrous results. The third is about a man being cruel to his kindly old neighbor. The fourth is an alternate take on the tale of the monkey's paw. And the fifth is about a man who takes up work as the head of a home for the blind, and his cruelty toward the residents. Whew, that's a busy movie, especially for the hour and a half run time. And I think that's kind of a problem. For example, the second story passes by so quickly it seems as though nothing happened at all. The first story is really good, but once again it was too brief, and oddly enough it would also become the first episode of the TV series years later. All of the stories are good, even though you have to suspend a lot of disbelief on the last one, and the acting and direction are well done overall. I just wish the movie was longer so a couple of the stories could have been fleshed out better. Flawed, but very satisfying in the end.

3.5/5

Tales from the Darkside: The Movie
Year – 1990
Director – John Harrison
Tags – Anthology, Mummies, Animals, Monsters

This anthology features 3 segments linked together by a wraparound story. The wraparound is about a woman planning a dinner party and has a little boy picked out for the main course. The first story is about some college kids and a reanimated mummy. The second is about a cat that refuses to die. And the last story is about a man who witnesses a gargoyle like creature commit a murder and then promises not to tell what he saw as long as he lives. This movie, much like the show it is based on is terribly uneven. None of the stories are really that great but if I had to pick a favorite, I would go with the third one. There's a lot of great talent here, but they're not put to good use. The direction is ok, but there's just not enough good content to keep the movie constantly interesting. The FX however, are pretty damn cool and definitely the highlight of the movie. None of the stories are bad per se, but they're not that great, making for a completely average anthology.

2.5/5

Tales from the Hood
Year – 1995
Director – Rusty Cundieff
Tags – Anthology, Ghosts, Monsters, Slasher / Survival, Suspense

This anthology has four segments and a wraparound story. The wraparound is about a bunch of gangbangers who visit a funeral home and listen to the caretaker tell stories of the dead. The first story is about a group of cops who kill an important political figure and receive the wrath of his ghost. The second is about a little boy who says he is abused by a monster. The third is about a politician who lives in a house where many slaves died, and now they have come back to rise against him. And the final story is about a convicted killer who receives some very drastic therapy. This is a fun anthology, my favorite story being the second, which is probably my favorite because it was the only story not to have overt racism in it. Seriously, every white person in this movie was a racist, but this was produced by Spike Lee, so I guess that's to be expected, but it was still way overdone. The acting was pretty bad for the most part, but the direction was good throughout. The FX were also really well done, especially in the end of the second story. The script is good, each story has its strong points but I really only consider the second one to be excellent, the rest just range from decent to good. But this is a nice anthology overall.

3/5

Tales of Terror
Year – 1962
Director – Roger Corman
Tags – Anthology, Suspense

This anthology based on the works of Poe is comprised of three stories. The first is about a man who blames his daughter for the death of his wife. The second is about a drunkard who neglects his wife and pays her no attention, until she seeks the affections of another man. And the last is about a sickly man who wishes to die and receives more than he bargained for. I just couldn't get into this movie. I did really appreciate Vincent Price's varied and well done performances in each story, but the stories themselves were hardly some of my favorites and just not that interesting when put to the screen. They came off slow and somewhat dull. But the sets, costumes and acting were all very much noteworthy, I just wish I was as pleased with the story picks and their execution.

2.5/5

Tamara
Year – 2005
Director – Jeremy Haft
Tags – Witchcraft

Tamara Riley is the girl in school that nobody really likes because she reads about witchcraft and rubs people the wrong way. But then a prank on her goes bad and she accidently dies, and the people involved cover it up. What they didn't expect was for her to come back from the grave and exact her revenge. The plot has been done before, and it has been done better, but it does have some interesting aspects to it, too bad there are so few that it ends up being slow as hell. The story is a half assed attempt at revenge horror and it just doesn't seem to have much thought put into it. The acting isn't very good either but it's not terrible. It does have some nice gruesome and twisted moments but that really is the only saving grace because everything is just so mundane.

2/5

Tattooist, The
Year – 2007
Director – Peter Burger
Tags – Ghosts

A young American tattoo artist sets up shop in New Zealand and unwittingly plays a part in the plans of a deadly spirit as everyone he tattoos suddenly dies, covered in ink. I have to give points to the filmmakers for trying something different, but it's just not an interesting enough subject. The actors involved aren't bottom barrel but they can't expect any lengthy careers in the movie business anytime soon. The story and direction are fairly dull but there is a slight upswing as the movie approaches its conclusion in terms of pacing. The death scenes are essentially the same and cool to see once but not beyond that. This is a somewhat interesting but ultimately forgettable horror movie that may be worth watching once but I wouldn't go out of your way to see it.

2/5

Tears of Kali
Year – 2004
Director – Andreas Marschall
Tags – Anthology

This movie features three stories with no real wraparound. The shorts that bookend the film are tied to all of the stories but are so short that saying anything about them would give it all away. The first story is about a woman set to be released from a mental home. The second is about a criminal who receives a new form of therapy. The third is about a bogus faith healer. To really give an in-depth synopsis of each section would give too much away because each relies on a very strange twist to make each story work. Each chapter starts out pretty slow but then quickly moves into some creepy and ultimately gory territory. Each section is capped off by some pretty graphic violence, which I really enjoyed. I just wish that each story could have been paced well throughout its runtime. The stories themselves are very good but I was left wanting a little more from the last one. Still, this is a very good anthology with lots of graphic visuals for all the gorehounds out there.

3.5/5

Ted Bundy

Year – 2002
Director – Matthew Bright
Tags – Serial Killer

This movie follows the exploits of true life serial killer Ted Bundy who killed an estimated 35 women between '74 and '78. He was known to have bludgeoned and strangled the women and also committed acts of rape and necrophilia. The guy who played Ted Bundy did such a wonderfully twisted job with the role that I knew he would be forever typecast in future roles. Seriously, he was excellent. The rest of the cast is a mix of good and bad. The way the story was told was very good, highlighting many of his misdeeds, but never really showing that much in detail. The direction was also very good, as the movie was paced well. This is a very good serial killer movie that lacks some really graphic content but is still a good display of one of the most notorious murderers in US history.

3.5/5

Teen Wolf

Year – 1985
Director – Rod Daniel
Tags – Werewolves

A teenage boy discovers he is a werewolf and uses his new found powers to lead his high school basketball team to victory. This is a very lighthearted werewolf movie that I've enjoyed since I was a kid. It has some genuinely funny moments and your typical life lesson in the end. The acting and direction are good, and the FX aren't bad either. The story, although similar to other non-horror teen movies of the era, still has quite a bit of charm to it. Maybe it's just because the lead character is a werewolf and I enjoyed it more because of that, but I just like this movie. Good fun and good nostalgia for those who grew up on movies like this.

3/5

Teen Wolf Too

Year – 1987
Director – Christopher Leitch
Tags – Werewolves

In this sequel we find the cousin of the original film's star afflicted with the same werewolf curse. Now I've seen a lot of sequels steal elements of the original for their own use, but I don't think I've ever seen someone steal the entire movie before. That's what happens here. The entire plot, everything that happens to the boy all the way to the ending, happens here. All they did here was tweak a few small things. Instead of high school it's college, and instead of basketball it's boxing and so on and so forth.

Ridiculous. This movie is a perfect example of a studio trying to cash in by forcing a sequel and not having any reason to do so. Avoid this movie completely, because if you've seen the original, you've seen this one, but you've just seen it done better.

1/5

Teeth
Year – 2007
Director – Mitchell Lichtenstein
Tags – Suspense

An abstinent young girl finds out she suffers from vagina dentata (her vagina has teeth) after she is raped by a young man in her abstinence club. While I absolutely love the concept, I figured this movie would be a one trick pony with not much substance to it. But in the end the movie turned out to be a completely hilarious and cringe-inducing flick that kept me glued to my seat until the end credits rolled. I think the writers and filmmakers did a wonderful job of turning this movie into much more than your typical rape revenge story, this is actually a multi-faceted coming of age story with a very dark sense of humor and a horror twist. The direction was really good and the acting was also good, especially for such a low budget flick. The FX work had me grabbing my crotch in response to certain scenes of amputation and was just very well done. And I'm also very glad to see them showing everything and not averting the camera. And this is the last place I expected to find such wonderful humor as well given the seriousness of the plot, but I laughed out loud on multiple occasions. This movie is far more than the one trick pony I expected, and I absolutely loved it.

4.5/5

Tenant, The (Le Locataire)
Year – 1976
Director – Roman Polanski
Tags – Suspense

A man moves into a new apartment where the previous tenant had attempted suicide. Soon he becomes obsessed with her and why she did it, all the while becoming exceedingly paranoid about the people he lives around and the new people who enter his life. This is a tale of madness, paranoia, and overall, incredible boredom. The movie is much too log and the direction is pretty shoddy. Things do pick up some time into the second half of the movie, where the story becomes much more interesting and things start to become pretty crazy, although it is inevitable that most people will figure out the ending about five minutes into the movie. The acting is great though, and the story does have its moments, but it was an overall disappointing thriller.

2.5/5

Terror Train

Ycar – 1980
Director – Roger Spottiswoode
Tags – Slasher / Survival

After a cruel prank performed years earlier, a group of college kids throw a party on a moving train. Now they are targeted by a masked killer and have nowhere to escape. I love the location of this movie because there is nowhere to run to, and you're pretty much stuck. And that's the highlight of this movie for me. The rest of the movie features off camera kills, very little blood and your typical slasher movie characters. Although David Copperfield plays the magician and that's pretty cool. The pacing is pretty good and there are a couple tense moments, but other than that this is just run of mill slasher flick. A good time.

3/5

Texas Chainsaw Massacre, The
Year – 1974
Director – Tobe Hooper
Tags – Slasher / Survival

Five youths, one of whom is wheelchair bound, encounter a masked madman and his twisted family after their van runs out of gas. The Texas Chainsaw Massacre is a classic for many reasons. First off, it is incredibly brutal and gruesome, but not very gory, which is quite a feat. The original story (inspired by serial killer Ed Gein) is well written and in turn, well directed. The harsh soundtrack increases the tension and the overwhelming madness that pervades the characters. The end of the movie is probably one of the most unique ever, suspense was kept in the air until the final frame of film, and after it ended, you could barely get your breath back. This movie is quite bizarre and that only helps it increase its legendary status, and meshes well with the gritty and dark feel of the movie. This is mandatory viewing for horror fans.

5/5

Texas Chainsaw Massacre 2, The
Year – 1986
Director – Tobe Hooper
Tags – Slasher / Survival

Fourteen years after the events of the first movie, the Sawyer family has still not been caught. But a man knows the truth and has hunted the family for years. With the help of a local DJ, he may just find the family and put an end to the killing. Long after the release of the first movie we get the first sequel, which is usually a sign that the movie will not be very good, but with Tobe Hooper back at the helm, we are treated to another worthwhile and bizarre experience. Undoubtedly this movie is less effective than its predecessor, but I'm not going to sit here and compare it, I'll judge the movie on its own merits, for which there are many. Bill Moseley is incredible in this movie and his creepy character is certainly one of a kind. The rest of the cast also does an admiral job, but his performance stands out. Also, there are some truly hilarious scenes like Dennis Hopper in the chainsaw store. The gore is amped up a bit from the last movie, and the set design is larger and more detailed. This is a great follow up to a classic movie and really I couldn't have asked for much more.

4/5

*The Texas Chainsaw Massacre 3 can be found under Leatherface: The Texas Chainsaw Massacre 3.

Texas Chainsaw Massacre 4: The Next Generation, The
Year – 1994
Director – Kim Henkel
Tags – Slasher / Survival

The fourth movie in The Texas Chainsaw Massacre franchise moves even further out of the range of continuity as the third one did, and on top of that, it's not even close to being as entertaining. The new family is just terrible, they don't make any sense and they're just boring. The acting is also pretty bad, which just makes things worse. The way the plot unfolds is beyond stupid, like they were trying to be as bizarre as the first, but the way it played out completely ruined everything. The direction isn't very good, the pacing could have definitely used a lot of work and there weren't even any good kills. The original compelled me to watch it, and this one compels me to turn it off. Terrible.

1.5/5

Texas Chainsaw Massacre, The [Remake]
Year – 2003
Director – Marcus Nispel
Tags – Slasher / Survival

This movie follows the original at its core with a few changes along the way. Remaking a classic is always tricky business, but I'm happy to say that the people behind this movie have made a very competent remake. The story stays essentially the same, the way it plays it however, is slightly different. The family is larger, there's no wheelchair bound victim, etc. The gore is definitely ramped up from the original, which is nice to see. The bizarre factor that made the original stand out so well is unfortunately absent here, but that is to be expected since this is a much more commercial release. The acting is great, and whoever decided to cast R. Lee Ermey deserves a lot of praise, he was perfect in his role. All told this is a very fine movie and I was more than pleased with the end product. Recommended to fans of the original.

4/5

Texas Chainsaw Massacre: The Beginning, The

Year – 2006
Director – Jonathan Liebesman
Tags – Slasher / Survival

Here we explore the origins of Leatherface and his family. Of course this movie was made pretty much for a quick buck, but it's still good. The brutal nature of this movie really lends to its entertainment value, including the graphic birth of Leatherface, so it's nice to see that filmmakers understand what was needed. In a lot of ways though, this is just more of the same, another rehash of the remake, as the two are very similar in tone and content. But the bloody kills are there, and that's what really counts, so despite the fact that this and the 2003 remake are way too similar, there is still a great deal of enjoyment here, you just have to turn your brain off to really enjoy it.

3.5/5

Them (Ils)
Year – 2006
Director – David Moreau, Xavier Palud
Tags – Suspense

A couple find themselves being stalked by a group of hooded assailants in and around their isolated country home. The fact that this is based on a true story, and who the assailants are, makes for one hell of a premise, fortunately it's also pulled off very well with only a few hiccups along the way. The 77 minute run time allows for a very brisk moviegoing experience, which is nice. It takes a short while to get to the meat of the story, but that's really the only time the movie is slow. After things start happening they never let up and there is a constant feeling of tension. The acting is very good as well, which lends to the overall suspense of the movie. It ended very strong and then gave further facts about the crimes that were committed and the ultimate outcome, which was a nice addition and just reminded you that what you were watching actually did happen. A very good movie.

3.5/5

They
Year – 2002
Director – Robert Harmon
Tags – Monsters

A group of people who suffered from night terrors as kids believe that they are being stalked by creatures that scared them as children, and now wish to devour them as adults. Well, it definitely sounds like an interesting movie, too bad it's actually a terrible piece of crap. The story just plain sucks and is as uneventful as it is uninteresting. When you do get to see the monsters, they are made of some very horribly rendered CGI that is not only poorly crafted, but poorly designed. The acting is ok but the direction is slow and boring. The movie does end strong, I'll give it that much, but that's hardly enough to make up for the hour and a half I just wasted watching this garbage.

1.5/5

They Live
Year – 1988
Director – John Carpenter
Tags – Aliens

A drifter looking for work stumbles upon an organization that knows a very big secret. Once the man puts on a special pair of sunglasses, he can see the aliens among humankind, and their subliminal messages meant to lull us into submission. Once again, Carpenter makes another unique and highly entertaining movie. The aliens look awesome, completely different from the norm. This movie also has the best fight scene ever filmed and involves Roddy Piper and Keith David. Seriously, watch it and tell me that's not awesome. Piper also has some really great, off the wall lines that he delivers perfectly. The acting is excellent, the story is superb, and the production as a whole is just about as good as it gets. This a funny, action packed, gun toting good time from a master filmmaker, and by far one of the most original and entertaining concepts for an alien movie ever created.

4.5/5

Thing, The
Year – 1982
Director – John Carpenter
Tags – Aliens

The Thing is based on the movie The Thing from Another World, and while it follows the general outline of the original, this version takes the story into different directions. This is one of my favorite movies of all time, it's flawless. The story is great, and while I enjoyed the original, this version improves upon it exponentially, which is an accomplishment by itself. Carpenter is at his best here and the direction is some of the tightest I have ever seen from him. The all male cast is well chosen as they perform their parts incredibly well and really give each character a unique personality. The FX work is mind boggling. The creatures that were created were nothing short of amazing and even seem to have a Lovecraftian feel, making them even creepier. The kills are exceptional, the blood and gore are stellar, and the set definitely feels cold and isolated. The feeling of total paranoia is unequalled, and the tension that permeates the film is really well done. This movie is as atmospheric as it is violent, which is another rare sight. I think this is the best sci-fi themed horror movies ever made (from what I've seen so far), topping even the incredible Alien. This movie is a masterpiece.

5/5

Thing from Another World, The
Year – 1951
Director – Christian Nyby
Tags – Aliens

A military squad, a journalist, and a group of scientists find an alien spacecraft under the ice in the North Pole. They also find an alien itself, ejected from the craft and now frozen in the ice. They take it back to their camp and it comes back to life, stalking and killing everyone it comes across. I had seen The Thing before this movie and having loved that one so much, I was very curious about the original. Now I see why Carpenter wanted to remake it, as it's a pretty damn good movie but it also strayed pretty far from the brilliant source material. The acting is great as was the direction. The alien itself looked wonderful, definitely something you would fear coming across in the isolated snowfields of the North Pole. The story is the highlight though, as it skillfully inserts scientists into the movie who can figure out just what the alien is and how to defeat it, it never felt convenient, which is a problem many similar movies of the era had suffered from. This is just a great alien movie made in the golden age of extraterrestrial cinema and if you're a fan of the sub genre, it's definitely worth your time.

4/5

Thinner
Year – 1996
Director – Tom Holland
Tags – Witchcraft

After an obese lawyer runs down a gypsy woman and gets away with it even though he was driving drunk, the woman's father puts a curse on him, causing him to lose weight at an uncontrollable rate. Yeah I know its gypsy magic and not witchcraft but I use that word to cover all of the black arts because it sounds cooler than saying black magic. Anyway, this movie, based on one of Stephen King's older books (When he wrote as Richard Bachman), is a very faithful adaptation of an ok story. The direction is good, keeping things interesting most of the time and it is supported by some good acting. There is some bad acting as well, but fortunately not from the characters with the most screen time. The FX are where the movie really stand out though, the transformation of the main character is really pretty amazing. In all this is a good movie of a less than stellar story and I wasn't disappointed by it.

3/5

To Let (Para Entrar a Vivar)
Year – 2006
Director – Jaume Balaguero
Tags – Slasher / Survival

This is part of the DVD box set "6 Films to Keep You Awake". A young couple with a baby on the way looking for a new place to live takes a tour of an apartment and notice that some of their own belongings already there. Then they realize that this is far from being a standard apartment showing. This is a very well done survival horror movie I must say, and if it wasn't for the sometimes terrible camera work, I could have easily loved this movie. The acting is great and the direction is very good with few pacing issues. There are also some excellent gore sequences and plenty of blood. The story is also great and not just your typical horror situation, this movie has more depth than most. Overall a very nice time, I just hate the use of shaky cam.

3.5/5

Tomie
Year – 1999
Director – Ataru Oikawa
Tags – Ghosts

A woman trying to uncover some lost memories through a psychiatrist ends up bringing forth the mystery of a girl named Tomie, the girl who will not die. What the hell did I just watch? This is a fairly nonsensical movie that's hurt even further by the very slow pacing. The story doesn't come together well at all and by the end I'm left with a lot of questions. This isn't a clever movie, nor is it a very entertaining one, but I will admit that during the second half things become more interesting and there were some creepy and bloody moments. But getting there is way too much of a chore. I feel I am being rather kind with my rating but it did have some moments I really dug, and I just hope that the rest of the series is a bit more cohesive.

2.5/5

Tomie 2: Another Face
Year – 1999
Director – Toshiro Inomata
Tags – Anthology, Ghosts

For some reason this second movie is split up like an anthology and simply features Tomie in three various tales about love and ultimately, death. Wow, there must have been no budget for the sequel because this one just feels cheap. The stories are also very light on interesting content and while having different protagonists eventually all feel the same. The movie is pretty boring and lacks much of the charm the original had, but it is watchable which is more than many other movies can claim. There are much better choices in the realm of Asian horror but I guess you could do worse.

2/5

Tomie 3: Replay
Year – 2000

Director – Tomijiro Mitsuishi
Tags – Ghosts

This movie doesn't seem to have a direct link to the original or the first sequel, so suffice to say, Tomie, the girl who will not die, is back. And the way she comes back is brilliant. The opening sequence is awesome and very memorable. Once again this movie has some great moments but is overall somewhat unsatisfying. It is better than the original mainly due to some awesome FX work and some extra creepy and bloody moments, as for everything else, pretty much the same. This movie is paced a little better though. Well, it's nice to see that this movie is better than the awkward original, but it isn't much of an improvement. Good, but still flawed.

3/5

Tomie 4: Rebirth

Year – 2001
Director – Takashi Shimizu
Tags – Ghosts

More Tomie, no continuity. I actually had some hope for this one since I like some of Shimizu's other films, and while this one is a bit better than the original Tomie, I still can't say I really liked it. It had some creepy, weird and bloody moments but in essence that's all it had and they were too few and far between to make the movie wholly interesting. The movie is ultimately pretty slow and the story is just a rehash of all the previous movies, just with different characters. This is a bizarre series because every movie plays out the same with some small tweaks here and there, and they all end in a similar manner, which is bizarre. Anyway, another average entry, nothing special here but may be worth a watch for a couple of cool scenes.

2.5/5

Tomie 5: Forbidden Fruit

Year – 2002
Director – Shun Nakahara
Tags – Ghosts

This fifth entry in the Tomie franchise is the first to really be noticeably different than the rest. Here a young girl gets involved with Tomie, who happened to the dead lover of her father many years ago and now has returned to be with him. I really liked the story here and this makes for the best of the series by far. This entry features some wonderfully bizarre moments that really work well and just need to be seen to get the full effect. The direction is also the best here as the movie moves along very well and doesn't slow down often. The series as a whole was pretty unremarkable but at least it wasn't too bad. This was meant to be the final chapter, but of course it wouldn't be. A very good movie and the best of the bunch so far.

3.5/5

Tommyknockers, The
Year – 1993
Director – Jim Power
Tags – Aliens

In a small town, a UFO that is buried under the ground begins affecting people, forcing them to build gadgets and unearth the craft. Now one man must put a stop to it or the entire town may be lost. The story is interesting but I never really liked it, it's a bit too slow and laborious for me. Same thing with this movie, the build up to the payoff is much too slow and when the pay off finally comes it just doesn't feel worth it. The acting is really great from a very diverse cast and I like the practical FX. Once again we have another Stephen King made for TV adaptation that should have just been a feature instead of a drawn out miniseries, which would have undoubtedly made it run smoother. I know I sound like I'm bashing this movie, but I don't hate it, I just didn't like it. The Tommyknockers has its strong points, there's just too few of them to really make me recommend this movie.

2.5/5

Tooth & Nail
Year – 2007
Director – Mark Young
Tags – Cannibals

This movie is set in a post apocalyptic world where the end did not come by any other means than we just simply ran out of gasoline. Here we follow one group of survivors as they hole up in an abandoned hospital and just try to live. Problem is that a group of men called "Rovers" have come ringing the dinner bell, and yep, they're cannibals. I was really looking forward to this movie in the '07 After Dark Horrorfest, and I have to admit, I was a little let down. I'm a sucker for post apocalyptic tales, but I just don't feel like the director did enough with this one. It's bloody, but it could have been bloodier, the Rovers are cool, but they could have been fleshed out more. The movie also lags in a few places and you just want something to happen. Even though I was a bit let down, I still like this movie. It's a good ride, just kind of a lazy production. Great visuals though.

3/5

Tower of Blood
Year – 2005
Director – Corbin Timbrook
Tags – Slasher / Survival

A group of friends decide to party on top of an abandoned building but little do they know that a crazed killer stalks the hallways. This movie blows. I can't say I was expecting much, but come on. I found it funny that the building supposedly had thirty floors when it was clearly only three or four stories tall. The acting was terrible and the direction was slow and uninteresting. The story is a complete throwaway with nothing at all to add to the genre, and not in the least bit entertaining. The soundtrack was highlighted in the movie but for what reason I am unsure because the music sucked. The kills were also pretty uninteresting but there was a beheading that made me laugh. Hardly any nudity either, with only a couple of misshapen boobs on display. And the killer was extremely boring. This is microbudget garbage and nothing more.

1/5

Trackman
Year – 2007
Director – Igor Shavlak
Tags – Slasher / Survival

Criminals and hostages make their escape into some underground tunnels that house a sadistic killer. I hope this movie isn't indicative of Russian horror, because I haven't been exposed to too much of it, and if this is the best they can do, it's pretty sad. This movie is so paint by numbers its ridiculous. You can pretty much guess who is going to die, when, and sometimes even how. The movie is slow and the kills are uninspired, dull and boring. And really, that's what will always make a break a slasher film, the story always comes second, it's the blood and guts that matter. This movie is a failure in almost every way it could be. I've seen worse, but not by much.

1/5

Trailer Park of Terror
Year – 2008
Director – Stephen Goldmann
Tags – Zombies

A group of troubled youths and their chaperon come across a trailer park that houses a group of redneck zombies. This movie had the potential to be awesome, but unfortunately fell flat on its face. Some of the zombies look incredibly lame as you can tell they are clearly wearing an appliance because their face will be bone but then you can see the skin around their eyes where the mask is applied. There are some cool FX shots and some of the make-up is ok, but there is a mix of really amateur looking stuff going on. The acting is passable I suppose, no one was really very good, but at least they weren't awful. The direction is another sticky point because the pacing was pretty bad. The story is interesting and I'm sure the comic book this movie is based off is good, but the script just isn't up to snuff. There are a lot of average things going on here that are mixed with some pretty bad parts and that makes this movie below average, which is a shame.

2/5

Transsiberian

Year – 2008
Director – Brad Anderson
Tags – Suspense

A couple boards the world famous Transsiberian railroad and meets another couple during their journey. And what happens to them next runs the gambit from deception to murder as a dire mystery unfolds before their very eyes. Much like a train itself, the movie is slow to get started, but once it hits its pace, it runs very smooth. This movie is very much like a work from Hitchcock, which is impressive to say the least. The direction is well done and features many beautiful shots. The acting is also very well done, but the true high point of the movie is the wonderfully tight woven story. You get a small inkling as to what is going on, but are never quite fully in the loop as to what is going to happen. Even when things do happen in the way you think they will, it still remains very satisfying. This is just a great movie and further solidifies Anderson's place as one of the great new suspense directors in the world of cinema.

4/5

Tremors

Year – 1990
Director – Ron Underwood
Tags – Monsters

Natives of an isolated desert town defend themselves against subterranean creatures the likes of which no one has ever seen. I love this movie, it's so much fun. The story is great and the monsters are really cool. This is definitely something new, and giant creatures that move underneath the ground are definitely a terrifying thought. The acting here is very good from a real hodge-podge cast. The monsters themselves are well conceived and well made, and I'm glad they opted for practical FX over CGI, as it looked really good. The movie also gets pretty funny at times, which works well. This is just good fun and a throwback to old monster movies (but with better FX). It's a modern day classic and should not be missed.

4.5/5

Tremors 2: Aftershocks

Year – 1996
Director – S.S. Wilson
Tags – Monsters

The creatures have returned, this time in Mexico, and now they're also evolving. The follow up to Tremors, while definitely not as good as the original, is still highly entertaining. Some familiar faces return for the sequel and the acting is good. The monsters still look great and their evolution is a nice addition to the storyline, avoiding the typical "Too similar story for the follow up movie" syndrome that plagues a lot of horror franchises. There's a lot more humor in this one including the standard comic relief character, which is ok, but it's been done better. All in all though, this is a very fun movie and a nice addition to the Tremors storyline.

3.5/5

Tremors 3: Back to Perfection
Year – 2001
Director – Brent Maddock
Tags – Monsters

The third movie is set back in Perfection Valley where the monsters magically reappear after being gone for eleven years. Yes, that's sarcasm in my synopsis. I think that if you can't think of a good reason to have another movie, maybe you just shouldn't have it. Still, this one isn't bad, it's just not good. The story is lame and the continued evolution of the monsters is just stupid. There are also some continuity errors which are just plain annoying. There are some familiar faces back from the first movie, but it doesn't matter too much. Here they also decided to use a lot of shots with CGI, which is just horrible looking. The direction is ok, the pacing is fine, but this installment just doesn't have anything interesting going for it.

2/5

Tremors 4: The Legend Begins
Year – 2004
Director – S.S. Wilson
Tags – Monsters

And now we get to a prequel since apparently no one could come up with even a stupid idea for a sequel. Although a prequel may be interesting, it certainly isn't here. There are more continuity errors here and I just find it hard to believe that if these creatures showed up in the old west that no one bothered to even write about them. The acting and direction are weak, the story is contrived and the FX seemed to get worse from the last movie, which is quite the feat. The series started out great but really went to hell quickly. End it already, besides, I'm sure the studio execs want to remake it already and all these sequels are just holing that up. Skip it.

1.5/5

Trilogy of Terror
Year – 1975
Director – Dan Curtis
Tags – Anthology, Suspense, Slasher / Survival

This anthology comprises of three segments with no wraparound story. Segment one is about a college student who blackmails the wrong teacher. Segment two is about a pair of sisters who hate one another. Segment three is about a woman who buys her boyfriend a Zuni fetish doll, and it comes to life and attacks her. This is some really good made for TV stuff here. Each segment runs smoothly and rarely lags. Karen Black stars in all three stories and really shows some range. I would say that probably the second story, while good, was probably my least favorite, but fortunately it is bookended by two very good stories, so it hardly matters. This is an entertaining watch for sure, hardly a masterpiece, but a good movie nonetheless.

3.5/5

Triloquist
Year – 2008
Director – Mark Jones
Tags – Slasher / Survival

This story follows a brother and sister who plan on traveling to Vegas to set up their ventriloquist act, murdering many people along the way with their animated dummy. I've got to be honest here, this movie kind of sucks. The story has many twisted elements to it, but almost everything is alluded to, and nothing is shown. There isn't much blood, off camera kills, all that crap that just annoys the hell out of me. The acting isn't that great either, but passable for the most part. The dummy looks cool but is under utilized and any FX work is pretty much non-existent. The movie also tries to be a dark comedy but doesn't have many funny moments. This is a below average offering that had some interesting ideas but never followed through with them.

2/5

Tripper, The
Year – 2006
Director – David Arquette
Tags – Slasher / Survival

A bunch of hippies congregate at a freedom music festival in the woods for some sex, drugs and rock and roll, only to be stalked by an axe wielding maniac dressed up like Ronald Reagan. This movie has a very fun concept behind it, which is perfect for a horror/comedy, and it ends up playing off very nicely. I believe this is the first time Arquette has directed, and he does an admirable job in his first outing, but there could have been a little bit of improvement. I still look forward to seeing more from him though because I think he'll only get better with time. The cast is a great mix of people that do a really good job. The story is good, but I think it could have used more laughs and more gore. Don't get me wrong, it's pretty funny and has some excellent kills and FX, but I was left wanting more. I think with a few improvements here and there this easily could have been one of the best slashers I've ever seen, but even as is it's pretty damn good and I enjoyed it quite a bit.

3.5/5

Trucks

Year – 1997
Director – Chris Thomson
Tags – Mechanical

This is a remake of Maximum Overdrive, and follows the same plot but has a different story. Why the hell anyone would remake Maximum Overdrive is beyond me, because you just can't get any better than the original. And to remake it so soon after the original also seems pointless. But hey, if it's anywhere near as good, I'm fine with it, but it's not. In fact it's pretty much god awful. The acting wasn't too bad, but the direction was painful. The changes in the story only complicated matters, which is stupid, because simplicity was the key element in the original. It does have some bloody moments, but the kills are fairly moronic. I can't decide which one was worse, the toy dump truck or the environmental suit filling up with air and killing. Yeah, it's the suit, because why would a phenomenon that gives machines a mind of their own give life to plastic and air? This movie is chock full of those dumb moments and I definitely don't recommend it to anyone.

1.5/5

Turistas

Year – 2006
Director – John Stockwell
Tags – Slasher / Survival

A group of backpackers are left marooned in the jungle after a bus accident, and despite the beautiful locale, they find only danger and death. Turistas is one a several similar movies pumped out after Hostel, but I had some faith in this one, too bad my faith was fairly short lived. The paint by numbers story is almost to be expected, as it goes hand in hand with the group of conventionally attractive people getting into trouble. The bonus here is some very graphic death scenes set in the backdrop of some very gorgeous locales. Add in a particularly good chase scene, and you have the good points of the movie, which unfortunately are not enough to have me rate this above average. Good for a clone, just don't expect much.

2.5/5

Twice Told Tales

Year – 1963
Director – Sidney Salkow
Tags – Anthology, Suspense, Ghosts

This anthology features three Nathaniel Hawthorne adaptations and no wraparound story. The first story is about two men who discover a fountain of youth, and when it brings back one of the men's dead wife, secrets of the past are revealed. The second is about a man who becomes infatuated with a woman he could never be with. And the third is about a cursed house and its new visitors. Hawthorne isn't exactly known for horror, but it's nice to see some of his more horrific tales put to the screen. I like this movie and it's always nice to see Vincent Price in multiple roles, but much this movie's counterpart, Tales of Terror, it's kind of dull. I do like the story selection here, all of which are pretty good but none completely satisfying. I did enjoy the end of the second story a great deal though. This is a very dry movie but not bad by any means.

3/5

Twilight Zone: The Movie
Year – 1983
Director – John Landis, Stephen Spielberg, Joe Dante, George Miller
Tags – Anthology, Suspense, Monsters

This movie based on the classic TV show is comprised of four stories and a wraparound. The wraparound story, well, I can't say much of anything because it would spoil it. The first is about a bigot who sees what its like to be on the other side. The second is about some senior citizens who want to relive their youth. The third is about a woman who discovers a boy with very special powers. And the fourth is about a man who swears he sees something on the wing of the plane he's riding. Some people may say the movie was unnecessary because the various segments were episodes of the TV series, but I say kiss my ass, this is a great movie. The first two segments are good, the third is great, but the fourth is the real winner. Throughout the entire movie, the acting is great, but John Lithgow not getting an Oscar nom for his work in the last segment is a travesty. I've never seen paranoia and utter madness performed so well. The collaborative direction is wonderful, the FX are great and this is just a well made horror anthology.

4/5

Two Thousand Maniacs!
Year – 1964
Director – Herschell Gordon Lewis
Tags – Slasher / Survival

Some people forced into a detour are sent to the small town of Paradise Valley, where they are invited to the town's centennial celebration. The problem is that instead of dealing with a friendly town of southern folk they're at the mercy of two thousand maniacs. I love the concept, too bad the movie sucks. I've seen many a slasher flick dealing with one killer, but 2000 of them is an overwhelming and brilliant idea. The acting is terrible and the direction is slow and plodding, making for a pretty boring movie. The FX are very cheap as well, looking way too fake. One thing I absolutely loved was the barrel roll, and once you see it, you'll know what I'm talking about, pretty damn cool. This movie definitely missed its mark, and that's unfortunate because there was a lot of potential here.

Ugly, The
Year – 1997
Director – Scott Reynolds
Tags – Serial Killer (Fictional)

A female psychologist visits a serial killer in a mental institution to try and understand why he killed so many people and to figure out how he picked his seemingly random victims. This is a damn good movie that only suffers from some relatively small issues. First off, I like the way it was shot between the present day, flashbacks, fantasy and reality. And while I liked that, at times it also hurt the movie because it was overused and made for some slight annoyances. The acting is really good and the direction is well done with some great shots and fairly solid pacing. The gore is interesting because all of the blood in the movie is black, as seen by this mentally disturbed person's eyes. The story is fascinating and jumps between being a very interesting look into the mind of a killer and being a very strong slasher movie. Overall a very appealing movie, The Ugly left me very pleased with its unique content and style.

3.5/5

Ultraviolet
Year – 2006
Director – Kurt Wimmer
Tags – Vampires

In the future there is a disease that turns humans into vampires, and a company is trying to eliminate the disease, by killing all of the vampires. Now it's up to one of the last vampires to steal their secret weapon and save her kind. I almost didn't put this movie in the book because even though it is about vampires, it's not really horror. But in the end I felt it should be to show another look at vampires because this is a very different story. And I like the story to some degree, it's just that's so poorly made that I couldn't really get into it. The movie is way too cartoonish for starters, extreme overuse of bad CGI and brain melting action sequences. And even with this flashy eye candy going on, the movie is exceedingly boring and poorly directed. Milla Jovovich is great in her role, but then again she's always good in these kinds of roles. Everyone else is decent. I liked the interesting angle placed on the vampires, and the story as a whole, but this is just not a good movie at all.

2/5

Unborn but Forgotten (Hayanbang)
Year – 2002
Director – Chang-Jae Lim
Tags – Ghosts

A cyber crimes cop and a reporter follow a series of deaths that seem to be tied to a website. The strange thing is that when the women die, they appear to have given birth. Okay, first off the translated title bothers me and it's supposed to be Unborn but Unforgotten, but I guess they screwed up on the DVD art and menu. Anyway, this movie is essentially just a rip-off of Ringu but here instead of dying seven days after watching a video, the people here die fifteen days after viewing a website. Even the main character in both movies is a reporter. That's pretty sad. There is an additional wrinkle to the story, which is interesting, but not enough for me to say that this still isn't a blatant rip-off. And to make matters worse the movie is incredibly slow. This movie is bad and really only for the hardcore fans of Asian cinema. Maybe you can look past the fact that this is a stolen idea, but I can't.

1.5/5

Unbreakable
Year – 2000
Director – M. Night Shyamalan
Tags – Suspense

A man becomes the sole survivor of a deadly train wreck and finds that there may be something extraordinary about him. This is a suspense movie with supernatural overtones, and I found it to be a perfect mix of both elements. The story is very original and well done, and I can always respect that. The acting is also pretty amazing. The direction is unique as the movie moves along great and has as much of an uplifting atmosphere as it has a dark and dreary one. This is a very human story even with the supernatural components, and that's where it shines. It manages to show the fragility of life in a light I don't think it has ever been shown. There is so much death in this movie but at the same time it manages to keep a tone of hope throughout it. This is a very unique movie that ends strong and stays with you long after you view it.

4.5/5

Undead
Year – 2003
Director – Michael Spierig, Peter Spierig
Tags – Zombies, Aliens

A small Australian village is bombarded with meteorites that cause the villagers to become ravenous zombies. But there is more at work here than just random occurrences. I love the way this movie is shot, it's very fun and stylish, and gives it the feel of being much older than it is. I could easily see this movie as being made back in the 80's as a double feature with Dead Alive or The Evil Dead. There are a couple points in the movie that lag, but they did not ruin my overall experience. What I did really like was over-the-top action and the subtle badass main character with his triple shotgun. The movie also has a thin line of humor running through it that feels just right, not overdone at all. The FX work is great in the practical sense, and while the CGI can get kind of shoddy, it actually works with the style of the movie. Overall a very inventive movie and just a good time, period.

4/5

Underworld

Year – 2003
Director – Len Wiseman
Tags – Vampires, Werewolves

This movie follows the war between vampires and werewolves to the present day where the werewolves are looking for a certain human, but the reason is unknown. In the rash of action/horror being pumped into theatres we have Underworld, which is a good, but not great addition to this budding sub genre. I have to get the werewolf transformations out of the way because they are just plain horrible. CGI all the way and they just look really bad. I also find it hard to believe that vampires out on the hunt would be covered in vinyl and leather, wearing giant Goth boots and a corset. I would imagine that there would be more appropriate attire for hunting werewolves. But that's just all a part of what this movie is: Flashy and no depth. And I'll review it as such, its good entertainment but nothing more. The direction and acting are fine, the CGI landscape work is nice but anything that moves, forget about it, it looks like crap. Underworld is good, dumb fun, and if that's all you're looking for in the video store on a Saturday night, you could do a lot worse.

3/5

Underworld: Evolution

Year – 2006
Director – Len Wiseman
Tags – Vampire, Werewolves

This movie takes place right after the events of the first movie. This movie is right in line with the original, but fortunately propels the story forward and doesn't just imitate it. I really liked the back story portion of the movie where it showed a pretty big battle between the Vamps and Lycans, but then it went back into the brainless, flashy style of the original. There's the same old crap CGI, bad transformations and whatnot, but this time there is more sex and violence, which would have been welcome, had they steered clear of CGI blood, which hardly ever looks good. But this is another entertaining movie just as good as the first and I like it just the same.

3/5

Unearthed

Year – 2007
Director – Matthew Leutwyler
Tags – Monsters

An ancient monster is unleashed against a small desert town and it's up to a disgraced sheriff and some random people to stop it. I'm always up for a good monster movie but this definitely isn't it. The story is trite and thrown together, offering up hardly anything interesting and conveniently explaining away everything. The acting isn't quite bottom barrel, but it's close. The direction is boring to say the least and the FX are pretty terrible. The monster itself is poorly designed and in the end, this movie just doesn't have much going for it. It may have just barely enough going for it to keep some people mildly entertained when nothing else is on, but if you're looking for a good monster movie, keep looking.

1.5/5

Unrest
Year – 2006
Director – Jason Todd Ipson
Tags – Ghosts

A young medical student suspects that the ghost of a cadaver housed in the morgue she works at is killing people who mishandle the body. This movie boasts that is was the first movie to use real dead bodies, not a good sign of quality here, as that is a pretty big gimmick. But fortunately it turned out to be a pretty good, if somewhat tame ghost story. There's really not much I can talk about here, it was just across the board average, acting, direction, blood, and atmosphere was all just decent. Nothing horrible, nothing spectacular. People will surely be disappointed if they go into this movie expecting great things, this is a time killer and nothing more. Enjoyable, at least for one viewing.

2.5/5

Untraceable
Year – 2008
Director – Gregory Hoblit
Tags – Serial Killer (Fictional)

The FBI engages in a deadly cat and mouse game with a serial killer who kidnaps his victims and then places them in front of the cameras on the World Wide Web. Everyone who logs on to the site brings the victim that much closer to death by various ways of torture which are activated by the viewer count. This is your typical run of the mill Hollywood thriller with little to no ingenuity to it. It's meant to be an entertainment piece and nothing more, and on that respect it is an accomplishment. But that doesn't excuse it from just being painfully average from the get-go and never trying to properly exercise the viewer's brain. The plot is nice, and it could have been an engaging tale of suspense, but the execution is so dumbed down that I tended to get bored with it. The acting is good, the torture sequences aren't bad but they are pretty tame for an R rating. There is no tension to speak of and the direction is poor, which puts Untraceable in league with all of the other average thrillers on the market today.

2.5/5

Urban Legend
Year – 1998
Director – Jamie Blanks
Tags – Slasher / Survival

Students at a college are subjected to a killer who kills his victims in a way consistent with urban legends. Another post-Scream clone, but with something a little different to add. The way the people are killed is interesting but at the same time it's pretty silly. The acting and direction are fine but it's a pretty underwhelming movie overall. It was nice to see a few genre vets in the movie, and it flows just fine, culminating with a decent twist. In a market flooded with teen slashers, there just isn't room for movies that don't put in much effort. Still, this isn't the worst one I've seen and it is somewhat entertaining so I guess it wouldn't be fair to call it bad.

3/5

Urban Legends 2: Final Cut
Year – 2000
Director – John Ottman
Tags – Slasher / Survival

This is only remotely related to the original. Here we have a group of film school students being stalked by a masked killer. See, it's totally different, before it was college students, and this is about another college. Lame. Anyway, the story here is not good at all and when you finally get to the reason why the killer is killing, it's pretty much the most pathetic reason for a slasher movie ever. The direction and acting are also pretty bad. The kills however… When the movie started and we got to see the first kill, it was awesome, an excellent, bloody, multi faceted kill. And then that was the end of good things for the movie. After that the kills were are very vanilla and boring. This movie sucks, plain and simple.

1.5/5

Urban Legends 3: Bloody Mary
Year – 2005
Director – Mary Lambert
Tags – Ghosts

This third movie in the series isn't even remotely related to the other two, thankfully. Here the ghost of woman murdered many years ago returns to wreak vengeance upon a new generation of kids attending the school where she was killed. I like that they took the franchise into a completely new direction because the old way was already well overdone and dumb after just two movies. This one isn't great by any means, but it definitely is a step above the last movie. The acting here isn't very good, or maybe I'm just annoyed by stupid high school kids. The direction is fairly good but there are some pacing issues. The story is nothing original but it's not too bad. It's the kills that make the movie stand out because even though there is some bad CGI usage, there are some bloody and inventive ways to die on display. I'll call this an average ghost flick, nothing more, nothing less.

2.5/5

Vacancy
Year – 2007
Director – Nimrod Antal
Tags – Suspense

A couple gets lost while attempting a shortcut and end up having car trouble to boot. They happen upon a hotel and decide to stay the night until the mechanic next door arrives in the morning. They soon discover that the hotel is part of a snuff film ring, and they're the next intended stars. I wasn't expecting much here, but the concept was cool, so I was intrigued by it. Luke Wilson and Kate Beckinsale really do a great job in conveying a couple whose marriage is on the rocks and the supporting cast does an equally great job throughout. The direction is well done and the movie is kept constantly moving forward from one scenario to the next, until the movie completely cops out in the end. Things were going along great but then the typical Hollywood ending ruined an otherwise fine film. Still enjoyed it for the most part though.

3.5/5

Vacancy 2: The First Cut
Year – 2009
Director – Eric Bross
Tags – Suspense

This is a prequel to the movie Vacancy and follows the first victims of the snuff film ring. The problem with a prequel like this is that you know how it's going to end so it better be interesting up until that point. The problem here is that not only is the movie boring as can be, but the ending really sucks. The story is as dull as it could be and the acting reflects this. The actors are either really bad in their roles or they appear to just be bored out of their skulls. The direction is also really bad and features some truly terrible pacing. There's a fair amount of blood, but the original didn't need that to be interesting and here it just doesn't fit. This is an awful movie, plain and simple.

1/5

Valentine
Year – 2001
Director – Jamie Blanks
Tags – Slasher / Survival

A group of young women are stalked by who they believe to be an old classmate who was ridiculed by them. I have one thing to say about this movie: Snore! The plot is derivative of many slasher flicks that came before it and this movie doesn't even attempt anything fun and original. It just plods along aimlessly with boring or off camera kills until it reaches the inevitably predictable ending and the credits roll. The direction is slow, the acting is bad and this is just one slasher that even the most hardcore fan shouldn't bother with. I've seen a lot of bad movies, and while this one definitely falls into that category, I can always say that I've seen worse. And that really does make me feel better about wasting an hour and a half of my life on this.

1.5/5

Vampire Hunters (The Era of Vampires)
Year – 2002
Director – Wellson Chin
Tags – Vampires

A group of monks hunting vampires come across the vampire king, and have more than a little trouble when attempting to dispose of him. I liked the lore behind the vampires of this movie because they actually start out as zombies and after eating the flesh of the living, they are transformed into vampires, and that's pretty cool. This martial arts infused horror flick is good, but really does come up short in both of the genres it is combining. The martial arts aspect is good but the choreography could have used more flair and a bit of tightening. The vampires are awesome looking and incredibly powerful, but the story that's going on in the midst of the fighting and bloodshed isn't the greatest. The pacing is also pretty slow. But in the end the fusion makes for a good movie with some great vampires.

3/5

Vampire Journals
Year – 1997
Director – Ted Nicolaou
Tags – Vampires

This is a spin-off prequel of the Subspecies franchise using some characters from Subspecies IV, even though this one seems to have been made before that movie. Anyway, no Radu, but some other interesting characters. As much as like the aforementioned franchise I just couldn't get into this one as much. It's very Anne Rice in a way but not as well constructed. The acting is pretty good and the direction is ok but it can get pretty slow at times. But much like Nicolaou did with his previous movies, he used great locales, these being even more grandiose at times than those used in the Subspecies movies. This is a comparable effort but not good enough to fully hold my interest.

2.5/5

Vampires
Year – 1998
Director – John Carpenter
Tags – Vampires

Vampires are real, and the Vatican financially backs various groups of vampire hunters to exterminate these unholy beasts from Earth. But during a routine clearing of a vampire nest, a team encounters what just might be the first vampire ever, and the most powerful. This is a pretty straightforward movie, especially for John Carpenter. There's a beginning, middle and an end. And that's it. That's not to say the movie isn't done well, as it is done very well, but it just feels a little mundane to me. James Woods is awesome as the master vampire slayer, and the direction is of course great. But everything else just feels too commercial and doesn't have a whole lot of appeal to me. It's a fun vampire movie with a fair amount of funny moments as well as a fair amount of bloody moments. It's entertaining, but fairly standard and doesn't do much for the sub genre.

3.5/5

Vampires: Los Muertos
Year – 2002
Director – Tommy Lee Wallace
Tags – Vampires

A new team of hunters set off to Mexico to hunt down a nest of vampires. A movie doesn't get much more average than this, I didn't love it, I didn't hate it, and I just felt it was ok. It's basically the same as the first movie, which I enjoyed, but just not done as well. You have the second string of actors, who really aren't likeable, they just have no personality and all feel very wooden. And I must say that Jon Bon Jovi is no James Woods, and while he wasn't bad, he couldn't pull the movie together like Woods did in the original. If you saw John Carpenter's Vampires, then you've already seen this movie, you've just seen it done better.

2.5/5

Vampires: Out for Blood
Year – 2004
Director – Richard Brandes
Tags – Vampires

A police detective with personal issues is bitten by a vampire, which in turn opens up the underground world of the undead to him. The story here is a complete throwaway, nothing worthwhile in the least. The acting isn't very good, despite having some worthwhile actors in it, but I'll blame the shallow character design first. The direction is god awful as well, but no excuses this time since the director also wrote this crap. The FX are fairly bad as well, so I guess there really isn't anything redeeming about this movie. Oh wait, there are tits, I'll give an extra point for some topless women. But that's pretty sad when that's the highlight of the movie.

1/5

Van Helsing
Year – 2004
Director – Stephen Sommers
Tags – Vampires, Werewolves, Monsters

Van Helsing, after a run in with Mr. Hyde, it dispatched to Transylvania to battle Dracula, who is using Dr. Frankenstein's research and a werewolf for some unknown purpose. Wow, as pathetic as this movie sounded, I didn't actually expect it to be so bad. There's very little good in this movie, so let me skip straight to the bad. First, the acting is laughable for the most part, as the guy playing Dracula gives probably the worst portrayal in the cinematic history of the character (barring some of the lesser known cinematic turds). Frankenstein's Monster is annoying, Kate Beckinsale's laughable accent is incredibly annoying and everyone else just seems bored in it. Kevin J. O'Connor is good though. The CGI isn't very good at all, and way too overused, practically the whole movie is computer generated. The story, while incredibly stupid from the onset, just tries to pack way too much into the movie and pretty much fails on every level. If you just want to watch something shiny, then I guess you could do worse, but when I go into a movie with low expectations, and they're still not met, that's pretty sad.

1.5/5

Van Helsing: The London Assignment
Year – 2004
Director – Sharon Bridgeman
Tags – Animation, Monsters

This animated short film is the prequel to the events leading up to the movie Van Helsing. It's no surprise to see that this is animated, seeing as how the movie itself is a lot like a cartoon. The funny thing is that this movie is better than its predecessor by leaps and bounds. Maybe the short runtime allowed it to feel smoother and better paced, but either way, it's a better watch. The animation is good and the story is good as well, even if we are forced to see Van Helsing swinging around London like Spiderman. There's some blood in this movie too, something that the full length movie was severely lacking, no doubt to increase its commercial appeal, but here in the straight to DVD world, you can make anything go. Fans of the original (if there are any), will probably enjoy this. And if you weren't a fan like me, you'll notice some similar crap going on between this movie and the other, but you'll probably find something to like in it. I know I did.

3/5

Vault of Horror

Year – 1973
Director – Roy Ward Baker
Tags – Anthology, Suspense

This anthology has five stories and a wraparound. The wraparound is about five men who find themselves trapped in the sub basement of a building and begin to tell each other their nightmares. The first story is about a man looking for his sister is a very curious town. The second is about an obsessively neat man who drives his new bride crazy. The third is about a magician that will do anything to possess a trick he has found in India. The fourth is about a man whose plot to bury himself alive for insurance goes wrong. And the last story is about an artist who has the power to make whatever happens to his paintings happen for real. This movie, much like Tales from the Crypt, jams many stories into a short run time, but it works better here and each story feels like it plays out to its full capacity. The first and last stories are the best but the ones in-between are still comparable. The acting is really good and the direction is great. Definitely one of my favorite anthologies.

4/5

Vengeance of the Zombies (La Rebelion de las Muertas)

Year – 1973
Director – Leon Klimovsky
Tags – Zombies

A man is murdering the young daughters of prominent families only to resurrect them with voodoo and make them his zombie slaves. This movie is so weird that I can't help but admire it. At the same time it just isn't a good movie. I don't know if it's too weird and senseless for its own good or if I was too distracted by the 70's porno music score, but this is hardly a lost classic of Spanish cinema. The story is somewhat interesting but its presentation is lackluster. The zombies are just pale women in sheer robes, so nothing special in the make-up department, but I do really like how when the zombies attacked, it was all shown in slow motion, it looked really cool. The FX weren't great either as the blood was way too bright. This isn't a good movie, this isn't a bad movie, and this ends up being just a weird little film from the 70's that amused me but didn't leave a particular mark on me.

2.5/5

Versus

Year – 2000
Director – Ryuhei Kitamura
Tags – Zombies

Two men escape from prison and travel into the forest to meet their pick up. When extenuating circumstances force one of the convicts to kill, they discover that they happen to be in the Forest of Resurrection, a mystical place that allows the dead to rise. While I do feel that this movie is way overhyped, it was a pleasant experience nonetheless. The movie is too long and comes off much too dull at times, but when the action sequences do hit, they hit like a ton a bricks. Loads of gore, bullets, slicing and dicing. The story is long winded but the back story portion of the movie is brilliant. The acting is great and I especially enjoyed some of the comedic performances. This is far from being a traditional zombie story, which is refreshing, and while this ambitious effort didn't work all the way for me, it was still very entertaining.

3.5/5

Vertigo
Year – 1958
Director – Alfred Hitchcock
Tags – Suspense

A detective who has a crippling fear of heights investigates an old friend's wife and begins to become dangerously obsessed with her, much to his own self destruction. I've always heard a lot of great things about Vertigo, but to be honest I was never all that impressed with it. Don't get me wrong, it's a great movie, but hardly a masterpiece. The performances are amazing but the first half of the movie was way too slow for my tastes. But once a certain plot twist occurs, the movie really picks up and the second half is nothing short of astounding with boundless suspense. The story is great, but it just takes too long to get to the meat of it. Vertigo is an outstanding film that could have been shorter to allow it to run smoother, and while I greatly enjoyed it, there's always this nagging feeling that I could have enjoyed it more.

4/5

Videodrome
Year – 1983
Director – David Cronenberg
Tags – Mechanical, Suspense

A man who runs a TV station devoted to sex and violence comes across a broadcast of torture and murder that not only begins to warp his mind, but his body as well. I wasn't really sure what to tag this as because it really does defy categorization, but since the TV is a big part of the movie, I just went with machines and also human horror. This movie is deliciously twisted with wonderful imagery and excellent FX, but I honestly could not get completely into it. The story is compelling and the direction is good, but there was just something about the way it unfolded that made me tune out at times. This is a very cerebral movie and thus will affect people differently, so it is kind of difficult to put roundabout words together in an effort to describe it. I'll just say that this movie is beautifully bizarre and unlike anything else that had come out before it, or even after it, and that's pretty impressive. While I couldn't fully get immersed by the movie I still greatly enjoyed it, but I know there are others out there who swear by it and the only way to find out where you would sit is by watching it yourself.

4/5

Village, The
Year – 2004
Director – M. Night Shyamalan
Tags – Monsters

Set in colonial America, The Village tells the tale of a group of settlers who built a small hamlet on the border of a forest. In that forest there are creatures that the villagers have struck an uneasy alliance with. After the indiscretion of a young man who invaded their territory, the creatures enter the village. This movie has a very dreary atmosphere that works incredibly well in the context of the story, and the woods themselves are very ominous. This movie is good, but there were some things I did not like about it. First off, the dialogue done in proper English feels forced when the actors recite, but other than that the acting is great. Second, the first big twist in the plotline left me disillusioned, but the end twist almost made up for it. The Village is a very well shot film, and I enjoyed it, I just wish it had continued on the path of creatures and darkness that it had started out as.

3.5/5

Village of the Damned
Year – 1960
Director – Wolf Rilla
Tags – Suspense

In the small English village of Midwich, everyone suddenly passes out without any reason. When they awaken, everything seems fine, until they realize down the road that many of the village's women are pregnant. Months later, on the same day, they all give birth to extraordinary children who grow up and advance their intelligence far above the levels of the peers, only to develop powers beyond the capabilities of mankind. This is a classic tale dealing with the taboo subject of killing children. When people around the village start to have "accidents", it begs the question of what to do, kill the children? Or let them continue on their path of domination? The acting and direction are great, all tied in with a wonderful story that carries one of the best endings I've ever seen. This is a very unique film that is remarkable in the fact that it is so old and yet it deals with such taboo subject matter. This is a must watch for fans of the genre.

4.5/5

*Village of the Damned 2 can be found under Children of the Damned.

Village of the Damned [Remake]

Year – 1995
Director – John Carpenter
Tags – Suspense

This movie, while not a shot for shot remake of the original by any means, follows the same story. Carpenter has done some truly awesome movies and wonderful remakes, so I was hopeful for this movie, but this is a definite miss. There's no real style to the movie and it just ends up following the original too closely for my tastes. Another thing is the runtime. The original worked so well because it was very short and ran so smooth, here the movie is much longer and features unnecessary sequences. The acting is very good though and the increased ability of the FX is definitely noticeable. This isn't a bad movie by any stretch of the word, but it's just not what it could have been. I still enjoyed it somewhat, but I don't love it.

3/5

Virgin Spring, The (Jungfrukallan)
Year – 1960
Director – Ingmar Bergman
Tags – Suspense

Set in medieval Sweden, this is the story of a young girl who while on her way to church is raped and murdered by some men who would later seek refuge at her father's house. When the men unwittingly try to sell the young girl's clothes back to her mother, her father is torn between vengeance and the Christian way of forgiveness. This movie is really impressive for the time period not only when it was written, but when it was eventually made into a film. The acting is great and the direction is well done, but please be forewarned that the pacing isn't exactly quick. But I liked the way it came off, it was slow, but that only built the tension in my mind. Don't expect anything graphic either, as it's very subdued, which also works for it. Had the rape and violence been extremely graphic, it would have only brought the movie down a level and made it less poignant. The movie isn't perfect but it's undeniably well made.

4/5

Virus
Year – 1999
Director – John Bruno
Tags – Mechanical

A salvage team comes across an abandoned Russian scientific ship in the ocean. Once they board it they discover that it is not abandoned, as there is an alien intelligence in the power system and it is making robots out of spare parts to deal with the new arrivals. This is an interesting movie that definitely has the possibility to be pretty cheesy given the nature of the story, but I found this movie to be a pretty good tale of horror personally. The acting is good, but even with some great actors beings present, they don't put on excellent performances and a couple even ham it up a bit. The story is good but you predict how it will progress much too easily. You can practically pick out who will die and when. The direction is ok but there are several lags in the pacing and the movie became a bit tedious at times. But then there's the FX, which were pretty damn cool. The robots looked great and there was a fair amount of blood as well. This is a good movie with heavy flaws but I still found enjoyment in it.

3/5

Viscera 2007
Year – 2007
Director – Multiple
Tags – Short Film Compilation

This DVD sold by The Chainsaw Mafia is a compilation of shorts gathered from the Viscera film festival, which is festival of horror featuring mainly women in the cast and crew roles. I think that's brilliant because women are not really a big part of the horror genre. Most people believe that women in horror serve one purpose, and that is for breast bearing, which is bullshit. I love women filmmakers because they almost always manage to bring something new to the table in a male dominated genre and women have created some of my favorite films to boot. And believing that women are able to bring something new to the genre is even further evidenced by this DVD. The shorts contained within are all uniquely done and from a perspective usually not seen in the genre, which automatically makes it a winner in my book because I favor originality so much. The shorts range from being average to phenomenal, my personal favorite being Wretched. And that's pretty cool, the worst short still isn't bad, which means we're dealing with a lot of talent in this film festival and hope to see everyone involved move onto big things. This compilation is a major achievement in the realm of horror and I hope to see more horror from women in the future.

4/5

Visions of Suffering
Year – 2006
Director – Andrey Iskanov
Tags – Vampires

A man becomes involved in a nightmarish world filled creatures called vampires. I know that's not much of a synopsis, but there isn't much of a plot here. And before someone says I didn't get it, let's be honest, there's nothing to get here. This movie is one giant tapestry of surreal nightmares, and I like it for that because the way it looks is really awesome. The movie reaches its downfall when an attempt at a story is entered into the equation. Had this just been a surreal nightmare of a film, I would have appreciated it more, especially since it contained such unique imagery and the vampires were not typical and pretty interesting to boot. Let me sum it up like this: A pretty pointless story mixed into some very artful direction of an overly long movie. A visual feast to say the least, but not fully satisfying in every sense.

3/5

Visiting Hours
Year – 1982
Director – Jean-Claude Lord
Tags – Slasher / Survival

A man tries to kill a reporter but only succeeds in wounding her greatly. Not being satisfied he continues to come after her, leaving a trail of death in his journey to end her life. The funny thing about this movie is that I really loved the killer and hated the victim. Michael Ironside is brilliant here and definitely one of the more memorable slashers in history. The rest of the acting is ok but nothing special as this is clearly Ironside's movie. Too bad the script isn't quite up to snuff, or the direction. They're not bad per se, but they did leave a lot to be desired. The kills could have also used a bit more flair since the killer had such personality. This is a good little 80's slasher flick that has its fair share of flaws but still comes out on the plus side.

3/5

Visitors
Year – 2003
Director – Richard Franklin
Tags – Suspense

A woman sailing solo across the world gets stuck near home without any wind for many days. During this time she begins hallucinating about people boarding her vessel. Is she losing her mind or is someone really out there with her? A single actor carrying a movie by his or her self is tough business that few have been able to do. And while Radha Mitchell is a great actor, she wasn't given much of a script to perform with. The story just isn't very interesting and everything suffers due to that fact. The direction is bumpy, the acting somewhat uneven. But I also didn't hate the movie and enjoyed it for what it is. It's an ambitious idea that just didn't pan out.

3/5

Voices (Du Saram-Yida)
Year – 2007
Director – Ki-Hwan Oh
Tags – Slasher / Survival

A family believe themselves to be cursed, as the women in their family have a habit of being killed by those close to them. After a young girl's aunt dies, the girl's friends and family members soon become overwhelmed with the need to kill her next. The story is pretty cool and really fills the viewer with a sense of dread as the lead character slowly begins to lose trust in everyone around her and no one can be sought for help. I only wish everything else about it was as good as the story. The acting is fine but the movie can really drag at times. There was also a good use of blood and a particularly violent kill scene, but I wished for more and didn't really get it. The movie does end strong with a very good third act but getting there was a chore at times. Still, this is a good movie overall, I just didn't love it.

3/5

Watcher, The
Year – 2000
Director – Joe Charbanic
Tags – Serial Killer (Fictional)

A burnt out detective who failed to catch a serial killer moves to Chicago but what he doesn't realize is that the killer followed him and is killing once again to get his attention. This is a pretty cool serial killer movie that may not be the most original or thought provoking movie out there but it sure does entertain, to some degree anyway. The acting is very good and the direction is passable. The story is good but doesn't really have anything great going for it because it really is a paint-by-numbers kind of plot. I still liked it though and while it just didn't resonate with me, but I definitely don't regret seeing it and found it to be a good movie.

3/5

Waxwork
Year – 1988
Director – Anthony Hickox
Tags – Vampires, Werewolves, Zombies, Mummies, Slasher / Survival, Monsters

In a small college town, a waxwork appears, but is not quite open for business, because they only have room for six, six souls that is. Each display in the waxwork is actually another world, controlled by the most sinister characters in history, and each display needs a soul. The displays are nearly full, and if each one acquires a soul, these evil beings will come back to life and destroy the world. Seriously, how awesome is that concept? Now the movie definitely has a massive cheese factor in the acting and the seemingly make-it-up-as-I-go-along plot, but that's just part of its fun. The set design, costume design and practical FX work are just amazing, and there's plenty of blood and great kills to satisfy most gorehounds. This movie really embodies the feel of 80's horror, and if you're a fan, you can really appreciate it. Of course things get a bit mixed up and you find yourself asking, "How is that possible, when it happened like this earlier?" more than once, it's undeniably entertaining, and even though is borrows heavily from other movies in its various display sequences, it manages to be an incredibly original movie. A gem of the decade without question.

4.5/5

Waxwork II: Lost in Time
Year – 1992
Director – Anthony Hickox
Tags – Monsters, Aliens, Ghosts, Zombies, Witchcraft, Vampires, Slasher / Survival

And here we have a very deserved and worthy sequel to the original Waxwork. This one has the survivors of #1 supposedly traveling through time, but really they're just traveling through classic movies. You'll notice Aliens, The Haunting, Frankenstein, Invasion of the Body Snatchers, Dawn of the Dead and more. But this movie does not rip them off, it's a complete homage. This movie is more about humor and silliness than the original, and it works, but there's also still plenty of gore. Once again the set designs and costumes are top notch, while the effects work is a mixed bag. There are some excellent practical FX mixed together with some horrendous old CGI. Notable supporting cast includes the late, great Buck Flower, the late great David Carradine, Bruce Campbell, and more. A bit more flawed than the first movie, but still incredibly fun.

3.5/5

Welcome to the Jungle
Year – 2007
Director – Jonathan Hensleigh
Tags – Cannibals

Two couples trek deep into the jungles of New Guinea searching for Michael Rockefeller (the heir to the Rockefeller fortune, who disappeared in 1961), when they find a cannibal tribe instead. Cannibal Holocaust set the bar for films of this type, and while I can appreciate the effort, the end result leaves much to be desired. This movie is shot in a similar style to the aforementioned movie, attempting the documentary look. The camera work on these kinds of movies must always be mentioned because it really can make or break it, and here, fortunately the camera movements are hardly jerky and fairly smooth. The story here just isn't very good. You don't even see your first cannibal until about an hour into the movie, and I could tell what the filmmakers were going for in having the two couples bicker endlessly, but they just didn't have the acting power behind the concept to pull it off. Another problem is that you never really get to see the violence happening, just some aftermath, making this actually a pretty tame movie for the most part. Welcome to the Jungle tried but didn't quite succeed its mission, it's not a bad movie, but it could have been a lot better.

2.5/5

What Lies Beneath
Year – 2000
Director – Robert Zemeckis
Tags – Ghosts

After her only daughter goes to college, a woman begins seeing a ghost around her house, and while everyone else thinks she's crazy, she sets out to discover who the woman is and how she died. This is what I consider geriatric horror. It's a little something for the older crowd out there that isn't too intense and made just right for them. The movie is hardly scary for a horror aficionado such as I am, but for a casual watcher it may be satisfactory. The story is good and has a nice climax to it, and the direction does reflect that, but at the same time the movie is long winded and could have much shorter. The acting is very good and the characters are more than just one dimensional cardboard cut-out figures, so that's nice. Overall I would say this is a good movie and if you prefer your horror tame then look not further, but if you're like me and you want the most intense experience possible, keep looking.

3/5

What's the Matter with Helen?
Year – 1971
Director – Curtis Harrington
Tags – Suspense

Two women move away together after their sons are convicted of murder and begin to receive threats against themselves. While one thrives in her new life, the other slowly descends into madness and paranoia. I really liked this movie because even though it's campy as hell, it has a really good story and some great acting. The direction leaves a bit to be desired though, as the movie is pretty poorly paced. But I did have to give the movie extra points for the great ending. This is a solid movie that really delves into some great areas of insanity but comes off much too dull in the in-between. The ending makes it all worth it though.

3.5/5

White Noise
Year – 2005
Director – Geoffrey Sax
Tags – Ghosts

After his wife dies, a man begins experiencing EVP, which is supposedly about the dead communicating with the living through electronic devices. The idea behind the movie is obviously a one trick pony and a pretty insubstantial one at that, and I'm sorry to say they just really didn't do anything with it. The story is about as vanilla as they come, with no scares and no suspense. They try to do the whole jump scare thing and are just incapable of using genuine scares, but you can see the jump scares coming from a mile away, so they couldn't even make those effective. The acting is really good though, and even though the direction is a struggle with the poor script, I can still sense an effort. This movie is nothing more than someone trying to cash in on whatever crap paranormal study groups are researching at the time, and it just isn't interesting. Hey, Elvis talks to me through my microwave and together we're writing a new hit record, let's make a movie out of that! I would like to see people try harder next time.

2/5

White Noise 2: The Light
Year – 2007
Director – Patrick Lussier
Tags – Ghosts

This movie involves different people from the first one. Here we follow a man who tries to kill himself after his wife and child are murdered and then afterward he is brought back from the dead and gains the ability to see people who are close to death. So this movie is only mildly related to the last one, which is good since the last movie wasn't very good. The acting here is very good and the direction is ok, not too slow. The FX are pretty awful though, especially when the main character is traveling toward the light after his suicide attempt. The story is decent enough to hold my attention but there isn't much in the way of ingenuity. This is a good ghost flick that surpasses the original easily, even though it's far from perfect.

3/5

White Zombie
Year – 1932
Director – Victor Halperin
Tags – Zombies

A man with the power to turn people into mindless zombie slaves steals a man's wife by turning her into a zombie so that he can use her for whatever he desires. This is an interesting movie with a nice premise, but I also feel that it is somewhat disjointed and it also feels hurried. The acting is typical for the times, overly dramatic and whatnot. The direction is good, but the movie does have some slow points. The set design is wonderful however, and the backgrounds looked very nice. The final showdown between the husband and the zombies is pretty cool though, just don't expect the flesh eating variety, this is way before Romero's time. I like this movie even if it does feel dated, and while it is by no means a lost masterpiccc, it's still a good watch.

3/5

Who Can Kill a Child? (Island of the Damned)
Year – 1976
Director – Narciso Ibanez Serrador
Tags – Slasher / Survival

A couple travel to an out of the way island off the coast of Spain to find some relaxation, instead they find nothing but dead adults as all of the children have turned into soulless killers. Whenever controversy surrounds a movie, I want to see it. Usually it's over some stupid bullshit that a bunch of crybabies can't handle, but every once in awhile it's due to some very disturbing content, and this movie has that. The subject of killing children if very taboo, and I always have to give points to filmmakers who have the balls to show it, because even though it's taboo, it happens. This film starts out displaying the results of war on the child population, both in words and actually showing the deaths of many real children, which is kind of shocking to the average viewer, but as I stated before, it happens, and you can't be afraid to show it. And that's an interesting catalyst to this movie, because here you'll see the children killing. The story is great, as is about everything else in this movie. It took a second viewing for this movie to really sink in before I could truly appreciate it, as it can be fairly slow, but after that second viewing the movie really stuck with me and made quite the impression. If you can't handle the death of children, just don't watch the movie, for the rest of us we will be treated to a very artistic and unflinching look at some very taboo subject matter.

4.5/5

Whoever Slew Auntie Roo?
Year – 1971
Director – Curtis Harrington
Tags – Suspense

A wealthy widow perpetually distraught over the death of her own child ends up kidnapping a young girl who looks similar to her deceased daughter. But her brother will do anything to get her back. What I really like about this movie is that we know the woman is emotionally unstable but the two kids involved in her mania are not saints and too quickly jump to conclusions, leaving the viewer wondering just who is to blame for the movie's climax. But to be honest, the movie isn't as engaging as I would have liked and times could be slow, but the well done acting and overall presentation won me over. Nothing great here but a solid addition to the suspense genre with this unusual take of Hansel and Gretyl.

3.5/5

Wicked Little Things
Year – 2006
Director – J.S. Cardone
Tags – Zombies

A family moves into a new home, but unbeknownst to them, nearby is the site where dozens of children were buried alive in a mining accident, and they're still there, but not quite human anymore. All I can say here is meh. Its ok, not your typical zombie movie by any means, and while it is nice to expand upon an oversaturated sub-genre, doing so here is actually more of hindrance than anything. They're not your conventional zombies and the new twist added to them actually only adds boredom, as this movie seems to drag on forever with nothing of significance occurring. The acting isn't that great, and the direction could have been better. The FX aren't bad though. It's not a terrible movie, just average at best.

2.5/5

Wilderness
Year – 2006
Director – Michael J. Bassett
Tags – Slasher / Survival, Animals

After a fellow inmate commits suicide, a group of young convicts are sent to a small island for some extreme rehabilitation. But once there they discover they are not alone and that a man and his pack of highly trained dogs begin hunting them down. I absolutely love this movie. Finally someone adds something of merit to the slasher sub genre. First off, the locale is perfect, such a beautiful island. The cast, a bunch of criminals, is a unique take. Usually you have innocent people in a slasher movie, and here you have a bunch of guys who are the dregs of society, which in a way makes you root for the killer. The cast is great and they really give life to their characters. Adding dogs is another interesting angle and very well done. The kills for the most part are extremely gory and well done, each having their own unique flair. The first third of the movie introduces you to the characters and sets the tone, while it does take a bit for the killing to start the initial stage of the movie is hardly dull and really is well performed. Once the killing does start though, the movie never really lets up from there, it is kept very tense and adds many pulse pounding moments. I can rave on and on about this movie, but why you don't just watch it already, you'll be glad you did.

4.5/5

Wishmaster
Year – 1997
Director – Robert Kurtzman
Tags – Demons

A magical being called a Djinn was imprisoned inside a fire opal back in twelfth century Persia. Now it has been unleashed into the modern world, granting wishes for people for the small price of their soul, all the while attempting to unlock the gate that bars its kind from Earth. This is a very fun movie with a great deal of innovation to it. It also doesn't hurt that the movie is bookended by some incredibly gory and unique FX sequences with huge body counts. The acting is very good, especially since there are a multitude of genre vets making appearances, and I mean a multitude. Buck Flower, Tony Todd, Reggie Bannister, Kane Hodder, Ted Raimi, Robert Englund and more. And these people know how to act in a horror movie. Andrew Divoff is brilliant as the Djinn and really gives the creature a ton of personality. I do wish they had a better female lead though, as there just really wasn't anything special about her. The direction was smooth and well done, and of course, the FX work was top notch. This is a bloody good show and a great addition to the genre.

Wishmaster 2: Evil Never Dies

Year – 1999
Director – Jack Sholder
Tags – Demons

This movie takes place a few years after the original. I have mixed feelings about this movie because it is a bit too similar to the original, but at the same time it tries to go about similar circumstances differently so I can appreciate that. The Djinn goes to prison for part of the movie, which is a pretty great idea since there is a lot of wishing going on there. The acting isn't that great this time around, but at least Divoff reprises his role and puts on a good show. The direction is decent, not bad, but could have been better. The FX are pretty good but they were much better in the original. This is a comparable follow up to a great movie, and while it lacked in a few areas, it was still a good time.

3/5

Wishmaster 3: Beyond the Gates of Hell

Year – 2001
Director – Chris Angel
Tags – Demons

This movie takes place sometime after the last one I guess, it doesn't seem to be related to the other two except by name. But it plays out the same. Only lamer! Wow, this movie was painful. It just kept getting worse. Just when I thought it couldn't get any more horrible, it did. The acting was bad, the new Djinn was lame, the direction was practically coma inducing, the FX were weak and the story was just a rip off of the previous two with some added garbage for good measure. This is a bona fide worthless movie, silly me for thinking that a franchise could be good for its entire run.

0.5/5

Wishmaster 4: The Prophecy Fulfilled

Year – 2002
Director – Chris Angel
Tags – Demons

This one, much like the last one, just follows similar events to a similar climax. After the last one I knew this one had to be better, but it just wasn't, this one is just as terrible and for the same reasons, everything about it is crap. So instead of droning on about how awful it was, just re-read the review for the third movie, it works here as well. Instead, I'll give an idea that just came off the top of my head, and what this movie should have been. How about we start the movie with someone making the third wish and unleashing the Djinn legions from their confines? Now we have hordes of demons killing people in gory fashion and collecting their souls, and now it's up to some survivors to find a way to send all of the Djinn back. That's not a bad idea, certainly better than the last two movies, and different to boot. Skip these last two abominations and do what I did, come up with your own movie in your head, you'll enjoy it more.

0.5/5

Witches of Eastwick, The
Year – 1987
Director – George Miller
Tags – Witchcraft

Three women use witchcraft to get the man of their dreams, and when a very flamboyant man enters their lives, they get much more than they ever expected. You have to love this movie for the great acting alone, Nicholson in particular puts on a very eccentric performance that I was very pleased with. There are also some great FX that are worth mentioning as well, especially during the final third of the movie. The direction is good but there are a few occasions when the movie drags. The story is an interesting one but feels a bit light on integral character development as well as a few other areas. Still, for the most part the story is very good and accompanied by great acting so while I don't love the movie, there's still a lot here to like.

3.5/5

Within the Woods
Year – 2005
Director – Brad Sykes
Tags – Slasher / Survival

In this third Camp Blood movie, we find the story taking place a few years after the last one. The budget is obviously much higher in this movie, but that actually works out to its detriment. Maybe Sykes can only pull off a decent movie with a nonexistent budget because here everything is nowhere near as good as the previous movies. The storyline went from pointless, to ludicrous, and now it's just downright atrocious. The acting is also somehow worse, and that's quite the feat given the acting in the previous movies. While Sykes showed improvement in his direction with the second movie, it is unfortunately all but gone here. This movie is just painful to watch. The FX are also garbage, and there's hardly any blood. This is just plain terrible.

1/5

Wizard of Gore, The
Year – 1970
Director – Herschell Gordon Lewis
Tags – Slasher / Survival

A journalist follows the exploits of a magician who brutally kills women on stage, only to have them up and walking by the end of the show. Then later on those women that were part of the act end up dead by the same means they were killed on stage. I like the concept of this movie, and it's interesting as to how it plays out, but this really is pretty crappy. The acting is bad even for a low budget movie, and the editing is bizarre, and not in a good way. The direction is as awful as ever but I actually liked the gore in this one quite a bit. It was a little more realistic than previous Gordon efforts and just looked better in general. The story is good, the blood certainly flows, but everything else is pretty much garbage, making for one very average and watchable movie, but really nothing more.

2.5/5

Wizard of Gore, The [Remake]
Year – 2007
Director – Jeremy Kasten
Tags – Slasher / Survival

The remake follows the original plot and story. I'm not a big fan of the original, but the idea is a pretty great one and would undoubtedly benefit from being remade, so how is it that the remake is actually worse than the original? Let's explore that. The direction is mind numbingly bad, this movie was pretty painful to sit through. It was so slow and boring that I could feel my own brain starting to decay while watching it. Now, it did have some good moments though, Crispin Glover was brilliant as The Wizard, Jeffrey Combs as The Geek played a small but excellent role, and there were a handful of naked Suicide Girls. But that's about it. The rest of the acting ranged from decent to awful, and this movie was just very poorly done. Maybe in the hands of a better director this could have been better but alas, the end product is just terrible.

1.5/5

Wolf
Year – 1994
Director – Mike Nichols
Tags – Werewolves

On his way back home one night, the editor-in-chief of a prestigious publishing house is bitten by a wolf and now he is beginning to change. I like this movie, but not so much for the werewolf aspects of it but instead for the human side and what the main character must do for his job. The werewolf half of the movie is good but there's just no depth to it. The movie is also much longer than it needs to be. But on the plus side, the acting is great, the story is very good, and the pacing only suffers mildly from the bloated runtime. This is a very good movie if you're in the mood for a more quasi horror type flick, focusing more on the normal aspects of the characters lives than the supernatural ones. Very nice.

3.5/5

Wolf Creek
Year – 2005
Director – Greg McLean
Tags – Slasher / Survival

Based on true events, Wolf Creek tells the tale of a trio of people who go hiking only to come back and find that their car won't start. A man comes along and offers to help, towing their car back to his house, but after they get there, they find out that helping them is the last thing on his mind. Let me get the bad out of the way right now. The first half of the movie is very slow and uneventful, so be prepared for that, but it does offer a great deal of character development, which comes in handy later. Besides that, this movie is pretty flawless. The story is wonderful and the direction is great. The characters act like real people and avoid the typical survival horror clichés, which is very refreshing. Like if you were to knock down the killer, would you run away like so much horror movie chum, or would you seize the moment and try to shoot him in the head while he's down? Out of ammo? Beat him with the gun! There are many great moments like that in the movie which really allows it to stand out in my eyes. Add to all this some great acting, lots of grisly imagery, brutality, blood, violence and tension, and you have yourself one hell of a movie.

4/5

Woods, The
Year – 2006
Director – Lucky McKee
Tags – Witchcraft

A troublesome girl with a hidden talent is sent to a private school in the woods by her parents. After some strange occurrences in the school and the woods surrounding it, the girl discovers that the women running it are not all that they seem. This is a very beautiful movie, and the way it was shot is the definite work of a master. The story is very original while still retaining a familiar feel to it. The build up to the end does feel a little slow, but it didn't ruin the overall enjoyment of the movie for me. The FX work really is something, the practical FX are real nice and even the CGI sequences look great and are not overdone in the least. The acting is excellent as well. This is just a great production and I can't understand why this sat on the shelf for years before getting released. Lucky McKee proves once again that he a new force to be reckoned with in the genre with this highly innovative and well done film.

4/5

Wrestlemaniac (El Mascarado Massacre)
Year – 2006
Director – Jesse Baget

Tags – Slasher / Survival

A van full of people shooting porn in Mexico come across an old ghost town that supposedly houses a genetically engineered Lucha Libre fighter (Mexican wrestler) after he began to kill his opponents. Only in horror will you find a plot like that folks. I have to give points out for the originality here in both the killer and the victims. I like this movie a lot but I wished there was more blood and a larger variety of kills. I like how the killer finishes his opponent off, but if he could have done some more interesting things beforehand, it would have enhanced this movie for me. And if they're out shooting porn, I want some more nudity too. But the direction is nice, the short run time allows for things to go smoothly, which I wish more people would get into and stop forcing their movies into the standard hour and a half run time. Even though I wanted more blood, there is still a fair amount of it to go around. This is just a very good slasher flick and it makes me want to see more from this director/writer. Good times.

3.5/5

Wrong Turn
Year – 2003
Director – Rob Schmidt
Tags – Slasher / Survival

After a car crash leaves them stranded in the woods, a group of people set off on foot to try and find help. But all they end up finding are some locals, happy to see them, but not for the reasons they would want, no, these locals are cannibals, and very hungry. Ok, so the plot is far from original, it's been done several times, but did this team make an entertaining movie? For the most part, yes. The inbred, backwoods folk look good, there's some nice kills, decent bloodshed, but it still feels half assed. Most of the cast looks bored to be in it, there's blood, but there could have been more to it, just more of everything. It's a fun movie, but with more effort, it could have been even better.

3/5

Wrong Turn 2: Dead End
Year – 2007
Director – Joe Lynch
Tags – Slasher / Survival

This movie plays out in a similar fashion to the first, but this time a group of people are filming a reality show in the woods. If you're going to make a sequel to Wrong Turn, your best bet is to just amp everything up. More blood, better kills, more kills, nudity, action, they need take everything up a level, and they did that, to some degree. This definitely feels like a much more fun production, even with some actors lagging behind the rest in terms of skill. Oh, and Henry Rollins is great in this movie. I definitely like the increase in bloodshed and the nice kills, but it is just more of the same. I like it better than the first, no classic here, but a solid movie nonetheless.

3.5/5

Zodiac

Year – 2007
Director – David Fincher
Tags – Serial Killer

This movie chronicles the exploits of the Zodiac Killer, a serial killer who terrorized various locations in California for years and was never caught. Making a movie like this is tricky business since there is no closure to the actual story, but the story here is rather good and I liked how it played out. The acting is also extremely good, and with a great director behind the helm, you just can't go wrong. But it did. This movie is just way too long, and actually even seems longer than it really is because the story drags through many a superfluous side story and never seems to end. That really is my only complaint about this movie, because everything else is stellar. Maybe I just don't have a good enough attention span for it, but I felt this movie was way overblown and would have benefitted from a much shorter runtime.

3.5/5

Zombie (Zombi 2)

Year – 1979
Director – Lucio Fulci
Tags – Zombies

After her father's boat shows up in New York City carrying a strange creature, a woman and a journalist travel to a remote island where her father was last seen alive. Once there they encounter hordes of the living dead, hungry for their flesh. Let me give you a little back story to the movie first. Dawn of the Dead was released in Italy as Zombi, and this movie was released as Zombi 2, a supposed sequel. Now there have been "sequels" that have nothing to do with the originals, and they usually suck something awful, but Zombi 2 was the exception. This ended up being a very well done zombie movie. It also features probably one of the most astonishing scenes in horror movie history. I am talking of course about Zombie vs. Shark. Yes, that's right, a guy made up like a zombie, underwater, fighting a real life shark. And it's not even cheesy, it's actually really cool. Aside from that the movie delivers good direction and loads of gore, along with some very decrepit looking zombies. I don't really feel the movie is a classic, but I love it nonetheless and this is a great depiction of Italian zombie movies.

4/5

Zombie 3 (Zombi 3)

Year – 1988
Director – Lucio Fulci
Tags – Zombies

Ok, so this series which technically started with number two has no relation to the other movies and here this movie is about a scientist who gets infected by a zombie virus and after being caught, a military screw up causes the virus to be released into the atmosphere, turning the dead into flesh hungry freaks. What an underwhelming movie for such a master of horror. He must have needed money or something. This is just a straight zombie movie that you've seen a hundred times, nothing special in the story. The direction is surprisingly inadequate and the movie is disjointed and slow. It does feature some good gore but the zombie action is too spread out and unexciting for the most part. I like everyday zombie flicks and this is just another one, it has its flaws but it's not all bad I guess.

2.5/5

Zombie 4: After Death (Oltre la Morte)
Year – 1988
Director – Claudio Fragasso
Tags – Zombies

This movie follows a woman as she unwittingly returns to the island where her parents were murdered by flesh eating zombies. Now the voodoo curse has been unleashed again and she must fight for her life. I guess the US isn't the only country that takes a movie and tacks on a franchise name for better recognition. This movie, not even remotely related to the other two, is pretty bad, but it does have some respectable moments. The acting is bad, the direction is slow as hell and the story is laughable. But that's just the thing, as it did make me laugh because it was just that poorly constructed. There was some awesome gore though, including a very well done face tearing. So while this movie had a lot of bad things going for it, I still found at least some enjoyment in it, but I will also say that I'm in no rush to watch it again.

2/5

Zombie 5: Killing Birds (Uccelli Assassinni)
Year – 1987
Director – Claudio Lattanzi
Tags – Zombies

Some students gather to study birds and then a zombie shows up for some reason and starts killing them off. Holy shit, this movie sucks! The story is an abomination, the acting is terrible, the direction is painful and the movie is just unbearably slow and senseless. There is some gore, some good gore in fact, not particularly special but enough to keep this movie out of the trash bin. I think it's pretty hilarious that this movie is called Zombie 5 even though it was made before Zombie 3, but hey, in the realm of terrible horror movies, I've learned to expect anything.

1/5

Zombie Honeymoon

Year – 2004
Director – David Gebroe
Tags – Zombies

While on their honeymoon, a couple is attacked by a zombie and it kills the husband. While at the hospital he miraculously comes back to life but slowly develops the need to devour human flesh. Will true love succeed or will the need for flesh consume him? After seeing the name of this movie, I just had to see it, but I must say that if you're expecting a horror/comedy, then you'll be pretty disappointed. This movie instead focuses on love and just how much a powerful bond between two people can endure. And for a microbudget movie, it's pretty well done. The acting is above par for the money spent, the story is good, not great, but it has its moments. The direction is pretty good with some well rounded pacing. This turned out to be more than I expected, which is nice, and while it's not the next great classic, it was pretty entertaining.

3/5

Zombie Night

Year – 2003
Director – David J. Francis
Tags – Zombies

Nuclear war erupts in the US and the radiation causes people to turn into flesh eating zombies. Survivors hole up in a school to escape the growing legions of undead. This is a microbudget movie, and the acting is on par with the budget. The script is just terrible. The timeline and events occurring are incredibly jumbled, especially in the beginning, but it does tend to smooth out as it goes along. There are also way too many characters and more just seem to appear out of nowhere. It's paced pretty well, but where the movie really shines is in the FX work. The zombies and dead bodies look great, and the blood and gore FX are almost at a professional level. This movie is very gory and even has a bit of nudity thrown in for good measure. It's not a bad movie, could have used more attention to detail though. There are some great things about it, unfortunately there are also an equal amount of bad things. But as far as microbudget zombie movies go, I've seen much worse.

2/5

Zombie Strippers

Year – 2008
Director – Jay Lee
Tags – Zombies

A stripper is attacked by a zombie in an underground strip club and soon becomes the hottest thing around. All the guys are dying to see her and the other strippers get jealous and one by one join the ranks of the undead while the owner of the club puts their zombified victims in a cage downstairs. You can't take a movie like this seriously I mean, look at title for crying out loud! This is a total horror/comedy and I like it a lot. There's plenty of gore, plenty of laughs and plenty of nudity, but it does have its share of issues as well. The acting is a mixed bag, on one end you have Robert Englund being absolutely brilliant and hilarious, and on the other end you have most of the rest of the cast. But the acting being so cheesy does kind of fit in with the theme of the movie. The CGI is pretty bad here as well, obvious green screen work and whatnot. The practical FX though, along with the make-up, are pretty great. This is a fun zombie movie with an interesting twist meant to make you laugh if nothing else.

3.5/5

Zombie Town
Year – 2007
Director – Damon Lemay
Tags – Zombies

A zombie uprising occurs in a small town and now the remaining residents are cut off from the rest of the world and must fight to survive. Yeah, the story isn't that great, it's just your standard low budget zombie stuff. But that's the only thing about this movie that's mundane. This is definitely what horror fans want: A low budget zombie movie that's extremely well done. The acting is very good, especially for a low budget flick. The movie has great characters as well as ones that aren't quite as one dimensional as we're used to seeing. The direction is great as well, the movie moves along nicely and never gets slow. There are also great FX, lots of blood and some good looking zombies. And as if that wasn't enough, the movie is also pretty damn hilarious as well. And not in that cheese factor way, the movie is just genuinely funny. This is kind of holy grail type of zombie movie, and if you're a fan of the sub genre, you definitely need to check this gem out immediately.

4/5

Zombies Anonymous (Last Rites of the Dead)
Year – 2006
Director – Marc Fratto
Tags – Zombies

Suddenly people stop dying and spend their afterlife with the living as zombies, or as they like to call themselves, "Mortally challenged". Terrorist groups have formed to eradicate the zombies even though they just want to lead normal unlives. But when they discover there is certain power to be gained from eating human flesh, the zombies fight back. Now that is a different kind of zombie movie right there and after watching dozens of paint by numbers low budget zombie movies, that's pretty refreshing. The acting is pretty good and the direction is well done. The movie not only features some gore but some pretty funny moments as well. This is a solid zombie flick that may not feature enough flesh eating for some zombie fans, but I really appreciated the different take and this ended up being just shy of greatness.

3.5/5

MOVIES BY YEAR

2009:
Against the Dark
Amusement
Butterfly Effect 3 – Revelations, The
Feast III – The Happy Finish
Friday the 13th [Remake]
His Name is Jason
My Bloody Valentine [Remake]
Perkin's 14
S. Darko
Silent Venom
Slaughter
Vacancy 2 – The First Cut

2008:
100 Feet
Alien Raiders
Alphabet Killer, The
Anaconda 3 – The Offspring
April Fool's Day [Remake]
Autopsy
Boogeyman 3
Broken, The
Cloverfield
Cottage, The
Dance of the Dead
Dark Floors
Day of the Dead [Remake]
Dead Space – Downfall
Doomsday
Dorothy Mills
Dying Breed
Eden Lake
Feast II – Sloppy Seconds
From Within
Happening, The
Haunting of Molly Hartley, The
Hellboy II – The Golden Army
Insanitarium
Joy Ride 2 – Dead Ahead
Killer Pad
Lakeview Terrace
Loch Ness Terror (Beyond Lock Ness)

Lost Boys II – The Tribe, The
No Man's Land – The Rise of Reeker
Organizm (Living Hell)
Otis
Outpost
Pathology
Poker Club, The
Prom Night [Remake]
Pulse 2 – Afterlife
Pulse 3 – Invasion
Red
Resident Evil – Degeneration
Rest Stop – Don't Look Back
Return to Sleepaway Camp
Ruins, The
Saw V
Shuttle
Solstice
Splinter
Strangers, The
Trailer Park of Terror
Transsiberian
Triloquist
Untraceable
Zombie Strippers

2007:
28 Weeks Later
30 Days of Night
1408
Aliens vs. Predator Requiem
American Crime, An
Awake
Awaken the Dead
Bats – Human Harvest
Believers
Beowulf
Blood and Chocolate
Bloodrayne 2 – Deliverance
Boogeyman 2
Borderland
Botched
Brotherhood of Blood
Brutal Massacre – A Comedy
Buried Alive
Buried Alive [Web Series]

Cadaverella
Captivity
Cave, The
Cellar Door, The
Chair, The
Days of Darkness
Dead Mary
Dead Moon Rising
Dead Silence
Deadwood Park
Death Proof
Death Sentence
Deaths of Ian Stone, The
Decoys – The Second Seduction
Diary of the Dead
Disturbia
Ed Gein – The Butcher of Plainfield
Eden Log
Empty Acre, The
First Born
Flight of the Living Dead – Outbreak on a Plane
Forest of the Dead
Frontiere(s)
Girl Next Door, The
Grim Reaper
Halloween [Remake]
Hannibal Rising
Headless Horseman
Hills Have Eyes 2, The
Hitcher, The [Remake]
Hostel Part II
I Am Legend
I Know Who Killed Me
Inside (A l'interieur)
Invasion, The
Jack Brooks – Monster Slayer
Joshua (2007)
Kaidan
Killing Gene, The (W Delta Z [WAZ])
Lake Dead
Lake Placid 2
Messengers, The
Mist, The
Mother of Tears, The (La Terza Madre)
Mr. Brooks
Murder Party

My Name is Bruce
Number 23, The
Orphanage, The (El Orfanato)
P2
Planet Terror
Primeval
Rage, The
Reaping, The
Resident Evil – Extinction
Return to House on Haunted Hill
Rise – Blood Hunter
Rise of the Dead
Rogue
Room 205 (Kollegiet)
Saw IV
Shrooms
Sick House, The
Sick Nurses (Suay Laak Sai)
Signal, The
Species IV – The Awakening
Spiral
Steel Trap
Stir of Echoes 2 – The Homecoming
Storm Warning
Stuck
Sublime
Substitute, The (Vikaren)
Sunshine
Tattooist, The
Teeth
Tooth & Nail
Trackman
Unearthed
Vacancy
Viscera 2007
Voices (Du Saram-Yida)
Welcome to the Jungle
White Noise 2 – The Light
Wizard of Gore, The [Remake]
Wrong Turn 2 – Dead End
Zodiac
Zombie Town

2006:
5ive Girls
13: Game of Death (13 Game Sayawng)

Abandoned, The
Abominable
Alone with Her
Altered
Automaton Transfusion
Baby's Room, The (La Habitacion del Nino)
Backwoods, The (Bosque de Sombras)
Bacterium
Basic Instinct 2
Behind the Mask – The Rise of Leslie Vernon
Beyond the Wall of Sleep
Big Bad Wolf
Black Christmas [Remake]
Black Sheep
Blame (La Culpa)
Bottom Feeder
Breed, The (2006)
Broken
Bug
Butterfly Effect 2, The
Cemetery Gates
Christmas Tale, A (Cuento de Navidad)
Crazy Eights
Creepshow 3
Dark Ride
Day Watch (Dnevnoy Dozor)
Deadlands – The Rising
Desperation
Devil's Chair, The
Driftwood
Entrance, The
Fido
Final Destination 3
Gravedancers, The
Graveyard, The
Grudge 2, The
Hamiltons, The
Hatchet
Hills Have Eyes, The [Remake]
Hollow Man 2
Host, The (Gwoemul)
I'll Always Know What You Did Last Summer
Jekyll + Hyde
Joshua (2006)
Lady in the Water
Last House in the Woods, The (Il Bosco Fuori)

Last Winter, The
Lost, The
Memory
Mulberry Street
Night of the Dead
Night of the Living Dead 3-D
Nightmare Detective (Akumi Tantai)
Nightmare Man
Omen, The [Remake]
Open Water 2 – Adrift
Other Side, The
Pan's Labyrinth (El Laberinto del Fauno)
Penny Dreadful
Perfect Creature
Plague, The
Plasterhead
Population 436
Pulse [Remake]
Quick and the Undead, The
Real Friend, A (Adivina Quien Soy)
Rest Stop – Dead Ahead
Retribution (Sakebi)
Return, The
Right at Your Door
Roman
Salvage
Savage Harvest 2 – October Blood
Saw III
See No Evil
Severance
Silent Hill
Slither
Snakes on a Plane
Spectre (Regreso A Moira)
Stay Alive
Subject Two
Texas Chainsaw Massacre – The Beginning, The
Them (Ils)
To Let (Para Entrar a Vivar)
Tripper, The
Turistas
Ultraviolet
Underworld – Evolution
Unrest
Visions of Suffering
Wicked Little Things

Wilderness
Woods, The
Wrestlemaniac (El Mascarado Massacre)
Zombies Anonymous (Last Rites of the Dead)

2005:
8MM 2
13 Tzameti
2001 Maniacs
All Soul's Day – Dia de los Muertos
Alone in the Dark
American Haunting, An
Apocalypse and the Beauty Queen
Bad Reputation
Beowulf & Grendel
Bloodrayne
Boogeyman
Boy Eats Girl
Call of Cthulhu, The [Silent]
Clawed – The Legend of Sasquatch
Constantine
Cry_Wolf
Cursed
Dark, The
Dark Hours, The
Dark Remains
Dark Water [Remake]
Day of the Dead 2 – Contagium
Dead Life
Dead Men Walking
Death Tunnel
Demon Pond (Yasha-Ga-Ike) [Stage]
Descent, The
Devil's Rejects, The
Dominion – Prequel to the Exorcist
Doom
Evil Aliens
Evil's City
Exorcism of Emily Rose, The
Feast
Feed
Fog, The [Remake]
Hammerhead
Hard Candy
Hellraiser VII – Deader
Hellraiser VIII – Hellworld

Horror Business
Hostel
House of 9
House of the Dead II
House of Wax [Remake]
Ice Queen
Isolation
J-Horror Anthology – Underworld
Jacket, The
Lady Vengeance (Chinjeolhan Geumjassi)
Land of the Dead
Legion of the Dead
Man-Thing
Mangler Reborn, The
Manticore
Mortuary
Prophecy IV – Uprising, The
Prophecy V – Forsaken, The
Red Eye
Reeker
Reincarnation (Rinne)
Return of the Living Dead 4 – Necropolis
Return of the Living Dead 5 – Rave to the Grave
Ring 2, The
Rise of the Undead
Roost, The
Saw II
Severed – Forest of the Dead
Single White Female 2 – The Psycho
Tamara
Tower of Blood
Urban Legends 3 – Bloody Mary
White Noise
Within the Woods
Wolf Creek

2004:
3 Extremes (Sam Gang Yi)
Aliens vs. Predator
Anacondas – The Hunt for the Blood Orchid
Blade – Trinity
Blood Gnome
Breaking Dawn
Butterfly Effect, The
Calvaire (The Ordeal)
Club Dread

Creep
Cube Zero
Dawn of the Dead [Remake]
Dead & Breakfast
Dead Birds
Dead End Road
Dead Man's Shoes
Dead Meat
Decoys
Evilenko
Exorcist – The Beginning
Feeding the Masses
Freak Out
Ginger Snaps 2 – Unleashed
Ginger Snaps Back – The Beginning
Grudge, The
Hellbent
Hellboy
Helter Skelter [Remake]
Hillside Strangler, The
Infection (Kansen)
Lightning Bug
Machinist, The
Malevolence
Marebito
Night of the Living Dorks (Die Nacht der Lebenden Loser)
Night Watch (Nochnoy Dozor)
Premonition (Yogen)
Resident Evil – Apocalypse
Riding the Bullet
Ring of Darkness
Salem's Lot [Remake]
Satan's Little Helper
Saw
Secret Window
Seed of Chucky
Shallow Ground
Shaun of the Dead
Skinned Deep
Species III
Starkweather
Tears of Kali
Tremors 4 – The Legend Begins
Vampires – Out for Blood
Van Helsing
Van Helsing – The London Assignment

Village, The
Zombie Honeymoon

2003:
Anatomy 2 (Anatomie 2)
Beyond Re-Animator
Bone Snatcher, The
Darkness Falls
Dead End
Diary of Ellen Rimbauer, The
Dreamcatcher
Final Destination 2
Flesh for the Beast
Freddy vs. Jason
Gacy
Ghouls, The
Gothika
High Tension (Haute Tension)
Hitcher II – I've Been Waiting, The
House of 1000 Corpses
House of the Dead
Identity
J-Horror Anthology – Legends
Jeepers Creepers 2
Ju-On 2
Leprechaun 6 – Back 2 tha Hood
Love Object
Mimic 3 – The Sentinel
Monster
Oldboy
Open Water
Razor Eaters
Red Riding Hood
Tale of Two Sisters, A (Janghwa, Hongryeon)
Texas Chainsaw Massacre, The [Remake]
Undead
Underworld
Visitors
Wrong Turn
Zombie Night

2002:
3 Extremes II (Saam Gaang)
28 Days Later
American Psycho 2 – All American Girl
Below

Blade II
Blood Feast 2 – All U Can Eat
Bubba Ho-Tep
Cabin Fever
Carrie [Remake]
Cube 2 – Hypercube
Dahmer
Dark Water (Honoguari Mizu No Soko Kara)
Darkness
Dead Above Ground
Deathbed
Deathwatch
Dog Soldiers
Eight Legged Freaks
Feardotcom
Ghost Ship
Halloween VIII – Resurrection
Hellraiser VI – Hellseeker
Ju-On
May
Miner's Massacre (Curse of the Forty-Niner)
Nightstalker
One Hour Photo
Queen of the Damned
Red Dragon
Resident Evil
Ring, The
Rose Red
Signs
Speck
Spider
Swimfan
Sympathy for Mr. Vengeance (Boksuneun Naui Geot)
Ted Bundy
They
Tomie 5 – Forbidden Fruit
Unborn but Forgotten (Hayanbang)
Vampire Hunters (The Era of Vampires)
Vampires – Los Muertos
Wishmaster 4 – The Prophecy Fulfilled

2001:
Along Came a Spider
Blood Moon (Wolf Girl)
Bones
Breed, The (2001)

Brotherhood of the Wolf (Le Pacte des Loupes)
Children of the Living Dead
Cradle of Fear
Dagon
Devil's Backbone, The (El Espinazo del Diablo)
Donnie Darko
Forsaken, The
Frailty
From Hell
Ghosts of Mars
Hannibal
Hole, The
Jason X
Jeepers Creepers
Joy Ride
Mangler 2, The
Meat Market 2
Mimic 2
Mulholland Dr.
Others, The
Plaga Zombie – Mutant Zone
Pool, The (Swimming Pool – Der Tod Feiert Mit)
Pulse (Kairo)
Session 9
Shaft, The (Down)
Slashers
Tomie 4 – Rebirth
Tremors 3 – Back to Perfection
Valentine
Wishmaster 3 – Beyond the Gates of Hell

2000:
American Psycho
Anatomy (Anatomie)
Book of Shadows – Blair Witch 2
Bruiser
Camp Blood 2
Ed Gein (In the Light of the Moon)
Final Destination
Flesh Freaks
Gift, The
Ginger Snaps
Hellraiser V – Inferno
Hollow Man
Island of the Dead
Leprechaun 5 – In the Hood

Meat Market
Pitch Black
Prophecy III – The Ascent, The
Ringu 0
Scream 3
Severed Head Network, The
Shadow of the Vampire
Soho Square
Tomie 3 – Replay
Unbreakable
Urban Legends 2 – The Final Cut
Versus
Watcher, The
What Lies Beneath

1999:
4th Floor, The
8MM
Audition (Odishon)
Bats
Blair Witch Project, The
Camp Blood
Candyman 3 – Day of the Dead
Deep Blue Sea
End of Days
Fear 2 – Halloween Night, The
From Dusk till Dawn 2 – Texas Blood Money
From Dusk till Dawn 3 – The Hangman's Daughter
Haunting, The [Remake]
House on Haunted Hill [Remake]
Idle Hands
Kolobos
Lake Placid
Ninth Gate, The
Rage – Carrie 2, The
Ravenous
Retro Puppet Master
Ring Virus, The
Ringu 2
Sixth Sense, The
Sleepy Hollow
Stir of Echoes
Storm of the Century
Tomie
Tomie 2 – Another Face
Virus

Wishmaster 2 – Evil Never Dies

1998:
Arrival II, The (The Second Arrival)
Bio-Zombie (Sun Faa Sau Si)
Blade
Bride of Chucky
Creature
Curse of the Puppet Master
Dark City
Deep Rising
Dentist 2 – Brace Yourself, The
Disturbing Behavior
Faculty, The
Halloween VII – H20
I Still Know What You Did Last Summer
Last Broadcast, The
Phantom of the Opera, The [Remake] (1998)
Phantoms
Progeny
Prophecy II, The
Psycho [Remake]
Rasen
Ringu
Shrieker
Species II
Sphere
Strangeland
Subspecies IV – Bloodstorm
Urban Legend
Vampires

1997:
Alien Resurrection
American Werewolf in Paris, An
Anaconda
Bleeders
Cube
Devil's Advocate, The
Edge, The
Event Horizon
I Know What You Did Last Summer
Kiss the Girls
Leprechaun 4 – In Space
Lost Highway
Mimic

Night Flier, The
Night of the Demons 3
Plaga Zombie
Quicksilver Highway
Relic, The
Scream 2
Shining, The [Remake]
Snow White – A Tale of Terror
Trucks
Ugly, The
Vampire Journals
Wishmaster

1996:
Arrival, The
Bad Moon
Beast, The
Bordello of Blood
Craft, The
Dentist, The
Fear (1996)
Frighteners, The
From Dusk till Dawn
Ghost and the Darkness, The
Hellraiser IV – Bloodline
Henry II – Portrait of a Serial Killer
Island of Dr. Moreau, The [Remake]
Lawnmower Man 2 – Jobe's War, The
Mary Reilly
Scream
Thinner
Tremors 2 – Aftershocks

1995:
Candyman 2 – Farewell to the Flesh
Castle Freak
Citizen X
Congo
Copycat
Demon Knight
Dolores Claiborne
Fear, The
Halloween VI – The Curse of Michael Myers
Haunted
Hideaway
Langoliers, The

Leprechaun 3
Lord of Illusions
Mangler, The
Outbreak
Prophecy, The
Screamers
Seven (Se7en)
Sleepstalker
Species
Tales from the Hood
Village of the Damned [Remake]

1994:
Cemetery Man (Dellamorte Dellamore)
Dark Angel – The Ascent
In the Mouth of Madness
Interview with the Vampire
Leprechaun 2
Lurking Fear
Mary Shelley's Frankenstein
Natural Born Killers
New Nightmare
Night of the Demons 2
Puppet Master V – The Final Chapter
Puppet Masters, The
Savage Harvest
Shatter Dead
Subspecies III – Bloodlust
Texas Chainsaw Massacre 4 – The Next Generation, The
Wolf

1993:
Arcade
Body Bags
Body Snatchers
Crush, The
Dark Half, The
Dark Waters
Good Son, The
Hidden 2, The
Jason Goes to Hell – The Final Friday
Kalifornia
Leprechaun
Maniac Cop 3 – Badge of Silence
Man's Best Friend
My Boyfriend's Back

Needful Things
Puppet Master IV – When Bad Puppets Turn Good
Return of the Living Dead 3
Subspecies II – Bloodstone
Tommyknockers, The

1992:
Alien 3
Army of Darkness
Bad Channels
Basic Instinct
Bram Stoker's Dracula
Buffy the Vampire Slayer
Candyman
Dead Alive (Braindead)
Hand that Rocks the Cradle, The
Hellraiser III – Hell on Earth
Innocent Blood
Lawnmower Man, The
Netherworld
Pet Sematary Two
Prom Night IV: Deliver Us from Evil
Raising Cain
Resurrected, The
Seedpeople
Single White Female
Sleepwalkers
Waxwork II – Lost in Time

1991:
Children of the Night
Child's Play 3
Freddy's Dead – The Final Nightmare
Howling VI – The Freaks, The
Omen IV – The Awakening, The
People Under the Stairs, The
Puppet Master II
Puppet Master III – Toulon's Revenge
Silence of the Lambs
Subspecies

1990:
Arachnophobia
Bride of Re-Animator
Child's Play 2

Fear (1990)
Flatliners
Gate II – Return to the Nightmare, The
Graveyard Shift
Gremlins 2 – The New Batch
It
Jacob's Ladder
Leatherface – The Texas Chainsaw Massacre 3
Maniac Cop 2
Misery
Night of the Living Dead [Remake]
Nightbreed
Pacific Heights
Predator 2
Prom Night III – The Last Kiss
Psycho IV – The Beginning
Shadowzone
Tales from the Darkside – The Movie
Tremors

1989:
Abyss, The
Church, The (La Chiesa)
Curse 2 – The Bite
Dead Calm
Dead Next Door, The
Dead Pit
Deepstar Six
Exorcist III, The
Friday the 13th Part VIII – Jason Takes Manhattan
Ghostbusters II
Halloween V – The Revenge of Michael Myers
House III – The Horror Show
Howling V – The Rebirth, The
Leviathan
Nightmare on Elm Street 5 – The Dream Child, A
Parents
Pet Sematary
Phantom of the Opera [Remake] (1989)
Puppet Master
Return of Swamp Thing, The
Shocker
Sleepaway Camp 3 – Teenage Wasteland

1988:
976-EVIL

Bad Dreams
Beetlejuice
Child's Play
Dead Heat
Dead Ringers
Friday the 13th Part VII – The New Blood
Gates of Hell II – Dead Awakening, The (Through the Fire)
Halloween IV – The Return of Michael Myers
Hellbound – Hellraiser II
Howling IV – The Original Nightmare, The
Killer Klowns from Outer Space
Maniac Cop
Night of the Demons
Nightmare on Elm Street 4 – The Dream Master, A
Poltergeist III
Psycho III
Return of the Living Dead 2
Scarecrows
Seventh Sign, The
Sleepaway Camp 2 – Unhappy Campers
Slugs
Sorority Babes in the Slime Ball Bowl-A-Rama
They Live
Waxwork
Zombie 3 (Zombi 3)
Zombie 4 (Oltre la Morte)

1987:
Angel Heart
Bay Cove (Bay Coven)
Creepshow 2
Curse, The
Evil Dead 2 – Dead by Dawn
Fatal Attraction
Flowers in the Attic
Gate, The
Ghoulies II
Hello Mary Lou – Prom Night II
Hellraiser
Hidden, The
House II – The Second Story
Howling III – The Marsupials, The
Its Alive 3 – Island of the Alive
Jaws – The Revenge
Lost Boys, The
Monster Squad, The

Near Dark
Nightmare on Elm Street 3 – Dream Warriors, A
Nightmare Sisters
Predator
Prince of Darkness
Running Man, The
Teen Wolf Too
Witches of Eastwick, The
Zombie 5 – Killing Birds (Uccelli Assassinni)

1986:

Aliens
April Fool's Day
Blue Velvet
Breeders
Chopping Mall
Deadly Friend
Demons 2 – The Nightmare Continues (Demoni 2 – L'incubo Ritorna)
Fortress
Friday the 13th Part VI – Jason Lives
From Beyond
Henry – Portrait of a Serial Killer
Hitcher, The
House
Manhunter
Maximum Overdrive
Neon Maniacs
Poltergeist II – The Other Side
Texas Chainsaw Massacre 2, The

1985:

Cat's Eye
Day of the Dead
Demons (Demoni)
Friday the 13th Part V – A New Beginning
Ghoulies
Hills Have Eyes Part II, The
Howling II – Your Sister is a Werewolf, The
Lifeforce
Nightmare on Elm Street 2 – Freddy's Revenge, A
Re-Animator
Return of the Living Dead, The
Silver Bullet
Stuff, The
Teen Wolf

1984:
C.H.U.D.
Friday the 13th Part IV – The Final Chapter
Ghostbusters
Gremlins
Mutant (Night Shadows)
Night of the Comet
Nightmare on Elm Street, A

1983:
Christine
Cujo
Hunger, The
Jaws 3
Psycho II
Sleepaway Camp
Twilight Zone – The Movie
Videodrome

1982:
Creepshow
Friday the 13th Part III
Halloween III – Season of the Witch
National Lampoon's Class Reunion
New York Ripper, The (Lo Squartatore di New York)
Poltergeist
Q – The Winged Serpent
Swamp Thing
Thing, The
Visiting Hours

1981:
American Werewolf in London, An
Beyond, The (E Tu Vivrai Nel Terrore – L'aldila)
Burning, The
Dead & Buried
Evil Dead, The
Eyes of a Stranger
Friday the 13th Part II
Halloween II
House by the Cemetery (Quella Villa Accanto al Cimitero)
Howling, The
My Bloody Valentine
Omen III – The Final Conflict, The
Scanners

1980:
Altered States
Cannibal Holocaust
City of the Living Dead (The Gates of Hell)
Fog, The
Friday the 13th
Hell of the Living Dead (Virus)
Inferno
Nightmare City (Incubo Sulla Citta Contaminata)
Prom Night
Shining, The
Terror Train

1979:
Alien
Brood, The
Salem's Lot
Zombie (Zombi 2)

1978:
Damien – Omen II
Dawn of the Dead
Halloween
Invasion of the Body Snatchers [Remake]
It's Alive 2 – It Lives Again
Jaws 2
Someone's Watching Me!
Summer of Fear (Stranger in Our House)

1977:
Deep, The
Exorcist II – The Heretic, The
Hills Have Eyes, The
Island of Dr. Moreau, The
Martin
Orca – The Killer Whale
Sentinel, The
Suspiria

1976:
Burnt Offerings
Carrie
Creature from Black Lake
Helter Skelter

Little Girl Who Lives Down the Lane, The
Omen, The
Tenant, The (Le Locataire)
Who Can Kill a Child? (Island of the Damned)

1975:
Deep Red (Profondo Rosso)
Jaws
Trilogy of Terror

1974:
Black Christmas
It's Alive
Texas Chainsaw Massacre, The

1973:
Badlands
Crazies, The
Exorcist, The
From Beyond the Grave
Vault of Horror
Vengeance of the Zombies (La Rebelion de las Muertas)

1972:
Deliverance
Frogs
Gore Gore Girls, The
Last House on the Left, The
Night of the Lepus
Raw Meat (Death Line)
Tales from the Crypt

1971:
Duel
Omega Man, The
What's the Matter with Helen?
Whoever Slew Auntie Roo?

1970:
Cry of the Banshee
Dunwich Horror, The
Wizard of Gore, The

1968:

Night of the Living Dead
Rosemary's Baby

1967:
Gruesome Twosome, The

1965:
Die, Monster, Die!

1964:
Children of the Damned
Last Man on Earth, The
Two Thousand Maniacs!

1963:
Birds, The
Blood Feast
Haunting, The
Twice Told Tales

1962:
Panic in the Year Zero!
Tales of Terror

1960:
Psycho
Village of the Damned
Virgin Spring, The (Jungfrukallan)

1959:
House on Haunted Hill

1958:
Vertigo

1956:
Bad Seed, The
Invasion of the Body Snatchers

1954:
Rear Window

1953:
House of Wax

1951:
Thing from Another World, The

1941:
Dr. Jekyll and Mr. Hyde [Remake]

1933:
Ghoul, The
Mystery of the House of Wax

1932:
Freaks
White Zombie

1931:
Dr. Jekyll and Mr. Hyde

1925:
Phantom of the Opera [Silent]

1922:
Nosferatu [Silent]

MOVIES BY DIRECTOR:

Abel Ferrara:
Body Snatchers

Adam Gierasch:
Autopsy

Adam Green:
Hatchet
Spiral

Adam Marcus:
Jason Goes to Hell – The Final Friday

Adam Mason:
Broken
Devil's Chair, The

Adrian Lyne:
Fatal Attraction
Jacob's Ladder

Agnes Merlet:
Dorothy Mills

Alan Parker:
Angel Heart

Alan Shapiro:
Crush, The

Alan Smithee:
Hellraiser IV – Bloodline

Albert Band:
Ghoulies II

Albert Hughes:
From Hell

Albert Pyun:
Arcade

Alejandro Amenabar:
Others, The

Alex Chandon:
Cradle of Fear

Alex de la Iglesia:
Baby's Room, The (La Habitacion del Nino)

Alex Proyas:
Dark City

Alex Turner:
Dead Birds

Alexander Witt:
Resident Evil – Apocalypse

Alexandre Aja:
High Tension
Hills Have Eyes, The [Remake]

Alexandre Bustillo:
Inside (A l'interieur)

Alfred Hitchcock:
Birds, The
Psycho
Rear Window
Vertigo

Allen Hughes:
From Hell

Ana Clavell:
Creepshow 3
Day of the Dead 2: Contagium

Andre de Toth:
House of Wax

Andreas Marschall:
Tears of Kali

Andrew Currie:
Fido

Andrew Fleming:
Bad Dreams
Craft, The

Andrew Leman:
Call of Cthulhu, The [Silent]

Andrey Iskanov:
Visions of Suffering

Andrzej Bartkowiak:
Doom

Andrzej Sekula:
Cube 2 – Hypercube

Angela Bettis:
Roman

Anthony C. Ferrante:
Headless Horseman

Anthony Hickox:
Hellraiser III – Hell on Earth
Waxwork
Waxwork II – Lost in Time

Anthony Perkins:
Psycho III

Anthony Waller:
American Werewolf in Paris, An

Anton Leader:
Children of the Damned

Antonia Bird:
Ravenous

Arch Nicholson:

Fortress

Arthur Speer:
Halloween V – The Revenge of Michael Myers

Asif Kapadia:
Return, The

Ataru Oikawa:
Tomie

Barbet Schroeder:
Single White Female

Barret J. Leigh:
Beyond the Wall of Sleep

Barry Levinson:
Sphere

Ben Rock:
Alien Raiders

Bennet Davlin:
Memory

Bernard Rose:
Candyman

Bill Condon:
Candyman 2: Farewell to the Flesh

Bill Paxton:
Frailty

Billy O'Brien:
Isolation

Bob Balaban:
My Boyfriend's Back
Parents

Bob Clark:
Black Christmas

Boris Sagal:
Omega Man, The

Boris Von Sychowski:
Pool, The (Swimming Pool – Der Tod Feiert Mit)

Brad Anderson:
Machinist, The
Session 9
Transsiberian

Brad Sykes:
Camp Blood
Camp Blood 2
Within the Woods

Brad Turner:
Species III

Brent Maddock:
Tremors 3 – Back to Perfection

Brett Leonard:
Dead Pit
Feed
Hideaway
Lawnmower Man, The
Man-Thing

Brett Piper:
Bacterium

Brett Ratner:
Red Dragon

Brett Sullivan:
Chair, The
Ginger Snaps 2 – Unleashed

Brian Avenet-Bradley:
Dark Remains

Brian Clement:
Meat Market

Brian de Palma:
Carrie
Raising Cain

Brian Gibson:
Poltergeist II – The Other Side

Brian Singleton:
Forest of the Dead

Brian Trenchard-Smith:
Leprechaun 3
Leprechaun 4 – In Space
Night of the Demons 2

Brian Yuzna:
Beyond Re-Animator
Bride of Re-Animator
Dentist, The
Dentist 2 – Brace Yourself, The
Progeny
Return of the Living Dead 3

Bruce A. Evans:
Mr. Brooks

Bruce Campbell:
My Name is Bruce

Bruce Hunt:
Cave, The

Bruce Pittman:
Hello Mary Lou – Prom Night Two

Bruno Mattei:
Hell of the Living Dead (Virus)

Bryan Bertino:
Strangers, The

Byron Werner:

Starkweather

C. Courtney Joyner:
Lurking Fear

Carl Bessai:
Severed – Forest of the Dead

Carl Schenkel:
Bay Cove

Carl Schultz:
Seventh Sign, The

Carter Smith:
Ruins, The

Chad Ferrin:
Ghouls, The

Chan-Wook Park:
3 Extremes (Sam Gang Yi)
Lady Vengeance (Chinjeolhan Geumjassi)
Oldboy
Sympathy for Mr. Vengeance (Boksuneun Naui Geot)

Chang-Jae Lim:
Unborn but Forgotten (Hayanbang)

Chris Angel:
Fear 2 – Halloween Night, The
Wishmaster 3 – Beyond the Gates of Hell
Wishmaster 4 – The Prophecy Fulfilled

Chris Fisher:
Nightstalker
S. Darko

Chris Gerolmo:
Citizen X

Chris Gorak:
Right at Your Door

Chris Kentis:
Open Water

Chris Sivertson:
I Know Who Killed Me
Lost, The

Chris Thomson:
Trucks

Christian Duguay:
Screamers

Christian James:
Freak Out

Christian Nyby:
Thing from Another World, The

Christophe Gans:
Brotherhood of the Wolf (Le Pacte des Loupes)
Silent Hill

Christopher Leitch:
Teen Wolf Too

Christopher P. Garetano:
Horror Business

Christopher Smith:
Creep
Severance

Chuck Bowman:
Dead above Ground

Chuck Parello:
Ed Gein (In the Light of the Moon)
Henry II – Portrait of a Serial Killer
Hillside Strangler, The

Chuck Patton:
Dead Space – Downfall

Chuck Russell:
Nightmare on Elm Street 3 – Dream Warriors, A

Chukiat Sakveerakul:
13: Game of Death (13 Game Sayawng)

Claudio Fah:
Hollow Man 2

Claudio Fragasso:
Zombie 4 – After Death (Oltre la Morte)

Claudio Lattanzi:
Zombie 5 – Killing Birds (Uccelli Assassinni)

Clay Borris:
Prom Night IV – Deliver Us from Evil

Clive Barker:
Hellraiser
Lord of Illusions
Nightbreed

Clive Saunders:
Gacy

Colin Strause:
Aliens vs. Predator Requiem

Conall Pendergast:
Flesh Freaks

Conor McMahon:
Dead Meat

Corbin Timbrook:
Tower of Blood

Courtney Solomon:
American Haunting, An

Craig R. Baxley:
Diary of Ellen Rimbauer, The
Rose Red

Craig Singer:
Dark Ride
Perkin's 14

Curtis Hanson:
Hand that Rocks the Cradle, The

Curtis Harrington:
What's the Matter With Helen?
Whoever Slew Auntie Roo?

Curtis Radcliffe:
Sick House, The

D.J. Caruso:
Disturbia

Damon Lemay:
Zombie Town

Damon Vignale:
Entrance, The

Dan Bush:
Signal, The

Dan Curtis:
Burnt Offerings
Trilogy of Terror

Dan O'Bannon:
Resurrected, The
Return of the Living Dead, The

Daniel Attias:
Silver Bullet

Daniel Farrands:
His Name Was Jason

Daniel Haller:
Die, Monster, Die!

Dunwich Horror, The

Daniel Liatowitsch:
Kolobos

Daniel Myrick:
Believers
Blair Witch Project, The
Solstice

Danny Boyle:
28 Days Later
Sunshine

Danny Cannon:
I Still Know What You Did Last Summer

Danny Draven:
Deathbed

Danny Pang:
Messengers, The

Danny Steinmann:
Friday the 13th Part V – A New Beginning

Dario Argento:
Deep Red (Profondo Rosso)
Inferno
Mother of Tears, The (La Terza Madre)
Phantom of the Opera [Remake] (1998)
Suspiria

Dario Piana:
Deaths of Ian Stone, The

Darren Lynn Bousman:
Saw II
Saw III
Saw IV

Dave Allen:
Puppet Master II

Dave Meyers:
Hitcher, The [Remake]

Dave Payne:
No Man's Land – The Rise of Reeker
Reeker

David Arquette:
Tripper, The

David Bruckner:
Signal, The

David Carson:
Carrie [Remake]

David Cronenberg:
Brood, The
Dead Ringers
Scanners
Spider
Videodrome

David DeCoteau:
Curse of the Puppet Master
Nightmare Sisters
Puppet Master III – Toulon's Revenge
Retro Puppet Master
Ring of Darkness
Shrieker
Sorority Babes in the Slime Ball Bowl-O-Rama

David Fincher:
Alien 3
Seven (Se7en)
Zodiac

David Flores:
Lake Placid 2

David Gebroe:
Zombie Honeymoon

David Grieco:
Evilenko

David Hackl:
Saw V

David J. Francis:
Zombie Night

David Jacobson:
Dahmer

David Keith:
Curse, The

David Koepp:
Secret Window
Stir of Echoes

David Lynch:
Blue Velvet
Lost Highway
Mulholland Dr.

David Morneau:
Them (Ils)

David Nutter:
Disturbing Behavior

David R. Ellis:
Final Destination 2
Snakes on a Plane

David S. Goyer:
Blade Trinity

David Schmoeller:
Netherworld
Puppet Master

David Slade:
30 Days of Night
Hard Candy

David Todd Ocvirk:

Kolobos

David Twohy:
Arrival, The
Below
Pitch Black

Dick Maas:
Shaft, The (Down)

Dominic Sena:
Kalifornia

Dominique Othenin-Girard:
Halloween V – The Revenge of Michael Myers
Omen IV – The Awakening, The

Don Coscarelli:
Bubba Ho-Tep

Don E. FauntLeRoy:
Anaconda 3: Offspring

Don Mancini:
Seed of Chucky

Don Siegel:
Invasion of the Body Snatchers

Don Taylor:
Damien – Omen II
Island of Dr. Moreau, The

Dong-Bin Kim:
Ring Virus, The

Douglas Cheek:
C.H.U.D.

Dwight H. Little:
Anacondas – Hunt for the Blood Orchid
Halloween IV – The Return of Michael Myers
Phantom of the Opera [Remake] (1989)

E. Elias Merhige:
Shadow of the Vampire

Edgar Wright:
Shaun of the Dead

Eduardo Sanchez:
Altered
Blair Witch Project, The

Edward Anderson:
Shuttle

Eli Roth:
Cabin Fever
Hostel
Hostel II

Ellory Elkayem:
Eight Legged Freaks
Return of the Living Dead 4 – Necropolis
Return of the Living Dead 5 – Rave to the Grave

Enrique Urbizu:
Real Friend, A (Adivina Quien Soy)

Eric Bress:
Butterfly Effect, The

Eric Bross:
Vacancy 2 – The First Cut

Eric Forsberg:
Night of the Dead

Eric Nicholas:
Alone With Her

Eric Red:
100 Feet
Bad Moon

Eric Stanze:
Deadwood Park

Erik Gardner:
Mangler Reborn, The

Ernest R. Dickerson:
Bones
Demon Knight

Ernie Barbarash:
Cube Zero
Stir of Echoes 2 – Homecoming

Ethan Wiley:
House II – The Second Story

F.W. Murnau:
Nosferatu [Silent]

Fabrice Canepa:
Dead End

Fabrice du Welz:
Calvaire (The Ordeal)

Farhad Mann:
Lawnmower Man 2 – Jobe's War, The

Fran Rubel Kuzui:
Buffy the Vampire Slayer

Francis Ford Coppola:
Bram Stoker's Dracula

Francis Lawrence:
Constantine
I Am Legend

Franck Khalfoun:
P2

Franck Vestiel:
Eden Log

Frank Darabont:
Mist, The

Frank Marshall:
Arachnophobia
Congo

Fraser Clarke Heston:
Needful Things

Fred Dekker:
Monster Squad, The

Fred Olen Ray:
Silent Venom

Fred Walton:
April Fool's Day

Freddie Francis:
Tales from the Crypt

Frederico Prosperi:
Curse 2 – The Bite

Fruit Chan:
3 Extremes (Sam Gang Yi)

Gabriel Bartalos:
Skinned Deep

Gabriele Albanesi:
Last House in the Woods, The (Il Bosco Fuori)

Gary Fleder:
Kiss the Girls

Gary Jones:
Boogeyman 3

Gary Marcum:
Gates of Hell II – Dead Awakening, The (Through the Fire)

Gary Sherman:

Dead & Buried
Poltergeist III
Raw Meat (Death Line)

Gary Ugarek:
Deadlands – The Rising

Gela Babluani:
13 Tzameti

Geoffrey Sax:
White Noise

George A. Romero:
Bruiser
Crazies, The
Creepshow
Dark Half, The
Dawn of the Dead
Day of the Dead
Diary of the Dead
Land of the Dead
Martin
Night of the Living Dead

George Bessudo:
Lake Dead

George McCowan:
Frogs

George Mihalka:
My Bloody Valentine

George Miller:
Twilight Zone – The Movie
Witches of Eastwick, The

George P. Cosmatos:
Leviathan

George Ratliff:
Joshua (2007)

Gerald Nott:

Quick and the Undead, The

Giacomo Cimini:
Red Riding Hood

Gilbert Adler:
Bordello of Blood
Demon Knight

Glen Morgan:
Black Christmas [Remake]

Glenn Standring:
Perfect Creature

Gordon Hessler:
Cry of the Banshee

Gore Verbinski:
Ring, The

Graham Baker:
Omen III – The Final Conflict, The

Grant Harvey:
Ginger Snaps Back – The Beginning

Greg McLean:
Rogue
Wolf Creek

Greg Spence:
Prophecy II, The

Greg Strause:
Aliens vs. Predator Requiem

Gregg Bishop:
Dance of the Dead
Other Side, The

Gregory Dark:
See No Evil

Gregory Hoblit:
Untraceable

Gregory Widen:
Prophecy, The

Gregory Wilson:
Girl Next Door, The

Guillermo del Toro:
Blade II
Devil's Backbone, The (El Espinazo del Diablo)
Hellboy
Hellboy II – The Golden Army
Mimic
Pan's Labyrinth (El Laberinto del Fauno)

Gus Van Zant:
Psycho [Remake]

Hal Masonberg:
Plague, The

Hans Horn:
Open Water 2 – Adrift

Hernan Saez:
Plaga Zombie
Plaga Zombie – Mutant Zone

Herschell Gordon Lewis:
Blood Feast
Blood Feast 2: All U Can Eat
Gore Gore Girls, The
Gruesome Twosome, The
Two Thousand Maniacs!
Wizard of Gore, The

Hideo Nakata:
Dark Water (Honoguari Mizu No Soko Kara)
Kaidan
Ring 2, The
Ringu
Ringu 2

Hope Perello:
Howling VI – The Freaks, The

Igor Shavlak:
Trackman

Ingmar Bergman:
Virgin Spring, The (Jungfrukallan)

Isaac Webb:
First Born

Ivan Reitman:
Ghostbusters
Ghostbusters 2

J. Mackye Gruber:
Butterfly Effect, The

J.R. Bookwalter:
Dead Next Door, The

J.S. Cardone:
8MM 2
Forsaken, The
Shadowzone
Wicked Little Things

J.T. Petty:
Mimic 3 – The Sentinel

Jack Bender:
Child's Play 3

Jack Sholder:
Hidden, The
Nightmare on Elm Street 2 – Freddy's Revenge, A
Wishmaster 2 – Evil Never Dies

Jacob Gentry:
Signal, The

Jake Kennedy:
Days of Darkness

Jake West:
Evil Aliens

James Cameron:
Abyss, The
Aliens

James Foley:
Fear (1996)

James Glenn Dudelson:
Creepshow 3
Day of the Dead 2: Contagium

James Gunn:
Slither

James Isaac:
House III – The Horror Show
Jason X

James K. Jones:
Crazy Eights

James Mangold:
Identity

James Wan:
Dead Silence
Death Sentence
Saw

James Watkins:
Eden Lake

James Wong:
Final Destination
Final Destination 3

Jamie Blanks:
Storm Warning
Urban Legend
Valentine

Jamie Dixon:
Bats: Human Harvest

Jan de Bont:
Haunting, The [Remake]

Jason Christ:
Savage Harvest 2 – October Moon

Jason Horton:
Rise of the Undead

Jason Todd Ipson:
Unrest

Jason Wulfsohn:
Bone Snatcher, The

Jaume Balaguero:
Darkness
To Let (Para Entrar a Vivar)

Jaume Collet-Serra:
House of Wax [Remake]

Jay Chandrasekhar:
Club Dread

Jay Lee:
Zombie Strippers

Jean-Baptiste Andrea:
Dead End

Jean-Claude Lord:
Visiting Hours

Jean de Segonzac:
Mimic 2

Jean-Pierre Jeunet:
Alien Resurrection

Jeannot Szwarc:
Jaws 2

Jeff Betancourt:
Boogeyman 2

Jeff Bleckner:
Beast, The

Jeff Broadstreet:
Night of the Living Dead 3-D

Jeff Brookshire:
Awaken the Dead

Jeff Buhler:
Insanitarium

Jeff Burr:
Leatherface – The Texas Chainsaw Massacre 3
Puppet Master IV – When Bad Puppets Turn Good
Puppet Master V – The Final Chapter

Jeff Burton:
Dead End Road

Jeff Crook:
Salvage

Jeff Lieberman:
Satan's Little Helper

Jeff Wadlow:
Cry_Wolf

Jeffrey Bloom:
Flowers in the Attic

Jeffrey Scott Lando:
Decoys – The Second Seduction

Jeremy Haft:
Tamara

Jeremy Kasten:
All Souls Day – Dia de los Muertos
Wizard of Gore [Remake]

Jeremy Rafn:
Soho Square

Jeremy Saulnier:
Murder Party

Jesse Baget:
Wrestlemaniac (El Mascarado Massacre)

Ji-Woon Kim:
3 Extremes II (Saam Gaang)
Tale of Two Sisters, A (Janghwa, Hongryeon)

Jim Gillespie:
I Know What You Did Last Summer

Jim Hemphill:
Bad Reputation

Jim Kaufman:
Night of the Demons 3

Jim Mickle:
Mulberry Street

Jim Power:
Tommyknockers, The

Jim Sonzero:
Pulse [Remake]

Jim Wynorski:
Chopping Mall
Return of Swamp Thing, The

Joby Harold:
Awake

Jody Dwyer:
Dying Breed

Joe Alves:
Jaws 3

Joe Berlinger:
Book of Shadows – Blair Witch 2

Joe Chapelle:
Halloween VI – The Curse of Michael Myers
Phantoms

Joe Charbanic:
Watcher, The

Joe Dante:
Gremlins
Gremlins 2 – The New Batch
Howling, The
Twilight Zone – The Movie

Joe Lynch:
Wrong Turn 2 – Dead End

Joel Moore:
Spiral

Joel Schumacher:
8MM
Flatliners
Lost Boys, The
Number 23, The

Joel Soisson:
Maniac Cop 3 – Badge of Silence
Prophecy IV – Uprising, The
Prophecy V – Forsaken, The
Pulse 2 – Afterlife
Pulse 3 – Invasion

John Boorman:
Deliverance
Exorcist II – The Heretic, The

John Bruno:
Virus

John 'Bud' Cardos:
Mutant (Night Shadows)

John Carl Buechler:
Friday the 13th Part VII – The New Blood
Miner's Massacre (Curse of the Forty-Niner)

John Carpenter:
Body Bags
Christine
Fog, The
Ghosts of Mars
Halloween
In the Mouth of Madness
Prince of Darkness
Someone's Watching Me!
They Live
Thing, The
Vampires
Village of the Damned [Remake]

John Dahl:
Joy Ride

John Fawcett:
Dark, The
Ginger Snaps

John Frankenheimer:
Island of Dr. Moreau, The [Remake]

John Gray:
Helter Skelter [Remake]

John Gulager:
Feast
Feast II – Sloppy Seconds
Feast III – The Happy Finish

John Harrison:
Tales from the Darkside – The Movie

John Hough:
Howling IV – The Original Nightmare, The

John Lafia:
Child's Play 2
Man's Best Friend

John Landis:
American Werewolf in London, An
Innocent Blood
Twilight Zone – The Movie

John Lechago:
Blood Gnome

John Maybury:
Jacket, The

John McNaughton:
Henry – Portrait of a Serial Killer

John McTierman:
Predator

John Ottman:
Urban Legends 2 – The Final Cut

John R. Leonetti:
Butterfly Effect 2, The

John Moore:
Omen, The [Remake]

John Pieplow:
Strangeland

John Polson:
Swimfan

John Schlesinger:
Pacific Heights

John Shiban:
Rest Stop – Dead Ahead

John Simpson:

Amusement

John Stockwell:
Turistas

Joji Iida:
Rasen

Jon Amiel:
Copycat

Jon Knautz:
Jack Brooks – Monster Slayer

Jonathan Demme:
Silence of the Lambs

Jonathan Hensleigh:
Welcome to the Jungle

Jonathan King:
Black Sheep

Jonathan Liebesman:
Darkness Falls
Texas Chainsaw Massacre – The Beginning, The

Joon-ho Bong:
Host, The (Gwoemul)

Jorge Montesi:
Omen IV – The Awakening, The

Joseph Mangine:
Neon Maniacs

Joseph Ruben:
Good Son, The

Joseph Sargent:
Jaws – The Revenge

Joseph Zito:
Friday the 13th Part IV – The Final Chapter

Josh Crook:
Salvage

Josh Klausner:
4th Floor, The

Joy N. Houck Jr.:
Creature from Black Lake

Juan Antonio Bayona:
Orphanage, The (El Orfanato)

Juan Carlos Fresnadillo:
28 Weeks Later

Juan Piquer Simon:
Slugs

Julien Maury:
Inside (l'interieur)

Karl Kozak:
Clawed – The Legend of Sasquatch (The Unknown)

Kathryn Bigelow:
Near Dark

Katja Von Garnier:
Blood and Chocolate

Katt Shea:
Rage – Carrie 2, The

Keith Samples:
Single White Female 2 – The Psycho

Keith Walley:
Speck

Ken Russell:
Altered States

Ken Wiederhorn:

Eyes of a Stranger
Return of the Living Dead 2

Kenneth Branagh:
Mary Shelley's Frankenstein

Kevin Connor:
From Beyond the Grave

Kevin Higgins:
Plasterhead

Kevin Tenney:
Arrival II, The (The Second Arrival)
Night of the Demons

Kevin Yagher:
Hellraiser IV – Bloodline

Ki-Hwan Oh:
Voices (Du Saram-Yida)

Kim Henkel:
Texas Chainsaw Massacre 4 – The Next Generation, The

Kit Ryan:
Botched

Kiyoshi Kurosawa:
Pulse (Kairo)
Retribution (Sakebi)

Koldo Serra:
Backwoods, The (Bosque de Sombras)

Kurt Wimmer:
Ultraviolet

Lamberto Bava:
Demons (Demoni)
Demons 2 (Demoni 2 – L'incubo Ritorna)

Lance W. Dreeson:
Big Bad Wolf

Lance Weiler:
Last Broadcast, The

Larry Cohen:
It's Alive
It's Alive 2 – It Lives Again
It's Alive 3 – Island of the Alive
Q – The Winged Serpent
Stuff, The

Larry Fessenden:
Last Winter, The

Lawrence Kasdan:
Dreamcatcher

Lee Tamahori:
Along Came a Spider
Edge, The

Len Wiseman:
Underworld
Underworld – Evolution

Leon Klimovsky:
Vengeance of the Zombies (La Rebelion de las Muertas)

Lewis Gilbert:
Haunted

Lewis Teague:
Cat's Eye
Cujo

Lex Halaby:
Snakes on a Plane

Linda Hassani:
Dark Angel – The Ascent

Louis Morneau:
Bats
Hitcher II – I've Been Waiting, The

Luca Bercovici:
Ghoulies

Lucio Fulci:
Beyond, The (Seven Doors of Death)
City of the Living Dead (The Gates of Hell)
House by the Cemetery (Quella Villa Accanto al Cimitero)
New York Ripper, The (Lo Squartatore di New York)
Zombie (Zombi 2)
Zombie 3 (Zombi 3)

Lucky McKee:
May
Red
Woods, The

Luis Camara:
Steel Trap

Luis Llosa:
Anaconda

M. Night Shyamalan:
Happening, The
Lady in the Water
Signs
Sixth Sense, The
Unbreakable
Village, The

Makoto Kamiya:
Resident Evil – Degeneration

Marc Fratto:
Zombies Anonymous (Last Rites of the Dead)

Marc Scholermann:
Pathology

Marcus Nispel:
Friday the 13th [Remake]
Texas Chainsaw Massacre , The [Remake]

Mariano Baino:
Dark Waters

Mark E. Poole:
Dead Moon Rising

Mark Edwin Robinson:
Breaking Dawn

Mark Goldblatt:
Dead Heat

Mark Jones:
Leprechaun
Triloquist

Mark Pavia:
Night Flier, The

Mark Romanek:
One Hour Photo

Mark Young:
Tooth & Nail

Martin Barnewitz:
Room 205 (Kollegiet)

Mary Harron:
American Psycho

Mary Lambert:
Pet Sematary
Pet Sematary Two
Urban Legends 3 – Bloody Mary

Masayuki Ochiai:
Infection (Kansen)

Mateo Gil:
Spectre (Regreso A Moira)

Mathias Dinter:
Night of the Living Dorks (Die Nacht der Lebenden Loser)

Mathieu Kassovitz:
Gothika

Matt Cunningham
Mangler Reborn, The

Matt Reeves:
Cloverfield

Matt Zettell:
Cellar Door, The

Matthew Bright:
Ted Bundy

Matthew Hastings:
Decoys

Matthew Leutwyler:
Dead & Breakfast
Unearthed

Maurice Devereaux:
Slashers

Mervyn LeRoy:
Bad Seed, The

Michael A. Simpson:
Sleepaway Camp 2 – Unhappy Campers
Sleepaway Camp 3 – Teenage Wasteland

Michael Anderson:
Orca – The Killer Whale

Michael Caton-Jones:
Basic Instinct 2

Michael Cohn:
Snow White – A Tale of Terror

Michael Curtiz:
Mystery of the House of Wax

Michael Feifer:
Ed Gein – The Butcher of Plainfield
Graveyard, The
Grim Reaper, The

Michael Gornick:
Creepshow 2

Michael Hamilton-Wright:
Mangler 2, The

Michael Hurst:
House of the Dead II

Michael J. Bassett:
Deathwatch
Wilderness

Michael Katleman:
Primeval

Michael Mann:
Manhunter

Michael Miller:
National Lampoon's Class Reunion

Michael Oblowitz:
Breed, The (2001)
Hammerhead

Michael Roesch:
Brotherhood of Blood

Michael Rymer:
Queen of the Damned

Michael Spierig:
Undead

Michael Weisz:
Hills Have Eyes 2, The

Michael Winner:
Sentinel, The

Michele Soavi:
Cemetery Man (Dellamorte Dellamore)
Church, The (La Chiesa)

Michelle Maxwell McLaren:
Population 436

Mick Garris:
Desperation
Psycho IV – The Beginning
Quicksilver Highway
Riding the Bullet
Shining, The [Remake]
Sleepwalkers

Mickey Liddell:
Haunting of Molly Hartley, The

Mikael Hafstrom:
1408

Mikael Saloman:
Salem's Lot [Remake]

Mike Mendez:
Gravedancers, The

Mike Nichols:
Wolf

Mitchell Altieri:
April Fool's Day [Remake]
Hamiltons, The

Mitchell Lichtenstein:
Teeth

Morgan J. Freeman:
American Psycho 2 – All American Girl

Nacho Cerda:

Abandoned, The

Narciso Ibanez Serrador:
Blame, The (La Culpa)
Who Can Kill a Child? (Island of the Damned)

Neal Sundstrom:
Howling V – The Rebirth, The

Neil Jordan:
Interview with the Vampire

Neil Kinsella:
Ice Queen

Neil LaBute:
Lakeview Terrace

Neil Marshall:
Descent, The
Dog Soldiers
Doomsday

Nelson McCormick:
Prom Night [Remake]

Nicholas Gessner:
Little Girl Who Lived Down the Lane, The

Nicholas Mastandrea:
Breed, The (2006)

Nick Hamm:
Hole, The

Nick Lyon:
Species IV – The Awakening

Nick Stillwell:
Jekyll + Hyde

Nimrod Antal:
Vacancy

Nonzee Nimibutr:
3 Extremes II (Saam Gaang)

Noria Tsuruta:
Premonition (Yogen)
Ringu 0

Ole Bornedal:
Substitute, The (Vikaren)

Oliver Hirschbiegel:
Invasion, The

Oliver Stone:
Natural Born Killers

Oxide Pang Chun:
Messengers, The

P.J. Pesce:
From Dusk till Dawn 3 – The Hangman's Daughter
Lost Boys II – The Tribe, The

Pablo Pares:
Plaga Zombie
Plaga Zombie – Mutant Zone

Paco Plaza:
Christmas Tale, A (Cuento de Navidad)

Paddy Breathnach:
Shrooms

Patrick Lussier:
My Bloody Valentine [Remake]
Prophecy III – The Ascent, The
White Noise 2 – The Light

Patrick Rae:
Empty Acre, The

Patty Jenkins:
Monster

Paul Andrew Williams:
Cottage, The

Paul Bales:
Legion of the Dead

Paul Etheredge:
Buried Alive [Web Series]
Hellbent

Paul Fox:
Dark Hours, The

Paul Lynch:
Prom Night

Paul Michael Glaser:
Running Man, The

Paul Schrader:
Dominion – Prequel to the Exorcist

Paul Verhoeven:
Basic Instinct
Hollow Man

Paul W.S. Anderson:
Aliens vs. Predator
Event Horizon
Resident Evil

Paul Ziller:
Loch Ness Terror (Beyond Loch Ness)

Pete Riski:
Dark Floors, The

Peter Burger:
Tattooist, The

Peter Chan:
3 Extremes II (Saam Gaang)

Peter Hyams:

End of Days
Relic, The

Peter Jackson:
Dead Alive (Braindead)
Frighteners, The

Peter Manoogian:
Seedpeople

Peter Medak:
Species II

Peter Mervis:
Dead Men Walking

Peter R. Simpson:
Prom Night III   The Last Kiss

Peter Scheerer:
Brotherhood of Blood

Peter Spierig:
Undead

Peter Svatek:
Bleeders

Peter Webber:
Hannibal Rising

Peter Yates:
Deep, The

Phedon Papamichael:
From Within

Phil Flores:
April Fool's Day [Remake]
Hamiltons, The

Philip Adrian Booth:
Death Tunnel

Philip Chidel:
Subject Two

Philip Kaufman:
Invasion of the Body Snatchers [Remake]

Phillip Noyce:
Dead Calm

Philippe Mora:
Howling II – Your Sister is a Werewolf, The
Howling III – The Marsupials, The

Piraphan Laoyont:
Sick Nurses (Suay Laak Sai)

Quentin Tarantino:
Death Proof

Rachel Talalay:
Freddy's Dead – The Final Nightmare

Ralph S. Singleton:
Graveyard Shift

Randy Daudlin:
Bottom Feeder

Ray Milland:
Panic in Year Zero!

Renny Harlin:
Deep Blue Sea
Exorcist – The Beginning
Nightmare on Elm Street 4 – The Dream Master, A

Richard Brandes:
Penny Dreadful
Vampires – Out for Blood

Richard Crudo:
Against the Dark

Richard Donner:

Omen, The

Richard Franklin:
Psycho II
Visitors

Richard Griffin:
Feeding the Masses

Richard Jeffries:
Organizm (Living Hell)

Richard Kelly:
Donnie Darko

Rick Bota:
Hellraiser VI – Hellseeker
Hellraiser VII – Deader
Hellraiser VIII - Hellworld

Rick Rosenthal:
Halloween II
Halloween VIII – Resurrection

Ridley Scott:
Alien
Hannibal

Rob Hedden:
Friday the 13th Part VIII – Jason Takes Manhattan

Rob Reiner:
Misery

Rob Schmidt:
Alphabet Killer, The
Wrong Turn

Rob Spera:
Leprechaun 5 – In the Hood

Rob Zombie:
Devil's Rejects, The
Halloween [Remake]

Robert Englund:
976-EVIL
Killer Pad

Robert Hall:
Lightning Bug

Robert Harmon:
Hitcher, The
They

Robert Hiltzik:
Return to Sleepaway Camp
Sleepaway Camp

Robert Kurtzman:
Buried Alive
Rage, The
Wishmaster

Robert Parigi:
Love Object

Robert Rodriguez:
Faculty, The
From Dusk till Dawn
Planet Terror

Robert Wilson:
Dead Mary

Robert Wise:
Haunting, The

Robert Zemeckis:
Beowulf
What Lies Beneath

Rockne S. O'Bannon:
Fear (1990)

Rod Daniel:

Teen Wolf

Rodman Flender:
Idle Hands
Leprechaun 2

Roger Corman:
Tales of Terror

Roger Donaldson:
Species

Roger Spottiswoode:
Terror Train

Roland Joffe:
Captivity

Rolfe Kanefsky:
Nightmare Man

Roman Polanski:
Ninth Gate, The
Rosemary's Baby
Tenant, The (Le Locataire)

Ron Oliver:
Prom Night III – The Last Kiss

Ron Underwood:
Tremors

Ronny Yu:
Bride of Chucky
Freddy vs. Jason

Rouben Mamoulian:
Dr. Jekyll and Mr. Hyde

Roy Knyrim:
Cemetery Gates

Roy Ward Baker:
Vault of Horror

Ruggero Deodato:
Cannibal Holocaust

Rupert Julian:
Phantom of the Opera [Silent]

Rupert Wainwright:
Fog, The [Remake]

Russell Mulcahy:
Resident Evil – Extinction

Rusty Cundieff:
Tales from the Hood

Ryan Schifrin:
Abominable

Ryuhei Kitamura:
Versus

S.S. Wilson:
Tremors 2 – Aftershocks
Tremors 4 – The Legend Begins

Sam Raimi:
Army of Darkness
Evil Dead, The
Evil Dead 2 – Dead by Dawn
Gift, The

Scooter McCrae:
Shatter Dead

Scott Derrickson:
Exorcism of Emily Rose, The
Hellraiser V – Inferno

Scott Glosserman:
Behind the Mask: The Rise of Leslie Vernon

Scott Reynolds:
Ugly, The

Scott Spiegel:
From Dusk till Dawn 2 – Texas Blood Money

Scott Thomas:
Flight of the Living Dead – Outbreak on a Plane

Sean Ellis:
Broken, The

Sean S. Cunningham:
Deepstar Six
Friday the 13th

Sebastian Gutierrez:
Rise – Blood Hunter

Seth Grossman:
Butterfly Effect 3: Revelations, The

Seth Pinsker:
Hidden 2, The

Shane Meadows:
Dead Man's Shoes

Shannon Hubbell:
Rise of the Undead

Shannon Young:
Razor Eaters

Sharon Bridgeman:
Van Helsing – The London Assignment

Shawn Papazian:
Rest Stop – Don't Look Back

Sheldon Winston:
Shallow Ground

Shinya Tsukamoto:
Nightmare Detective (Akumi Tantai)

Shun Nakahara:
Tomie 5 – Forbidden Fruit

Sidney Salkow:
Twice Told Tales

Simon Boyes:
Broken

Stanley Kubrick:
Shining, The

Stefan Avalos:
Last Broadcast, The

Stefan Ruzowitsky:
Anatomy (Anatomie)
Anatomy 2 (Anatomie 2)

Stephen Ayromlooi:
Leprechaun 6 – Back to tha Hood

Stephen Bradley:
Boy Eats Girl

Stephen Chiodo:
Killer Klowns from Outer Space

Stephen Frears:
Mary Reilly

Stephen Goldmann:
Trailer Park of Terror

Stephen Hopkins:
Ghost and the Darkness, The
Nightmare on Elm Street 5 – The Dream Child, A
Predator 2
Reaping, The

Stephen King:
Maximum Overdrive

Stephen Norrington:

Blade

Stephen Sommers:
Deep Rising
Van Helsing

Stephen Spielberg:
Duel
Jaws
Twilight Zone – The Movie

Stephen T. Kay:
Boogeyman

Stevan Mena:
Brutal Massacre – A Comedy
Malevolence

Steve Barker:
Outpost

Steve Beck:
Ghost Ship

Steve Miner:
Day of the Dead [Remake]
Friday the 13th Part II
Friday the 13th Part III
Halloween VII – H20
House
Lake Placid

Steven C. Miller:
Automaton Transfusion

Steven R. Monroe:
House of 9

Stewart Hopewell:
Slaughter

Stuart Gillard:
Creature

Stuart Gordon:
Castle Freak
Dagon
From Beyond
Re-Animator
Stuck

Stuart Orme:
Puppet Masters, The

Sturla Gunnarsson:
Beowulf & Grendel

Sylvain White:
I'll Always Know What You Did Last Summer

T. Hayes Hunter:
Ghoul, The

Takashi Miike:
3 Extremes (Sam Gang Yi)
Audition (Odishon)
Demon Pond (Yasha-Ga-Ike) [Stage]

Takashi Shimizu:
Grudge, The
Grudge 2, The
Ju-On
Ju-On 2
Marebito
Reincarnation (Rinne)
Tomie 4 – Rebirth

Taylor Hackford:
Devil's Advocate
Dolores Claiborne

Ted Nicolaou:
Bad Channels
Subspecies
Subspecies II – Bloodstone
Subspecies III – Bloodlust
Subspecies IV – Bloodstorm
Vampire Journals

Terrence Malcik:
Badlands

Terry West:
Flesh for the Beast

Thodsapol Siriwiwat:
Sick Nurses (Suay Laak Sai)

Thom Eberhardt:
Night of the Comet

Thom Fitzgerald:
Blood Moon (Wolf Girl)

Thom Mauer:
Beyond the Wall of Sleep

Thomas Smugala:
Apocalypse and the Beauty Queen

Ti West:
Roost, The

Tibor Takacs:
Gate, The
Gate II – Return to the Nightmare, The

Tim Burton:
Beetlejuice
Sleepy Hollow

Tim Kincaid:
Breeders

Tim McCann:
Poker Club, The

Tim Southam:
Island of the Dead

Tim Sullivan:
2001 Maniacs
Driftwood

Timothy Friend:
Cadaverella

Timur Bekmambetov:
Day Watch (Dnevnoy Dozor)
Night Watch (Nochnoy Dozor)

Tobe Hooper:
Body Bags
Lifeforce
Mangler, The
Mortuary
Poltergeist
Salem's Lot
Texas Chainsaw Massacre, The
Texas Chainsaw Massacre 2, The

Toby Wilkins:
Splinter

Tod Browning:
Freaks

Tom Gries:
Helter Skelter

Tom Holland:
Child's Play
Langoliers, The
Thinner

Tom Lewis:
Evil's City

Tom McLoughlin:
Friday the 13th Part VI – Jason Lives

Tom Savini:
Night of the Living Dead [Remake]

Tom Shankland:
Killing Gene, The (W Delta Z [WAZ])

Tomijiro Mitsuishi:
Tomie – Replay

Tommy Lee Wallace:
Halloween III: Season of the Witch
It
Vampires – Los Muertos

Tommy O'Haver:
American Crime, An

Tony Krantz:
Otis
Sublime

Tony Maylam:
Burning, The

Tony Randel:
Children of the Night
Hellbound – Hellraiser II

Tony Scott:
Hunger, The

Tor Ramsey:
Children of the Living Dead

Toshiro Inomata:
Tomie 2 – Another Face

Travis Betz:
Joshua (2006)

Tripp Reed:
Manticore

Trygve Allister Diesen:
Red

Turi Meyer:
Candyman 3: Day of the Dead
Sleepstalker

Ubaldo Ragona:
Last Man on Earth, The

Umberto Lenzi:
Nightmare City (Incubo Sulla Citta Contaminata)

Uwe Boll:
Alone in the Dark
Bloodrayne
Bloodrayne 2: Deliverance
House of the Dead

Victor Fleming:
Dr. Jekyll and Mr. Hyde [Remake]

Victor Garcia:
Return to House on Haunted Hill

Victor Halperin:
White Zombie

Victor Salva:
Jeepers Creepers
Jeepers Creepers 2

Vincent Robert:
Fear, The

Vincenzo Natali:
Cube

Walter Salles:
Dark Water [Remake]

Warren P. Sonoda:
5ive Girls

Wellson Chin:
Vampire Hunters (The Era of Vampires)

Wes Craven:
Cursed
Deadly Friend
Hills Have Eyes, The

Hills Have Eyes II, The
Last House on the Left, The
New Nightmare
Nightmare on Elm Street, A
People Under the Stairs, The
Red Eye
Scream
Scream 2
Scream 3
Shocker
Summer of Fear (Stranger in Our House)
Swamp Thing

William Brent Bell:
Stay Alive

William Castle:
House on Haunted Hill, The

William F. Claxton:
Night of the Lepus

William Friedkin:
Bug
Exorcist, The

William Lustig:
Maniac Cop
Maniac Cop 2
Maniac Cop 3 – Badge of Silence

William Malone:
Feardotcom
House on Haunted Hill, The [Remake]

William Peter Blatty:
Exorcist III, The

William Victor Schotten:
Dead Life

William Wedig:
Rise of the Dead

William Wesley:

Scarecrows

Wilson Yip:
Bio-Zombie

Wolf Rilla:
Village of the Damned

Wolfgang Petersen:
Outbreak

Xavier Gens:
Frontiere(s)

Xavier Palud:
Them (Ils)

Zack Snyder:
Dawn of the Dead [Remake]

Zev Berman:
Borderland

Multiple:
J-Horror Anthology – Legends
J-Horror Anthology – Underworld
Severed Head Network, The
Viscera 2007

MOVIES BY SUB-GENRE

Aliens:
Abyss, The
Alien
Alien 3
Alien Raiders
Alien Resurrection
Aliens
Aliens vs. Predator
Aliens vs. Predator Requiem
Altered
Arrival, The
Arrival II, The (The Second Arrival)
Bad Channels
Breeders
Dark City
Dead Space – Downfall
Decoys
Decoys – The Second Seduction
Dreamcatcher
Evil Aliens
Faculty, The
Hidden, The
Hidden 2, The
Killer Klowns from Outer Space
Predator
Predator 2
Progeny
Puppet Masters, The
Signs
Slither
Species
Species II
Species III
Species IV – The Awakening
Substitute (Vikaren)
They Live
Thing, The
Thing from Another World, The
Tommyknockers, The
Undead
Waxwork II – Lost in Time

Animals:

Anaconda
Anaconda 3 – The Offspring
Anacondas – The Hunt for the Blood Orchid
Arachnophobia
Bats
Bats – Human Harvest
Beast, The
Birds, The
Black Sheep
Bone Snatcher, The
Breed, The (2006)
Congo
Creepshow
Cujo
Deep Blue Sea
Edge, The
Eight Legged Freaks
Frogs
Ghost and the Darkness, The
Isolation
Jaws
Jaws 2
Jaws 3
Jaws – The Revenge
Lake Placid
Lake Placid 2
Man's Best Friend
Night of the Lepus
Orca – The Killer Whale
Primeval
Rogue
Roost, The
Silent Venom
Slugs
Snakes on a Plane
Tales from the Darkside – The Movie
Wilderness

Animated:
Beowulf
Dead Space – Downfall
Resident Evil – Degeneration
Van Helsing – The London Assignment

Anthology:
3 Extremes (Sam Gang Yi)

3 Extremes II (Saam Gaang)
Body Bags
Cat's Eye
Cradle of Fear
Creepshow
Creepshow 2
Creepshow 3
From Beyond the Grave
Quicksilver Highway
Tales from the Crypt
Tales from the Darkside – The Movie
Tales from the Hood
Tales of Terror
Tears of Kali
Tomie 2 – Another Face
Trilogy of Terror
Twice Told Tales
Twilight Zone – The Movie
Vault of Horror

Biological:
Bacterium
Body Snatchers
Creepshow
Creepshow 2
Curse, The
Die, Monster, Die!
Happening, The
Invasion, The
Invasion of the Body Snatchers
Invasion of the Body Snatchers [Remake]
Organizm (Living Hell)
Ruins, The
Seedpeople
Stuff, The

Cannibals:
Cannibal Holocaust
Doomsday
Ravenous
Raw Meat (Death Line)
Tooth & Nail
Welcome to the Jungle

Cults:

Bay Cove (Bay Coven)
Believers
Borderland
Gates of Hell II – Dead Awakening, The (Through the Fire)
Haunting of Molly Hartley, The
Helter Skelter
Helter Skelter [Remake]
Lord of Illusions

Demonic Possession:
5ive Girls
976-EVIL
Army of Darkness
Dead Mary
Deathbed
Demon Knight
Desperation
Dominion – Prequel to the Exorcist
Evil Dead, The
Evil Dead II – Dead by Dawn
Exorcism of Emily Rose, The
Exorcist, The
Exorcist II – The Heretic, The
Exorcist III, The
Exorcist – The Beginning
Idle Hands
Night of the Demons
Night of the Demons 2
Night of the Demons 3
Nightmare Sisters
Prince of Darkness
Savage Harvest
Savage Harvest 2 – October Blood
Sorority Babes in the Slime Ball Bowl-A-Rama

Demons:
Church, The (La Chiesa)
Constantine
Dark Angel – The Ascent
Demon Knight
Demons (Demoni)
Demons 2 – The Nightmare Continues (Demoni 2 – L'incubo Ritorna)
Doom
Entrance, The
Evil's City
Flesh for the Beast

Gate, The
Gate 2 – Return to the Nightmare, The
Ghoulies
Ghoulies II
Hellbound – Hellraiser II
Hellboy
Hellboy II – The Golden Army
Hellraiser
Hellraiser III – Hell on Earth
Hellraiser IV – Bloodlines
Hellraiser V – Inferno
Hellraiser VI – Hellseeker
Hellraiser VII – Deader
Hellraiser VIII – Hellworld
Killer Pad
Other Side, The
Prom Night III – The Last Kiss
Wishmaster
Wishmaster 2 – Evil Never Dies
Wishmaster 3 – Beyond the Gates of Hell
Wishmaster 4 – The Prophecy Fulfilled

Devil:
Damien – Omen II
Devil's Advocate, The
End of Days
Needful Things
Ninth Gate, The
Omen, The
Omen III – The Final Conflict, The
Omen IV – The Awakening, The
Omen, The [Remake]

Ghosts:
3 Extremes II (Saam Gaang)
100 Feet
1408
Abandoned, The
American Haunting, An
Baby's Room, The (La Habitacion del Nino)
Beetlejuice
Below
Blair Witch Project, The
Bones
Boogeyman
Boogeyman 3

Book of Shadows – Blair Witch 2
Chair, The
Crazy Eights
Creepshow 3
Dark, The
Dark Floors
Dark Remains
Dark Water (Honoguari Mizu No Soko Kara)
Dark Water [Remake]
Darkness
Darkness Falls
Dead Birds
Dead Silence
Deadwood Park
Death Tunnel
Deathwatch
Devil's Backbone, The (El Espinazo del Diablo)
Diary of Ellen Rimbauer, The
Driftwood
Event Horizon
Feardotcom
Fog, The
Fog, The [Remake]
Frighteners, The
From Beyond the Grave
Ghost Ship
Ghostbusters
Ghostbusters II
Ghost of Mars
Gothika
Gravedancers, The
Grudge, The
Grudge 2, The
Haunted
Haunting, The
Haunting, The [Remake]
Hello Mary Lou – Prom Night II
House
House on Haunted Hill
House on Haunted Hill [Remake]
Ju-On
Ju-On 2
Kaidan
Messengers, The
Orphanage, The (El Orfanato)
Others, The

Poltergeist
Poltergeist II – The Other Side
Poltergeist III
Pulse (Kairo)
Pulse [Remake]
Pulse 2 – Afterlife
Pulse 3 – Invasion
Rasen
Reincarnation (Rinne)
Retribution (Sakebi)
Return to House on Haunted Hill
Ring, The
Ring 2, The
Ring Virus, The
Ringu
Ringu 0
Ringu 2
Rise of the Dead
Room 205 (Kollegiet)
Rose Red
Sick Nurses (Suay Laak Sai)
Sixth Sense, The
Sleepy Hollow
Solstice
Stay Alive
Stir of Echoes
Stir of Echoes 2 – The Homecoming
Tales from the Hood
Tattooist, The
Tomie
Tomie 2 – Another Face
Tomie 3 – Replay
Tomie 4 – Rebirth
Tomie 5 – Forbidden Fruit
Twice Told Tales
Unborn but Forgotten (Hayanbang)
Unrest
Urban Legends 3 – Bloody Mary
Waxwork II – Lost in Time
What Lies Beneath
White Noise
White Noise 2 – The Light

Horror Related:
Brutal Massacre – A Comedy
His Name Was Jason

Horror Business
Lightning Bug

Infection:
28 Days Later
28 Weeks Later
Alien Raiders
Cabin Fever
Crazies, The
Curse 2 – The Bite
Dead Space – Downfall
Doomsday
Dreamcatcher
Ghost of Mars
Infection (Kansen)
Insanitarium
Island of the Dead
Leviathan
Mulberry Street
Mutant (Night Shadows)
Nightmare City (Incubo Sulla Citta Contaminata)
Outbreak
Plague, The
Rage, The
Signal, The
Splinter

Mechanical:
Arcade
Chopping Mall
Christine
Creepshow 3
Cube
Cube 2 – Hypercube
Cube Zero
Deadly Friend
Mangler, The
Mangler 2, The
Mangler Reborn, The
Maximum Overdrive
Screamers
Shaft, The (Down)
Trucks
Videodrome
Virus

Monsters:

Abominable
Alone in the Dark
Beowulf
Beowulf & Grendel
Bleeders
Blood Gnome
Bottom Feeder
Brood, The
Brotherhood of the Wolf (Le Pacte des Loupes)
C.H.U.D.
Call of Cthulhu, The [Silent]
Castle Freak
Cat's Eye
Cave, The
Cemetery Gates
Clawed – The Legend of Sasquatch (The Unknown)
Cloverfield
Creature from Black Lake
Creepshow
Dagon
Dark Floors
Deaths of Ian Stone, The
Demon Pond
Descent, The
Eden Log
Feast
Feast II – Sloppy Seconds
Feast III – The Happy Finish
From Beyond
Graveyard Shift
Gremlins
Gremlins 2 – The New Batch
Hammerhead
Host, The (Gwoemul)
House II – The Second Story
Ice Queen
In the Mouth of Madness
Island of Dr. Moreau, The
Island of Dr. Moreau, The [Remake]
It
It's Alive
It's Alive 2 – It Lives Again
It's Alive 3 – Island of the Alive
Jack Brooks – Monster Slayer
Jeepers Creepers

Jeepers Creepers 2
Lady in the Water
Langoliers, The
Lurking Fear
Man-Thing
Manticore
Mary Shelley's Frankenstein
Mimic
Mimic 2
Mimic 3 – The Sentinel
Mist, The
Monster Squad, The
My Name is Bruce
Nightbreed
Pan's Labyrinth (El Laberinto del Fauno)
Pitch Black
Q – The Winged Serpent
Relic, The
Resident Evil
Resident Evil – Apocalypse
Resident Evil – Degeneration
Resident Evil – Extinction
Return of Swamp Thing, The
Shadowzone
Shrieker
Silent Hill
Sleepwalkers
Sorority Babes in the Slime Ball Bowl-A-Rama
Splinter
Swamp Thing
Tales from the Darkside – The Movie
Tales from the Hood
They
Tremors
Tremors 2: Aftershocks
Tremors 3: Back to Perfection
Tremors 4: The Legend Begins
Twilight Zone – The Movie
Unearthed
Van Helsing
Van Helsing – The London Assignment
Village, The
Waxwork
Waxwork II – Lost in Time

Mummies:

Bubba Ho-Tep
Legion of the Dead
Monster Squad, The
Tales from the Darkside – The Movie
Waxwork

Sea Monsters:
Creature
Deep Rising
Deepstar Six
Leviathan
Loch Ness Terror (Beyond Loch Ness)

Serial Killer:
Alphabet Killer, The
Citizen X
Dahmer
Ed Gein (In the Light of the Moon)
Ed Gein – The Butcher of Plainfield
Evilenko
From Hell
Gacy
Helter Skelter
Helter Skelter [Remake]
Henry – Portrait of a Serial Killer
Hillside Strangler, The
Monster
Nightstalker
Speck
Starkweather
Ted Bundy
Zodiac

Serial Killer (Fictional):
American Psycho
American Psycho 2 – All American Girl
Badlands
Basic Instinct
Basic Instinct 2
Copycat
Creepshow 3
Dead End Road
Deep Red (Profondo Rosso)
Eyes of a Stranger
Fear (1990)

Feed
Gore Gore Girls, The
Hannibal
Hannibal Rising
Hideaway
Kalifornia
Killing Gene, The (W Delta Z [WAZ])
Kiss the Girls
Manhunter
Memory
Mr. Brooks
Natural Born Killers
New York Ripper, The (Lo Squartatore di New York)
Otis
Razor Eaters
Red Dragon
Seven (Se7en)
Silence of the Lambs
Soho Square
Ugly, The
Untraceable
Watcher, The

Short Film Compilation:
J-Horror Anthology – Legends
J-Horror Anthology – Underworld
Severed Head Network, The
Viscera 2007

Slasher / Survival:
2001 Maniacs
Amusement
Anatomy (Anatomie)
April Fool's Day
April Fool's Day [Remake]
Autopsy
Bad Dreams
Behind the Mask – The Rise of Leslie Vernon
Black Christmas
Black Christmas [Remake]
Blood Feast
Blood Feast 2 – All U Can Eat
Body Bags
Boogeyman 2
Botched
Bride of Chucky

Bruiser
Buried Alive
Burning, The
Calvaire (The Ordeal)
Camp Blood
Camp Blood 2
Candyman
Candyman 2 – Farewell to the Flesh
Candyman 3 – Day of the Dead
Child's Play
Child's Play 2
Child's Play 3
Club Dread
Cottage, The
Creep
Creepshow 2
Cry_Wolf
Curse of the Puppet Master
Dark Hours, The
Dark Ride
Dead Above Ground
Death Proof
Dentist, The
Dentist 2 – Brace Yourself, The
Devil's Rejects, The
Dying Breed
Fear, The
Fear 2 – Halloween Night, The
Final Destination
Final Destination 2
Final Destination 3
Fortress
Freak Out
Freddy vs. Jason
Freddy's Dead – The Final Nightmare
Friday the 13th
Friday the 13th Part II
Friday the 13th Part III
Friday the 13th Part IV – The Final Chapter
Friday the 13th Part V – A New Beginning
Friday the 13th Part VI – Jason Lives
Friday the 13th Part VII – The New Blood
Friday the 13th Part VIII – Jason Takes Manhattan
Friday the 13th [Remake]
Frontiere(s)
Graveyard, The

Grim Reaper
Gruesome Twosome, The
Halloween
Halloween II
Halloween IV – The Return of Michael Myers
Halloween V – The Revenge of Michael Myers
Halloween VI – The Curse of Michael Myers
Halloween VII – H20
Halloween VIII – Resurrection
Halloween [Remake]
Hatchet
Headless Horseman
Hellbent
High Tension (Haute Tension)
Hills Have Eyes, The
Hills Have Eyes Part II, The
Hills Have Eyes, The [Remake]
Hills Have Eyes 2, The
Hitcher, The
Hitcher II – I've Been Waiting for You, The
Hitcher, The [Remake]
House III – The Horror Show
House of 1000 Corpses
House of Wax [Remake]
I Know What You Did Last Summer
I Still Know What You Did Last Summer
Identity
I'll Always Know What You Did Last Summer
Inside (A l'interieur)
Jason Goes to Hell – The Final Friday
Jason X
Joshua (2006)
Joy Ride
Joy Ride 2 – Dead Ahead
Kolobos
Lake Dead
Last House in the Woods, The (Il Bosco Fuori)
Leatherface – The Texas Chainsaw Massacre 3
Leprechaun
Leprechaun 2
Leprechaun 3
Leprechaun 4 – In Space
Leprechaun 5 – In the Hood
Leprechaun 6 – Back 2 tha Hood
Malevolence
Maniac Cop

Maniac Cop 2
Maniac Cop 3 – Badge of Silence
Miner's Massacre (Curse of the Forty-Niner)
Murder Party
My Blood Valentine
My Blood Valentine [Remake]
National Lampoon's Class Reunion
Neon Maniacs
New Nightmare
Nightmare Detective (Akumi Tantai)
Nightmare Man
Nightmare on Elm Street, A
Nightmare on Elm Street 2 – Freddy's Revenge, A
Nightmare on Elm Street 3 – Dream Warriors, A
Nightmare on Elm Street 4 – The Dream Master, A
Nightmare on Elm Street 5 – The Dream Child, A
No Man's Land – The Rise of Reeker
Penny Dreadful
People Under the Stairs, The
Perkin's 14
Plasterhead
Pool, The (Swimming Pool – Der Tod Feiert Mit)
Prom Night
Prom Night IV – Deliver Us from Evil
Prom Night [Remake]
Psycho
Psycho II
Psycho III
Psycho IV – The Beginning
Psycho [Remake]
Puppet Master
Puppet Master II
Puppet Master III – Toulon's Revenge
Puppet Master IV – When Bad Puppets Turn Good
Puppet Master V – The Final Chapter
Red Riding Hood
Reeker
Rest Stop – Dead Ahead
Rest Stop – Don't Look Back
Retro Puppet Master
Return to Sleepaway Camp
Running Man, The
Satan's Little Helper
Scarecrows
Scream
Scream 2

Scream 3
See No Evil
Seed of Chucky
Severance
Shocker
Shrooms
Shuttle
Sick House, The
Skinned Deep
Slashers
Sleepaway Camp
Sleepaway Camp 2 – Unhappy Campers
Sleepaway Camp 3 – Teenage Wasteland
Sleepstalker
Steel Trap
Storm Warning
Tales from the Hood
Terror Train
Texas Chainsaw Massacre, The
Texas Chainsaw Massacre 2, The
Texas Chainsaw Massacre 4 – The Next Generation, The
Texas Chainsaw Massacre, The [Remake]
Texas Chainsaw Massacre – The Beginning, The
To Let (Para Entrar a Vivar)
Tower of Blood
Trackman
Trilogy of Terror
Triloquist
Tripper, The
Turistas
Two Thousand Maniacs!
Urban Legend
Urban Legends 2 – The Final Cut
Valentine
Visiting Hours
Voices (Du Saram-Yida)
Waxwork
Waxwork II – Lost in Time
Who Can Kill a Child? (Island of the Damned)
Wilderness
Within the Woods
Wizard of Gore, The
Wizard of Gore, The [Remake]
Wolf Creek
Wrestlemaniac (El Mascarado Massacre)
Wrong Turn

Wrong Turn 2 – Dead End

Suspense:
3 Extremes (Sam Gang Yi)
3 Extremes II (Saam Gaang)
4th Floor, The
8MM
8MM 2
13 – Game of Death (13 Game Sayawng)
13 Tzameti
Abyss, The
Alone With Her
Along Came a Spider
Altered States
American Crime, An
Anatomy 2 (Anatomie 2)
Angel Heart
Apocalypse and the Beauty Queen
Audition (Odishon)
Awake
Backwoods, The (Bosque de Sombras)
Bad Reputation
Bad Seed, The
Beyond the Wall of Sleep
Blame, The (La Culpa)
Blood Moon (Wolf Girl)
Blue Velvet
Body Bags
Breaking Dawn
Broken
Bug
Buried Alive [Web Series]
Burnt Offerings
Butterfly Effects, The
Butterfly Effect 2, The
Butterfly Effect 3 – Revelations, The
Captivity
Carrie
Carrie [Remake]
Cat's Eye
Cellar Door, The
Children of the Damned
Christmas Tale, A (Cuento de Navidad)
Cradle of Fear
Crush, The
Dark Half, The

Dead Calm
Dead Man's Shoes
Dead Ringers
Death Sentence
Deep, The
Deliverance
Disturbia
Dolores Claiborne
Donnie Darko
Dorothy Mills
Dr. Jekyll and Mr. Hyde
Dr. Jekyll and Mr. Hyde [Remake]
Duel
Eden Lake
Edge, The
Empty Acre, The
Fatal Attraction
Fear (1996)
First Born
Flatliners
Flowers in the Attic
Frailty
Freaks
Gift, The
Girl Next Door, The
Good Son, The
Hand that Rocks the Cradle, The
Hard Candy
Henry II – Portrait of a Serial Killer
Hole, The
Hollow Man
Hollow Man 2
Hostel
Hostel Part II
House of 9
House of Wax
I Know Who Killed Me
Jacket, The
Jacob's Ladder
Jekyll + Hyde
Joshua (2007)
Lady Vengeance (Chinjeolhan Geumjassi)
Lakeview Terrace
Last Broadcast, The
Last House on the Left, The
Lawnmower Man, The

Lawnmower Man 2 – Jobe's War, The
Little Girl Who Lived Down the Lane, The
Lost, The
Lost Highway
Love Object
Machinist, The
Mary Reilly
May
Misery
Mulholland Dr.
Mystery of the House of Wax
Number 23, The
Oldboy
One Hour Photo
Open Water
Open Water 2 – Adrift
P2
Pacific Heights
Panic in Year Zero!
Pathology
Phantom of the Opera, The [Silent]
Phantom of the Opera, The [Remake] (1989)
Phantom of the Opera, The [Remake] (1998)
Poker Club, The
Population 436
Premonition (Yogen)
Prophecy, The
Prophecy II, The
Prophecy III – The Ascent, The
Prophecy IV – Uprising, The
Prophecy V – Forsaken, The
Quicksilver Highway
Rage – Carrie 2, The
Raising Cain
Real Friend, A (Adivina Quien Soy)
Reaping, The
Rear Window
Red
Red Eye
Return, The
Riding the Bullet
Right at Your Door
Roman
S. Darko
Salvage
Saw

Saw II

Saw III

Saw IV

Saw V

Scanners

Secret Window

Session 9

Seventh Sign, The

Shining, The

Shining, The [Remake]

Single White Female

Single White Female 2 – The Psycho

Slaughter

Someone's Watching Me!

Spectre (Regreso A Moira)

Sphere

Spider

Spiral

Storm of the Century

Strangeland

Strangers, The

Stuck

Subject Two

Sublime

Swimfan

Sympathy for Mr. Vengeance (Boksuneun Naui Geot)

Tale of Two Sisters, A (Janghwa, Hongryeon)

Tales from the Crypt

Tales from the Hood

Tales of Terror

Teeth

Tenant, The (Le Locataire)

Them (Ils)

Transsiberian

Trilogy of Terror

Twice Told Tales

Unbreakable

Vacancy

Vacancy 2 – The First Cut

Vault of Horror

Vertigo

Videodrome

Village of the Damned

Village of the Damned [Remake]

Virgin Spring, The (Jungfrukallan)

Visitors

What's the Matter with Helen?
Whoever Slew Auntie Roo?

Vampires:
30 Days of Night
Against the Dark
Blade
Blade II
Blade – Trinity
Bloodrayne
Bloodrayne 2 – Deliverance
Bordello of Blood
Bram Stoker's Dracula
Breed, The (2001)
Brotherhood of Blood
Buffy the Vampire Slayer
Children of the Night
Day Watch (Dnevnoy Dozor)
Forsaken, The
From Dusk till Dawn
From Dusk till Dawn 2 – Texas Blood Money
From Dusk till Dawn 3 – The Hangman's Daughter
Hunger, The
I Am Legend
Innocent Blood
Interview with the Vampire
Last Man on Earth, The
Lifeforce
Lost Boys, The
Lost Boys II – The Tribe, The
Martin
Meat Market
Meat Market 2
Monster Squad, The
Near Dark
Night Flier, The
Night Watch (Nochnoy Dozor)
Nosferatu [Silent]
Omega Man, The
Perfect Creature
Queen of the Damned
Rise – Blood Hunter
Salem's Lot
Salem's Lot [Remake]
Shadow of the Vampire
Subspecies

Subspecies II – Bloodstone
Subspecies III – Bloodlust
Subspecies IV – Bloodstorm
Ultraviolet
Underworld
Underworld – Evolution
Vampire Hunters (The Era of Vampires)
Vampire Journals
Vampires
Vampires – Los Muertos
Vampires – Out for Blood
Van Helsing
Visions of Suffering
Waxwork
Waxwork II – Lost in Time

Werewolves:
American Werewolf in London, An
American Werewolf in Paris, An
Bad Moon
Big Bad Wolf
Blood and Chocolate
Cursed
Dog Soldiers
Ginger Snaps
Ginger Snaps 2 – Unleashed
Ginger Snaps Back – The Beginning
Howling, The
Howling II – Your Sister is a Werewolf, The
Howling III – The Marsupials, The
Howling IV – The Original Nightmare, The
Howling V – The Rebirth, The
Howling VI – The Freaks, The
Monster Squad, The
Silver Bullet
Teen Wolf
Teen Wolf Too
Underworld
Underworld – Evolution
Van Helsing
Waxwork
Wolf

Witchcraft:
Craft, The
Cry of the Banshee

Dunwich Horror, The
From Beyond the Grave
Inferno
Mother of Tears, The (La Terza Madre)
Netherworld
Snow White – A Tale of Terror
Summer of Fear (Stranger in Our House)
Suspiria
Tamara
Thinner
Waxwork II – Lost in Time
Witches of Eastwick, The
Woods, The

Zombies:

All Souls Day – Dia de los Muertos
Army of Darkness
Automaton Transfusion
Awaken the Dead
Beyond, The (Seven Doors of Death)
Beyond Re-Animator
Bio-Zombie (Sun Faa Sau Si)
Boy Eats Girl
Bride of Re-Animator
Cadaverella
Cemetery Man (Dellamorte Dellamore)
Children of the Living Dead
City of the Living Dead (The Gates of Hell)
Creepshow
Creepshow 2
Dance of the Dead
Dawn of the Dead
Dawn of the Dead [Remake]
Day of the Dead
Day of the Dead 2 – Contagium
Day of the Dead [Remake]
Days of Darkness
Dead & Breakfast
Dead & Buried
Dead Alive (Braindead)
Dead Heat
Dead Life
Dead Meat
Dean Men Walking
Dead Moon Rising
Dead Next Door, The

Dead Pit
Deadlands – The Rising
Diary of the Dead
Feeding the Masses
Fido
Flesh for the Beast
Flesh Freaks
Flight of the Living Dead – Outbreak on a Plane
Forest of the Dead
Ghoul, The
Ghouls, The
Hell of the Living Dead (Virus)
House II – The Second Story
House by the Cemetery (Quella Villa Accanto al Cimitero)
House of the Dead
House of the Dead II
Land of the Dead
Meat Market
Meat Market 2
Mortuary
My Boyfriend's Back
Night of the Comet
Night of the Dead
Night of the Living Dead
Night of the Living Dead [Remake]
Night of the Living Dead 3-D
Night of the Living Dorks (Die Nacht del Lebenden Loser)
Outpost
Pet Sematary
Pet Sematary Two
Plaga Zombie
Plaga Zombie – Mutant Zone
Planet Terror
Quick and the Undead, The
Re-Animator
Resident Evil
Resident Evil – Apocalypse
Resident Evil – Degeneration
Resident Evil – Extinction
Resurrected, The
Return of the Living Dead, The
Return of the Living Dead 2
Return of the Living Dead 3
Return of the Living Dead 4 – Necropolis
Return of the Living Dead 5 – Rave to the Grave
Rise of the Undead

Roost, The
Severed – Forest of the Dead
Shatter Dead
Shaun of the Dead
Slither
Trailer Park of Terror
Undead
Vengeance of the Zombies (La Rebelion de las Muertas)
Versus
Waxwork
Waxwork II – Lost in Time
White Zombie
Wicked Little Things
Zombie (Zombi 2)
Zombie 3 (Zombi 3)
Zombie 4 – After Death (Oltre la Morte)
Zombie 5 – Killing Birds (Uccelli Assassinni)
Zombie Honeymoon
Zombie Night
Zombie Strippers
Zombie Town
Zombies Anonymous (Last Rites of the Dead)

[Hidden to Conceal Spoilers]:

Broken, The
Dark Waters
Dead End
Devil's Chair, The
Disturbing Behavior
From Within
Halloween III – Season of the Witch
Hamiltons, The
Last Winter, The
Marebito
Parents
Phantoms
Ring of Darkness
Rosemary's Baby
Sentinel, The
Shallow Ground
Sunshine

MOVIES ACCORDING TO RANK

5:
28 Days Later
Alien
Aliens
American Psycho
Bram Stoker's Dracula
Candyman
Dawn of the Dead
Descent, The
Evil Dead, The
Feast
Ginger Snaps
Halloween
Hellraiser
Invasion of the Body Snatchers [Remake]
Jaws
Lightning Bug
Lost Boys, The
May
Mist, The
Murder Party
Natural Born Killers
Near Dark
Night of the Living Dead
Night of the Living Dead [Remake]
Oldboy
Omen, The
Pan's Labyrinth (El Laberinto del Fauno)
Psycho
Red
Seven (Se7en)
Shaun of the Dead
Shining, The
Silence of the Lambs, The
Spiral
Texas Chainsaw Massacre, The
Thing, The

4.5:
13 Tzameti
28 Weeks Later

Alone With Her
American Werewolf in London, An
Army of Darkness
Basic Instinct
Beyond, The (E Tu Vivrai Nel Terrore – L'aldila)
Blair Witch Project, The
Blue Velvet
Burning, The
Call of Cthulhu, The
Cannibal Holocaust
Carrie
Child's Play
Christmas Tale, A
City of the Living Dead
Cloverfield
Creepshow
Dagon
Dawn of the Dead [Remake]
Day of the Dead
Dead Alive (Braindead)
Deadwood Park
Demon Knight
Demons (Demoni)
Devil's Advocate, The
Devil's Backbone, The (El Espinazo del Diablo)
Dog Soldiers
Event Horizon
Evil Dead II: Dead by Dawn
Exorcist, The
Freaks
From Beyond
From Dusk till Dawn
Gate, The
Ginger Snaps Back: The Beginning
Girl Next Door, The
Ghostbusters
Halloween II
Hatchet
In the Mouth of Madness
Inside (A l'interieur)
Interview with the Vampire
Invasion of the Body Snatchers
Lady Vengeance
Lost, The
Lost Highway
Machinist, The

Martin
Misery
Monster Squad, The
Night of the Demons
Nightmare on Elm Street, A
Orphanage, The (El Orfanato)
Other Side, The
Parents
Phantom of the Opera, The [Silent]
Planet Terror
Prophecy, The
Re-Animator
Rear Window
Resurrected, The
Return of the Living Dead, The
Saw II
Sentinel, The
Signal, The
Silent Hill
Sixth Sense, The
Splinter
Subspecies
Suspiria
Teeth
They Live
Tremors
Unbreakable
Village of the Damned
Waxwork
Who Can Kill a Child? (Island of the Damned)
Wilderness

4:
3 Extremes (Sam Gang Yi)
8MM
13: Game of Death
30 Days of Night
Abominable
Alien Raiders
Angel Heart
Audition (Odishon)
Baby's Room, The (La Habitacion del Nino)
Bad Reputation
Bad Seed, The
Badlands
Beetlejuice

Behind the Mask: The Rise of Leslie Vernon
Birds, The
Black Christmas
Black Sheep
Blade
Blade: Trinity
Body Snatchers
Borderland
Brotherhood of the Wolf (Le Pacte des Loupes)
Brutal Massacre: A Comedy
Butterfly Effect, The
Calvaire (The Ordeal)
Castle Freak
Cemetery Man (Dellamorte Dellamore)
Chair, The
Christine
Citizen X
Constantine
Copycat
Cradle of Fear
Cube
Cujo
Damien: Omen II
Dark Hours, The
Dark Remains
Dark Waters
Day Watch (Dnevnoy Dozor)
Dead & Buried
Dead Calm
Dead End
Dead Man's Shoes
Dead Next Door, The
Dead Ringers
Death Proof
Death Sentence
Deathwatch
Deep Red (Profondo Rosso)
Demon Pond (Yasha-Ga-Ike) [Stage]
Dentist, The
Devil's Rejects, The
Dolores Claiborne
Donnie Darko
Doomsday
Dr. Jekyll and Mr. Hyde
Exorcist III, The
Faculty, The

Feed
Fido
Final Destination
Final Destination 2
Fortress
Frailty
Friday the 13th
Friday the 13th Part IV: The Final Chapter
Frighteners, The
From Hell
Gift, The
Ginger Snaps 2: Unleashed
Gremlins
Gremlins 2: The New Batch
Grudge, The
Halloween III: Season of the Witch
Hard Candy
Hellbound: Hellraiser II
Hellboy
Hellboy II: The Golden Army
Hellraiser III: Hell on Earth
Helter Skelter
Helter Skelter [Remake]
Henry – Portrait of a Serial Killer
Hideaway
High Tension (Haute Tension)
Hills Have Eyes, The [Remake]
Hillside Strangler, The
Hitcher, The
Horror Business
Host, The
Hostel Part II
House of 9
House of 1000 Corpses
House of Wax
House on Haunted Hill
Howling, The
Hunger, The
Insanitarium
Jacob's Ladder
Jeepers Creepers
Joshua (2007)
Ju-On
Kalifornia
Last House on the Left, The
Lord of Illusions

Love Object
Maniac Cop 2
Marebito
Mulberry Street
Mulholland Dr.
My Bloody Valentine
My Boyfriend's Back
New York Ripper, The
Night Watch (Nochnoy Dozor)
Nightmare City (Incubo Sulla Citta Contaminata)
Nightmare on Elm Street 3: Dream Warriors, A
Nosferatu
Otis
Pet Sematary
Poker Club, The
Poltergeist
Predator
Pulse (Kairo)
Razor Eaters
Real Friend, A (Adivina Quien Soy)
Resident Evil: Apocalypse
Return of the Living Dead 3
Ring, The
Ringu
Rogue
Roman
Rosemary's Baby
Savage Harvest
Saw
Saw III
Scanners
Scream
Severance
Shuttle
Silver Bullet
Sleepaway Camp
Slither
Spectre (Regreso A Moria)
Stir of Echoes
Storm Warning
Strangers, The
Stuck
Subspecies II: Bloodstone
Subspecies III: Bloodlust
Sunshine
Sympathy for Mr. Vengeance (Boksuneun Naui Geot)

Tale of Two Sisters, A (Janghwa, Hongryeon)
Texas Chainsaw Massacre 2, The
Texas Chainsaw Massacre, The [Remake]
Thing from Another World, The
Transsiberian
Twilight Zone: The Movie
Undead
Vault of Horror
Vertigo
Videodrome
Virgin Spring, The (Jungfrukallan)
Viscera 2007
Wishmaster
Wolf Creek
Woods, The
Zombie (Zombi 2)
Zombie Town

3.5:
100 Feet
1408
2001 Maniacs
Abandoned, The
Alien 3
Alien Resurrection
Altered States
American Crime, An
Anatomy (Anatomie)
Anatomy 2 (Anatomie 2)
Arachnophobia
Autopsy
Beowulf
Beowulf & Grendel
Beyond Re-Animator
Big Bad Wolf
Bio-Zombie (Sun Faa Sau Si)
Blade II
Blame, The (La Culpa)
Blood Moon
Body Bags
Botched
Boy Eats Girl
Bride of Chucky
Bride of Re-Animator
Broken, The
Bubba Ho-Tep

C.H.U.D.
Children of the Night
Church, The (La Chiesa)
Congo
Cottage, The
Crazies, The
Creep
Creepshow 2
Crush, The
Cry of the Banshee
Cube 2: Hypercube
Dance of the Dead
Dark City
Dark Water (Honoguari Mizu No Soko Kara)
Dead Birds
Dead Meat
Dead Space: Downfall
Deep, The
Deep Rising
Diary of the Dead
Dr. Jekyll and Mr. Hyde [Remake]
Driftwood
Duel
Eden Lake
Eden Log
Empty Acre, The
Evil Aliens
Evilenko
Exorcism of Emily Rose, The
Exorcist: The Beginning
Fatal Attraction
Feeding the Masses
Flatliners
Flight of the Living Dead: Outbreak on a Plane
Fog, The
Forsaken, The
Freddy vs. Jason
From Within
Frontiere(s)
Gacy
Ghost and the Darkness, The
Ghostbusters II
Ghoul, The
Ghouls, The
Graveyard Shift
Hamiltons, The

Hannibal

Haunting, The

Hellbent

Hello Mary Lou: Prom Night II

Hellraiser V: Inferno

Hidden, The

His Name Was Jason

Hollow Man

Hostel

House

House of Wax [Remake]

Howling V: The Rebirth, The

Identity

Infection (Kansen)

Inferno

Island of Dr. Moreau, The [Remake]

Isolation

It

J-Horror Anthology: Legends

Jack Brooks: Monster Slayer

Jacket, The

Joy Ride

Kaidan

Killer Klowns from Outer Space

Killer Pad

Kiss the Girls

Kolobos

Land of the Dead

Last Broadcast, The

Leatherface: The Texas Chainsaw Massacre 3

Leprechaun

Leviathan

Lifeforce

Little Girl Who Lives Down the Lane, The

Malevolence

Manhunter

Maniac Cop

Mary Shelley's Frankenstein

Maximum Overdrive

Meat Market 2

Memory

Mimic

Monster

Mother of Tears, The (La Terza Madre)

Mr. Brooks

New Nightmare

Night Flier, The
Nightbreed
Nightmare Detective
Nightmare on Elm Street 4: The Dream Master, A
Omega Man, The
Omen III: The Final Conflict, The
One Hour Photo
Outpost
Pacific Heights
Panic in Year Zero!
Pathology
People Under the Stairs, The
Phantom of the Opera, The [Remake] (1989)
Pitch Black
Primeval
Prince of Darkness
Prophecy V: Forsaken, The
Psycho II
Puppet Master
Puppet Master III: Toulon's Revenge
Puppet Masters, The
Red Dragon
Reeker
Relic, The
Resident Evil
Resident Evil: Degeneration
Return to Sleepaway Camp
Rise: Blood Hunter
Roost, The
Rose Red
Ruins, The
Running Man, The
Salem's Lot
Salvage
Savage Harvest 2: October Blood
Saw IV
Scarecrows
Screamers
Secret Window
See No Evil
Seed of Chucky
Severed: Forest of the Dead
Severed Head Network, The
Shadow of the Vampire
Shadowzone
Shatter Dead

Shrooms
Signs
Single White Female
Sleepwalkers
Someone's Watching Me!
Sorority Babes in the Slime Ball Bowl-A-Rama
Species
Sphere
Spider
Strangeland
Stuff, The
Subspecies IV: Bloodstorm
Substitute, The
Swamp Thing
Tales from the Crypt
Tears of Kali
Ted Bundy
Texas Chainsaw Massacre: The Beginning, The
Them (Ils)
To Let (Para Entrar a Vivar)
Tomie 5: Forbidden Fruit
Tremors 2: Aftershocks
Trilogy of Terror
Tripper, The
Ugly, The
Vacancy
Vampires
Versus
Village, The
Waxwork II: Lost in Time
What's the Matter with Helen?
Whoever Slew Auntie Roo?
Witches of Eastwick, The
Wolf
Wrestlemaniac
Wrong Turn 2: Dead End
Zodiac
Zombie Strippers
Zombies Anonymous

3:
4th Floor, The
5ive Girls
976-Evil
Abyss, The
Along Came a Spider

Alphabet Killer, The
April Fool's Day
Arcade
Awaken the Dead
Backwoods, The (Bosque de Sombras)
Bay Cove (Bay Coven)
Beast, The
Below
Black Christmas [Remake]
Bone Snatcher, The
Book of Shadows: Blair Witch 2
Broken
Brood, The
Buffy the Vampire Slayer
Bug
Buried Alive [Web Series]
Butterfly Effect 3: Revelations, The
Cabin Fever
Camp Blood
Cat's Eye
Child's Play 2
Chopping Mall
Club Dread
Craft, The
Curse 2: The Bite
Dark Angel: The Ascent
Dark Floors
Dark Half, The
Darkness
Dead Heat
Dead Mary
Dead Men Walking
Dead Pit
Deadlands: The Rising
Deadly Friend
Decoys
Deepstar Six
Deliverance
Demons 2: The Nightmare Continues (Demoni 2: L'incubo Ritorna)
Dentist 2: Brace Yourself, The
Devil's Chair, The
Disturbing Behavior
Dominion: Prequel to the Exorcist
Dorothy Mills
Dunwich Horror, The
Dying Breed

Edge, The
Eight Legged Freaks
Fear (1996)
Fear, The
Feast III: The Happy Finish
Final Destination 3
Flowers in the Attic
Forest of the Dead
Freddy's Dead: The Final Nightmare
Friday the 13th Part V: A New Beginning
Frogs
From Beyond the Grave
Gate II: Return to the Nightmare, The
Good Son, The
Gore Gore Girls, The
Halloween 4: The Return of Michael Myers
Halloween [Remake]
Hand that Rocks the Cradle, The
Hellraiser IV: Bloodline
Henry II – Portrait of a Serial Killer
Hills Have Eyes, The
Hole, The
House II: The Second Story
House by the Cemetery
I Know What You Did Last Summer
I Know Who Killed Me
Innocent Blood
Island of Dr. Moreau, The
It's Alive 2: It Lives Again
It's Alive 3: Island of the Alive
Jason Goes to Hell: The Final Friday
Jaws 2
Jeepers Creepers 2
Jekyll + Hyde
Ju-On 2
Killing Gene, The (W Delta Z [WAZ])
Lakeview Terrace
Langoliers, The
Last Man on Earth, The
Lawnmower Man, The
Leprechaun 3
Leprechaun 5: In the Hood
Leprechaun 6: Back 2 tha Hood
Lurking Fear
Maniac Cop 3: Badge of Silence
Man's Best Friend

Mary Reilly
Meat Market
Mutant (Night Shadows)
Mystery of the House of Wax
Needful Things
Neon Maniacs
Night of the Comet
Night of the Living Dorks (Die Nacht der Lebenden Loser)
Nightmare on Elm Street 5: The Dream Child, A
Number 23, The
Open Water 2: Adrift
Orca: The Killer Whale
Outbreak
Perfect Creature
Pet Sematary Two
Phantoms
Poltergeist II: The Other Side
Pool, The (Swimming Pool – Der Tod Feiert Mit)
Population 436
Progeny
Psycho III
Q: The Winged Serpent
Quick and the Undead, The
Rage: Carrie 2, The
Raising Cain
Ravenous
Raw Meat (Dead Line)
Retribution (Sakebi)
Right at Your Door
Ring Virus, The
Ringu 2
Salem's Lot [Remake]
Satan's Little Helper
Scream 2
Session 9
Seventh Sign, The
Shrieker
Sick Nurses
Silent Venom
Slashers
Sleepaway Camp 3: Teenage Wasteland
Sleepstalker
Sleepy Hollow
Starkweather
Tales from the Hood
Teen Wolf

Terror Train
Thinner
Tomie 3: Replay
Tooth & Nail
Twice Told Tales
Underworld
Underworld: Evolution
Urban Legend
Vampire Hunters
Van Helsing: The London Assignment
Village of the Damned [Remake]
Virus
Visions of Suffering
Visiting Hours
Visitors
Voices (Du Saram-Yida)
Watcher, The
What Lies Beneath
White Noise 2: The Light
White Zombie
Wishmaster 2: Evil Never Dies
Wrong Turn
Zombie Honeymoon

2.5:

Aliens vs. Predator
American Psycho 2: All American Girl
Anaconda
Anacondas: The Hunt for the Blood Orchid
Arrival, The
Bacterium
Bad Dreams
Bad Moon
Bats
Blood Gnome
Boogeyman 2
Bordello of Blood
Bottom Feeder
Breed, The (2006)
Breeders
Bruiser
Buried Alive
Burnt Offerings
Camp Blood 2
Candyman 2: Farewell to the Flesh
Cave, The

Cellar Door, The
Cemetery Gates
Children of the Damned
Child's Play 3
Clawed: The Legend of Sasquatch (The Unknown)
Creature
Cube Zero
Curse, The
Dahmer
Dark Ride
Darkness Falls
Days of Darkness
Dead End Road
Deaths of Ian Stone, The
Decoys: The Second Seduction
Deep Blue Sea
Die, Monster, Die!
Doom
Dreamcatcher
Ed Gein
Eyes of a Stranger
Feast II: Sloppy Seconds
Flesh Freaks
Freak Out
Friday the 13th Part II
Friday the 13th Part III
Friday the 13th Part VII: The New Blood
Ghosts of Mars
Gravedancers, The
Grim Reaper
Grudge 2, The
Gruesome Twosome, The
Hannibal Rising
Haunting, The [Remake]
Hitcher II: I've Been Waiting, The
House III: The Horror Show
House on Haunted Hill [Remake]
It's Alive
J-Horror Anthology: Underworld
Jason X
Lake Placid
Loch Ness Terror
Lost Boys II: The Tribe
Mangler, The
Mimic 3: The Sentinel
My Bloody Valentine [Remake]

My Name is Bruce
Netherworld
Night of the Demons 2
Night of the Lepus
Nightmare Man
Nightmare on Elm Street 2: Freddy's Revenge, A
No Man's Land: The Rise of Reeker
Organizm
Others, The
P2
Penny Dreadful
Plaga Zombie: Mutant Zone
Plasterhead
Poltergeist III
Premonition (Yogen)
Prom Night
Prom Night III: The Last Kiss
Prophecy II, The
Pulse [Remake]
Puppet Master IV: When Bad Puppets Turn Good
Queen of the Damned
Rage, The
Reincarnation (Rinne)
Resident Evil: Extinction
Return of Swamp Thing, The
Ringu 0
Rise of the Dead
Rise of the Undead
Saw V
Slugs
Snakes on a Plane
Snow White: A Tale of Terror
Storm of the Century
Tales from the Darkside: The Movie
Tales of Terror
Tenant, The (La Locataire)
Tomie
Tomie 4: Rebirth
Tommyknockers, The
Turistas
Unrest
Untraceable
Urban Legends 3: Bloody Mary
Vampire Journals
Vampires: Los Muertos
Vengeance of the Zombies (La Rebelion de las Muertas)

Welcome to the Jungle
Wicked Little Things
Wizard of Gore, The
Zombie 3 (Zombi 3)

2:

3 Extremes II (Saam Gaang)
8MM 2
Altered
American Werewolf in Paris, An
Automaton Transfusion
Bad Channels
Bleeders
Blood Feast
Blood Feast 2: All U Can Eat
Bones
Boogeyman 3
Butterfly Effect 2, The
Cadaverella
Carrie [Remake]
Cursed
Dark, The
Dark Water [Remake]
Dead & Breakfast
Dead Life
Dead Silence
Desperation
End of Days
Fear (1990)
Friday the 13th Part VI: Jason Lives
Ghost Ship
Ghoulies
Gothika
Graveyard, The
Halloween V: The Revenge of Michael Myers
Halloween VII: H20
Happening, The
Haunted
Hell of the Living Dead
Hellraiser VII: Deader
Hills Have Eyes 2, The
Hitcher, The [Remake]
Hollow Man 2
Howling II: Your Sister is a Werewolf, The
I Am Legend
I Still Know What You Did Last Summer

Idle Hands
Invasion, The
Island of the Dead
Jaws 3
Joshua (2006)
Joy Ride 2: Dead Ahead
Lady in the Water
Lake Dead
Last Winter, The
Leprechaun 2
Man-Thing
Manticore
Mimic 2
Mortuary
National Lampoon's Class Reunion
Nightmare Sisters
Nightstalker
Omen IV: The Awakening, The
Open Water
Phantom of the Opera, The [Remake] (1998)
Plaga Zombie
Plague, The
Prophecy III: The Ascent, The
Prophecy IV: Uprising, The
Psycho IV: The Beginning
Puppet Master II
Puppet Master V: The Final Chapter
Quicksilver Highway
Rasen
Reaping, The
Red Riding Hood
Return of the Living Dead 2
Return of the Living Dead 5: Rave to the Grave
Return to House on Haunted Hill
Room 205 (Kollegiet)
S. Darko
Scream 3
Shallow Ground
Shocker
Sleepaway Camp 2: Unhappy Campers
Soho Square
Species II
Speck
Stay Alive
Stir of Echoes 2: The Homecoming
Subject Two

Sublime
Summer of Fear (Stranger in Our House)
Tamara
Tattooist, The
Tomie 2: Another Face
Trailer Park of Terror
Tremors 3: Back to Perfection
Triloquist
Two Thousand Maniacs!
Ultraviolet
White Noise
Zombie 4: After Death (Oltre la Morte)
Zombie Night

1.5:
Aliens vs. Predator Requiem
American Haunting, An
Amusement
Apocalypse and the Beauty Queen
Basic Instinct 2
Believers
Bloodrayne
Boogeyman
Breaking Dawn
Breed, The (2001)
Captivity
Children of the Living Dead
Crazy Eights
Creature from Black Lake
Cry_Wolf
Curse of the Puppet Master
Day of the Dead [Remake]
Deathbed
Diary of Ellen Rimbauer, The
Ed Gein: The Butcher of Plainfield
Fear 2: Halloween Night, The
Feardotcom
First Born
Friday the 13th Part VIII: Jason Takes Manhattan
Friday the 13th [Remake]
From Dusk till Dawn 2: Texas Blood Money
Ghoulies II
Halloween 6: The Curse of Michael Myers
Headless Horseman
Hellraiser VI: Hellseeker
Hidden 2, The

Hills Have Eyes Part II, The
Howling IV: The Original Nightmare
Ice Queen
Jaws: The Revenge
Last House in the Woods, The (Il Bosco Fuori)
Miner's Massacre (Curse of the Forty-Niner)
Night of the Dead
Night of the Demons 3
Ninth Gate, The
Perkin's 14
Predator 2
Prom Night IV: Deliver Us from Evil
Rest Stop: Dead Ahead
Retro Puppet Master
Return of the Living Dead 4: Necropolis
Riding the Bullet
Seedpeople
Shaft, The (Down)
Sick House, The
Skinned Deep
Species III
Swimfan
Texas Chainsaw Massacre 4: The Next Generation, The
They
Tremors 4: The Legend Begins
Trucks
Unborn but Forgotten (Hayanbang)
Unearthed
Urban Legends 2: Final Cut
Valentine
Van Helsing
Wizard of Gore, The [Remake]

1:
Against the Dark
All Souls Day: Dia de los Muertos
Alone in the Dark
Anaconda 3: The Offspring
April Fool's Day [Remake]
Arrival II, The (The Second Arrival)
Awake
Bloodrayne 2: Deliverance
Brotherhood of Blood
Candyman 3: Day of the Dead
Dead Above Ground
Disturbia

Entrance, The
Evil's City
Exorcist II: The Heretic
Fog, The [Remake]
From Dusk till Dawn 3: The Hangman's Daughter
Gates of Hell II: Dead Awakening, The (Through the Fire)
Halloween Resurrection
Hammerhead
Hellraiser VIII: Hellworld
House of the Dead II
Howling VI: The Freaks, The
I'll Always Know What You Did Last Summer
Lake Placid 2
Legion of the Dead
Leprechaun 4: In Space
Mangler Reborn, The
Messengers, The
Night of the Living Dead 3-D
Omen, The [Remake]
Prom Night [Remake]
Pulse 3: Invasion
Red Eye
Rest Stop: Don't Look Back
Return, The
Ring 2, The
Slaughter
Solstice
Species IV: The Awakening
Teen Wolf Too
Tower of Blood
Trackman
Vacancy 2: The First Cut
Vampires: Out for Blood
Within the Woods
Zombie 5: Killing Birds (Uccelli Assassinni)

0.5:

Bats: Human Harvest
Beyond the Wall of Sleep
Blood and Chocolate
Creepshow 3
Day of the Dead 2: Contagium
Dead Moon Rising
Death Tunnel
Flesh for the Beast
Haunting of Molly Hartley, The

House of the Dead
Howling III: The Marsupials, The
Lawnmower Man 2: Jobe's War, The
Mangler 2, The
Psycho [Remake]
Pulse 2: Afterlife
Ring of Darkness
Shining, The [Remake]
Single White Female 2: The Psycho
Steel Trap
Wishmaster 3: Beyond the Gates of Hell
Wishmaster 4: The Prophecy Fulfilled

TV SHOW ANNEX

What would a book on horror be without highlighting some of the horror themed television shows that have graced the small screen over the years? I decided to include ten shows whose run has now ended and of course, much like the movies are available in their entirety on DVD. A lot of horror shows never make it past season one because they usually don't have the mass appeal that other shows do, which is unfortunate, so you'll see a lot of one off shows here. There are two kinds of shows, free running and anthology. For the anthology shows, each episode has no relation to the other, so I'll give my thoughts on each episode individually and for the free running shows I'll discuss it by season. Everything else is pretty much set up just like the movies, so hopefully you'll discover a new favorite show here and then immediately be disappointed when you find out it only existed for one mere season.

Dracula – The Series
Season 1
Year: 1990-1991
Tags: Vampires

In this series, two brothers move to Europe to live with their uncle and soon realize that not only are vampires real, but Dracula himself lives in the same town. Fortunately for them, their uncle is a descendant of the Van Helsing bloodline and quite an accomplished vampire hunter. This is not your typical vampire from ancient lore however, here Dracula has established a billion dollar empire and is quite the businessman, going by the name Alexander Lucard (A. Lucard, get it?!). I remember watching this show a few times as a kid and I really liked it, but then again, horror shows were not readily available back then. When I saw it was on DVD, I just had to get it and see if it still holds up to my childhood fondness of it. And it really doesn't. At first I didn't like this series at all due to the ultra cheesy set-up for each episode and the incredibly hammy acting, but as I continued to watch I started to dig the ham and cheese sandwich that was Dracula – The Series. It's pretty hilarious at times because each episode has the same underlying factors: Kids get into shenanigans, elder Van Helsing comes along to save the day, and Dracula is foiled again. The series also features more hilarity because at several points Dracula could just win and kill everyone easily, but not just that, there are also several occasions where the vice versa is true. Honestly, this series could have been summed up in two episodes. Episode one: kids discover vampires are real and that Dracula lives nearby. Episode two: Dracula rips their dumbass heads off and drinks their blood, series concluded. I also enjoyed how everyone could just come and go to Dracula's castle because a billionaire vampire just couldn't afford any kind of security or guards, or even a door that locks. It may seem like I'm saying a lot of bad things about the series but I really did enjoy it on some level. It's far from being anything brilliant and falls into the cliché trap in just about every episode, but its cheesiness is somewhat endearing. It was hard to get into at first but I definitely enjoyed it more as it went on and found Dracula – The Series to be a nice addition to my collection. I just don't anticipate that I'll be watching it often, but maybe when I need a good laugh, I'll pop it in.

Fear Itself
Season 1
Year: 2008-2009
Tags: Anthology

This anthology show is essentially Masters of Horror 2.0 as it has the same people behind it and kind of the same concept in having different directors handle each episode. After the untimely death of Masters of Horror, I was glad to see it get revitalized, but the other side of the coin is that it would be aired on network television, so essentially we would be saddled with a very watered down Masters of Horror. Still could be cool though, especially since I am talking about the DVD versions of each episode, and in the DVD world, anything goes. So let's see how things go.

Chance
Director – John Dahl
Tags – Suspense

A man trying to make deal on an antique vase ends up failing in his quest and is offered much less money for it than what he paid. In a rage he kills the art dealer and ends up finding a double of himself in the art shop after looking into a curious mirror. I guess that's what it's about, but I'm not sure because the story is garbage. And since it is crap, the direction is also very slow and convoluted. The acting is good though, especially from Ethan Embry who plays dual roles very well. But there aren't many compliments I can pay this turd beyond that.

1.5/5

Circle, The
Director – Eduardo Rodriguez
Tags – Infection

A writer is having a conference at his cabin with his agent and publisher when a knock comes at the door. Two girls deliver a book that was supposedly written by him, and now everything contained within its pages is coming true, including an unnatural darkness outside that transforms people into crazed creatures. This is probably the best of the series. A cool story, great acting and some pretty smooth direction to boot. I like how it played out at first but honestly I didn't really care for the climax, it did end well though. But all in all it was fun and I liked it as a whole.

3.5/5

Community
Director – Mary Harron
Tags – Suspense

A couple trying to conceive a child score an invitation to live in an upscale community that's just too good to be true. Of course it is, when they find out that private matters between family members end up as public affairs because in this community, nothing is sacred. I was excited for this episode being a fan of the director (I can say this line for many of the episodes), and unfortunately the director was saddled with a very unimpressive story (which, sadly I can also say of many of the episodes). Everything about it is very transparent and that's probably because it's extremely derivative of many similar movies (Bay Cove comes to mind, as well as many others). The way the story is laid out doesn't allow for much creative flair and I wish Harron had a more original tale to tackle. The acting is fine, and in truth the episode isn't all bad but I was still very disappointed by the whole affair.

2/5

Eater
Director – Stuart Gordon
Tags – Cannibals

A notorious cannibalistic serial killer is housed at a small precinct for the night. But one of the officers on duty senses something is amiss and learns that her prisoner may be much more than just a cannibal. A cannibal with mystical powers? Sounds cool to me! I'll be honest in that I'll watch anything Stuart Gordon makes because I think he's a genuinely talented director, so I was really looking forward to this episode. And I wasn't really let down either. It wasn't his finest moment but it was pretty damn entertaining nonetheless. The episode moved along nicely, had some good bloodshed and the story was solid. Honestly, my only complaint was the ending, which is cool in its own way but I don't think it would actually work, and that's the only thing that really irked me. Still, pretty cool.

3.5/5

Echoes
Director – Rupert Wainwright
Tags – Suspense

A man begins having déjà-vu that involves a man and woman and possibly murder. Soon their lives begin to take over his own life and he begins to manifest another personality. To quote a new favorite movie of mine: Now I know what the visual representation of a dial tone looks like. Bad story, bad acting, bad direction, everything stunk. And one woman insisted on singing the same song over and over, just absolutely brutalizing it with her terrible voice. But that was just one annoyance in this pile of slop.

0.5/5

Family Man
Director – Ronny Yu
Tags – Suspense

A family man has a near fatal accident and ends up switching bodies with a known killer. Now the killer has his family and the man is behind bars with no one who believes him. The idea here is interesting but the lack of information as to how such an event could occur strikes me as a cop-out. But that's not the least of the episode's problems. First off, it's just not that interesting and the acting isn't very good, quite frankly I was pretty bored by the whole thing. The ending could be seen coming from a mile away but that's ok because it did end how it should have and I liked it. Unfortunately that's one of the few things I did like about it. This episode isn't completely worthless but it really isn't very good either.

2/5

In Sickness and In Health
Director – John Landis
Tags – Serial Killer (Fictional)

On her wedding day a woman is passed a note from an anonymous person saying that the person she is about to marry is a serial killer. Landis definitely delivered when he worked on Masters of Horror so it's kind of a surprise to me that the same man delivered such an absolute turd here. There is really nothing good I can say about this episode. The acting was bad, the story was lame, and the pacing was terrible, everything was very much off its mark. In fact, I have trouble even remembering anything about the episode right after viewing it which means it was just instantly forgettable. Disappointing to say the least.

1/5

New Year's Day
Director – Darren Lynn Bousman
Tags – Zombies

A woman wakes up on New Year's Day with more than just a hangover. It appears as though overnight the whole city has become overrun with zombies. I was looking forward to this episode because I love zombies and I think Bousman is a talented guy, I mean, he made me care about the Saw series when he was behind the helm, so imagine how pissed off I was when this turned out to be the worst of the series. The acting was horrendous, the story was nonexistent, the editing was painfully annoying, the pacing was terrible and the ending was downright stupid. And the zombies, I don't think I've ever seen zombies quite this annoying. I'm not even going to go on because it just pisses me off further to relive what a wretched piece of shit this episode was. Absolutely worthless in every sense of the word.

0.5/5

Sacrifice, The
Director – Breck Eisner
Tags – [Hidden to conceal spoilers]

Four criminals take refuge in an old fort after their car breaks down, thinking it empty. But then they find out that three women live there, and they're not the only ones. I was looking forward to this because it sounded like it could be pretty cool, but I was let down once again. It's not really bad so much as it was just mundane. The acting was fine and the direction was ok, the story wasn't anything special though and the whole production just felt very bland. I did like the fort, but I have a sneaking suspicion that it was the same fort that was used in Ginger Snaps Back. Anyway, the twist in the storyline isn't much of a twist and it all ended being a very predictable and average episode.

2.5/5

Skin and Bones
Director – Larry Fessenden
Tags – [Hidden to conceal spoilers]

Some men become lost in the mountains one winter, and with hope all but gone, one man returns home emaciated and frostbitten, but that's not the only change. It's pretty easy to figure out what's going on if you've read any Native American folklore, and that's my main issue with the story, it's incredibly formulaic. You know what's going to happen, who's going to die and all that jazz. But there were some shining spots. The lead actor is great and his make-up is extremely well done. The episode also moves along decent enough. Unfortunately everything else about it is pretty mundane. It's a shame really.

2/5

Something with Bite
Director – Ernest R. Dickerson
Tags – Werewolves

A veterinarian is bitten by a werewolf and starts to feel the change. But when people he knows begin to die in the night under the claws of a wild beast, he starts to wonder if he is the killer himself. This is a pretty fun episode, and after all of the garbage episodes, it was very welcome. It has some humorous moments and good horror elements backed up by some good acting and direction. And that's really all I have to say about it. It wasn't anything great that blew me away but it was far from being terrible as well. Just a very solid horror/comedy that I enjoyed but wasn't wowed by.

3/5

Spirit Box, The
Director – Rob Schmidt
Tags – Ghosts

Two girls construct a spirit box to commune with the dead and end up drudging up an old mystery about a schoolmate who supposedly killed herself, but now is believed to have been murdered. Five minutes in I could tell this would be one of the worst episodes, and it definitely was. The acting was terrible, the story was predictable and boring and the direction was slow. If you can stay awake long enough you'll be treated to a stupid ending and then the credits will finally role. That's forty minutes I'll never get back.

0.5/5

Spooked
Director – Brad Anderson
Tags – Ghosts

A police officer who was the hero of the day one moment for saving a young boy and then fired the next for using too much force on the job begins a new career as a private investigator. But his latest job dredges up the ghosts of his past, both literally and figuratively. Always excited to see something by Anderson, but this episode is repugnant. The story is absolute garbage and not the least bit scary, interesting and at times, it doesn't even make sense. The acting is ok and there are a couple of cool FX shots, but I was bored to death by this episode and hated it on practically every level.

1.5/5

I didn't expect Fear Itself to top Masters of Horror, but I didn't expect it to be this bad either. I can clearly see now why this show was cancelled before the full season even ran. It was terrible story after terrible story, bad acting, poor direction, everything. There were just as many good episodes as worthless ones, with everything else falling between average and bad. Not a single episode I would call great. I actually hated this show and it didn't really even suffer from being watered down for network television, it was just bad. A grave disappointment indeed.

Season Score: 1.5/5

Harper's Island
Season 1
Year: 2009
Tags: Slasher / Survival

Two young lovers are about to tie the knot at Harper's Island with several guests in tow. But as their numbers begin to mysteriously thin out, there might just be a killer on the loose. And it wouldn't be the first time that a killer has been on the island. Who could it be, and who will survive. This show, as opposed to others that were cancelled during or after their first season, was only meant to run one season. While on the outside this show may seem like familiar fare, I can tell you that the show is really as much about human drama and mystery as it is about being a slasher, and that is a very good thing. Essentially this is like a ten hour epic movie with so many twists and turns you may just find yourself going way out into left field to try and find out who is behind the killings. I had many "out there" theories. And speaking of the killings, they are pretty damn graphic at times, especially considering that the show aired on CBS. There's a lot more aftermath gore that initial killing, but both are extremely well done. Also well done is the acting, everything is very natural and each character is given a specific and unique personality, which is pulled off by the actors splendidly. The direction varies from episode to episode but most are paced very well and while it does get slow a couple of times, it never really hindered my viewing experience. I do think that the show could have been pared down to 12 episodes instead of thirteen because the biggest story reveal comes on episode 12 and I would say that only about half of the last episode was necessary. But again, that's pretty minor. The story is the absolute highlight here because the relationships between the characters is great, you are constantly kept guessing as to who could be killing because there are excellent red herrings that pop up throughout the show. There's just a lot going on amidst the horror that really allows you to get to know the characters and care about their lives. Definitely one of the best horror shows out there and I really hope that the writers craft another show together because I would love to see them in action again. Great stuff.

Season Score: 4.5/5

Invasion
Season 1
Year: 2005-2006
Tags: Aliens

A hurricane hits the small community of Homestead, but more than just a hurricane, it brings something with it. Some people went missing during the hurricane only to turn up nude without a scratch on them. It seems as though this hurricane brought with it some strange luminescent creatures that now live in the water around the community, and they have gotten a hold of some people and changed them. The single season show, you never quite know if the appeal is only for a few people or if the show really just sucked. Well this show is unfortunately pretty great. I say unfortunately because there is only one season of the show and that is all there will ever be. And for such a great show, I feel that's pretty unfortunate. I hear a lot of reasons as to why the show was cancelled but the one that seems to make the most sense is that the studio just kept moving it around in their schedule to different days and time slots, and it's pretty hard to gather an audience when you do that. Anyway, onto the show. The characters are great, which is very important since this is such a character driven show. But what about these weird orange creatures? Well, they're pretty cool too, I really like the stingray/jellyfish design and the CGI is pretty good, mainly because it's not overused. I really enjoyed the progression of the story and felt that the show definitely had legs and could have easily progressed into a few more seasons, but I must warn you that if you do get attached to the show, there is no nicely wrapped up finale and instead it is a huge cliffhanger into the second season that would never come to pass. There are a bunch of unanswered questions, so just prepare yourself for that. The show isn't quite perfect though. Sometimes it could get a little slow and not all of the actors are really good, fortunately most are great but there are a few that annoyed me, like the youngest kid, she wasn't very good. But those are minor complaints in a very substantial series that treads familiar ground but definitely manages to go into its own unique direction. This may sound like Invasion of the Body Snatchers – The Series, and while it does have a sometimes similar feel, it goes way beyond that and manages to be just a great character based show revolving around an extraterrestrial invasion of sorts. Just a well done show that should have at least had two more seasons, but what we have it still really entertaining.

Kolchak – The Night Stalker
Season 1
Year: 1974-1975
Tags: Vampires, Werewolves, Zombies, Aliens, Serial Killer (Fictional), Ghosts, Demonic Possession, Demons, Monsters, Mechanical, Witchcraft, Cults, Suspense

A news journalist investigates strange deaths that seem to plague Chicago, with each one seeming to have a paranormal figure at the center of it. So as you can see, during the show's single season, it covered damn near every sub genre of horror it could. I'll start by saying that Kolchak is easily one of the single greatest characters ever written. He's a sneaky reporter, intelligent, a smart ass and funny as hell. He's also portrayed by a great actor who really understood the character and played him perfectly. I also greatly enjoyed the variety of villains he tangled with, because not only did he take on the traditional horror fare, but the writers also delved into the mythology of a wide variety of cultures to look for new kinds of opposition for the wily reporter. Also, they didn't do the whole Scooby-Doo thing and make each creature just some dude pretending to be the werewolf or vampire and instead actually made Kolchak go up against the real thing (as it were). That being said, I really enjoyed this show but it's not without its problems. First off, there's no long running storyline and instead each episode stands on its own, almost like an anthology, and I would have called it an anthology, but every episode is exactly the same. The show is so formulaic it's ridiculous. Murder, Kolchak investigates, stays ahead of the cops, pulls tricky maneuvers, more deaths, discovers creature, seeks out how to destroy it, more deaths, Kolchak destroys it, no one believes him. Seriously, that's every episode and it isn't even a spoiler because that's how you would expect it to play out, and it does, every time. And some episodes are better than others, some getting rather slow at times. That said, it's still a really well done show, sure every episode follows the same exact formula to a tee, but the great variation in creatures that Kolchak tangles with keeps it interesting. I was highly entertained by this but I'm not surprised it didn't last more than one season because if it had, it would have quickly devolved into Kolchak chasing Leprechauns.

Masters of Horror
Season 1
Year: 2005-2006
Tags: Anthology

This anthology show is the brainchild of Mick Garris and the idea behind it is to gather prolific horror directors and have them create one hour films with few restrictions put on themselves, essentially allowing them to make films that they want to make. Now that's one hell of an idea and definitely one I can get behind, but also calling it "Masters of Horror" also allows it to be under extreme scrutiny from mega dork horror fans… like me. So in addition to my thoughts on each episode, I'll also judge the merits and resume of each director involved. Now, onward!

Chocolate
Director – Mick Garris
Tags – Suspense

My distaste for Mick Garris is pretty obvious. Sure, he's done a lot of genre movies, but most of them are bad. I think his best work is Sleepwalkers but I know I'm pretty much in the minority on that one. I respect him for getting the show up and running but I just don't care for his body of work. Maybe he would be better off behind the scenes instead of behind the camera.

Here a lonely man begins to experience life through a beautiful woman, feeling everything she feels as well as just seeing. Soon he develops an obsession for her and focuses all of his energy on finding her. Honestly I don't know why this was made into a Masters of Horror episode because there really aren't any horror moments at all and I only tagged it as suspense because I didn't know what else to do. This is more of a fantasy movie with strong sexual overtones, and it's a pretty boring one at that. The idea isn't all that interesting to me. Ok, he feels what she feels, and then? It never really goes anywhere interesting and doesn't belong in this series. Had it been made elsewhere and not branded as a genre work, I may have more respect for it, because it is well acted and it does look good, but in the end it's just a boring episode and didn't fit the series in the least.

1/5

Cigarette Burns
Director – John Carpenter
Tags – Suspense

It's John Carpenter people! Easily one of my favorite directors of all time, if he wasn't involved in the Masters of Horror, it would have been a travesty.

A man known to be able to find rare cinema items is employed by an eccentric man to find the granddaddy of all lost films, rumored to have caused madness and murder during its first and only screening. As he attempts to locate the legendary film, he embarks on a dark odyssey amongst shady figures in the hope that one will be able to point him in the right direction. Let me lay things out like this: This is an incredible story performed by an amazing director and backed by some great performances, need I say more? This is easily the best episode of the season as it is a wonderfully unique and engrossing tale that is pulled off in a pitch perfect manner. It is a dialogue heavy piece, which works for it, but also features some heavy gore and I think that a dialogue piece with gore is just so cool. This is definitely something that genre fans should go out of their way to see.

4.5/5

Dance of the Dead

Director – Tobe Hooper
Tags – Zombies

Tobe Hooper has definitely spent some time in the genre. From his groundbreaking work on The Texas Chainsaw Massacre into more mainstream fare such as Poltergeist, he has made a tremendous mark on the genre. Even if all of his movies haven't been the best, he's still done quite a lot of good.

Set in a post apocalyptic world, this episode explores a night club where the dead are brought back to life by a wicked MC and forced to dance for the patrons. This is a really weird tale penned by Richard Matheson and while I can appreciate weirdness in stories, I don't think it fully comes together to make for a gripping tale. The way the movie is shot has a strange, flashy tone that feels more disjointed than stylish. The majority of the acting is pretty good and I like certain aspects of the episode but as a whole I couldn't really get into it. I tagged it as "Zombies" due to the undead aspect but it plays out more like an apocalyptic, cyber-punk, sexual sleaze kind of movie. It's worth checking out for the FX alone, namely the nude burning bodies, which was pretty extraordinary, but it's still fairly average.

2.5/5

Deer Woman
Director – John Landis
Tags – Monsters

When I think of John Landis I really don't think about horror, but really, I guess he would be a master after all. An American Werewolf in London is an undeniable classic and he's done some more horror that's very respectable. If nothing else this show has helped me to recognize that he has been influential on the genre and a good addition here.

A police detective is assigned to a series of murders where men appear to have been trampled to death by a deer. The tricky thing is that the murders have occurred where no deer could go, allowing for some very interesting theories as to who the murderer could be. The first time I watched this episode I wasn't really into it but the second time around I really enjoyed it. It's pretty funny at times while still being a definite horror movie, a Landis mark. The acting is also pretty good and I liked the deer woman because she didn't have any lines but her facial expressions spoke volumes. Beyond it being an original tale for the screen, it's highly entertaining and really makes me want to see Landis do more work in the genre.

4/5

Dreams in the Witch-House
Director – Stuart Gordon
Tags – Witchcraft

Gordon was another obvious pick to be part of this show, having multiple excellent genre films over the years, his most famous likely being Re-Animator. He may not be a household name but his Lovecraft adaptations and more have proven him to be a force in the genre.

A student takes up residence at an old boarding house that was rumored to have been the residence of a witch in the 17th century. He begins to have strange dreams and feels that there still may be an evil presence in the house. Gordon taps into Lovecraft again for this episode and makes yet another story come to life. I was really glad to see Ezra Godden return after working with Gordon in Dagon, because he's a pretty damn good actor and he puts on another great performance here. This episode is almost entirely his show, but the supporting cast does a great job as well. The story is well done and may even be a little crazier than the source material. It is very much Lovecraft and something that just needs to be seen to fully realize it. Another great episode.

4/5

Fair Haired Child, The
Director – William Malone
Tags – [Hidden to Conceal Spoilers]

William Malone. The name doesn't exactly illicit the words master of horror. His most well known movies in the genre are probably the House on Haunted Hill remake, which was average at best, and Feardotcom, which sucked, so I have no idea why he would be involved. No offense, but his past history is not the best.

Here a sweet but outcast girl is kidnapped for nefarious reasons that are revealed as the episode goes on. Saying more would reveal too much for the first time viewer. I thought this episode was ok, but it certainly wasn't anything that would define the series. The acting was decent and the story itself took a little too long to get going. The Fair Haired Child itself was pretty cool looking in a Rubber Johnny kind of way. I didn't love the episode but it wasn't bad, it had some originality to it and it was satisfying as a short horror film, but I can also live without it.

2.5/5

Haeckel's Tale
Director – John McNaughton
Tags – Zombies

McNaughton directed Henry – Portrait of a Serial Killer, which is pretty badass, but he has not really done anything else in the genre, so his inclusion here was strange, but then I read that he was replacing George A. Romero, so I guess he was a last minute choice. No offense, he's good, but a master of horror he is not.

A man obsessed with bringing the dead back to life ends up staying with an old man and his young wife and discovers that they share a horrible secret. Well, this is definitely a different zombie tale, heavy on sensuality, which I can appreciate, but the story is ultimately unappealing.

It has its moments of greatness but as a whole it is mediocre. The acting is ok, but again, ultimately mediocre. There are some cool FX here and there and the episode moves along decent enough with a heavy mix of sex and gore but I was kind of off put by it all and didn't really enjoy it that much.

2.5/5

Homecoming
Director – Joe Dante
Tags – Zombies

Dante definitely epitomizes being a master of horror with several great genre offerings under his belt. Not only is he a great filmmaker but he's also consistently good, which I really appreciate. I'm glad he was included in this series.

Set during the Bush Jr. White House reign (of terror, haha), this movie shows the soldiers who have died overseas coming back to life not for human brains, but for the right to vote. Wait a minute, what? While I can appreciate the political nature of this episode as it will undoubtedly cause controversy among crybaby individuals who can't fathom that this is a work of fiction, I honestly think it kind of sucks. I can agree with the statements presented here but this is a horror show, and despite the presence of zombies, it's very light on horror and just doesn't belong here. When I watch a show called "Masters of Horror", I want horror, not a political piece. Honestly I was kind of bored by this episode, and unimpressed by the acting. I felt this was well below Dante's usual level of talent. I did like the political aspects, but I don't think it worked at all in the horror setting. Disappointing.

1.5/5

Imprint
Director – Takashi Miike
Tags – Suspense

Miike may not have been around as long as many of the veterans, but his mark has been made with some wonderfully dark and unique films. Films that deal with a lot that has never before been seen on the screen and his episode is no different.

A man travels to an island inhabited by whores in search of a woman he swore he would come back for. But what he finds is that she's dead and the woman who tells her tale has a mighty tale indeed. This movie was banned from broadcast due to subject matter, and while I have no issue watching it and rather enjoyed the risks Miike took, I can see why it was not aired. He deals with many taboo and controversial subjects here, not just a couple, but several, and the beauty behind it is that he doesn't include them just for shock value, and they actually work in each their own way. This episode does have a lot of crazy shit going on and honestly, you just have to see it to believe it. Wonderfully acted and beautifully shot, this unique tale is definitely one that I will remember and treasure for a long time to come. Brilliant.

4.5/5

Incident On and Off a Mountain Road
Director – Don Coscarelli
Tags – Slasher / Survival

Don Coscarelli may not have had a long career in the genre but he is responsible for the entire Phantasm series and the highly entertaining Bubba Ho-Tep so I'm glad to see him included here. I like Coscarelli and really wish he would do more in the genre.

Here a woman is assaulted on a mountain road (shocker) by a killer known simply as Moonface and now she fights for survival against him and has a few tricks up her sleeve. I like that this isn't your typical cliché slasher flick. Sure there's a female protagonist, but she doesn't turn from weak kneed woman to survivor girl like all the others. Here we see through flashbacks that she was married to a survival nut and she has skills from the get go. Very fresh and great to see. The acting is well done and the man himself Angus Scrimm puts on a very entertaining performance. Aside from the survivalist aspect this episode is a lot like your typical slasher flick, but a damn good one and the ending is just icing on the cake. Definitely a damn fine addition to the season.

3.5/5

Jenifer
Director – Dario Argento
Tags – Demons

Argento really doesn't need any introduction as he has crafted not only a multitude of horror films but a large number of great horror films. I like that this series didn't make the mistake of hiring only American filmmakers as well.

A cop shoots a maniac to death in order to save a woman's life. The woman's face is horribly disfigured but he slowly builds an obsession for her nonetheless. His life falls apart as he obsesses further and when he finds out that she has extreme murderous tendencies and a taste for human flesh, he is torn between doing the right thing and fulfilling his sexual appetites. I tagged this as a demon flick because it's pretty clear to me that Jenifer is some sort of succubus. Anyway, this episode is pretty damn good. Loads of gore and sex, very solid acting and a brisk pace make for a rather entertaining time. I like the story but it does feel pretty formulaic with the steady pace of gore, sex, gore, gore, sex, but I'm definitely not complaining. Good stuff.

3.5/5

Pick Me Up
Director – Larry Cohen
Tags – Serial Killer (Fictional)

I definitely agree with Cohen's inclusion in this series because even though he hasn't really created what I would call any classics of the genre, his work in horror is definitely very good and he has created a number of genre films and I can honestly say there hasn't been anything he's done that I didn't enjoy on some level.

Here a bus breaks down in the middle of the wilderness and one woman decides to walk to the nearest hotel. Being a strong individual she feels that she can take care of herself. She could probably even handle a serial killer, but can she handle two? The idea of dueling serial killers is a pretty cool one and this episode does a good but not great job of exploring it. There are some veteran actors involved that do a great job but some of the people in lesser roles are kind of bad. The direction is nice and the episode moves along nicely with some good blood to boot. The story is well written in a round about way but kind of unfulfilling, especially with the predictable and far fetched ending. But it's still a good watch and definitely works with the rest of Cohen's catalog providing a good but ultimately unremarkable effort.

3/5

Sick Girl
Director – Lucky McKee
Tags – Animals, Infection

McKee is not exactly a household name and only has a couple of genre films under his belt, but they are pretty damn incredible so while he is a youngster amongst the veterans, I'm really glad to see that he is a part of this series.

A woman obsessed with bugs is sent a rather unusual specimen around the time she engages in a new relationship with a young woman. The bug infects her new girlfriend and changes not only her personality, but changes her physically as well. This is a pretty damn cool story. McKee superbly crafts a rather bizarre story while still managing to keep it grounded in reality by adding some excellent human touches. The acting is amazing and the pacing is very tight. The whole insect angle gets pretty out there and may not appeal to everyone, but I love the weirdness and how the whole episode plays out. And it has some kick ass FX too.

4/5

In a way I'm kind of disappointed with the first season of the show, but then I slap myself in the back of the head and realize that not every episode could have been gold and instead realize that most of the episodes were above average with only a couple of episodes that I would have called bad. So that's pretty good. Personally I would have liked to have seen George A. Romero, Wes Craven, Clive Barker, David Cronenberg, Neil Marshall and Guillermo del Toro involved to name a few, but I'm sure there were scheduling conflicts and maybe payment issues associated with some of them. But still, that would have probably been pretty cool. Romero is a legend, Craven is inconsistent but still delivered the goods on many occasions, Barker is thought of more as a writer but has still created some great movies in the director's chair, Cronenberg is another legend but is in the realm of fringe horror, Marshall may be new but much like McKee has already created some amazing movies and has already proven himself, and del Toro, well, the man is just a genius and has proven he can not only make independent and artistic horror, but incredibly respectable Hollywood budget horror as well. Kudos to Garris for pulling this together and I greatly look forward to season two. As a whole I enjoyed the season and my season score at the bottom reflects it as a whole.

Season Score: 4/5

Masters of Horror
Season 2
Year: 2006-2007
Tags: Anthology

Here we see the series return for a second season with some familiar faces behind the helm and some new ones to boot. So let's just dive right in.

Black Cat, The
Director – Stuart Gordon
Tags – Animals

Stuart Gordon returns from season one.

This is not exactly an adaptation of Poe's "The Black Cat", rather it focuses on Poe himself and how he deals with a shortcoming in finances, alcoholism, writer's block, his wife's illness and her devious cat who would end up providing the inspiration for one his most beloved stories. This is an interesting idea, to focus on Poe himself instead of another adaptation but I must admit I didn't like it the first time I watched it. But that's what second viewings are for. I really liked it the second time and while I still found it be a little slow I really appreciated it more. Jeffrey Combs puts on an immaculate performance and even looks a great deal like Poe. I really got sucked into the era and the story and liked how everything turned out, but to say more would reveal too much.

3.5/5

Damned Thing, The
Director – Tobe Hooper
Tags – Suspense

Tobe Hooper returns from season one.

Years ago a malevolent force found a man's father and he killed his wife, with the boy barely escaping with his life. Now, years later, the damned thing has found him and as the town he lives in burns to the ground and the townsfolk begin to go into murderous rages, will he find away to overcome it or will it destroy the world? I was intrigued by this episode but after watching it I just couldn't fully get into the story. It was heavy on gore but I think that was there to more or less make up for the tale's shortcomings and it did help, but not really enough. The bulk of the episode is kind of slow but really picks up the pace toward the end. It's well acted and not completely unsatisfying, but really not as great as I would have hoped.

Dream Cruise

Director – Norio Tsuruta
Tags – Ghosts

Norio Tsuruta is new to this season but not to the genre. His genre works however, are not the best. I like the inclusion of Asian filmmakers to give the series some cultural diversity and while I do like Tsuruta's work on some level, I honestly would have much rather preferred someone like Takashi Shimizu.

A man with a dreadful fear of boats and the water ever since he saw his brother drown is forced by a client to accompany him and his wife on his yacht. There is something between the man and his client's wife and he fears the client knows, but on the open sea he finds out that there is more to worry about and that the dead never forget. Dream Cruise is the one episode that has an uncut version making it a full length movie instead of an hour long one and I think that's where the episode went wrong. The story is pretty good and I like the idea of a haunting on a yacht with other underlying elements, but it is just too long and the pacing suffers from it. It does get plenty creepy and atmospheric, especially in the third act but I think I really would have preferred a cut version. If it was smoother this may have been the best of the season, but it's still pretty good.

3/5

Family

Director – John Landis
Tags – Slasher / Survival

John Landis returns from season one.

A couple moves into a new neighborhood and strike up a friendship with a neighbor who harbors a deadly secret. It appears as though he is fond of kidnapping people and dissolving the flesh from their bones to create his ideal family. And now he has his eyes on a possible new bride. Landis returns to deliver another morbidly dark comedy and succeeds once again. The story is pretty good, I can't say I really loved it but I did enjoy it a great deal, especially the twist in the storyline. The acting is very good, especially from George Wendt, who was brilliant. This is a pretty fun episode in the end and a nice break from the more serious episodes.

3.5/5

Pelts

Director – Dario Argento
Tags – Animals

Dario Argento returns from season one.

A sleazy fur trader gets his hands on some priceless raccoon pelts that are beyond perfection. But it seems as though everyone who handles them is compelled to commit suicide, so they may not just be priceless, but cursed. Cursed raccoons? That's uh… interesting. I think in anyone else's hands this would be pure schlock, but when Argento packs it to the gills with gore and sex, it makes for a damn good time. Hell, there was even a period when I completely forgot about the pelts. The story isn't so much good as it is a set-up for massive amounts of boobs and blood, and while not great, hell, it was good enough for me.

3.5/5

Pro-Life
Director – John Carpenter
Tags – Suspense

John Carpenter returns from season one.

A young girl heads to an abortion clinic with her heavily religious father following close behind, and he'll do anything to stop her from terminating her pregnancy. But while in the clinic the doctors discover that her pregnancy is anything but normal. Making this episode is pretty ballsy given the subject matter, but it's far from being political, so those who were offended really missed the point. This is horror and I won't say what kind of horror because that would reveal too much, but suffice to say when a certain plot device rears its head, even pro-lifers will want the girl to have an abortion. Once again Carpenter takes top honors in crafting the best episode of the season and while not quite as brilliant as Cigarette Burns, Pro-Life is beautifully paced, wonderfully acted, especially by Ron Pearlman who is amazing in his role and the story comes together in a very unique fashion and allows the FX guys to really stretch their legs. Great stuff all around.

4/5

Right to Die
Director – Rob Schmidt
Tags – Ghosts

At the time of this season, the only thing Schmidt had really created was Wrong Turn, which is good, but seriously, no one else was available? Nothing against him at all, but the show is called Masters of Horror and he really doesn't fit the bill.

After a grisly car accident, a man barely escapes alive but his wife is burned horribly in the process. He wants to pull her off of life support and becomes embroiled in a battle against his mother-in-law for the right to do so. But when his wife dies briefly, only to be resuscitated, he sees her vengeful ghost and she has turned against the living. This is an interesting take on the ghost genre. I like the idea of her dying in the hospital and being resuscitated and during those brief times, she is one pissed off, burned up ghost. The acting and FX are good and the direction is solid. This is another one of those episodes that has nothing really bad about it and it's just a good time.

3.5/5

Screwfly Solution, The
Director – Joe Dante
Tags – Suspense

Joe Dante returns from season one.

A virus quickly spreads across the world, affecting only men. Now when they become sexually aroused they no longer wish to have sex with women, but to kill them. Scientists race for a cure while women continue to die in droves. Will this be the extinction of the human race? I'm sure this had women's rights groups all up in a tizzy due to its misogynistic nature, but I'm intelligent enough to realize that this show is based on works of fiction and fictitious circumstances don't bother me. Anyway, this is Dante's second Masters of Horror episode and both have their controversy, but the difference between this one and the last one is that this one is really good. It was actually on the road to becoming my favorite until the incredibly stupid ending. But anyway, up to that point it's very cool with a lot of graphic kills and the story reaches a very apocalyptic tone in a way that hasn't been done before. Great acting and pacing make for a great episode, torn down only by the ending. Who knows, you may like it but I found it to make me feel very disillusioned.

3.5/5

Sounds Like
Director – Brad Anderson
Tags – Suspense

Brad Anderson is another newcomer and more for the suspense genre than the horror one, but he is really talented and I think he has the potential to be the next Hitchcock so I was glad to see him involved.

A man with uncanny hearing coping with the loss of his young child continues to have his life spiral out of control, and the further his life gets out of hand, the more his madness takes over. In continuing with the theme of the season, here we have another wildly original theme. No one displays madness quite like Anderson and this unique tale shows that off quite well. I know if I could hear like this guy I would go pretty nuts too. The acting is great and the pacing is very good but this is another episode I just couldn't love all the way. Still entertaining but not my favorite.

3.5/5

V Word, The
Director – Ernest R. Dickerson
Tags – Vampires

Dickerson is new to this season and a curious addition. From what I can tell, he's only done two genre movies: Bones, which was pretty lackluster, and Demon Knight, which really is one of my all time favorites. So while I love Demon Knight, his inclusion in the show is strange to me.

Two youths sneak into a funeral home to see a real dead body and get much more than they bargained for when a vampire sets his sights on their necks. This is a pretty cool episode. The story is different from most vampire tales and the vampire itself is far from the norm, which is always really cool. The acting is solid and the direction is well done, add some gore and you have the makings of a very good episode. This is a nice movie that I enjoyed and while it didn't blow me away there was nothing about it that I could really say was bad.

3.5/5

Valerie on the Stairs
Director – Mick Garris
Tags – Demons

Mick Garris returns from season one.

A man moves into a house for unpublished writers in the hope that it will give him the opportunity to finally break into the industry, but shortly after moving in he is distracted by a mysterious woman who is assaulted by a demon like figure. The more he investigates, the more he discovers that the other writers in the house know more about her than they let on. While disappointed with the Barker adaptation from season one and Garris' episode from season one, I ended up being pleasantly surprised here. It's not great and it does feel convoluted, but it's still satisfying and well acted. I like the story but don't feel it was executed as well as it could have been. I believe that really the best person to adapt Clive Barker stories is Barker himself and this probably could have been better if he did.

3/5

Washingtonians, The
Director – Peter Medak
Tags – Cannibals

Peter Medak has a long history in filmmaking and has also done a lot of TV, so his inclusion here makes sense. He has made really good movies like The Changeling but then again he also made Species II, so I guess we'll just have to see what he does here.

A man finds an interesting artifact in his dead grandmother's basement that links George Washington to cannibalism. When the letter he finds proves to be authentic, a group known simply as The Washingtonians who carry on his legacy of cannibalism attempt to get it back by any means necessary. Medak has definitely crafted a damn fine episode here. Sure it's weird, but unique, and very well done. It's also well acted even with some hammy moments, but we are talking about George Washington and cannibalism here and it's bound to get a bit silly at times. Strange for sure, but oddly satisfying.

3.5/5

We All Scream for Ice Cream
Director – Tom Holland
Tags – Ghosts

I'm surprised Tom Holland wasn't in the first season with his work on Child's Play, Fright Night and a couple of other genre films. Again, he's not a huge name in horror but has definitely made a mark.

Years after a prank results in the death of a mentally challenged ice cream man, the boys who were involved are now grown and have children of their own. But now it appears as though the ice cream man is back as a vengeful spirit (almost a zombie) and is getting his revenge through their children. This episode is kind of silly but then again, so was Child's Play and the director did wonders with it, and while he doesn't quite work the same magic here, he does enough to make it enjoyable. I love the death scenes because the guys essentially melt into pools of ice cream and once again, while it sounds silly, it's actually pretty gory and really works. Oh and since the ice cream man is a creepy clown, that should really get to people with coulrophobia. It's well acted and well made and despite its glaring absurdity, it works as a horror piece and I rather enjoyed it.

3.5/5

This would be the last season of Masters of Horror for some reason. I read once that this was Showtime's #2 series but it still got cancelled and that really blows. I actually prefer the first season over this one because nothing here blew me away but on the plus side there wasn't a single episode I would call bad and it was consistently good. R.I.P. Master of Horror, your run was much too short but I appreciate the two seasons I was given.

Season Score: 3.5/5

Nightmares and Dreamscapes
Season 1
Year: 2006
Tags: Anthology

This is more of a miniseries than a show and the concept behind it was simple. Eight episodes based on Stephen King short stories. So each episode clocks in at under an hour (except Battleground which was aired without commercials). So let's just get to it!

Autopsy Room Four
Director – Mikael Salomon
Tags – Suspense

A man finds himself in a morgue but still completely aware of his surroundings. Is he just conscious after death or is he still alive but no one realizes it? This story was never one of my favorites because I never found it to be all that interesting. It's a good concept for a short film so that it doesn't get too boring, but this episode is still kind of slow. The acting is good but some of the things the "dead" guy says in his narration are just senseless and weird. This episode is ok, not bad at all given the subject matter, which I feel is weak, and not what I would call a waste of time, but it is not great either.

2.5/5

Battleground
Director – Brian Henson
Tags – Slasher / Survival

A hit man performs a contract kill on a toy maker and later receives a strange package at his home. When he opens it, he discovers a small footlocker filled with green army men, but these are no regular toys, they're alive. Living army men sounds kind of lame, but the story is badass and the adaptation even better. I like how they filmed the army men action sequences and the FX are very well done. I also like William Hurt in the lead role, but I don't think he even had any lines, which worked because he could really act out the part with just his facial expressions. If nothing else this is a very unique survival horror tale with quick pacing and a very high entertainment factor.

4.5/5

Crouch End
Director – Mark Haber
Tags – Monsters

A lawyer and his new wife on their honeymoon in London become lost in a strange part of the city. This place has thin spots the locals say, allowing creatures from an alternate dimension to spill over in our reality. Here Stephen King taps directly into the Lovecraft mythos for this tale and crafts a very nightmarish story. I love the story but there were a couple things about the adaptation that I didn't like. Obviously the first is the CGI, which is bad by Sci-Fi channel standards. I really wish they had invested the time in practical FX. And also the style of filming, which I imagine was done to lay credence to the nightmarish reality, didn't work all the time and was a bit overused. Still, it's pretty damn enjoyable because like I said, the story is great and it's well acted. Fun stuff.

4/5

End of the Whole Mess, The
Director – Mikael Salomon
Tags – Biological

A documentary filmmaker chronicles the life of his genius brother and how he was disillusioned with the state of the world. So he decided to do something about it and devised a way to create world peace through water. But things go horribly wrong. Of course they went wrong, and things would be pretty boring if everything was all peaceful and nice. I really like the story and the adaptation was spot on with great acting and wonderful pacing. This is a great apocalyptic tale that really strays from the norm by allowing humanity to fail with not a bang, but a whimper. Pretty awesome.

4/5

Fifth Quarter, The
Director – Rob Bowman
Tags – Suspense

A con is released from jail and promises to lead a straight life but when an old friend of his shows up bleeding at his home, he gets drawn into a robbery and seeks not only revenge, but his friend's quarter of the money. This is a well crafted story that keeps the viewer guessing as to what's going on and heaps on plenty of suspense in the process. The acting is really good and the pacing is pulled off well. When the end comes, it's pretty good, just like everything leading to it. It all feels a little rushed though and maybe could have used a longer runtime, but it's still very good and I enjoyed it.

3.5/5

Road Virus Heads North, The
Director – Sergio Mimica-Gezzan
Tags – Slasher / Survival

A best selling horror author buys a creepy painting whose creator committed suicide. Now as he travels back home the painting begins to change and a man begins to kill the people he has shown the painting to, and now the man is coming for him. The premise is pretty cool and ends up being somewhat interesting, but still falls short in my eyes. I did enjoy the way the conclusion was made and how it was left pretty clear the road the author was going to be forced to take. It's a good episode but maybe too abrupt in its storytelling to leave a lasting impression. Not bad though.

3/5

Umney's Last Case
Director – Rob Bowman
Tags – Suspense

A private eye's life is turned upside-down when everything normal in his life changes. Soon afterward he discovers that he is a fictional character and the man who created him wants to swap lives. This is a pretty cool story and William H. Macy in the lead role was a great choice. But I can't say I loved it. It was a little slow and overblown at times. I understand it was supposed to be a 30's set piece and that's how many 30's era movies were but the fast talking and overacting was just overdone. Anyway, it's different and fun and worth checking out but I'm definitely a fan of the more horrific stuff.

3/5

You Know They Got a Hell of a Band
Director – Mike Robe
Tags – Suspense

A couple take a wrong turn on the road and end up in the idyllic town of Rock n' Roll Heaven which just happens to house some uncanny look-a-likes for some of Rock n' Roll's most iconic deceased musicians. But are they really look-a-likes? And what dark secret does this town hold (It is an idyllic small town after all, they're never quite right)? I always liked this story because it was a very unusual and welcome take on the typical weird small town. Its adaptation here however, is a little less memorable. First off, I wish the "look-a-likes", actually looked like the artists they were representing. A couple of them do, but for the most part, you have to be told who they are so that you can actually realize who they're supposed to be. The acting is ok, nothing great, the direction is fine I guess, a little slow, but nothing horrible. I would have liked to have seen this story given a better treatment but as it stands this is a pretty average episode.

2.5/5

Not a bad a miniseries at all, but honestly I could think of many different stories I would have liked to have seen adapted than a few here. But we are talking about Stephen King and I do firmly believe that everything he has written will be adapted for the big or small screen eventually. So I liked Nightmares and Dreamscapes, but despite some great episodes, I can't say I loved it. Definitely worth viewing for King fans though.

Season Score: 3.5/5

Night Stalker
Season 1
Year: 2005
Tags: Serial Killer (Fictional), Monsters, Suspense

This show is a remake of Kolchak – The Night Stalker (yes, they remake shows as well). Here Kolchak is looking for who or what killed his wife and travels into the seedy underworld as a journalist to try and find answers. I can see why this was cancelled mid season. It's not a bad series by any means but just about all of the charm of the original has been completely stripped away here. Kolchak was an awesome character but now the original character has been tweaked and spread across three characters, and that's the first big issue I have with this show. The new Kolchak in dark and brooding (boring), and he will fight against the evil of the world. The camera man is the comic relief and not very funny. And the lead journalist is the consummate professional in it for the story. Kolchak used to be all three, he wanted the story, he was hilarious, and he fought the evil creatures. Now it's three people and that's pretty lazy. At least here the show isn't as formulaic as its predecessor and there is an ongoing story. But once again, the story isn't all that great. By the time I actually became somewhat interested in it, the show was over. It only lasted six episodes and the DVD release has ten, just enough to wet your palate but not receive any real kind of pleasure from it. The acting was good but not that great and I was kind of bored during some parts of each episode. The occasionally silly rubber suits of the original were replaced with bad CGI and still they call it a progression in technology. It's pretty bad when a rubber suit looks better than your technological advancement. There also didn't seem to be much thought put into the creatures and people Kolchak would face. Another interesting side note I have to talk about is in regards to corporate greed. Each original series episode clocked in a just over 51 minutes, and this was back in the seventies. Now the episodes in this series are just over 41 minutes, meaning that there has been an additional ten full minutes of commercials added to hour long TV shows nowadays. That's pretty ridiculous. Now nearly a full third of your TV shows are commercials, a third! It used to comprise of less than one sixth and has doubled over the course of thirty short years. This is why I don't have cable and instead buy TV shows that interest me on DVD, that way I don't have to be subject to twenty minutes of commercials, crap shows I have no interest in watching and ridiculous bills for a service that's barely worthwhile. Anyway, that's my little rant. As for the show, it's completely watchable, but I just couldn't fully get into it.

2.5/5

Surface
Season 1
Year: 2005
Tags: Sea Monsters

A marine biologist discovers a new species of marine life only to have it covered up by the government. Still she continues to prove the existence of the creatures, much to her own peril as government agents first discredit her and then try to kill her. At the same time an insurance agent watches his brother die at the hands (fins?) of one of the creatures and a teenage boy finds a strange egg and raises a creature in secret. A show about sea monsters? You can immediately sign me up. I'm always wary about shows that only run for a single season, but I absolutely loved Surface. And of course now I'm really disappointed that I will never get any more episodes. It took a few episodes to get really immersed in the show but by the time I had inserted disc 2 of my set, I was definitely hooked. The characters are great and definitely have a great deal of depth to them. The scenarios are superb and just keep getting better, and while you definitely have to suspend disbelief several times throughout the series, it still makes for a rather compelling watch. The series features several CGI sequences, but I wouldn't exactly call it CGI heavy because the human drama definitely takes the front seat. Now the CGI is far from being great, but honestly I didn't really mind it because the CGI was appropriate and never really overused, instead it was used in places where practical FX just were not an option. But the CGI is definitely much better than what you would see in your typical Sci-Fi channel original movie. As for what longevity the show may have had, I feel it could have gone on for quite a long time. The show, as compelling as it was, barely even scratched the surface of its potential and instead the whole first season (only season), acted as a set-up for the many story arcs that could have followed. Let's just say that show ends in a jaw dropping way with unanswered questions and many possible routes for it to continue. Because of this I am incredibly annoyed that there will never be another episode, but that's life, eventually something will happen to something you love watching that will leave a bad taste in your mouth. A show goes south, or a movie franchise takes a nosedive, etc. Only on rare occasions can you be fully satisfied. Still, the first season was just damn good TV that had a couple flaws but were relatively minor in the grand scheme of excellent acting, grand storytelling and a unique concept for a TV show that I appreciated on many levels. Surface is definitely a great show and I recommend that everyone give it a chance. And don't give up on it after the first disc of four, as it becomes even better to watch as it moves along.

4/5

Tales from the Crypt
Season 1
Year: 1989
Tags: Anthology

Based on not only the horror comic that the show takes its name from, but also uses stories from other similar comics. Each half hour show is bookended by some commentary by the Cryptkeeper, a rather decrepit looking individual who hasn't seen life in a long time. This anthology series made quite a name for itself during its run so let's start at the beginning shall we?

And All Through the House
Director – Robert Zemeckis
Tags – Slasher / Survival

A woman makes the mistake of killing her husband in the same night that a crazed madman in a Santa Claus suit has escaped from the local asylum, with ax in hand. This is an awesome episode because it holds your typical slasher feel, but it also has the added bonus of a greedy woman killing her husband, which opens up all kinds of suspense since now she doesn't have anyone else in the house to help protect her and her daughter, as well as the added fact that the police are out and about looking for the killer and may just find another killer. Awesome episode, and probably my favorite of the season.

4/5

Collection Completed
Director – Mary Lambert
Tags – Suspense

A man retires after a very dedicated career and finding nothing to do, and he decides to take up a hobby that doesn't go well with his wife's love of animals. Conflict arises soon into his retirement. This episode reminds me of my parents even though my dad has no hobbies and my mom dislikes animals. I'm reminded of them because the man here is a colossal pain in the ass. Just kidding dad! Kind of… Anyway, the story is pretty fun and backed by some great acting and very good direction. It's hilarious at times and ends well. Great episode.

4/5

Dig that Cat… He's Real Gone
Director – Richard Donner
Tags – Suspense

A bum gains the ability to resurrect himself through an experimental procedure that a scientist has created by transferring a cat's nine lives into a human. He then uses his new found power to make a lot of money for himself, but runs into complications along the way. This is a fun episode and even though you can see the direction it's heading in with its conclusion, it's still a fun ride getting there. Joe Pantoliano is great in the lead role and adds a ton of personality to the character. Good story, direction, this episode has it all and makes for a very entertaining (and somewhat silly) time.

3.5/5

Lover Come Hack to Me
Director – Tom Holland
Tags – Slasher / Survival

A man who married a wealthy woman for her bank account alone goes on a honeymoon with his new bride and she wants everything to be perfect. And she'll do anything to get her way. I like this story because it seems to straightforward but then it gets really weird and off the wall, which is pretty cool. The acting is well done, especially by Amanda Plummer and the direction is pretty spot-on throughout. A definitely fun tale with a hint of weirdness, ok, maybe more than a hint. Good times.

3.5/5

Man Who Was Death, The
Director – Walter Hill, Kevin Yagher
Tags – Serial Killer (Fictional)

When the death penalty is abolished, the man who threw the switch suddenly not only loses his job, but his purpose in life. But he finds new purpose in executing those who he feels got away with murder. This is a pretty cool way to kick off the series because the story is a fun slice of serial killer with morals. William Sadler plays the lead role and does a great job with his character. Overall a good but not too great episode. Certainly enough fun to keep me entertained and I don't need much beyond that.

3.5/5

Only Sin Deep
Director – Howard Deutch
Tags – Witchcraft

A beautiful hooker strikes a deal with a pawn broker that she will sell him her beauty in the form of a plaster mask in exchange for $10,000. But months later when her beauty begins to fade, she realizes that it wasn't just a mask of her beauty that the man took. This story is kind of cool, definitely not one of my favorites, but I still dig it. The acting is pretty good and the direction is fine but I wasn't really thrilled with the episode. Not bad at all but probably the weakest of the season.

3/5

So I'm a little disappointed that there were only six episodes in the first season but I guess it started out as a tester season and performed well enough to get a full run. Still, it was six very respectable episodes with not a bad one in the lot and I would look forward to all the full seasons that would come.

Season Score: 3.5/5

Tales from the Crypt
Season 2
Year: 1990
Tags: Anthology

Season two is the first full season of the show, with eighteen episodes.

Cutting Cards
Director – Walter Hill
Tags – Suspense

Two hardcore gamblers at war with one another amp up the stakes in a game of chance that could be their last. This is an awesome episode. This episode rests on the shoulders of Lance Henriksen and Kevin Tighe, who play their parts perfectly. The story and direction are near perfection and the episode flies by so quickly you would swear it was only five minutes long. It manages to be very suspenseful and even ends up being pretty funny at times. A landmark episode in the season.

4/5

Dead Right
Director – Howard Deutch
Tags – Suspense

A woman seeks fast cash by looking for a rich man to marry. When she entrusts her future to a psychic, things go from bad to worse as she marries a huge slob who is supposed to inherit a fortune. I love this episode and it's a great way to kick off the season. There's a nice twist in the storyline, and the story as a whole is very fun. This is backed up further by some great acting and smooth direction. Nothing much else I can say, one of the best of the season right here.

4/5

Fitting Punishment
Director – Jack Sholder
Tags – Zombies

A cheap undertaker is forced to take in his nephew, much to his disdain. But when an "accident" relieves him of his burden, his nephew seeks revenge from beyond the grave. I love this episode because the undertaker is just such a piece of shit that you want something to happen to him. I like shows and movies that really drive home how terrible some people are. And when the boy comes back, it's pretty creepy and features some awesome FX work. Great acting and direction overall with a pleasing, straightforward story. Excellent.

4/5

For Cryin' Out Loud
Director – Jeffrey Price
Tags – Suspense

A concert promoter is trying to steal the profits from his benefit show but has a problem: His inner monologue has gained a mind of its own and it attempting to dissuade him. If that's not enough, someone is blackmailing him for half of the cash. This episode is more humorous than anything, but it does have a fair share of suspense as well. It's just really good. Great cast, fun story, solid direction. No real scares, but there really didn't need to be, it was funny and enjoyable. Plus, Iggy Pop was performing, which was awesome.

3.5/5

Four-Sided Triangle
Director – Tom Holland
Tags – Suspense

A farmhand is lusting after a beautiful young woman but she rejects his advances, because she's in love with the scarecrow. Yeah, it sounds weird but I really love this episode. It mainly consists of Patricia Arquette looking hot and Chelcie Ross acting like a rather horny old man, but the road to the conclusion is a very enjoyable one, mainly because Patricia Arquette was looking hot. I kid of course, that wasn't the only reason. The acting as a whole is great, and the story, while weird, ends very cool and I just love this episode.

4/5

Judy, You're Not Yourself Today
Director – Randa Haines
Tags – Witchcraft

A woman is duped by a witch into switching bodies and now must convince her husband that she is not an old lady and instead his loving wife, all while trying to find a way to get her body back. Here's another fun episode that relies more on laughs than scares, but it still works. The acting is overdone but really it's meant to be given the overall feel of the episode. The story is a good one despite its silliness and the direction is very smooth. Once again, another winning episode for season two.

3.5/5

Korman's Kalamity
Director – Rowdy Harrington
Tags – Monsters

A comic book illustrator realizes that his newest horrific creations are coming to life, all while he tries to deal with his overbearing wife. This episode has always been one of my favorites. There are several monsters on display and all of them are pretty awesome. Despite that, this episode is fairly light on horror and instead opts more for humor, which completely works for it. I love the acting, direction, overall story, just every aspect of this one. One of my favorites of this season or any other.

5/5

Lower Berth
Director – Kevin Yagher
Tags – Mummies

A side show main attraction (a man with two faces), falls in love with the latest attraction, a 4000 year old mummy that supposedly carries a deadly curse, but first he must get past his cruel owner. Tales from the Crypt fans will surely enjoy this episode for the ending alone, but all over it is a very enjoyable one. It's typical "freaks are more human than humans" tale but it certainly is a well conceived one. Well acted, directed and all that jazz. Another highlight to the season.

4/5

Mute Witness to Murder
Director – Jim Simpson
Tags – Suspense

A woman witnesses her neighbor kill his wife and the sudden shock causes her to fall mute, now the killer wants to end her life before she regains the ability to tell anyone of his crime. I like the concept and the episode but it really isn't anything special. The acting and direction are fine and the story is ok but it really plays out in a somewhat mundane way. It's still enjoyable after all is said and done but it didn't leave much of a positive impression on me in the end.

3/5

My Brother's Keeper
Director – Peter S. Seaman
Tags – Suspense

This episode follows a pair of conjoined twins, one who is a pompous ass and the other who is more refined. The ass wants an operation to split them, but the other brother is afraid. But when he finds a woman he can love, he reconsiders, even though his brother is hiding something. This is a fun episode that flows well up to the nice if not somewhat predictable twist ending. The acting is good and the pacing is nice. Good times.

3.5/5

Sacrifice, The
Director – Richard Greenberg
Tags – Suspense

A man and his new lover devise a way to kill her husband so they can be together. Unfortunately someone saw them and blackmails them, not for money, but for the woman. Nice episode. It begins like many others, new lovers, one attached, murder and more, but this one has a little something extra. The story is really well done, the acting is good and the direction is good as well. This is a solid little suspense tale, nothing major but definitely fills the entertainment quota, for me at least.

3.5/5

Secret, The
Director – J. Michael Riva
Tags – [Hidden to conceal spoilers]

A boy is adopted from an orphanage by a well to do couple, who lavish toys and food upon him, but they are not the loving new parents he thought they would be, because they have a secret. I remember watching this as a kid and the ending just blew my little mind, it was amazing! I had never seen anything like it and while it still gives me enjoyment today, it may be a little easier to figure out nowadays, but it still sure does pack a punch. The acting is great, the direction is flawless, and this has always been my absolute favorite episode of all time. Brilliant!

5/5

Switch, The
Director – Arnold Schwarzenegger
Tags – Suspense

A lonely, elderly rich man is in love with a younger woman but doesn't want her to love him just for his money so he expends some of his fortune to give him a new youthful appearance by switching his face with a younger man's. But it may not be enough. This is a cool episode, even if you can see where it's going from a mile away. The acting is a bit cheesy too at times. But I still liked it because it was paced well and just plain fun. And it was directed by Schwarzenegger, which is pretty badass since it marked his directorial debut. I think it was a right of passage for all the Hollywood stars to be involved in an episode of Tales from the Crypt or something.

3/5

Television Terror
Director – Charlie Picerni
Tags – Ghosts

A pompous television talk show host visits a home that was the sight of a string of grisly murders in a ratings stunt. But the long deceased residents are not happy with this at all. A lot of Tales from the Crypt episodes have some great humor in them, but this one was always a different beast. This one was just a straight up dark horror tale, and it's brilliant. Part of it is shot in a cinema verite style from the camera man's perspective, which heightens the scares. This episode is pretty creepy and genuinely scary, and with the great acting and direction, it makes for another one of my all time favorite episodes.

5/5

Thing from the Grave, The
Director – Fred Dekker
Tags – Zombies

A photographer and a model fall in love, much to the chagrin of the model's abusive boyfriend. But when he takes revenge on the photographer, the photographer ends up wanting revenge back. Here's another fun episode aided by Miguel Ferrer playing his typical prick character with excellence. The rest of the cast does an admirable job too. This is another good episode that didn't wow me with anything but didn't really disappoint me either. And hey, Dekker makes a rare directorial showing in the genre, which has always been a good thing.

3.5/5

Three's a Crowd
Director – David Burton Morris
Tags – Suspense

A man is convinced that his wife is cheating on him with her friend, and during their anniversary he plans on taking revenge on them both. This all starts as a fairly mundane but still enjoyable revenge thriller. The acting is good and so is the direction, making it fully watchable. But as the episode progressed, and the husband became ever more insane with his jealousy, it started to get even more enjoyable and then when the end hit, wow, that was a good one. So the episode was average but ended so strong that it almost became great.

3.5/5

'Til Death
Director – Chris Walas
Tags – Witchcraft

A man on the verge of losing everything seeks out a wealthy woman to help him protect his assets, but when she rejects him he decides to dabble in voodoo in order to win her over, which has consequences of its own. So why is it that when an outsider seeks out black magic, that they always disregard the warnings of the person issuing it to them? I guess clichés like this are what makes horror sometimes. Anyway, this episode is pretty good, definitely not a bad one, but not the most memorable of the season either. The acting isn't bad and the direction is pretty solid. The story however, I didn't really care for as much. It falls into the cliché trap one too many times. But still completely watchable.

3/5

Ventriloquist's Dummy, The
Director – Richard Donner
Tags – Suspense

A man trying to break into the ventriloquist business seeks out his idol, the greatest ventriloquist in the world, but his idol has a dark secret that had made him the best. This is another pretty funny episode that does get a bit silly at times but still manages to entertain, especially when the ventriloquist reveals his secret, it's pretty awesome. Bloodshed ensues, more hilarity, you know. So yeah, this is really good stuff. Great acting, a solid story and very good direction. Can't ask for much more.

3.5/5

What a season! Not a single bad episode, in fact, every episode was above average and that includes a trio of masterpieces. The first short season may have been a nice jumping off point but this season really set the series into motion. It was also this season that really made me watch the show religiously as a kid. Great stuff all around.

Season Score: 4.5/5

Tales from the Crypt
Season 3
Year: 1991
Tags: Anthology

Tales from the Crypt returns for a third season with an additional fourteen episodes.

Abra Cadaver

Director – Stephen Hopkins
Tags – Suspense

A med student plays a trick on his brother and it results in him having a heart attack. Years later his brother has a little something planned for him. Here's a fun episode. I like how it plays out and features more than one plot twist, which is always fun when it works, and it definitely works here. The acting and direction are well done and this was just quite simply a good episode worth a watch or two.

3.5/5

Carrion Death

Director – Steven E. de Souza
Tags – Suspense

A serial killer who escaped from prison and is on his way to Mexico is pursued by a cop who ultimately handcuffs himself to the killer and swallows the key with his dying breath. This episode is pretty cool but the thing that really irks me is that the killer is freaking out because he can't get free from the dead cop. Are you serious? You're in the desert, could just pick up a big rock and break the guy's arm off or cut open his stomach and get the key, so I had a big problem believing that he would drag this corpse all around the desert. But I guess they couldn't take the common sense route or the ending wouldn't work. Other than that it was cool and the acting and direction were great, but I just couldn't get past that issue.

3/5

Dead Wait

Director – Tobe Hooper
Tags – Suspense

A criminal gets involved with a man he intends to rob and also gets involved intimately with his wife. But will voodoo interfere with his plans? This episode starts out pretty dull and continues in that tradition for most of the runtime. The acting is ok but I just couldn't get into the story or direction at all. Towards the end there was a nice little gruesome twist and it does end well, so it's not all bad, but it does end up just being an average episode.

2.5/5

Deadline

Director – Walter Hill
Tags – Suspense

An alcoholic journalist is having trouble finding work and is determined to clean up his act, but just how far we he go for a story in the hopes that he'll be back on top of the reporter's game? This is a rather lackluster episode that really didn't have much going for it. The acting is good but the story just isn't very worthwhile and the episode ends up being rather slow. And then when the ending came I must say that I still didn't really care.

2/5

Easel Kill Ya
Director – John Harrison
Tags – Serial Killer (Fictional)

A painter unable to create good art anymore takes to murder for artistic inspiration and cold hard cash. I like the idea of an artist resorting to murder in the name of art and this is enhanced further by some very good acting that supports a well conceived story with a brilliant ending. The direction is also very good. The death scenes, especially the second one, are well made. A very well done episode.

3.5/5

Loved to Death
Director – Tom Mankiewicz
Tags – Suspense

A man practically becomes obsessed with a woman in his apartment building but she wants nothing to do with him so he resorts to using a love potion, but it ends up working a little too well. There's something pretty damn entertaining about Mariel Hemingway playing the love stricken woman to the nth degree, but beyond that I didn't really dig this episode. The acting is fine but it ends up being fairly dull. I did enjoy the ending though. Just ok in my book.

2.5/5

Mournin' Mess
Director – Manny Coto
Tags – [Hidden to conceal spoilers]

A reporter on his last legs in the business desperately tries to uncover a story that may show a relation between a serial killer of the homeless and a new charity foundation. This episode takes a bit too long to really get going and while it definitely ended strong (as most episodes do) it just took its time getting there. But the acting and direction as a whole are fine I just couldn't fully get into the story until the end.

3/5

Reluctant Vampire, The
Director – Elliot Silverstein

Tags – Vampires

A good natured vampire doesn't want to kill people and instead takes a night job at a blood bank so he can satisfy his urges, but things don't quite work out the way he wants them to. This is a pretty fun episode, showing a very different side to your typical vampire. Good acting, a few laughs, nice direction and a solid story make for a well rounded episode. And it's nice to see Michael Berryman as a good guy AND with a real role.

3.5/5

Split Second
Director – Russell Mulcahy
Tags – Suspense

A lonely waitress marries a lumberjack who shows his terrible jealousy streak when she begins his eyeing the new young lumberjack on the job. So I figured this would be a typical jealously followed by revenge type tale and for the most part it was but the ending was something I really didn't see coming, well not all of it anyway. There's also a nice cast of genre actors who have appeared in many movies but none of them really made it big as leads. A very good episode.

3.5/5

Spoiled
Director – Andy Wolk
Tags – Suspense

A woman wants to live out her life like a trashy soap opera, but when her husband doesn't have time for her as he is on the brink of a medical breakthrough, so she seeks the affections of another man. I like how this episode played out like the soap opera this woman was trying to emulate, complete with over the top acting. Besides that the episode was pretty unremarkable up until the ending, which was a brilliant revenge retort. Not bad, it just is what it is.

3/5

Top Billing
Director – Todd Holland
Tags – Suspense

An actor who just doesn't have "the look" finds it difficult to find work and his life is falling apart all around him. But he has one more chance in a theatre production of Hamlet, and he'll do anything to get the role. Here's a favorite of mine from this season. The episode moves along nicely with great acting and a smooth story, making it a good but not great episode. And then the twist ending comes and automatically makes it brilliant. Seriously, just watch it and you'll see what I mean.

4/5

Trap, The
Director – Michael J. Fox
Tags – Suspense

A jobless man tries to get one over on his insurance company by faking his own death with the aid of his doctor brother, but things don't end up quite as planned. So the episode started out as your typical take on a familiar tale but I did like how it ended up in the end as it was very fitting. Good acting, good direction, nothing exemplary per se but just a well done episode with definite entertainment value.

3/5

Undertaking Palor
Director – Michael Thau
Tags – Suspense

Four boys discover that the local mortician has a scam going with the local pharmacist to drudge up some business by poisoning the medications of some locals and they try to catch him in the act. I like how this episode took a cinema verite style during the final portion of the episode but beyond that there wasn't much I really dug about it. Well, the way the mortician dealt with his clients was pretty crazy. The acting and direction were decent enough and this ended up being a good episode.

3/5

Yellow
Director – Robert Zemeckis
Tags – Suspense

Set in World War I, this story is about a young man who is tried for cowardice, but his commanding officer, who also happens to be his father. Will his father be able to do the right thing or will he stick by his son? This doesn't seem to fit in the Tales from the Crypt universe but it is still definitely a welcome addition and pretty suspenseful in nature. It's also gruesome, being a very accurate and well done portrayal of war. It also has great acting and ends up being the best of the season.

4/5

This is a pretty unremarkable season for Tales from the Crypt, especially considering that it followed a very remarkable season. There just wasn't much going for it but I do have to say that it wasn't completely unenjoyable by any means. It was pretty solid the whole way through with only a couple of hiccups but not really any stand-out episodes. Good, but I definitely have high hopes that season four will rebound the series back on track.

Season Score: 3/5

Tales from the Crypt
Season 4
Year: 1992
Tags: Anthology

Tales from the Crypt delivers another fourteen episodes in its fourth season.

Beauty Rest
Director – Stephen Hopkins
Tags – Suspense

An aging actress has yet to hit her big break and is beginning to lose hope, so when her roommate gets a very big opportunity she makes sure that the roommate will be indisposed so that the opportunity will be hers instead. I really liked this episode mainly because I liked most of the actors involved and it was a very interesting watch. I knew it was all going to be leading toward something but I wasn't quite sure what that something was. So when the ending hit, I got to admit, I wasn't very happy. I just said to myself: "Really, that's it?" And it was also way too similar an ending to an episode from the previous season. I still really liked it for the aforementioned reasons, but it just kind of petered out in the end.

3.5/5

Curiosity Killed
Director – Elliot Silverstein
Tags – Suspense

Two elderly couples head out for a trip in the woods, but when the men start acting a little strange, one of the women starts to think that they may plan to kill her. Probably the best thing about this movie is Margot Kidder and her old person make-up, not that anyone else is bad, everyone is quite good but she really does steal the show. The story isn't all that great and when the reveal comes for what's really happening, I can't say I really cared. But the whole end sequence was pretty cool.

2.5/5

King of the Road
Director – Tom Holland
Tags – Suspense

A young street racer blackmails an old street racer turned cop with the threat of exposing his past, which included a manslaughter charge he successfully evaded. He wants to pull the old timer out of retirement for one last race. Ok, here we have another episode that just doesn't fit in the Tales from the Crypt schematic, but as the episode Yellow from last season kind of stepped out of the genre, at least it was good, which this episode is not. The acting is really good but the story is a definite stinker and it just really had no kind of excitement. I guess maybe if I was a car guy I would have enjoyed it more, but there just wasn't much here for me.

2/5

Maniac at Large
Director – John Frankenheimer
Tags – Serial Killer (Fictional)

A librarian overreacts after hearing that there is a serial killer on the loose and begins to suspect that everyone around her is the killer. Well, this episode is good for what it is but I didn't really like it all that much. I think it was made a little too obvious who the killer is but the acting and direction were fairly good. Another weak episode in the season but not a complete loss I suppose, just an average installment.

2.5/5

New Arrival, The
Director – Peter Medak
Tags – Suspense

A child psychologist takes his radio show on the road and visits a woman who is having trouble with her out of control daughter, but this is anything but a typical by the book case. I'm glad that the late, great Zelda Rubinstein received a good role in this show because I've always felt that she was a great actor that was just terribly underused in her career. And David Warner was just icing on the cake. So yeah, the acting is great and the direction is ok, honestly it took a little too long to get to the meat of the story, but when it hit its stride mid way through the episode, it really moved forward well to the great ending.

3.5/5

None but the Lonely Heart
Director – Tom Hanks
Tags – Suspense

A con man marries older woman only to ensure that they die and leave all of their money to him. But as he gets closer to becoming indicted for his crimes, he tries to pull off one more marriage, but will things unfold as planned? What I really like about this episode is that it seems to be heading in one direction and then goes somewhere else completely, which is very welcome. The acting is great and the direction is really good, along with some nicely done FX. I don't love this episode but its ending definitely pulled it off the crap heap.

3.5/5

On a Deadman's Chest
Director – William Friedkin

Tags – Suspense

The lead singer of a rock band gets a special tattoo on his chest, unfortunately for him, the face of a woman he hates is what he gets and he decides that the only way to get rid of the tattoo is to get rid of her. This had the potential to be pretty cool but I really wasn't all that impressed by it. The acting wasn't the best and as a whole the story wasn't all that interesting, but like most Crypt episodes, it ended very strongly. Just an ok episode.

2.5/5

Séance
Director – Gary Fleder
Tags – Suspense

A pair of con artists tried to juke a man out of his money with blackmail, but when that doesn't quite work they must resort to other methods. To be honest I was pretty bored with this episode but I did like the acting and rather enjoyed the ending quite a bit as it definitely went against the grain of the story before the climax hit. There was also some very surprising gore, which was nice to see. Still not impressed by the episode, but it wasn't bad at all.

2.5/5

Showdown
Director – Richard Donner
Tags – Ghosts

Set in the old west, an outlaw finds himself confronted with all the men he has killed. That's pretty much the extent of the story, which I really didn't care for. The way it's presented is fine and it is definitely well acted, but I just didn't really like it and found it to be kind of dull. Maybe this is why we don't see many horror/westerns, because sometimes they just flat out do not work, which is definitely the case here.

2/5

Split Personality
Director – Joel Silver
Tags – Suspense

A conman comes across a pair of rich twins, but being unsatisfied with only half their fortune, he devises a way that he can marry both of them, but will it work out for him? Of course not, this is Tales from the Crypt. Anyway, I really like this episode. Joe Pesci really hams it up and the story definitely has its moments with a very memorable ending. Nothing all that spectacular, just a good time, which is enough for me.

3.5/5

Strung Along

Director – Kevin Yagher
Tags – Suspense

An aging puppeteer is planning a comeback but the thought that his young wife may be having an affair is getting in the way. Here's a good episode that didn't leave any particular lasting impressions on me but it didn't leave any bad impressions either. The acting was fine, direction was ok and the story was decent enough, brought up from mediocrity by the ending. Just a good time, no more, no less.

3/5

This'll Kill Ya

Director – Robert Longo
Tags – Suspense

A blowhard manager of a medical research facility leaks news about their new wonder drug being ready for human trials when it isn't, so the employees decide to test it on him, with disastrous consequences. Wow, what a completely predictable piece of crap we have here. The acting is mostly bad, the story is weak and it's fairly dull as well. This is a bona fide bad episode with very little redeeming value.

1.5/5

Werewolf Concerto

Director – Steve Perry
Tags – Werewolves

A group of people are trapped in a resort and begin turning up dead one by one, all the victims of a werewolf. Fortunately for the people, there is a werewolf hunter among them, but then again, so is the werewolf. Gee, I wonder who the werewolf and the hunter are. Aside from the obvious nature of the twist ending, this is a great episode. A cool looking werewolf, great acting, smooth direction and a solid story make for one of the better episodes of the season. There's also a fair amount of gore as well.

3.5/5

What's Cookin'

Director – Gilbert Adler
Tags – Suspense

A couple is having trouble keeping their restaurant afloat until a young drifter comes along with a very special steak recipe that manages to strike up some new business. So the episode doesn't waste much time in telling you what's going on, which is very smart since it's easy to figure out, and instead focuses on a rather large moral dilemma, allowing the episode to play out like a dark comedy, which works wonders. The story works beautifully with a great ending, there are fantastic actors and it's all wrapped up with great direction. The best episode of the season.

4.5/5

Well, I was hoping for a rebound and what I received was even more of a dud than last season. Season four definitely had its ups and downs (mostly downs it seems), and while there were some enjoyable episodes, there were also just as many unenjoyable ones. This makes for an average season and now I'll repeat myself and say that I hope the series can get back on track next season.

Season Score: 2.5/5

Tales from the Crypt
Season 5
Year: 1993
Tags: Anthology

Tales from the Crypt comes back with thirteen more episodes. Why are the seasons getting shorter?

As Ye Sow
Director – Kyle McLachlan
Tags – Suspense

A man that suspects his young wife is cheating on him will do anything to prove that she is, even though she may not be. Some guys have jealousy that is just way out of control and this episode definitely plays on that. I am getting a little tired of the cheating spouse tales though. This one does vary it up a bit but I wouldn't exactly call it great. What it does have going for it is that it is well acted and directed and it certainly is enjoyable, just not all that memorable.

3/5

Came the Dawn
Director – Uli Edel
Tags – Suspense

A man offers a woman on the run a place to stay in his cabin, but when a jealous lover enters the scene, things start to get crazy. I was figuring on another standard lover's triangle story but this one definitely had a twist that would alleviate my previous misconceptions. The acting and direction are very good but as far as the story goes, it does all balance on that twist ending because everything else about is fairly mundane. Still, what a way to end it.

3.5/5

Creep Course
Director – Jeffrey Boam
Tags – Mummies

A nerdy girl tries to help a jock pass an Egyptology course but the teacher, who is a rabid collector of Egyptian antiquity, has more suitable plans for her. This is a fun episode that isn't exactly brilliance in horror but it does have some great things going for it. The acting is pitch perfect and the mummy looks pretty damn cool. It also has a great, morbid sense of humor. So while I didn't particularly love the story, it was entertaining.

3.5/5

Death of Some Salesman
Director – Gilbert Adler
Tags – Slasher / Survival

A con man tries to scam the wrong family and ends up having to try and seduce their hideous daughter for his life. This is just a brilliant episode. First off the casting is great, especially Tim Curry playing not one, not two, but three roles with his patented creepiness. And there are some especially creepy moments here, not to mention some good and bloody ones. This was the first episode of the new season and it really kicked things off with a bang. Great stuff.

4.5/5

Food for Thought
Director – Rodman Flender
Tags – Suspense

An old psychic travels in a carnival with his girlfriend, and is obsessively jealous when another man looks her way. So how can she keep her affair secret from a psychic? While I stated earlier that I am tired of the whole cheating on a lover episode, this one is quite different. The carnival and psychic aspect add a lot to the story. The acting is great and the direction is good. I really did like the ending as well. Solid.

3.5/5

Forever Ambergris
Director – Gary Fleder
Tags – Infection

An over the hill photographer is jealous of his protégé's talent and covets his girlfriend so he tricks him into going into a village that was ravaged by disease so he too will become infected and he'll be able to get back on top. This awesome tale once again features great acting and direction with a very solid story, but the main highlight is the FX work. When the protégé becomes infected, it's pretty gnarly and the FX get even better for the stellar ending which features some great gore. An excellent episode.

Half-Way Horrible
Director – Gregory Widen
Tags – Zombies

A man whose corporation is about to release a super preservative is forced to revisit his past when his associates begin to die. And now the key ingredient for his preservative, which is derived from the Amazon, may bring back some dead issues to light. Voodoo zombies still provide a lot of enjoyment for me in the post-Romero world and I really liked this episode. You have your typical asshole character thinking he can throw money at a supernatural problem and this episode falls into a few clichés like that, but I still dug it. Really good acting, direction and gore make up a solid episode.

3.5/5

House of Horror
Director – Bob Gale
Tags – [Hidden to conceal spoilers]

Three fraternity pledges have to go to a supposedly haunted house as part of their initiation, but is this house just more than a local legend. I have always loved this episode because it really is creepy. You are left wondering as to what is really going on. Is it all a prank? Is there really a ghost? Is there a madman in the house? The ending will definitely surprise you. And that's all I'm going to say. Besides that the acting and direction are great all around. One of the best out of not only the season but the series as well.

4.5/5

Oil's Well that Ends Well
Director – Paul Abascal
Tags – Suspense

A con woman teams up with a man to pull off a scam on some rubes who think that there's oil in a graveyard, but just who is playing who? This typical scam episode plays out in a fairly straightforward manner with many twists and turns but most of them can easily be seen coming. But the acting and direction are good and it was an entertaining yarn so despite it being not particularly impressive, I still enjoyed it.

3/5

People Who Live in Brass Hearses
Director – Russell Mulcahy
Tags – Suspense

Two brothers plan on robbing an ice cream man but things go all wrong and in the process, they learn the ice cream man's dark secret. First off, the casting. Brilliant. We get Brad Dourif and Bill Paxton as the brothers? Wow, it doesn't get much better than that. And everyone else is great too. The story is really good but the highlight is the crazy storyline twist and very gory FX work. This is an incredibly weird episode and I loved it.

4/5

Till Death Do We Part
Director – W. Peter Iliff
Tags – Suspense

Not really all that much horror, this is more of a suspenseful mob tale. Here a mob woman's trophy husband is fooling around with a younger woman and she wants her dead. I like how the story was told because it was pretty unorthodox and I was wondering where they would go with it. Well, I liked where they went and the nice double twist was great. Good acting and direction is a nice episode would close out the season here.

3.5/5

Two for the Show
Director – Kevin Hooks
Tags – Suspense

A man kills his wife after she says she going to leave him, but now he is posed with a problem because how can he get rid of the body with a cop following him around? This episode has a ton of great, suspenseful moments sprinkled all throughout and it leads up to one of the more memorable twist endings in the series. The acting and direction are very well done and this is an all around great episode.

4/5

Well Cooked Hams
Director – Elliot Silverstein
Tags – Suspense

A magician who is failing at his craft witnesses an amazing trick by another magician and is determined to possess it at any cost. This is a typical tale that you can see unfolding just how you imagined and for that I didn't like the episode, but it does fortunately have some great acting and despite it being way too predictable, I was entertained by it. Probably the worst episode of the season but it's still an above average attempt.

3/5

Yes! The show rebounds in the fifth season by adding lots of gore and a bit more nudity too. The episodes this time were more horror related and there were less of the typical suspense tales, which I also felt helped the season be what it is. I definitely feel that this is one of the top seasons and I hope they can carry this momentum into season six.

Season Score:
4/5

Tales from the Crypt
Season 6
Year: 1994-1995
Tags: Anthology

The show returns with fifteen episodes (maybe an extra to make up for last year being one short?).

99 & 44/100% Pure Horror
Director – Rodman Flender
Tags – Suspense

A despicable wife who owes everything to her husband becomes angry with him and looks for a way out when he can longer provide her with what she wants. I don't know what's going on with the title either. The episode is entertaining but fairly mundane up until the ending, which features one of my favorite FX shots of series and I just had to give this episode another point for that. The acting is fine and the story is fine despite the whole cheating spouse being incredibly redundant by now. But like I said, at least the end makes up for it.

3.5/5

Assassin, The
Director – Martin von Haselberg
Tags – Suspense

A housewife is pitted against three CIA agents who suspect that her husband is an assassin who has gone AWOL. This episode is so stupidly predictable but it's also stupid fun. The acting is pretty good but the story seems to be a poor fit for the series. But like I said, it's still stupid fun and I was definitely entertained by this episode. But come on people it's time to pick some horror stories for the horror show.

3/5

Bribe, The
Director – Ramon Menendez
Tags – Suspense

A fire marshal intent on shutting down a seedy strip club is instead forced to take a bribe from the owner when financial difficulties come his way, but being unable to live with the deal, he devises another way to shut it down. This across the board average offering doesn't really illicit any kind of love or hatred from me, it's just dull, but strangely satisfying, it doesn't stand out, but it's still entertaining. You get what I'm saying? It's average, that's all.

2.5/5

Comes the Dawn
Director – John Herzfeld
Tags – [Hidden to conceal spoilers]

Two ex-soldiers wish to do some poaching in Alaska and hire a guide to aid them but everything is not as it seems and their wicked past comes back to haunt them. I've always thought that this episode was the inspiration for the story behind a fairly recent movie I greatly enjoyed, and you'll know what I mean when you watch this. The episode is great and features some great actors alongside a not so good one. The story unfolds splendidly and features a great twist that will go down as one of the best in the series. Just a great episode.

4/5

Doctor of Horror
Director – Larry Wilson
Tags – Suspense

Two security guards aid a doctor in acquiring dead bodies so that he can try and search for the human soul. And through this the doctor realizes he needs much fresher specimens. So this story is pretty fun and features some good acting and it all culminates into rather enjoyable ending. This episode shows what makes Tales from the Crypt episodes good: It has horror and it has humor, I can't ask for much more than that.

3.5/5

In the Groove
Director – Vincent Spano
Tags – Suspense

A struggling radio show host spices his sex show up with a new assistant but must still be under the thumb of his sister, who runs the station, and he desperately searches for a way to get rid of her. Well, this episode is ok I guess. I don't really dig the story as I was kind of bored with it, but the acting was good and the conclusion, although predictable, was satisfying. It's a good time, but fairly unremarkable.

3/5

Let the Punishment Fit the Crime
Director – Russell Mulcahy
Tags – Suspense

A hot shot lawyer gets stuck in small town with unusually harsh sentences for even the most minor crime. Love this episode. Catherine O' Hara was perfection is her role and the rest of the cast is also admirable. What a great way to kick off the season! I won't reveal too much but suffice to say that this is one place you wouldn't want to litter or shoplift because I can only imagine what the punishment would be. Hilarious and awesome episode and you just have to love the ending.

4/5

Only Skin Deep
Director – William Malone
Tags – Suspense

A man goes to a Halloween party to confront his ex but instead ends up spending the night with another woman who carries a very unusual and dark secret. This is another great episode that takes awhile to get to the horror of the tale, but in the meantime you get some sex and creepy atmosphere, so that's pretty cool. And the woman's mask is just so awesome looking. Nice acting and a great ending make for another highly enjoyable episode.

4/5

Operation Friendship
Director – Roland Mesa
Tags – Suspense

A lowly computer programmer finally gets a woman into his life but his imaginary friend objects and tries to get him to dispose of her. What an underwhelming episode. There's hardly any horror to it and it just comes off fairly lame. The acting is good but I just quickly became bored with it and it never really got interesting. The ending was ok but once again, I was just unimpressed by the story.

2/5

Pit, The
Director – John Harrison
Tags – Suspense

Two equally matched fighters agree to a cage fight to the death at the behest of their naggy wives. This is another episode that just doesn't seem to belong on Tale from the Crypt. That's not to say it's bad though, it's ok, but where's the horror? It's a fairly entertaining watch but the twist is completely predictable. Not impressive by any stretch of the word but still completely watchable.

2.5/5

Revenge is the Nuts
Director – Jonas McCord
Tags – Suspense

A cruel man runs a home for the blind and constantly torments them and deprives them of basic necessities. Until one day they fight back and hatch a devious plan against him. So this was better in the movie but this episode is still pretty damn good. The cruelty of the owner is just ridiculous and it really allows you to fully hate him to the point where his punishment isn't even good enough (even though it is pretty good). Nice acting and some solid direction round out a very well done episode.

3.5/5

Staired in Horror
Director – Stephen Hopkins
Tags – Suspense

A killer on the run finds refuge in a strange house that is inhabited by an old woman with a dark secret. This episode is pretty weird and doesn't make the most sense, but I still kind of liked it. The acting was solid and the FX were really good. The direction was ok but the episode could get rather dull in places. And to top off a rather weird episode, it had a rather weird ending that didn't really do much for me.

3/5

Surprise Party
Director – Elliot Silverstein
Tags – [Hidden to conceal spoilers]

A man inherits his father's property but is warned to stay away, when he goes anyway, he finds a group of people having a party there, and they appear to have been waiting for him. So just who are these people? Well that's pretty easy to figure out but that doesn't make the episode unenjoyable, it just makes it another in a line of fairly mundane offerings. Still good but lacking the big punch of the better episodes.

3/5

Whirlpool
Director – Mick Garris
Tags – Suspense

A woman keeps reliving the same terrible day over and over, and no matter what she does, it keeps turning out the same. And that's what makes the episode so lame, what a crap story! You get the same thing over and over again for the duration of the episode and then it ends. What the hell? Who thought this was good? Completely boring with only a couple instances of being mildly humorous.

1.5/5

You, Murderer
Director – Robert Zemeckis
Tags – Suspense

A murderer has had plastic surgery to change his appearance but finds out that he may have been figured out, which leads him to find the person who knows his true identity before it's too late. Ok, the whole Humphrey Bogart thing is lame and it just looks terrible, which is a shame seeing as how this episode features some great actors who are not put to good use by the below par story. I was just disappointed by this episode and felt it was a bad way for the season to go out.

2/5

Well, it wasn't as good as last season, but still not bad. There were some stinkers but it also featured some really good episodes that made it a slightly better than average season. I think there was just too little straight out horror in this season and they began to use some digital FX here which just looked terrible. But hey, it wasn't a complete disappointment and that's what matters the most.

Season Score: 3/5

Tales from the Crypt
Season 7
Year: 1996
Tags: Anthology

Tales from the Crypt moves to London for the final thirteen episodes of the iconic horror series.

About Face
Director – Thomas E. Sanders
Tags – Suspense

An amorous priest discovers that he has twin daughters as the result of a past indiscretion. But life is not as happy as he would like due to one of the twins hating him. And that's all I'm going to say. This episode is definitely one of the best of the season because you just have to love that ending and the fact that the episode revolves around a very horny priest, which is always good for some laughs. Well acted and directed, this is a very solid episode.

3.5/5

Cold War
Director – Andrew Morahan
Tags – [Hidden to conceal spoilers]

Two thieves always fighting with one another have a new person enter their lives and cause some rather unexpected trouble. This fairly entertaining episode has key horror elements to it but uses them more for comedy instead of horror, which kind of works. The acting is pretty fun and the direction moves things along nicely. This is good stuff, with a nice sense of humor, nothing overly grand, but it's enjoyable.

3.5/5

Confession
Director – Peter Hewitt
Tags – Serial Killer (Fictional)

An accomplished screenwriter is accused of being a serial head chopper and is interrogated by a tough cop. Even though this episode is predictable as can be, I was still highly entertained by it. The acting is great and the direction allowed it to run very smoothly. It was also very humorous and just a pleasure to watch unfold. Even though I knew how it would end, I was still interested in seeing what path the episode would take to get there. Great stuff.

4/5

Ear Today... Gone Tomorrow
Director – Christopher Hart
Tags – Suspense

A compulsive gambler is given one last chance to wipe his debt by cracking a safe, but since his ears aren't as good as they used to be, he uses a different method to get ahead. This weird as hell episode definitely moments of being entertaining and honestly does have good acting and direction but it's just too senseless to really be all that great. But it wasn't bad in the least, so I guess that makes it ok in my book.

3/5

Escape
Director – Peter MacDonald
Tags – Suspense

Set during World War II, a German officer is stuck into a POW camp and tries to lead an escape before a secret about him that can cost him his life is told. This episode, although well acted and featuring a great location for the material, is quite dull. I just didn't care for how the story unfolded and then it ended just as I expected it to, time to move on to the next episode, nothing much to see here.

2/5

Fatal Caper

Director – Bob Hoskins
Tags – Suspense

An ill man changes his will so that his sons may be cut off from his money and one will do anything to claim his inheritance. The story here is somewhat interesting, definitely not a grand event but more than adequate. The twist here is definitely interesting. The acting is pretty good and the direction is fine. This definitely didn't turn out to be a killer start to the final season but hey, it wasn't bad either.

3/5

Horror in the Night
Director – Russell Mulcahy
Tags – [Hidden to conceal spoilers]

A man decides to rip off some gems and hole up in a hotel until he can fence his stolen goods and find a way out, but he picked the wrong hotel. Now this is more like it, an actual horror episode, which seems to be rarity in the last couple seasons. I won't say too much and risk revealing the twist, which is a good one. Let's just say there is some well done acting, excellent FX, and while it can be a little slow it still had a solid story.

3.5/5

Kidnapper, The
Director – James H. Spencer
Tags – Suspense

A lonely man gets no attention from his girlfriend and all of it is instead lavished upon her baby, so he devises a plan to make sure there is nowhere else for her attention to go. This is another average episode that I garnered some enjoyment from but once again, it failed to impress me. The acting was good and the story had some moments of being interesting but ultimately it still felt pretty flat.

2.5/5

Last Respects
Director – Freddie Francis
Tags – Suspense

This episode is basically just another take on the classic story of the Monkey's Paw. A pretty boring one at that. It just lacks any great big surprise or wonderful twisting of wishes. The acting is ok, the direction is fine but I just could not get into the story or the characters. I guess I could say that it is completely watchable but I wasn't really entertained by it and instead I just wanted the next episode.

2.5/5

Report from the Grave
Director – William Malone
Tags – Ghosts

A man trying to commune with the dead through his own invention ends up killing his girlfriend, and he will do anything to get her back. At least I think that's what he was trying to do. Look into the minds of dead serial killers or something. It's pretty poorly laid out. The acting is ok and the killer that the movie focuses on had a pretty interesting past but beyond that there isn't much good to be said about this episode.

2/5

Slight Case of Murder, A
Director – Brian Helgeland
Tags – Suspense

A mystery writer must deal with her annoying neighbor at the same time someone is trying to kill her. Whatever. This is just another boring episode that once again didn't really do anything for me and I just patiently waited for the next episode to come on. But again, it's not bad and it's easy to watch, it just did not do anything for me. Decent acting and direction but no real twist or interesting plot device to really propel the story forward.

2.5/5

Smoke Wrings
Director – Mandie Fletcher
Tags – Suspense

An advertising executive hires a young man with no experience for what he believes are his good looks but there is a dark ulterior motive behind it all. This is a rather mundane episode that once again was completely watchable but really failed to impress. The acting was good and I like how the story ended but up to that point I found it to be fairly dull and not very memorable. Oh well, another forgettable episode.

2.5/5

Third Pig, The
Director – Bill Kopp, Patrick A. Ventura
Tags – Animated, Animals

This animated episode is a pretty different take on The Three Little Pigs tale. This is an interesting way to end the series. The last episode goes for straight gory humor in a cartoon way, and that worked for me. Bobcat Goldthwait voicing the wolf was an excellent choice and the way the episode played out was not only very unorthodox, but it was fun. It's not great by any means, but still a good time.

Well that's it folks, the end of the series, and it didn't exactly end on high note, no, quite the opposite, instead it ended with the worst season of them all, but honestly, it still really wasn't all that bad. There were definite good times in this show and while not every episode was a winner (how could they be?), there was still far more good than bad, and when it was good, it was really freakin' good. Not the best way to end an overall great series but even in the lackluster episodes we had one of the greatest horror hosts ever in the Cryptkeeper. His puns will not soon be forgotten.

Season Score: 2.5/5

I want to comment on directors because many have shown trends in their filmmaking, in on direction or the other. For example, whenever someone like John Carpenter, Neil Marshall or Guillermo del Toro release a new movie, I'll be going to watch it promptly because they have proven track records of creating great movies. Of course that's just a short list because there are several directors that fall under that category. Now someone like Wes Craven I'm a little more wary about because even though he has created some amazing movies, he's delivered several turds as well. Of course on the other side of the spectrum we have people like Uwe Boll, Chris Angel and Rick Bota, who have delivered nothing but shit, so I tend to avoid their movies until I can acquire them practically for free. Although I do think Uwe Boll is capable of making a good movie. He hasn't done it yet, and I know I'm in the minority in thinking that way, but I think one day he'll deliver an awesome genre movie. But he does suck right now. Anyway, some people are just naturally talented, and some need a good script or proper conditions to perform well. Some should never get behind the camera and some are just studio whores that will never create anything wonderful and unique but instead just do as they're told, never showing one iota of creativity. I'm talking to you Steve Miner.

I know a lot of people complain about three things in particular when it comes to horror: Remakes, PG-13 and sequels. First things first, I'll tackle remakes. Remaking horror is common practice, especially nowadays, and the reason for this is quite simple. Hollywood is a business and they feel that what worked for them once will work again, even though they don't usually have to be of high quality. The truth is that execs are scared of putting anything new out because they don't want to lose money, and that's the bottom line. By remaking all of the old classics, they can ensure that most people who liked the original will go and see an update as well as appealing toward a younger generation. A new movie doesn't have that instant name recognition. Sure, for every Dawn of the Dead remake there's a dozen Prom Nights but it's never going to change so you have to wait for that great remake and wade through the shit (it's pretty easy to tell which is going to be which). The same thing goes for sequels. Any movie that makes even a slight return for the execs will see a sequel because once again, it's all about name recognition. The (somewhat) good news is that since so many of the remakes are so terrible, odds are that the sequels can't be much worse. Yeah I know it still sucks. And as for PG-13 movies, they appeal to a wider audience by allowing younger audiences into the theater, and once again, that aids the execs bottom line. But once again, they're not all bad. Sure, many are watered down and won't appeal to die hard horror fans, but a movie like Jaws was merely PG, and that's one of the greatest horror movies ever made in my opinion. So once again, for every Jaws you'll have probably two dozen copies of The Haunting of Molly Hartley. It's never going to change because it's a business plan that works for Hollywood, and we'll just have to put up with it, and by putting up with it I mean I won't be seeing it in the theater and I'll only watch them when I can pick up a used copy in the bargain bin, because honestly that's all they deserve. You don't have to patronize their movies if you don't want to and there's always the alternative of foreign films and independent cinema, which also isn't perfect, but does have a better track record. Either way there is no use in complaining about it because it's never going to change. Just roll with the punches, find what you like and stick with it. The masses will always keep Hollywood in business and that's fine because I like being the guy who watches all the obscure stuff and shows it to his friends, promptly blowing them away with awesome movies instead of the humdrum garbage they're used to. Don't lose respect for the genre because so many have none at all for it, because there are plenty of people who love it and try their best to support it with great films and wonderful ideas. Don't let one bad apple spoil the whole damn bunch.

So, a thousand movies, that's a lot, but it's also only the beginning. So what have I learned from watching so many genre films? Well… Let's discuss. First off, don't ever have children, they'll either end up killing you or becoming a liability and either way, you're screwed. Next, if the military gets involved in an unknown situation their first and only idea will be to "blow the shit out of" whatever is attacking, and that's usually the wrong course of action. Third, always carry some kind of knife with you, I don't know how many people could have been saved if they all just carried around some kind of edged weapon to either fend off an attacker or cut themselves free from a sticky situation. Lastly, don't ever go into the woods, an old house, any large body of water, a cemetery, hell, just stay at home, unless it's haunted, which it most likely is. Looks like just about everyone is shit out of luck actually, but if you fortify your home against zombies and keep your distance from the psycho who appears to be dead but rarely ever is, you may just survive after all. So that's the first volume of this book series, I hope you found some use for it, whether it be discovering new movies or having some handy rolling papers when you run out of Zig Zags. I may sounds like an asshole, and I am, because that's my right and if something sucks, I'm really going to elaborate on it. Until next time boils and ghouls, I'll keep watching and keep being an asshole, because Volume II is on the way. Keep it gory!

-Eric Myford

Made in the USA
Lexington, KY
05 December 2011